W9-AZS-827

FIRST NATIONS OF NORTH AMERICA

SUBARCTIC PEOPLES

ROBIN S. DOAK

HEINEMANN LIBRARY
CHICAGO, ILLINOIS

www.heinemannraintree.com
Visit our website to find out
more information about
Heinemann-Raintree books.

To order:
☎ Phone 888-454-2279
🖥 Visit www.heinemannraintree.com
to browse our catalog and order online.

© 2012 Heinemann Library
an imprint of Capstone Global Library, LLC
Chicago, Illinois

Original illustrations © Capstone Global Library, Ltd.
Illustrated by Mapping Specialists, Ltd.
Originated by Capstone Global Library, Ltd.
Printed by China Translation and Printing Company

15 14 13 12 11
10 9 8 7 6 5 4 3 2 1

Library of Congress Cataloging-in-Publication Data
Doak, Robin S. (Robin Santos), 1963-

  Subarctic peoples / Robin S. Doak.

    p. cm.—(First nations of North America)

  Includes bibliographical references and index.

  ISBN 978-1-4329-4954-9 (hc)—ISBN 978-1-4329-4965-5
(pb) 1. Indians of North America—Canada, Northern—Juvenile literature. 2. Indians of North America—Alaska—Juvenile
literature. I. Title.

  E78.C2D53 2012

  971.9'01—dc22   2010042643

Acknowledgments

The author and publisher are grateful to the following for
permission to reproduce copyright material:

Alamy: p. 24 (© INTERFOTO); AP Photo: p. 40 (Jeffrey
Ulbrich); Corbis: 14 (© National Geographic Society), 29
(© Christopher J. Morris), 35 (© Corbis), 39 (© Laurent
Gillieron/epa); Getty Images: pp. 5 (Danita Delimont), 10
(Stephen J. Krasemann), 19 (Bert Garai), 31 (Emily Riddell);
istockphoto: p. 36 (© Dan Driedger); Library of Congress
Prints and Photographs Division: p. 4; Nativestock.com: pp.
15 (© Marilyn Angel Wynn), 16 (© Marilyn Angel Wynn),
26 (© Marilyn Angel Wynn), 27 (© Marilyn Angel Wynn),
28 (© Marilyn Angel Wynn), 33 (© Marilyn Angel Wynn);
Photolibrary: pp. 11 (Nativestock Pictures/Marilyn Angel
Wynn), 13 (The Print Collector), 17 (Nativestock), 22
(Thorsten Milse), 23 (Marilyn Angel Wynn), 30 (Nativestock
Pictures), 38 (Thorsten Milse), 41 (Brian Summers);
Shutterstock: p. 21 (© Morgan Lane Photography); SuperStock:
pp. 18 (IndexStock / SuperStock), 34 (© Christie's Images,
Ltd.); The Granger Collection, NYC: pp. 12, 20, 32.

Cover photograph of a Cree quilled hide pouch reproduced
with permission from SuperStock (© Christie's Images, Ltd.).

We would like to thank Peter Collings,Ph.D., for his invaluable
help in the preparation of this book.

Contents

Some words are shown in bold **like this**. You can find out what they mean by looking in the glossary.

Who Were the First People in North America?

In 1980 native peoples throughout Canada adopted a **resolution**. It said, in part:

> We, the original people of this land know the Creator put us here.... The Creator gave us our spiritual beliefs, our languages, our **culture**, and a place on Mother Earth which provided us with all our needs.... The rights and responsibilities given to us by the Creator cannot be altered or taken away by any other **Nation**.

More than 12,000 years ago, people lived throughout North America. The earliest peoples made their homes in every part of the continent, from icy northern regions to hot, humid regions in the southern part of the continent. But, after European explorers began arriving there in the late 1400s, other groups began laying claim to North America.

◄ Some of the earliest peoples in North America settled in the Subarctic region of the continent.

◄ The descendants of the first peoples to live in the Subarctic region of Alaska and Canada continue to follow long-standing traditions.

Native Americans or American Indians?

In 1492 Italian explorer Christopher Columbus arrived in the Americas. Believing he had found Asia, which was then called the Indies, he used the name "Indian" for the peoples who were living in the region. For centuries, all of the first peoples of the Americas were known as Indians.

The term "American Indian" was used for many years. "Native American" was introduced in the late 1900s honoring the fact that these were the first humans to live in the region. Most native peoples, however, would rather be identified by their **tribe** or nation—for example, Ojibwa.

Today, **descendants** of the earliest Subarctic peoples live and work in the same areas where their **ancestors** first settled. In Alaska, these people are known as Alaskan Native. In Canada, they are the First Nations people.

Who were the first people in North America?

The first people to settle in North America **migrated** from Asia. Scientists believe they arrived on foot, following the herds of mammoths, reindeer, and other large animals they hunted for food and clothing. They traveled from one continent to the other over the **Bering Land Bridge**, a 1,000-mile (1,600-kilometer) stretch of land that connected Asia to North America. This pathway existed during the last Ice Age, between 10,000 and 25,000 years ago.

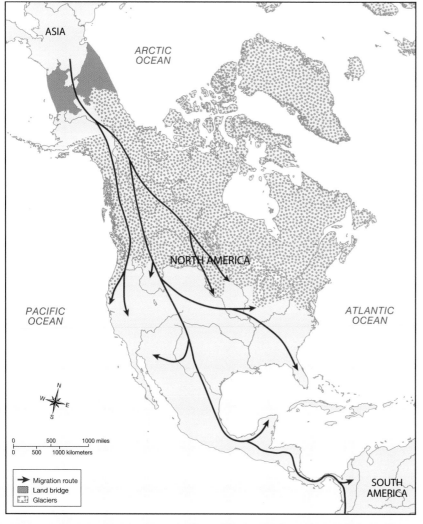

◄ This map shows some of the routes early peoples took as they spread across North America.

The new arrivals, known today as **Paleo-Indians**, spread throughout North America. Some headed into present-day Mexico and beyond. Other groups made their homes on the **plains**. Still others settled on the east and west coasts of the continent, becoming farmers and cultivating crops of squash, corn, and beans.

The Subarctic

Scientists believe that the Subarctic region was one of the first areas to be settled in North America. The Subarctic is a 3,000-mile (4,800-kilometer) band of **boreal forests** stretching across the northern part of the continent. It includes most of present-day Canada and parts of Alaska. Fewer early peoples lived in the Subarctic than in other regions in North America.

The Ice Age came to an end and temperatures rose. Ice glaciers melted and ocean levels rose. The Bering Land Bridge eventually disappeared. People, animals, and plants stopped migrating from Asia to North America.

Who Are the Peoples of the Subarctic?

In the Subarctic, the first settlers lived together in small groups called **bands**. Each band was made up of one or more families. A band might have as many as 30 people. Bands that lived in the same area were known as a **tribe**. Bands within the tribe shared the same language and customs. They also shared hunting territories and sometimes lived together in seasonal camps.

In recent years, some tribes have banded together and formed **nations**. They did this in order to protect their land and customs. For example, the Dene Nation is made up of tribes in the **Northwest Territories**, an area in northern Canada.

Major groups

There are two major groups of Subarctic peoples within the region. Those who live in the eastern part of the region (see the map at right) speak Algonquian languages. They include the Cree, Innu, Ojibwa, and Algonquin peoples. In the western part of the region, many Subarctic peoples spoke Athabaskan languages. These groups include the peoples of the Dene Nation as well as Alaskan Athabaskan people.

Another distinct group within the Subarctic region is the **Métis**. They are the **descendants** of both First Nations people and Europeans. The Métis speak a language that includes native, French, and English words.

▲ Subarctic bands lived throughout central Alaska and much of Canada.

LANGUAGE

What's in a Name?

The word "Dene" is an Athabaskan term that means "the people." The Dene call their homeland Denendeh, which means "the Creator's Spirit flows through this Land."

The boreal forest

The Subarctic region is made up of the **boreal forest** of North America. The boreal forest, sometimes called the taiga, stretches across the interior of Alaska and Canada. It is wedged between two areas. To the north is the Arctic **tundra**. Tundra is flat, frozen, treeless land. To the south are **plains**, forests, and mountains.

The boreal forest is made up of evergreen trees, including spruce, birch, pine, and fir. Winters in the forest are long, cold, and snowy. Temperatures average around 14°F (-10°C). In many places the ground is covered with a layer of permanently frozen soil called **permafrost**. Summers are short, with temperatures hovering around 72°F (22°C).

▲ The Subarctic region is made up of lakes, rivers, and forests filled with evergreen trees such as pines and firs.

▲ Subarctic bands adapted to their local surroundings.

Surviving in the boreal forest

Because of the long winters, farming was not possible for early Subarctic peoples. Instead, they relied on hunting and gathering to survive. The forests were home to many different kinds of animals. Large **game** included moose and caribou. Early peoples trapped smaller animals, such as beavers, rabbits, fox, and otters, for food and clothing. They also hunted birds.

The many rivers and lakes throughout the region were a source of fish, including trout, salmon, and pike. During the summer, bands would camp together by the water and fish and hunt together. People also gathered berries and roots to eat.

What Was an Early Subarctic Village Like?

Early Subarctic peoples did not live in permanent villages. Instead, they traveled between winter and summer camps. They moved from one place to the other to take advantage of the most plentiful food sources. In the winter, many **bands** hunted the **migrating** caribou. In the summer, they traveled to rivers and lakes to fish.

Because they were constantly on the move, early Subarctic peoples had few possessions. Most of their goods were things that were necessary, such as clothing, hunting tools, and the items they needed to build their next shelters. When they left one camp for the next, they had to pack up and carry all of their belongings.

▲ Subarctic families lived together in groups called bands.

▲ Family life was very important to early Cree Indians, as it is to modern Crees today.

Families in the Subarctic

The family was the most important unit for Subarctic bands. Families included grandparents, a husband and wife, and children. In some bands, two families that were related to one another lived together in one dwelling. If members of a band were too closely related, they were not allowed to marry one another.

The villages did not have a **chief**. Instead, the members of a band or **tribe** looked to the person who was the wisest and who could lead the others in times of trouble. This leader might make decisions about warfare and trading. However, his power came from the entire band. If members of the band did not agree with the leader, they did not have to follow his advice.

Subarctic tipis and lean-tos

People in the Subarctic used the resources available in the **boreal forest** to construct their houses. Most homes were constructed of wood, animal **hides**, and dirt. All of the homes were fast and simple to build and take down.

One of the most common types of Subarctic homes was the **tipi**. Tipis were tentlike dwellings that were made with a frame of wooden poles or branches. The frame was then covered with either animal hides or tree bark. Some tipis were cone-shaped, while others were dome-shaped. All tipis were portable and easy to put up, take down, and transport.

Another type of summer home was the **lean-to**. This open-faced, temporary shelter was made with branches and leaves. Larger families might build a double lean-to, with two lean-tos facing each other. A single fire, lit in the center, was used for warmth, light, and cooking.

▲ Among the Cree, women made and owned the tipis.

▲ This Cree home is covered with caribou skins.

Log houses, pit houses, and sweathouses

In the winter, some bands moved into sturdy, cone-shaped log houses. These homes had roofs of dirt and snow. Subarctic peoples wedged moss in the gaps of the logs to keep the cold and wind from entering. Other groups built **pit houses** in the winter. These were dug partially into the ground and covered with a roof of dirt, snow, and branches.

A **sweathouse** was a special dome-shaped structure covered with robes and blankets. A hole dug in the middle of the house was filled with hot stones and covered with wet moss. The steam was believed to cure illnesses and purify the body.

What Did Early Subarctic Peoples Eat?

The early peoples of the Subarctic were hunters and gatherers. Among their chief sources of food were the caribou and moose that lived in the region. Some groups, like the Chipewyan, depended upon caribou completely. They were **nomadic**, following the animals as they **migrated** from place to place.

Because the caribou were difficult to successfully hunt, **bands** of Subarctic peoples often came together to share hunting grounds. They would camp at the same sites and work together to make sure that their people did not go hungry. Bands hunted, fished, and lived side by side.

▲ Several bands of Subarctic hunters would often work together to corral and kill caribou.

▲ In addition to trapping and fishing, women also cut up, prepared, and stored food for their band.

Who hunted for food?

Men were in charge of hunting and killing the big animals. Sometimes they built pens called **corrals** out of tree branches. Some groups scared the caribou into the corrals, where the hunters used spears, bows and arrows, and knives to kill them. After Subarctic peoples began trading with French and English fur traders (see pages 32 to 35), they used guns to kill the animals.

Women played an important role in finding and preparing food. They hunted smaller animals, including rabbits, birds, and fish. They created traps to catch small **game**, and they wove nets and baskets to trap and store fish. Cree women followed the men as they hunted buffalo. When a buffalo was killed, the women would go to work. They cut up the animal and carried it back to camp.

17

▲ The hides of animals were scraped free of fur, then used to make clothing and baskets.

Respecting nature

The Subarctic peoples believed that to be successful hunters, they must respect the animals they hunted. All animals were believed to have a soul or spirit. Many bands performed **rituals** before and after the hunt to calm the animal spirits. During the rituals, they thanked the animal for allowing itself to be caught and killed.

Early peoples put nearly every part of the dead animal to use. They used the meat and organs for food. They turned furs and **hides** into clothing, blankets, and tent coverings. They used bones and antlers to make tools, or they carved them into pieces of art. They even used the animals' stomach lining as storage containers for berries and other items.

Gathering and storing food

Although they did not farm, the peoples of the Subarctic collected the many berries and edible plants that grew throughout the region. They ate blueberries, cranberries, raspberries, and strawberries, along with roots, barks, and herbs. Sometimes they mixed the berries with fat and dried fish or meat. This food, which lasted for months, was called **pemmican**. Berries and roots were also used to make medicines to cure diarrhea and other ailments.

Subarctic peoples stored food to help them survive the long winters. They placed dried fish, caribou, and other meats in storage places called **caches**. Some caches were pits dug into the ground. Others were platforms built high in the branches of a tree.

◄ Subarctic peoples caught fish using woven baskets and nets, as well a hooks and lines.

How Did Early Subarctic Peoples Travel?

Travel was the key to survival for most Subarctic **bands**. The most common form of travel was by foot. When the time came to move to a new camp, all of the band's goods— clothing, tents, and hunting tools—were packed up and loaded to be transported. In Chipewyan groups, the women were responsible for toting all the goods. This left the men free to hunt as they traveled.

Because of large amounts of standing water, summertime travel could be difficult. Subarctic peoples used the rivers and lakes as pathways. They built sturdy **canoes** out of birch bark. Birch bark is hard, lightweight, and waterproof. The bark was attached to cedar pieces that had been soaked in water and shaped to form the canoe's skeleton. Canoes were also used for fishing and hunting caribou.

▲ To carry heavy loads, some Subarctic peoples used a **tumpline**. This is a headband that is used to support a load and make it easier to carry.

▲ Each region of the Subarctic had its own style of snowshoe. Most were narrow, with the toe turned up.

Winter travel

Early Subarctic peoples created special equipment to help them get around in the winter. The Subarctic peoples invented sleds called **toboggans** to carry goods through the snow. Other groups made snowshoes out of birch and animal **hides**. The hides were used to create the snowshoe netting. Early Subarctic peoples wore the snowshoes while hunting and gathering food. They also created snow goggles to cut down on the glare of sunlight on snow.

What Clothing Did Early Subarctic Peoples Wear?

Like other native peoples, early Subarctic **bands** used the animals they hunted to make clothing. Moose and caribou **hides** were among the most common sources of shirts, dresses, **tunics**, leggings, and **moccasins**. Women prepared the hides for sewing by scraping them first to remove the hair. Then some bands soaked the skins in animal brains to make them soft.

While summer clothing was lightweight, winter fashions were warmer and heavier. Women made fur coats, robes, and sleeping garments out of beaver and rabbit fur. Moccasins were replaced with fur-lined boots.

▶ Winter clothing was designed to protect people from the cold and snow.

Decorating clothes and bodies

The clothes of early Subarctic peoples were functional. But many things they wore were also beautiful. Women decorated their clothing with porcupine quills, animal teeth, and beads made out of seeds they collected. They dyed their clothes with berries and clay. Some bands wore hats and jewelry. Subarctic jewelry was made out of shells, antlers, and even bear claws.

Subarctic peoples took great pride in their appearance. Men plucked the hair from their faces. Men and women alike rubbed animal fat into their hair and skin to make it soft and shiny. Some **tribes** tattooed or painted their faces and other parts of the body. Body paint was made of clay mixed with fat.

Baby fashion

In some areas, Subarctic babies wore diapers made of animal hides. The diapers were stuffed with moss to absorb wetness. Infants throughout the Subarctic spent the first months of their lives strapped into a **cradleboard**. This was a board with a sack for the baby that was worn on the mother's back.

▶ Subarctic groups often decorated their clothing. These clothes are made from caribou hide and then painted with designs.

23

What Did Early Subarctic Peoples Believe?

Early Subarctic peoples believed that all living things in the world around them had spirits. They believed that these spirits could help or harm them—depending upon whether the spirit was good or bad. They prayed to the spirits for health, successful hunting, and protection from evil.

A spiritual leader helped connect people to the unseen world. The leader was believed to have been given special powers by the spirits.

▲ This Chippewa healer sucks disease out of a patient with a bone.

"How Wisagatcak Flooded the World": A Cree Folktale

The following is a Cree story that explains the creation of the world. Wisagatcak, the Cree trickster, wanted to capture the Great Beaver. The trickster threw his spear at the animal, but missed. Beaver wanted revenge. He created a huge dam, which caused a flood that destroyed the world.

As the water levels rose, Wisagatcak built a raft and put all the animals of Earth on it. After spending several days floating, the trickster placed moss on the surface of the raft. The moss grew and grew until it created a whole new world.

The spiritual leader used his or her powers to communicate with the spirits and also to heal the sick. During healing **ceremonies**, he or she sang and danced. He or she might massage or blow on the suffering person. The spiritual leader also knew which berries, roots, and barks to use for medicines.

Spirits, heroes, and tricksters

Some groups believed in a supreme spirit that created Earth and all things in it. Algonquian-speaking groups called this spirit the Great Manitou. Other **bands** also believed in both a hero and trickster character. The hero was the first powerful person in the world. The trickster was a mischievous spirit that could cause trouble for humans. Both the hero and the trickster helped form the world.

What Did Early Subarctic Peoples Do to Celebrate?

Subarctic **bands** often came together seasonally to share good hunting and fishing grounds. But these meetings were about more than just work. Subarctic peoples used the gatherings as a chance to hold festivals, **ceremonies**, and **rituals** and to celebrate being together.

One important celebration for the Alaskan Athabaskan people was the **potlatch**. This was a ceremony of feasting and gift giving. It could be held to honor the dead. A potlatch also marked a special occasion, such as when a boy took part in his first hunt. Other potlatches were held by one band to show visiting bands how prosperous they were. Alaskan Athabaskan people continue this celebration today.

▲ Seasonal hunting camps brought people from different bands together for work and for play.

In the past, potlatch ceremonies could last for up to a week. During that time, native peoples sang, danced to the beat of drums, and ate. The Alaskan Athabaskan people even built a special building for the potlatch. Potlatches are still held by Alaskan Athabaskan people today.

The Sun Dance

Another important ceremony was the Sun Dance, also called the Thirst Dance. During this ritual, men of the **tribe** did not eat or drink anything for several days. They stayed out in the hot Sun until they had a vision. In Cree bands, the men pierced their own skin with a horn and attached themselves to a pole. They danced, tugged, and twisted until the horn ripped free from their skin. Sun Dances are still held in Canada today.

▶ This Chippewa man dances in a traditional celebration. Subarctic peoples today carry on the traditions of their **ancestors**.

A DAY IN THE LIFE OF A CREE YOUNG PERSON

Today is a special day for the teen. Like his father and grandfather before him, the boy will begin his **vision quest**. The vision quest is a **ritual** that all boys must undergo. When it is over, he will no longer be considered a boy. Instead, his **band** members will look at him as a man.

The boy has been preparing for this moment all his life. As a child, he watched and listened as the band's **elders** taught him how to survive in the forest. His uncle taught him how to find his way home when he was lost. His father told him about the caribou and moose. He explained the animals' habits and where to find them.

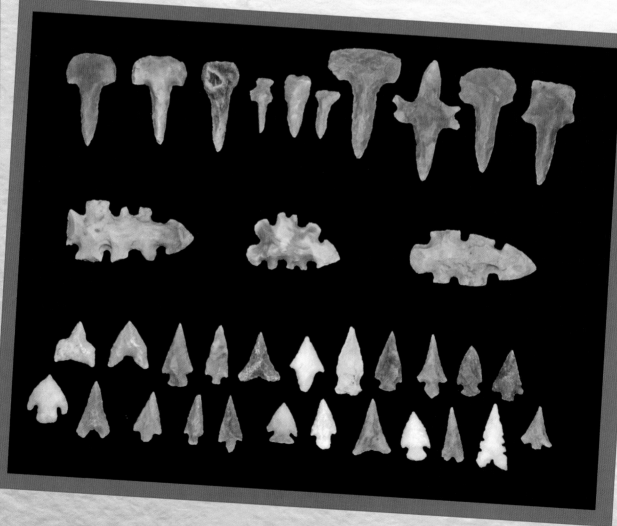

▲ Cree boys were taught to create arrowheads and other weapons for hunting.

▲ Subarctic children of today are learning to preserve their heritage.

The boy and his friends also practiced the skills they would need as adults. While his sister learned to sew and to cut up rabbits and other small **game**, he shot bows and arrows at a target. Games like stickball, played with a caribou-**hide** ball stuffed with moss, helped the boy become well coordinated.

Now, the boy and his father have arrived at the abandoned bear den. The two smoke a pipe together. The boy is left alone. He will stay here, **fasting** and praying, for days. If he is successful, the young man will eventually have a vision. He will find his spirit helper. He believes this spirit will help him get through life without harm. Only then will he return home and take his place—as an adult—among his band.

What Art and Music Did Early Subarctic Peoples Create?

The items early Subarctic peoples chose to move from camp to camp were often both useful and beautiful. They decorated clothing, tents, and other everyday items, making them works of art.

▲ This Chippewa woman weaves a mat for the inside of her home.

A Subarctic Art Form

Subarctic artists are best known for their elaborate embroidery and beading. In earlier times, the Dene, Alaskan Athabaskan, and other groups sewed geometric patterns and pictures of flowers and animals onto their clothing.

They also decorated shirts, robes, and coats with fringes, porcupine quills, animal teeth, and the seeds of local plants. After contact with Europeans, they began making artwork with the glass beads they got from trading.

▲ Cree and other Subarctic peoples continue to create beautiful beaded items today.

Early craftspeople made baskets with animal **hides**, reeds, and other items. These baskets were used for storage and to carry goods. But many were also decorated with woven patterns and colorful dyes. Subarctic peoples throughout the region continue to craft baskets today.

Painting is another traditional form of Subarctic art. Early peoples in the region painted on hides, birch bark, clothing, and even their **tipis**. They used paints and dyes made of berries and clay.

Music

Music is important to the Subarctic peoples, too. Drums made of animal hide and wood were the most common early musical instrument. They were used during religious **ceremonies** as well as festive occasions such as the **potlatch**. Later, Subarctic peoples were introduced to fiddles by French and Scots traders. They soon incorporated fiddling into their ceremonies and began creating their own folk songs, which are still sung today.

How Did Subarctic Peoples Interact with Nonnatives?

Europeans first entered the Subarctic region in the early 1500s. These first visitors were French and English explorers and fur traders. They came looking for the **hides** of foxes, rabbits, caribou, and especially beavers. People in Europe used the furs for hats, coats, boots, and other items.

In 1608 French explorer Samuel de Champlain founded Quebec City, the first permanent European settlement in present-day Canada. French fur traders, called **voyageurs**, set out from there and from other later settlements to trade with the peoples of the Subarctic. In 1611 English explorer Henry Hudson came into contact with the Cree people in the James Bay region of Canada. He then staked an English claim to the area.

▲ This illustration depicts Pierre-Esprit Radisson, a French explorer and trader, meeting Subarctic traders.

Trade

In the early 1670s, an English company called the Hudson's Bay Company set up trading posts throughout the region. Several Algonquian-speaking groups moved from their traditional campsites to be closer to the trading posts. They began to change their seasonal patterns of hunting and fishing, to have better opportunities to trade with the Europeans.

In the coming years, both the Cree and Ojibwa would serve as important **middlemen** between the Europeans and native **bands** throughout the region. They carried weapons, clothing, and beads to Subarctic peoples, trading them for the furs that the Europeans prized.

▲ Subarctic peoples traded animal furs such as these for goods such as beads and items made from metal.

Major changes

The arrival of European settlers and traders changed the way most Subarctic bands lived. Many **tribes** began to rely on the European trade goods they received in exchange for animal skins and furs. Bands began using guns to hunt animals instead of the traditional spears, and bows and arrows. Many Subarctic peoples stopped wearing the traditional animal-hide clothing, preferring instead to make their garments out of the cloth supplied by European traders.

◄ European goods changed some aspects of Subarctic peoples' lives such as how they dressed.

The Europeans also tried to influence relations within and between bands. Traders attempted to set up **chiefs** within each native band. They hoped that this would make it easier for them to control trade through the chief they had chosen. Some Europeans even took up arms in native conflicts. In 1609, for example, Champlain and French troops helped the Algonquin defeat their enemy, the Iroquois.

Problems

The contact with Europeans came at a cost. In the 1800s and 1900s, peoples throughout the region suffered from **discrimination**, or unfair treatment. They lost their lands to nonnative settlers. They also faced pressure from **missionaries**, politicians, and educators to give up their native religions, languages, and customs and adopt the ways of the Canadian and U.S. people.

BIOGRAPHY

Louis Riel: Métis Champion

Louis Riel (1844-1885) was the **descendant** of native and French-Canadian people. In 1869 Riel organized **Métis** people living in the Red River Settlement in present-day Manitoba, Canada.

Together, Riel and the Métis prevented the Canadian government from taking control of Métis land. In 1885 Riel was hanged after leading a second, less successful rebellion.

▶ Louis Riel helped found the **province** of Manitoba and served as one of its leaders.

What Have Subarctic Peoples Contributed to the World?

Subarctic peoples have left their mark on other **cultures** since the first Europeans arrived. The earliest French and English traders to visit the region adopted native **canoe**, snowshoe, and clothing designs in order to better adapt to life in their new homes. They relied on native peoples to guide them through the region. They needed to learn about the animals of the **boreal forests** and about the local rivers and lakes.

▲ Some of the first people to use toboggans were the First **Nations** people of Canada. Now people all over the world use **toboggans**.

LANGUAGE

Native Names

Places throughout Canada and Alaska still bear the names given to them by the native peoples of the Subarctic region. Here are just a few:

Manitoba: This comes from a Cree or Ojibwa word meaning "strait of the spirit."

Quebec: This comes from an Algonquian word meaning "where the river narrows."

Saskatchewan: This comes from a Cree word meaning "swift-flowing river."

Saskatoon: This comes from a Cree word meaning "early berries."

Winnipeg: This comes from Cree words meaning "muddy water."

Yukon: This comes from a Gwich'in word meaning "great river."

People today still use gear that was originally designed by Subarctic peoples. In the winter, for example, adults and children alike enjoy using snowshoes and toboggans for fun. In the summer, people paddle canoes that are still very similar in design to early Subarctic ones.

Language

Many words of the Subarctic peoples have been adopted into the English language and are used today. These words include "canoe," "chipmunk," "toboggan," and "totem."

Arts and crafts

Subarctic arts and crafts are popular with people near and far. The **Métis's** capes, purses, jewelry, and clothing are highly valued. Cree artists also create popular pieces of art made by chewing a pattern onto birch bark. A number of Subarctic artists have recently attracted worldwide attention.

Where Are Subarctic Peoples Today?

People who are **descendants** of early Subarctic peoples continue to make their homes in Canada and Alaska. In the **Northwest Territories**, half of all people living there are descendants of native peoples. In all, nearly 4 percent of Canada's population is made up of descendants of the region's first peoples.

Reserves

Less than half of all native peoples in Canada live on **reserves**. A reserve is an area of land that has been set aside by the Canadian government. There are more than 2,000 such areas throughout Canada, covering more than 6 million acres (2.4 million hectares) of land.

▲ Some reserves are far away and difficult to reach.

▲ These Cree representatives attend a meeting at the United Nations headquarters in Geneva, Switzerland.

On the reserves, people work to balance modern ways with the older, more traditional ways. **Canoes** have been replaced in some areas by boats with motors. Instead of sled dogs, some Subarctic peoples use snowmobiles to drag **toboggans** to help them get around in the winter.

Keeping traditions alive

The Cree people make up the largest native group in Canada. They keep their **culture** alive by teaching Cree ways to the young and the Cree language in schools. Some Cree have gained positions in government in order to make their voices heard.

Most Subarctic peoples live in towns and cities throughout Canada. It is often easier to find jobs and earn a living there. But away from other members of their **tribe**, it is also easier for them to forget the old ways. It is a challenge for these people to keep long-standing traditions alive.

Taking care of the land

One of the challenges native peoples face today is protecting their lands from development. As the demand for natural resources like wood, oil, and electricity increases, non-natives have tried to **exploit** the land where native peoples have lived for centuries. Many Subarctic peoples have joined forces to fight for protection of their lands.

▲ The James Bay Project is destroying lands that once belonged to native peoples. The Grand Council of the Crees was formed to help fight for Crees' rights to their lands.

▲ Subarctic young people are taught traditional customs, as well as modern technology.

In Canada, some **bands** are working with mining, timber, and power companies. The Innu in some regions, for example, are making agreements that ensure their land is used carefully and respectfully. They also want to benefit from any use of their land.

First Nations

Canada's native peoples have banded together to make sure their concerns are heard. More than 600 bands call themselves the First **Nations**. (The term does not include the Inuit or the **Métis**.) The term emphasizes the common background and traditions that the bands and tribes share. It also highlights their desire to be recognized as the native peoples of the region. By standing together, First Nations people have successfully stopped development that would have harmed the land they have lived on for centuries.

In the coming years, the people of the Subarctic region will continue to face challenges from people who want to use their land. They must find ways to make sure that the ancient ways are remembered and passed on to future generations.

Timeline

about 10,000 BCE	People from Asia cross the **Bering Land Bridge** to North America.
1492 CE	Christopher Columbus reaches the Americas. He calls the people he meets there Indians, a name that is still used in some areas today.
1608	French explorer Samuel de Champlain founds Quebec City, the first permanent European settlement in Canada.
1609	Champlain and French troops help the Algonquin defeat their enemy, the Iroquois.
1611	Henry Hudson, on his last voyage to North America, comes into contact with the Cree of James Bay.
early 1670s	The Hudson's Bay Company sets up trading posts throughout the Subarctic region.
1869	**Métis** leader Louis Riel organizes a successful resistance in present-day Manitoba, Canada.
1885	After leading an unsuccessful armed rebellion in the **Northwest Territories**, Riel is hanged for treason (being disloyal) by the Canadian government.
mid-1900s	Many Subarctic peoples move to cities, seeking work after the fur trade ends.
1971	The Alaska Native Claims Settlement Act gives land and money to Native Alaskans.

1985   Canada revises its Indian Act to remove sections that caused **discrimination** and to give back native rights and status.

1994   Cree and other native peoples temporarily halt a massive **hydroelectric** project in Quebec called the James Bay Project.

2001   Cree people, Quebec officials, and government officials sign an agreement to use native land to create hydroelectric power.

2007   First **Nations** people organize a demonstration called the Aboriginal Day of Action to bring attention to poverty, lack of health care, and other native issues.

Glossary

ancestor family member from the distant past

band Indian family group that lived together

Bering Land Bridge stretch of land, 1,000 miles (1,600 kilometers) long, that once connected Asia to North America

boreal forest northern forest made up of coniferous and evergreen trees

cache place to store food and other goods

canoe light, narrow boat

ceremony religious event or observance

chief leader of a group of people

corral pen used to capture animals like caribou

cradleboard device made from a board and a sack and worn on the back for carrying an infant

culture shared ways of life and beliefs of a group of people

culture area region of North America in which Indians traditionally had a similar way of life

descendant offspring of an earlier group

discrimination act of being unfair to a person or group

elder older person

exploit use unfairly

fast to go without food

game wild animals hunted for food

hide animal skin

hydroelectric electricity created by channeling moving water

lean-to open-faced, temporary shelter made with branches and leaves

Métis people in Canada who are the descendants of both native and European people

middleman person or group who acts as a go-between for two other groups

migrate move from one place to another

missionary person who tries to persuade others to adopt his or her religion

moccasin ankle-length shoe made of animal skin

nation group of tribes that have banded together

nomadic moving from place to place without a fixed home

Northwest Territories territory in northern Canada that includes Nunavut

Paleo-Indians first people to enter and live in the Americas

pemmican long-lasting food made of berries mixed with fat and dried fish or meat

permafrost layer of permanently frozen soil

pit house home dug partially into the ground and covered with a roof of dirt, snow, and branches

plain flat stretch of land

potlatch feast held by some American Indian tribes, during which the host offers gifts to his or her guests

province administrative division of a country, similar to a state in the United States

reserve area of land given back to the native peoples of Canada by the government

resolution formal expression of opinion

ritual formal acts or series of acts performed according to a set of rules, often having to do with religion

sweathouse hut heated with steam

tipi portable, tentlike dwelling made with wooden poles and animal skins

toboggan long, flat sled with a curved front end

tribe group of American Indians who share a culture

tumpline headband used to support a load and make it easier to carry

tundra frozen plain in the Arctic regions

tunic long shirt made out of animal skins

vision quest ritual that marks the beginning of adulthood for some American Indian boys

voyageur French-Canadian fur trader

Find Out More

Books

Doherty, Craig A., and Katherine M. Doherty. *Subarctic Peoples*. New York: Chelsea House, 2010.

Howse, Jennifer. *Métis*. Calgary, Canada: Weigl, 2010.

King, David C. *First People: An Illustrated History of American Indians*. New York: Dorling Kindersley, 2008.

Murdoch, David H. *North American Indian*. New York: Dorling Kindersley, 2005.

Websites

Alaska History and Cultural Studies
www.akhistorycourse.org
This website includes information on Native Alaskans.

Innu Nation
www.innu.ca
Visit the website of the Innu nation.

Virtual Museum of Canada
www.museevirtuel-virtualmuseum.ca
This website includes the early history of Subarctic peoples.

Virtual Museum of Métis History and Culture
www.metismuseum.ca
Visit this website to learn more about the Métis people.

DVDs

Native Art of Canada. Vancouver: Daval, 2008.

Ontario, Canada's Far North—Moose Factory First Nation People. Directed by Tom Geagan. Marina del Rey, Calif.: Travelscope, 2010.

Visions from the Wilderness: The Art of Paul Kane. Directed by John Bessai. Toronto: Cinefocus, 2006.

Places to visit

Alaska Native Heritage Center
Heritage Center Dr.
Anchorage, AK
www.alaskanative.net

Canadian Museum of Civilization
Gatineau, Quebec, Canada
www.civilization.ca/cmc/home/cmc-home

National Museum of the American Indian
Fourth Street and Independence Avenue, SW
Washington, D.C.
www.nmai.si.edu

Further research

What parts of the Subarctic lifestyle did you find the most interesting? How does life for native peoples in the boreal forest compare to the way native peoples live today in other regions? How did the peoples who first lived in your area contribute to life today? To learn more about the Subarctic or other culture areas, visit one of the suggested places on these pages or head to your local library for more information.

Index

Issues for
Debate in American
Public Policy,
13th Edition

Issues for
Debate in American
Public Policy,

**THIRTEENTH
EDITION**

Los Angeles | London | New Delhi
Singapore | Washington DC

SELECTIONS FROM **CQ RESEARCHER**

Los Angeles | London | New Delhi
Singapore | Washington DC

FOR INFORMATION:

CQ Press
An Imprint of SAGE Publications, Inc.
2455 Teller Road
Thousand Oaks, California 91320
E-mail: order@sagepub.com

SAGE Publications Ltd.
1 Oliver's Yard
55 City Road
London EC1Y 1SP
United Kingdom

SAGE Publications India Pvt. Ltd.
B 1/I 1 Mohan Cooperative Industrial Area
Mathura Road, New Delhi 110 044
India

SAGE Publications Asia-Pacific Pte. Ltd.
3 Church Street
#10-04 Samsung Hub
Singapore 049483

Acquisitions Editor: Charisse Kiino
Associate Editor: Nancy Loh
Production Editor: Brittany Bauhaus
Typesetter: C&M Digitals (P) Ltd.
Cover Designer: Judy Meyers
Marketing Manager: Jonathan Mason
Permissions Editor: Adele Hutchinson

Printed in the United States of America

Library of Congress Control Number: 2012938703

This book is printed on acid-free paper.

SFI Certified Sourcing
www.sfiprogram.org
SFI-00453

12 13 14 15 16 10 9 8 7 6 5 4 3 2 1

Contents

EDUCATION

SOCIAL WELFARE

HEALTHCARE

Annotated Contents

FOREIGN AFFAIRS AND NATIONAL SECURITY POLICY

Rising Tension Over Iran

Successive U.S. presidents have insisted that a nuclear-armed Iran is "unacceptable." Iran's Islamic leadership insists that its nuclear program is for peaceful purposes only, but even as U.N. inspectors headed to Tehran in late January 2012, the body of evidence from earlier inspections raised nagging questions that the Iranians have failed to answer, such as why facilities for a peaceful program would be buried hundreds of feet underground. A nuclear Iran would alter the strategic balance in the tense Middle East and, some say, possibly trigger a regional atomic arms race. Although the United States and Europe have imposed tough economic sanctions on Iran, the Iranians have not stopped enriching uranium or begun operating their nuclear program with more transparency. But with Israel reportedly considering a pre-emptive strike on nuclear facilities in Iran—which has vowed to destroy Israel—the question of the sanctions' effectiveness may be moot.

Foreign Aid and National Security

The Sept. 11, 2001, attacks and subsequent wars in Iraq and Afghanistan prompted U.S. leaders to increase U.S. aid in the belief that improved global stability ultimately undergirds U.S. security. Secretary of State Hillary Clinton is among those calling for elevating international development assistance and diplomacy to the same status as defense. But budget debates on Capitol Hill could block aid-reform efforts. The Republican-led House calls for drastically reducing international affairs funding, but the Democratic-led Senate and the Obama administration are resisting. Complicating the arguments are questions about the efficiency of America's aid bureaucracy and, ultimately, the effectiveness of the aid itself. While aid supporters point to improved accountability, it's unclear whether future aid requests can withstand the pressure of budget cutters.

ENVIRONMENT, SCIENCE, AND TECHNOLOGY

Fracking Controversy

Environmental groups and the Obama administration have long promoted natural gas as a domestic energy source that is cleaner and cheaper than oil and offers a way for the United States to break its dependence on foreign energy suppliers. But a drilling method being used to unlock gas deposits deep inside the Earth has led to widespread protests. Hydraulic fracturing, or "fracking," involves injecting massive amounts of water, chemicals, sand and other material under high pressure into shale formations to break the rock and release the gas trapped inside. Critics say fracking fouls drinking water, pollutes the atmosphere with toxic methane gas and turns rural communities into ugly industrial zones. Energy executives say, however, that the technique is safe and efficient and is creating thousands of jobs. In Congress, lawmakers have introduced bills to tighten environmental regulation of fracking, and some states have banned the procedure while they study its impact.

Water Crisis in the West

Across the West, water is becoming an endangered resource as a warming climate adds new stress to an already strained supply. Drought is devastating Texas; flows of the Colorado River—vital to a seven-state region—have become more uncertain; and important underground aquifers are being depleted in several states. As concern about shortages grows, conflicts among housing developers, farmers and environmentalists are increasing. Agriculture is in the spotlight because it accounts for about 80 percent of Western water consumption. Farmers say they're far more careful about conservation than many suburban residents, with their swimming pools and thirsty lawns. Water conflicts go

back a long way in the nation's most arid region. But a growing number of Western water-policy experts say cooperation, compromise and conservation offer the only practical approaches to cope with rising demands on the region's water supply.

Space Program

More than 40 years after astronauts first walked on the moon, the U.S. space program is in search of direction. With the end of the space shuttle program in 2011, the United States must rely on Russian *Soyuz* rockets to send Americans into space. Private contractors are building spacecraft to ferry astronauts to the International Space Station and beyond, but those won't be ready for years. Meanwhile, budget cutters have pared NASA spending, and President Obama has angered some space enthusiasts by proposing to shift funds from two international Mars missions to a new telescope slated to replace the aging Hubble observatory. Mars remains a tantalizing destination, and a sophisticated rover is scheduled to land there in August 2012 to search for signs of life. But a human landing may be decades away. Obama has rejected returning to the moon as a stepping stone to Mars, preferring to send astronauts to an asteroid.

BUSINESS AND THE ECONOMY

Financial Misconduct

The United States is slowly coming out of the worst financial crisis since the Great Depression, but many Americans want tougher law enforcement against the companies and executives they say created the mess. Four years after the crisis began in 2008, no prominent financial executives have been prosecuted. Civil charges were brought against major banks for misleading investors by packaging subprime mortgages with insufficient disclosure, but a federal judge recently rejected a proposed settlement as too lenient. Meanwhile, major mortgage lenders are negotiating a potential multibillion-dollar settlement over allegations of improper home foreclosures. Some states, however, are balking at banks' request for protection from subsequent lawsuits. Many experts say the government has failed to devote adequate resources to prosecuting wrongdoers. But some also acknowledge that certain activities that triggered the crisis were not necessarily illegal.

Reviving Manufacturing

The United States is losing its place as the global leader in high-tech innovation and manufacturing, say many business and Obama administration officials. They point to a steady decline in manufacturing's share of the U.S. economy—and the corresponding erosion of a key source of well-paying jobs. Most worrisome, they say, is the outsourcing of key high-tech products, including certain semiconductors, screens for some electronic reading devices and batteries for portable electronics. Defenders of globalized manufacturing argue that U.S.-based inventors and engineers devised most of those outsourced products and that high-end manufacturing will survive in the United States even if more factories are built abroad. Yet, both advocates and critics of globalization agree that young Americans aren't getting the training needed to keep the United States competitive in the high-tech arena.

Attracting Jobs

Tax-supported subsidies aimed at luring companies to relocate or retain offices and factories in specific locations have proliferated. Local and state governments, engaged in fierce competition for jobs, are giving businesses up to $70 billion annually in tax breaks, new roads and training facilities and other incentives. Economic-development officials and companies that have relocated for subsidies say the incentives have spurred employment growth and helped some businesses stay profitable. But critics, who include many economists, argue that the incentives generate relatively few new jobs and instead lead many companies merely to shift operations from one place to another, depending on where they can broker the best deal. Among the most controversial subsidies are those supporting professional-sports stadiums. Supporters say new sports facilities help cities raise their profile and attract growth, while critics charge the subsidies fail to pay for themselves.

EDUCATION

Digital Education

Digital technology is becoming increasingly commonplace in K-12 education, and many researchers argue that it will save money and transform schools into more effective institutions. But other experts contend that the evidence so far is slim on exactly what computers can accomplish in the classroom. The dominance of standardized testing means digital technologies must raise students' test scores to levels administrators and policymakers deem significant. But computer-based learning may not be well suited for that task, and further efforts to computerize education may require schools to shift away from standardized testing, experts say. Until now, most successful computer-learning initiatives have required specialized training for teachers. But experts say developing technology that will be easy for nonspecialists to use remains a challenge. Meanwhile, despite the debate over the effectiveness of computerized education, all-online K-12 schools are proliferating nationwide, and enrollment in online courses is soaring.

Student Debt

As Congress tries to reduce the federal debt, it is forcing federal loan and grant programs for higher education to fight for scarce dollars. In negotiations over the debt ceiling in the summer of 2011, lawmakers shifted money from loan programs for students who borrow for graduate and professional school and students who pay back loans on time to Pell Grants for low-income students. The government has implemented several new programs to make the loan system fairer, including making payments easier for lower-wage earners and providing federal loans directly to borrowers rather than through banks, to avoid subsidizing commercial institutions. However, some consumer advocates say unless education debt can be forgiven through bankruptcy proceedings, as most other debt can, the system will never be fair to student borrowers. Meanwhile, tuition continues to rise, and total higher-education debt has surpassed credit-card debt for the first time, rising to $830 billion in mid-2010 and continuing to climb.

Youth Volunteerism

After Hurricane Katrina hit New Orleans in 2005, Tulane University made volunteering for community projects in the ravaged city, such as restoring parks or tutoring grade-school students, a requirement for graduation. Since then, applications to Tulane have shot up. Schools and colleges nationwide have increased volunteer opportunities for students, and nearly 90 percent of colleges offer service-learning programs that tie class work with volunteer activities. Researchers see ample evidence that at least some service programs encourage students to participate in civic life as they grow older. Experts worry, however, that volunteer opportunities are far more prevalent for middle-class and affluent students than for those from low-income families. Meanwhile, many school districts continue to mull whether to require volunteer service for high school graduation. Courts have upheld the constitutionality of such requirements, but some students and parents resist them.

SOCIAL WELFARE
Occupy Movement

Demonstrators protesting income inequality and corporate greed have taken over parks and other public places across the country in the wake of the Occupy Wall Street protest launched in September 2011 near New York City's Financial District. Police have shut down many camps following mass arrests, occasional violence and heavy-handed police tactics, including in New York and Oakland, Calif. Still, while top Republicans have condemned the protesters as divisive and dangerous, some Democratic politicians have voiced sympathy for their message. The movement's main claim—that the U.S. political and economic system benefits the richest 1 percent to the detriment of the other 99 percent—has put the issue of economic fairness front and center in the presidential race. But the Occupy movement faces a long, cold winter and a pair of daunting challenges: defining its long-term goals and forming a leadership structure that can chart a sustainable course for the protest effort.

Child Poverty

One in five American children lives in a household with income below the poverty line—$22,050 for a family of four. Not only are the daily lives of poor children difficult, but experts worry that many will suffer lifelong effects from early deprivation. Concern about child poverty has grown especially strong amid a push in Congress for sweeping budget cuts, including reductions in spending on food stamps and other anti-poverty programs. As child poverty continues to rise amid the nation's persistent

economic woes and high unemployment, a long-simmering debate over the problem's root causes is heating up. Liberals argue that fewer children would fall into poverty if the government safety net were stronger and more jobs were available for struggling parents. Conservatives, on the other hand, say child poverty largely stems from parental behavior—particularly a growing tendency to have children out of wedlock.

Immigration Conflict

Americans are very concerned about illegal immigration but ambivalent about what to do about it—especially the 11 million aliens currently in the United States illegally. Frustrated with the federal government's failure to secure the borders, several states passed laws allowing state and local police to check the immigration status of suspected unlawful aliens. Civil rights organizations warn the laws will result in ethnic profiling of Latinos. The Obama administration is suing to block several of the laws for infringing on federal prerogatives. Advocates of tougher enforcement say undocumented workers are taking jobs from U.S. citizens, but many business and agricultural groups say migrant workers are needed to fill jobs unattractive to U.S. workers. In 2010, the U.S. Supreme Court upheld an Arizona law providing stiff penalties for employers that knowingly hire illegal aliens. Now, the justices are preparing to hear arguments on the controversial, new Arizona law that inspired other states to crack down on illegal immigration.

HEALTHCARE
Preventing Disease

The U.S. health care system faces spiraling costs from chronic, or noncommunicable, illnesses such as diabetes, heart disease and preventable cancers. But public health experts are discovering that just pushing people to change bad habits isn't working. Instead, they are placing more focus on "making the healthy choice the easy choice" through such efforts as reformulating processed foods and making streets safe for walkers and bikers. Some in Congress and the Obama administration made a big push for community-based disease prevention approaches, but concerns over the budget deficit could result in major cuts to the Prevention and

Public Health Fund enacted as part of the 2010 health reform act. However, some say the government is over-reaching in its war on obesity, and studies show that some prevention efforts add to health care costs. The fight against preventable disease is not a U.S. problem alone. In poor countries, the biggest threats are the same ones afflicting Americans: lack of exercise, smoking and unhealthy diets.

Aging Population

The oldest of the 78 million Americans born during the post-World War II baby boom generation turned 65 in 2011, while the share of the population older than 85 is growing even faster. The flood of elderly Americans is putting severe financial stress on programs that benefit older citizens. The number of people covered under Medicare will increase by more than 30 million over the next 20 years. So far, congressional proposals for constraining Medicare spending have encountered stiff resistance. But economists say the country's deficits will become unmanageable if entitlement programs aren't scaled back. The United States is not aging as rapidly as other developed countries and will continue to have a growing population of working-age people. But as longevity and spending on health care increase, many seniors will outlive their retirement savings.

Preface

Should Congress expand welfare funding? Can technology replace classroom teachers? Should states crack down on unlawful aliens? These questions—and many more—are at the heart of American public policy. How can instructors best engage students with these crucial issues? We feel that students need objective, yet provocative examinations of these issues to understand how they affect citizens today and will for years to come. This annual collection aims to promote in-depth discussion, facilitate further research and help readers formulate their own positions on crucial issues. Get your students talking both inside and outside the classroom about *Issues for Debate in American Public Policy.*

This thirteenth edition includes sixteen up-to-date reports by *CQ Researcher,* an award-winning weekly policy brief that brings complicated issues down to earth. Each report chronicles and analyzes executive, legislative, and judicial activities at all levels of government. This collection is divided into six diverse policy areas: foreign affairs and national security policy; environment, science, and technology; business and the economy; education; social welfare; and healthcare—to cover a range of issues found in most American government and public policy courses.

CQ RESEARCHER

CQ Researcher was founded in 1923 as *Editorial Research Reports* and was sold primarily to newspapers as a research tool. The magazine was renamed and redesigned in 1991 as *CQ Researcher.* Today, students are its primary audience. While still used by hundreds of journalists and newspapers, many of which reprint portions of the reports, the *Researcher's* main subscribers are now high school, college and public libraries. In 2002, *Researcher* won the American Bar Association's coveted Silver Gavel award for magazine excellence for a series of nine reports on civil liberties and other legal issues.

Researcher staff writers—all highly experienced journalists—sometimes compare the experience of writing a Researcher report to drafting a college term paper. Indeed, there are many similarities. Each report is as long as many term papers—about 11,000 words—and is written by one person without any significant outside help. One of the key differences is that writers interview leading experts, scholars and government officials for each issue.

Like students, staff writers begin the creative process by choosing a topic. Working with the *Researcher's* editors, the writer identifies a controversial subject that has important public policy implications. After a topic is selected, the writer embarks on one to two weeks of intense research. Newspaper and magazine articles are clipped or downloaded, books are ordered and information is gathered from a wide variety of sources, including interest groups, universities and the government. Once the writers are well informed, they develop a detailed outline, and begin the interview process. Each report requires a minimum of ten to fifteen interviews with academics, officials, lobbyists and people working in the field. Only after all interviews are completed does the writing begin.

CHAPTER FORMAT

Each issue of *CQ Researcher,* and therefore each selection in this book, is structured in the same way. Each begins with an overview, which briefly summarizes the areas that will be explored in greater detail in the rest of the chapter. The next section chronicles important and current debates on the topic under discussion and is structured around a number of key questions, such as "Is foreign aid necessary for national security?" and "Are students incurring too much education debt?" These questions are usually the subject of much debate among practitioners and scholars in the field. Hence, the answers presented are never conclusive but detail the range of opinion on the topic.

Next, the "Background" section provides a history of the issue being examined. This retrospective covers important legislative measures, executive actions and court decisions that illustrate how current policy has evolved. Then

the "Current Situation" section examines contemporary policy issues, legislation under consideration and legal action being taken. Each selection concludes with an "Outlook" section, which addresses possible regulation, court rulings, and initiatives from Capitol Hill and the White House over the next five to ten years.

Each report contains features that augment the main text: two to three sidebars that examine issues related to the topic at hand, a pro versus con debate between two experts, a chronology of key dates and events and an annotated bibliography detailing major sources used by the writer.

CUSTOM OPTIONS

Interested in building your ideal CQ Press Issues book, customized to your personal teaching needs and interests? Browse by course or date, or search for specific topics or issues from our online catalog of over 150 *CQ Researcher* issues at http://custom.cqpress.com.

ACKNOWLEDGMENTS

We wish to thank many people for helping to make this collection a reality. Thomas J. Billitteri, managing editor of *CQ Researcher,* gave us his enthusiastic support and cooperation as we developed this thirteenth edition. He and his talented staff of editors and writers have amassed a first-class library of *Researcher* reports, and we are fortunate to have access to that rich cache. We also thankfully acknowledge the advice and feedback from current readers and are gratified by their satisfaction with the book.

Some readers may be learning about *CQ Researcher* for the first time. We expect that many readers will want regular access to this excellent weekly research tool. For subscription information or a no-obligation free trial of *Researcher,* please contact CQ Press at www.cqpress.com or toll-free at 1–866–4CQ-PRESS (1–866–427–7737). We hope that you will be pleased by the thirteenth edition of *Issues for Debate in American Public Policy.* We welcome your feedback and suggestions for future editions. Please direct comments to Charisse Kiino, Publisher, College Publishing Group, CQ Press, 2300 N Street, NW, Suite 800, Washington, D.C. 20037, or *ckiino@cqpress.com.*

—The Editors of CQ Press

Contributors

Nellie Bristol is a veteran Capitol Hill reporter who has covered health policy in Washington for more than 20 years. She now writes for *The Lancet, Health Affairs* and *Global Health* magazine. She recently earned a master's degree in public health/global health from The George Washington University, where she earned an undergraduate degree in American studies.

Marcia Clemmitt is a veteran social-policy reporter who previously served as editor in chief of *Medicine & Health* and staff writer for *The Scientist.* She has also been a high school math and physics teacher. She holds a liberal arts and sciences degree from St. John's College, Annapolis, and a master's degree in English from Georgetown University. Her recent reports include "Income Inequality" and "Financial Industry Overhaul."

John Felton has been a journalist for more than 40 years, specializing primarily in international affairs. After covering education and politics for newspapers in Ohio and Delaware, he covered foreign policy for Congressional Quarterly, then was a foreign editor at National Public Radio. He is now a freelance writer and editor, living in the Berkshires of Western Massachusetts.

Roland Flamini is a Washington-based correspondent who specializes in foreign affairs. Fluent in six languages, he was *Time* bureau chief in Rome, Bonn, Beirut, Jerusalem and the European Common Market and later served as international editor at United Press International. While covering the 1979 Iranian Revolution for

Time, Flamini wrote the magazine's cover story—in which Ayatollah Ruhollah Khomeini was named Man of the Year—and was promptly expelled because authorities didn't like what they read. His books include a study of Vatican politics in the 1960s, *Pope, Premier, President.* His most recent report for *CQ Global Researcher* was "Turmoil in the Arab World."

Alan Greenblatt covers foreign affairs for National Public Radio. He was previously a staff writer at *Governing* magazine and *CQ Weekly,* where he won the National Press Club's Sandy Hume Award for political journalism. He graduated from San Francisco State University in 1986 and received a master's degree in English literature from the University of Virginia in 1988. For the *CQ Researcher,* his reports include "Confronting Warming," "Future of the GOP" and "Immigration Debate." His most recent *CQ Global Researcher* reports were "Attacking Piracy" and "Rewriting History."

Kenneth Jost graduated from Harvard College and Georgetown University Law Center. He is the author of the *Supreme Court Yearbook* and editor of *The Supreme Court from A to Z* (both *CQ Press*). He was a member of

the *CQ Researcher* team that won the American Bar Association's 2002 Silver Gavel Award. His previous reports include "States and Federalism" and "Bilingual Education vs. English Immersion." He is also author of the blog *Jost on Justice* (http://jostonjustice.blogspot.com).

Peter Katel is a *CQ Researcher* staff writer who previously reported on Haiti and Latin America for *Time* and *Newsweek* and covered the Southwest for newspapers in New Mexico. He has received several journalism awards, including the Bartolomé Mitre Award for coverage of drug trafficking, from the Inter-American Press Association. He holds an A.B. in university studies from the University of New Mexico. His recent reports include "Child Poverty" and "Reviving Manufacturing."

Daniel McGlynn is a California-based independent journalist who covers science and the environment. His work has appeared in *The New York Times Magazine, Earth Island Journal, Bay Citizen,* and other publications. He has a master's degree in journalism from the University of California, Berkeley. His last report for *CQ Researcher* was "Mine Safety."

Issues for Debate in American Public Policy, 13th Edition

1

Rising Tension Over Iran

Roland Flamini

Two Iranian protesters try to pry a British coat of arms from the wall surrounding the British Embassy in Tehran, as rioters stormed the facility on Nov. 29, 2011. The assault recalled the 1979 attack and hostage-taking at the American Embassy in the same city. The November mob was protesting Britain's agreement to support beefed-up Western sanctions on Iran over its disputed nuclear program.

AP Photo/Vahid Salemi

From *CQ Researcher*,
Feb. 7, 2012

When angry students, upset that London had cut off financial ties with Iran, attacked the British embassy in Tehran last November, Amb. Dominick Chilcott could only stand by, holding his quivering dog Pumpkin as attackers rampaged through offices and grounds. The marauders smashed furniture and portraits of Queen Elizabeth II, tore up documents and torched parked cars. Iranian riot police also watched, making no move to halt the destruction.[1]

An outraged British government withdrew its diplomats and closed the embassy in protest.[2]

Inevitably, the assault revived memories of the 1979 U.S. hostage crisis, when hard-line supporters of Iran's new Islamic Revolution stormed the American Embassy and took 52 staffers and Marine guards captive for more than a year. Since then the United States has had no diplomatic relations with the regime — a theocracy ruled by conservative Shiite clerics, surrounded by mostly Sunni Arab neighbors.

The striking similarities between the two embassy attacks reflect Iran's reputation for irrational behavior, fanaticism and disdain for the rules of international conduct — all of which helps explain why the possibility that Iran may be building nuclear weapons has caused consternation in the international community.

In November the U.N.'s nuclear monitoring organization said Iran probably has a nuclear weapons program. Iran has carried out activities "relevant to the development of a nuclear explosive device," the International Atomic Energy Agency (IAEA) said. "These activities took place under a structured programme" before 2003 and "may still be ongoing."[3]

Tensions Rise in Volatile Gulf Region

The wars in Iraq and Afghanistan have garnered most of the world's attention in the past decade. But with the fighting in those countries winding down, the spotlight is turning to their neighbor — Alaska-size Iran. The Western powers worry that Iran is developing weapons at its numerous nuclear facilities, some buried deep underground, which Iran says are strictly for peaceful purposes. In an effort to force Iran to halt its nuclear program, the European Union on Jan. 23 voted to join with the United States in embargoing Iranian oil exports. Iran responded by threatening to close the crucial Strait of Hormuz, located in the Persian Gulf on Iran's southern border, through which nearly 40 percent of the world's seaborne oil is shipped.

Types of Nuclear Facilities in Iran

Source: map by Lewis Agrell

The West has long suspected that Tehran's ruling ayatollahs were trying to develop nuclear bombs. Now, the IAEA report "destroys Iran's pretention that its nuclear activities have been purely peaceful," says Mark Fitzpatrick, director of the Nonproliferation and Disarmament Program at London's International Institute of Strategic Studies (IISS). Now that suspicion "has the imprimatur of the IAEA."

If Iran develops a nuclear weapon, it would violate the U.N. Nuclear Nonproliferation Treaty (NPT), which Tehran signed in 1968, and change the strategic equation in the Middle East, an unstable region on which the industrialized world depends for its oil lifeline. "This is not a question of [Middle Eastern] security," declared German Foreign Minister Guido Westerwelle recently. "It is a question of the whole world."[4]

Israel, the Middle East's sole nuclear power, strongly opposes Iran joining the nuclear club, given Tehran's open hostility to the Jewish state. Indeed, Israel sees a nuclear-armed Iran as an existential threat. On Feb. 3, Iran's Supreme Leader Ayatollah Ali Khamenei denounced tightening oil sanctions and renewed Israeli threats of an attack on his nation's nuclear facilities by vowing to retaliate in a way that "would be 10 times worse for the interests of the United States" than for Iran. In an unusually blunt warning, Khamenei said Iran would support militant opponents of Israel. His speech came one day after Israel's leaders delivered their own blunt warning that they might pre-emptively strike Iran's nuclear enrichment sites, possibly as soon as this spring. Israel has long contended that if the West waits to see if sanctions work, Iran will have time to bury key nuclear facilities deep inside mountain bunkers, making them inaccessible to even the most powerful bombs.[5]

Iran at a Glance

The Islamic Republic of Iran is the size of Alaska but with a population that is three times that of Texas. It has a predominantly Persian population and a Shiite theocracy, surrounded by mostly Sunni-dominated countries with Arab populations. Iran's per capita income is on a par with South Africa's.

Quick Facts About Iran

Area: 636,371 sq. miles (about the size of Alaska)

Population: 77,891,220* (about the same as Turkey, or three times the population of Texas)

Chief of state: Supreme Leader Sayyid Ali Khamenei (since June 1989)

Head of government: President Mahmoud Ahmadinejad (since August 2005)

Government type: Theocratic republic; Supreme Leader appointed for life by the Assembly of Experts; president elected by popular vote for up to two four-year terms; legislative members elected by popular vote for four-year terms

Ethnic groups: Persian 61%, Azeri 16%, Kurd 10%, Lur 6%, Baloch 2%, Arab 2%, Turkmen and Turkic tribes 2%, other 1% (2008 est.)

Religion: Muslim (official religion) 98% (Shiite 89%, Sunni 9%), other (includes Zoroastrian, Jewish, Christian and Baha'i) 2%

Infant mortality rate: 42.26 deaths/1,000 live births (60th in the world)

GDP: $818.7 billion**

GDP per capita: $10,600** (about the same as South Africa)

Unemployment rate: 13.2%**

Industries: petroleum, petrochemicals, fertilizers, caustic soda, textiles, cement and other construction materials, food processing, metal fabrication, armaments

July 2011 estimate

** *2010 estimate*

Source: The World Factbook, Central Intelligence Agency, 2012, https://www.cia.gov/library/publications/the-world-factbook/geos/ir.html.

Moreover, the United States apparently hasn't ruled out a strike of its own. Concerned for the stability of the region and pressured by Israel and its supporters in Congress, two successive U.S. presidents have repeatedly said a nuclear Iran was "unacceptable" and that — as President Obama warned during his Jan. 24 State of the Union address —"no options" are off the table.

And in a U.S. presidential election year, talk of military action and war with Iran provides sound-bite ammunition for the various candidates. Republican Mitt Romney vowed, if elected, to "do everything in my power to assure that Iran doesn't become a nuclear nation [and] threaten Israel, threaten us and threaten the entire world."[6]

Going nuclear would boost Iran's ambition to be a major international player. Some argue that it also would

Iranian Women Lost Rights Under the Mullahs

One Million Signatures Campaign seeks major changes.

During the Arab Spring uprisings last year, Iranian women's groups circulated a cautionary video, "Message from Iranian Women for Tunisian and Egyptian Women." The film depicted how Iranian women's lives changed dramatically after the Islamic Revolution of 1979 and warned Tunisian and Egyptian women that the same thing could happen to them if the religious party, the Muslim Brotherhood, gained majorities in their countries.[1]

During the reign of Shah Reza Pahlavi, Iranian women had made progress in the traditionally male-oriented region. They wore whatever they wanted in public and have been allowed to vote since 1963.

Under the ayatollahs, however, the *hijab* — the headscarf worn by Muslim women — immediately became mandatory, and Islamic law was introduced and strictly enforced.[2] For example, the minimum age of marriage for women was changed from 18 to nine — although it has since been raised to 13 after protests by activists.

Polygamy has increased, as has the so-called temporary marriage (*mut'a*), a verbal, short-term relationship for a predetermined period, with no divorce necessary to end it. Permitted under Shiite Muslim law, the *mut'a* is seen by many as prostitution under another name, because a dowry is one of its prerequisites.*[3]

The changes helped to spark the One Million Signatures Campaign, a grass-roots Iranian feminist effort to convince Iran's parliament to change marriage, divorce, custody and inheritance laws that discriminate against women.

The movement also wants to improve the legal position of women who are sex-crime victims. A married Iranian woman who is raped is considered to have committed adultery and can be stoned to death. If she kills her aggressor, she can be tried for murder. If she is unmarried, she could end up being killed by a male family member to avoid bringing shame on the family name. Such so-called honor killings are more a patriarchal custom than a practice condoned by the Quran.[4]

But that's not the full picture, according to Sussan Tahmasebi, an American-born Iranian who helped launch the campaign. "We have female doctors, we have politicians, MPs (members of parliament)," she said. "It's paradoxical that, despite these achievements, discrimination against women is embedded in the legal system, and that lawmakers justify it by saying it's based on religion."[5]

However, CNN broadcaster and columnist Fareed Zakaria says Iranian women fare better than women in Saudi Arabia. He was struck while on a recent visit, he writes, "by how defiantly [Iranian] women try to lead normal and productive lives. They wear the headscarves and adhere to the rules about covering their bodies, but do so in a very stylish way. They continue to go to college in large numbers, to graduate school and to work."[6]

Iranian women can vote, he added, while women in Saudi Arabia —"another country . . . run along strict Islamic lines" — cannot. And in Saudi Arabia, he noted, women "are not well integrated into the workforce or mainstream life."[7]

Even so, Iranian women face a litany of constraints. A daughter still needs her father's permission to marry; a wife must obtain her husband's written permission to travel abroad or get a passport. An Iranian woman can't sing in public or attend sports events where men are present.

In 1979, thousands of women protested in the streets against the shah — only to be repressed by Ayatollah Ruhollah Khomeini as soon as he assumed power. In 2009, women were a strong presence in the "Green" protests against the disputed re-election of President Mahmoud Ahmadinejad. Neda Agha Soltan, a 26-year-old music student, was shot dead in a Tehran street during the demonstrations. The bloody video of her death went viral on the

---

* Depending on the culture, a dowry is the money or property that a bride's family pays to the groom's family or that a groom pays to a bride.

enable Iran to wreak havoc, by, for instance, giving a portable nuclear device to one of its proxies, such as the Lebanese Shiite fundamentalist movement Hezbollah or the radical Palestinian Sunni party, Hamas, which controls the Gaza Strip — both listed as terrorist organizations by Washington.

Neighboring Arabs aren't crazy about the idea of the region's two non-Arab countries having the only nuclear weapons in the Middle East. If Iran gets the bomb, warned Prince Turki Al-Faisal Al Saud, former head of Saudi Arabian intelligence, it would "unleash a cascade of [nuclear] proliferation that would significantly destabilize the region."[7]

Internet, making her what *The New York Times* called "the public face" of those who died in the protests.[8]

In 2002, the European Union lobbied to help persuade the Iranian courts to declare a moratorium on death by stoning, of either gender. The moratorium was extended in 2008 — although according to reports, four men and one woman were executed by stoning, a method usually reserved for convicted adulterers. In 2008, a spokesman for the judiciary confirmed that two of the men had been stoned, saying that the moratorium had no legal weight, and judges could ignore it. However, draft legislation to abolish death by stoning is being considered.[9]

The United Nations also has pressured Iran to reform its discriminatory laws, most of which violate the U.N.'s 1979 Convention of the Elimination of All Forms of Discrimination Against Women, which the mullahs say undermines Islamic teaching.[10]

The regime is particularly vigilant with regard to cultural activities. In 2011, the Iranian actress Marzieh Vafamehr was sentenced to a year in jail and 90 lashes for her role in the film "My Tehran for Sale," an internationally acclaimed underground movie about life in Tehran. She was never lashed, however, and was released after serving three months.[11]

It was a case of life imitating art. Vafamehr played a young theater actress trying to pursue her career against the backdrop of Iran's repressive regime. But the film's director, the Australian-Iranian poet Granaz Moussavi, says the movie, which was filmed in Iran, actually had the regime's approval.

"Nobody can deny that we are working with restrictions when it comes to writing and film making," she says. "But in Iran, and especially in Tehran, everything can be risky, even crossing the road."

— *Roland Flamini*

Female supporters of Mir Hossein Mousavi, Iran's reformist candidate in the 2009 presidential election, show off their fingers and nails — painted green, the color of Mousavi's campaign — during a Tehran rally on June 9, 2009. Iranian women, who have been able to vote since before the 1979 Islamic Revolution, played a big part in the so-called Green Movement — anti-government demonstrations that challenged Mousavi's defeat by President Mahmoud Ahmadinejad. The movement was brutally suppressed by the government.

AFP/Getty Images/Atta Kenare

[1]Dina Sadek, "Women in Egypt Heed Warning From Iranian Women on Rights," Global Press Institute, Jan. 10, 2012, www.globalpressinstitute.org/global-news/africa/egypt/women-egypt-heed-warning-iranian-women-rights.

[2]For background, see Sarah Glazer, "Sharia Controversy," *CQ Global Researcher*, Jan. 3, 2012, pp. 1-28.

[3]Donna M. Hughes, "Women in Iran: A look at President Khatami's first year in office," *Z Magazine*, October 1998, www.uri.edu/artsci/wms/hughes/khatami.htm.

[4]For background, see Robert Kiener, "Honor Killings," *CQ Global Researcher*, April 19, 2011, pp. 183-208.

[5]"Fighting for Women's Rights," Human Rights Watch, Oct. 11, 2011, www.hrw.org/news/2011/10/31/fighting-women-s-rights-iran.

[6]Fareed Zakaria, "Zakaria: Comparing the status of women in Iran and Saudi Arabia," CNN.com, Dec. 27, 2011, http://globalpublicsquare.blogs.cnn.com/2011/10/27/zakaria-comparing-the-status-of-women-in-iran-and-saudi-arabia%E2%80%A8/.

[7]*Ibid.*

[8]Nazla Fathi, "In a death seen around the world, a symbol of Iranian protests," *The New York Times*, June 22, 2009, www.nytimes.com/2009/06/23/world/middleeast/23neda.html.

[9]"Chaknews" (Iranian human rights blog), undated, www.chaknews.com/English/print.php?type=N&item_id=365.

[10]Christina Hoff Sommers, "Feminism by Treaty," American Enterprise Institute, June 1, 2011, www.aei.org/article/society-and-culture/race-and-gender/feminism-by-treaty/.

[11]"Concerns Iran film star Marzieh Vafamehr 'to be lashed,' " BBC News, Nov. 11, 2011, www.bbc.co.uk/news/world-asia-pacific-15262071.

But while the Sunni Saudis would certainly want to match the nuclear capability of their Shiite regional rival, most experts believe an arms race would be unlikely. "No countries went nuclear after Israel went nuclear, so why would they want to now?" asks Iran specialist Vali Nasr, a professor of international politics

at the Fletcher School of Law and Diplomacy at Tufts University in Medford, Mass.

Defense Secretary Leon Panetta said recently that a nuclear Iran was a "red line" for the United States and for Israel. But he seems to differentiate between being *capable* of making nuclear weapons and actually *making*

Most Iranian Oil Ends Up in Asia

Nearly two-thirds of the 2.2 million barrels of oil exported daily by Iran goes to Asia, with one-fifth of it destined for China. Asian buyers have not signed onto new, tougher sanctions against Iranian oil purchases — imposed by the European Union on Jan. 23. For that reason, some observers doubt that the new restrictions will succeed in forcing Iran to halt its uranium enrichment program, seen as a possible precursor to the development of nuclear weapons.

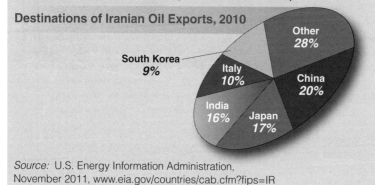

Destinations of Iranian Oil Exports, 2010

Other 28%
China 20%
Japan 17%
India 16%
Italy 10%
South Korea 9%

Source: U.S. Energy Information Administration, November 2011, www.eia.gov/countries/cab.cfm?fips=IR

them. "Are [the Iranians] trying to develop a nuclear weapon?" Panetta asked, rhetorically, on CBS's "Face the Nation" on Jan 8. "No. But we know that they're trying to develop a nuclear capability. And our red line to Iran is: Do not develop a nuclear weapon. That's a red line for us."[8]

The Iranians consistently have denied trying to do either. Last year, Iran's foreign minister, Ali Akbar Salehi, told Euronews that Supreme Leader Khamenei had decreed that holding, producing or using nuclear weapons "is against the principles of our religion." And a decree by the supreme leader, Salehi pointed out, "is both religious and governmental."[9]

Iran insists it is enriching uranium for only peaceful purposes, such as power generation. According to the IAEA, the Iranians now have enough 3 percent enriched uranium that, if further enriched to weapons-grade 90 percent strength, would allow them to make at least two nuclear bombs. Some uranium already has been converted to 20 percent strength — a higher level than is needed for civilian use. The report also warned that Iran may have other "undeclared nuclear facilities and material."[10] Iran also is moving at least one of its uranium-processing facilities to a location deep underground, an odd thing to do if the program's purpose is peaceful.

The West reacted to the report by ratcheting up long-running economic sanctions in an effort to force Iran into serious negotiation about halting its enrichment program. On Dec. 31, President Obama signed a law that "cuts off from the U.S. financial system foreign firms that do business with Iran's central bank."[11] Then on Jan. 23, the 27 members of the European Union (EU) agreed to embargo Iranian oil imports — starting in July — and froze the Iranian central bank's assets in Europe.[12]

Iran reacted by threatening to close the Strait of Hormuz, the Persian Gulf bottleneck through which up to 40 percent of the world's seaborne oil is shipped.[13] Washington said it would be forced to act to keep the vital shipping lanes open. Experts said Iran's belligerence indicated sanctions are pushing the country's economy into a nosedive.[14]

Frederick W. Kagan, a defense and security specialist at the conservative American Enterprise Institute, a Washington think tank, contends there is no question Iran wants the bomb. "The Iranian regime intends to acquire nuclear weapons," he says, "and it's bizarre that we continue to say, 'Well, maybe they don't mean it.'"

Still, others aren't so sure. David Aaron, who tracks Iran developments for the RAND Corporation think tank in Palo Alto, Calif., says, "The picture is one of a country that has technology and some physical capacity to produce nuclear weapons, but they still haven't taken the next step of stockpiling material capable of being turned into nuclear weapons. There seems to be internal disagreement in the Iranian leadership on the issue." He cites Khamenei's recent declaration that nuclear weapons are *haram*, or forbidden in Islam, and the fact that the influence of President Mahmoud Ahmadinejad, who talks the most about developing a nuclear program, "seems to be in decline."

The regime's insistence that its program is for peaceful purposes has "helped to build up support domestically for the nuclear program, and everyone is committed as a matter of national pride," says Riccardo Alcaro, a foreign policy analyst at the Italian Institute of International Affairs in Rome. "If the regime was now seen to be producing nuclear weapons, it would lose credibility with its own people. Crossing that threshold would be difficult — unless Iran were attacked. In that case Iranians would be much more understanding."

As 2011 ended, Iran's navy announced that it had successfully tested long- and short-range missiles, but they weren't able to carry nuclear payloads.[15]

"Iran is very dangerous," Israeli President Shimon Peres said, but "there's no need to get hysterical about the threat that it poses." Israel's nuclear arsenal, he implied, would deter the Iranians from bombing Israel.[16]

Experts say the international sanctions — along with the killings of at least five Iranian nuclear scientists and a 2010 cyber attack that temporarily crippled the nuclear program's computers — have delayed Iran's nuclear program. It would now take anywhere from less than two to as long as five years to produce a bomb, experts say.

As the West and Iran's neighbors fret over the nuclear threat posed by the Iranian regime, here are some of the questions being debated:

Can economic sanctions stop Iran from building a nuclear weapon?

On Jan. 23 the 27 members of the European Union, striking at what *The Guardian* newspaper called "the Islamic republic's lifeblood," agreed to embargo Iranian oil imports. The EU also froze the Iran central bank's assets in Europe and banned transactions involving gold, precious metals and diamonds. The measures amounted to "an unprecedented package of sanctions on Iran," said a joint statement issued by the British, German and French leaders.

"Until Iran comes to the table, we will be united behind strong measures to undermine the regime's ability to fund its nuclear programme," the statement said.[17]

"To avoid any military solution, which could have irreparable consequences, we have decided to go further down the path of sanctions," Alain Juppé, France's foreign minister, told reporters. "It is a good decision that sends a strong message and which I hope will persuade Iran that it must change its position, change its line and accept the dialogue that we propose."[18]

A month earlier, the United States had passed legislation making it illegal for any U.S. bank to do business with any foreign institution transacting business with Iran's central bank.

Whether the latest round of sanctions will achieve what earlier constraints have not remains to be seen. The United States first launched sanctions against Iran in 1979 and has been tightening the economic screws ever since. In 2006, in an effort to force fuller compliance with the IAEA, the U.N. Security Council adopted the first of four economic sanctions resolutions.

Iran today finds it increasingly difficult "to do business with any reputable bank internationally" or to conduct transactions in either euros or U.S. dollars, said White House national security official Tommy Vietor.[19]

Moreover, "the oil and gas sectors are not drawing anywhere near the international capital they need," wrote William C. Ramsay, energy adviser at the French Institute of Foreign Affairs (IFRI) in Paris.[20]

Yet Iran's nuclear program is well advanced, and progress — while slow at times — has never halted for very long. "Sanctions haven't failed in squeezing Iran and making it suffer, but they have failed in their objective" to halt Iran's enrichment program, says Middle East specialist Nasr of Tufts University.

That's because many countries enforce the sanctions poorly or refuse to abide by them — creating holes in the sanctions net big enough to drive an oil tanker through. For instance, despite a raft of U.S. and U.N. sanctions, EU trade with Iran in 2010, totaled $33.4 billion ($14.6 billion in European exports and $18.8 billion in imports).[21] The same year, about 60 companies in Germany — Iran's second-largest trading partner after the United Arab Emirates — registered to attend an international gas and oil refining convention in Tehran, an action that "violated international law," according to a German official. In addition, German Chancellor Angela Merkel's retired official jet, embarrassingly, was somehow sold to the sanctioned Iranian airline Mahan.[22]

Under pressure from the U.S. and Israeli governments, Berlin last year began to tighten controls on its Iran trade, according to *Der Spiegel* magazine. The Israelis provided the names of companies and individuals who "help prop up the Iranian regime," and some German exports were being used "for dubious purposes," the article said. When the Israelis showed that Daimler heavy trucks were being converted into rocket launchers, Berlin banned exports of heavy trucks.[23]

AFP/Getty Images/Atta Kenare

Demonstrators hold portraits of assassinated Iranian nuclear scientist Majid Shahriari during a protest in front of the British Embassy in downtown Tehran on Dec. 12, 2010. At least five Iranian nuclear scientists have been killed in recent years in an apparent effort to slow Iran's nuclear program. Iranians have blamed the killings on British, U.S. or Israeli intelligence services.

Taken together with Washington's latest sanctions, Europe's strong action on Jan. 23 raised the stakes dramatically, prompting Iran's sharp response. "If any disruption happens regarding the sale of Iranian oil, the Strait of Hormuz will definitely be closed," declared Mohammed Kossari, deputy head of Iran's parliamentary Foreign Affairs and National Security Commission.[24]

But even if the EU action succeeds in plugging European gaps in Iran's sanctions net, it's still riddled with Asian holes. For example, the new rules will not affect Iran's trade with China, which imported a fifth of Iran's oil exports in 2010, nor will it disrupt trade with Japan, which bought 17 percent of Iran's oil in 2010. India bought another 16 percent and South Korea, 9 percent. By comparison, Italy bought 10 percent in 2010.[25]

Indeed, skepticism is rife that the sanctions won't work. "Sanctions tend to punish citizens more than they do the regime," observes Kuwait-based Alanoud Al Sharekh, corresponding senior fellow for Middle East politics at London's International Institute of Strategic Studies.

But that's partly the point, said a senior administration official. "The question is whether people in the government feel pressure from the fact that there's public discontent," the unnamed official told *The Washington Post* recently.[26]

That isn't happening, according to Al Sharekh. "In spite of the problems, there's belief in the [Iranian] leadership and the ideology," she says.

Russia, which opposes the sanctions, called the latest EU action a mistake. "Under this kind of pressure, Iran will not agree to any kind of concessions or change in its policies," the Russian Foreign Ministry said in a statement.[27]

Would a nuclear Iran trigger an arms race in the Middle East?

Saudi Prince Turki's belief that a nuclear-armed Iran would lead to "a cascade of nuclear proliferation" in the Middle East is widely held. British Foreign Secretary William Hague said in a recent interview that an Iranian breakthrough in producing nuclear weapons "threatens the whole region with nuclear proliferation."

The U.S. National Intelligence Council expressed the same concern in its "Global Trends 2025" report. A nuclear Iran, it said, could well encourage other nations "to consider their own nuclear ambitions."[28]

Shmuel Bar, director of studies at the Institute of Policy Studies think tank in Herzliya, Israel, asked the question: Could "a polynuclear Middle East be avoided in the wake of Iran's acquisition of nuclear weapons?" The answer, he concluded, "seems to be clearly negative." Rather, he wrote, a nuclear Iran would "undoubtedly intensify the drive of other states in the region for nuclear weapons."[29]

Not so, counters Tufts University's Nasr. The threat of nuclear proliferation is "more a talking point than a reality," he says. "No Middle East countries went nuclear when Israel went nuclear. Egypt and Turkey would have no motivation to follow suit. Besides, it takes time to build up a nuclear arsenal of say 20 to 30 nuclear warheads — perhaps 10 years or more."

Some experts point out that when Communist China went nuclear in the 1950s, Beijing's neighbors were dissuaded from following suit because the United States offered to protect them from a nuclear attack. The same thing happened after North Korea developed nuclear weapons.

But that approach was less likely to work in this instance, argues Bar, because of "the decline of American stature in the region after the withdrawal from Iraq" — and Washington's apparent failure, at least so far, to keep Iran from developing nuclear weapons.

C H R O N O L O G Y

1950s-1960s *U.S. consolidates influence in Iran by helping to remove nationalist leader and installing pro-Western monarch.*

Aug. 20, 1953 After Prime Minister Mohammed Mossadegh nationalizes Iran's oil industry, he is overthrown with help of U.S. and British intelligence agencies. . . . Shah Mohammed Reza Pahlavi is put in power.

January 1963 Shah launches campaign to modernize Iran, including land and economic reform and improving conditions for women — which alienates religious clergy.

1970s-1980s *Rising discontent forces shah from office. Shiite Islamic theocracy is established. Hostage- taking at U.S. Embassy sours U.S.-Iran relations for decades. Iraq and Iran go to war.*

1978 Civil unrest against shah's dictatorial rule breaks out, inflamed by taped sermons by exiled Shiite clergyman Ayatollah Ruhollah Khomeini. Shah imposes martial law.

1979 Shah leaves Iran on Jan. 16. . . . Khomeini returns, and Islamic republic is established following referendum.

Nov. 4, 1979 Iranian militants storm U.S. Embassy in Tehran, demanding shah's return to Iran to stand trial. Fifty-two Americans are taken hostage and held for 444 days, leading to ongoing animosity.

September 1980 Iraq attacks Iran, triggering eight-year war.

Aug. 20, 1988 U.N. brokers peace in Iran-Iraq war.

1990s-2000s *Iran resumes abandoned nuclear program. West suspects Iran wants to develop nuclear weapons and imposes sanctions to pressure Iran to accept U.N. inspections. Iranian regime suppresses reform.*

Aug. 25, 1992 Iran re-starts nuclear program begun under shah's rule.

1995 U.S. imposes oil and trade embargo because of Iran's efforts to acquire nuclear arms, hostility toward Israel and alleged sponsorship of "terrorism." Iran denies the charges; says its nuclear program is for peaceful use.

Aug. 15, 2002 Iranian exiles say Iran is building two secret nuclear sites — a secret uranium-enrichment plant at Natanz and another in Arak.

Nov. 12, 2003 Iran agrees to suspend uranium enrichment, allows tougher U.N. inspections. International Atomic Energy Agency (IAEA) finds no evidence of weapons program.

Nov. 14, 2004 Britain, France Germany and Iran sign Paris accord, reaffirming Iran's commitment not to acquire nuclear weapons.

Nov. 16, 2005 Iran reverses course and resumes enrichment program, breaking IAEA seals at Natanz nuclear facility.

Dec. 23, 2006 U.N. Security Council imposes sanctions on Iran's trade in nuclear materials and technology.

Oct. 25, 2007 U.S. slaps toughest-yet sanctions on Iran.

2009 Five Security Council members plus Germany offer to enrich Iran's uranium. Iranians refuse. Government cracks down on protests over disputed presidential election.

2010-Present *Despite persistent U.N. requests for more transparency in its nuclear program, Iran remains defiant and evasive. West increases sanctions. Danger rises of possible military intervention to halt Iran's uranium enrichment.*

2011 Iran strongly denies IAEA report saying it could be secretly trying to develop nuclear weapons. . . . United States bars any foreign bank that does business with Iran Central Bank from dealing with U.S. financial institutions.

2012 European Union agrees on Jan. 23 to embargo Iranian oil imports, starting in July. . . . Tehran threatens to block critical Strait of Hormuz oil-shipping lanes if Europeans put sanctions in place.

Decades of Sanctions, But No Surrender

Some companies still find ways to get around them.

"*A nation boycotted is a nation that is in sight of surrender. Apply this economic, peaceful, silent, deadly remedy, and there will be no need for force.*"

The speaker was not President Obama grappling with the Iran conundrum, or even one of his immediate predecessors. It was President Woodrow Wilson, who believed "no modern nation could resist" the power of economic sanctions.[1]

But in reality, sanctions have a poor record of bringing recalcitrant nations to heel. Sanctions failed to topple the late Iraqi leader Saddam Hussein, former Serbian President Slobodan Milosevic or longtime Libyan dictator Moammar Gadhafi. And although the West has been piling on sanctions against Iran for more than 30 years, the regime doesn't seem to be in sight of surrender — at least not yet.[2] Some say sanctions worked in ending apartheid in South Africa because they hurt the middle class, which was able to pressure the government. But there were other factors at play, as well, such as frustration at being excluded from international sporting events, a younger generation more sensitive to the injustices of the system and political pressure from the British Commonwealth.

The Obama administration retains its faith in sanctions, coupled with diplomacy, to convince the Iranians to halt their uranium enrichment effort and agree to more transparency for their nuclear program. "The path we're on — the economic sanctions and the diplomatic pressure — does seem to me to be having an effect," Gen. Martin Dempsey, chairman of the Joint Chiefs of Staff, said recently. "It's premature to be deciding that the economic and diplomatic approach is inadequate."[3]

Sanctions also have been imposed on Iran by the U.N. Security Council, Canada and the 27-member European Union.

After the American Embassy in Tehran was seized along with 52 hostages more than 30 years ago, President Jimmy Carter froze all Iranian assets in U.S. banks. In 1984, after Iran was implicated in bombings of French and U.S. military bases in Beirut that killed 299, export controls were imposed on dual-use products and a long list of products, from helicopters to scuba gear.[4]

Tougher U.S. trade restrictions were imposed when Iran appeared interested in developing nuclear weapons: the Iran-Iraq Arms Non-Proliferation Act of 1992 and the Iran, North Korea and Syria Nonproliferation Act of 2000. Taken together, they banned the transfer of equipment or technology that could be used to "make a material contribution to the development of weapons of mass destruction."[5]

In 1995, President Bill Clinton banned U.S. trade and investment with Iran, making it virtually impossible for American companies to do business in Tehran. Then the Iran and Libya Act (ILSA) of 1996 banned energy investments in either country by foreign companies. Libya was removed from ILSA after it renounced its nuclear program in 2003.

The U.S. Treasury Department administers the American sanctions program. Its website lists sanctions covered by successive laws, executive orders and other decisions, right down to a ban on importing Persian carpets. It also lists scores of banks and other organizations affected by the sanctions.[6]

Many companies have figured out ways to get around the sanctions, even tlthough the United States imposes prison sentences and fines of up to $100 million on convicted "sanction busters."

The United States recently listed four shipping companies in the Mediterranean island-state of Malta that allegedly fronted for the Islamic Republic of Iran Shipping Lines.[7] The Gulf emirate of Dubai has long been a transit point for goods to Iran, legal and otherwise, but Dubai calls the process "re-exporting" rather than "sanctions busting." Iranian firms open offices in Dubai and import the prohibited goods ostensibly to the emirate. But then cargo planes and Gulf freighters transport the goods across the water to nearby Iran.[8]

In one of the highest-profile cases against sanction violators, Britain's Lloyds TSB Bank paid the U.S. government

$350 million in 2009 to settle a case involving cash transfers out of the country for clients in Iran, Libya and Sudan.[9] Sanctions were imposed on Sudan in 1997 for its alleged support of terrorism and persecution of its Christian minority.

The United States also has frozen the financial assets and property of members of the elite Iranian Revolutionary Guard Corps, Quds commando forces and several leading military officers. On Dec. 31, the United States went one step further and banned financial institutions from doing business with the Iran central bank.

International Sanctions

Since 2006, the U.N. Security Council has passed four resolutions imposing sanctions on Iran — each tied to requests for better access for IAEA inspectors and the halting of Iran's uranium enrichment. The first banned the shipment of arms, nuclear materials or technology to Iran. The second and third — in 2007 and 2008, respectively — froze the assets of organizations and some individuals involved in Iran's nuclear program.

But the toughest sanctions came in 2010, when the Security Council tightened the arms embargo, banned international travel for those involved in Iran's nuclear program and froze the funds, businesses and other assets of the Iranian Revolutionary Guard and the Islamic Republic of Iran Shipping Lines.[10] The Security Council listed 41 Iranian individuals subject to travel bans and assets freeze and of 75 entities subject to assets freeze.[11]

As for the European Union, in June 2008 it moved away from a policy of negotiation with Iran and froze the assets of 40 individuals and entities doing business with Bank Melli, Iran's biggest bank. This began what the Congressional Research Service, Congress' nonpartisan research arm, called "a narrowing of past differences between the United States and its allies on the issue."[12]

By June 2010, the EU had adopted many of the major U.S. sanctions, including a ban on investment in the Iranian oil and gas industries and doing business with the Iran central bank. It also published the names of 442 entities on its sanctions list.

Then in January the EU embargoed crude oil, petroleum and petrochemical products from Iran, starting in July. Contracts concluded before Jan. 23, 2012, were allowed to be executed — but only until July.[13]

Given that the EU is Iran's second-largest trading partner — some observers ask: If European sanctions don't bring the Iranians to the table, what will?[14]

— *Roland Flamini*

[1] Barry C. Hufbauer, "Economic Sanctions: America's Economic Folly," Council on Foreign Relations, Oct. 10, 1997, www.cfr.org/trade/economic-sanctions-americas-folly/p62.

[2] Simon Jenkins, "Why is Britain ramping up sanctions against Iran?" *The Guardian*, Jan. 3, 2012, www.guardian.co.uk/commentisfree/2012/jan/03/britain-ramoing-sanctions-against-iran-washington.

[3] Elad Benar, "Obama: Our Sanctions on Iran 'Had a Lot of Bite,' " IsraelNationalNews.com, Jan. 27, 2012, www.israelnationalnews.com/News/News.aspx/152169#.TybRi9VLaf8.

[4] Greg Bruno, "The Lengthening List of Iran Sanctions," Council on Foreign Relations, Nov. 22, 2011, www.cfr.org/iran/lengthening-list-iran-sanctions/p20258.

[5] "Iran, North Korea and Syria Nonproliferation Act Sanctions," www.state.gov/t/isn/inksna/index.htm.

[6] "An Overview of OFAC Regulations Governing Sanctions against Iran," U.S. Treasury, www.treasury.gov/resource-center/sanctions/Programs/Documents/iran.pdf.

[7] "Malta companies on Iran sanctions busting list," *Times of Malta*, Aug. 27, 2010, www.timesofmalta.com/articles/view/20101027/local/us-lists-malta-based-companies-individuals-involved-in-iran-sanctions-busting.333387.

[8] Raymond Barrett, "Sanctions busting is in Dubai's DNA," *The Guardian*, April 20, 2010, www.guardian.co.uk/commentisfree/2010/apr/20/iran-sanctions-busting-dubai.

[9] Gil Montia, "Lloyds TSB settles US sanctions case with $250 million," *Banking Times*, Jan. 11, 2009, www.bankingtimes.co.uk/tag/sanctions/.

[10] Kenneth Katzman, "Iran Sanctions," Congressional Research Service, Jan. 6, 2012, www.fas.org/sgp/crs/mideast/RS20871.pdf.

[11] "Individuals and entities designated as subject to travel ban and assets freeze, etc.," United Nations Security Council, August 2010, www.un.org/sc/committees/1737/pdf/1737ConsolidatedList.pdf.

[12] Kenneth Katzman, "Iran Sanctions," Congressional Research Service, April 9, 2010, http://fpc.state.gov/documents/organization/141587.pdf.

[13] "EU publishes updated list of sanctions on Iran," Kuwait News Agency, Jan. 30, 2012, www.kuna.net.kw/ArticleDetails.aspx?id=2217118&language=en.

[14] Najimeh Bozorgmehr and Geoff Dyer, "China overtakes EU as Iran's top trading partner," *Financial Times*, Feb. 8, 2010, www.ft.com/intl/cms/s/0/f220dfac-14d4-11df-8f1d-00144feab49a.html#axzz1l6Bbzi00.

Al Sharekh of IISS contends that a nuclear Iran "doesn't make much difference to the Gulf Arabs. There's a lot of antagonism towards Iran in the Gulf, but Iran is the 'frenemy,' " she says, meaning a friend who can still create problems. "We share a waterway, and we're too close to be a nuclear target. This is a very crowded neighborhood. From the neighbors' point of view, a nuclear Iran is more a flexing of the muscles."[30]

There's also a cost factor, she says. "At the end of the day it's also an economic issue. Kuwait is still paying for the [1991] invasion of Iraq, and we're in the middle of a world-wide recession."[31]

However, many think the predominantly Sunni Saudis would likely want to assume a more responsive posture to a nuclear-armed Shiite Iran. In June, Prince Turki told NATO officials that if Iran developed nuclear weapons, Saudi Arabia would have no choice but to do likewise, according to a British press report.[32]

That wouldn't necessarily mean the kingdom would have to produce its own bombs, says Kagan of the American Enterprise Institute. "It could order them from Pakistan," he says. "The Saudis financed the Pakistani stockpile," which amounts to having "purchased" them.

Is military action against Iran inevitable?

"No doubt there is a danger there, but the Obama administration doesn't want to go there," says Iran expert Nasr, at Tufts University. And anyway "we may have passed the point" when attacking the Iranian nuclear facilities will make any lasting difference. The danger, he says, is from "the chances of war happening as a result of escalating the sanctions."

Both the Obama administration, with its action against the Iran central bank, and the European Union with its Iran oil embargo, have ratcheted up the sanctions to a level that might cause too much economic pain, potentially forcing the Iranians to take military action.

Tehran's threats to close the Strait of Hormuz are one result, says Nasr. Not that the Iranians would deliberately take on the U.S. Navy: Some covert action through surrogates in Afghanistan or Pakistan is more likely. But an incident in the strait could spark a shooting war; and mines and small gunboats could do a lot of damage before American warships asserted their superiority.

Furthermore, U.S. spy chiefs warned Congress on Jan. 31 that, if pushed hard enough, Iran might launch terrorist attacks inside the United States. They said the alleged plot, uncovered last October, to assassinate the Saudi Arabian ambassador in Washington might foreshadow other attempts.

"Sanctions were once enthusiastically embraced because they were free and stable, but they have become a factor of instability," Nasr says.

Others recommend more aggressive action by the West. The United States should "conduct a surgical strike against Iran's nuclear facilities, pull back and absorb the inevitable round of retaliation and then seek to quickly de-escalate the crisis," says Matthew Kroenig, an assistant professor of government at Georgetown University and a fellow of the Council on Foreign Relations. Prior to the attack, he adds, the United States would embark on a diplomatic effort to assure the Iranians that the strike was not an attempt to destroy the regime.

But even he concedes that military action is unlikely to halt Iran's nuclear program. At best it will "significantly" set it back from three to 10 years, "buying a lot more time for diplomacy."

For the Israelis, however, waiting for sanctions to succeed means time is running out for a pre-emptive strike. "It is still possible from the Israeli point of view to launch an attack within a few months," says Israeli military commentator Ron Ben-Yishai. While the nuclear facility in Natanz is vulnerable to air assault with penetration bombs, a newer facility near the holy city of Qom — built up to 450 feet deep inside a mountain —"is not so susceptible to air strike," he says, even with bunker-busting bombs. And the Iranians are moving their main uranium-enrichment operation to that underground site.

Unlike the Iraqi or Syrian nuclear facilities — both of which the Israelis bombed out of existence — a unilateral attack on the Iranian facilities would not be "an easy option," says Nasr, because Iran's facilities are widespread and would require "sustained aerial bombing."

Indeed, Iran's nuclear program is spread across a country the size of Britain and Germany combined, says Alcaro, of the Institute of International Affairs in Rome. Thus, no one thinks an attack will destroy the program, he says. Rather than deterring the Iranians, "The program is more likely to go forward underground," he contends.

Should the United States and/or Israel attack Iran, they likely would become locked into "a cycle of facing the same problem every three to 10 years," Alcaro adds.

The only reason to attempt an attack would be to weaken the regime so as to create the conditions for a coup or insurrection that would install a government more responsive to U.S. demands, he says. But that probably won't happen, he adds, because, "the nuclear program is an issue of national pride; even a reformist government acceptable to the West would still want one."

Thus, a surgical strike, says Nasr, would probably only "encourage the Iranians to accelerate their program."

And Denis Bauchard, Middle East specialist at the French Institute of International Relations, points out that Iran's determination to establish its "nuclear sovereignty" is total, leaving little hope for a negotiated solution.

"History teaches that engagement and diplomacy pay dividends that military threats do not," Thomas R. Pickering and William H. Luers, two former senior U.S. diplomats, wrote recently. "Deployment of military force can bring the immediate illusion of 'success' but always results in unforeseen consequences and collateral damage that complicate further the achievement of America's main objectives."[33]

BACKGROUND

Persian Roots

Persia was the center of Sunni learning until the rise of the conservative Safavid empire, a militant Shiite theocracy that governed the country from 1501-1732 and established a Shiite branch of Islam as the official religion. The predominantly Sunni population had no choice but to convert or leave.[34]

When the empire ended in the 18th century, Shiism survived as the dominant religion. For the next 200 years the country "lay in decay" as "[b]andit chiefs and feudal lords plundered it at will, [and] people yearned for strong central rule and stability."[35]

In 1921 Reza Khan Pahlavi, a Persian army officer, overthrew the reigning house, set up secular dynastic rule and — to differentiate his people from their Arab neighbors — changed the name of the country to Iran, which means Land of the Aryans.

The Shiite clergy "accepted the legitimacy of the rule of monarchs so long as they did not violate religious law [or] harm Shiism," explains Tufts' Nasr.[36]

The discovery of oil in Iran early in the 20th century drew the interest of the British and Americans. Until the early 1950s, the dominant Western presence in Iran was British. The Anglo-Iranian Oil Co. gave the British a majority interest in Iran's oil, and London exercised considerable political influence in Tehran. But in 1951, Iran's popular, newly elected liberal-democrat prime minister, Mohammad Mossadegh, nationalized the oil industry, at considerable financial loss to British interests.[37] Two years later, he was ousted in a coup organized jointly by the CIA and British Intelligence, mainly to safeguard Anglo-American oil interests.[38] America's role in Mossadegh's removal generated anti-American feeling in the region for the first time.

Shah Mohammad Reza Pahlavi gained control over the country, with growing U.S. support. During the 1950s, Iran was a frontline state in America's Cold War with the Soviet Union and the most important U.S. ally in the Middle East. About the size of Alaska, Iran shared a 1,200-mile border with the Soviet Union and served as an Allied listening post into the Soviet bloc. It also was one of the few Muslim countries to recognize Israel and to sell it oil. U.S. military aid to Iran increased from $10 million in 1960 to its highest level of just over $5 billion in 1977.[39]

But the Pahlavi regime was autocratic and tightly controlled by SAVAK, the nation's hated, CIA-trained, national security organization, notorious for its arrests and torture of political opponents and dissidents. The shah did introduce some reforms — agrarian reform, increased literacy, greater participation by women in society — but corruption was rife, and most citizens did not benefit from the country's oil wealth.

Shiite Radicalism

Social unrest grew, fomented by the Shiite clergy, which opposed Iran's secularization. Cassettes of anti-government sermons by exiled cleric and spiritual leader, Ayatollah Ruhollah Khomeini, were sold in the bazaars. Khomeini's violent rhetoric called the shah "the Jewish agent, the American serpent whose head must be smashed with a stone."[40]

By 1978, mosques had become centers of opposition to the regime. Huge anti-regime demonstrations erupted across the country, and up to a million protesters swarmed the streets of Tehran, including many women in chadors, the head-to-toe black covering mandated by the mullahs.

President Jimmy Carter pressured the shah to avoid bloodshed, so the army did not intervene. Even after some demonstrations turned into violent clashes with security forces, the Carter administration continued to urge the shah to try to ease tensions by bringing moderate opposition figures into the government and calling for elections.

On Jan. 16, 1979, the shah left Iran — ostensibly to seek medical treatment abroad. He would never return. Instead, Khomeini came home in triumph less than a month later, and Iran was declared an Islamic republic, with Khomeini as its supreme leader. Within less than a year, all members of the secular government had been purged, and the clerics were in control. A new age of Shiite radicalism had begun.

On Nov. 4, 1979, a group of student followers of Khomeini stormed and occupied the U.S. Embassy in Tehran, in retaliation for President Carter allowing the deposed shah to enter the United States for cancer treatment.[41] Khomeini publicly approved the takeover, calling the embassy "a nest of spies."

Eventually, 52 American diplomats, staff and Marine guards were held captive for 444 days, despite a failed rescue attempt in April 1980.[42] Negotiations to free the hostages — mediated by Algeria — continued, even as the Carter administration froze $8 billion in Iranian assets in U.S. banks and embargoed Iranian oil exports — the first of a long series of sanctions. The United States has not bought Iranian oil since.

On Jan. 20, 1981, the hostages were released within minutes of President Ronald Reagan's inauguration as Carter's successor, a move designed to cause Carter the most humiliation. In return, the United States agreed not to interfere in Iranian politics.[43] By then, the shah was dead, and Iran had been attacked by Iraq in a conflict that was to last eight years.

War With Iraq

The previous September, Iraqi leader Saddam Hussein had taken advantage of Iran's domestic turmoil to take possession of Shatt al-Arab, a waterway disputed by both countries that flows into the Persian Gulf, and some adjacent oil fields. Centuries-old Sunni-versus-Shia and Arab-versus-Persian religious and ethnic tensions contributed to the outbreak of hostilities, as did a personal animosity between Saddam and Khomeini. Ten years

earlier, Saddam had expelled the ayatollah after he had taken refuge in Iraq.[44]

Iran threw waves of young men and boys against Saddam's heavy armor in a conflict that developed into trench warfare reminiscent of the bloody fighting in World War I. And, like the Germans in WWI, Saddam even used mustard gas against the Iranians. In Tehran, fountains ran water dyed red to symbolize the blood of martyred Iranian soldiers.

In 1988, exhausted, economically battered and deadlocked, both sides agreed to a U.N.-brokered cease fire. Iraq's territorial gains were returned to Iran. More than a million soldiers and civilians perished in what was essentially an exercise in futility.

As the war was winding down, two incidents served to further sour U.S.-Iranian relations. In 1988, the *USS Samuel B. Roberts*, an American frigate, hit an Iranian mine in the Strait of Hormuz. In retaliation, U.S. forces destroyed two offshore oil platforms, sank two Iranian frigates and damaged a third. "The aim was to teach the Iranians a lesson," the BBC recalled in a recent analysis. "The conclusion was clear — Iran's conventional naval forces were no match for U.S. sea power in a straight fight."[45]

Weeks later, the *USS Vincennes*, a guided missile cruiser, shot down an Iranian commercial jet carrying 290 passengers and crew. Washington said the *Vincennes* mistook the plane for a military aircraft, and refused to apologize or admit any wrongdoing.[46]

Driven by anti-U.S. sentiment and its perceived mission to spread Shiism, Iran between 1980 and 1996 strongly supported Islamist terrorist groups such as Hezbollah (in Lebanon), Hamas, Palestinian Islamic Jihad, the Supreme Council for Islamic Revolution in Iraq (SCIRI), the Afghan Northern Alliance and its precursors and groups in Bahrain, Saudi Arabia, Kuwait, Egypt, Algeria and elsewhere. But since then, as Iran's revolutionary fervor has dissipated somewhat, Tehran's support for terrorist organizations has became more focused on its own strategic interests. By the mid- and late-1990s, the Iranians had reduced their support to Hezbollah and Hamas.[47]

That may have been in part because Iran was at a kind of political cross-roads. In the summer of 1989, Ayatollah Khamenei had succeeded Khomeini as supreme leader, and progressives were making inroads in

Iranian politics. In 1997, the moderate Mohammad Khatami won the presidential election with 70 percent of the vote, beating the conservative ruling elite.

Stronger Sanctions

Beginning in the mid-1990s, Iran's efforts to resume its stalled nuclear program would escalate tensions between Tehran and the West.

In 1995, President Bill Clinton imposed new, stricter sanctions on Iran, arguing that Iran supported international terrorism, was trying to undermine the Middle East peace process and was acquiring weapons of mass destruction.[48] The new restrictions blocked trade in technology, goods or services to or from Iran and prohibited U.S. citizens from investing in Iranian projects.

In August 1996 Congress tightened the screws even further by passing the Iran-Libya Sanctions Act (ILSA), which extended restrictions on energy-related investments to foreign-owned companies. The new law, said a report by Chatham House, a British foreign affairs think tank, was designed to force foreign companies to decide whether they wanted to "do business with Iran and Libya or the United States."[49]

Despite the sanctions, U.S.-Iran relations appeared ready to thaw a bit in September 2000, when Iranian President Khatami remained in the hall at the annual opening of the U.N. General Assembly to listen to President Clinton address the body.[50] Later, Clinton reciprocated, breaking a tradition since 1979 of U.S. officials leaving the chamber when an Iranian leader spoke. Some American import restrictions were removed, including on Iranian carpets, but not on oil. And Secretary of State Madeleine Albright met with the Iranian foreign minister Kamal Kharrazi — the first such meeting since the United States broke off diplomatic ties with Tehran in 1979.

Then, after the Sept. 11, 2001, terrorist attacks in the United States, Iran quietly offered support for the U.S. campaign in Afghanistan, for example, by blocking the retreating Taliban from crossing into Iranian territory. That November, Secretary of State Colin Powell shook hands with Kharrazi — a simple yet historic gesture.

But in his Jan. 29, 2002, State of the Union address, President George W. Bush declared Iran a member of "an axis of evil" (along with North Korea and Syria) that was "arming to threaten the peace of the world."[51] Two days

later, National Security Adviser Condoleezza Rice said, "Iran's direct support of regional and global terrorism and its aggressive efforts to acquire weapons of mass destruction belie any good intentions." Her statement was reinforced by a CIA report claiming that Tehran was "attempting to develop a domestic capability to produce various types of weapons — chemical, biological and nuclear — and their delivery systems."[52]

Nuclear Program

Iran has always claimed it needed nuclear power in order to shift from its over-reliance on oil for domestic energy. With oil exports accounting for 50-76 percent of the Iranian government's revenues, the country prefers to sell as much oil as possible rather than burn it for electricity.[53]

With the help of the Germans and the Americans — before the revolution — and the Russians after it, Iran built a nuclear power station in Bushehr on the Persian Gulf. Enriched uranium is needed to run a nuclear power station, but only enriched to single-digit percentage levels. To make a nuclear weapon, uranium must be enriched to 90 percent or higher. Although Iran has not yet enriched uranium to weapons-grade levels, it has enriched some up to 20 percent of the strength needed, according to the IAEA.

In short, for nearly a decade Western governments have tried using negotiations, threats and U.N. sanctions to persuade the Iranians to either import their enriched uranium from elsewhere or make their enrichment operation more transparent. So far, the Iranians have refused to comply.

Talks between Iran and Britain, France and Germany got off to a promising start in 2004, when the Iranians agreed to suspend all uranium enrichment activities while negotiations continued and to allow the IAEA to inspect its nuclear sites. Some observers linked Tehran's concessions to the U.S. invasion of Iraq the previous year. The Iranian leadership had been cowed into cooperating by the proximity of a strong U.S. fighting force across the border, they said.

The most optimistic moment came in March 2005, when the United States joined the negotiations, and the Western team became known as 3+1 (and eventually as 3+2 when Russia was added, and then 5+1 with the inclusion of China). As a goodwill gesture the United States offered to supply spare parts for Iran's civil aviation fleet.

EU Trade with Iran Rose, Despite Sanctions

Even though the United States and the U.N. had imposed sanctions on trade with Iran, the European Union (EU) increased its trade with Iran more than 17 percent between 2009 and 2010. In January, the EU adopted its own sanctions against trade with Iran, increasing international pressure designed to stop the regime from enriching uranium, considered a precursor to the production of nuclear weapons.

Value of EU Trade (Imports and Exports) with Iran, 2009-2010

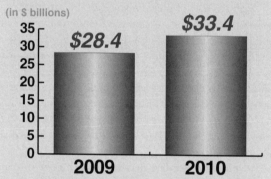

Source: "Iran: EU Bilateral Trade and Trade With the World," Directorate General for Trade, European Commission, January 2012, trade.ec.europa.eu/doclib/docs/2006/september/tradoc_113392.pdf

Then the Iranians insisted on resuming uranium enrichment as a condition for continuing negotiations, and the talks collapsed.[54]

The election of Ahmadinejad, then mayor of Tehran, as president in 2005 — when negotiators had hoped for the more pragmatic Akbar Hashemi Rafsanjani — further hardened Iran's position.

The battle then moved to the U.N. Security Council, which between 2006 and 2010 passed four resolutions, starting with an IAEA resolution demanding more inspections. Each subsequent resolution piled on more economic sanctions and restrictions, including freezing the assets of the Republic of Iran Shipping Lines and the powerful Iranian Revolutionary Guard Corps and authorizing the inspection and seizure of shipments violating the sanctions.

The Iranian facilities in question included the nuclear plant at Bushehr, the Isfahan plant, where "natural" uranium is converted into uranium hexafluoride — a gas used in centrifuges to create weapons-grade uranium — and Natanz, an enrichment facility where the Iranians were said to be installing centrifuges. In 2009, Iran revealed the existence of another heavily fortified plant near the holy city of Qom, where the Iranians told the IAEA it was transferring its operations to enrich uranium to 20 percent levels.

In 2009, the world reacted with shock when the Iranian regime brutally suppressed huge "Green" protest demonstrations that erupted after Ahmadinejad, who had trailed badly in the polls, somehow won an overwhelming re-election victory over his progressive challenger, Mir Hussein Mousavi.[55] Youthful supporters of Mousavi called for a more stable economy, greater freedom at home and a friendlier foreign policy.

The Obama administration had remained aloof from the international chorus of criticism of the regime. "We do not interfere in Iran's internal affairs," Obama said at the time. But in December 2011, as his re-election campaign began heating up, his GOP challengers criticized Obama for not supporting the Iranian protesters in 2009. The White House promptly issued sanctions against two senior members of the Iranian military for their part in "the violent crackdown in the summer of 2009."[56]

Inevitably, Iran's nuclear ambitions have spurred war talk. Both the United States and Israel are rumored to have contingency plans for a military strike against Tehran's nuclear facilities. For some years the accepted version of events was of Washington restraining an increasingly apprehensive Jerusalem and urging that sanctions be given a chance to work.

"Everybody says a military attack should be a last resort," says Ben-Yishai, the Israeli military affairs expert. "The question is, 'When is the last resort?' " The notion of a nuclear Israel and a nuclear Iran creating a system of mutual deterrence doesn't wash in Israel because of Iran's declared hostility to the Jewish state's very existence.

"Deterrence worked during the Cold War, because both sides were rational and responsible centers with fresh memories of World War II," argues Ben-Yishai.

"The Iranian leaders are fanatic clerics with visions of martyrdom. We don't know what they'll do, and we can't live under the threat of doomsday."

Tensions rose again in November, when the IAEA reported for the first time that the Iranians could be working on a nuclear explosive device — although the agency did not say they were already capable of producing a bomb.[57]

"The Americans and the Europeans . . . have succeeded in turning Iran's nuclear program into an issue of international security," says Alcaro of the Italian Institute of International Affairs. What happens next, he adds, will depend largely on whether the Americans and Europeans can maintain a united front with Russia and China.

"Under pressure from all the major powers, Iran may be willing to give in on the question of enriching uranium — provided a mechanism can be found to save appearance," Alcaro says.

CURRENT SITUATION

Tightening Sanctions

IAEA inspectors were in Iran in late January for their first visit in three years, during which time the Iranians have refused to even discuss allegations that they were developing nuclear weapons. "We're looking forward to the start of a dialogue," the agency's deputy director, Herman Nackaerts, declared, "a dialogue that is overdue since very long."[58]

The three-day visit — during which the IAEA team was expected to inspect several locations, including the new underground facility deep inside a mountain near Qom, could greatly influence the direction and urgency of the U.S.-led efforts to halt Iran's nuclear program.

Both the Obama administration and the EU have followed up their most robust economic moves so far against the Iranian regime with a strong barrage of rhetoric on both sides of the Atlantic.

Obama used his State of the Union address to warn that "America is determined to prevent Iran from getting a nuclear weapon, and I will take no options off the table to achieve that goal." He added, however, that, "A peaceful resolution of this issue is still possible."[59]

And in a rare joint statement, German Chancellor Angela Merkel, French President Nicolas Sarkozy and

Prime Minister David Cameron of Britain cautioned that Tehran would face economic isolation unless it "immediately" abandoned its nuclear ambitions. "We will not accept Iran acquiring a nuclear weapon," they said emphatically.[60] Meanwhile, U.S., British and French warships steamed into the Strait of Hormuz, testing the freedom of passage.

Faced with rising tension, Major Gen. Mohammad Ali Asoudi of the Islamic Revolution Guards Corps said Iran's armed forces "are at the height of their powers and military prowess, and threats by the U.S. and Israel are (part of) a psychological warfare campaign."[61]

Meanwhile, Ahmadinejad played down the impact of the EU oil embargo: "Today, we have attained a status that we need not sell oil to Europe, and we are following our path determinedly," he said. And the freezing of the Iran central bank's European assets, he continued, would have minimal effect, because only $24 billion of Iran's $200 billion in foreign exchange are in Europe.[62]

Economic Pain

The Iranian economy is in shambles because the U.N. sanctions block outside investment and development. In the last three months, the value of the Iranian rial has plunged 40 percent against the dollar, according to the French newspaper *Le Monde*.[63]

Several European countries had been worried that an embargo would cause oil prices to spike, exacerbating the EU's serious economic problems. But the EU governments fell into line, in part because they have good prospects for alternative supplies.

"The French strategy is to confront Iran with a choice: The future of the regime, or the nuclear bomb," said *Le Monde*.[64]

But will it work? Turkey, China and India — major importers of Iranian oil — say they will not honor the embargo, although Japan agreed to cut back its Iranian oil purchases after a personal visit by U.S. Treasury Secretary Timothy Geithner. While Beijing "adamantly opposes Iran developing and possessing nuclear weapons," Prime Minister Wen Jiabao declared recently, it will continue to import Iranian oil.[65]

In December, Obama wrote to Ahmadinejad urging him to resume negotiations with the 5+1, after nearly a year-long break. The daily *Tehran Times* said Obama's request "announced readiness for negotiation and the

Is Iran planning to build nuclear weapons?

YES
Frederick W. Kagan
Resident Scholar and Director Critical Threats Project American Enterprise Institute

Written for *CQ Global Researcher*, February 2012

Iran's leaders are seeking the ability to produce an arsenal of atomic weapons. No other explanation fits their behavior. Claiming that Iran needs nuclear power to meet its energy needs in order to strengthen its economy and raise its people's quality of life, the Iranian leadership has brought crushing sanctions on its country.

In addition to constraining Iran's economy, the sanctions have badly undermined its currency and harmed its population. The international community — including Russia, one of Iran's most trusted allies — has offered to provide Iran with nuclear fuel, yet the regime persists in its enrichment program. If the regime sought to improve Iran's economic well-being, it would have abandoned the nuclear program long ago.

The regime claims it has a right to the full nuclear fuel cycle, however, and insists that its program is nothing more than the pursuit of that right. Indeed, Iran could develop a nuclear program in accord with the international laws its leaders cite — if it complied fully with the inspections regime established by those laws and embodied in the International Atomic Energy Agency (IAEA).

Instead, the regime has consistently refused to answer questions from the IAEA, let alone provide the agency with full access and transparency to its program, which other signatories do.

The Iranian regime is not only pursuing a nuclear program to the enormous detriment of its people but it is doing so in violation of the very treaties it claims allow it to pursue the program in the first place.

One could add the disturbing fact that Iran has buried an enrichment facility (which it did not declare until others discovered it) under a small mountain — not the behavior of a regime seeking peaceful nuclear power. Numerous reports also show that Iran has tried to acquire and build atomic weapons devices, detonators and testing facilities and already has a large arsenal of ballistic missiles ready to have atomic warheads fitted.

But the reality already should be clear. The facts support only one rational explanation: Iran's leaders are building a nuclear program to support an arsenal of atomic weapons. All other explanations are rationalizations.

NO
Riccardo Alcaro
Research Fellow, Istituto Affari Internazionali, Rome and Fellow, European Foreign and Security Policy Studies Program

Written for *CQ Global Researcher*, February 2012

It is true that Iran has gone the extra mile to divert international checks on its nuclear program, but uncertainty still clouds its ultimate objective. Meanwhile, there simply is not enough evidence to argue that Iran is determined to leave the Nuclear Non-Proliferation Treaty, test a nuclear device and declare itself a nuclear state.

If Iran were to go openly nuclear, it would have a hard time persuading its mostly opportunistic partners (like China) to resist American and European demands to isolate it. In theory, Iran could go nuclear without telling anyone. In practice, however, keeping the construction of a nuclear arsenal secret is an increasingly difficult, costly and risky option, and Iran is under almost unprecedented scrutiny from the International Atomic Energy Agency (IAEA) and Western powers.

Iran's behavior so far has seemed to fit the strategy of approaching but not crossing the nuclear threshold. While resisting what it considers excessive intrusions into its nuclear program, it has avoided severing ties with the IAEA. Defiance of Western pressure — as well as of IAEA and U.N. Security Council resolutions — seems to have paid off for the Iranian leadership. Domestically, it has given the regime a narrative around which popular support could coalesce. Internationally, it has forced a re-appraisal of Iran's role in the strategic calculus of the United States. And thanks to the nuclear dispute, Iran potentially is in a better position to extract concessions from what Ayatollah Ruhollah Khomeini labeled the "Great Satan" than it was before the nuclear standoff.

From that point of view, the nuclear program is more a means to get U.S. acceptance of the clerical regime and recognition of Iran's regional interests than an end in itself. If that is the case, there still is room for settling the nuclear dispute, as Iran may decide that compromise rather than continued defiance can ultimately deliver its strategic objective of climbing the region's hierarchy.

However, if it has no way out but bowing to U.S. demands or — worse — if attacked by the United States and/or Israel, Iran might instead calculate that isolation with an H-bomb is better than isolation without it. Grownup diplomacy, not teenage muscle flexing, can spare the world another unnecessary crisis.

resolution of mutual disagreements." However, the last session, in January 2011, lasted only a day-and-a-half and ended without agreeing on either an agenda or a date for another session.

Each side accuses the other of delaying the start of new talks. The Iranians insist there should be no preconditions. In a separate account the *Tehran Times* quoted Iranian Foreign Minister Salehi as saying, "If the West has a sincere intention, a date should be decided, and negotiations should start."[66]

Yet, when Salehi said on Jan. 18 that, "Negotiations are going on about venue and date. We would like to have these negotiations," an EU spokesman denied that any discussions were under way on new talks.[67]

Ray Takeyh, a senior fellow at the Council on Foreign Relations, said skepticism abounds regarding Tehran's sincerity. "By threatening the disruption of global oil supplies, yet dangling the prospect of entering talks," he wrote recently, "Iran can press actors such as Russia and China to be more accommodating." But any concessions made by Iran at a negotiating table "are bound to be symbolic and reversible."[68]

Meanwhile, Israel says the window of opportunity for a successful military operation is rapidly closing. "There's a very vivid and very bitter dispute going on between the Israeli and U.S. governments" over timing, says the Israeli commentator Ben-Yishai. "It is still practicable, from an Israeli point of view, to launch an attack, but the Americans say, 'Give sanctions time to work.'" Isareli Defense Minister Ehud Barak, however, said recently that any decision on attacking Iran is "very far off."[69]

Some say a covert war to derail Iran's nuclear program already is underway. On Jan. 11, Iranian chemist Mostafa Ahmadi Roshan, head of the Natanz enrichment facility, was killed after a motorcyclist attached a magnetic bomb to his car in Tehran's rush-hour traffic. He was the fifth Iranian nuclear scientist killed in the past two years. The Iranians blame his killing on U.S. and/or Israeli intelligence agents, but the United States adamantly denied any role in the killing.

In 2010, work had to be suspended for a while at the Natanz nuclear facility after a computer worm called Stuxnet caused large numbers of centrifuges to malfunction. The operating system was restarted a few days later, but the centrifuges remained less efficient.[70]

No one took credit for the cyber attack.

OUTLOOK
Diplomacy and Provocation

"The next few months will look pretty much like the last few months," predicts Takeyh, at the Council on Foreign Relations. "There'll be diplomacy, incremental gains and, occasionally, a degree of provocation, with all parties invested in not having full-scale conflict."

However, he believes Iran would be open to "an arrangement with the United States," under "certain circumstances." For instance, if Iran were allowed to join the World Trade Organization, it could mean a quantum leap in the Iranian economy.[71]

The EU oil embargo won't begin until the summer, allowing European importers time to organize alternative suppliers, such as possibly Libyan oil production, badly damaged during the civil war. Saudi Arabia also is expected to fill the gap, despite Tehran's warning not to increase capacity for its defecting clients.

As for the effectiveness of the oil embargo, experts say the international oil market is too complex, with too many options. "History is littered with failed oil embargoes ranging from Cuba, Rhodesia [today's Zimbabwe] and South Africa to the Arab oil embargo [of 1973], and the embargo against Iraq in 1990," Paul Stevens of London's Chatham House wrote recently.[72]

Moreover, he continued, "some form of [Iranian] retaliatory action against the EU countries . . . could also be expected. There could even be a Lockerbie-type response prompted by elements from within Iran," he continued, referring to Libya's 1988 bombing of a Pan American jet liner over Scotland.[73]

The endgame, according to Julian Lee, an energy expert at the London-based Centre for Global Energy Studies, is to get the Iranians to agree to "proper monitoring of their nuclear industry. The sanctions aren't an end in and of themselves."[74]

Meanwhile, Israel's intentions are unclear, and there is uncertainty about how the Iranian regime will respond to the latest sanctions. The more immediate concern is Iran's threat to close the Strait of Hormuz, which could easily spark a broader conflict. As for hopes of a breakthrough in the negotiations, "No amount of sanctions can pressure Iran into U-turning on its nuclear program," The *Arab News* commented recently.[75]

"Iran knows where the whole world stands; we know where Iran stands; the situation will continue that way," Saudi Prince Turki said recently. "None of us want to engage in military conflict, and I think the Iranians themselves . . . fear that they will be the target of military strikes either by Israel or the United States or both."[76]

In Israel, meanwhile, talk of war rises and subsides. "There's no realistic hope in Israel that the Iranians will suspend their enrichment program altogether," says commentator Ben-Yishai. "If the sanctions work, they might say, 'We suspend enrichment at 20 percent.' That, in itself, would be a big gain."

NOTES

1. "British ambassador: "I had to leave my dog in Iran," BBC News, Dec. 2, 2011, www.bbc.co.uk/news/uk-16009838.

2. Robert F. Worth and Rick Gladstone, "Iran Protesters Attack British Embassy," *The New York Times*, Nov. 29, 2011, www.nytimes.com/ 2011/11/ 30/world/middleeast/tehran-protesters-storm-british-embassy.html.

3. "Implementation of the NPT Safeguards Agreement and relevant provisions of Security Council Resolutions in the Islamic Republic of Iran," International Atomic Energy Agency, Nov. 8, 2011, p. 10, http://isis-online.org/uploads/isis-reports/ documents/IAEA_Iran_8Nov2011.pdf.

4. Don Melvin, "EU formally adopts Iran oil embargo," *Arab News*, Jan. 23, 2012, http://arabnews.com/ middleeast/article567075.ece?comments=all.

5. Ronen Bergman, "Will Israel Attack Iran?" *The New York Times Magazine*, Jan. 29, 2012, p. 22. Robert F. Worth, "Iran's Supreme Leader Threatens Retaliation Against Attack," *The New York Times*, Feb. 3, 2012; and Joel Greenberg and Joby Warrick, "Israel: Iran must be stopped soon," *The Washington Post*, Feb. 3, 2012, p. 1.

6. "Remarks by the President in State of the Union Address," Office of the Press Secretary, The White House, Jan. 24, 2012, www.whitehouse.gov/the-press-office/2012/01/24/remarks-president-state-union-address. Also see "Remarks by Mitt Romney," The Israel Project, www.theisraelproject.org/site/ apps/nlnet/content2.aspx?c=ewJXKcOUJlIaG&b=7 721235&ct=11521353#.TyNrUWNSSkM.

7. Ghazanfar Ali Khan, "Attack on Iran would have 'calamitous' consequences, says Prince Turki," *Arab News*, Dec. 13, 2011, http://arabnews.com/saudi-arabia/article547026.ece.

8. Transcript, "Face the Nation," CBS News, Jan. 8, 2012, www.cbsnews.com/8301-3460_162-57354647/ face-the-nation-transcript-january-8-2012/.

9. "Iran's foreign minister on protests and nukes," *Euronews*, March 3, 2011, www.euronews.net/2011/03/03/ interview-with-irans-foreign-minister/.

10. "Implementation of the NPT Safeguards Agreement and relevant provisions of Security Council Resolutions in the Islamic Republic of Iran," *op. cit.*

11. "Obama signs Iran Sanctions Bill into Law," BBC News, Dec. 31, 2011, www.bbc.co.uk/news/world-us-canada-16376072.

12. Stephen Castle and Alan Cowell, "Europe and U.S. Tighten Vise of Sanctions on Iran," *The New York Times*, Jan. 23, 2012, www.nytimes.com/2012/ 01/24/world/middleeast/iran-urged-to-negotiate-as-west-readies-new-sanctions.html?ref=world.

13. Dan Murphy, "Iran's Threats over Strait of Hormuz? Understandable, but not easy," *The Christian Science Monitor*, Dec. 28, 2011, www.csmonitor.com/ World/Backchannels/2011/1228/Iran-s-threats-over-Strait-of-Hormuz-Understandable-but-not-easy.

14. Fareed Zakaria, "Iran: Growing state of desperation," *The Washington Post*, Jan. 4, 2012, www .fareedzakaria.com/home/Articles/Articles.html.

15. Armin Arefi, "Iran-Etats-Unis: jusqu;ou iront les deux meilleurs ennemis?" Le Point.fr, Jan. 2, 2012, www .lepoint.fr/monde/iran-etats-unis-jusqu-ou-iront-les-deux-meilleurs-ennemis-02-01-2012-1414517_ 24.php.

16. "President Shimon Peres says 'Iran is very dangerous, but there is no need to get hysterical,' " Youtube,

Dec. 27, 2011, www.youtube.com/watch?v=x3e8 QgAHv9g.

17. "PM, Merkel, Sarkozy: We call on Iran to suspend nuclear activities and abide by international obligations," Number 10 (official site of the British Prime Minister's Office), Jan. 23, 2012, www.number10. gov.uk/news/iran-sanctions/.

18. *Ibid.*

19. V. Vera, *et al.*, "Sanctions on Iran: Reactions and Impact," *AEI Iran Tracker*, Nov. 1, 2011.

20. William C. Ramsay, "Punish Iran Not Each Other," French Institute of International Relations, September 2009, www.ifri.org/?page=detail-contribution&id= 5412&id_provenance=97.

21. Indira A. R. Lakshmanan, "Bank Tejarat Banned by U.S., EU Move Stifling Iran Trade," Bloomberg News, Jan. 24, 2012, www.bloomberg.com/ news/2012-01-24/bank-tejarat-banned-by-u-s-eu-in-move-stifling-iran-s-trade.html.

22. Kristen Allen, "Iranian Airline Buys Chancellor Merkel's Retired Jet," *Der Spiegel*, Nov. 21, 2011, www.spiegel.de/international/world/0,1518, 798973,00.html.

23. Bastian Berlner, "U.S. and Israel Demand Greater Measures against Israel," *Der Spiegel*, Nov. 14, 2011, www.spiegel.de/international/europe/0,1518, 797570,00.html.

24. Hossein Jaseb and Justyna Pawlak, "WRAPUP 3: Iran slams EU oil embargo, warns could hit U.S.," Reuters, Jan. 23, 2012, www.reuters.com/article/ 2012/01/23/nuclear-iran-idUSL5E8CN223201 20123.

25. "Iran exports by country, 2010," United States Energy Information Administration, www.eia.gov/ countries/country-data.cfm?fips=IR.

26. Karen de Young and Scott Wilson, "Public ire is one goal of sanctions against Iran, U.S. official says," *The Washington Post*, Jan.11, 2012, www.washingtonpost .com/world/national-security/goal-of-iran-sanctions-is-regime-collapse-us-official-says/2012/01/10/ gIQA0KJsoP_story.html.

27. Castle and Cowell, *op. cit.*

28. "Global Trends 2025: A Transformed World," National Intelligence Council, November 2008, www.dni.gov/nic/PDF_2025/2025_Global_ Trends_Final_Report.pdf.

29. Shmuel Bar, "Can Cold War Deterrence Apply to a Nuclear Iran?" *Strategic Perspectives*, Jerusalem Center for Public Affairs, November 2011, www.jcpa.org/ text/cold_war_deterrence_nuclear_iran.pdf.

30. "Saudi Arabia may need nuclear weapons to fend off threat from Iran and Israel, says former intelligence chief," *Daily Mail*, Dec. 6, 2011, www.dailymail .co.uk/news/article-2070704/Saudi-Arabia-need-nuclear-weapons-fend-threat-Iran-Israel-says-prince .html#ixzz1kOpRWhKh.

31. For background, see Patrick G. Marshall, "Calculating the Costs of the Gulf War," *Editorial Research Reports*, March 19, 1991, pp. 145-155, available in *CQ Researcher Plus Archive.*

32. "Saudi Arabia may need nuclear weapons to fend off threat from Iran and Israel, says former intelligence chief," *op. cit.*

33. William H. Luers and Thomas R. Pickering, "Military action isn't the only solution to Iran," *The Washington Post*, Dec. 30, 2012, www.washington-post.com/opinions/military-action-isnt-the-only-solution-to-iran/2011/12/29/gIQA69sNRP_story .html.

34. "History of Iran, Persian Empire," http://docmv .co.uk/Documents/History%20of%20iran.pdf.

35. See "Safavid Empire (1501-1722)," "Religions," BBC online, www.bbc.co.uk/religion/religions/ islam/history/safavidempire_1.shtml.

36. Quoted in Mike Shuster, "Shia Rise Amid Century of Mideast Turmoil," Part 2 of the series, "Partisans of Ali," NPR, Feb. 13, 2007, www.npr.org/templates/ story/story.php?storyId=7371280.

37. David Painter, "The United States, Great Britain, and Iran," Georgetown University Institute for the Study of Diplomacy, 1993, www.princeton.edu/~bsimpson/ Hist%20725%20Summer%202006/The%20 US%20and%20Mossadegh%201951-1953.pdf.

38. Mark Gasiorowski and Malcolm Byrne (eds.), "Mohammed Mossadeq and the 1953 Coup in

Iran," National Security Archive, June 2004, www
.gwu.edu/~nsarchiv/NSAEBB/NSAEBB126/index
.htm. "The CIA, with help from British intelligence,
planned, funded and implemented the operation."

39. "Arms exports to Iran," Stockholm International
Peace Research Institute, http://armstrade.sipri.org/
armstrade/page/values.php.

40. "Ruhollah Mousavi Khomeini, Part 3: Life in Exile,"
Medlibrary.org, http://medlibrary.org/medwiki/
Ruhollah_Mousavi_Khomeini#Life_in_exile.

41. "The American Experience: The Iranian Hostage
Crisis," PBS, www.pbs.org/wgbh/americanexperience/
features/general-article/carter-hostage-crisis/.

42. "On This Day, 1980: Tehran Hostage Rescue Mission
Fails," BBC, April 25, 2005, http://news.bbc.co.uk/
onthisday/hi/dates/stories/april/25/newsid_
2503000/2503899.stm.

43. "Timeline: U.S.-Iran Contacts," Council on Foreign
Relations, March 9, 2007, www.cfr.org/iran/timeline-
us-iran-contacts/p12806/.

44. "Iran-Iraq War (1980-1988)," Global Security, Nov. 7,
2011, www.globalsecurity.org/military/world/war/
iran-iraq.htm.

45. Jonathan Marcus, "Is a U.S.-Iran maritime clash
inevitable?" BBC News, Jan. 10, 2012, www.bbc
.co.uk/news/world-middle-east-16485842.

46. Lionel Beehner, "Timeline: U.S.-Iran Contacts,"
Council on Foreign Relations, March 9, 2011, www
.cfr.org/iran/timeline-us-iran-contacts/p12806#p5.

47. Mark Gasiorowski, "Evidence to the National
Commission on Terrorist Attacks Upon the United
States: Iranian Support for Terrorism," National
Commission on Terrorist Attacks Upon the United
States, July 2003, www.9-11commission.gov/hearings/
hearing3/witness_gasiorowski.htm.

48. B. J. Rudy, "The Future of U.S. Unilateral Sanctions
and the Iran-Libya Sanctions Act," Chatham House,
Feb. 12-13, 2001, www.google.com/search?q=
chatham%20house%3A%20clinton%20administra-
tion%20imposes%20sanctions%20on%20
iran&ie=utf-8&oe=utf-8&aq=t&rls=org.mozilla:en-
US:official&client=firefox-a&source=hp&channel=np.

49. *Ibid*. Libya was removed from ILSA after Libyan
leader Moammar Gadhafi renounced the development of nuclear weapons.

50. Scott McLeod, "Diplomacy: Clinton and Khatami
Find Relations Balmy," *Time*, Sept. 18, 2000, www
.time.com/time/magazine/article/0,9171,997984,00
.html.

51. "Bush State of the Union Speech," CNN transcript,
Jan. 20, 2002, http://edition.cnn.com/2002/
ALLPOLITICS/01/29/bush.speech.txt/.

52. "How Iran entered the Axis," PBS "Frontline,"
undated, www.pbs.org/wgbh/pages/frontline/shows/
tehran/axis/map.html.

53. "Firms Reported in Open Sources as Having
Commercial Activity in Iran's Oil, Gas, and
Petrochemical Sectors," Government Accountability
Office, April 22, 2010, www.gao.gov/products/
GAO-10-515R.

54. "Iran 'ready for nuclear talks,' " BBC News, June 8,
2006, http://news.bbc.co.uk/2/hi/middle_
east/5059322.stm.

55. "Ahmadinejad wins Iran presidential election," BBC
News, June 12, 2009, news.bbc.co.uk/2/
hi/8098305.stm.

56. Joel Gehrke, "894 days: Now Obama stands up for
the Greens," *The Examiner*, Dec. 14, 2011, http://
campaign2012.washingtonexaminer.com/blogs/
beltway-confidential/894-days-now-obama-stands-
green-revolution/257116.

57. "Q and A: Iran nuclear issue," BBC News, Nov. 9,
2011, www.bbc.co.uk/news/world-middle-east-
11709428.

58. "IAEA nuclear inspection gets under way in Iran,"
Daily Telegraph, Jan. 31, 2012, www.telegraph.co.uk/
news/worldnews/middleeast/iran/9048556/IAEA-
nuclear-inspection-gets-under-way-in-Iran.html.

59. "Obama uses State of Union speech to warn Iran to
'change course' as Europe sends battleships to Gulf,"
Daily Mail, Jan. 25, 2012, www.dailymail.co.uk/
news/article-2091450/Obama-uses-State-Union-
speech-warn-Iran-change-course-nuclear-ambitions.
html.

60. *Ibid*.

61. "US, Israeli threats are empty: IRGC official," *Tehran Times*, Jan. 25, 2012, http://tehrantimes .com/politics/94816-us-israeli-threats-are-empty-irgc-official.

62. *Ibid.*

63. "Le EU décide de geler les avoirs de la Banque Central d'Iran," *Le Monde*, Jan. 18, 2012, www .lemonde.fr/proche-orient/article/2012/01/18/l-ue-decide-de-geler-les-avoirs-de-la-banque-centrale-d-iran_1631366_3218.html.

64. Natalie Nougayrede, "Paris redoute des frappes sur Iran pendant l'ete," *Le Monde*, Jan. 19, 2012, www .lemonde.fr/proche-orient/article/2012/01/19/ paris-redoute-des-frappes-sur-l-iran-pendant-l-ete_1631865_3218.html.

65. "Chinese Premier Wen Jiabao defends Iran oil imports," *Daily Telegraph*, Jan. 19, 2012, www.telegraph.co.uk/ news/worldnews/middleeast/iran/9024517/Chinese-Premier-Wen-Jiabao-defends-Iran-oil-imports.html.

66. "Tehran-5+1 dialogue should start if West has intention — Salihi," *Tehran Times*, Jan. 21, 2012, http:// tehrantimes.com/politics/94724-tehran-51-dialogue-should-start-if-west-has-sincere-intention-salehi.

67. Robin Pomer and Ramin Mostafavi, "Iran says it is in touch with powers on new talks, EU denies," *News Daily* (Reuters), Jan. 18, 2012, www.newsdaily .com/stories/tre80h15z-us-iran/.

68. *Ibid.*

69. *Ibid.*

70. Julian Borger, "West's previous attempts to derail Iran's nuclear program," *The Guardian*, Nov. 2, 2011, www.guardian.co.uk/world/2011/nov/02/previous-attempts-iran-nuclear-programme?intcmp=239.

71. "The Manama Dialogue," Fifth Plenary Session, International Institute of Strategic Studies, Dec. 4, 2010, www.iiss.org/conferences/the-iiss-regional-security-summit/manama-dialogue-2010/plenary-sessions-and-speeches/fourth-plenary-session/ fourth-plenary-qa-session/.

72. Paul Stevens, "An Embargo on Iranian Crude Oil Exports: How likely and with what Impact?" Chatham House, January 2012, www.chatham house.org/sites/default/files/public/Research/

Energy,%20Environment%20and%20Development/ 0112pp_stevens.pdf.

73. *Ibid.*

74. Stephen Mufson, "Oil prices, Iran are increasingly sources of concern," *The Washington Post*, Jan. 14, 2012, www.washingtonpost.com/business/economy/ increasing-concern-over-oil-prices-iran/2012/01/13/ gIQAP98PzP_story.html.

75. Linda Heard, "U.S. and Iran: Wheels within wheels," *Arab News*, Jan. 17, 2012, http://arabnews .com/opinion/columns/article564103.ece.

76. "Fifth Plenary Session — HRH Prince Turki Al Faisal: The Changing Nature of Regional Security Issues," 7th IISS Regional Security Summit, The Manama Dialogue, The International Institute for Strategic Studied, Dec. 4, 2010, www.iiss.org/con ferences/the-iiss-regional-security-summit/manama-dialogue-2010/plenary-sessions-and-speeches/ fifth-plenary-session/hrh-prince-turki-al-faisal/.

BIBLIOGRAPHY
Selected Sources
Books

Brumberg, David, *Reinventing Khomeini: The Struggle for Reform in Iran*, University of Chicago Press, 2001.
An associate professor of government at Georgetown University examines Ayatollah Khomeini's often contradictory ideas about government and how they led to competing institutions and ideologies in today's Iranian leadership.

Kamrava, Mehran, *Iran's Intellectual Revolution*, Cambridge University Press, 2008.
The director of Georgetown University's Qatar-based Center of International Studies examines the strengths and weaknesses of the three major intellectual currents in Iran — religious conservative, religious reformist and secular modernist.

Nasr, Vali, *The Shia Revival: How Conflicts Within Islam Will Shape the Future*, W. W. Norton, 2006.
A noted authority on the Arab world and a professor of international politics at the Fletcher School of Law and

Diplomacy at Tufts University argues that Operation Iraqi Freedom set the scene for a "new" Middle East fueled by the sectarian struggle between the majority Sunnis and minority Shiites.

Takeyh, Ray, *Hidden Iran: Paradox and Power in the Islamic Republic*, Times Books, 2006.
A senior fellow for Middle Eastern studies at the Council on Foreign Relations in Washington explains why we fail to understand Iran and offers a new strategy for redefining this crucial relationship.

Wright, Robin, ed., *The Iran Primer: Power, Politics and U.S. Policy*, United States Institute for Peace Press, 2010.
A distinguished American foreign correspondent well versed in Middle Eastern affairs pulls together 50 seasoned experts from around the world to compile a comprehensive primer on Iran today — its politics, society, military and nuclear program.

Articles

Bergman, Ronen, "Will Israel Attack Iran?" *The New York Times Magazine*, Jan. 29, 2012, p. 22.
An Israeli journalist and author of *The Secret War With Iran* concludes, along with several other Israeli politicians, that Israel will attack Iran in 2012.

Escobar, Pepe, "The Myth of 'Isolated' Iran," *Le Monde Diplomatique*, Jan. 24, 2012, http://monde-diplo.com/openpage/the-myth-of-isolated-iran.
An Al Jazeera analyst says Tehran, which is adept at "Persian shadow play," has no intention of provoking a suicidal Western attack.

Esfandiary, Dina, "It's Time to Deal With Nuclear Iran," *The Huffington Post*, Nov. 16, 2011, www.iiss .org/whats-new/iiss-experts-commentary/its-time-to-deal-with-nuclear-iran/.
A research analyst and project coordinator at the Non-Proliferation and Disarmament Programme at London's International Institute for Strategic Studies warns against jumping to conclusions about a 2011 IAEA report on Iran's nuclear ambitions.

Gelb, Leslie H., "Leslie H. Gelb on How President Obama Should Handle Iran," *The Daily Beast*, Jan. 30, 2012, www.thedailybeast.com/articles/2012/01/30/leslie-h-gelb-on-how-president-obama-should-handle-iran.html.
A former strategic arms reduction negotiator during the Carter administration says President Obama should offer a robust peace proposal now that toughest-ever sanctions are pressuring Iran to halt its nuclear program.

Kahl, Colin, "Not Time to Attack Iran," *Foreign Affairs*, Jan. 17, 2012, www.foreignaffairs.com.
An associate professor in security studies at Georgetown University explains why a military intervention to halt Iran's nuclear program would be ill-judged.

Kroenig, Matthew, "Time to Attack Iran," *Foreign Affairs magazine*, Jan/Feb 2012, www.foreignaffairs .com.
A nuclear security fellow at the Council on Foreign Relations says attacking Iran is the "least bad option."

Reports and Studies

Fitzpatrick, Mark, "Iran's Nuclear, Chemical, and Biological Capabilities —A Net Assessment," Institute of International Strategic Studies, Feb. 3, 2011, www.iiss.org/publications/strategic-dossiers/irans-nuclear-chemical-and-biological-capabilities/.
The London-based institute's detailed technical assessment of Iran's weapons of mass destruction programs concludes that Iran does not have a nuclear weapon and, "won't have one tomorrow, or next week, or next month or a year from now."

Kerr, Paul, "Iran's Nuclear Program: Tehran's Compliance with International Obligations," Congressional Research Service, Dec. 21, 2011, http://fpc.state.gov/documents/organization/180686.pdf.
A specialist reviews Iran's nuclear program and details the legal basis for actions taken by the IAEA and U.N. Security Council.

Pletka, Danielle, *et al.*, "Containing and Deterring a Nuclear Iran," American Enterprise Institute, December 2011.
Experts from the conservative think tank contend that Iran already is a nuclear state and outline a containment strategy.

For More Information

Chatham House, The Royal Institute of International Affairs, 10 St. James's Square, London SW1Y4LE, United Kingdom; 44 207 957 5710; www.chathamhouse.org. A leading source of independent analysis on global and domestic issues.

Council on Foreign Relations, The Howard Pratt House, 58 East 68th St., New York, NY 10065; 212-434-9400; www.cfr.org. An independent think tank that "promotes understanding of foreign policy and America's role in the world."

International Atomic Energy Agency, P.O. Box 100, 1400 Vienna, Austria; 431 2600-0; www.iaea.org. The U.N. agency charged with promoting the development of "safe, secure, peaceful nuclear science and technology."

King Faisal Center for Research and Islamic Studies, P.O. Box 51049, Riyadh 11548, Saudi Arabia; 966 1 465 2255; www.kff.com. Furthers Islamic civilization by supporting continuing research and cultural and scientific activities in a variety of fields.

National Iran-American Council, 1411 K St., Washington, DC 20005; 202-386-6325; www.niacouncil.org/site/PageServer?pagename=NIAC_index. A nonprofit, nonpartisan organization dedicated to furthering the interests of the Iranian-American community and providing information about Iran.

University of Tehran, 16 Azur St., Tehran 14174, Iran; 9821 664 05047; www.ut.ac.ir/en. Offers courses in most academic fields, including foreign policy.

Voices From Abroad:

BENJAMIN NETANYAHU

Prime Minister, Israel

A threat to all

"The significance of the (IAEA) report is that the international community must bring about the cessation of Iran's pursuit of nuclear weapons, which endangers the peace of the world and of the Middle East."

Al Jazeera (Qatar), November 2011

ALI AKBAR SALEHI

Foreign Minister, Iran

A peaceful program

"We have repeatedly announced that we are just after a peaceful use of the nuclear energy and we consider production or use of nuclear bombs as Haram (religiously banned). The European Union should think about the real threat of the atomic bombs stockpiled in Europe instead of presenting a deceitful and unreal image of Iran's peaceful nuclear program."

Fars News Agency (Iran), October 2011

MAHMOUD AHMADINEJAD

President, Iran

Building other things

"The Iranian nation is wise. It won't build two bombs against 20,000 [nuclear] bombs you (the West) have. But it builds something you can't respond to: ethics, decency, monotheism and justice."

National televised speech, November 2011

VLADIMIR EVSEYEV

Center for Public Policy Research, Russia

Japan's footsteps

"Iran is likely to follow Japan's way now, that is, it creates the opportunities for the production of nuclear weapons, but it does not produce it. It creates technical potential,

Riber Hansson/Sweden

which can allow it this. But it is difficult to restrict the creation of this potential."

Trend News Agency (Azerbaijan), May 2011

JOSCHKA FISCHER

Former Vice Chancellor, Germany

Endangering balance

"An Iran armed with nuclear weapons (or one political decision away from possessing them) would drastically alter the Middle East's strategic balance. At best, a nuclear-arms race would threaten to consume this already-unstable region, which would endanger the NPT, with far-reaching global consequences."

Korea Times (South Korea), December 2011

AFZAL BUTT

President, National Press Club, Pakistan

Double standards

"Iran will go ahead with its nuclear activities which are the country's right. They (the United States) cannot see a Muslim state following independent policy and not paying any attention to American threats. They must stop adopting dual standards against Iran . . . [the] U.S. knows that Iran is not developing a weapon-oriented nuclear program."

Philippine News Agency, February 2011

MEHDI GHAZANFARI

Minister of Industries, Mines, and Commerce, Iran

Meaningless sanctions

"Some people think that sanctions have reached a damaging point and if the sanctions include the Central Bank, Iran will be finished off. But we think differently because this is their last ploy and test, and after this, sanctions will become meaningless."

Mehr News Agency (Iran), January 2012

UZI EILAM

Senior Research Fellow Institute for National Security Studies, Israel

Uncertainty

"If they have enough . . . enriched uranium, they (Iran) will have to come up with a good design for the bomb. Then again, nobody knows how far they went in this field."

Trend News Agency (Azerbaijan), December 2011

AYATOLLAH SEYED AHMAD KHATAMI

Senior cleric, Iran

The U.S. is finished

"Today Iran is mighty, strong and powerful and retaliates against any plot so powerfully that it would become a lesson for others. . . . [T]he United States is a finished superpower . . . an empty drum."

Sermon during the Muslim Feast of Sacrifice, November 2011

2

Foreign Aid and National Security

Nellie Bristol

Workers in Rwanda learn to install solar panels at health clinics under a project funded by the U.S. Agency for International Development. Defense Secretary Robert Gates has endorsed efforts by President Obama to increase U.S. foreign assistance, but congressional Republicans are calling for reductions.

U.S. Agency for International Development

From *CQ Researcher*, June 17, 2011

F ormer Marine Capt. Rye Barcott is no stranger to suffering. When he was a University of North Carolina undergraduate, even before he joined the Marines, he and two Kenyans founded a leadership-building youth center and health clinic in the infamous Kibera slum in Nairobi.

But it was while he was serving in Iraq, as he watched kids playing soccer on a dusty field at Abu Ghraib prison, that he fully grasped the potential of economic and social development assistance in struggling countries.

As Barcott watched an 11-year-old accused killer kick a goal, he realized the connection between the boy and his 15-year-old accomplice and many of the youths he knew in Kenya. "As troubled as I was by the [Iraqi] boys' situation, I had still viewed them as the enemy," he wrote in his just-published memoir, *It Happened on the Way to War: A Marine's Path to Peace.* "Now, they had confessed and were playing soccer, and I was seeing them again for who they were. Kids. They were just boys."

It dawned on him with particular clarity that separating his two callings — soldier and humanitarian worker — wasn't possible. "They were different means toward the same goal: peace and stability in a violent world," he wrote. "Surely we would always need a strong military, though there had to be a better way toward peace than this: our detention at Abu Ghraib of two kids almost half my age."

Barcott is now out of the military and working with U.S. groups pushing to give a larger role to U.S. foreign aid, for both humanitarian and national security reasons. The boys in Iraq, Barcott learned, had been coerced into murdering an Iraqi leader, caught up in forces far beyond their control. And that, he says today,

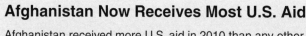

Afghanistan Now Receives Most U.S. Aid

Afghanistan received more U.S. aid in 2010 than any other country, and nearly twice as much as Israel. A decade ago, Israel by far was the biggest aid recipient, and Afghanistan was not even on the list.

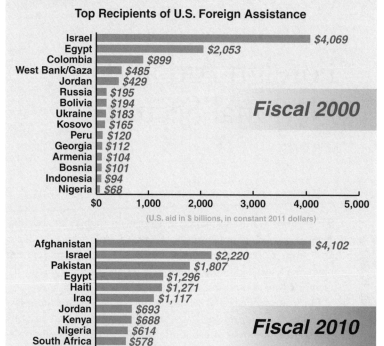

Top Recipients of U.S. Foreign Assistance

Fiscal 2000

Country	Aid
Israel	$4,069
Egypt	$2,053
Colombia	$899
West Bank/Gaza	$485
Jordan	$429
Russia	$195
Bolivia	$194
Ukraine	$183
Kosovo	$165
Peru	$120
Georgia	$112
Armenia	$104
Bosnia	$101
Indonesia	$94
Nigeria	$68

(U.S. aid in $ billions, in constant 2011 dollars)

Fiscal 2010

Country	Aid
Afghanistan	$4,102
Israel	$2,220
Pakistan	$1,807
Egypt	$1,296
Haiti	$1,271
Iraq	$1,117
Jordan	$693
Kenya	$688
Nigeria	$614
South Africa	$578
Ethiopia	$533
Colombia	$507
West Bank/Gaza	$496
Tanzania	$464
Uganda	$457

(U.S. aid in $ billions, in constant 2011 dollars)

Source: Curt Tarnoff and Marian Leonardo Lawson, "Foreign Aid: An Introduction to U.S. Programs and Policy," Congressional Research Service, February 2011, assets.opencrs.com/rpts/R40213_20110210.pdf

improve living conditions, rather than deal with the consequences after the situation has deteriorated. Poverty and poor governance can spur violence and instability anywhere in the world, the argument goes, spawning terrorism, desperation and disease that may come to haunt the United States or need to be addressed through a larger military investment.

After the terrorist attacks on the United States on Sept. 11, 2001, the George W. Bush administration pushed the connection between long-term economic and social development assistance and national security, a link the Obama administration has continued.

"We need an integrated civilian-military national security budget," said Secretary of State Hillary Rodham Clinton. "[I]t's now so important to have diplomats and development experts working side by side [with the military]." Clinton said civilian efforts led by the State Department and the U.S. Agency for International Development (USAID) were especially crucial in the "front-line states" of Pakistan, Iraq and Afghanistan as the U.S. military reduces its forces.

U.S. foreign aid is designed to help increase government stability and develop reliable services, including water and schools, making citizens less dissatisfied with their government and less apt to seek or be susceptible to alternatives. "Too many people on Capitol Hill and throughout the country say, 'Okay, so the military's gone, we don't need to spend any money,' which would be a terrible mistake," Clinton said. "It would make Iraq even more vulnerable to outside interference from Iran."[1]

But House Republicans are pushing for sharp cuts in foreign aid as they seek to slash federal spending and reduce the size of the government. To many of them,

"shows me there are just clearly dramatic limitations to what the military can do, and at that particular moment it wasn't going to be any type of positive force in these kids' lives."

Barcott is not alone in his belief that U.S. foreign policy would be more effective by putting greater emphasis on the civilian tools of diplomacy and development, rather than military force. It is far preferable, he says, to work proactively with faltering countries to

and others, the bigger threat to national security is out-of-control government spending and the massive federal debt. The projected $9.7 trillion national debt over the next decade not only will make the United States more dependent on foreign creditors and international financial markets but also could force cuts to the defense budget that could weaken the military.[2]

Although he also supports a greater role for development aid and diplomacy, Joint Chiefs of Staff Chairman Adm. Mike Mullen said, "The more significant threat to our national security is our debt." He added, "That's why it's so important the economy move in the right direction, because the strength and the support and resources that our military uses are directly related to the health of our economy over time."[3] The defense spending reauthorization bill in the House this year calls for a study of the security risks associated with the U.S. debt held by China.[4]

Complicating the argument is aid's uneven past. Advocates of international assistance point to numerous successes over the years — increased agricultural yields for millions of hungry people, reduced disease worldwide and improved childbirth safety for vulnerable women. But even advocates of aid acknowledge its shortcomings. The United States devoted more than $50 billion to projects in Iraq, for example, including construction of police stations, government buildings and health facilities.[5] Yet poor management, corruption and security problems resulted in billions in cost overruns, and many projects may never be finished.[6]

Afghanistan is another example. While remarkable aid-driven improvements have been made in the country in the last several years, the Senate Foreign Relations Committee released a report on June 8 showing that efforts to push money toward short-term development projects in volatile areas have been counterproductive and may result in an economic crisis in the country when the United States withdraws. It suggests the Obama administration overhaul its approach to ensure projects are "necessary, achievable and sustainable before funding is allocated." The report is sure to play into continuing debates both on the value of foreign aid and the U.S. role in Afghanistan.[7]

In addition, foreign aid may be the most misunderstood piece of the federal budget. According to a 2010 poll, Americans think 25 percent of the federal budget goes to foreign aid and that a more appropriate percentage would be 10 percent.[8] In reality, foreign aid constitutes only around 1.1 percent of the budget.

Another complicating factor is the confusing nature of aid, which is used for a variety of purposes. Slightly more than half of the 2010 foreign aid budget was directed at humanitarian and development projects.[9] The remainder was intended for strategic purposes or to bolster civilian law enforcement or militaries and never intended to improve economic growth in a country. Still, in the eyes of the public, the accounts often are lumped together.

"If we give money to a friendly dictator, 10 years later not much development comes of it, and people say 'Oh, well foreign aid doesn't work,' " says David Beckmann, president of the anti-hunger group Bread for the World. "But the point was to buy an air force base, it wasn't to help people, so we shouldn't be surprised later that it doesn't help people."

As lawmakers on Capitol Hill debate the size of the federal budget. USAID Administrator Rajiv Shah, widely viewed as a dynamic, progressive leader, is trying to convince members of Congress of the value of aid in an era of tight budgets. Shah is making the agency and its aid recipients more accountable, working more closely with developing countries and better tracking effectiveness.

"Like an enterprise, we're focused on delivering the highest possible value for our shareholders — in this case, the American people and the congressional leaders who represent them," Shah said. "We will deliver that value by scaling back our footprint to shift resources to critical regions, rationalizing our operations and vigilantly fighting fraud, waste and abuse."[10]

As the debate over foreign aid and the federal deficit heats up, here are some of the questions being asked:

Is foreign aid necessary for national security?

The importance of the connection between non-military foreign aid and national security is being supported strongly by what may be a surprising group: former and active members of the U.S. military. And the message is coming from the top: Secretary of Defense Robert Gates. "It has become clear that America's civilian institutions of diplomacy and development have been chronically undermanned and underfunded for far too

Foreign Aid Is Tiny Part of U.S. Budget

Foreign assistance accounted for 1.1 percent of U.S. federal budget outlays in fiscal 2010. Foreign aid spending has represented, on average, just over 1 percent of total budget authority annually since 1977.

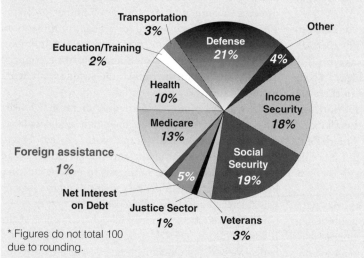

* Figures do not total 100 due to rounding.

Source: Curt Tarnoff and Marian Leonardo Lawson, "Foreign Aid: An Introduction to U.S. Programs and Policy," Congressional Research Service, February 2011, assets.opencrs.com/rpts/R40213_20110210.pdf

long relative to what we spend on the military, and more important, relative to the responsibilities and challenges our nation has around the world," Gates said in 2008.[11]

Gates sees civilian tools of "persuasion and inspiration" as indispensable to a stable world. "We cannot kill or capture our way to victory," he said. "What the Pentagon calls 'kinetic' operations should be subordinate to measures to promote participation in government, economic programs to spur development and efforts to address grievances that often lie at the heart of insurgencies and among the discontented from which the terrorists recruit."

Retired Adm. James M. Loy, former deputy secretary of Homeland Security and Coast Guard commandant, traces the shift in approach to September 11. Since the attacks, he says, "the very definition of national security is much broader in scope." While pre-9/11 security operations might have involved the White House, the National Security Council and the State and Defense departments, they now include participants ranging

from the Treasury and Justice departments to the Agriculture Department and Environmental Protection Agency.

"Who would have thought we'd ever pine for the good old days of the Cold War, with the simplistic notion of a couple of superpowers keeping client states under their wing and in order, all fostered by the notion of mutually assured destruction?" says Loy, now co-chair of the National Security Advisory Council at the U.S. Global Leadership Coalition, a network of business and nongovernmental leaders that advocates increased use of civilian power. In today's more complicated world, he adds, "We're still trying to understand it."

Investment in civilian operations is considered a "best buy" by J. Stephen Morrison, senior vice president at the Center for Strategic and International Studies (CSIS). It is much cheaper to send specialists in health or elections to a country than to fund a military intervention, not to mention saving the lives and limbs of soldiers, he notes. Supporters of development as a national security tool acknowledge that definitive results for the approach are hard to find, mostly because it's difficult to measure what would have happened absent the aid. But, Morrison argues, "there's the kind of presumptive, wise, forward investment in creating a form of human security, accountability and transparency that will make for a better-functioning world."

Afghanistan is frequently cited as an example of how aid would have protected the United States. When the Russians left in 1989, after nearly 10 years of war and occupation, the United States didn't follow through in rebuilding. Such actions can have serious consequences, comments Adm. Loy, who says, "Often when we've watched [foreign aid] fall, we've paid the price shortly thereafter."

But not everyone agrees. James Roberts, a research fellow for economic freedom and growth at the Heritage Foundation, a conservative think tank, warned that "out of control federal spending" leads to a national security threat and that traditional development assistance "does not work, at least not if the goal is to foster sustainable development in poor countries."[12] He said development is better accomplished through private organizations. He did, however, laud humanitarian aid delivered under U.S. global HIV/AIDS programs.

Justin Logan, associate director of foreign policy studies at the Cato Institute, a libertarian think tank, says strategic aid is unnecessary and counterproductive. "I think we're secure, independent of these efforts to try to tinker with the balance of power in other regions," he says. He calls a lot of aid, especially to problematic allies such as Egypt and Pakistan, "bribery." "I don't buy the Rube Goldberg theory that regional instability everywhere will always come back to bite us, [a view] I think is quite prevalent in Washington," he adds.

U.S. willingness to engage throughout the world has made other countries less motivated to provide services for their citizens or even shore up their own defenses, Logan says. The U.S. tendency to pick and choose when and how to get involved in conflicts internationally "taints the image of America as a beacon of liberalism and democracy to the rest of the world and in some cases causes actual animosity and terrorism against the United States," he adds.

Significantly, among those not fully convinced by the development aid-as-national security argument are lawmakers influential in budget matters. House Budget Committee Chairman Paul Ryan, R-Wis., developed a 2012 budget plan that would have cut international affairs funding, which includes foreign aid, by as much as 28 percent.[13]

And Rep. Kay Granger, R-Texas, chair of the House Appropriations Committee's State, Foreign Operations and Related Programs Subcommittee, said that given the country's constrained economic circumstances, foreign aid needs to be focused on "direct national security."[14]

While she acknowledged the connection between foreign aid and national security in long-term U.S. commitments to Israel, Iraq, Afghanistan, Pakistan and Mexico, she suggested other, less pressing development investments would be a lower priority in the current climate. "We have to look at our national security, particularly in foreign aid, and say, What is in our national security interest?" she said.

Sen. Rand Paul, R-Ky., makes the most extreme case against foreign aid, saying all aid should be cut, even to longtime ally Israel. Citing a Reuter's poll, Paul said, "71 percent of the American people agree with me that when we're short of money, when we can't do the things we need to do in our country, we certainly shouldn't be shipping the money overseas." In making his case, Paul said that while he's sympathetic to challenges faced by developing countries, aid money too often goes to unscrupulous leaders. "You don't want to just keep throwing money to corrupt leaders who steal it from their people," he argued.

Moreover, Paul said, U.S. aid to Israel is matched by aid to Islamic countries, possibly contributing to an arms race in the region. "I don't think that funding both sides of an arms race, particularly when we have to borrow the money from China to send it to someone else — we just can't do it anymore. The debt is all-consuming, and it threatens our well-being as a country."[15]

Does the U.S. benefit from foreign aid spending?

Foreign aid has always been a hard sell, but in the current political and economic climate, it's harder still. While much of official Washington considers aid vital, the value is often lost on everyday Americans, many of whom are struggling to hold on to their houses, find new jobs and educate their kids.

"It's really important that you all know this committee is extremely supportive of programs that really will save the lives and positively impact the developing world," Rep. Jerry Lewis, R-Calif., a member of the Foreign Operations Subcommittee, told USAID and State Department officials March 31. "In turn, our public just plain doesn't believe it, and they wonder why, for God's sake, we're spending this money when we don't actually sense there's any positive result for the American taxpayer."[16]

Calculating the ultimate value of aid to the donor is difficult to begin with. Further, examples of misspent, ineffective and even harmful aid are plentiful. Several prominent economists, including William Easterly of New York University, author of *The White Man's Burden: Why The West's Efforts to Aid the Rest Have Done So Much Ill and So Little Good*, and Dambisa Moyo, author of *Dead Aid: Why Aid Is Not Working and How There Is a Better Way for Africa*, have harshly criticized Western

The ABC's of Foreign Assistance

U.S. foreign assistance totaled $39.4 billion, or 1.1% of the federal budget in fiscal 2010, the highest amount since 1985. Aid has three primary rationales: enhancing national security, bolstering commercial interests and addressing humanitarian concerns. U.S. aid falls into several categories based on the goal and form of the aid:

- **Bilateral Development Assistance** totaled $12.3 billion in 2010, or 34 percent of foreign aid appropriations, and is largely administered by USAID. It is used for long-term projects supporting economic reform, private-sector development, democracy promotion, environmental protection and human health.

- **Multilateral Development Assistance** made up 7 percent of the 2010 budget, totaling $2.6 billion. It is combined with contributions from other donor nations and implemented by international organizations such as the United Nations.

- **Humanitarian assistance** was allotted $5.1 billion in 2010, or 13.5 percent of the assistance budget. Funding is used to help victims of earthquakes, floods and other crises. A large portion addresses issues related to refugees and internally displaced persons.

- **Assistance serving both development and special political/strategic purposes** includes the Economic Support Fund, which now largely goes to countries key to the war on terrorism. Several other programs in this category are aimed at Europe and Asia. These funds totaled $9.6 billion in 2010, or 25 percent of total assistance.

- **Civilian Security Assistance** focuses on terrorism, illicit narcotics, crimes and weapons proliferation and totaled 9 percent of the foreign aid budget in 2010.

- **Military Assistance** is provided to U.S. friends and allies to help them purchase U.S. military equipment and training. In 2010, Congress appropriated $4.7 billion for this account, or 12.5% of total foreign aid.

Note: Totals do not add to 100 due to rounding.

Source: Curt Tarnoff and Marian Leonardo Lawson, "Foreign Aid: An Introduction to US Programs and Policy," Congressional Research Service, Feb. 10, 2011, www. fas.org/sgp/crs/row/R40213.pdf.

steadily, particularly in the last decade, to document program effectiveness.[17] For example, the *Oportunidades* program in Mexico was proven to successfully alleviate poverty and ill health by providing payments to families to keep their kids in school and take them to health clinics.[18] Similar programs have been established in Brazil and Nicaragua.[19] Other successful interventions include deworming, immunization, vitamin supplements and oral rehydration solutions to treat diarrhea in areas in the developing world with high child mortality rates.

But when it comes to specific programs, determining value is "a little bit tricky," says Christopher J. L. Murray, director of the Institute for Health Metrics and Evaluation at the University of Washington in Seattle. The health arena boasts several obvious winners, Murray says, including programs providing insecticide-treated bed nets to prevent mosquito-borne malaria in Africa and HIV/AIDS treatments to millions of sufferers, also particularly in Africa. "Pretty much anyone would say there's been a real benefit, and the U.S. has played an important role in both," Murray says. But with other programs, he says, "evaluating value for money is much harder."

It's not that aid isn't having an effect, Murray adds, but that it's harder to pinpoint exactly what is creating the positive result. For example, while there has been marked progress recently in reducing child morality in the poorest countries, it's hard to prove with certainty which factors are most responsible. "So many things contribute to reductions in child mortality . . . rising incomes contribute at the household and community level, better housing, better water, etc. Probably half of

attempts at poverty alleviation. Some experts urge a move toward expanded trade opportunities with developing countries rather than continued direct assistance.

To counter theories that aid is akin to pouring money down a rat hole, development professionals have worked

the decline in child mortality is related to improvements in educating young girls. So the challenge here is teasing out the effect of, let's say, vaccination programs versus these broader development trends," Murray notes. "I think it's likely that development assistance has contributed to that. Can I prove that in a rigorous, scientific way like we can for bed nets or [HIV/AIDS therapies]? Much harder to do," he says.

Dean Karlan, a professor of economics at Yale University and president and founder of Innovations for Poverty Action, a consulting firm that evaluates poverty programs, thinks at least partial evaluation of programs is possible. When asked if the U.S. gets value for its foreign aid dollars, Karlan says, "The answer is, sort of. Some things work, and some things don't."

Both Karlan and Murray see the development sector as much more motivated and able now to examine specific programs, largely because more tools have become available to collect and analyze data, and more development organizations, including governments, the U.N. and private donors, are demanding transparency and accountability of both funding and data.

But objectivity has its limitations. Karlan favors randomized evaluations to rigorously examine intervention effectiveness. The method works for discrete programs, including health services, and is being adopted vigorously by USAID and other U.S. government programs. However, Karlan says, the method doesn't work for everything.

U.S. Contributes Most Aid

The United States contributed nearly $29 billion in official development assistance (ODA) in 2009, the most in the world and more than twice the amount of France, which ranked second (top graph). As a percentage of gross national income (GNI), however, the U.S. contributed only 0.2 percent to such assistance, ranking far behind Nordic countries such as Sweden and Norway, each of which gave more than 1 percent (bottom graph).

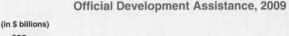

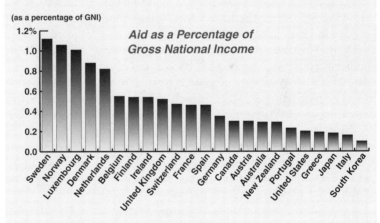

Source: "Net Official Development Assistance in 2009," Organisation for Economic Co-operation and Development, April 2010, www.oecd.org/dataoecd/17/9/44981892.pdf

Efforts such as judicial reform, democracy building or even road construction are more difficult to evaluate for their impact on local citizens.

Whether projects result in goodwill and enhanced security for Americans is even more difficult to measure.

"There are some areas of aid that still elude us in terms of establishing good, clear, rigorous evaluation," Karlan says. Without clear evidence, "all we can do is fire rhetoric and bad data at each other, but no one's ever going to convince the other side on it."

A U.S. military helicopter delivers cement to Pakistan's flooded Swat Valley last October. Slightly more than half of the U.S. foreign aid budget for 2010 supported humanitarian and development projects. The remainder was allocated for strategic purposes, including military aid.

Does the United States give too much aid to authoritarian governments?

America has long bestowed aid to win friends and influence people — and not always to the most savory individuals. Despots who have received U.S. aid include Ferdinand Marcos in the Philippines, "Baby Doc" Duvalier in Haiti, and even Saddam Hussein in Iraq. During the Cold War, the practice of supporting harsh, non-democratic governments, while roundly criticized, was viewed as a necessary evil in ensuring regional stability and keeping countries from turning to communism. But the doctrine has come under renewed scrutiny during the recent "Arab Spring" unrest, when the United States was criticized for being on the wrong side of several democratic uprisings, most notably in Egypt.

Egypt is a top recipient of U.S. aid — more than $70 billion since 1948 — mostly for weapons.[20] The Egyptian-Israeli Peace Treaty of 1979 cemented U.S. backing.[21] From America's perspective, the aid increases Egypt's stability, raises regional support for the United States and helps Egypt stay at peace with Israel. But the recent protests in Cairo's Tahrir Square against the now-ended regime of Hosni Mubarak put the United States in the difficult position of having to denounce a government it had financially helped for many years, and the administration's lukewarm initial reaction to the uprisings generated widespread criticism.

"The Obama administration now appears to be wavering on whether America really backs the demands of the Egyptian people, or just wants to return to stability with a façade of change," Rep. Gary Ackerman, D-N.Y., said in February.[22]

The Obama administration's experiences with the Egyptian upheaval and others in the Middle East may prompt a re-evaluation of its strategies toward countries with autocratic leaders, such as Yemen and Bahrain.[23]

Anthony Kim, a policy analyst at the Heritage Foundation, says it's about time. "In the name of stability the United States has been giving out a lot of taxpayers' money to a lot of authoritarian regimes, and as we know now better than before, in countries like Egypt and Pakistan political freedom is very limited," Kim says. "We blindly, without thinking through the true effect of foreign aid, have been wasting our money on those countries."

Referring largely to the billions of dollars of non-military aid to Egypt over the years, Kim said the funding did little for economic development. "Year after year, the data show economic development has been at best cosmetic" and has not reached citizens, he says. "So basically we end up empowering and enriching those corrupt powers in the government" and perhaps contributing to the longevity of non-democratic regimes. "The money we paid hasn't paid off for the United States," he says.

An even more complicated situation is occurring in Pakistan, according to Molly Kinder, a senior policy analyst at the Center for Global Development, a development think tank in Washington. The United States has aided the country for many years, but it stepped up funding after 9/11 to enlist Pakistan's anti-terrorism help. The assistance started out heavily weighted toward military aid, but Congress forced a more balanced approach in 2009, tripling the amount designated for economic development.[24]

Overall, U.S. aid for Pakistan has been largely based on U.S. strategic needs rather than the needs of the people of Pakistan, says Kinder. "The ebbs and flows of foreign aid are contingent on what's going on in the world," she says. "So when Pakistan is needed as an ally in the war on terror or the Cold War, our aid to Pakistan spikes, often corresponding with military regimes [there]. So I think it's a very fair criticism to say Pakistanis view the United States as putting money disproportionately to non-democratic regimes" in Pakistan, Kinder says.

While such a policy may endear the United States to ruling authoritarian powers and give it at least the illusion of an ally, the U.S. ends up looking bad to the citizenry, Kinder says. "There's a real ethical conundrum and a real foreign policy challenge because it certainly can breed resentment toward the United States, which we're seeing now in Pakistan," she says. A recent poll by the Pew Research Center showed that only 11 percent of Pakistanis have favorable views of the United States, one of the lowest levels in Muslim countries surveyed.[25]

"My big question about aid to countries we're not quite comfortable with is whether we are just keeping a lid on things and hoping that the governments stay in power to do the things we want them to do?" Kinder asks. "Is the aid just blunting pressure for reform or pressure for change, giving the government resources to just kind of survive against the will of the people? That's something that I think requires a lot of soul-searching from the U.S. perspective."

But Roberts of the Heritage Foundation said that while development aid is ineffective in Egypt and many other places, military aid paid big dividends for the United States during the Egyptian revolt. He cited the U.S.-supported Egyptian military as having succeeded in "holding the line against virulently anti-U.S. elements."[26] That view is echoed by Secretary of State Hillary Rodham Clinton, who said U.S. support of the Egyptian military "was one of the best investments America made" because the relationship facilitated communication between the United States and the Egyptian military during the protests.[27]

Joint Chiefs Chairman Mullen made a similar argument, noting military aid to Egypt has been of "incalculable value" in transforming the country's army into a capable force. "Changes to those relationships — in either

U.S. Aid Tracks Events, Presidential Initiatives

Foreign aid funding in recent decades can be attributed to specific foreign policy events and presidential initiatives. Since the Sept. 11, 2001, terrorist attacks, funding has been closely tied to U.S. strategy in Iraq and Afghanistan. Global health initiatives by the Bush and Obama administrations, including the Global Health Initiative, the Millennium Challenge Corp., and the PEPFAR HIV/AIDS program, also drove increases. Aid to the Middle East also rose, especially in nations viewed as vital partners in America's War on Terror.

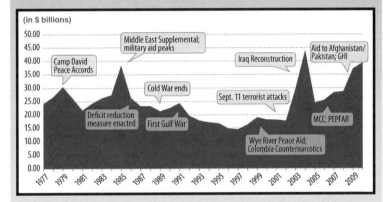

Source: Curt Tarnoff and Marian Leonardo Lawson, "Foreign Aid: An Introduction to U.S. Programs and Policy," Congressional Research Service, Feb. 10, 2011

aid or assistance — ought to be considered only with an abundance of caution and a thorough appreciation for the long view, rather than in the flush of public passion and the urgency to save a buck," he added.[28]

BACKGROUND

Rise of Modern Aid

Foreign assistance became a key component of U.S. foreign policy during and after World War II. The United States began providing support for war-devastated European countries in 1945. Those diffuse efforts were centralized when Secretary of State George C. Marshall and other officials called for a massive, coordinated effort to rebuild Europe's infrastructure. The European Recovery Program, known as the Marshall Plan, pumped $12.5 billion into Western Europe over a three-year period beginning in 1948. The aid was designed to advance U.S. interests as well as help Europe.

C H R O N O L O G Y

1940s-1960s *United States begins a tradition of foreign assistance.*

June 5, 1947 Economic assistance for postwar Europe proposed by Secretary of State George C. Marshall. "Marshall Plan" plays key role in stimulating Western Europe's economic revival.

Jan. 30, 1961 Citing concerns about the spread of communism, President John F. Kennedy announces plans for a new aid program: "Our role is essential and unavoidable in the construction of a sound and expanding economy for the entire noncommunist world, helping other nations build the strength to meet their own problems, to satisfy their own aspirations — to surmount their own dangers."

Sept. 4, 1961 Congress passes Foreign Assistance Act, separating military and non-military aid.

Nov. 3, 1961 Kennedy establishes U.S. Agency for International Development as the first foreign-assistance organization focused primarily on long-range economic and social development.

1970s *U.S. foreign aid focuses on Middle East, begins to decline.*

1970 U.N. calls for "economically advanced countries" to progressively increase their development assistance to 0.7 percent of gross national product.

1971 Senate rejects foreign-assistance funding for fiscal 1972 and 1973.

1973 Congress passes amendments to the Foreign Assistance Act that break aid into targeted sectors including food and nutrition, population planning and health and education and human resources.

1979 Camp David Accords boost U.S. aid to Israel and Egypt to encourage the peace process. Most of the aid is military assistance to buy U.S. weapons.

1990s *U.S. foreign aid continues to decline.*

1990 U.S. spending on foreign aid peaks at $65.5 billion and begins a 20 percent decline to $53.1 billion by 2000.

1997 Sen. Jesse Helms, R-N.C., makes unsuccessful attempt to downsize USAID and place it fully in the State Department.

2000s *Terrorist attacks on Sept. 11, 2001, renew U.S. interest in stabilizing "failing states"; U.S. becomes a leader in global health funding.*

Sept. 8, 2000 World's nations adopt U.N. Millennium Declaration vowing to reduce extreme poverty by half and address other inequities by 2015.

March 14, 2002 President George W. Bush creates a new aid mechanism, the Millennium Challenge Account, which offers assistance only to countries that adopt reforms and effective policies. He pledges $5 billion a year for the effort.

Jan. 28, 2003 President Bush announces the $15 billion, five-year President's Emergency Plan for AIDS Relief (PEPFAR), which becomes the largest international commitment by any country dedicated to a single disease.

Jan. 18, 2006 Secretary of State Condoleezza Rice announces move toward transformational diplomacy, or elevating the role of diplomacy and development in U.S. foreign policy.

2008 Democratic presidential candidate Barack Obama pledges to double U.S. foreign assistance to $50 billion by 2012, a promise that runs headfirst into the global economic collapse.

Dec. 8, 2010 Incoming House Foreign Affairs Committee Chairwoman Ileana Ros-Lehtinen, R-Fla., pledges to "restore fiscal discipline to foreign affairs."

Dec. 16, 2010 Secretary of State Hillary Rodham Clinton releases long-awaited Quadrennial Diplomacy and Development Review, a blueprint for making U.S. foreign policy more coherent and calling for greater engagement of "civilian power" in advancing national interests.

April 15, 2011 House passes budget resolution that would cut international affairs budgets by as much as 28 percent in 2012.

A primary driver of the efforts was concern that a Europe on its knees would allow westward expansion of the Soviet Union and the spread of communism. The plan also advanced U.S. economic interests by requiring the purchase of U.S. goods.

The Marshall Plan was considered by most to be a success, although some would argue other factors contributed to the recovery, notably a 32 percent increase in Western Europe's gross national product, spurred by an 11 percent rise in agricultural production and a 40 percent increase in industrial output over pre-war levels.[29]

Inspired by the success in Europe, President Harry S Truman proposed aid to developing countries. Nonetheless, foreign aid spending was stagnant during the costly Korean War (1950-53) and the Eisenhower administration (1953-61).

Much of the modern architecture of foreign aid was developed during the foreshortened presidency of John F. Kennedy (1961-1963). On Nov. 3, 1961 Kennedy consolidated assistance programs into the United States Agency for International Development (USAID). Its creation was mandated by the Foreign Assistance Act of 1961, which for the first time separated military and non-military aid. It was the first U.S. assistance organization to focus on long-range economic and social development and to offer direct support to developing countries. Even then, the threat of global economic disparity weighed heavily in arguments for foreign aid.

"[W]idespread poverty and chaos lead to a collapse of existing political and social structures which would inevitably invite the advance of totalitarianism into every weak and unstable area," Kennedy said in 1961. "Thus our own security would be endangered and our prosperity imperiled. A program of assistance to the underdeveloped nations must continue because the nation's interest and the cause of political freedom require it."[30]

Although the stated goal of foreign aid was development, during the Vietnam War era, concerns arose that it was too focused on short-term military goals. In 1971, as the conflict was nearing its end, the Senate defeated foreign assistance funding for 1972 and 1973; it was the first time since the start of the Marshall Plan that either chamber of Congress had rejected aid funding. In 1973, Congress amended the Foreign Assistance Act to steer funds into specific, functional categories including education, agriculture and family planning. The aid structure developed by the amendments remains largely intact today.

Controversies have cropped up since the United States began handing out foreign assistance. One of the most contentious occurred during Ronald Reagan's presidency (1981-1989), when anti-abortion groups complained that taxpayer money was supporting abortion in foreign countries, particularly in China. That prompted Reagan, through a 1984 executive order, to bar government funding for family planning to any foreign, non-governmental organizations that "perform or actively promote" abortions or conduct research to improve abortion methods.[31]

Known by opponents as the "global gag rule," it targeted groups providing "abortion as a method of family planning." The ban applied to groups even using their own funds for abortion-related activities. Reaction to the rule reflected the politics of the abortion debate: Democratic President Bill Clinton rescinded the policy, Republican George W. Bush reinstated it and Democrat Obama again rescinded it.

Organizational dysfunction and lack of clear successes also plagued foreign aid. Programs were criticized as being too dispersed and U.S. bureaucracies too hidebound to be effective. The intermingling of aid used to curry friends — mostly in the form of military and strategic accounts — and aid aimed at long-term development made it difficult to determine whether the aid was achieving the goal of poverty alleviation.

Congressional requirements for the use of U.S. commodities, goods and services also kept aid administrators from pursuing the most effective interventions. Dissatisfaction with the program both among the public and in Congress led to a decline in USAID funding. Foreign Service permanent staffing declined from a high of about 4,500 in 1970 to a low of 1,000 in 2000. The level is projected to be around 2,000 in 2012.[32]

Moreover, several unsuccessful efforts were made to reform the Foreign Assistance Act, including a move to abolish USAID. In 1991, President George H. W. Bush proposed a comprehensive rewriting of the act, but Congress did not seriously consider it. President Clinton also tried his hand at reform through the 1994 Peace, Prosperity and Democracy Act, but it too failed to gain traction in Congress.

New Approach

The 9/11 terrorist attacks put foreign aid back in the spotlight. While little evidence suggested that poverty in

China's Growing Aid to Africa

Does it undermine U.S. influence?

With U.S. foreign aid budgets threatened on Capitol Hill, the Obama administration is warning that decreasing American influence abroad could lead to greater influence for China. "Let's put aside the moral, humanitarian, do-good side of what we believe in, and let's just talk, you know, straight realpolitik," Secretary of State Hillary Rodham Clinton told the Senate Foreign Relations Committee on March 2. "We are in competition with China."[1]

China has increased its foreign aid significantly over the past few years, particularly in Africa, where it grew from $300 million in 2001 to $2.1 billion in 2009.[2] Most of the aid is in the form of loans. The rise has caused alarm from some who say China is baldly seeking influence in developing countries by, among other things, constructing high-profile buildings such as hotels, conference centers and soccer stadiums.[3]

"These highly visible investments, seemingly unavoidable across Africa, are designed to buy influence with governments," writes *Washington Post* columnist Michael Gerson.[4] The move seems to be working, at least among the public. In a recent poll, developing nations had more positive than negative views of China, especially Nigeria (82 percent) and Kenya (77 percent).[5] China has been active in both countries for several years.[6]

China's growing aid budget raises concerns about:

- The general threat of another power seeking influence in the developing world;

- A lack of transparency associated with Chinese aid;
- Extraction of natural resources without much return for the host country, and
- Aid without regard to a country's governance record that will weaken attempts to encourage countries to reform.

But China expert Deborah Brautigam, a professor of international relations at American University in Washington, sees the situation differently. "There are a lot of myths out there about China's aid program," she says, pointing out that China focuses more on export credits, which foster exports and business, while the United States emphasizes outright aid. China's focus on exports stems from the affordability of its goods in Africa, unlike those from the United States, she explains.

As for China locking up all Africa's natural resources, "that's really unrealistic," she says. She acknowledges Chinese aid programs lack transparency but says that's not unusual for countries relatively new to the foreign-assistance arena. Nonetheless, she notes, China recently released a white paper outlining some of its activities.[7] While it was not the detailed, country-by-country data that would have been expected from a more experienced donor country, Brautigam says, "I thought for them this was a very big step. Expecting this kind of transparency to happen immediately, people are bound to be disappointed."

Meanwhile, critics complain that despite China's deep pockets, reflected in both its growing aid efforts

the Arab world had motivated the terrorists, U.S. officials noted that al-Qaida, the group behind the attacks, was based in Afghanistan, one of the world's poorest countries.

Concern about the link between poverty and terrorism led to a focus on stabilizing other fragile and "failing states" to minimize the number of places where terrorist groups could flourish as well as to attract allies in the war against Islamic extremists. A reshuffling of U.S. foreign aid followed. While Israel and Egypt had been the top aid recipients in fiscal 2000, Afghanistan was in the No. 1 spot in 2010, and Pakistan, Haiti, Iraq and Kenya had become major recipients as well.[33]

The attacks also fostered a new approach to foreign policy, which Secretary of State Condoleezza Rice termed "transformational diplomacy." The goal, Rice said in 2006, was "to work with our many partners around the world to build and sustain democratic, well-governed states that will respond to the needs of their people and conduct themselves responsibly in the international system."[34]

The effort included a new post: director of foreign assistance, who served concurrently as USAID administrator.

and ability to put on costly events like the 2008 Olympics, it continues to receive aid from the Global Fund to Fight AIDS, Tuberculosis and Malaria — $539 million since 2003.

"China's aggregate award from the fund is nearly three times larger than that of South Africa, one of the most affected countries from these three diseases," wrote Jack Chow, a former assistant director general of the World Health Organization, now a professor at Carnegie Mellon University.[8] A fund spokesman said China isn't usurping money from other needy countries because the fund so far has been able to approve all applications "of quality."[9]

The question may soon be moot. The fund recently froze its grants to China over a dispute about management of the money and funding of community organizations, a move likely to intensify the debate over whether China should be receiving grants at all.[10]

— *Nellie Bristol*

Masai tribesmen perform a traditional dance as a Chinese hospital ship departs Mombasa, Kenya, after providing residents with free medical help.

[1]Transcript of Senate Foreign Relations Committee hearing on the Proposed Fiscal 2012 Budget for the State Department, March 2, 2011, http://micevhill.com/attachments/immigration_documents/hosted_documents/112th_congress/TranscriptOfSenateForeignRelationsCommitteeHearing OnTheProposedFiscal2012ForeignAffairsBudget.pdf.

[2]Benedicte Vibe Christensen, "China in Africa: A Macroeconomic Perspective," The Center for Global Development, Dec. 22, 2010.

[3]Michael Gerson, "China's African Investments: Who Benefits?" *The Washington Post*, March 28, 2011, www.washingtonpost.com/opinions/chinas-african-investments-who-benefits/2011/03/28/AF8G7mqB_story.html.

[4]*Ibid.*

[5]Andrew Walker, "China's New Economic Power Fans Fear, BBC Poll Finds," BBC, March 27, 2011, www.bbc.co.uk/news/business-12867892.

[6]"China's Hu boosts Kenyan Business," BBC, April 28, 2006, http://news.bbc.co.uk/2/hi/africa/4953588.stm, and "Chinese Engagement in Nigeria Would Aid the Industrialization of the Country," Pan-African News Wire, May 30, 2009.

[7]Sven Grimm, "China's Aid Policy White Paper: Transparency Now?" *Devex*, May 20, 2011, www.devex.com/en/blogs/full-disclosure/china-s-aid-policy-white-paper-transparency-now.

[8]Jack C. Chow, "China's Billion-Dollar Aid Appetite: Why is Beijing Winning Health Grants at the Expense of African Countries," *Foreign Policy*, July 2010, www.foreignpolicy.com/articles/2010/07/19/chinas_billion_dollar_aid_appetite.

[9]Gillian Wong, "China Rises and Rises, Yet Still Gets Foreign Aid," *The Daily Journal*, Oct. 1, 2010, www.smdailyjournal.com/article_preview.php?id=142573&title=China%20rises%20and%20rises,%20yet%20still%20gets%20foreign%20aid.

[10]Sharon LaFraniere, "AIDS Funds Frozen for China in Grant Dispute," *The New York Times*, May 20, 2011, www.nytimes.com/2011/05/21/world/asia/21china.html.

The goal was to better coordinate foreign assistance programs, which spanned more than 20 government agencies, and better align foreign assistance with national security goals.

The effort also was aimed at increasing America's civilian capability to address instability and crisis abroad. Over time, responsibility for foreign operations increasingly had fallen to the military, and it began to ask for help. Secretary of Defense Gates in 2007 called for "a dramatic increase in spending on the civilian instruments of national security — diplomacy, strategic communications, foreign assistance, civic action and economic reconstruction and development."[35]

While the development and humanitarian communities applauded the increased focus on civilian efforts, they also had a fundamental concern. Many worried that folding USAID more tightly into the State Department linked foreign assistance too closely with short-term policy goals, leaving little room for sustainable development and poverty alleviation. The USAID administrator post was appointed as a separate position in the Obama administration.

More Aid Sought for Women and Girls

Secretary Clinton: "They represent potential that goes unfulfilled."

A majority of the planet's poor, jobless, illiterate, hungry and uneducated people are females.[1] They are subject to domestic violence, child marriage and poor reproductive health services that result in unwanted pregnancies and pregnancy-related death and disability. Yet, women and girls receive only 2 cents of every development dollar, according to some estimates, despite evidence that investing in females creates broad social gains.[2]

For example, an extra year of secondary school increases wages by 15-25 percent; girls who stay in school longer than seven years marry later and have fewer children, and women are more likely than men to reinvest their incomes in their families.[3]

Special attention to the needs of women and their connection to broader development progress was underscored at a 1994 United Nations Conference on Population and Development in Cairo, Egypt.[4] Then-first lady Hillary Rodham Clinton was a prominent leader of the U.S. delegation. While goals for achieving better health care for women became mired in anti-abortion politics during the Bush years, the issue has become popular again now that Clinton is secretary of State.

"When a girl becomes a mother before she becomes literate, when a women gives birth alone and is left with a permanent disability, when a mother toils daily to feed her large family but cannot convince her husband to agree to contraception, these struggles represent suffering that can and should be avoided," Clinton said on the 15th anniversary of the Cairo conference. "They represent potential that goes unfulfilled. And they also represent an opportunity to send critical help to women worldwide and the children who depend on them."[5]

Opportunities and health care for woman and girls are centerpieces of several Obama administration assistance programs, including the secretary's International Fund for Women and Girls and the Global Health Initiative (GHI). The fund, a public-private effort started by Clinton, invests in organizations with innovative ideas to combat violence and create economic and political opportunities for women and girls. A focus on women, girls and gender equality is one of the first principles of the GHI, which proposes a $63-billion, six-year expansion of U.S. programs addressing infectious disease, nutrition, maternal and child health, neglected tropical disease and other issues.

In addition, as HIV/AIDS began to affect more women than men in high prevalence regions, the United States global HIV/AIDS program PEPFAR began to shift resources to address mother-to-child transmission of the disease and develop female-controlled prevention strategies.

Bush's Initiatives

But Bush also instituted programs to benefit countries that were not key to U.S. political strategy. Calling the fight against poverty a moral imperative, Bush in a speech to the Inter-American Development Bank in Monterrey, Mexico, in 2002 pledged increases in core development assistance by 50 percent over three years.[36] The funds would be administered through a newly developed Millennium Challenge Account, separate from USAID. The approach was approved by Congress in 2004 and is administered by a State Department arm, the Millennium Challenge Corporation (MCC).

Before doling out funds, the MCC requires countries to prove they are well-governed and have the administrative capacity to effectively use them. In addition, countries have to show progress in fighting corruption, educating girls, building democracy and other actions. Instead of deciding in Washington which projects would be funded, MCC sponsors programs suggested by the countries themselves. But sluggish appropriations from Congress and difficulties in getting projects off the ground have slowed MCC's progress. Bush originally envisioned the agency receiving $5 billion per year, but MCC has approved only $7.4 billion in development programs in the seven years since its inception.[37]

Some aid experts worried that the MCC's strict approach would result in further suffering by poor people in countries with ineffective or corrupt leaders. Meanwhile, some U.S. beneficiaries, including Afghanistan and Pakistan, were not meeting many of the MCC criteria.

Obama is pushing combining HIV treatment with family planning and other health services.

The shift responds to recent research showing that supporting the development of women and girls has a multiplier effect. Ensuring a basic education for girls, for example, helps them control their fertility better, allows them more opportunities in the workplace and gives them the knowledge they need to keep their families healthier, according to Nandini Oomman, a senior program associate at the Center for Global Development in Washington. "If development and foreign assistance that's supposed to support development doesn't address gender differentials, then you're not going to make a lot of progress in human development no matter how much economic development you have," she says.

Reaching women with aid is difficult in many places, especially rural areas. Women tend to be mostly at home, out of the public sphere, and bear a disproportionate share of the family burden. Girls, for example, are more likely than boys to carry out household chores rather than go to school. "When you don't think specifically about how you can bring services to women, then they can't avail themselves of those services," said Oomman. In other words, she says, aid for women can only be effective when it focuses on their circumstances.

"If you start with a man as a norm, you leave off women," agrees Serra Sippel, president of the Center for Health and Gender Equity in Washington.

But raising the issue of gender is difficult in countries where discrimination is firmly entrenched. USAID recently stripped several gender-equity provisions from large projects in Afghanistan.[6] When asked at a congressional hearing about the change, Clinton acknowledged that promoting opportunities for women in the country "is really hard. And there are deep cultural challenges to doing this work." Nonetheless, Clinton reaffirmed America's commitment to gender equality. "We believe strongly that supporting women and girls is essential to building democracy and security," she told the panel.[7]

— *Nellie Bristol*

[1]Ritu Sharma, "Written Testimony: House Subcommittee on State Foreign Operations, and Related Programs," April 14, 2011, http://appropriations.house.gov/_files/041411WomenThriveWorldwideTestimony.pdf.

[2]Nancy Gibbs, "To Fight Poverty, Invest in Girls," *Time*, Feb. 14, 2011, www.time.com/time/magazine/article/0,9171,2046045,00.html.

[3]*Ibid.*

[4]Lori S. Ashford, "What Was Cairo? The Promise and Reality of ICPD," Population Reference Bureau, September 2004, www.prb.org/Articles/2004/WhatWasCairoThePromiseandRealityofICPD.aspx.

[5]Hillary Rodham Clinton, "Remarks on the 15th Anniversary of the International Conference on Population and Development," Jan. 8, 2010, www.state.gov/secretary/rm/2010/01/135001.htm.

[6]Rajiv Chandrasekaran, "In Afghanistan, US Shifts Strategy on Women's Rights as it Eyes Wider Priorities," *The Washington Post*, March 14, 2011, www.washingtonpost.com/wp-dyn/content/article/2011/03/05/AR2011030503668.html?nav=emailpage.

[7]Rajiv Chandrasekaran, "Clinton: US Will Keep Helping Afghan Women," *The Washington Post*, March 11, 2011, www.washingtonpost.com/wp-dyn/content/article/2011/03/10/AR2011031005181.html.

The biggest aid effort of the George W. Bush administration was the President's Emergency Plan for AIDS Relief (PEPFAR). After an initially slow response to the burgeoning global HIV/AIDS epidemic, Bush proposed the plan in his 2003 State of the Union address, promising $15 billion over five years. Congress enthusiastically approved the U.S. Leadership Against HIV/AIDS, Tuberculosis and Malaria Act with the goal of providing HIV/AIDS care, treatment and prevention to specific hard-hit countries. PEPFAR is the largest single disease program ever supported by one nation. It has provided antiretroviral drugs to millions of HIV sufferers in poor countries, helped develop key prevention programs and prevent the transmission of the disease from mothers to newborns.[38] The U.S Office of the Global AIDS coordinator, housed at the State Department, oversees the program. The act was reauthorized in 2008, allowing funding of up to $39 billion for the program over five years. Bush also developed the freestanding President's Malaria Initiative.

In addition, Bush authorized major U.S. contributions to multilateral efforts to improve global health. In 2001, the U.S. appropriated $100 million for the fledgling Global Fund to Fight AIDS, tuberculosis and Malaria, which helps low- and middle-income countries. As of late last year, donors have pledged $30 billion to the fund, which has approved nearly $20 billion in grants to more than 140 countries.[39] The United States has pledged $9.7 billion and had contributed 28 percent of the fund's total contributions as of October 2010. But the fund is facing

An Israeli tank guards the border with the Gaza Strip. U.S. military aid to Israel dropped to $2.2 billion last year from $4 billion in 2000. According to a 2010 poll, most Americans think 25 percent of the federal budget goes to foreign aid. In reality, foreign aid constitutes only about 1.1 percent of the budget.

criticism and potential budget cuts in Congress as it works through a fraud investigation of some of its grants.[40]

Through PEPFAR and other efforts, Bush established the United States as a leader in foreign assistance through global health programs, a tradition that President Obama continued but may now be threatened by concerns over the budget deficit.

As foreign aid increased in the United States in the last decade, other countries were embracing it as well. In 2001, the United Nations adopted the Millennium Development Goals (MDGs), eight measures for reducing poverty in the developing world by 2015. The MDGs offered concrete targets in areas including poverty and hunger reduction, universal education, gender equality and improved health. The purpose was to galvanize nations and development experts toward meeting specific goals with a set timeline. While solid progress is being made on some of the goals, others are proving more difficult. Many regions have improved access to primary school for girls, for example, while there is less progress in the areas of women's paid employment and reductions in deaths related to childbirth.[41]

Also during this heady time for international assistance, the developed country members of the Organisation for Economic Co-operation and Development (OECD) began increasing their funding for foreign aid. While amounts for development, known as Official Development Assistance (ODA), rose steadily from 1960 to 1992, they faltered

through the mid-1990s. Then they started to climb again and rose from $67.9 billion in 1997 to $127 billion by 2010.[42] The United States is by far the largest donor in dollar terms, contributing $28 billion in 2009, followed by France, Germany, the United Kingdom and Japan. Nonetheless, the United States contributes only 0.2 percent of its gross national income to development assistance while Denmark, Luxembourg, the Netherlands, Norway and Sweden each exceeded the United Nations target of 0.7 percent in 2009.[43] Many are concerned that the global economic downturn will diminish foreign assistance.

While governmental foreign aid boomed in the 2000s, private aid rose as well. The leader in funding for global health and development was the Bill & Melinda Gates Foundation. Since 1994, the foundation has donated $3.3 billion to global development and another $14.5 billion to global health activities.[44] InterAction, an umbrella group for non-government organizations, estimates that aid provided by foundations, corporations, NGOs, universities and religious organizations totaled $49 billion worldwide in 2007, almost half the amount of aid provided by governments that year. In the United States, InterAction says, private aid to developing countries exceeded U.S. government assistance that year, totaling $33.4 billion compared with $21.8 billion.[45]

Obama's Initiatives

Global health and development were key features of the presidential campaigns of both Obama and Hillary Clinton. Both followed the Bush administration in advocating development as one of the three pillars of United States foreign policy along with defense and diplomacy. Obama, whose father was Kenyan, was considered to have a personal interest in the welfare of developing countries, especially those in Africa. In August 2006, Obama and his wife Michelle were both publicly tested for HIV/AIDS in an attempt to reduce stigmas associated with the procedure. Obama called for increased funding for PEPFAR, creation of stronger health systems globally to help combat AIDS and other diseases and increased funding for multilateral organizations involved with global health.

Obama came into office determined to double yearly foreign aid funding to $50 billion by 2012. But the global economic crisis, followed by a battle in Congress over health care reform, and foreign assistance fell down the priority list. Development experts and supporters in Congress saw

Does foreign aid help governments and their societies?

YES
Samuel A. Worthington
President and CEO, InterAction

Written for *CQ Researcher*, June 13, 2011

Robust foreign assistance helps governments in developing nations build more stable, prosperous societies and can be a catalyst in pulling a country out of poverty. Such an investment by the United States, in turn, makes our nation more secure and may create new economic partners, as was the case with former aid recipient South Korea.

Cash-strapped governments in developing nations often leverage foreign assistance to supplement their own health, education, infrastructure and other programs that enable a society to grow and prosper. This assistance — which for the United States amounts to less than 1 percent of the federal budget — saves lives.

Programs like USAID's Feed the Future initiative, for example, help boost agricultural capacity and enable a family to get nutritious food. The President's Emergency Plan for AIDS Relief (PEPFAR) has provided help to tens of millions of people suffering from HIV and AIDS, via the delivery of retroviral drugs and counseling.

In many countries, disaster risk-reduction programs funded by USAID build on existing preparedness efforts. Experts estimate that for every dollar invested in such programs, $7 is saved in disaster-response costs later on. Often implemented in partnership with nongovernmental organizations (NGOs), this assistance strengthens local and national governments and better prepares them to deal with future disasters.

The best U.S. foreign-assistance programs involve a range of stakeholders, including civil society groups and the private sector, who should work together to achieve measurable goals. Some Millennium Challenge Corporation (MCC) programs reward good governance and encourage civil society involvement as well as that of the private sector.

The debate over U.S. foreign aid and how it helps developing governments and their people takes place amid efforts to make this assistance more effective and better aligned with the priorities of the societies we are trying to help.

Aid given to governments without active citizen engagement serves only to create dependency, particularly if a government views aid solely as a way to develop the state instead of improving the lives of its people. That is why assistance should be aligned with a country's broader development strategies that have been developed in consultation with citizens and their communities.

There will always be those who argue that foreign assistance is a luxury, particularly as we are trying to balance our own budget. But for economic, moral and security reasons, the opposite is true. We can't afford not to do it.

NO
Anthony B. Kim
Policy Analyst, Center for International Trade and Economics, The Heritage Foundation

Written for *CQ Researcher*, June 13, 2011

President Obama recently unveiled a new foreign aid package for the Middle East and North Africa. The announcement has conveyed a "feel-good" public diplomacy message that the United States is willing to help the region. But can foreign aid, in general, effectively deliver much-needed economic vitality and development?

Real-world cases strongly indicate that development assistance has a dismal record in catalyzing economic growth. Indeed, recipients of large amounts of aid tend to become dependent on it — and more likely to founder than to prosper.

All too often over the decades, U.S. foreign aid has wound up enriching corrupt and anti-democratic governments that have severely undermined economic development for ordinary people in their countries. Perhaps it's not surprising, then, that U.S. foreign aid has come under more intensive scrutiny in recent months.

Instead of following an approach that has repeatedly failed, the United States, as well as aid-recipient nations, would benefit from a re-evaluation of their foreign assistance agendas, which should be focused on real reforms and advancing economic freedom.

Numerous studies indicate that policy changes that create a more conducive environment for economic transactions are far more important to development than the amount of aid a country receives. Such changes, in turn, bolster a free and fair legal system while strengthening government accountability and responsiveness.

In other words, entrepreneurship encouraged by greater economic freedom leads to innovation, economic expansion and overall human development. A fresh case in point is Rwanda, now undergoing an entrepreneurial revolution. According to The Heritage Foundation's 2011 *Index of Economic Freedom*, Rwanda had notable improvements in half of the 10 indicators of economic freedom, achieving the largest score gain among 179 economies examined.

It's no coincidence that Rwanda's gross domestic product per capita increased to more than $1,000 in 2009, from less than $350 in 1994. Along with solid economic growth backed by sound economic policies, social indicators are rising fast, too. For example, primary-school enrollment has risen 50 percent.

As the index noted, "in pursuing sustainable prosperity, both the direction of policy and commitment to economic freedom are important." Indeed, over the last decade, the countries with greater improvements in economic freedom have achieved much higher reductions in poverty.

To successfully revamp foreign aid programs to provide more effective development assistance, we need to employ the principles of economic freedom.

their best opportunity for reform in decades fade away as the United States grappled with enormous debt and a sluggish economy. While many thought a foreign assistance reform bill could pass the Democratic-controlled House and Senate and be signed by Obama, the November 2010 elections brought in a large class of conservatives to the House and turned control of the chamber to the Republicans. The shift not only put reform efforts suddenly out of reach, but also resulted in foreign assistance coming under attack in a way it hadn't been for many years.

Nonetheless, Obama thrilled global development advocates when he brought the issue front and center in a speech at the United Nations in September 2010. He announced a Presidential Policy Directive that officially made global development a part of national security and realigned its goals.

"My national security strategy recognizes development as not only a moral imperative, but a strategic and economic imperative," Obama said.[46]

He proposed revitalizing USAID, and after years of having its mission outsourced to other parts of the government, ensured the agency was the lead development focus for the United States. Obama followed the directive in December 2010 with release of the first ever Quadrennial Diplomacy and Development Review (QDDR), a State Department document aimed at giving civilian leadership a greater role in advancing national interests and working with the military. "The QDDR is a blueprint for how we can make the State Department and USAID more nimble, more effective and more accountable," Secretary of State Clinton said in announcing the plan.[47] A key goal of the effort is to bolster the use of "soft power," encompassing a non-military approach to improve global stability. "Leading through civilian power means directing and coordinating the resources of all America's civilian agencies to prevent and resolve conflicts; help countries lift themselves out of poverty into prosperous, stable and democratic states; and build global coalitions to address global problems," State Department documents explain.[48]

CURRENT SITUATION

Modest Reforms

While wholesale reform of America's foreign assistance apparatus is seen as unlikely in the foreseeable future, development nonetheless remains a key goal of the Obama administration, which is pushing modest changes on several fronts.

First and foremost, USAID is transforming itself to become more businesslike and efficient, largely to improve its functional status, but also in an effort to stave off conservative efforts to trim it. Administrator Shah has embarked on a number of efforts to transform the agency it into what he called a "modern development enterprise."[49] The effort includes the "USAID Forward" initiative, which Shah hopes will allow countries to eventually graduate from needing U.S. aid. The reforms include changing the way USAID works with contractors, increasing and improving the technical capability of local staff and recreating USAID policy and budget bureaus. In addition, technology and innovation will be emphasized, and monitoring and evaluation of aid's effectiveness will be made more rigorous.

The Obama administration is also championing two global development programs in particular, one promoting sustainable agriculture in the developing world and the other addressing health issues. Obama is seeking $3.5 billion from Congress to be spent over three years for Feed the Future, a new program aimed at increasing agricultural productivity, expanding markets and trade and bolstering economic resilience in poor, rural areas.[50]

He also proposed $63 billion over six years for the Global Health Initiative (GHI), which broadens and builds on President George W. Bush's PEPFAR program. While continuing its primary focus on combating AIDS, tuberculosis and malaria, the initiative also targets neglected tropical diseases; maternal, newborn and child health; and nutrition and health systems improvement.[51] The program is led by USAID, the Centers for Disease Control and Prevention and the U.S. Global AIDS coordinator and seeks to ensure fairness and effectiveness by focusing on:

- Gender equality;
- Allowing countries to choose which projects the United States will invest in;
- Increased integration and coordination in providing aid; and
- Improved monitoring and evaluation.

Even with efforts to improve efficiency and accountability, foreign aid faces a tough battle for funding in the new Congress. Several key House Republicans began indicating as early as last year that foreign assistance would be a prime target in future deficit-reduction talks. "I have identified and will propose a number of cuts to the State Department and foreign aid budgets," House Foreign Affairs Committee Chairwoman Ileana Ros-Lehtinen, R-Fla., said last December. "There is much fat in these budgets, which makes some cuts obvious. Others will be more difficult, but necessary, to improve the efficiency of U.S. efforts and accomplish more with less."[52]

In January, the conservative Republican Study Committee, a group of more than 175 House Republicans, proposed a spending reduction act that gutted USAID funding.[53] In a continuing resolution proposed by Republicans in February, foreign aid received the third-largest percentage of cuts out of the 12 appropriations subcommittees, according to State and Foreign Operations Subcommittee Chairwoman Kay Granger, R-Texas.[54] Cuts proposed by the House mainly target international development, not assistance to conflict zones.

Ros-Lehtinen is also using her leadership post to blast another traditional target of conservatives: the United Nations. Some in Congress are dismayed with the international organization over allegations of sexual abuse committed by U.N. peacekeepers in Africa and reports of abuse of the oil for food program in Iraq in 2004. The U.N.'s Human Rights Council regularly has been accused of anti-Semitism and being comprised of member countries with spotty human rights records.[55] However, initial efforts to cut funding to the organization failed in February to gain the two-thirds House majority needed to pass under an expedited consideration process.[56]

Senators, particularly Democrats, are more supportive of foreign assistance funding. The Senate Appropriations Committee, chaired by Hawaii Democrat Daniel K. Inouye, preserved funding for foreign aid, echoing the Obama administration position that aid is vital in supporting national security. Still, Senate Democrats proposed a $6.5 billion reduction to the State Department and foreign operations budget compared to the amount requested by the Obama administration. This compares to an $11.7 billion reduction outlined by the House.

OUTLOOK
Budget Battle

The inevitable all-out war on the federal budget means lawmakers on Capitol Hill and administration officials

can expect an especially long and hot summer this year in Washington.

House Republicans have shown willingness to take on even the most popular programs, including Medicare, in the name of government and deficit reduction. While the international-affairs funding cuts outlined by the House Appropriations Committee are not as drastic as those suggested in the Republican's budget resolution, they are worrisome to economic development advocates.

"The core programs (non-war-related funding) are certainly being reduced with serious long-term funding implications," said the U.S. Global Leadership Coalition, a broadbased group of business leaders and NGOs that advocates increased foreign aid.[57] The group estimates the allocations would cut some programs by 12-16 percent. The House Appropriations Committee also is considering cuts to international agriculture programs.[58]

The Senate appears to be taking a different course, having rejected the House-passed budget proposal as well as the president's fiscal 2012 budget request. It also overwhelmingly rejected, 90-7, the budget cuts proposed by Sen. Paul.[59]

Indeed, foreign assistance as a means of enhancing national security has strong bipartisan support in the Senate, notably from South Carolina's Lindsey Graham, the ranking Republican on the State, Foreign Operations and Related Programs Subcommittee.

"If you don't want to use military force any more than you have to, count me in," said Graham. "State Department, USAID, all of these programs, in their own way, help win this struggle against radical Islam. The unsung heroes of this war are the State Department officials, the [Department of Justice] officials and the agricultural people who are going out there."

Graham added: "To those members [of Congress] who do not see the value of the civilian partnership in the war on terror, I think they are making a very dangerous decision."[60]

Aid supporters are lining up to make their case. Seventy top military leaders signed a recent letter to Congress stressing the importance of foreign assistance.[61] Global health advocates are particularly concerned about future funding for flagship programs like PEPFAR and other global health initiatives and are hitting the Hill with their support.

While acknowledging that the current budget environment is "very, very tough," Nora O'Connell, senior director of policy development and advocacy for the international welfare-advocacy group Save the Children, says she sees important support for foreign assistance.

"If you talk to congressional leaders and particularly those that are charged with oversight of foreign affairs, the Foreign Relations Committee and the Appropriations Committee, there's actually very strong bipartisan support for foreign affairs, and it comes from this fundamental belief that this is critical for our national security," she says. "What we're hoping for is that members of Congress can sort of stay strong to what the facts show . . . that this is a tiny percent of our budget, that the U.S. gets a lot out of this money and that some of these programs are serving some of the poorest and most vulnerable people in the world."

But the pressure from Republicans is fierce, especially for other Republicans who stray from the party line. Newly elected Florida Republican Sen. Marco Rubio got a taste of that intensity when he made some positive comments about foreign aid: "Foreign aid serves our national interests, and by the way, foreign aid is not the reason why we're running trillions of dollars of debt."[62] He was soon attacked for the comment on a political website. "This man ran under the Tea Party bandwagon just to get elected. He puts other countries [sic] interest before our own. Why would a supposed Tea Party candidate do this?"[63]

NOTES

1. "Hillary Clinton on Foreign Aid, Secretary of State insists on a link between foreign assistance and national security," ABC News Extra, Feb. 2, 2011, http://abcnews.go.com/ThisWeek/video/web-extra-hillary-clinton-foreign-aid-12959689.

2. Gerald F. Seib, "Deficit Balloons into National Security Threat," *The Wall Street Journal*, Feb. 2, 2010, http://online.wsj.com/article/SB1000142405 274870342290457503917363348289 4.html.

3. "Mullen: Debt is Top National Security Threat," CNN, Aug. 27, 2010, http://articles.cnn.com/2010-08-27/us/debt.security.mullen_1_pentagon-budget-national-debt-michael-mullen?_s=PM:US.

4. Pete Kasperowicz, "GOP Bill Would Study Security Threat Posed by Chinese-Held Debt," *The Hill*, May 10, 2011, http://thehill.com/blogs/floor-action/house/160163-house-defense-bill-treats-us-debt-held-by-china-as-possible-security-risk.

5. Kim Gamel, "US wasted billions in rebuilding Iraq: Hundreds of Infrastructure projects are incomplete or abandoned," The Associated Press, Aug. 8, 2010, www.msnbc.msn.com/id/38903955/ns/world_news-mideastn_africa/.

6. *Ibid.*

7. Majority Staff Report, "Evaluating U.S. Foreign Assistance to Afghanistan," Prepared for the Committee on Foreign Relations, United States Senate, June 8, 2011.

8. "American Public Opinion on Foreign Aid," WorldPublicOpinion.org, Nov. 30, 2010, www.worldpublicopinion.org/pipa/pdf/nov10/ForeignAid_Nov10_quaire.pdf.

9. Curt Tarnoff and Marian Leonardo Lawson, "Foreign Aid: An Introduction to US Programs and Policy," Congressional Research Service, Feb. 10, 2011, www.fas.org/sgp/crs/row/R40213.pdf.

10. Dr. Rajiv Shah, "The Modern Development Enterprise," Center for Global Development, Jan. 19, 2011, www.usaid.gov/press/speeches/2011/sp110119.html.

11. Robert Gates, speech to the U.S. Global Leadership Campaign, July 15, 2008, Washington, D.C., www.defense.gov/speeches/speech.aspx?speechid=1262.

12. James Roberts, "Not All Foreign Aid is Equal," Backgrounder, The Heritage Foundation, March 1, 2011.

13. "The Path to Prosperity: Restoring America's Promise, Fiscal Year 2012 Budget Resolution," House Committee on Budget, http://budget.house.gov/UploadedFiles/PathToProsperityFY2012.pdf.

14. Kay Granger, "PBS NewsHour," March 10, 2011, www.pbs.org/newshour/bb/world/jan-june11/foreignaid_03-10.html.

15. Matt Schneider, "Sen. Paul Rand: We Should End all Foreign Aid to Countries, Including Israel," *Medialite*, Jan. 30, 2011, www.mediaite.com/tv/rand-paul-we-should-end-all-foreign-aid-to-countries-including-israel/.

16. "House Appropriations Subcommittee on State, Foreign Operations and Related Programs Holds Hearing on Proposed Fiscal Year 2012 Appropriations

for Global Health and HIV/AIDS Programs, March 31, 2001.

17. Steven Radelet, "Bush and Foreign Aid," *Foreign Affairs*, September/October 2003, www.cgdev.org/doc/commentary/Bush_and_Foreign_Aid.pdf.

18. Theresa Braine, "Reaching Mexico's Poorest," *Bulletin of the World Health Organization*, 2002, www.scielosp.org/scielo.php?script=sci_arttext&pid=S0042-96862006000800004&lng=pt&nrm=iso&tlng=en.

19. Hyun H. Son, "Conditional Cash Transfer Programs: An Effective Tool for Poverty Alleviation?" Asian Development Bank, July 2008, www.adb.org/Documents/EDRC/Policy_Briefs/PB051.pdf.

20. Jeremy M. Sharp, "Egypt in Transition," Congressional Research Service, March 29, 2011, www.fas.org/sgp/crs/mideast/RL33003.pdf.

21. "Background Note: Egypt," Department of State, Nov. 10, 2010, www.state.gov/r/pa/ei/bgn/5309.htm.

22. Ashish Kumar, Sen., "Lawmakers Criticize Obama's Response to Egypt Crisis," *The Washington Times*, Feb. 9, 2011, www.washingtontimes.com/news/2011/feb/9/republican-and-democratic-lawmakers-criticized-the/.

23. David Francis, "Foreign Aid Dilemma: Dictators on Our Dole," *The Fiscal Times*, March 16, 2011, www.thefiscaltimes.com/Articles/2011/03/16/Foreign-Aid-Dilemma-Dictators-on-our-Dole.aspx?p=1.

24. "Aid to Pakistan by the Numbers," Center for Global Development, www.cgdev.org/section/initiatives/_active/pakistan/numbers.

25. "Obama's Challenge in the Muslim World: Arab Spring Fails to Improve US Image" Pew Research Center, May 17, 2011, http://pewglobal.org/files/2011/05/Pew-Global-Attitudes-Arab-Spring-FINAL-May-17-2011.pdf.

26. James Roberts, "Not all Foreign Aid is Equal," Backgrounder, The Heritage Foundation, March 1, 2011, www.heritage.org/Research/Reports/2011/03/Not-All-Foreign-Aid-Is-Equal.

27. "ABC News Extra," *op. cit.*

28. "US Military: Aid to Egypt has 'Incalculable Value,' " Reuters, Feb. 16, 2011, www.reuters.com/article/2011/02/16/us-usa-budget-egypt-idUSTRE71F4CO20110216.

29. Diane B. Kunz, "The Marshall Plan Reconsidered, A Complex of Motives," *Foreign Affairs*, May/June 1997.

30. "About USAID, USAID History," USAID, www.usaid.gov/about_usaid/usaidhist.html.

31. Richard P. Cincotta and Barbara B. Crane, "The Mexico City Policy and US Family Planning Assistance," *Science*, Oct. 19, 2002.

32. "USAID Foreign Service Permanent Workforce & USAID Managed Program Dollars," USAID, www.usaid.gov/press/speeches/2011/ty110330b.pdf.

33. Tarnoff and Lawson, *op. cit.*

34. Condoleezza Rice, remarks at Georgetown School of Foreign Service, Jan. 18, 2006, www.unc.edu/depts/diplomat/item/2006/0103/rice/rice_georgetown.html.

35. Thom Shanker, "Defense Secretary Urges More Spending for US Diplomacy," *The New York Times*, Nov. 27, 2007, www.nytimes.com/2007/11/27/washington/27gates.html?_r=1.

36. Radelet, *op. cit.*

37. "About MCC," Millennium Challenge Corporation, www.mcc.gov/pages/about.

38. The President's Emergency Plan for AIDS Relief, "Latest Results," www.pepfar.gov/results/index.htm.

39. "The US & The Global Fund to Fight AIDS, Tuberculosis and Malaria," Kaiser Family Foundation, November 2010, www.kff.org/globalhealth/upload/8003-02.pdf.

40. John Heilprin, "AP Enterprise: Fraud Plagues Global Health Fund," The Associated Press, Jan. 23, 2011, http://news.yahoo.com/s/ap/20110123/ap_on_re_eu/eu_aids_fund_corruption.

41. *Ibid.*

42. "Net ODA Disbursements, Total DAC Countries," Organisation for Economic Co-operation and Development, http://webnet.oecd.org/dcdgraphs/ODAhistory/.

43. *Ibid.*

44. "Foundation Fact Sheet," Bill & Melinda Gates Foundation, www.gatesfoundation.org/about/Pages/foundation-fact-sheet.aspx.

45. "Private Aid Flows," *InterAction*, www.interaction.org/private-aid-flows.

46. Barack Obama, "Statement by the President at the Millennium Development Goal Summit in New York, New York," Sept. 22, 2010, www.whitehouse.gov/the-press-office/2010/09/22/remarks-president-millennium-development-goals-summit-new-york-new-york.

47. "Leading Through Civilian Power: Quadrennial Diplomacy and Development Review," *DipNote*, Dec. 15, 2010, http://blogs.state.gov/index.php/site/entry/civilian_power_qddr.

48. *Ibid.*

49. Shah, *op. cit.*

50. Angela Rucker, "$3.5B US Hunger Plan to Feed 40 Million People," "Frontlines," USAID June 2010, www.usaid.gov/press/frontlines/fl_jun10/p01_hunger100601.html.

51. The US Global Health Initiative, www.ghi.gov/.

52. Nicole Gaouette, "Ros-Lehtinen To Seek Cuts in Diplomatic, Foreign Aid Funding," Bloomberg, Dec. 9, 2010, www.bloomberg.com/news/2010-12-09/ros-lehtinen-to-seek-cuts-in-diplomatic-foreign-aid-funding.html.

53. Emily Cadei, "Proposed Cuts Thrust Foreign Aid Into Center of Spending Debate," *CQ Today*, Jan. 21, 2011.

54. Emily Cadei, "In Fiscal 2011 Bill, Senate Democrats Take a Broader view of Security Spending," *CQ Today*, March 4, 2011.

55. Emily Cadei, "Key Post Gives Ros-Lehtinen a Platform to Hammer U.N." *CQ Today*, Jan. 7, 2011.

56. Frances Symes, "Effort to Cut U.N. Funding Over Tax Payments Falls Short on House Floor," *CQ Today*, Feb. 9, 2011.

57. Stuart B. Baimel, "International Affairs Budget Update, 5-12-11," US Global Leadership Coalition, May 24, 2011, www.usglc.org/2011/05/24/international-affairs-budget-update-5-12-2011-2/.

58. Stuart B. Baimel, "International Affairs Budget Update, 5-27-11," US Global Leadership Coalition, May 27, 2010, www.usglc.org/2011/05/27/international-affairs-budget-update-5-27-11/.

59. "Senate Rejects Rand Paul Budget Plan," Kentucky Politics, May 25, 2011, http://cincinnati.com/blogs/nkypolitics/2011/05/25/senate-rejects-rand-paul-budget-plan/.

60. Josh Rogin, "Lindsey Graham to the Rescue for State and USAID," *The Cable*, Feb. 1, 2011, http://thecable.foreignpolicy.com/posts/2011/02/01/lindsey_graham_to_the_rescue_for_state_and_usaid.

61. "Military Leaders Letter to Congress," US Global Leadership Coalition, March 30, 2011, www.usglc.org/wp-content/uploads/2011/03/NSAC-letter-2011.pdf.

62. "Sen. Marco Rubio: 'Foreign Aid Serves Our National Interest," YouTube, "Your World with Neil Cavuto," March 30, 2011, www.youtube.com/watch?v=KAcfaXEDem8.

63. "Tea Party Has Been Swindled by Marco Rubio," The Truth Stings, April 8, 2011, http://truthstings.com/tea-party-has-been-swindled-by-marco-rubio/.

BIBLIOGRAPHY

Selected Sources

Books

Brautigam, Deborah, *The Dragon's Gift: The Real Story of China in Africa*, Oxford, 2009.
A noted China expert at American University in Washington explains China's African aid strategy.

Easterly, William, *The White Man's Burden: Why the West's Efforts to Aid the Rest Have Done So Much Ill and So Little Good*, Penguin Books, 2006.
A New York University economics professor argues that Western attempts to alleviate poverty have been futile.

Moyo, Dambisa, *Dead Aid: Why Aid is Not working and How There is a Better Way for Africa*, Farrar, Straus and Giroux, 2009.
An African economist argues that African countries are worse off as a result of foreign aid.

Sachs, Jeffrey, *The End of Poverty: Economic Possibilities for Our Time*, Penguin, 2005.
A Columbia University economist contends that extreme global poverty can be eliminated through development aid by 2025.

Karlan, Dean, *More than Good Intentions: How a New Economics is Helping to Solve Global Poverty*, Penguin, 2011.
A Yale University economics professor discusses behavioral economics and worldwide field research to explore what works in development aid.

Calderisi, Robert, *The Trouble with Africa: Why Foreign Aid Isn't Working*, Palgrave, Macmillan, 2006.
A former World Bank international spokesman on Africa discusses the shortcomings of foreign aid.

Articles

Ali, Ambreen, "Tea Party: Unimpressed — and Angry as Ever," *CQ Weekly*, March 7, 2011.
Ali examines the Tea Party's insistence on smaller government.

Cadei, Emily, "Proposed Cuts Thrust Foreign Aid Agency into Center of Spending Debate," *CQ Today Online News*, Jan. 21, 2011.
Cadei outlines House Republican criticism of the U.S. Agency for International Development.

Kunz, Diane B., "The Marshall Plan Reconsidered: A Complex of Motives," *Foreign Affairs*, May/June 1997.
Kunz argues that the posts-World War II aid effort paid huge dividends for the United States and that similar efforts can be justified today.

McKenzie, A. D., "Parliamentarian ask G8 to focus on Women," *Guardian Development Network*, May 19, 2011.
Countries at the G8 conference in France call for an increased focus on the role of women and girls in development.

Norris, John, "Five Myths about Foreign Aid," *The Washington Post*, April 28, 2011.
The executive director of the sustainable security program at the Center for American Progress discusses foreign aid budget cuts proposed by Republicans and misconceptions about economic development.

Pennington, Matthew, "Clinton Says US in Direct Competition With China," *The Associated Press*, March 2, 2011.
Pennington recounts Secretary of State Hillary Rodham Clinton's comments to the Senate Foreign Relations Committee.

Reports and Studies

"A Woman-Centered Approach to the US Global Health Initiative," *Center for Health and Gender Equity*, February 2010.
Explains and supports "woman-centered" approach in the US global health policy.

Epstein, Susan, "Foreign Aid Reform, National Strategy, and the Quadrennial Review," *Congressional Research Service*, Feb. 15, 2011.
An analyst for the nonpartisan agency details congressional and administration efforts to reform foreign-assistance programs.

Levine, Ruth, Cynthia B. Lloyd, Margaret Greene and Caren Grown, "Girls Count: A Global Investment and Action Agenda," *Center for Global Development*, December 2009.
The authors detail the disadvantages faced by girls in developing countries and make a case for gender equality.

Sharp, Jeremy M., "Egypt in Transition," *Congressional Research Service*, March 29, 2011.
Sharp gives an overview of the transition occurring in Egypt and outlines U.S. foreign aid to the country.

Tarnoff, Curt, and Marian Leonardo Lawson, "Foreign Aid: an Introductory Overview of US Programs and Policy," *Congressional Research Service*, Feb. 10, 2011.
CRS analysts present an overview of the types and goals of U.S. foreign assistance.

Williams-Bridgers, Jacquelyn, "Foreign Operations, Key Issues or Congressional Oversight," *Government Accountability Office*, March 3, 2011.
The author reviews a GAO study of weaknesses in U.S. foreign assistance programs.

For More Information

Bread for the World, 425 Third St., S.W., Suite 1200, Washington, DC 20024; (800) 822-7323; www.bread.org. Christian citizens' movement dedicated to ending hunger domestically and abroad.

Cato Institute, 1000 Massachusetts Ave., N.W., Washington, DC 20001; (202) 842-0200; www.cato.org. Libertarian think tank opposing strategic foreign aid and promoting economic freedom as a solution to problems overseas.

Center for Global Development, 1800 Massachusetts Ave., N.W., Third Floor, Washington, DC 20036; (202) 416-4000; www.cgdev.org. Independent and non-partisan research institute working to reduce global poverty.

Heritage Foundation, 214 Massachusetts Ave., N.E., Washington, DC 20002; (202) 546-4400; www.heritage.org. Conservative think tank advocating for policies that oppose traditional development assistance.

InterAction, 1400 16th St., N.W., Suite 210, Washington, DC 20036; (202) 667-8227; www.interaction.org. Alliance of U.S.-based nongovernmental organizations focusing on disaster relief and sustainable development.

Millennium Challenge Corporation, 875 15th St., N.W., Washington, DC 20005; (202) 521-3850; www.mcc.gov. Bilateral U.S. foreign aid agency distributing funds through a process of competitive selection.

Modernizing Foreign Assistance Network, 425 Third St., S.W., Suite 1200, Washington, DC 20024; (202) 688-1087; www.modernizeaid.net. Coalition of foreign policy practitioners advocating for a larger U.S. leadership role in reducing poverty and suffering around the world.

U.S. Agency for International Development, 1300 Pennsylvania Ave., N.W., Washington, DC 20523; (202) 712-0000; www.usaid.gov. U.S. federal agency primarily responsible for administering civilian foreign aid.

U.S. Global Leadership Coalition, 1129 20th St., N.W., Suite 600, Washington, DC 20036; (202) 833-5555; www.usglc.org. Coalition of American businesses and NGOs promoting greater U.S. diplomatic and development efforts.

3

Fracking Controversy

Daniel McGlynn

An engineer adjusts the drill on a natural gas platform in Fort Worth. Nearly 500,000 natural gas wells are spread across 34 states; 90 percent use fracking, in which thousands of gallons of water and chemicals are injected below ground to release gas trapped in shale. Industry officials say fracking is environmentally friendly, but critics argue it poses health and safety risks.

From *CQ Researcher*,
Dec. 16, 2011

N atalie Brant says she was "scared, shocked and very disturbed" when her husband, Gino, lit the water from their kitchen faucet on fire.

"I thought, that's not normal," Brant told a New York State Senate hearing last August investigating a controversial new natural gas-drilling technique called hydraulic fracturing, or "fracking."

The Brants live in Springville, N.Y, a rural village 35 miles south of Buffalo that sits atop one of the world's richest natural gas fields. In 2008 their landlord leased property near their house to the U.S. Energy Corp., which began employing fracking to extract gas trapped in rock thousands of feet below the surface. Used throughout the United States and worldwide, the technique has unlocked trillions of cubic feet of gas in recent years, but it has spurred intense debate over whether it releases pollutants into the atmosphere and fouls local drinking-water supplies.

"Soon after the drilling began," Natalie Brant told lawmakers, "we started getting really sick." The family suspected the gas drilling, she said, but "didn't know what was going on for two-and-a-half years."

Then, in July 2010, Brant's husband watched the Oscar-nominated documentary film "Gasland," a highly critical examination of the gas-drilling industry. In one of the film's dramatic scenes, a man in northeastern Colorado — like New York state, a fracking hotbed — lights the well water from his kitchen faucet on fire. "We realized everything that was happening in the film was happening in our life, too," Natalie Brant said.[1]

Shale-Gas Deposits Span U.S.

Twenty-six productive shale-gas formations stretch across the continental United States, from the Northeast to Utah and Montana. Among the most active are the massive Marcellus Shale, a 575-mile-long formation undergirding New York, Pennsylvania, West Virginia and Ohio; the Haynesville/Bossier formation in Louisiana and Texas; the Barnett Shale in Texas; and the Antrim formation in Michigan.

Shale Basins in the United States

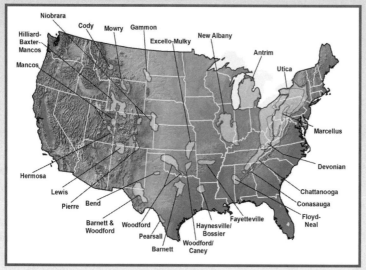

Source: "Modern Shale Gas Development in the United States: A Primer," U.S. Department of Energy, April 2009, www.netl.doe.gov/technologies/ oilgas/ publications/epreports/shale_gas_primer_2009.pdf

Complaints have dogged the natural-gas industry since the mid-2000s, when hydraulic fracturing took off worldwide amid rising demand for cleaner-burning fuel.[2] Fracking not only has sparked discord in towns and rural areas beset by drillers, it has cast a shadow over an energy source that environmental groups and the Obama administration once touted as a clean, cheap way to reduce U.S. reliance on foreign oil.[3]

Critics and proponents are far apart on whether hydraulic fracturing is a benefit or bane for the environment. To reach underground gas pockets, drillers inject tens of thousands of gallons of water and chemicals under high pressure into shale rock formations thousands of feet below the surface to crack the rock and

release "shale gas." * In a technique called directional drilling, which evolved from oil exploration, drills go straight down a mile or more, then turn horizontally to reach gas pockets.

Industry officials say fracking is safe, precise and environmentally friendly, in part because it reduces the number of wellheads needed to produce large quantities of gas. "The technology rivals NASA," says Travis Windle, a spokesman for the Marcellus Shale Coalition, an industry lobbying group in Canonsburg, Pa. "Drillers can hit a coffee can at a mile down and a mile over."

But environmentalists and residents who live near drilling sites argue that hydraulic fracturing poses potentially huge health and safety risks and that its long-term effects are unknown.[4] In a study released earlier this month, the Environmental Protection Agency established the first scientific links between fracking and pollution of nearby drinking water. And critics complain that fracking is exempt from most major environmental laws, including the Safe Drinking Water Act and parts of the Clean Air Act. Key among their claims: that fracking fouls underground and surface water with cancer-causing chemicals, pollutes the air near drilling sites and turns quiet villages like Springville into industrial zones.

Concern also is growing that fracking can touch off earthquakes. Geologists in Arkansas and Oklahoma are studying a spike in recent years of seismic activity at fault lines near new fracturing projects.[5] In November, a gas driller in the United Kingdom said fracking near Blackpool in northwest England probably caused two

_____

* Shale is a fine-grained dense rock that often is saturated with fossil fuels such as oil or gas. Shale gas is natural gas, primarily methane, that is trapped in such rock. The word shale refers to the granular nature of the rock, not necessarily a specific variety of stone.

minor earthquakes. The company blamed a geological fluke, but British authorities have halted fracking nationwide pending further study.[6]

Moreover, Mayor Michael Bloomberg, I-N.Y., expressed concern to the state's Department of Environmental Conservation (DEC) that underground cement tunnels supplying the city's drinking water could crack if fracturing were allowed nearby.[7]

"Everywhere around the world, people are thinking this [fracking] is crazy," says Bruce Ferguson, an organizer with Catskill Citizens for Safe Energy, a grassroots anti-fracking group in upstate New York. "We are being presented with a very new and potentially dangerous technology."

For decades natural gas was regarded as a secondary fuel and often extracted as a byproduct of oil drilling. But demand for natural gas has surged as oil prices have risen sharply and geopolitical turmoil has put foreign sources at risk. In the United States, meanwhile, production — most of it through fracking — is booming from the Texas Panhandle and eastern plains of Colorado to the vast Marcellus Shale deposit, a 575-mile-long formation undergirding New York, Pennsylvania, West Virginia and Ohio.[8]

As the financial and environmental costs associated with burning oil and coal for energy have risen, natural gas has become attractive for everything from running power plants to fueling a new breed of energy-efficient autos. Gas also is being liquefied for export to energy-hungry markets in Europe and Asia.

One-fourth of the nation's energy supply came from natural gas last year.[9] And as gas has risen in prominence, so too has hydraulic fracturing. It accounts for nearly a third of the U.S. gas supply, up from a mere 1 percent in 2000.[10] By 2035, nearly half of the nation's natural gas production will be done through fracking, the U.S. Energy Information Agency (EIA) forecasts.

The number of active gas wells reflects that fore-casted growth. Nearly 500,000 wells — double the

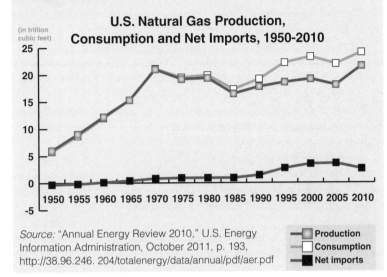

Domestically Produced Gas Fuels U.S. Market

The United States consumed 24 trillion cubic feet of natural gas in 2010, 90 percent of it produced domestically. Consumption has increased fourfold over the past 60 years, while domestic production has more than tripled. Imports have grown but remain a small part of U.S. gas consumption.

U.S. Natural Gas Production, Consumption and Net Imports, 1950-2010

(in trillion cubic feet)

Source: "Annual Energy Review 2010," U.S. Energy Information Administration, October 2011, p. 193, http://38.96.246. 204/totalenergy/data/annual/pdf/aer.pdf

Production
Consumption
Net imports

number in 1990 — are spread across 34 states.[11] Ninety percent use fracking.[12]

At the start of the fracking boom, many mainstream environmental groups saw natural gas as a cleaner alternative to oil or coal. When burned, it releases less carbon dioxide, a "greenhouse" gas associated with global climate change. Natural gas also is considered a so-called bridge fuel that the nation can use until alternative-energy sources such as wind and solar power are widely available.

Once a well is drilled, the shale rock, often compared to a slab of concrete in density, is fractured using tens of thousands of gallons of water injected under high pressure. The water is laden with chemicals and sand called "proppants" that help keep the fractures open and allow gas to escape to the surface through the well opening.[13]

But reports of underground water contamination, chemical spills and other problems have been frequent. At the same time, scientists have begun to document the release of methane — another greenhouse gas and a major component of natural gas — during the drilling, extracting and transportation phases of natural gas production.

If not contained properly during drilling, methane can migrate through the ground to water sources or be released into the atmosphere once above ground. Yet the reports haven't been conclusive. Studies from some leading universities and research teams have concluded that natural gas, when properly extracted and handled, is still cleaner then coal or oil.[14]

While the environmental impact of hydraulic fracturing technology continues to be debated, regulators are trying to figure out how best to manage the drastic increase of natural gas wells. In March 2010 the U.S. Environmental Protection Agency (EPA) began a massive study of fracking's impact on groundwater. The study, which may influence future federal natural gas legislation, will not be complete for several years.[15]

In the absence of clear federal guidelines, it remains up to state regulators to figure out how best to proceed with hydraulic fracturing. In New York, fracturing was halted while the Department of Environmental Conservation considers the environmental and health impacts.

"New York finds itself in the middle of the national debate," says DEC Commissioner Joe Martens. "We didn't just dive right into high-volume hydraulic fracturing. We are moving slow and taking our time, and I think we have come up with the most stringent and fair regulations out there."

As industry groups, regulators and communities debate the future of natural gas production, here are some of the questions they are asking:

Is natural gas a clean fuel?

Policymakers, environmentalists and the business community support natural gas as a low-carbon alternative to coal and oil. The International Energy Agency predicts that by 2030 natural gas will surpass coal as an energy source and provide a fourth of the world's energy.[16]

But critics argue that large-scale fracking cancels any environmental benefits that the use of natural gas as a fossil fuel may have over oil or coal.

Gas contains 25 percent less carbon than oil and half as much as coal, according to the Worldwatch Institute, an environmental research group in Washington. "Planned and proposed federal and state actions to curb greenhouse gas emissions — from stricter requirements for emissions-control technology to renewable or clean-energy portfolio standards to an [emission] cap on carbon — all expose oil and coal investments to much higher risk than natural gas," it says.[17]

The EPA says natural gas-fired power plants produce half as much carbon dioxide, less than a third as much nitrogen oxides and 1 percent as much sulfur oxides as coal-fired plants.[18] But recent research into the complete life cycle of natural gas emissions raises questions about its relative cleanliness.

Earlier studies focused mainly on the amount of carbon dioxide and other traditional air pollutants, such as sulfur dioxide and nitrogen oxides, that were released into the atmosphere when gas was burned at power plants. But scientists have begun taking a closer look at the effects of methane, which leaks from fractured wells or is otherwise released during natural gas drilling, transportation and power-plant combustion.

An EPA study completed in November 2010 found that natural gas may be less than 25 percent cleaner than coal and oil.[19] The World Bank estimates that natural gas production is responsible for 20 percent of human-induced methane at the current rates of production.[20]

Robert Howarth, a Cornell University ecologist, said in a recent study that extraction of natural gas from the Marcellus Shale deposit "could do more to aggravate global warming than mining coal."[21] Methane, he said, has "105 times more [global] warming impact pound for pound than carbon dioxide." Howarth estimated that 8 percent of the methane in shale gas escapes during the lifetime of a fractured well, twice as much as from a traditionally drilled well.[22]

But other researchers disagree with Howarth's conclusions. In a study released in August, researchers from Carnegie Mellon University in Pittsburgh said producing electricity from Marcellus Shale gas is 25 to 50 percent cleaner than using coal, even when factoring in the energy needed to drill, transport and clean wastewater produced at fracturing sites.

"Shale gas is better than coal when it comes to electricity generation," said one of the study's authors, Paulina Jaramillo, an assistant research professor in Carnegie Mellon's Engineering and Public Policy Department. "We looked at the life cycle of gas and coal emissions, and even though methane emissions from gas are higher than from coal, the combustion emissions from coal really overwhelm them."[23]

Is extracting natural gas from shale safe?

Besides the Marcellus Shale, several other major U.S. shale deposits have been explored for natural gas in recent decades, including the Barnett Shale in Texas, Fayetteville Shale in Arkansas, Haynesville Shale in Louisiana and Niobrara Shale in Colorado, Utah and Wyoming.

Before natural gas can be unlocked from the shale, the rock formations must be fractured. "Hydraulic fracturing is absolutely necessary to develop shale gas," says Mike Nickolaus, special projects director at the Ground Water Protection Council, a group in Oklahoma City that studies water issues and provides policy guidance to state water regulators throughout the United States. Fracking uses a combination of chemicals that act as a lubricant for the underground drilling equipment and keep the fractures open so gas can escape. These additives are combined with tens of thousands of gallons of water and then injected, at high pressure, underground. Well holes are drilled vertically and then horizontally up to several miles in multiple directions.

The pressurized water, chemicals and material such as sand that work their way into the fractures unlock the gas from the shale. Once the drilling water and chemicals are pumped back out of the well, the gas from the surrounding fractured rock travels to the surface through the openings and then through metal pipe inserted and cemented into the well.[24]

Fracking opponents say the technique is potentially dangerous because the millions of gallons of water used in the process can contaminate underground drinking water supplies. But the natural gas industry says the process has been used in oil and gas fields for decades and has a proven track record.

Nickolaus downplays the risk. "Even in the worst-case scenarios, we have never seen a case where chemicals from hydraulic fracturing get into groundwater," he says. "The regulations over the years have developed tremendously."

Indeed a 2004 EPA study found no evidence that chemicals used in hydraulic fracturing have contaminated drinking water.[25] This year researchers at the Massachusetts Institute of Technology corroborated the study, concluding that fracking's environmental impacts "are challenging but manageable." The researchers acknowledged "concern that these fractures can . . . penetrate shallow freshwater zones and contaminate them with fracturing ?uid," but found "no evidence that this is occurring."[26]

Still, a growing number of anecdotal stories have surfaced around the country of drinking-water contamination near fracking operations. In the documentary "Gasland," filmmaker and activist Josh Fox gathered evidence from places such as Dimock, Pa., Pavillion, Wyo., and Fort Worth, Texas, that tap water in homes near drilling sites was polluted with toxins and carcinogens. In some cases the water coming out of faucets was flammable.[27]

In December 2011 the EPA released data from two environmental monitoring water wells drilled near Pavillion. For years residents had complained that nearby fracking by Encana, a Canadian natural gas company, had contaminated their drinking water. Encana supplied trucked-in water to 42 homes with foul water but denied responsibility for the contamination. Water samples from the EPA's monitoring wells, however, showed that the aquifer supplying Pavillion contains high levels of cancer-causing chemicals and at least one chemical compound linked to fracking.[28]

While water-well contamination near fracking operations is being investigated nationwide, gas-well construction is sometimes cited as a cause.[29] Once a well is drilled, a casing is cemented in the well shaft. This is a crucial step to ensure that gas or other contaminates do not leak from the well as they travel to the surface, particularly through layers of rock closer to the surface that contain aquifers.[30]

But the casings are put under enormous pressure and sometimes fail. Because the work is done thousands of feet underground, verifying the structural integrity of the casing installation is challenging. State regulations require that casings be monitored and that well operators install warning and safety equipment, such as a blow-out preventer. Still, well failures sometimes occur.

The natural gas industry says many areas, including Dimock and Pavillion, have a history of substandard water-well construction — such as wells drilled directly into pockets of methane — and that there are documented instances of methane and other forms of contamination in the groundwater before gas drilling began. In some parts of Pennsylvania, says Windle of the Marcellus Shale Coalition, "People have been lighting their faucets on fire since before I was born."

But the EPA's environmental monitoring wells in Pavillion rule out pollution from shallower, naturally occurring methane pockets and agricultural runoff.[31]

How Fracking Captures Natural Gas in Rock

Hydraulic fracturing, or fracking, is used to extract natural gas trapped in shale layers thousands of feet below the surface. Drills go straight down a mile or more, then turn horizontally to reach gas pockets. Drillers then inject thousands of gallons of water and chemicals into the shale under high pressure to crack the rock and release the gas.

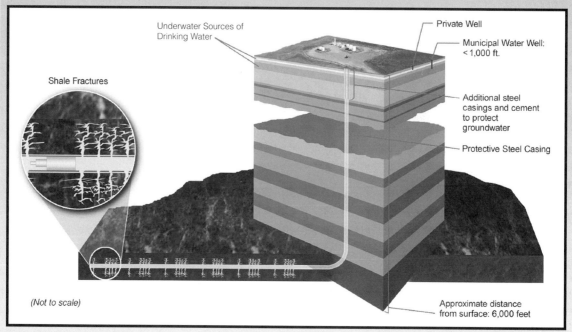

Source: Department of Energy

A 2011 Duke University study that sampled water from 68 private wells in New York and Pennsylvania found "evidence for methane contamination of drinking water associated with shale-gas extraction."[32] The study also found that water wells closest to drilling activities had higher rates of methane contamination. The methane levels at the sites nearest natural gas drilling platforms were within the range set by the U.S. Interior Department for requiring immediate "hazard mitigation" action.[33]

The Duke study, however, did not find instances of hazardous fracking chemicals migrating into drinking water supplies, a second pathway for contamination. Thus, the study has been used to support both sides of the fracking debate.

In addition to the concerns about contamination of underground water sources, there also is debate about what to do with the briny, chemical-laden wastewater once a fracturing job is complete. About 85 percent of the wastewater is left underground; the rest is pumped back to the surface and stored in holding ponds or trucked off-site for disposal.[34] State regulators are struggling with how to cope with fracking wastewater that is not only salty and toxic but also sometimes radioactive.

In October, 250 medical professionals in New York state asked Democratic Gov. Andrew Cuomo to do a "full assessment of the public-health impacts of gas exploration and production" in other states where fracking has occurred before approving high-volume hydraulic fracturing in New York. The state's Departments of Environmental Conservation and Public Health are both researching the issue.[35]

In response, the New York Independent Oil and Gas Association said, "regulations and permit conditions have been and will be in place to prevent pathways to humans and the environment, similar to those in effect for many other industries."[36]

Is natural gas regulation too lax?

While the federal government has been heavily involved in regulating natural gas prices over the past 70 years, states have been responsible for most of the environmental regulation of gas exploration and development. Industry officials and state regulators say that arrangement works well because each state has its own unique geological formations, environmental considerations and drilling techniques.

"Hydraulic fracturing was never regulated by the EPA," says Windle, the Marcellus Shale Coalition spokesman. "It is, however, aggressively regulated by state environmental regulators" with whom "we work closely and collaboratively."

But fracking opponents want federal guidelines. "There should be some sort of minimal standard," says Jesse Thomas-Blate, associate director of river protection at American Rivers, an environmental group based in Washington. Natural gas companies are exempt from seven of 15 major environmental laws that apply to most other industries, including the Safe Drinking Water, Clean Air and Comprehensive Environmental Response, Compensation, and Liability ("Superfund") Acts.[37]

Fracking critics also complain that state regulatory agencies lack the funding and human resources to adequately oversee thousands of new drilling projects in states such as Pennsylvania that have seen recent booms in fracking.[38]

But the natural gas industry and the Ground Water Protection Council say adding federal regulations will slow gas development and make it more expensive at a time when finding new energy resources is important.[39]

Windle agrees. "It doesn't make sense to give Washington carte blanche to regulate natural gas," he says. He adds that the industry is not opposed to working with state regulators or raising permitting fees.

In New York state, where fracking has been banned while the Department of Environmental Conservation develops regulatory guidelines, Windle says that "the uncertainty in Albany has been a wet blanket on investment."

www.gaslandthemovie.com

AP Photo/Alex Brandon

Water Issues

Drinking water in Colorado containing methane is ignited in a scene from the award-winning 2010 documentary "Gasland" (top). Jean Carter uses bottled water by the case for her home in Dimock, Pa., because of methane contamination (bottom). Residents and environmentalists blame fracking throughout the region for the contamination, but industry officials say residents' water wells were improperly drilled into pockets of methane before the fracking began.

Gas Wells Nearly Doubled in Two Decades

The number of natural gas wells in the United States increased to nearly half a million from 1989 to 2009. Many environmental groups promote natural gas as a cleaner energy source than oil and coal, but critics say hydraulic fracturing used in many wells has fouled drinking water and created other health hazards.

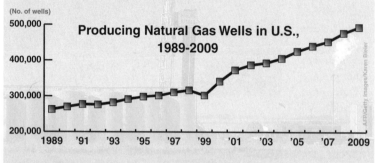

(No. of wells)

Producing Natural Gas Wells in U.S., 1989-2009

Source: "Natural Gas," U.S. Energy Information Administration, November 2011, http://38.96.246.204/dnav/ng/hist/na1170_nus_8a.htm

Meanwhile, the EPA is studying seven hydraulic fracturing sites across the country, each with different shale formations and well-site conditions. Five sites already have been fractured and two others are in development. A draft of the study's results is expected in 2012, and a final version by 2014.[40]

Congressional lawmakers have reintroduced the Fracturing Responsibility and Awareness of Chemicals Act, which would eliminate fracking's exemption from the Safe Drinking Water Act.

"Families, communities and local governments are upset that the safety of their water has been compromised by a special-interest exemption, and we join them in that frustration," said Rep. Jared Polis, D-Colo, a co-sponsor of the legislation. "The problem is not natural gas or even hydraulic fracturing itself. The problem is that dangerous chemicals are being injected into the Earth, polluting our water sources, without any oversight whatsoever."[41]

Regulators also are trying to figure out how to deal with the increased use of freshwater in the fracking process and what to do with the water once it is pumped out of the wells.

Most of it is taken to wastewater treatment plants. But such plants may not be equipped to adequately clean

the water. Studies by the EPA and the drilling industry, which were never made public but were obtained by *The New York Times,* show that treatment at wastewater facilities does not always work, meaning that some of the naturally occurring radioactivity in treated fracking waste cannot be adequately diluted in rivers and streams used for drinking water.[42]

While no federal regulations apply to fracking wastewater, New York, Pennsylvania and other states are scrambling to develop controls.

"We're burning the furniture to heat the house," said John Quigley, former secretary of Pennsylvania's Department of Conservation and Natural Resources. "In shifting away from coal and toward natural gas, we're trying for cleaner air, but we're producing massive amounts of toxic wastewater with salts and naturally occurring radioactive materials, and it's not clear we have a plan for properly handling this waste."[43]

BACKGROUND

Gas Pockets

Natural gas often is presented as a newcomer compared with fuel sources such as coal and oil, but it has been harnessed for millennia.

About 1400 B.C., ancient Greeks built a temple for the Oracle of Delphi on a natural gas pocket that was used to feed a small flame in the temple. About a thousand years later, the Chinese invented a crude drilling technique to harness gas to boil seawater and create salt. In 1626, French explorers were the first to document natural gas in North America. They noted that Native Americans around Lake Erie were igniting pockets of natural gas. By the 1700s cities in Europe were using natural gas in streetlights.[44]

In 1821, William Hart, a gunsmith in Fredonia, N.Y., created a catch basin for a pocket of escaping natural gas. Then residents built a crude wooden pipeline to deliver

C H R O N O L O G Y

1820s-1930s *Early drilling and pipeline technologies lay the groundwork for future innovation*

1825 Natural gas is extracted from shallow-rock pools in Fredonia, N.Y., which harnesses the gas for lighting.

1891 First interstate gas pipeline spans more than 100 miles from gas fields in Indiana to Chicago.

1892 Thomas Edison builds the first coal-powered electricity generator in New York City, rapidly ending demand for gas lighting.

1908 Wisconsin Public Utility Commission switches the energy value for natural gas from candlepower to the British Thermal Unit (BTU), reflecting the transition of gas from a fuel source for lighting to a heating fuel.

1930s-1950s *Interstate natural gas pipelines begin crisscrossing the nation, and the federal government restricts pipeline companies from becoming monopolies.*

1931 Peoples Gas Light and Coke Co. in Chicago builds a large pipeline to gas fields in southwestern Kansas, then one of the nation's largest gas-producing regions.

1937 Natural gas explosion in Texas kills 300 students near their school.

1954 Supreme Court rules in *Phillips Petroleum v. Wisconsin* that the Federal Power Commission (FPC) must regulate natural gas prices at the wellhead.

1970s-1990s *Natural-gas shortages hit some parts of the country. And price deregulation follows.*

1978 Passage of the Natural Gas Policy Act replaces the FPC with the Federal Energy Regulatory Commission (FERC).

1989 Natural Gas Wellhead Decontrol Act lifts remaining wellhead price controls.

1992 The first horizontal natural gas well is hydraulically fractured in the Barnett Shale formation near Fort Worth, Texas, making shale gas suddenly profitable.

2000s-Present *Hydraulic fracturing of shale gas takes off nationwide, raising concerns about the speed of the gas boom and its impacts.*

2004 Environmental Protection Agency concludes that injecting fracking fluids underground does not contaminate drinking water, but scientists question the study's conclusions.

2005 Drilling begins in the Marcellus Shale Deposit in Pennsylvania, setting off the current shale-gas boom. . . . Congress passes the 2005 Energy Act, which exempts hydraulic fracturing from the Safe Drinking Water Act.

2009 Environmental and safety problems in Dimock, Pa., and at other drilling sites draw national attention. . . . New York state temporarily bans hydraulic fracturing to study its full environmental and health consequences; other states and countries follow suit.

2010 The documentary film "Gasland," highly critical of the hydraulic fracturing industry, is released.

2011 Two proposals — the Fracturing Responsibility and Awareness of Chemicals Act (FRAC Act) that tightens regulation of fracking, and the New Alternative Transportation to Give Americans Solutions Act (NAT GAS) to create subsidies for vehicles using natural gas — are introduced in Congress. . . . FERC approves construction of U.S. liquefied natural gas export terminals. . . . New York state continues to uphold the ban on fracking pending an environmental study. . . . residents of Dimock sue drilling company Cabot Oil and Gas in federal court, alleging damages to their water wells from fracking. . . . Delaware River Basin Commission postpones decision to allow fracking in watershed serving 15 million people in Delaware, Pennsylvania, New York and New Jersey. . . . EPA documents the first linkage between fracking and underground water contamination at two monitoring water wells in Pavillion, Wyo.

Gas Producers Eye Export Market

"The shale story just kept building and building."

So much natural gas has been produced in the United States from hydraulic fracturing — or fracking — of shale formations that the industry is looking to foreign markets to soak up the vast new supply.

North American ports are switching from importing gas from other major producing regions, such as Russian and the Middle East, to exporting it to energy-hungry markets such as Europe and Asia.[1]

The glut of U.S.-produced shale gas also is affecting other aspects of the international gas market. In the late 1990s, countries such as Russia and Qatar spent heavily to build facilities to store liquefied natural gas (LNG) — gas that has been converted to liquid for ease of storage and transport — in hopes of selling it to the United States. Now they may have to compete with the United States for a share of the growing overseas market.[2]

The change in natural gas markets has geopolitical implications. It is estimated that Iran has 15.8 percent of the world's natural gas reserves, second only to Russia. Iran plans to develop six offshore gas-drilling sites in the Persian Gulf.[3]

Still, despite access to one of the largest gas fields in the world, Iran has been slow to develop its gas resources because international sanctions have hindered foreign investment. The sanctions were imposed because of Iran's development of nuclear-weapons technology. In October, however, a Chinese company expressed interest in investing in Iran's natural gas projects.[4]

Exporting natural gas is a complex process. Before it can be loaded onto a tanker and shipped overseas, gas arriving via pipeline must be cooled to a liquid, which requires not only special infrastructure but also Department of Energy approval under an extensive permitting process.

In Oregon, officials of the Jordan Cove Energy Project are deciding whether to build a $3.5 billion terminal at the international port of Coos Bay to ship U.S.-produced gas overseas. The terminal, which would make Oregon the western export gateway for LNG, would tap into gas pipelines along the California border that in turn connect to suppliers in the Rocky Mountains.

But the terminal faces potential competition. A joint venture backed by three large energy companies — Apache, Encana, and EOG Resources — was granted a license in October by Canada's National Energy Board to build an LNG export terminal at the deepwater port of Kitimat, British Columbia. The terminal is expected to be completed by 2015 and have the capacity to ship 1.4 billion cubic feet of natural gas per day.[5]

the gas to homes for lighting and cooking. The Fredonia gas well was the first in the United States and launched the Fredonia Gas Light Co.[45]

In 1859 American Edwin Drake developed a new oil-drilling method. By inserting a metal pipe into the drill hole, he was able to drill deeper and more productive wells because the insert prevented the well holes from collapsing on themselves. The method later was also used to tap deep pockets of natural gas.[46] The first interstate natural gas pipeline was built in 1891 from Indiana to Chicago.[47]

By the late 1800s, however, electricity generated mainly by burning coal was becoming popular, and gas lamps were being replaced by electric lights.

In the 1920s, with the construction of adequate pipelines, natural gas began to affect the national energy market as new appliances and technologies were developed to use natural gas for cooking and heating. But with coal inexpensive and easier to transport, natural gas did not play a significant role in power generation until after World War II.[48]

Regulating Gas

As natural gas slowly emerged on the energy scene in the late 1800s and early 1900s, it was regulated at the state level, but the focus was on production, prevention of monopolies and avoidance of wild boom-bust cycles, not environmental protection.

Laws and guidelines required oil and natural gas drillers to cap and case wells and permitted only a certain number of wells in a producing field. States also regulated transportation of gas through pipelines because of concerns

Proponents of the West Coast projects say terminals will be cost-effective because they are convenient to the Asian market.[6] But states in other U.S. regions also are moving forward with export terminals.

Along the Gulf Coast, Houston-based Cheniere Energy plans to build a $6 billion terminal in Louisiana to ship gas to Europe and Asia. And Freeport LNG is proceeding with a $2 billion project on the Texas coast with a goal of exporting 1.4 billion cubic feet of LNG per day, or about $4 billion to $6 billion of gas annually, to Europe and Asia. Both locations are close to major shale-gas production areas in Texas, Arkansas and Louisiana.[7]

Freeport's terminal opened in 2008 to import LNG. But Michael Smith, Freeport's CEO, said the time was right to convert the facility for export. "The shale story just kept building and building over the past few years until, finally, we did the engineering and it just made sense," he said.[8]

— *Daniel McGlynn*

Jordan Cove Energy Project, L.P.

An artist's rendering shows the proposed Jordan Cove liquefied natural gas facility in Coos Bay, Ore.

[1]Tom Fowler, "Glut prompts project to chill natural gas for export," *Houston Chronicle*, Nov. 23, 2010, www.chron.com/business/energy/article/Glut-prompts-project-to-chill-natural-gas-for-1697992.php.

[2]"Qatar shifts gas plan as U.S. output grows," United Press International, Oct. 14, 2011, www.upi.com/Business_News/Energy-Resources/2011/10/14/Qatar-shifts-gas-plan-as-US-output-grows/UPI-33401318608222/?spt=hs&or=er.

[3]*Ibid.*

[4]Landane Nasseri, "China may invest in Iran LNG plant construction, official says," Bloomberg, Oct. 25, 2011, www.bloomberg.com/news/2011-10-25/china-may-invest-in-iran-lng-plant-construction-official-says.html.

[5]Edward Welsch, "Canada approves plan for BC LNG shipments to Asia," Dow Jones Newswire, Oct. 13, 2011, www.foxbusiness.com/industries/2011/10/13/canada-approves-plan-for-british-columbia-lng-shipments-to-asia/.

[6]Ted Sickinger, "Backers of Coos Bay site to apply for federal export license," *The Oregonian*, Sept. 22, 2011, www.oregonlive.com/business/index.ssf/2011/09/coos_bay_lng_backers_to_apply.html.

[7]Christopher Swann and Neil Unmack, "Outlook Brightens for U.S. gas exports," *The New York Times*, Oct. 13, 2011, www.nytimes.com/2011/10/14/business/outlook-brightens-for-us-gas-exports.html?_r=1.

[8]Fowler, *op. cit.*

that producers would use interstate pipelines to control supplies and prices.[49]

Pipeline technology improved enough between 1927 and 1931 to permit construction of larger lines. During that time about a dozen major transmission systems were built, piping natural gas over hundreds of miles.[50]

The federal government first began regulating natural gas in 1938. The Natural Gas Act, which charged the Federal Power Commission with regulating hydroelectric projects and interstate electric utilities, also authorized the commission to set rates for interstate gas sales and restrict interstate pipeline construction. At the time, members of Congress were concerned that gas producers were overcharging to ship gas and that a few producers could easily control the market across several states.[51]

During the 1940s Congress was divided over whether the Natural Gas Act applied only to control of the transportation and sale of gas or was intended to regulate producers by setting prices at the wellhead. In 1954 the U.S. Supreme Court ruled in *Phillips Petroleum v. Wisconsin* that the FPC applied to wellhead prices for producers who sold gas to interstate pipelines.[52]

Producers argued that the price controls kept natural gas prices artificially low and reduced incentives for exploration and development of new reserves and conservation of existing ones.

In 1966, natural gas was available to consumers in every state but Hawaii, and in 1970 it accounted for 30 percent of the U.S. energy supply. But domestic oil and natural gas drilling slowed in the late 1970s, and government price

New EPA Study Links Fracking, Water Pollution

Drilling chemicals were found in a Wyoming town's water.

The Environmental Protection Agency (EPA) has established the first scientific links between hydraulic fracturing and pollution of nearby drinking water.

In a draft report released Dec. 8, the EPA said chemicals found in a drinking-water aquifer near the central Wyoming farming town of Pavillion are consistent with the kinds of chemicals used in nearby fracking operations. The widely anticipated study presents the first scientific evidence that chemicals used in natural gas fracking can migrate from drilling sites deep below the surface into shallower drinking-water wells and aquifers.[1]

Pavillion residents first noticed water-well problems, such as water that smelled and tasted like chemicals, in 2005 and suspected that some of the 200 gas wells drilled in the area since the mid-1990s might be to blame.[2]

"There's nothing else going on there except oil and gas development," says Deb Thomas, an organizer for the Powder River Basin Resource Council, an environmental organization that works with Pavillion Area Concerned Citizens, a grassroots water-quality group.

For the past three years the EPA has been testing 42 residential drinking-water wells in Pavillion and has drilled two deeper wells to monitor the underlying aquifers.[3]

Encana, a Canadian natural gas company that owns and operates the Pavillion-area gas wells, rejected the EPA's findings conclusions and said the draft report is inconclusive.

"We strongly disagree with the conclusions of the draft report because they couch them as likely and maybe," says company spokesman Doug Hock. He contends the study was poorly constructed and that any contamination found in the EPA's deep monitoring wells could have resulted from the EPA's own drilling to test the aquifers.

The EPA said, however, that it had been careful to avoid contaminating the aquifer.

Encana planned to sell its Pavillion gas-field operations to Texas-based Legacy Reserves for $45 million.[4] As part of the deal, Encana was to retain liability for any underground water contamination, Hock says. But Legacy abandoned the deal in late November, when it learned what would be in the EPA draft report, he says. "Legacy felt that the level of scrutiny and attention of the study wasn't worth it," Hock says.

In hydraulic fracturing, chemicals — such as the carcinogen benzene — along with water and sand are injected under strong pressure into shale-rock formations to open fissures and release the gas.

Fracking proponents have long defended the method's safety record, saying there had never been a documented case of fracking chemicals entering aquifers underground.

controls discouraged additional exploration and development. Consequently, the market share of natural gas began to decline, and major natural gas shortages hit some states in 1976 and '77.[53]

Deregulation

During the 1970s, Congress debated whether to deregulate natural gas pricing. In 1977, lawmakers passed the Department of Energy Organization Act and in 1978 the Natural Gas Policy Act as part of the larger National Energy Act. The Energy Act replaced the Federal Power Commission with the Federal Energy Regulatory Commission (FERC), which was put in charge of regulating natural gas. The new law also began phasing out price controls at gas wellheads in an effort to equalize supply and demand. Many policymakers viewed controls aimed at protecting against high prices and industry monopolies as detrimental to consumers, arguing that the regulations created gas shortages.

Passage in 1989 of the Natural Gas Wellhead Decontrol Act repealed all remaining price controls at

But opponents have voiced concern about the potential of chemicals to foul drinking water.

The EPA said "health and safety values for several contaminants were exceeded" in its two monitoring wells in Pavillion. The EPA also said it found benzene concentrations that were "orders of magnitude" above the standards set by the federal Safe Drinking Water Act and that pH levels were high enough in alkalinity to pose skin-contact or drinking hazards.

No known geologic barrier separates the contamination found in the monitoring wells from water in nearby drinking water wells, the EPA said. But without more information on flow direction and movement of contaminants, the agency cautioned, "significant uncertainty exists regarding specific future impacts to drinking water wells," the agency says. The EPA draft report will be open for public comments for 45 days and must be peer reviewed by scientists before it is finalized.

The EPA said the results are relevant only to Pavillion because of the region's unique geology and drilling history. But the report could help shape a much larger study of fracking's effects on groundwater that the EPA is conducting at seven drilling sites in North Dakota, Texas, Pennsylvania and Colorado. The results of the national study are not expected for several years.

Meanwhile, for residents of Pavillion who have complained that they can't drink from their faucets, the newly released draft report offers some peace of mind, Thomas says. "They are just so happy that now they are getting some answers," she says.

— *Daniel McGlynn*

Residents of the central Wyoming farming town of Pavillion first noticed water problems in 2005. Since the mid-1990s, 200 gas wells have been drilled in the area.

ALeqM5jVjSCLUeua_nbBiWJ3GZBfrD8Xrw?docId=0f23e155503d4990b0a0c787f6b3bc69. The EPA's draft report is: "Investigation of Ground Water Contamination near Pavillion, Wyoming," December 2011, www.epa.gov/region8/superfund/wy/pavillion/EPA_ReportOnPavillion_Dec-8-2011.pdf.

[2]For background see, Abrahm Lustgarten, "Hydrofracked? One man's mystery leads to a backlash against natural gas drilling," *ProPublica*, Feb. 25, 2011, www.propublica.org/ article/hydrofracked-one-mans-mystery-leads-to-a-backlash-against-natural-gas-drill/single.

[3]"Pavillion Area Groundwater Investigation," United States Environmental Protection Agency, Superfund Technical Assessment and Response Team 3 — Region 8, Jan. 6, 2010, www.epa.gov/region8/superfund/wy/pavillion/Pavillion_GWInvestigationFSP.pdf.

[4]Dina O'Meara, "Fracking concerns scuttle Encana asset sale," *Calgary Herald*, Dec. 7, 2011, www.calgaryherald.com/business/Fracking+concerns+scuttle+Encana+asset+sale/5821030/story.html.

[1]Mead Gruver, "EPA theorizes fracking-pollution link," The Associated Press, Dec. 12, 2011, www.google.com/hostednews/ap/article/

the wellhead. In addition, FERC separated the rules and responsibilities for gas pipeline operators from those for companies that sold gas to utility districts. According to the Natural Gas Supply Association, the final restructuring rule issued by FERC in 1992 was "the culmination of deregulation" of the interstate natural gas industry.

"Distilled to its main purpose," the association said, the order gave "all natural gas sellers equal footing in moving natural gas from the wellhead to the end-user." It allowed "the complete unbundling of transportation,

storage and marketing." Customers could choose "the most efficient method of obtaining gas."[54]

As demand for natural gas reached a plateau in the 1970s and '80s, mainly because of federal regulations and doubts about long-term supply, other energy sources became cheaper in comparison.

As many federal regulations were lifted from natural gas in the 1990s, concerns grew about the consequences of burning coal and oil for energy. Environmentalists touted gas as a cleaner burning fossil fuel, boosting demand for it and sparking new efforts to find additional reserves.

In 1990, gas accounted for 12 percent of the U.S. energy supply — a far cry from the 30 percent registered in 1970 but beginning to rebound.[55]

Also during the 1990s, 65 percent of the capacity added to the U.S. power grid came from newly designed, efficient gas-fired power plants, while only 2 percent of new capacity was added from coal-fired plants. Natural gas prices remained high, the result of market controls in prior decades and limitations in production capacity.

Natural gas was imported from Canada to help meet the growing demand. In addition, energy companies began to propose building liquefied natural gas terminals to handle imports from overseas.

By 2009, the price of gas in the United States had dropped, in part because of the discoveries of shale-gas deposits in such areas as the Marcellus and Barnett formations.[56]

Hydraulic Fracturing

The recent spike in U.S. demand for natural gas is in large part fueled by the exploration and development of massive deposits of what are called "unconventional" natural gas reservoirs. In previous decades, natural gas was extracted from pockets of gas trapped between layers of impermeable rock, usually with oil. Now it can be extracted from geological formations such as shale and sand.

Standard Oil pioneered hydraulic fracturing in 1949. Since then, almost 2.5 million wells have been fractured around the world. The method was first used to stimulate oil wells when their flow was slowing because of blockages in the well hole or when a well was near the end of its production cycle.

Stimulating oil wells has a long history. In the 1860s, drillers poured nitroglycerin down hard-rock wells to enhance performance. By the 1930s, while looking for a non-explosive way to stimulate wells, drillers began using acid to break up underground rock formations that contained oil. The acid dissolved harder parts of the rock and let the liquid oil pass through.[57]

In 1947, a mixture of napalm thickened with gasoline was injected into the Hugoton gas field in Kansas. More tests were conducted, and the process, called Hydrafrac, was patented in 1949. The Halliburton Oil Well Cementing Co. was granted the exclusive license to use the new technology.[58]

In the first year of production, Halliburton treated 332 wells, increasing productivity by 75 percent. By the mid-1950s Halliburton was fracturing 3,000 wells a month.[59]

When fracturing first began, the average job required 750 gallons of water and chemicals and 400 pounds of sand. Today, because of the vast scale of hydraulic fracturing operations, wells typically use 60,000 gallons of fluid and 100,000 pounds of chemical additives to lubricate well holes and break up underground geological formations. Instead of crude oil or napalm, drillers are using roughly 750 different kinds of chemicals as fracturing fluids. Some large-scale fracturing operations can use up to 1 million gallons of fluid.[60]

Initially, river sand was used as a proppant to keep the fractures open. Early experiments also included everything from nutshells to instant coffee. While most concerns over hydraulic fracturing now focus on the number of chemical additives, hundreds of thousands of pounds of sand is still used. Some of it flows out of the well during the process, creating a chemical-laden slurry that needs disposal.[61]

Besides growing in chemical complexity, contemporary fracturing allows wells to be drilled vertically deep into the ground and then secondary wells to be drilled horizontally away from the main shaft. Advocates say that approach reduces the number of wells drilled from the surface while allowing more gas to be extracted. Opponents say the underground tunneling increases the likelihood of contaminating aquifers.

In 1992 high-volume horizontal hydraulic fracturing accessed natural gas in the Barnett Shale in Texas.[62] In the 2000s, producers started buying land and setting up similar drilling operations in Pennsylvania and New York, atop the Marcellus Shale.

Hydraulic fracturing got a boost with passage of the Energy Act of 2005, which exempted the process from regulation under the Safe Water Drinking Act. Fracking opponents call the exemption the "Halliburton Loophole" because all other underground injection activities are regulated by the federal government. Opponents claim that former Vice President Dick Cheney, who was Halliburton's CEO before serving in the George W. Bush administration, spearheaded the exemption's passage.[63]

In 2009, House and Senate Democrats from Colorado, New York and Pennsylvania introduced the Fracturing Responsibility and Awareness of Chemicals Act (FRAC Act) to close the exemption. The bill also sought to compel drilling companies to fully disclose the chemicals used in their operations.[64] The legislation failed to pass but was reintroduced this year.

CURRENT SITUATION
Oceans of Gas

Initial estimates of the size and scope of the nation's natural gas reserves, particularly in the Marcellus Shale, are under intense review, even as the controversy over fracking continues.[65]

In 2002, geologists estimated the Marcellus Shale would yield 2 trillion cubic feet (TCF) of economically recoverable natural gas.[66] But the rapid development of underground imaging to examine the shale and improvements in hydraulic fracturing techniques led to a higher estimate in 2007 — 50 TCF, according to Terry Engelder, a professor of geosciences at Pennsylvania State University.[67]

By 2009, Engelder's number had grown to 489 TCF, and drillers rushed to purchase leases on Marcellus Shale land.[68] In July 2011 the U.S. Energy Information Administration put Marcellus Shale gas reserves at 410 TCF.[69]

In 2011, however, the U.S. Geological Survey found that only 84 TCF of Marcellus natural gas is economically recoverable with existing fracturing technology.[70] The shifting estimates point to uncertainty about the future of natural gas — and fracking in particular — from economic, environmental and health perspectives.

In 2009, the Center for American Progress, a liberal think tank in Washington, called natural gas "the biggest game changer for climate action in the next two decades." But as more attention focuses on the environmental effects of fracking and the lack of federal oversight, public support for natural gas here and abroad may be shifting.[71]

Fracking has been banned in Quebec, Canada, France, Germany and South Africa until it can be studied further. And New York, New Jersey and Maryland have imposed moratoria on fracking while state environmental agencies examine environmental and health impacts.[72]

But the New York moratorium could be ending as the two-year environmental assessment nears completion. "I think it is safe to say that the Department [of Environmental Conservation]'s position is that, given the proposed regulations, high-volume hydraulic fracturing

can be undertaken safely with adequate oversight," says Commissioner Martens.

Meanwhile, the natural gas industry is trying to figure out how to repair fracking's damaged reputation. "We have not done a very good job explaining where and how hydraulic fracturing fits into the shale-gas development process," said Jack Williams, the president of Exxon's shale-gas division, XTO Energy. "We must do all we can to restore the public's trust. . . . Our industry depends on it."[73]

In addition to studying the environmental and health risks associated with hydraulic fracturing, individual states are trying to deal with the economic and infrastructure impacts. Chief among the concerns: the lack of staff and resources at state environmental regulators' offices and the damage to roads and bridges resulting from heavy equipment and tanker trucks used in hydraulic fracturing.

"In the Fayetteville Shale region, in Arkansas, the state Highway Department reported that the gas industry has caused $455 million worth of damage to highways," said economist Jannette Barth, a member of the anti-fracking group Catskill Citizens for Safe Energy. "Insufficient funds are collected from the industry, and even with a severance tax, it appears that the taxpayers of Arkansas will have to pay more than $400 million of the road-repair costs."[74]

To address such concerns, states are discussing tax structures and permitting requirements for new drilling operations. Martens, for example, says New York is considering charging gas drillers "a permit fee based on how deep a well is drilled. We are also looking into a severance tax, which other states with gas drilling have." (A severance tax is a fee that state governments charge companies for removing nonrenewable resources.)

Pennsylvania has no severance tax or other kind of levy on the gas industry. "The Marcellus is a resource, a source of potential wealth," said Republican Gov. Tom Corbett. "It is the foundation of a new economy, not just something new to tax."[75]

Like federal regulators, state regulators are also asking for more information about what exactly drilling companies are injecting into the ground. To address concerns about the full disclosure of the chemicals used in fracturing, the Ground Water Protection Council has created a database called FracFocus in which drilling companies can voluntarily report which chemicals they are using.[76]

Is hydraulic fracturing good for the economy?

YES

Aubrey K. McClendon
Co-Founder, Chairman and CEO, Chesapeake Energy Corp.

Keynote address before the Marcellus Shale Insights Conference, Philadelphia, Sept. 7, 2011

According to a newly released study of Marcellus natural gas development by Penn State University, the shale-gas revolution is the biggest opportunity to hit Pennsylvania since the steel industry more than 100 years ago. . . .

Consider these numbers:

- Marcellus natural gas development generated $11 billion in value-added regional gross domestic product last year. That number will rise to $13 billion in 2011 and reach $17 billion in 2015. . . .
- Chesapeake [Energy Corp.] has 2.4 million acres under lease in the Marcellus and has already paid almost $2 billion in lease bonus and royalties to farmers, families and townships across Pennsylvania.
- Direct and indirect employment from this economic boom has already surpassed 140,000 jobs. . . . Chesapeake alone has about 2,100 employees in the Marcellus and about 1,700 of them were hired regionally. According to Penn State, further development of the Marcellus will support 216,000 jobs in 2015. . . .
- If you think this shale discovery and development is like hitting the lottery, you are right, especially if you happen to be the budget director for Pennsylvania. State and local taxes paid will total about $1.2 billion this year and are projected to reach $1.4 billion in 2012. . . .
- Nationally, the numbers only get bigger. Natural gas exploration and development supports about 3.5 million jobs across the country and with continued investment can easily add 500,000 more. By way of example, Chesapeake has added about 3,000 direct employees nationwide in the first eight months of 2011 alone.

But the benefits don't stop there. Chesapeake has 1 million mineral owners in 16 states. To put that in perspective, about one in every 300 Americans has an oil and natural gas lease with Chesapeake. And they have been very well rewarded. We've paid out $9 billion in lease bonuses over the past five years, about $5 billion in royalties over the past four years and another $2 billion in taxes over the past five years.

And every one of those numbers is going up daily. The lives of millions rest on us getting this issue right and utilizing this American Treasure. . . .

And remind me, what value [have] these shale gas protestors created? What jobs have they created? You know the answer, and so do I, and it's time that we contrast what we do for a living [versus] what they do for a living.

NO

Jannette M. Barth
Economist, Pepacton Institute, and member, Catskill Citizens for Safe Energy

Testimony before public hearing of state Sen. Greg Ball, R-N.Y., Aug. 23, 2011

The gas industry is seriously misleading the public and our politicians. They ignore costs and exaggerate benefits. . . . The oil and gas industry is 10 times more capital-intensive than the average industry. Capital-intensive industries, by definition, are not major job creators. It would be far better for our economy, and in particular for job creation, to encourage a more labor-intensive industry.

The studies that claim a positive economic impact from gas drilling tend to be biased, dated, seriously flawed or inapplicable to our region. It's critical to examine what has been left out of these studies. What costs have not been taken into account? . . .

The studies funded by the gas industry ignore declines in other industries that are likely to result from a combination of pollution, a shift to an industrial landscape and "crowding out." Examples of industries likely to be negatively affected include agriculture, tourism, organic farming, wine making, hunting, fishing and river recreation.

The industry-funded studies ignore the fact that there will be damage to infrastructure, especially roads and bridges. In the Fayetteville Shale region, in Arkansas, the state Highway Department reported that the gas industry has caused $455 million worth of damage to highways. Insufficient funds are collected from the industry, and even with a severance tax it appears that the taxpayers of Arkansas will have to pay more than $400 million of the road-repair costs.

The costs of drinking-water contamination and land, stream and air pollution are ignored in the economic impact studies. The cost of mitigation is ignored and so is the cost in terms of health. . . .

Costs to communities are ignored, including costs due to the increased demand on hospitals, police, fire departments and emergency health services. . . .

Likely declines in property values are ignored. Supporters of gas drilling say that property values will increase. Rental rates will probably increase due to the influx of transient workers, and hotel occupancy rates may increase. We have seen this happen in Pennsylvania. The value of large tracts of land may increase, but single-family homes and small lots will probably decline in value. . . . Also, some insurance companies are refusing to issue policies on homes with gas wells.

The industry-funded studies take a myopic view. They don't address what happens when the gas is gone, and we may be left with contaminated drinking water, pollution, an industrial landscape, a population with failing health and vanished employment opportunities.

States including New Mexico, Louisiana and Texas are using FracFocus as a permitting requirement. "So far there are 60 participating companies and 4,300 hydraulic-fracturing records of individual wells," says the council's Nickolaus. However, fracking opponents point out that FracFocus has limits: Participation is voluntary, drilling companies that participate don't have to disclose all chemicals used in every well and they aren't required to disclose proprietary information.

Federal Initiatives

While state regulators are preparing for an increase in natural gas exploration and development, the federal government is trying to figure out the best way to create enforceable regulations within the context of existing legislation. Some members of Congress have introduced a bill that targets fracturing directly.

The 2011 Fracturing Responsibility and Awareness of Chemicals Act (FRAC Act), a reintroduction of a measure that failed to pass in 2009, would give the EPA more authority to regulate hydraulic fracturing by closing the exemption to the Safe Drinking Water Act. The legislation also would require companies to fully disclose the kinds of chemicals used in fracking. However, observers say the bill lacks broad support in Congress.

Meanwhile, the EPA is trying to develop new regulatory standards using existing legislation. For example, the agency is studying air quality at natural gas drilling and other production sites and proposing new air-quality standards for producers. There is concern that natural gas production might be releasing not only methane but also high levels of smog-forming volatile organic compounds and the carcinogen benzene into the air. The new rules would affect approximately 25,000 gas wells and require special equipment to filter emissions before they escape from drilling rigs.[77] The EPA claims the new rules would save the industry money because more natural gas would be delivered to market instead of leaking into the environment.[78]

Howard Feldman, director of scientific and regulatory policy at the American Petroleum Institute, said the trade group would review the proposed rules "to ensure that they don't inadvertently create unsafe operating conditions, are cost effective and truly provide additional public health benefits, and don't stifle the development of our abundant natural resources."[79]

Getty Images/Robert Nickelsberg

High-pressure fracking pumps are monitored by a Halliburton Co. engineer at a natural gas well near Hope, N.M. Twenty-six productive shale-gas formations stretch across the United States, from the Northeast to Utah and Montana. The Barnett Shale formation in Texas is among the largest.

Gas Economics

Development of natural gas not only is widely seen as a cleaner way to produce energy but also touted as a potential economic engine for local regions. Production can generate jobs in the construction and service industries as well as the gas industry. But critics argue that gas development will lead to boom-and-bust economic cycles and permanently damage other, more sustainable economic activities, such as agriculture, tourism and recreation.

The pace and scope of natural gas development is tied to the overall health of the national economy. According to the Energy Information Administration, "economic activity is a major factor influencing natural gas markets. When the economy improves, the increased demand for goods and services for the commercial and industrial sectors generates an increase in natural gas demand."[80] But during the second half of 2010, natural gas prices declined significantly. "These lower prices were accompanied by a steep decline in the number of rigs drilling for gas," the agency said.[81]

The drop in natural gas prices reflected the effect of fracturing, which flooded markets with cheap gas even as overall economic growth slowed. The combination of high supply and slowing demand could retard the speed of gas development in the near future, experts say.

Getty Images/Spencer Platt

Opponents and supporters of fracking attend a public hearing in New York City on proposed fracking regulations in upstate New York, where much of the city's drinking water comes from. If the regulations are approved, drilling in New York state's portion of the Northeast's vast Marcellus Shale formation could begin in 2012.

To encourage shale-gas development, a bipartisan group of House members introduced the New Alternative Transportation to Give Americans Solutions Act of 2011, which would provide tax incentives to the makers and purchasers of natural gas vehicles. Texas energy magnate and financier T. Boone Pickens lobbied heavily for the measure, and three of its four original co-sponsors hail from energy-rich Oklahoma and Texas.[82] But several Republican congressional members have withdrawn their support, objecting to using taxes to favor specific industries.[83]

While some Marcellus Shale states are divided over how to proceed with hydraulic fracturing, others, such as North Dakota, which sits atop the Bakken Shale, are encouraging fracking to fuel economic growth. But the high-volume fracturing operations in North Dakota are targeting oil, not gas. As in previous decades of oil exploration, the natural gas that is found in the same geological pockets is simply burned off. Building the equipment, such as pipelines and compressor stations, to handle the natural gas would be too expensive and slow the Bakken oil rush.

Meanwhile, in a move that parallels earlier natural gas regulation, the Securities and Exchange Commission (SEC) has begun investigating the industry.

The SEC, which oversees publicly traded companies, is concerned that natural gas companies are inflating estimates of the amount of gas that is economically extractable and minimizing the potential financial liabilities from lawsuits, environmental cleanup and compliance with future regulations.

The SEC has asked publicly traded gas companies to provide it with confidential information, such as the proprietary chemicals used in their fractured wells. Depending on its findings, the SEC might require some of the information to be disclosed to the public. Until the information is disclosed, however, the SEC cannot share its findings with other federal regulators, such as the EPA or the Departments of Energy or Interior, all of which also are requesting similar information from the industry.[84]

OUTLOOK
More Fracking Likely

For reasons ranging from national security to environmental concern to economics, domestic production of natural gas is likely to grow sharply in the near future. The Energy Information Administration predicts that shale gas will supply 45 percent of the country's natural gas supply by 2035, up from the current 24 percent.[85]

Because most of the currently explored natural gas reserves are locked up in "unconventional" geological structures such as shale, it is likely that hydraulic fracturing will become more pervasive. Given the rate of development, some forecasts show shale gas supplying half of the nation's natural gas in 10 years, up from close to a third today.

In New York state, where the fracturing debate is especially contentious, Department of Environmental Conservation Commissioner Martens says, "I think it could play a significant role in the future of New York. We could have thousands of wells drilled in the next 10 years." And, Martens adds, "It's a responsible way to go if you consider New York is a large consumer of natural gas. It's cleaner than other fossil fuels."

But Ferguson of Catskill Citizens for Safe Energy says fracking has a cost. "We are going to export natural gas to an area of Canada that doesn't allow fracking. China is buying shale gas in the U.S. In a sense we are becoming the new third world."

As fracking accounts for a larger share of the nation's energy supply, fracturing technology is likely to continue to develop, allowing access to even deeper pockets of gas. Although the current attention is focused on accessing the Marcellus Shale, companies are researching another gas-rich field in the area — the Utica Shale.[86]

Like the Marcellus, the Utica Shale is enormous, extending from Canada to Kentucky. It too has been called "a game changer." In most places the Utica Shale is tucked a few thousand feet below the Marcellus Shale. The Utica is larger and deeper than the Marcellus, but so far there are no estimates of how much natural gas it contains. Some companies have begun exploration and drilling in Ohio, where the Utica appears to be the shallowest.[87]

Whether drilling companies will be compelled to fully disclose their fracking fluids, a move they say could damage individual companies' intellectual-property rights, remains uncertain. However, companies are investing in the research and development of more benign drilling practices.

David Burnett, a petroleum engineer and director of technology at Texas A&M University's Petroleum Research Institute, is developing a system that studies and recommends new drilling technologies that reduce environmental impact. Burnett points to a gas well that operates in a hospital parking lot in Amsterdam, Netherlands, with virtually no detectable emissions.[88]

Natural gas companies also are working on less toxic hydraulic fracturing chemicals. Halliburton recently announced that it developed a fracking agent called CleanStim, made of compounds used in the food industry.

But the public perception of hydraulic fracturing risks persists. In November 2011 the Delaware River Basin Commission, a federal agency charged with protecting a watershed that supplies 15 million people with drinking water in New York, New Jersey, Pennsylvania and Delaware, postponed plans to approve fracking and set drilling regulations in the basin.

The commission is divided on how to proceed. Without its approval widespread drilling within the watershed remains uncertain. Environmentalists and anti-fracking activists celebrated the postponement as a victory with a rally in Trenton, N.J.[89] And as of December 2011, the meeting to approve fracking in the watershed had not been rescheduled.

NOTES

1. New York State Senate Public Hearing on Veterans, Homeland Security and Military Affairs, Aug. 23, 2011, www.youtube.com/watch?v=tstGKhNobCc&feature.

2. For background, see the following *CQ Researcher* reports: Peter Katel, "Water Crisis in the West," Dec. 9, 2011, pp. 1025-1048; Jennifer Weeks, "Energy Policy," May 20, 2011, pp. 457-480; and Weeks, "Water Shortages," June 18, 2010, pp. 529-552.

3. Amanda Little, "Should enviros embrace liquefied natural gas?" *Grist*, Nov. 6, 2003, www.grist.org/article/assets.

4. For background, see Jeff McMahon, "Fracking study may expose natural gas industry to regulation," *Forbes*, May 5, 2011, www.forbes.com/sites/jeffmcmahon/2011/05/10/fracking-study-exposes-natural-gas-industry-to-regulation/2/.

5. Charles Q. Coi, "Did fracking cause Oklahoma's largest recorded earthquake?" *Scientific American*, Nov. 14, 2011, www.scientificamerican.com/article.cfm?id=did-fracking-cause-oklahomas-largest-recorded-earthquake.

6. Garry White, "Cuadrilla admits drilling caused Blackpool earthquakes," *The Telegraph*, Nov. 2, 2011, www.telegraph.co.uk/finance/newsbysector/energy/8864669/Cuadrilla-admits-drilling-caused-Blackpool-earthquakes.html.

7. Ilya Marritz, "At city fracking hearing new questions about quake danger," WNYC, Nov. 30, 2011, www.wnyc.org/articles/wnyc-news/2011/nov/30/bloomberg-administration-fracking-induced-quakes-could-damage-water-system/.

8. For background, see Jonathan D. Silver, "The Marcellus boom/origins: the story of a professor, a gas driller and Wall Street," *Pittsburg Post-Gazette*, March 20, 2011, www.post-gazette.com/pg/11079/1133325-503.stm; and, Eliza Griswold, "The Fracturing of Pennsylvania," *The New York Times Magazine*, Nov. 17, 2011, www.nytimes.com/2011/11/20/magazine/fracking-amwell-township.html?hp.

9. U.S. Energy Information Administration, Washington, D.C., "Natural gas explained: use of natural gas,"

www.eia.gov/energyexplained/index.cfm?page= natural_gas_use.

10. David Brooks, "Shale gas revolution," *The New York Times*, Nov. 3, 2011, www.nytimes.com/2011/11/04/ opinion/brooks-the-shale-gas-revolution.html.

11. Richard L. Gaw, "Fighting fracking in the Hudson Valley: Actor Mark Ruffalo leads the movement to stop hydraulic fracturing for New York's natural gas," *Hudson Valley Magazine*, July 2011, www.hvmag .com/core/pagetools.php?pageid=8612&url=%2F Hudson-Valley-Magazine%2FJuly-2011%2FFighting- Fracking-in-the-Hudson-Valley-Actor-Mark-Ruffalo- Leads-the-Movement-to-Stop-Hydraulic-Fracturing- for-New-Yorks-Natural-Gas%2F&mode=print.

12. Ian Urbina, "Regulation lax as gas wells' tainted water hits rivers," *The New York Times*, Feb. 26, 2011, www .nytimes.com/2011/02/27/us/27gas.html? page wanted=all.

13. For background, see "What is hydraulic fracturing?" *ProPublica*, www.propublica.org/special/hydraulic- fracturing-national.

14. For background, see Mohan Jiang, *et al.*, "Life cycle greenhouse gas emissions of Marcellus shale gas," *Environmental Research Letters*, Vol. 6, No. 3, July- September 2011, http://iopscience.iop.org/1748- 9326/6/3/034014/fulltext/; and, "The Future of Natural Gas: An Interdisciplinary Study," Massachusetts Institute of Technology, 2011, http:// web.mit.edu/mitei/research/studies/naturalgas.html.

15. "Hydraulic Fracturing," U.S. Environmental Protection Agency, http://water.epa.gov/type/ground- water/uic/class2/hydraulicfracturing/index.cfm.

16. "Coming Soon to a Terminal Near You: Shale Gas Should Make the World a Cleaner Safer Place," *The Economist*, Aug. 6, 2011, www.economist.com/ node/21525381.

17. Christopher Flavin and Saya Kitasei, "The role of natural gas in a low-carbon energy economy," Worldwatch Institute, April 2010, p. 3.

18. "Natural Gas: Electricity from Natural Gas," U.S. Environmental Protection Agency, www.epa.gov/ cleanenergy/energy-and-you/affect/natural-gas.html.

19. "Greenhouse Gas Emissions Reporting from the Petroleum and Natural gas Industry: Background Technical Support Document," U.S. Environmental Protection Agency, Climate Change Division, www .epa.gov/climatechange/emissions/downloads10/ Subpart-W_TSD.pdf.

20. Abrahm Lustgarten, "Climate benefits of natural gas may be overstated," *ProPublica*, Jan. 25, 2011, www .propublica.org/article/natural-gas-and-coal-pollu tion-gap-in-doubt.

21. See Robert W. Howarth, Renee Santoro and Anthony Ingraffea, "Methane and the greenhouse-gas foot- print of natural gas from shale formations," *Climate Change Letters*, March 2011, www.acsf.cornell .edu/2011Howarth-Methane.

22. Stacey Shackford, "Natural gas from fracking could be 'dirtier' than coal, Cornell professors finds," *Chronicle Online*, Cornell University, April 11, 2011, www .news.cornell.edu/stories/April11/GasDrillingDirtier .html.

23. Don Hopey, "Marcellus Shale gas cleaner than coal, CMU study says," *Post-Gazette* (Pittsburgh), Aug. 20, 2011, www.post-gazette.com/pg/11232/1168671- 503-0.stm#ixzz1aKGI2Xv3.

24. "What is hydraulic fracturing?" *ProPublica*, www .propublica.org/special/hydraulic-fracturing-national.

25. Ian Urbina, "Pressure limits efforts to police drilling for gas," *The New York Times*, March 3, 2011, www.nytimes .com/2011/03/04/us/04gas.html?pagewanted=all.

26. "The Future of Natural Gas: An Interdisciplinary Study," Massachusetts Institute of Technology, 2011, http://web.mit.edu/mitei/research/studies/naturalgas. html.

27. Josh Fox, Gasland, released December 2010, http:// gaslandthemovie.com.

28. Abrahm Lustgarten, "EPA finds compound used in fracking in Wyoming aquifer," *ProPublica*, Nov. 10, 2011, www.propublica.org/article/epa-finds-fracking- compound-in-wyoming-aquifer/single.

29. Jeremy Fugleberg, "Buyer nixes deal for controversial natural gas assets," *Casper Star-Tribune*, Nov. 28, 2011, http://billingsgazette.com/news/state-and-regional/ wyoming/buyer-nixes-deal-for-controversial-natural- gas-assets/article_51a46b5c-fe93-5962-acda- 1b66af49a802.html.

30. Louis Bergeron, "Extracting natural gas from shale can be done in an environmentally responsible way, says Stanford researcher on government panel," *Stanford Report*, Aug. 30, 2011, http://news.stanford.edu/news/2011/august/zoback-fracking-qanda-083011.html.

31. Lustgarten, "EPA Find Compound. . . ," *op. cit.*

32. Mark Clayton, "Fracking for natural gas is polluting ground water, study concludes," *The Christian Science Monitor*, May 9, 2011, www.csmonitor.com/Environment/2011/0509/Fracking-for-natural-gas-is-polluting-ground-water-study-concludes.

33. Abrahm Lustgarten, "Scientific study links flammable drinking water to fracking," *ProPublica*, May 9, 2011, www.propublica.org/article/scientific-study-links-flammable-drinking-water-to-fracking/single.

34. Abrahm Lustgarten, "In new wells, more drilling chemicals remain underground," *ProPublica*, Dec. 27, 2009, www.propublica.org/article/new-gas-wells-leave-more-chemicals-in-ground-hydraulic-fracturing.

35. Mireya Navarro, "Doctors urge NY to weigh health risks of fracking," *The New York Times*, Green blog, Oct. 5, 2011, http://green.blogs.nytimes.com/2011/10/05/doctors-urge-n-y-to-weigh-health-risks-of-fracking/.

36. Quoted in *ibid.*

37. Urbina, *op. cit.*, March 3, 2011.

38. Ian Urbina, "A tainted water well, and concern there may be more," *The New York Times*, Aug. 3, 2011, www.nytimes.com/2011/08/04/us/04natgas.html?pagewanted=all.

39. Groundwater Protection Council, "State oil and natural gas regulations designed to protect water resources, a report prepared for the U.S. Department of Energy, Office of Fossil Energy, National Energy Technology Laboratory," May 2009, p. 37.

40. "Hydraulic Fracturing," Environmental Protection Agency, http://water.epa.gov/type/groundwater/uic/class2/hydraulicfracturing/index.cfm#curstud.

41. Abrahm Lustgarten, "FRAC Act — Congress introduces bills to control drilling," *ProPublica*, June 9, 2009, www.propublica.org/article/frac-act-congress-introduces-bills-to-control-drilling-609.

42. Urbina, *op. cit.*, Feb. 26, 2011.

43. *Ibid.*

44. For background, see the history section of natural-gas.org, which is maintained by the Natural Gas Supply Association.

45. Seamus McGraw, *The End of Country* (2011), pp. 32-35.

46. Byron W. King, "The Ghost of Colonel Drake," Post Carbon Institute, Energy Bulletin, Nov. 6, 2004, www.energybulletin.net/node/8295.

47. "The history of natural gas," U.S. Department of Energy, http://fossil.energy.gov/education/energylessons/gas/gas_history.html.

48. Ann Chambers, *Natural Gas and Electric Power in Non-Technical Language* (1999), p. 4.

49. "State oil and natural gas regulations designed to protect water resources, a report prepared for the U.S. Department of Energy, Office of Fossil Energy, National Energy Technology Laboratory," The Ground Water Protection Council, May 2009, p. 13.

50. Chambers, *op. cit.*, p. 5.

51. "The history of natural gas regulation," Naturalgas.org, www.naturalgas.org/regulation/history.asp.

52. *Ibid.*

53. Flavin and Kitasei, *op. cit.*, p. 2.

54. "The history of natural gas regulation," Naturalgas.org, *op. cit.*

55. *Ibid.*

56. Flavin and Kitasei, *op. cit.*, p. 4.

57. Carl T. Montgomery and Michael B. Smith, "Hydraulic Fracturing: History of an Enduring Technology," Society of Petroleum Engineers, December 2010, p. 27, www.spe.org/jpt/print/archives/2010/12/10Hydraulic.pdf.

58. *Ibid.*

59. *Ibid.*

60. *Ibid.*

61. "Committee Democrats Release New Report Detailing Hydraulic Fracturing Products," United States House of Representatives, Committee on Energy and Commerce, April 16, 2011, http://democrats.energy

commerce.house.gov/index.php?q=news/committee-democrats-release-new-report-detailing-hydraulic-fracturing-products.

62. Sarah Hoye and Steve Hargreaves, "Fracking yields fuel, fear in Northeast," CNN, Sept. 3, 2010, www.cnn.com/2010/US/09/02/fracking/index.html.

63. Kara Cusolito, "The next drilling disaster?" *The Nation*, June 3, 2010, www.thenation.com/article/next-drilling-disaster.

64. Lustgarten, *op. cit.*, June 9, 2009.

65. Ian Urbina, "Insiders sound an alarm amid a natural gas rush," *The New York Times*, June 25, 2011, www.nytimes.com/2011/06/26/us/26gas.html?pagewanted=all.

66. "Assessment of undiscovered oil and gas resources of the Appalachia Basin Province," U.S. Geological Survey Fact Sheet 009-03, http://pubs.usgs.gov/fs/fs-009-03/.

67. Ira Glass, "Game changer," "This American Life," July 8, 2011, www.thisamericanlife.org/radio-archives/episode/440/game-changer.

68. Mike Orcutt, "How much US shale gas is there really?" *MIT Technology Review*, Aug. 31, 2011, www.technologyreview.com/energy/38463/page1/.

69. "Review of Emerging Resources: U.S. Shale Gas and Shale Oil Plays," U.S. Energy Information Administration, Washington DC, July 8, 2011, www.eia.gov/analysis/studies/usshalegas/.

70. Tom Fowler, "New estimate raises Marcellus gas estimate forty-fold," *Houston Chronicle*, Aug. 24, 2004, www.chron.com/business/article/New-estimate-raises-Marcellus-gas-estimate-2139925.php. The final estimate is the mean of estimates ranging from 43 trillion to 144.1 trillion cubic feet.

71. Joe Romm, "Climate Progress," Center for American Progress, http://thinkprogress.org/romm/2009/06/03/204193/climate-action-game-changer-unconventional-natural-gas-shale, and John D. Podesta and Timothy E. Wirth, "Natural Gas: A Bridge Fuel for the 21st Century," Center for American Progress, Aug. 10, 2009, www.eia.gov/forecasts/aeo/chapter_executive_summary.cfm#domestic.

72. Steve Hargreaves, "The fracking public relations mess," CNN Money, June 21, 2011, http://money.cnn.com/2011/06/21/news/economy/fracking_public_relations/index.htm.

73. *Ibid.*

74. Jannette Barth, testimony at New York State Senate Public Hearing on Veterans, Homeland Security and Military Affairs, Aug. 23, 2011, www.youtube.com/watch?v=tstGKhNobCc&feature=youtube.

75. Quoted in Glass, *op. cit.*

76. For background, see FracFocus, http://fracfocus.org/.

77. Deborah Solomon and Tennille Tracy, "EPA unveils air quality rules for natural gas fracking," *The Wall Street Journal*, July 29, 2011, http://online.wsj.com/article/SB10001424053111904800304576474462644360884.html.

78. Dina Cappiello, "Fracking: EPA targets air pollution from natural gas drilling boom." The Associated Press, July 28, 2011, www.huffingtonpost.com/2011/07/28/fracking-epa-air-pollution-natural-gas-drilling_n_912564.html.

79. Solomon and Tracy, *op. cit.*

80. U.S. Energy Information Administration, *op. cit.*

81. *Ibid.*

82. "The NAT GAS Act," Rep. John Sullivan, http://sullivan.house.gov/perspectives/natgasact.htm. the measure originally was co-sponsored by Reps. John Sullivan, R-Okla., Dan Boren, D-Okla., Kevin Brady, R-Texas, and John Larson, D-Conn. At its peak it had 76 other sponsors.

83. Dan Berman and Patrick Reis, "Republicans withdraw support for Pickens bill," *Politico*, May 26, 2011, www.politico.com/news/stories/0511/55800.html.

84. Deborah Solomon, "SEC bears down on fracking," *The Wall Street Journal*, Aug. 25, 2011, http://online.wsj.com/article/SB10001424053111904009304576528484179638702.html.

85. "Annual Energy Outlook, 2011," U.S. Energy Information Administration, www.eia.gov/forecasts/aeo/chapter_executive_summary.cfm#domestic.

86. Glenn Coin, "Utica shale is the nest fracking frontier," *The Post Standard* (Syracuse), Oct. 10, 2011, www.syracuse.com/news/index.ssf/2011/10/utica_shale_is_the_next_fracki.html.

87. Ryan Dezember, "Utica Shale energizes deal frenzy in Ohio," *The Wall Street Journal*, Sept. 27, 2011, http://online.wsj.com/article/SB10001424052970204010604576592783750697202.html.

88. "Forum: Just how safe is fracking of natural gas?" *Yale360*, June 20, 2011, http://e360.yale.edu/feature/forum_just_how_safe__is_fracking_of_natural_gas/2417/.

89. "Key Delaware River gas drilling vote postponed," The Associated Press, Nov. 18, 2011, http://online.wsj.com/article/APa11d7405f6524fcaba568158a09764df.html.

BIBLIOGRAPHY

Selected Sources

Books

McGraw, Seamus, *The End of Country*, Random House, 2011.
A journalist documents the leasing of his family's farm to a natural gas company in rural Pennsylvania.

Yergin, Daniel, *The Quest: Energy, Security and the Remaking of the Modern World*, Penguin Press, 2011.
An energy analyst explains how natural gas fits into the global quest for energy.

Articles and Series

Bateman, Christopher, "A Colossal Fracking Mess: The Dirty Truth Behind the New Natural Gas," *Vanity Fair*, June 21, 2010, www.vanityfair.com/business/features/2010/06/fracking-in-pennsylvania-201006.
A reporter examines what went wrong with natural gas drilling in Dimock, Pa.

Griswold, Eliza, "The Fracturing of Pennsylvania," *The New York Times Magazine*, Nov. 20, 2011, www.nytimes.com/2011/11/20/magazine/fracking-amwell-township.html?scp=1&sq=situation%20normal%20all%20fracked%20up&st=cse.
A writer examines Amwell Township in southwest Pennsylvania and "the dividing line . . . between those who are getting rich" from fracking "and those who are paying the price."

Lustgarten, Abrahm, and Nicholas Kusnetz, "Fracking," *ProPublica*, www.propublica.org/series/fracking.
A team of journalists at the nonprofit investigative-reporting outlet provides ongoing coverage of the natural gas industry.

Lustgarten, Abrahm, "Hydrofracked? One Man's Mystery Leads to a Backlash Against Natural Gas Drilling," *ProPublica*, Feb. 25, 2011, www.propublica.org/article/hydrofracked-one-mans-mystery-leads-to-a-backlash-against-natural-gas-drill/single.
A reporter profiles Wyoming resident Louis Meeks and problems with his drinking water after nearby gas drilling in the town of Pavillion.

Urbina, Ian, "Drilling Down Series," *The New York Times*, www.nytimes.com/interactive/us/DRILLING_DOWN_SERIES.html?ref=us.
A reporter covers the environmental impacts and regulatory challenges associated with natural gas. The controversial series has been heavily criticized by the natural gas industry as unbalanced. *The Times* has defended its coverage and released hundreds of corroborating documents on its website.

Reports and Studies

"Investigation of Ground Water Contamination near Pavillion, Wyoming," Environmental Protection Agency, Draft Report, December 2011, www.epa.gov/region8/superfund/wy/pavillion/EPA_ReportOn Pavillion_Dec-8-2011.pdf.
For the first time, the EPA links fracking to groundwater contamination.

Andrews, Anthony, *et al.*, "Unconventional Gas Shales: Development, Technology, and Policy Issues," Congressional Research Service, Oct. 30, 2009, www.fas.org/sgp/crs/misc/R40894.pdf.
The nonpartisan research group provides background on a wide range of gas issues.

"Plan to Study the Potential Impacts of Hydraulic Fracturing on Drinking Water Resources," Environmental Protection Agency, November 2011, http://water.epa.gov/type/groundwater/uic/class2/hydraulicfracturing/upload/hf_study_plan_110211_final_508.pdf.

The EPA outlines plans for a comprehensive study of hydraulic fracturing and groundwater contamination.

Flavin, Christopher, and Saya Kitasei, "The Role of Natural Gas in a Low Carbon Energy Economy," Worldwatch Institute, April 2010, www.worldwatch .org/files/pdf/Worldwatch%20Gas%20Paper%20 April%202010.pdf.
A think tank examines the relationship between natural gas and energy policy.

"Modern Shale Gas Development in the United States: A Primer," The Ground Water Protection Council, April 2009, www.fossil.energy.gov/programs/oilgas/publications/ naturalgas_general/Shale_Gas_Primer_2009.pdf.
A group representing state water regulators gives an overview of shale gas development.

"The Future of Natural Gas: An Interdisciplinary Study," Massachusetts Institute of Technology, 2011, http://web.mit.edu/mitei/research/studies/naturalgas .html.
Researchers on all sides of the natural gas debate say phasing out coal and increasing natural gas energy can cut U.S. carbon dioxide emissions by 8 percent.

Documentary Film

"Gasland," released December 2010, www.gasland themovie.com.
Filmmaker and activist Josh Fox traveled across the country to find answers about fracking. The film has won accolades from audiences and protests from the gas industry.

For More Information

America's Natural Gas Alliance, 701 Eight St., N.W., Suite 800, Washington, DC 20001; 202-789-2642; http://anga .us. Industry group representing 30 major North American natural gas companies.

Catskill Citizens for Safe Energy, P.O. Box 103, Fremont Center, NY 12736; 845-468-7063; http://catskillcitizens.org. Coalition of residents of New York state's Catskill region who are concerned about the growth of hydraulic fracturing in the area.

Damascus Citizens for Sustainability, P.O. Box 147, Milanville, PA 18443; www.damascuscitizens.org. Citizen group formed to protest natural gas drilling in Pennsylvania.

Energy Information Administration, 100 Independence Ave., S.W., Washington, DC 20585; 202-586-8800; http:eia .doe.gov. Federal agency that provides statistics and information on natural gas use.

Food & Water Watch, 1616 P St., N.W., Suite 300, Washington, DC 20036; 202-683-2500; www.foodandwater watch.org. Watchdog group proposing a ban on fracturing.

Frack Action, c/o Sustainable Markets, 45 West 36th St., 6th Floor, New York, NY 10018; 347-709-3585; www.frackaction .com. Activist group fighting hydraulic fracturing.

Ground Water Protection Council, 13308 N. MacArthur Blvd., Oklahoma City, OK 73142; 405-516-4972; www.gwpc .org. Studies water issues and suggests policy guidance for state water regulators.

Independent Petroleum Association of America, 1201 15th St., N.W., Suite 300, Washington, DC 20005; 202-857-4722; www.ipaa.org. Trade group representing independent oil and natural gas producers and service companies.

Interstate Natural Gas Association of America, 20 F St., N.W., Suite 450, Washington, DC 20001; 202-216-5900; www.ingaa.org. Advocacy organizations for the natural gas pipeline industry on regulatory and legislative issues.

Marcellus Shale Coalition, 4000 Town Center Blvd., Suite 310, Canonsburg, PA 15317; 724-745-0100; www.marcel luscoalition.org. Lobbying group for gas drilling companies and operators working in the Marcellus Shale.

Natural Gas Supply Association, 1620 Eye St., N.W., Suite 700, Washington, DC 20006; 202-326-9300; www .ngsa.org. Trade group representing natural gas producers and marketers.

4

Water Crisis in the West

Peter Katel

Farmer Jerry Gannaway surveys his barren cotton field in Hermleigh, Texas, on July 27, 2011. Most of the state's dry-land growers (those with non-irrigated fields) have seen their crops fail because of the severe drought devastating the Southwest. Experts warn that the drought seems likely to continue in 2012.

From *CQ Researcher*,
Dec. 9, 2011

A s an unprecedented drought blisters Texas and parts of other Western states, scientists are telling the country's most arid region that the worst may be yet to come. Water, they warn, could become even scarcer — much scarcer.

"The megadroughts currently believed by scientists and water managers alike to be the worst case possible may not be as bad as it could get," Jonathan Overpeck, a geoscientist and co-director of the University of Arizona's Institute of the Environment, told the Senate Natural Resources Committee last April, describing newly analyzed climate data covering two millennia. "We now have reason to believe that a drought as long as 49 years interrupted by only one wet year happened in recent history; and thus, this could happen in the future."[1]

"Recent," to an Earth scientist means about 2,000 years ago. Still, in the country's most arid region, the new findings and related research were enough to prompt the Senate committee's chairman, Jeff Bingaman, D-N.M., to convene the hearing. He held it in Santa Fe, N.M., in the heart of a seven-state region that depends for much of its drinking and irrigation water on a single waterway, the Colorado River. The river's flow has declined for most of the past 10 years.

Against this worrisome backdrop, signs of a warming climate have introduced a new factor into the equation. The U.S. Bureau of Reclamation — the West's top federal water-management agency — reported last April that temperatures in the Western states are projected to rise this century by 5 to 7 degrees Fahrenheit, depending on location. "Droughts on top of climate change," Overpeck told the

Water Shortages Affect Vast Area

Concerns about water supplies are widespread throughout the West but especially acute in the seven-state Colorado River Basin and Texas, a vast swath of territory that includes the entire Southwest. For most of the 20th century, massive dams, reservoirs and canals helped sustain the region's water supply, but now the combination of drought, climate change and new scientific data on ancient drought patterns is prompting scientists to worry about water shortages. In many states, aquifers are losing billions of gallons of water annually, in part because they aren't being recharged by rainfall.

Colorado River Basin Supplies 7 States

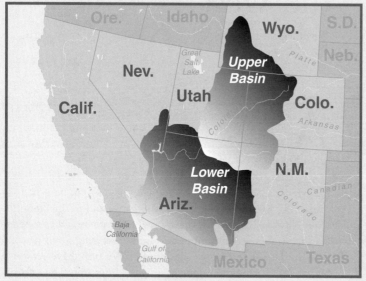

Source: "Climate Change and Water," U.S. Bureau of Reclamation, April 2011

are the answer. In Texas, the water level is down 80 feet in the Trinity Aquifer, which lies under the state's central section, in part because it's not getting recharged by rainfall. This year Texas has received less than 25 percent of its normal annual precipitation. In Idaho, the Eastern Snake Plain Aquifer, a giant natural reservoir often compared in size to Lake Erie, has been losing an estimated 79 billion gallons a year.[3]

Actual or projected shortages threaten to expand the number of conflicts between holders of older —"senior" — water rights, which have priority under Western water laws, and those with more recently acquired "junior" rights. Already, competition is looming between agricultural users, who tend to have "senior" rights and account for about 80 percent of Western water consumption, and the cities and suburbs that are "junior" rights holders.[4]

In simplest terms, the competition comes down to alfalfa versus swimming pools — or one of the West's biggest and thirstiest crops, used in livestock feed, versus pell-mell housing development.

Grady Gammage Jr., a senior research fellow at Arizona State University's Morrison Institute for Public Policy in Phoenix, advocates an end to alfalfa cultivation in Arizona. But he acknowledges that conserving water hasn't exactly been a priority in the urban area where he lives. "If we wanted to have an impact, we'd say, 'Quit building private swimming pools,' or, 'Let's not have grass lawns any more,' " Gammage says.

But banning alfalfa isn't as simple a solution — at least in some parts of the West — as it may appear. "There's a lot of alfalfa grown in northern New Mexico because it allows people to keep their land," says Consuelo Bokum of Santa Fe, a board member of New Mexico Water Dialogue, a water-policy advocacy group in Albuquerque. "For people living at subsistence level, they can grow alfalfa and always have a job."

committee, "will likely be a double whammy — much worse than drought alone and much worse than just climate change alone."[2]

The confluence of drought, climate change and new scientific data on the region's natural history is prompting a wave of concern in a region where massive dams, reservoirs and canals were thought for most of the 20th century to have solved water problems in the region. Worries are widespread throughout the West but especially acute in the sprawling seven-state Colorado River Basin and in Texas, a swath of territory that includes the entire Southwest.

Underground basins — aquifers — that supply drinking and irrigation water to many areas no longer

Meanwhile, competition over water rights has led to legislative and court battles in Montana and New Mexico over whether states should continue to exempt individual land-owners' wells from water-rights per-mits — exemptions that developers have used in providing water for new subdivisions. And a legal dispute in Idaho pits competing groups of food producers against each other.

"If your water resource is declin-ing, with more and senior water-right holders injured, eventually you're going to be like other aquifers — [in] a race to the bottom," says Randy MacMillan, vice president for research and environmental affairs at Clear Springs Foods in Buhl, Idaho, which raises trout in spring water from the Eastern Snake Plain Aquifer. Clear Springs has clashed in court with farmers drawing water from the same aquifer. Settlement talks are in the works.

"You can grow if you can conserve water and make it available for new people to come along," MacMillan says. "But if you can't, you're going to be robbing Peter to pay Paul; that's where you get into water-rights conflicts."

That conclusion likely wouldn't have surprised one of the pioneer explorers of Western rivers, who warned toward the end of the 19th century that nature had placed insurmountable limits on growth in the West. "There is not sufficient water to supply the land," John Wesley Powell, then director of the U.S. Geological Survey, told the Second International Irrigation Conference in Los Angeles in 1893.[5]

Scorn and outrage greeted his dissent from the nation's prevailing faith in engineering solutions. Only a few decades earlier, the majority conviction had been that "rain follows the plow." Because a wave of settle-ment in the 1860s and 1870s coincided with a period of above-average rainfall, opinion leaders proclaimed that the trends were related. According to one notion, plow-ing released moisture from the Earth into the upper atmosphere.[6]

Powell also warned that with too many people lined up to use an insufficient resource, the West would be torn

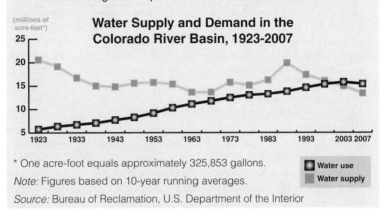

Water Use Strains Colorado River

Demand for water for residential, agricultural and industrial use has exploded in the Southwest over the past century, putting massive strains on the Colorado River, a key water source for the region. Water use from the Colorado River Basin has tripled since 1923, outpacing its capacity to satisfy demand. Rapid population growth and climate change are expected to continue the imbalance.

Water Supply and Demand in the Colorado River Basin, 1923-2007

(millions of acre-feet*)

* One acre-foot equals approximately 325,853 gallons.

Note: Figures based on 10-year running averages.

Source: Bureau of Reclamation, U.S. Department of the Interior

■ Water use
■ Water supply

by legal clashes over water. "You are piling up a heritage of conflict and litigation over water rights," he said.[7]

The accuracy of that prediction is indisputable. Arizona even mobilized its National Guard in 1934 to block construction of a dam that would hold water for a California aqueduct.[8]

Though no troops are on the march these days, water experts in the Southwest are focusing on how to keep cities, suburbs and farms supplied while also ensuring enough water to maintain environmental health.

Environmentalists contend that the key to ensuring continued availability of water lies in reducing wasteful-ness — with agriculture a priority because it accounts for most water consumption. "To keep doing what we've been doing clearly isn't going to work," says Peter H. Gleick, president of the Pacific Institute, an environ-mental think tank in Oakland, Calif. "There are a lot of ways of improving agricultural efficiency that include both responsibilities of government and responsibilities of individual farmers. You can use tools like pricing, you can use tools like regulation and you can use tools like education."

The California Farm Bureau, the state's major agri-cultural lobby, cites efficiency improvements that farm-ers have made on their own. It argues that what the water

Ancient Trees Augur Extreme Drought

"We need to be prepared for a big water shortage."

In the rugged San Juan Mountains of southwestern Colorado four years ago, Cody Routson peered through his binoculars and spotted what he was looking for — a living stand of ancient bristlecone pine trees. Thanks to Routson's sharp eyes, he and other scientists say they've been able to push Southwestern climate records back 2,200 years — two millennia past the previous limit on their data.

Routson, a doctoral candidate in paleoclimatology at the University of Arizona, and his colleagues say tree rings from dead bristlecone pines found near the live ones showed that the Southwest's climate, historically, has been even drier than scientists had thought.

"Even the worst Southwestern droughts of the last 1,200 years" — including a so-called megadrought in the 12th century —"were eclipsed by a drought in the 2nd century A.D. that lasted 49 years in the headwaters of the Rio Grande," Jonathan Overpeck, co-director of the university's Institute of the Environment, told the Senate Energy and Natural Resources Committee last April.[1]

Previously, scientists in the region were working on tree-ring data going back slightly more than 1,000 years. As Overpeck testified, that evidence showed a 12th-century drought lasting from 1146 to 1155 AD, but with some effects starting earlier and lasting later — a span running from 1140 to 1159.[2]

Bristlecone pines were essential to both climate-history projects. "Gnarled and bent, bristlecone pines are the world's oldest living organisms," according to the American Chemical Society, and are known to survive for longer than 5,000 years. Great Basin National Park in Nevada has two stands of the rare trees, which by federal law may not be cut.[3]

The live trees that Routson found were about 1,000 years old. He and his colleagues also found 2,000-year-old dead bristlecone pines nearby, which enabled them to collect another full millennium's worth of data.

These put the experience accumulated since 2000 in perspective. "We've experienced 10 years of drought," Routson says, contrasting that record with a 50-year drought the Southwest endured from 122 A.D. to 172 A.D. "The drought we're looking at is 50 consecutive years of pretty severe drought surrounded by pretty dry intervals. We need to be prepared for a big water shortage."

The ancient 50-year drought stretched from southern New Mexico into Idaho, Routson and his colleagues conclude in a paper scheduled for publication by the American Geophysical Union. His coauthors are Connie A. Woodhouse, a paleoclimatologist in the University of Arizona's School of

users need most are more reservoirs to capture some river runoff that now flows into the Pacific. "If we focus solely on conserving the maximum amount of water," says Daniel Merkley, a water specialist with the Farm Bureau, "we have hardened demand and we have nowhere else to go. We're boxing ourselves into a corner."

It's been argued for years that conserving as much water as possible makes emergency measures during a drought impossible because demand has "hardened" so much that people resist efforts to reduce consumption further. A study last year by a group of California state agencies on how to significantly reduce water use over 10 years called demand-hardening a legitimate concern but added, "California will still have ample conservation opportunity even after statewide per capita use is reduced by 20 percent."[9]

Debate over conservation and drought emergencies reflect the growing concern over water availability.

"We can't meet all the water demands we now meet," says Bradley H. Udall, director of the Western Water Assessment, a joint project of the University of Colorado and the National Oceanic and Atmospheric Administration (NOAA). "We are going to have to rethink how we do lots of things — where we live, how we use crops."

As Western states struggle to find and allocate enough water to satisfy residential and agricultural needs, here are some of the questions policymakers, environmentalists and scientists are asking:

Geography who was the principal author of the 1,200-year study, and Overpeck.[4]

The paper also notes that evidence from ocean sediment and elsewhere indicate that La Niña, the Pacific weather pattern associated with modern drought, may have played a role both in the 12th-century megadrought and its longer second-century antecedent. "Dating uncertainty and limited other records make these assessments less than robust," Routson and his collaborators added.[5]

Nevertheless, the paper concludes, data accumulated so far provide plenty of reason to prepare for the worst in southern Colorado and northwest New Mexico, where two of the Southwest's major rivers originate. The worst, they say, likely includes higher temperatures than those that prevailed during the medieval and ancient droughts. "Until the climate dynamics of megadrought are thoroughly understood, managers of water and natural resources in the Four Corners, Rio Grande and Colorado regions should take note that megadroughts as long, or longer, than 50 years could [recur], with the caveat that future droughts will be even warmer than those in the past."[6]

Overpeck warned in his Senate testimony that conditions today, including those originating with human behavior, seem to be adding to the region's water challenges. "Poor land use and desertification in the Southwest could further reduce stream flow in snow-dominated systems like the Colorado/Rio Grande by allowing greater amounts of dust to blow out of lower elevations and into our headwaters, where the dust is known to speed the melting of snow and reduce the flow in our rivers."[7]

Routson suggests that whatever preparations Southwesterners are making may fall short of the conditions that nature could — once again — impose. "My guess would be," Routson says, "that if we experience one of these droughts today, we would encounter severe shortages."

— *Peter Katel*

[1]"Drought and Climate Change on Water Resources," Senate Committee on Energy and Natural Resources, April 27, 2011, pp. 34-35, www.gpo.gov/fdsys/pkg/CHRG-112shrg6645 5/pdf/CHRG-112shrg66455.pdf.

[2]Connie A. Woodhouse, *et al.*, "A 1,200-year perspective of 21st century drought in southwestern North America," *Proceedings of the National Academy of Science*, Dec. 14, 2010, www.pnas.org/content/107/50/21283 .full.

[3]"CAS Colors of Chemistry — Bristlecone Pine," American Chemical Society, updated Jan. 26, 2009, www.cas.org/aboutcas/colors/redbristlecone09.html; Max Bearak, "In Ancient Pines, a Startling Shift in Tree Rings," *Green* (environment blog), *The New York Times*, Sept. 19, 2011, http://green.blogs.nytimes.com/2011/09/19/in-ancient-pines-a-startling-shift-in-tree-rings/.; "Bristlecone Pines," Great Basin National Park, National Park Service, undated, www.nps.gov/grba/planyourvisit/identifying-bristlecone-pines.htm.

[4]Cody C. Routson, *et al.*, "Second century megadrought in the Rio Grande headwaters, Colorado: How unusual was the medieval drought?" *Geophysical Research Letters* (forthcoming).

[5]*Ibid.*

[6]*Ibid.*

[7]"Drought and Climate change, *op. cit.*, p. 33.

Will water shortages limit growth in the West?

The West's major population growth was a 20th-century phenomenon. Massive dams, reservoirs and aqueducts made it possible for cities such as Phoenix to blossom in the desert, for Los Angeles to spread north and east into once-arid scrubland and for California and Arizona to become world-class agricultural producers.

But some scientists are skeptical about the possibility of continuing that growth at anywhere near the torrid pace of the past century. "The capacity for water to support cities, industry, agriculture and ecosystems in the U.S. West is near its limit under current management practices," a group of environmental scientists wrote last December.[10]

Yet, others project the growth to continue. Glen M. MacDonald, director of the Institute of the Environment and Sustainability at the University of California, Los Angeles, notes that the U.S. Census Bureau projects the population of the Southwest (by this definition Arizona, New Mexico, Colorado, Nevada and Utah), plus California, will reach 67 million by 2030, up from 49 million in 2000. Arizona would gain 5 million people, becoming one of the nation's 10 most populous states.[11]

But worries about water supply are prompting questions about whether growth of that magnitude is possible. With drought hitting much of the West and fears of global warming widespread, concerns about the sufficiency of the water supply are spreading.

Arizona and other desert states are among the most nervous. But worries also are echoing among other members of the Colorado River Basin, the seven-state region for which the river is an indispensable water source. "We can't meet all the water demands that we now meet," says Udall of the Western Water Assessment. "We have a slightly declining supply in the Colorado River. The supply and demand lines crossed in the early 2000s, so demand exceeds supply for the first time ever."

Growth "potentially" can continue, Udall says, but only if conservation becomes part of the Western way of life. That, in turn, depends on raising water bills, he argues. "If you underprice a resource," he says, "you get two outcomes: overconsumption and underinvestment in ways to use the resource more efficiently. People don't invest in more efficient irrigation techniques, low-flow toilets and lawn watering that's less wasteful."

But Gammage of Arizona State University agrees that higher water prices would allow continued growth in the Phoenix-Tucson area. "Particularly for Phoenix and to a lesser degree for Tucson, we are in fairly good shape and can support fairly steady sustained growth for some time," he says.

Nevertheless, Gammage says Arizona's growth possibilities are more limited outside of the Phoenix-Tucson corridor. And even there, he says, growth depends on residents' capacity to conserve more water than they do now — especially in Phoenix — and on decreasing the share of water used by the agricultural industry.

DeWayne Justice, who grows organic citrus and raises cattle as co-owner of the 360-acre Justice Brothers Farms in Waddell, Ariz., argues, however, that urban areas can waste more water than farms do. "They have developed thousands of acres in the desert, on ground that never had water," he says.

Justice agrees that water supplies in the West are tight. But, he says, farmers' excess irrigation water soaks back into aquifers in a way that doesn't happen on cities' concrete expanses. In Phoenix, he adds, people "move out from Ohio and still want it to look like Ohio."

Gleick of the Pacific Institute maintains that compromise and conservation could allow cities to coexist with agriculture, even as growth continues. But, he says, "if we are going to grow, that means not taking any more water out of the Colorado River. It means rethinking what we are doing with the water we're already using."

The key, Gleick argues, lies in ensuring that water doesn't go to waste, in farms or cities. "Farmers say, 'Why should I change the way I use water so that cities can fill their swimming pools?' Cities say, 'Why should I constrain my high-value industries so that farmers can grow alfalfa?' Both of them are right, and both of them are wrong. It's time for an honest conversation about how we're going to use scarce water resources."

Should states expand regulatory power over water use?

In the absence of a debate on conservation throughout the region, groups in several parts of the West are turning to state courts and legislatures to resolve water-use issues.

In southern Idaho, crop farmers are fighting with two acquaculture companies that raise trout. The concrete canals where the trout swim are fed by a spring that rises from the Eastern Snake Plain Aquifer, which encompasses about 10,000 square miles. The aquifer is believed to hold as much as 300 million acre-feet of water. (Idaho's Department of Water Resources may revise that estimate, based on a new study under way).[12]

Farmers also use water from that aquifer to irrigate their fields, and the aquaculture companies argue that their own water resources are diminished as a result. Last March, the Idaho Supreme Court ruled for the aquaculture firms, concluding that the state's Water Resources Department had been correct in limiting water-pumping by the farmers. The court said the state had caused "material injury" to the trout companies' senior water rights and rejected farmers' arguments that the state had overstepped its authority.[13]

"The State has the duty to supervise the appropriation and allotment of both surface and ground waters to those diverting such waters for any beneficial purpose," it ruled.[14]

In New Mexico and Montana, real estate developers and environmentalists are fighting over whether state authority over water rights should extend to an individual homeowner's or farmer's well on his or her own land.

"Exempt wells are very appropriate for dispersed places in rural areas," says Sarah Bates, a senior associate of the University of Montana's Center for Natural Resources and Environmental Policy in Helena.

But, she adds, developers have used such exemptions to cover entire housing subdivisions. State Department of Natural Resources data show a 129 percent rise in the number of exempt wells from 1,875 in 1991 to 4,299 in 2006. The exemptions "have been used for subdivisions with 50 or 100 houses which are not being regulated as they would be if [the wells formed] a little water system for the development," she says.

Bates and others advocate a "mitigation" approach now being tested in Washington state.[15] Homebuilders in rural areas who plan to use exempt wells are required to pay into a fund that finances purchases of senior water rights in the aquifer supplying water to the wells. "A bucket-for-bucket exchange is made," Bates says. "It's really straightforward for the homeowner."

Montana laid the groundwork for that system with a 2007 law that required small water-rights applicants to prove that taking water from aquifers wouldn't reduce surface water flows.[16]

The Montana Association of Realtors blocked a 2009 attempt to expand that law by requiring well owners to replace water taken from the aquifer. "We were concerned that that was going too far," says Glenn Oppel, the association's government affairs director. The association argued that drawing down an aquifer does not automatically have a negative effect on surface-water flows, and therefore on rights to that water.

"When you look at the science of it, these exempt wells do not have much impact on surface water flows, and therefore on senior water rights," Oppel says. "Any water shortages or stream-flow reductions occurring in Montana water basins in high-growth areas are due to drought, not to the proliferation of exempt wells."

That argument may not be catching on. Nathan Bracken, legal counsel for the Western States Water Council in Murray, Utah, and author of a comprehensive regional study of exempt-well laws, says that throughout the West, "If there's one common thing I found, the biggest concern is with developers using exemptions to install subdivisions."

Lawns and Pools Drain California Water Supplies

About half the water consumed in California's urban areas is used for lawn watering, swimming pools, golf course maintenance and other landscaping purposes (left). Nearly half of the water comes from local surface-water sources, such as small rivers and storm runoff. Most of the rest is from underground aquifers, the Colorado River and other in-state and out-of-state sources (right).

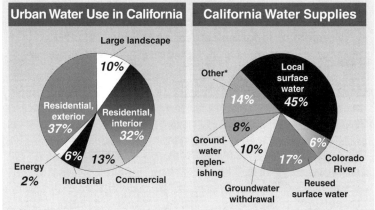

Urban Water Use in California
- Large landscape 10%
- Residential, exterior 37%
- Residential, interior 32%
- Energy 2%
- Industrial 6%
- Commercial 13%

California Water Supplies
- Other* 14%
- Local surface water 45%
- Ground-water replenishing 8%
- Groundwater withdrawal 10%
- Reused surface water 17%
- Colorado River 6%

* Includes State Water Project deliveries, Central Valley Project deliveries, local imported deliveries, recycled water and other federal deliveries.

Source: Ellen Hanak, et al., "Managing California's Water: From Conflict to Reconciliation," Public Policy Institute of California, 2011, pp. 77, 97, www.ppic.org/content/pubs/report/R_211EHR.pdf

Mitigation procedures that compensate for water withdrawals can play a valuable role in resolving the issue, Bracken says. The result of what should be a "collaborative" process, not an adversarial one, he says, should be that water availability is an element of all land-management decisions.

Some westerners, however, argue that imposing new regulations on land use would raise real estate prices in rural areas that traditionally have been affordable. "I think a lot of the cities are trying to utilize these arguments to direct growth where and how they want," says Marvin Magee, president of the New Mexico Ground Water Association and a well driller in Las Cruces. If rural landowners had to pay for water rights, well-drilling costs would skyrocket, he says. "Any growth will be limited to urban areas, and the process will be detrimental to rural land prices."

Magee acknowledges a personal stake in the issue. If ending or limiting exemptions were to lead to a decline

Conservation Curbs Consumption in Arizona

The amount of water delivered to Arizona residents grew sharply in the past two decades as the state's population boomed. At the same time, conservation and efficiency measures eased per capita consumption. In Phoenix, the capital and largest city, for example, population grew 57 percent from 2000 to 2008, but the amount of water delivered to the city from all sources rose at a more modest 10 percent as per capita usage fell by nearly a third.

Growth in Population, Water Deliveries and Daily Water Consumption for Select Arizona Cities, 1990-2008*

City	Population growth	Change in water delivered	Change in daily per capita water consumption
Phoenix	57%	10%	-30%
Tucson	44%	26%	-13%
Mesa	63%	37%	-16%
Chandler	163%	159%	-2%
Glendale	67%	47%	-12%
Scottsdale	86%	71%	-8%
Gilbert	621%	509%	-16%
Yuma	70%	15%	-32%
Tempe	22%	-2%	-19%
Peoria	241%	169%	-21%

* Water-delivery figures may be higher than reported.

Source: Michael J. Cohen, "Municipal Deliveries of Colorado River Basin Water," Pacific Institute, June 2011, pp. 14, 16, www.pacinst.org/reports/co_river_municipal_deliveries/crb_water_8_21_2011.pdf

in well drilling, as he predicts it would, many drilling firms would go out of business, he says.

Is large-scale energy development endangering water supplies?

Concerns about the West's water supply are intersecting with efforts to expand domestic oil and gas production, which uses large quantities of water and also may threaten water quality.

The major potential threat to quality comes from the production technique known as hydraulic fracturing —"fracking" — in which a mixture of water, sand and chemicals is directed under high pressure at rock formations to unlock oil or gas deposits. With the practice spreading, fracking has prompted concern that the process uses too much water and threatens to contaminate drinking-water wells and surface water near discharges of fracking liquids.[17]

Energy companies are fracking in a number of Eastern and Western states, including Texas, Colorado, Wyoming and New Mexico. Idaho recently approved rules for proposed fracking projects in that state.

Water arguably also is threatened by a different form of petroleum production, one that some companies want to establish in parts of the Mountain West. The objective is to release oil from shale rock by applying heat as high as 1,000 degrees Fahrenheit to the rock, either when it's underground or after it's been mined and brought to the surface. The process, conceived more than 100 years ago and now in small-scale use in China and elsewhere, uses substantial amounts of water, though experts disagree on the magnitude.[18]

Super-heating isn't close to being employed in the United States. Currently, a handful of companies are holding "research, development and demonstration" leases on federal land. But shale deposits in Colorado, Utah and Wyoming contain an estimated 3 trillion barrels of oil — an amount equivalent to the world's proven reserves of liquid oil, the Government Accountability Office (GAO) reported last year.[19]

The report raised the question of whether the cost in water would be worth the output in oil. "The size of an industry in Colorado or Utah may eventually be limited by water availability," the GAO said. The report noted that estimates of water consumption range widely: from between one and 12 barrels of water for every barrel of oil produced if the shale-heating takes place underground, to two to four barrels of water per barrel of oil if the shale is mined, then heated aboveground.[20]

In addition, runoff from super-heating operations could contain sediment, salts or chemicals that could migrate into rivers and creeks, potentially harming fish and plants, the GAO reported.[21]

Industry critics of the GAO report say it overestimated water-use requirements. "In actuality, the real numbers coming from industry experts were in the range of three barrels of water for one barrel of oil, and some people are saying it's lower than that," says Glenn Vawter, a petroleum engineer in Glenwood Springs, Colo., and executive director of the National Oil Shale Association.

Vawter adds that the discussion of possible excessive water consumption from the super-heating process has a special resonance in western Colorado, where he lives and where the Colorado River begins. "Ironically, in our part of the state," he says, "our water is being taken one way or other, either going to the eastern slope of our state, where the population growth is occurring, or going downstream to users in Nevada and California."

But Udall of the Western Water Assessment calls the shale water-usage estimates "a little scary." In any event, he says, "I have trouble believing that oil shale makes any long-term environmental sense in a carbon-constrained world. I don't believe we're going to be dumb enough to develop this resource. I don't think it's a path we can afford to take in the long term."

As for fracking, Udall says the apparently high productivity of gas wells in which that process is used may act as a disincentive for energy companies to use super-heating. Still, he says fracking may be a mixed blessing. "There is some worry that it has the potential to harm underground aquifers."

The University of Texas' Energy Institute has started what it describes as a comprehensive examination of fracking, including possible effects on groundwater. In November, the study's director, geology professor Chip Groat, told the *Dallas Morning News* that preliminary data indicated no pollution of deep underground water sources. He added that the preliminary results involved underground water sources only. "There are many other [fracking] activities going on at the surface and at the shallow areas," he said, "that could potentially affect shallow [water] supplies."[22]

The Environmental Defense Fund helped design Groat's study and will review the final report before publication. Possible effects of fracking on water safety remain a major concern nationwide. Most recently, the

Bleached sandstone — the "bathtub ring" — on a canyon wall at Arizona's Lake Powell in March 2007 shows the effects of a six-year drought that hit the region early in the decade.

Environmental Protection Agency reported apparent fracking-related contamination of underground water sources in Wyoming.[23]

Water-quality issues aside, fracking also has raised questions about its water-intensiveness. Even in a state with deep loyalties to the oil and gas industry, intense drought is prompting residential areas to restrict frackers' water usage. In Texas, Grand Prairie quit selling water to drillers; Arlington raised water prices to fracking firms and Fort Worth and other cities asked energy firms to use reclaimed water instead of drinking water for fracking.[24]

Drillers used 463.6 million gallons of water in Fort Worth last year, the *Star-Telegram* reported. In Arlington, fracking consumed 395.4 million gallons. But that amounted to less than 4 percent of total usage in Arlington; and drilling in Fort Worth accounted for 1 percent of overall water consumption there.[25]

Industry officials were quick to defend their consumption record. "When you look at the total used by gas-drilling companies, it is not on the upper end," Ed Ireland, executive director of the Barnett Shale Energy Education Council, told the newspaper.[26]

But Libby Willis, president of the Forth Worth League of Neighborhoods, argued that most water used for domestic needs is then recycled for other purposes. But water used in fracking can't be reused, because it contains chemicals used in the process. "The impact is larger because we are losing so much of it forever," Willis says.[27]

BACKGROUND

Early Irrigators

The first known residents of the desert West recognized that their existence depended on a steady water supply. The Hohokam (a name derived from a later Indian description, huhu-kam, or "all used up") settled in central Arizona about 3,000 years ago. They did everything they could to capture, divert and store water. Archaeological remains include evidence of 900 miles of canals, one of which provided irrigation for 10,000 acres of crops. Eventually, however, the Hohokams' ingenuity proved no match for drought cycles.[28]

In the late 1500s, Spanish colonists, the first Europeans to settle in the West, brought a small-scale irrigation system developed during more than 700 years of Muslim Arab rule of Spain. *Acequias* — irrigation ditches — that the Spanish began building in 1598 in the northern Rio Grande valley of today's New Mexico numbered about 164 by 1800. *Acequias* remain in operation, maintained by user commissions. At last count, in 1987, there were 721 commissions.[29]

The Spanish also imported a system of laws designed to protect collective rights to water — among farm villages, for example.

Spanish colonists' water management allowed only small-scale agriculture. A Mormon colony that established itself in the late 1840s in the arid territory that later became Utah had bigger ambitions. As historians acknowledge, Mormons pioneered modern Western water development.

Working with only the most primitive tools and knowledge, the Mormon settlers worked with astounding speed and industry to build dams and irrigation channels. These, they had concluded, were essential to the farm-based society they were determined to build.

They built the biggest dams that their resources allowed. The strategy worked. By 1850, the Mormons were farming 16,333 irrigated acres by 1850, having plowed their first field just three years earlier. By 1890, more than 250,000 acres of Mormon land, divided into about 10,000 farms, were irrigated. And by 1902, Mormons in the three principal states in which they'd settled — Nevada and Arizona as well as Utah — were farming 6 million irrigated acres.[30]

Acclaimed environmental writer Marc Reisner noted in an influential work on Western water history that

Mormon water engineering became the model for the federal irrigation agency — the U.S. Bureau of Reclamation, founded in 1902.[31]

Nevertheless, the Mormon colony, which established itself in one relatively small part of a very big region, wasn't the only influence on Western water policy.

Historian Donald Worster attributes Western water legal doctrine to two water-intensive mining booms — the California and Colorado gold rushes of 1849 and 1859, respectively. That doctrine, called "prior appropriation," holds that the first person to use a quantity of water has top priority to the resource. The principle reflected the inescapable reality that water was scarce in the West and that a latecomer who wanted to use water might be reducing its availability to someone who was first on the scene.

Appropriative water law broke with British "riparian" water law, under which only someone living alongside a river had rights to it.

In the British Isles, those who didn't own riverside property had no problem obtaining water, which was so plentiful that it was available to anyone who dug a well. But riparian law didn't seem to fit the Western United States landscape, where rivers often flowed through inaccessible and uninhabited canyons.

Western states' water laws added a provision stating that water rights are limited by the amount that the owner puts to "beneficial use." That provision ensures that state governments have the power to determine whether a water-rights applicant should be approved, based on the applicant's plans for the water.[32]

Overall, Worster writes, appropriative law reflected and perpetuated a philosophy that people should shape nature to their purposes — divert and dam up rivers, for instance, instead of letting them flow.[33]

Dividing the Waters

Nevertheless, by the late 1800s, leaders of all the Western states agreed that big water-engineering projects were the key to growth. California, in particular, wanted to develop a steady supply of water to a stretch of Sonoran desert in Southern California.[34]

With a reliable water source, that arid expanse could support year-round farming on a big scale, land developers had concluded by the end of the 19th century. One of them took the first public-relations step in 1901 by naming the parched landscape the Imperial Valley.[35]

C H R O N O L O G Y

1500 B.C.-1902 *Ancient Indians and Spanish colonists build numerous small irrigation canals; Mormons expand exploitation of water resources.*

1500 B.C.-1500 A.D. Hohokam Indians use irrigation.

1850 Dams and canals in Mormon settlements in today's Utah allow irrigation of more than 16,000 acres.

1901 Developer renames stretch of Southern California desert Imperial Valley, laying public-relations groundwork for massive irrigation project.

1902 Mormons irrigate 6 million acres.

1905-1968 *Enormous federal investment in dams, reservoirs and canals fosters development of West.*

1905 Colorado River diversion channel fails, flooding Imperial Valley and leading engineers to conclude that dams and reservoirs are needed for reliable water supply.

1911 Wyoming sues Colorado over plans to divert water from Laramie River before it crossed into Wyoming.

1922 U.S. Supreme Court upholds Colorado diversion on grounds that the first user of water acquires the right to it. . . . Colorado River Basin states rely on the decision to seek major portion of Colorado's flow. . . . Agreement on sharing the river's waters uses data that overstate river's future flow.

1935 Massive Hoover Dam and its reservoir, 247-square-mile Lake Mead, are completed.

1956 Congress approves series of new Colorado Basin dams following long debate over environmental value of one proposed site.

1968 Congress authorizes Central Arizona Project, major series of canals and pumping stations to supply Colorado River water to Phoenix and Tucson.

1986-2011 *Concerns about water grow amid droughts and indicators of climate change.*

1986 Marc Reisner's *Cadillac Desert* prompts debate about whether dams and reservoirs merely postponed the West's reckoning with water scarcity.

1995 Possibility raised of "severe, sustained drought" on Colorado River.

1997 With the 20th century's water-engineering work complete, federal dams divert as much as 85 percent of major Western river systems.

1999 Two-year drought begins in Texas.

2000 Colorado River drought begins, with flows into Arizona, Nevada and California falling to 62 percent of 30-year average.

2002 The year is one of the 11 driest over the past 100 in the Southwest.

2004 Colorado River flow falls to 49 percent of 30-year average.

2005 Water in Lake Powell, on the Colorado, falls to one-third capacity.

2008 Western Governors Association says region's water resources are under stress, seeks federal funds for research on ways to expand supply by desalination, recycling, weather modification and other techniques.

2009 Texas suffers second year of a drought that is the most severe on record in some parts of the state.

2010 Interior secretary says past 10 years set record for driest period in Colorado River Basin. . . . Scientists warn that sustained warming is reducing flow of Colorado. . . . Most severe one-year period of drought in Texas begins. New Mexico court upholds exempting domestic wells from regulation.

2011 University of Arizona geoscientist suggests possibility of five-decade drought. . . . U.S. Bureau of Reclamation reports that Southwestern temperatures are projected to rise 5 to 7 degrees Fahrenheit in present century. . . . Retiring U.S. District Judge Oliver Wanger says politicians are letting courts decide major California water-policy issues that lawmakers should tackle. . . . Texas state climatologist says another year of drought probable.

Prayers Help Texans Cope With Drought

"I thank God for this truck of hay."

Texas State Climatologist John W. Nielsen-Gammon has bad news for anyone expecting a quick end to a drought that has devastated a state that's mostly hot and dry even in the best of times.

"Substantial improvement of drought conditions between now and the end of April 2012, while possible, is not likely," Nielsen-Gammon, a professor of atmospheric sciences at Texas A&M University in College Station, told the Texas legislature in October. "The drought . . . seems likely to continue for at least another year."[1]

So far, the drought registers as more intense on a scale that combines various effects (precipitation, water in soil and temperature) than its most recent — and, so far, longer-lasting — predecessor, which ran from 1950 through 1957.[2]

Already, after less than a year, the drought that began in September 2010 has seen lakes and reservoirs drop, prompted Midwestern states to send hay to desperate ranchers and spurred Republican Gov. Rick Perry to ask Texans to pray for rain.[3]

"Throughout our history . . . Texans have been strengthened, assured and lifted up through prayers," said a proclamation that Perry issued last April, asking Lone Star residents to pray for rain for three days ending on Easter Sunday. "It seems right and fitting that the people of Texas should join together in prayer to humbly seek an end to this devastating drought and these dangerous wildfires," Perry explained.[4]

The prayers brought no relief. By summer, average temperatures exceeded the previous state record by at least 2 degrees. Many parts of Texas suffered at least 100 days of 100-plus-degree temperatures. Most of the state's 200 reservoirs were far below capacity. And at least two (in West Texas and the Panhandle) completely dried up. By late October, 96 percent of the reservoirs were below 60 percent capacity.[5]

Groesbeck, a town of 4,300 east of Waco in north-central Texas, has run a 3.3-mile pipeline to a water-filled abandoned rock quarry in an attempt to tap the only nearby source of water. The Navasota River, where Groesbeck draws its water in normal times, has dried up. So has Fort Parker Lake, the nearest reservoir. Mayor Jackie Levington told state lawmakers in early November that the town was facing extinction. "Gentlemen," she said, "there will never be anybody coming to Groesbeck if there is no water. And the people that are there are not going to stay."[6]

Groesbeck may be an extreme case, but not a unique one. The Texas Commission on Environmental Quality said in November that 11 cities and towns face the prospect of running out of water within the next six months.[7]

Grateful ranchers, meanwhile, were receiving hay donated by Midwestern farmers. "I thank God for this truck of hay," said the Rev. Diane Eggemeyer, pastor of Trinity Evangelical Church in Miles, "and for the generous farmers willing to grow these crops and share with others." She arranged the donation with the pastor of St. John Lutheran Church in Luana, Iowa.[8]

In a statewide — though non-philanthropic — attempt to grapple with the same problem, the Texas Department of Agriculture set up a "Hay Hotline" on which more than 1,000 hay producers from 42 states posted their prices to give Texas ranchers a place to shop for replacement feed.

The obvious source for the irrigation project was the Colorado River, upon which California had long depended. But the landlocked mountain and desert states upriver also had plans for the Colorado's waters.

The river ended its run in Southern California or in Mexico — the end-point varied depending on how much silt blocked one channel or another. But early attempts to channel Colorado water west to the Imperial Valley foundered. First, so much silt clogged one channel that it was abandoned. Then, in 1905, the river broke through another channel, with the resulting flood forming the Salton Sea but also ruining 12,000 acres of farmland. After another flood in 1910, Congress spent $1 million to bail out the company trying to develop the Imperial Valley.

Meanwhile, Mexico, where one of the canals to the valley began, was demanding the right to half the water from the river. In response, U.S. farmers began lobbying for an "all-American" canal, entirely located north of the

The hotline also supplies information on hay-hauling services. "Texas is the national leader in cattle production," state Agriculture Commissioner Todd Staples said in a press release, "so it is critical that we preserve the herds on which all of America relies."[9]

Perhaps the only realistic possibility is that if the drought continues, its intensity could lessen. "Though a second year of drought is expected, the lack of rainfall will almost certainly not be as extreme as it was during the first year," Nielsen-Gammon hypothesized.[10]

A possible confirmation of that projection has come from neighboring states, which have been hit by the same drought.

Oklahoma, for example, enjoyed as much as 6.6 inches of rain over two days in November. And in northern New Mexico, ski areas were reporting healthy snowfall — enough to allow Thanksgiving weekend openings at Taos Ski Valley, Red River and elsewhere. In the state's far north, snowpack was reported 20 percent above normal.[11]

But, as in Texas, experts in New Mexico caution that even an early-December snowstorm that was especially heavy in the northern mountains may not signal a major break in the drought. "Several snowstorms can't overcome the kind of spring we've had," says Ed Polasko, the National Weather Service's hydrologic program manager in Albuquerque. "We're guardedly optimistic, but in terms of whether we're in a water boom, it's still too early to make that call."

How much comfort Texans will take from New Mexico ski reports is an open question, especially given emergency conditions at high school football fields. "One of the practice fields has become so dry there are cracks in the surface that are two or three inches wide," Justin Wiley, coach of the Smithville Tigers, told the *Austin American-Statesman.* "We joke with our freshmen that they have to use the buddy system when crossing the field in case someone gets lost in the cracks."[12]

— *Peter Katel*

[1]John W. Nielsen-Gammon, "The 2011 Texas Drought," Office of State Climatologist, Oct. 31, 2011, pp. 11, 41, http://atmo.tamu.edu/osc/library/osc_pubs/2011_drought.pdf.

[2]*Ibid.*, pp. 35,39.

[3]Patricia Kilday Hart, "Gov. asks Texans to pray for rain," *San Antonio Express-News*, April 21, 2011, www.mysanantonio.com/news/local_news/article/Gov-asks-Texans-to-pray-for-rain-1347623.php; "More than 1,000 Hay Producers Listed on Hay Hotline Stand Ready to Help Drought-Stricken Ranchers With Needed Hay," States News Service, Nov. 2, 2011.

[4]Quoted in *ibid.* (Hart).

[5]"Drought continues to lower Texas reservoirs," The Associated Press, Nov. 18, 2011, www.kcbd.com/story/16076989/drought-continues-depleting-texas-reservoirs; "Drought Impacts on Texas Reservoirs Mounting," Texas Parks & Wildlife, July 21, 2011, www.tpwd.state.tx.us/newsmedia/releases/?req=20110721a.

[6]Quoted in Susannah Jacob, "A Small Town, Almost Waterless, Takes a Big Gamble," *The New York Times*, Sept. 12, 2011, www.nytimes.com/2011/11/13/us/a-small-town-almost-waterless-takes-a-big-gamble.html; Susannah Jacob, "Groesbeck, Nearly Out of Water, Hopes to Build Pipeline," *Texas Tribune*, Nov. 17, 2011, www.texastribune.org/texas-environmental-news/water-supply/groesbeck-adopts-new-solution-water-shortage/; "Groesbeck Mayor: Town Will Run Out of Water in Two Weeks," The Associated Press, Nov. 24, 2011, http://houston.cbslocal.com/2011/11/24/groesbeck-mayor-town-will-run-out-of-water-in-two-weeks/.

[7]Ryan Murphy, "Interactive Map: Texas Cities at Risk of Running Out of Water," *Texas Tribune*, updated Nov. 30, 2011, www.texastribune.org/library/data/tceq-high-priority-water-locations/.

[8]Jane Jeschke, "650 Bales Brighten Spirits," *San Angelo Standard-Times* (Texas), Sept. 28, 2011, p. V4.

[9]"More than 1,000 Hay Producers . . . ," *op. cit.*

[10]Nielsen-Gammon, *op. cit.*, p. 41.

[11]Susan Montoya Bryan, "NM ski season off to stellar start despite drought," The Associated Press, Nov. 26, 2011, www.msnbc.msn.com/id/45466129/ns/travel-seasonal_travel/t/nm-ski-season-stellar-start-despite-drought.

[12]Quoted in Rick Cantu, "Prolonged drought drying up support for costly grass fields," *Austin American-Statesman*, Oct. 11, 2011, p. C6.

border — a project deemed too expensive for anyone but the federal government.

The Bureau of Reclamation's director noted that a new canal alone would not solve the problem. Dams and reservoirs were needed so that water could be controlled in a steady flow.

In 1922, a serious legal issue intruded, culminating in a U.S. Supreme Court decision. Wyoming had sued Colorado in 1911 over plans by a Colorado irrigation company to divert water from the Laramie River before it flowed north into Wyoming. Essentially, Wyoming argued that lessening the amount of water available to water-rights holders in Laramie, Wyo., violated the prior-appropriation doctrine.[36]

The Supreme Court rejected that argument and upheld the validity of prior-appropriation.[37]

By then, legislation was planned to authorize a major dam and canal that were keys to reliable irrigation of the

Imperial Valley. Colorado Basin states upriver from California realized that the effect of the Supreme Court ruling would be to uphold California's senior rights to Colorado water.

A negotiated deal between all the Colorado Basin states seemed preferable to lengthy litigation that could end up with California getting the lion's share of the Colorado flow. Anticipating the high court ruling, Congress had already formed a Colorado River Commission, with Commerce Secretary (and future president) Herbert Hoover in charge.

Meeting in Santa Fe in 1922, commissioners representing each of the seven Colorado River states forged an agreement. It was based on a division between the upper and lower basins, rendered according to a line drawn in Arizona, near the Utah border, at a spot called Lees Ferry (sometimes spelled Lee's Ferry). Arizona, California, and Nevada formed the lower basin; and Colorado, New Mexico, Utah and Wyoming, the up-river counterpart.

But unbeknownst to the commissioners, the data underlying the deal were flawed. Measurements of Colorado flow had been taken during an unusually wet period that began in 1896.

The river carried about 18.5 million acre-feet a year during that period, experts told the commissioners. With that data in hand, they allocated each basin 7.5 million acre-feet a year.

In 1963, measurements collected for a lawsuit between Arizona and California that also went to the Supreme Court showed that the flow in 1922-1956 averaged 14 million acre-feet a year. The bottom line, writes historian Norris Hundley Jr., is that the upper-basin states had obliged themselves to deliver 1 million acre-feet more a year to the lower basin than they could keep for themselves.[38]

Damming the River

Lawmakers in states involved in the agreement — formally called the Colorado River Compact — didn't rubber-stamp the deal. In the upper basin, legislatures in Wyoming and Colorado worried that their states had come out behind. Indian tribes, for their part, were completely ignored in the agreement — an omission eventually corrected in some of the more than 40 court decisions and congressional and executive-branch actions involving Colorado River water rights that

extend to 2007 and are known collectively as "the law of the river."[39]

Suspicion of California ran strongest in neighboring Arizona, at one point leading to that state's symbolic 1934 declaration of martial law over construction of Parker Dam, a project straddling the Arizona-California border that was designed to provide more water to Southern California. Given Arizona's resistance, the remaining six states agreed that the deal could take effect without the holdout state's approval. Arizona finally ratified it in 1944.

By then, the compact had set off a burst of dam building by the Bureau of Reclamation, focusing on projects that benefited California.

The most notable of these was Hoover Dam, west of the Grand Canyon, at the border between Arizona and Nevada. At 726.4 feet, Hoover was the tallest structure of its kind in the world when it was completed in 1935. Alongside the dam came Lake Mead, at 247 square miles then and now the largest reservoir in the United States.[40]

Federal dam and reservoir construction projects resumed after World War II.

The Bureau of Reclamation and some Western politicians and businesspeople had long argued that a new dam and reservoir on the upper Colorado was essential to ensuring that water delivery requirements to the lower basin could be met consistently. Without it, the argument went, upper-basin states might have to restrict their own consumption in dry years. Growing electricity needs (beyond those claimed for nuclear weapons testing in Nevada and Utah) were part of the picture as well.

Arizona strongly supported the proposed Colorado River Storage Project (CRSP). But in yet another sign of how complicated water politics can be, California politicians opposed the plan because they saw it as a way to divert water that would otherwise reach their state.

As debate raged in the early 1950s, project backers in the bureau and Congress gave up on the idea of siting one of the six proposed CRSP dams at scenic Echo Canyon. The Sierra Club, emerging on the national scene for the first time, played a major role in the shift, though its leaders came to regret relocating the dam to the also beautiful Glen Canyon.

Congress finally passed the CRSP legislation in 1956. Construction soon began on the massive series of installations on the Colorado and two of its tributaries, the Green River in Utah and the San Juan in New Mexico. In Arizona, Glen Canyon Dam created the country's second-biggest reservoir, Lake Powell. All the installations include hydropower plants.[41]

The next major piece of water engineering in the Colorado Basin was designed to expand the water-supply system for the growing desert cities of Phoenix and Tucson. The Central Arizona Project is a 336-mile series of canals and pumping plants. It channels about 1.5 million acre-feet a year of Arizona's share of the Colorado River from the Lake Havasu reservoir (created by the 1938 construction of Parker Dam). The project was authorized in 1968, began functioning in 1985 and was completed in 1993.[42]

Dam-building continued into the 1960s. California — the West's and the nation's agricultural powerhouse — had 1,251 major reservoirs by the late 1970s. And by 1997, Bureau of Reclamation projects diverted between 40 percent and 85 percent of the annual flow of major river systems, including the Rio Grande, Snake, Sacramento and San Joaquin, in addition to the Colorado.[43]

Scarcity

Throughout the 1990s, awareness of climate change was growing in the scientific community and among environmentalists. One impetus was environmental writer Reisner's widely acclaimed 1986 book, *Cadillac Desert: The American West and Its Disappearing Water*, which argued that big dams and reservoirs had made people forget that most of the West was a desert.

Reisner wrote before "global warming" or "climate change" had entered the nation's everyday vocabulary. By the 1990s, water experts were starting to call attention to the possibility that conditions in the West had entered a new phase that would strain the water supply.

In 1995, the "Water Resources Bulletin" (now the *Journal of the American Water Resources Association*) devoted an entire issue to the question of how "severe, sustained drought" would affect the Colorado River.[44]

Until then, and even for a few years afterward, discussions of Colorado River supply had centered on how to manage surplus water, a group of experts noted in a separate 2010 study.[45]

But projections of the possible effects of drought turned out to have been optimistic, given actual

Sprinklers spray crops in California's Imperial Valley with Colorado River water and recovered runoff. A vast network of canals and irrigation channels has turned the valley, once a vast desert, into an agricultural oasis. Growers in the region use 70 percent of California's allotted river water.

conditions in the first years of the 21st century. The amount of water stored at Lake Mead dropped sharply in 1999-2007, to about one-half the 24 million acre-feet that the Bulletin's specialists had projected. At Lake Powell, the reservoir was at one-third capacity by early 2005.[46]

Colorado River flows into the so-called "lower-basin" states fell to 62 percent of the 30-year average in 2000, 59 percent in 2001, 51 percent in 2003 and 49 percent in 2004 before rebounding to 102 percent in 2007. Interior Secretary Ken Salazar said last December that the 2000-2010 period had been the driest decade in the Colorado River Basin in the 102 years of record-keeping. "There are no clear signs of an end to this drought," he added.[47]

Salazar went on to note that intense drought from sharply decreased rainfall represented only one danger. The warming of the region threatened to bring a sustained reduction in the Colorado's flow, a group of specialists wrote in 2010, partly because of increased evaporation.[48]

Experts contributing to the *Proceedings of the National Academy of Sciences* (PNAS) in 2010 noted, among other findings, that three of the 11 driest years during the past century had occurred in the 2000s (2002, 2007 and 2008). Moreover, "The drought

Getty Images/Brent Stirton

appears to be part of a longer-term trend of strong dry-ing that began around 1979," wrote UCLA's MacDonald, summarizing some of his colleagues' stud-ies. "As bad as things might seem, they have the demon-strated potential to become much worse."[49]

By then, the drought in the Colorado River Basin that was the backdrop to the PNAS studies, as well as similar conditions elsewhere in the region, had contrib-uted to a general sense that the Western water system was facing major challenges.

Texas was especially hard hit, suffering a string of two-year droughts in 1999-2002, 2005-2006 and 2007-2009. The latter "may well have been the worst drought on record up to that point" in parts of south-central and south Texas, State Climatologist John W. Nielsen-Gammon, a professor of atmospheric sciences at Texas A&M University, said in a report last October.[50]

The Western Governors Association noted in 2008 that the region's water sources had "become stressed" and called for federal financing of research on desalination of ocean water, water recycling, "weather modification" and other strategies to expand supply. "Undefined and un-definable climate and other variables," the association said, "mean continuing uncertainty."[51]

CURRENT SITUATION

Ruling on Wells

Water-policy experts and landowners in New Mexico and throughout the West are waiting for the New Mexico Supreme Court to rule on a lawsuit challenging the state's exemption of private landowners' wells from regulation.

The case, under way since 2006, tests the modern viability of the traditional doctrine that private wells don't fall under state regulatory authority — even in water-scarce areas. Some argue that exempting private wells benefits housing developers rather than individual homeowners.

Jesse J. Richardson, research and policy adviser to the Water Systems Council, a trade association of well-drill-ing equipment manufacturers and related businesses, urged attendees at a conference last May on well exemp-tions in the Pacific Northwest to follow the litigation, which began with a lawsuit by southern New Mexico farmer Horace Bounds Jr. and his wife. "Other states

[are] looking at Bounds with great interest," he said in an outline of his remarks, noting that it could affect deci-sions in other states though it wouldn't apply directly outside New Mexico.[52]

Hoping to influence the outcome, Richardson filed a supporting brief for the council on behalf of the New Mexico state engineer, the state's top water authority and the target of the lawsuit challenging well exemptions.

The Boundses, who farm in southwest New Mexico, sued State Engineer John D'Antonio in 2006. They argued that their farm's water rights — which date back to 1869 — were potentially endangered by 45 exempt wells dug in the Mimbres River Basin since 1972. In that year, the basin was closed to grants of new water rights.

In 2008, a district court judge ruled for the Boundses on grounds that the well exemptions contradicted the state constitution's requirement that water rights be awarded according to the doctrine of prior appropria-tion. The exemption law "lacks any due process provi-sions to protect senior water rights from out-of-priority . . . domestic well applications," Robinson wrote.[53]

The New Mexico Court of Appeals reversed Robinson's opinion in October 2010. In ruling for the state engineer, the court said the domestic well exemp-tion "does not on its face violate the priority doctrine." Prior appropriation is only a "broad principle," which state lawmakers are responsible for applying. "We must presume that the Legislature understands the criticality of and balance needed for resolving the tension and clash between unavailability of water in fully appropriated basins and the declared need to provide well water for new domestic use," the appeals court wrote.[54]

The Boundses then took the case to the state's highest court, where lawyers argued the matter last October. "Domestic wells should not have a free pass," Beverly J. Singleman, a lawyer for the farming couple, told the jus-tices. Housing developers, she said, can easily use the exemption to bypass regulatory proceedings involved in installing community water systems.[55]

Bracken of the Western States Water Council reported in a comprehensive examination of well exemptions in the West that some New Mexico subdivision developers have used the exemptions to provide water to develop-ments that otherwise had no water rights.[56]

Do federal water-management policies aimed at protecting fish species in the California Delta hurt farmers?

YES
Thomas Birmingham
General Manager, Westlands Water District, western Fresno and Kings Counties, Calif.

From testimony prepared for delivery to House Subcommittee on Water and Power field hearing, Fresno, Calif., April 11, 2011

We are living under a federal regulatory regime that has made droughts more frequent and their impacts more severe. And those same regulations are reducing many of the natural benefits we used to derive from periods of high precipitation.

The Central Valley Project Improvement Act (CVPIA) has been implemented by the Department of the Interior in a manner that has reallocated more than 1 million acre-feet of water away from farms, ranches and business to the environment — for the restoration and enhancement of fish and wildlife.

In 2009, dry conditions did contribute to reduced water supplies. However, restrictions imposed on CVP operations under the Delta smelt biological opinion exacerbated the impact of those dry conditions. . . .

The most severe impact of the restrictions imposed under the CVPIA and the Endangered Species Act occurred in 2009, the first year in which the CVP was operated under the Delta smelt biological opinion. As a result of the combined effects of dry hydrologic conditions and regulatory restrictions, the final allocation for south-of-Delta agricultural water service contractors was 10 percent. Hundreds of thousands of acres of productive farmlands had to be fallowed, and millions of dollars' worth of permanent crops were destroyed. . . .

The allocation for south-of-Delta Central Valley Project agricultural water service contractors is 75 percent of the water we have contracted for. However, in 2011 these same regulations reduced the initial allocation for south-of-Delta CVP agricultural water service contractors to 50 percent. And although that allocation has incrementally increased, so that today our farmers can expect to receive 75 percent so long as farmers cannot rely on receiving an adequate supply of water, they are unable to efficiently plan their annual operations and are unable to secure crop loans until very late in the growing season.

California's water system was designed to enable us to live within the extremes of flood and drought. In the past it gave us the flexibility to adjust to these changing conditions and move our water supplies around to the places where and when they are needed most. That flexibility is what the current federal regulatory regime has taken away.

The harm these regulations have done to our communities, our economy and the environment would be bad enough, but what is worse, they have produced no demonstrable benefits for at-risk species.

NO
Michael L. Connor
Commissioner, U.S. Bureau of Reclamation

From testimony prepared for delivery to House Subcommittee on Water and Power field hearing, Fresno, Calif., April 11, 2011

California has been experiencing a twofold crisis over the past several years — one related to water supply and the other related to the collapsing Bay-Delta ecosystem. The issues, of course, are inextricably linked. Acres of land have been fallowed, once productive fisheries have been shut down and many communities within the Delta itself and in coastal California are concerned about their long-term survival.

The commercial and recreational salmon fishing season in California was completely closed in 2008 and 2009, and the Delta smelt population has continued to decline.

The U.S. Fish and Wildlife Service and National Marine Fisheries Service, respectively, determined that the Central Valley Project and the State Water Project, as proposed, would jeopardize fish species protected under the Endangered Species Act. . . . As a result, water exports through the Delta have been modified to protect at-risk fish species and the overall aquatic ecosystem, which affects water deliveries to urban and agricultural water users.

As of March 31 this year, the biological opinion for Delta smelt has not resulted in any restrictions on pumping. With respect to the biological opinion for salmon and other species, to date it has caused some restrictions on pumping, but only in an amount of approximately 10,000 acre-feet.

The subcommittee and some of our customers are asking a very reasonable question: How can [the Bureau of] Reclamation announce agricultural water supply allocations south of the Delta of only 75 percent? Since 1990, however, these contracts have been allocated at 100 percent only three times. This phenomenon did not develop overnight. It has been driven by a host of factors, including drought conditions, listing of numerous fish species under the Endangered Species Act, state-imposed flow and water-quality requirements [and] state water-rights priorities.

Understanding the need of farm operators to make early planting decisions, Reclamation also developed a series of actions for the 2011 water year to help support water allocations earlier and higher and intended to be used to respond to dry-year conditions as necessary. The water supply and Delta conditions have declined over several decades, and the long-term solution needs to be thoughtful, implementable and supported by the public.

We understand the very real ramifications of water shortage and declining fish populations on peoples' businesses, on families and on communities. We will continue to work to maximize our reliability in light of the challenges presented by hydrologic droughts, environmental conditions or regulatory actions.

But lawyers defending the exemption noted that the Boundses hadn't produced any evidence that the exempt wells had diminished their water supply.

Absence of actual harm had been an issue since the case began. Robinson had written in deciding for the Boundses that no evidence of damage was needed in order to conclude that exempting private wells from regulation was unconstitutional. "It will do little good for Bounds, and others similarly situated, to sit idly and wait for actual impairment," Robinson wrote. "When the water is gone, it will be too late."[57]

But that reasoning has been under attack ever since. "We have no doubt that the courts of New Mexico should play a role in vigorously protecting water rights, but that protection is only necessary where a scientifically proven threat exists to those rights," the National Groundwater Association had said in a brief supporting the state engineer.[58]

At the Supreme Court hearing last October, the justices paid close attention to the absence of actual harm, according to a synopsis by Richardson, who supports the state engineer's position. "The Justices repeatedly referred to the Boundses' lack of injury, calling it 'hypothetical' and 'theoretical' on numerous occasions," he wrote.[59]

Farms and Fish

A long-running dispute over California water-management schemes designed to protect salmon and other fish has entered a new phase following a California federal judge's rejection last September of federal fish-protection plans based on what he called "bad science." But U.S. District Judge Oliver Wanger didn't dispute a need for federal water-management orders designed to ensure viability of salmon and other species affected by the re-plumbing of the Sacramento-San Joaquin Delta.[60]

Wanger's sharply worded 279-page decision was taken as a victory by farmers' organizations long opposed to federal fish-protection plans. The plans, authorized by the federal Endangered Species Act, have led to restrictions on the amount of runoff from the rivers of the Sierra Nevada allowed into the farmland of the Delta. Instead, the water is channeled into the ocean to maintain the ecosystem that keeps the fish alive.

Wanger ordered scientists from the National Marine Fisheries Service, a wing of NOAA, to rewrite the section of their 844-page plan — known as a "biological

opinion," or BiOp — that concern the magnitude of river flows and the flow rate of pumps that push water to Southern California. Wanger said the plan lacked sufficient supporting evidence.[61]

Legal and political battles over water-management plans in the Delta go back decades. The conflicts, which have tended to pit farmers and irrigation district managers against environmentalists and federal regulators, have helped shape the debate over how to manage California's water resources, especially water that's pumped to the arid southern part of the state. Southern California's water demand — about half met from snowmelt-fed rivers in Northern California and half from the Colorado River — has played a central part in determining Western water policy.[62]

The decision by the Fresno-based Wanger amounted to a declaration that there is a "better way to serve the needs of fish and the needs of the people who rely on the water supplied by these projects," Tom Birmingham, general manager of the Westlands Water District, told *The Fresno Bee.*[63]

Birmingham acknowledged that the ruling was not a sweeping victory for opponents of the federal wildlife-protection plans. A summary of the decision by a lawyer with Pacific Legal Foundation, a conservative organization that litigates against federal regulatory actions, noted that Wanger concluded that water flows do have to be regulated to protect the salmon and other species involved. "There is record support for some form of action designed to prevent large numbers of fish from being killed or harmed," lawyer Brandon Middleton wrote in paraphrasing Wanger's ruling.[64]

A supporter of the federal plan emphasized that element of the ruling. "We are pleased that he still recognizes that, in fact, pumping in the Delta at the wrong times and in the wrong amounts can really hurt the fish," Zeke Grader, executive director of the Pacific Coast Federation of Fishermen's Associations, a trade group for commercial salmon fishermen, told *The Fresno Bee.*[65]

Indeed, last year, Wanger issued a similar ruling concerning federal protective plans for the tiny Delta smelt. He concluded that the law requires California's water system to be managed in a way that protects the smelt. But he rejected a federal protective plan. "The public cannot afford sloppy science and uni-directional prescriptions that ignore California's water needs," the judge wrote.[66]

Despite Wanger's consent to the substance of the federal plan, two spokesmen for Valley farmers applauded his harsh words for government scientists, whom he accused of tailoring their testimony to suit the objectives of their protection plan. "[W]e are worried about the loss of large amounts of water the [scientists'] biological opinion would do not only to our ag economy, but also to our tourist economy, our recreational economy and to our business economy as a whole," irrigation district managers Jeff Shields and Steve Knell wrote in the *Modesto Bee*. "In our area, where we live, less water means fewer jobs."[67]

Nevertheless, some Delta farmers have failed in an attempt to have federal protection for the smelt discarded. Three farmers — represented by the Pacific Legal Foundation — had argued that because the species doesn't cross state borders and has no commercial value, it doesn't fall under the purview of the Commerce Clause of the Constitution.[68]

Like the 20th-century water conflicts between Arizona and California, the fish-protection conflicts in California have reached the U.S. Supreme Court. In late October, the court effectively upheld Wanger's decision that the smelt deserves protection under the Endangered Species Act. Trent Orr, a lawyer with Earthjustice, a nonprofit law firm, told Environmental News Service, "After five lower courts found that it's in the national interest to preserve all of America's wildlife, including species that happen to exist only within the confines of a single state, the top court in the land agrees."[69]

Nevertheless, further conflicts lie ahead over the specifics of species-protection plans and the water-management measures involved.

OUTLOOK

"Legislative Failure"

Judge Wanger, a key figure in California water policy, retired at the end of September. Before stepping down, he took the opportunity to note that he owed the large role he has played to federal and state lawmakers' failure to adapt water policy to changing times. "The world is upside down in water in California, because the courts have had to assume such a role because the political system is impotent," Wanger told the *Contra Costa Times*.[70]

He was echoing a point he had taken the trouble to include in his 2010 decision on protective measures for the Delta smelt. On that occasion, he said that existing laws aren't adequately balancing competing needs for water in California. He cited a "legislative failure to provide the means to assure an adequate water supply for both the humans and the species dependent on the Delta." And, he warned, "The law alone cannot afford protection to all the competing interests at stake in these cases."[71]

Correct or not in his view of the court system's inadequacy as water-policy decision-maker, Wanger is one of many in the West who argue that the time for fundamental decisions on how to share water has arrived — and that courtrooms may not always be the best forum for those determinations.

In New Mexico, says Bokum of New Mexico Water Dialogue, "Communities should have the ability to decide what happens to them." She adds, acknowledging intense regional debate over agricultural water use, "If people in a community value agriculture, then the system should work to support that decision."

Sarah Bates, a senior associate of the University of Montana's Center for Natural Resources and Environmental Policy, says she's confident that negotiated solutions to water conflicts are possible. "Conditions are likely to get worse, but western water policy is incredibly dynamic, and innovation pops up out of crisis."

Similarly, Gleick of the Pacific Institute says new technology will help farmers and communities deal with water needs, even if, as expected, the climate grows hotter and drier. "Without a doubt we will be growing food and meeting urban needs with more efficient technologies and practices," he says.

These include expanding use of drip irrigation; scheduling irrigation times more precisely, based on climate and soil conditions; and using less water at certain times for certain crops, including almonds, pistachios and wine grapes, which accept water limitations at some stages of development.[72]

Stark necessity is the reason, Gleick says. "There simply isn't enough new supply to satisfy growing demands at an economic or environmental price we can afford."

Precedent exists elsewhere for necessity forcing change. Albuquerque, N.M., changed its entire water-use policy in the 1990s after learning that it could no longer count on an endless supply from the city's aquifer. The U.S. Geological Survey reported in 1993 that the city was using up that underground supply three times faster than it could be replaced by water from the Rio Grande.[73]

The following year, the Albuquerque Bernalillo County Water Utility Authority set a goal of cutting per capita use by 40 percent by 2015. By 2008, the city's residents used 34 percent less water than in 1994. Albuquerque prohibits outdoor watering during the hottest parts of the day in spring and summer — drip irrigation systems exempted — and grants water-bill credits of $1.50 per square foot of lawn replaced by drought-resistant landscaping known as "xeriscaping."[74]

Establishing financial incentives for conservation and efficiency is a method with enormous promise that needs far more use, says Udall of the Western Water Assessment.

Such basic techniques aside, Udall argues that the West should learn from the arid continent of Australia.

"They began water reforms in 1994, driven by the need at the time to have their utility industry be as efficient as it could be," he says. "They look through the lens of a limited and constrained water supply. They have a whole bunch of people at the table trying to answer the question of how to have a healthy society, a health environment and healthy economy given the constraint. Here, that debate is not being held. We have a complex system that is resistant to change, difficult to modify and very suboptimal."

NOTES

1. "Drought and Climate Change on Water Resources," Senate Committee on Energy and Natural Resources, April 27, 2011, pp. 31-32, www.gpo.gov/fdsys/pkg/CHRG-112shrg6645 5/pdf/CHRG-112shrg66455 .pdf.

2. *Ibid.*, p. 31; "Climate Change and Water," U.S. Bureau of Reclamation, April 2011, p. vii; www.usbr.gov/climate/SECURE/docs/SECUREWaterReport.pdf.

3. Lauren Drewes Daniels, "Sucking Up Water and Sand in the Quest for Natural Gas," *Dallas Observer*, Sept. 15, 2011; "Idaho Hydrologist aims to measure aquifer," The Associated Press, June 22, 2011; John

4. "Western Irrigated Agriculture," U.S. Department of Agriculture, updated July 20, 2004, www.ers .usda.gov/Data/WesternIrrigation/.

5. Quoted in Donald Worster, *Rivers of Empire: Water, Aridity, and the Growth of the American West* (1985), p. 132.

6. Marc Reisner, *Cadillac Desert: The American West and its Disappearing Water* (1993 edition, revised), pp. 35-37.

7. Quoted in Worster, *op. cit.*

8. Norris Hundley Jr., *Water and the West: The Colorado River Compact and the Politics of Water in the American West* (2nd ed., 2009), pp. 293-295; Timothy Farrington, "Arizona fends off a water 'invasion,' " *The Daily*, Feb. 19, 2011, www.thedaily.com/page/2011/02/19/021911-opinions-history-hoover-dam-farrington-1-3/.

9. Richard Pinkham and Bill Davis, "North Central Arizona Water Demand Study," Grand Canyon Trust, June 2002, p. 95, www.grandcanyontrust.org/documents/gc_ncazWaterDemandStudy.pdf; "20x2020 Water Conservation Plan," California Department of Water Resources, *et al.*, February 2010, p. 2, www.water.ca.gov/wateruseefficiency/sb7/docs/20x2020plan.pdf.

10. John L. Sabo, *et al.*, "Reclaiming freshwater sustainability in the Cadillac Desert," Proceedings of the National Academy of Sciences, p. 21269, www.pnas .org/content/107/50/21263.full.

11. Glen M. MacDonald, "Water, climate change, and sustainability in the southwest," *Proceedings of the National Academy of Sciences*, Dec. 14, 2010, p. 21258, pnas.org/content/107/50/21256.full.pdf+html; "Resident Population of the 50 States, the District of Columbia, and Puerto Rico: Census 2000," U.S. Census Bureau, Dec. 28, 2000, www.census.gov/population/www/cen2000/maps/files/tab02.pdf.

12. "Eastern Snake River Plain Aquifer," Digital Geology of Idaho, Idaho State University, updated August 2007, http://geology.isu.edu/Digital_Geology_

W. Nielsen-Gammon, "The 2011 Texas Drought," Office of State Climatologist, Oct. 31, 2011, pp. 3, 41, http://atmo.tamu.edu/osc/library/osc_pubs/2011_ drought.pdf.

Idaho/Module15/mod15.htm; "Idaho hydrologist aims to measure aquifer," *op. cit.*

13. Quoted in *Clear Springs Foods, et al. v. Spackman, Idaho Ground Water Appropriators, et al.*, Opinion 32, March 17, 2011, www.isc.idaho.gov/opinions/ CLEAR%20SPRINGS%2037308.pdf; "Major water rights ruling upheld: Idaho Supreme Court sides with trout farms," The Associated Press, (*Lewiston Morning Tribune*), March 19, 2011, www .vcstar.com/news/2011/mar/22/idaho-high-court-rules-on-major-water-rights/?print=1.

14. Quoted in Clear Springs Foods . . . , *ibid.*

15. "Conference White Paper — Exempt Wells: Problems & Approaches in the Northwest," Washington State University et seq., May 17-18, 2011, http://water center.montana.edu/pdfs/Exempt_Wells_ Conference_Report_FINAL.pdf.

16. "Comments on Water Policy Interim Committee draft legislation and reports," Montana Association of Realtors, July 30, 2008, http://leg.mt.gov/content/ Committees/Interim/2007_2008/water_policy/ staffmemos/wpicreportcomments.pdf.

17. For background see Jennifer Weeks, "Energy Policy," *CQ Researcher*, May 20, 2011, pp. 457-480; "Hydraulic Fracturing," U.S. Department of Energy, undated, www.netl.doe.gov/technologies/oil-gas/ publications/eordrawings/Color/colhf.pdf; "Hydraulic Fracturing — Fact Sheet," Chesapeake Energy, September 2011, www.chk.com/Media/Educational-Library/Fact-Sheets/Corporate/Hydraulic_ Fracturing_Fact_Sheet.pdf; Anthony Andrews, *et al.*, "Unconventional Gas Shales: Development, Technology, and Policy Issues," Congressional Research Service, Oct. 30, 2009, www.fas.org/sgp/ crs/misc/R40894.pdf.

18. "Energy-Water Nexus: A Better and Coordinated Understanding of Water Resources Could Help Mitigate the Impacts of Potential Oil Shale Development," Government Accountability Office, October 2010, summary and p. 7, www.gao.gov/ new.items/d1135.pdf.

19. *Ibid.*, summary page.

20. *Ibid.*

21. *Ibid.*, pp. 11-12.

22. Quoted in Elizabeth Souder, "University of Texas researchers find no evidence that fracking contaminates groundwater," *Dallas Morning News*, Nov. 10, 2011, www.dallasnews.com/business/energy/20111109-university-of-texas-researchers-find-no-evidence-that-fracking-contaminates-groundwater.ece.

23. Abrahm Lustgarten, "EPA Finds Compounds Used in Fracking in Wyoming Aquifer," *ProPublica*, Nov. 10, 2011, www.propublica.org/article/epa-finds-fracking-compound-in-wyoming-aquifer/single.

24. Susan Schrock and Bill Hanna, "Parched Tarrant County cities moving to control water usage by drillers," *Fort Worth Star-Telegram*, Aug. 30, 2011, www .star-telegram.com/2011/08/29/3321900/parched-tarrant-county-cities.html.

25. *Ibid.*

26. Quoted in *ibid.*

27. Quoted in *ibid.*

28. Brigitte Buynak, "Basic Water Law Concepts," in "Water Matters!," Utton Transboundary Resources Center, University of New Mexico School of Law, 2011, http://uttoncenter.unm.edu/pdfs/Water_ Matters_2011.pdf; Donald Worster, *Rivers of Empire: Water, Aridity, and the Growth of the American West* (1985), pp. 75-76; Paul Saavedra, "Surface Water Irrigation Organizations in New Mexico," New Mexico State Engineer Office, March 1987, www.nmacequiacommission.state.nm.us/ Publications/ose-acequia-rpt1987.pdf.

29. *Ibid.*

30. Worster, *op. cit.*, pp. 76-77.

31. Reisner, *op. cit.*, p. 2.

32. Worster, *op. cit.*, pp. 89-91; Dan Tarlock, *et al.*, "Water in the West: Challenge for the Next Century," *Western Water Policy Review Advisory Commission*, June 1998, pp. 4-3, 5-20, www.prevention web.net/files/1785_VL102318.pdf.

33. Worster, *ibid.*, pp. 91-93.

34. Except where otherwise indicated, this subsection is drawn from Powell, *op. cit.*

35. For the differing accounts, see Marc Reisner, *Cadillac Desert: The American West and Its Disappearing Water* (1993), pp. 122-123; James Lawrence Powell, *Dead*

Pool: Lake Powell, Global Warming, and the Future of Water in the West (2008).

36. Frank Gibbard, "Wyoming v. Colorado: A 'Watershed' Decision," *The Colorado Lawyer*, March 2005, www.cobar.org/tcl/tcl_articles.cfm?articleid=4063. The decision is *Wyoming v. Colorado*, 259 U.S. 419 (1922), http://supreme.justia.com/us/259/419/.

37. *Ibid.*

38. Norris Hundley Jr., *Water and the West: The Colorado River Compact and the Politics of Water in the American West* (2009 edition), pp. 307-309; *Arizona v. California*, 373 U.S. 546 (1963), http://supreme.justia.com/us/373/546.

39. *Ibid.*, pp. 302-304; "Law of the River," Central Arizona Project, 2011, www.cap-az.com/AboutUs/LawOfTheRiver.aspx.

40. "Hoover Dam — Frequently Asked Questions, Lake Mead," U.S. Bureau of Reclamation, updated December 2008, www.usbr.gov/lc/hooverdam/faqs/lakefaqs.html.

41. "Colorado River Storage Project," updated Nov. 25, 2008, www.usbr.gov/uc/rm/crsp/index.html.

42. "Arizona Water Atlas, Vol. 1, Appendix C, p. 128," Arizona Department of Water Resources, updated Oct. 28, 2011, www.azwater.gov/AzDWR/Statewide Planning/WaterAtlas/documents/appendix_c.pdf.

43. Marca Weinberg, "Water Use Conflicts in the West: Implications of Reforming the Bureau of Reclamation's Water Supply Policies," Congressional Budget Office, August 1997, p. 11, www.cbo.gov/ftpdocs/0xx/doc46/wateruse.pdf.

44. Quoted in Doug Kenney, *et al.*, "Rethinking Vulnerability on the Colorado River," *Journal of Contemporary Water Research & Education*, March 2010, www.ucowr.org/updates/144/2.pdf; James Lawrence Powell, *Dead Pool: Lake Powell, Global Warming, and the Future of Water in the West* (2008), pp. 18-19.

45. *Ibid.*

46. *Ibid.*

47. "Remarks prepared for the Colorado River Water Users Association annual meeting," Dec. 17, 2010, www.doi.gov/news/speeches/Colorado-River-Water-Users-Association-Annual-Meeting.cfm.

48. Kenney, *et al.*, *ibid.*; N. Christiansen and D. P. Lettenmaier, "A multimodal ensemble approach to assessment of climate change impacts on the hydrology and resources of the Colorado River basin," Hydrology and Earth System Sciences Discussion, Nov. 28, 2006, wwa.colorado.edu/climate_change/docs/christensen_multimodel_06.pdf.

49. MacDonald, *op. cit.*, p. 21259.

50. Nielsen-Gammon, *op. cit.*, p. 9.

51. "Water Needs and Strategies for a Sustainable Future: Next Steps," Western Governors' Association, June 2008, pp. 9, 31, www.westgov.org/wga/publicat/Water06.pdf.

52. Jesse J. Richardson, Jr., "Legal Aspects to Exempt Wells: A National Review," May 17, 2011, www.eiseverywhere.com/file_uploads/896ac80383dca2ca62f5356fc23f5611_Richardson.pdf; "Exempt Wells: Problems & Approaches in the Northwest, Conference Paper," Washington State University, *et al.*, May 17-18, 2011, http://watercenter.montana.edu/pdfs/Exempt_Wells_Conference_Report_FINAL.pdf.

53. "Domestic Wells," Water Matters!, Utton Transboundary Resources Center, University of New Mexico, Updated 2010, http://uttoncenter.unm.edu/pdfs/WM_Domestic_Wells.pdf; *Bounds v. State of New Mexico*, Sixth Judicial District, State of New Mexico, July 10, 2008.

54. *Horace Bounds Jr., et al., v. State of New Mexico*, New Mexico Court of Appeals, No. 28,860, Oct. 29, 2010, p. 32, [emailed to *CQ Researcher*].

55. Quoted in Staci Matlock, *The New Mexican*, Oct. 13, 2011, www.santafenewmexican.com/localnews/High-court-ponders--domestic-well-rights.

56. Nathan Bracken, "Exempt Well Issues in the West," *Environmental Law*, Lewis and Clark Law School, March 8, 2010, p. 222, http://aquadoc.typepad.com/files/exempt_wells_in_the_west_n_bracken.pdf.

57. *Bounds, et al., v. State of New Mexico*, Sixth Judicial District, *op. cit.*

58. *Bounds, et al., v. State of New Mexico*, Amicus Curiae Brief, National Ground Water Association, July 29, 2011, p. 18, www.ngwa.org/Media-Center/press/2011/Pages/New-Mexico-Brief.aspx.

59. "More Exempt Wells — Bounds v. State of New Mexico: Oral Arguments before NM Supreme Court," *WaterWired* (blog), Oct. 18, 2011, http://aquadoc.typepad.com/waterwired/2011/10/bounds-v-state-of-new-mexico-oral-arguments-before-nm-supreme-court.html.

60. Quoted in Bettina Boxall, "Judge orders U.S. to revise salmon safeguards," *Los Angeles Times*, Sept. 21, 2011, http://articles.latimes.com/2011/sep/21/local/la-me-water-salmon-20110921; Consolidated Salmonid Cases, 1:09-CV-01053 OWW DLB, Memorandum Decision, U.S. District Court, Eastern District of California, Sept. 20, 2011, http://plf.typepad.com/files/salmonbiopsept2011decision.pdf.

61. John Ellis, "Parts of Delta salmon plan invalidated in court," *The Fresno Bee*, Sept. 20, 2011, www.fresnobee.com/2011/09/20/2546254/parts-of-salmon-plan-invalidated.html.

62. "Sacramento-San Joaquin Delta . . . Resolving a Crisis," Metropolitan Water District of Southern California, updated Oct. 11, 2011, www.mwdh2o.com/mwdh2o/pages/yourwater/supply/delta/index.html.

63. Quoted in Ellis, *op. cit.*

64. Brandon Middleton, "2009 salmonid biop found to be unlawful," *PLF Liberty Blog*, Pacific Legal Foundation, Sept. 20, 2011, http://plf.typepad.com/plf/2011/09/author-brandon-middleton-conclusion-for-all-the-reasons-set-forth-above-a-plaintiffs-and-dwrs-motions-for-summar.html.

65. Quoted in Ellis, *op. cit.*

66. Quoted in Colin Sullivan, "Judge Discards 'Sloppy Science' by FWS on Delta Smelt," *Greenwire* (in *The New York Times*), Dec. 15, 2010, www.nytimes.com/gwire/2010/12/15/15greenwire-judge-discards-sloppy-science-by-fws-on-delta-75600.html.

67. Jeff Shields and Steve Knell, "How ruling affects New Melones," *Modesto Bee*, Nov. 25, 2011, www.modbee.com/2011/11/25/1961222/how-ruling-affects-new-melones.html#ixzz1erVYW911.

68. Michael Doyle, "Federal protections will remain for smelt," *The Fresno Bee*, Nov. 1, 2011, p. A3.

69. Quoted in "U.S. Supreme Court Allows Delta Smelt Protection to Stand," Environmental News Service, Oct. 31, 2011, www.ens-newswire.com/ens/oct2011/2011-10-31-091.html.

70. Quoted in Mike Taugher, "Powerful figure in California's water wars steps down," www.mercurynews.com/news/ci_19006234.

71. "Delta Smelt Consolidated Cases," U.S. District Court for the Eastern District of California, Dec. 14, 2010, pp. 218-219, www.eenews.net/assets/2010/12/15/document_gw_01.pdf.

72. Heather Cooley, *et al.*, "Sustaining California Agriculture in an Uncertain Future," Pacific Institute, July 2009, www.pacinst.org/reports/california_agriculture/final.pdf.

73. Bruce Selcraig, "Albuquerque learns it really is a desert town," *High Country News*, Dec. 26, 1994, www.hcn.org/issues/26/728.

74. "Protecting the Lifeline of the West: How Climate and Clean Energy Policies Can Safeguard Water," Western Resource Advocates, Environmental Defense Fund, 2010, p. 18, www.westernresourceadvocates.org/water/lifeline/lifeline.pdf; "Double-Rebate Xeriscape Program Extended," Albuquerque Bernalillo County Water Utility Authority, Aug. 18, 2011, www.abcwua.org/content/view/533/63.

BIBLIOGRAPHY

Selected Sources

Books

Hundley, Norris Jr., *Water and the West: The Colorado River Compact and the Politics of Water in the American West*, University of California, 2009 ed. Originally published in 1975, this updated edition of a major work by an emeritus professor of history at UCLA tells the story of the single most important western water-rights agreement.

Powell, James Lawrence, *Dead Pool: Lake Powell, Global Warming, and the Future of Water in the West,* **University of California, 2008.**
Geologist/science author Powell (also director of the National Physical Science Consortium) sounds an alarm over the effects of climate change on the West.

Reisner, Marc, *Cadillac Desert: The American West and Its Disappearing Water,* **Penguin, 1993 ed.**
An acclaimed environmental writer combines an enormous volume of historical and scientific material in a book that influences debate on Western water and growth to this day.

Worster, Donald, *Rivers of Empire: Water, Aridity, and the Growth of the American West,* **Oxford University, 1985.**
A University of Kansas scholar and environmental-history pioneer offers a masterful account of Western water development.

Articles

Barringer, Felicity, "Officials Back Plan to Restore California Bay Delta," *The New York Times,* **Dec. 16, 2010, p. A30, http://www.nytimes.com/2010/12/16/us/16delta.html?scp=1&sq=Officials%20Back%20Plan%20to%20Restore%20California%20Bay%20Delta&st=cse.**
An environmental correspondent reports on federal approval of new infrastructure to channel water from Northern California to the southern part of the state.

Finley, Bruce, "Farms push to save water," *Denver Post,* **Jan. 30, 2011, p. B-1.**
Colorado irrigation systems turn to computer-controlled devices to control and monitor water discharges.

Fleck, John, "N.M. Tied to Water Questions in California," *Albuquerque Journal,* **June 28, 2011, p. A1.**
A water specialist with New Mexico's statewide daily lays out the deep and consequential connections between the water supply systems of his state and California.

Hargrove, Brantley, "The Long Dry Fall of the Texas Rancher," *Dallas Observer,* **Sept. 29, 2011, www.dallasobserver.com/2011-09-29/news/the-long-dry-fall-of-the-texas-rancher/.**

A Dallas weekly chronicles at length and in detail the devastating effects of drought on one of Texas' signature industries.

Hazlehurst, John, "Western states edge ever-closer to water conflicts," *Colorado Springs Business Journal,* **Nov. 26, 2010.**
A reporter offers a concise summation of the reasons to expect water scarcity in the West and competition for the shrinking supply.

McKinnon, Shaun, "Arizona challenge: Water for the next 100 years," *Arizona Republic,* **March 19, 2011, p. A1.**
Concern over water supply is growing in a major desert state, an Arizona's statewide daily reports.

Reports and Studies

Canessa, Pete, *et al.,* "Agricultural Water Use in California, a 2011 Update," **Center for Irrigation Technology, Fresno State University, November 2011, www.californiawater.org/docs/CIT_AWU_Report_v2.pdf.**
A team of agricultural experts from California farm country argues that agriculture makes careful, non-wasteful use of water.

Gammage, Grady Jr., *et al.,* "Watering the Sun Corridor: Managing Choices in Arizona's Megapolitan Area," **Morrison Institute for Public Policy, Arizona State University, http://morrisoninstitute.asu.edu/publications-reports/2011-watering-the-sun-corridor-managing-choices-in-arizonas-megapolitan-area.**
A public-policy expert analyzes Arizona water use as a means to encourage debate over options facing the state.

Gleick, Peter H., "Roadmap for sustainable water resources in southwestern North America," **Proceedings of the National Academy of Sciences, Dec. 14, 2010, www.pnas.org/content/107/50/21300.full.pdf+html.**
A leading environmentalist argues for widespread adoption of water-use efficiency techniques in order to adapt to climate changes already under way.

"Reclamation, Climate Change and Water, 2011," U.S. Bureau of Reclamation, April 2011, www.usbr.gov/climate/SECURE/docs/SECUREWater Report.pdf.
As required by a 2009 law, the major federal water-management agency in the West reports in detail on the current and projected effects of climate change.

Nielsen-Gammon, John W., "The 2011 Texas Drought, a Briefing Packet for the Texas Legislature," Oct. 31, 2011, http://atmo.tamu.edu/osc/library/osc_pubs/2011_drought.pdf.
The state climatologist lays out details of drought in Texas' regions and analyzes possible future developments, which tend toward the unfavorable.

For More Information

California Farm Bureau Federation, 2300 River Plaza Dr., Sacramento, CA 95833; 916-561-5500; www.cfbf.com. Major trade association for state's agricultural industry; provides information on water issues affecting farmers.

Center for Natural Resources and Environmental Policy, University of Montana, 516 N. Park Ave., Helena, MT 59601; 406-457-8475; www.cnrep.org. Think tank that promotes cooperative methods to solve water-rights conflicts.

Institute of the Environment, University of Arizona, P.O. Box 210158b, Tucson, AZ 85721; 520-626-4345; www.environment.arizona.edu. Research by institute members includes analysis of paleoclimatological evidence for indicators of lengthy droughts in past centuries.

Metropolitan Water District of Southern California, P.O. Box 54153, Los Angeles, CA 90054; 213-217-6000; www.mwdh2o.com/index.htm. Major drinking-water system; maintains a vast and complicated supply system.

Pacific Institute, 654 13th St., Preservation Park, Oakland, CA 94612; 510-251-1600; www.pacinst.org. Science-oriented environmental research and advocacy organization; focuses on sustaining water resources.

U.S. Bureau of Reclamation, 1849 C St., N.W., Washington DC 20240; 202-513-0501; www.usbr.gov. Major federal water-management agency; provides detailed information on Western dams, reservoirs and associated infrastructure.

Western Water Assessment, NOAA Earth System Research Laboratory, R/PSD 325 Broadway, Boulder, CO 80305; (fax only) 303-497-6449; wwa.colorado.edu. Joint federal and University of Colorado think tank specializing in climate-change effects on the water supply.

5

Space Program

John Felton

NASA's Mars Science Laboratory, carrying the rover Curiosity, is lifted into position before being attached to an Atlas rocket at Cape Canaveral on Nov. 3, 2011. The mission to Mars was launched on Nov. 26 and is due to arrive at the "red planet" Aug. 6. Critics say the Obama administration's proposed withdrawal from participation with the European Space Agency on two unmanned follow-up expeditions to Mars threatens U.S. leadership in space research. But NASA says it is considering future Mars missions.

From *CQ Researcher*,
Feb. 24, 2012

I
f all goes as planned next August, a NASA rover about the size of a small SUV will be gently lowered from a spacecraft onto the surface of Mars and begin searching for signs that the "red planet" once supported life — and perhaps still does.

The $2.5 billion mission — the most ambitious to Mars ever mounted — marks a bright spot on an otherwise cloudy horizon for the U.S. space program. Beset by disagreements over the next destination for human spaceflight and squeezed by budget cuts, the U.S. space program faces more uncertainty than at any time in its storied history.[1]

"We are in a real mess right now with our space program, and it's not clear how we're going to get out of it," says Alex Roland, a professor emeritus of history at Duke University and longtime critic of NASA, where he was an historian in the 1970s.

Some critics are especially upset at cancellation of the space shuttle program, leaving the United States to depend on Russian *Soyuz* spacecraft to bring Americans to the International Space Station (ISS), the only current destination for American astronauts.

"I am not at all happy with some of the directions the space program is going, in particular retiring the space shuttles before we have a new heavy-lift launching system in place," pioneering astronaut John Glenn, who became the first American to orbit Earth 50 years ago this month, told *The New York Times*. "If the Russians had a hiccup with *Soyuz*, our manned space program would be ended, maybe for years."[2]

Indeed, China and Russia are the only countries currently capable of putting humans into Earth orbit.[3] Private companies, operating

National Aeronautics and Space Administration

A *Falcon 9* rocket lifts off from Cape Canaveral, Fla., on Dec. 8, 2010, carrying the Dragon space capsule. The launch was sponsored by SpaceX, the firm founded by PayPal co-founder Elon Musk. SpaceX (Space Exploration Technologies) is one of two firms NASA has contracted with to build rockets and spacecraft that will take food, fuel, scientific equipment and other supplies to the space station. The Hawthorne, Calif., firm has a $1.6 billion contract for 12 cargo flights through 2016.

under NASA contracts, might begin taking cargo to the space station this year, but commercial flights to ferry astronauts to the station are several years away.

Spaceflight emerged as an issue in the Republican presidential primaries in January when former House Speaker Newt Gingrich, campaigning in Florida, proposed a major commitment to colonize the moon. A small number of space advocates have pushed such a plan, but Gingrich's political opponents mocked it, and his appeal for votes along Florida's Space Coast, where NASA has launched rockets since the 1950s, failed to help him win the Florida primary.[4]

A much more serious debate about the future of the space program likely will take place this year in Congress. The starting point will be President Obama's fiscal 2013 budget request, submitted Feb. 13, which would continue most current programs and give NASA about the same amount — $17.8 billion — as for the current fiscal year. However, the administration would eliminate two unmanned scientific missions to Mars, scheduled for 2016 and 2018, that had been high-profile examples of cooperation in space between the United States and Europe.

Roger Handberg, a political science professor at the University of Central Florida who has written extensively about space policy, is deeply skeptical about NASA's ability to continue its programs without reshaping them to fit a new era of reduced budgets. "I don't think NASA will survive doing what it is doing — and wants to do on the scale it has been at — because the money won't be there," he says.

NASA has courted members of Congress by scattering installations and contracts around the country, Handberg says, but "the problem is that they don't have the kind of public support they need to survive a major cutback in the budget."

NASA officials say, however, that the space program is well-charted for years to come. NASA and private contractors are spending billions of dollars on research and other programs that NASA says could return Americans to deep space as early as 2025.

Citing a series of recent decisions, notably the selection of a design for a new launch vehicle intended eventually to take humans to Mars and beyond, NASA Administrator Charles Bolden said last September that "NASA is not only alive and well" but is "poised to take the next big leaps into both human space exploration and scientific discovery."[5]

Scientific discovery is the one aspect of the U.S. space program that has continued relatively unabated. NASA currently runs more than 90 unmanned scientific missions, some operated with other countries. One of the most famous is the spunky golf cart-sized *Opportunity* rover on Mars, which is still roaming eight years past its original 90-day lifespan. *Opportunity*'s twin, the *Spirit*, got mired in sand in 2009 and went silent in 2010. The *Mars Odyssey* has been orbiting the "red planet" since 2001; among its achievements is the detection of hydrogen just beneath the Martian surface, suggesting the presence of frozen water.[6]

The new Mars mission, the Mars Science Laboratory, with its bigger, more complex rover, *Curiosity*, launched last Nov. 26, is due to arrive at Mars Aug. 6.[7] However, the Obama administration has decided, for budget reasons, to withdraw U.S. participation from two unmanned follow-up scientific expeditions to Mars, both in cooperation with the European Space Agency. Outraged advocates of planetary science missions say the United States risks losing its leadership in an important area of research. Bolden, however, said NASA is not abandoning scientific exploration of Mars and suggested that some kind of mission might be possible in 2018-20, when the planet will be relatively close to Earth.[8]

NASA also has two telescopes in space that have produced copious information. The orbiting Kepler telescope has discovered more than 1,000 planet candidates.[9] The better-known Hubble Space Telescope, repaired in space four times because of design and production flaws, has looked into remote areas of the universe; it has been capturing light emitted 13 billion years ago and discovered the largest black holes yet observed.[10] NASA plans to replace Hubble in 2018 with the much more powerful James Webb Space Telescope — that is, if Congress continues funding it. The House of Representatives tried unsuccessfully to kill the Webb program in 2011, but Obama has called on Congress to keep it alive.

The single biggest and most expensive space endeavor ever — the International Space Station — is still operating. The ISS, a $100 billion project by the United States, Russia, Europe, Japan and others, was finally completed last year and has been occupied by astronauts since 2000. Current plans call for it to continue operating at least until 2020 and possibly as late as 2028.[11]

Russia also is active in Mars exploration but has failed 17 times compared with two partial successes.[12] The latest failure came when its Phobos-Grunt mission failed to push past Earth orbit last November and crashed into the Pacific Ocean Jan. 15.[13] The mission was supposed to land on the Martian moon Phobos and send a small soil

Many See U.S. Space Leadership as Essential

Nearly 60 percent of Americans say it is crucial for the United States to remain a world leader in space exploration. The highest percentages with that view are Republicans and those with annual household income of more than $75,000.

Views on U.S. Space Leadership, June 2011

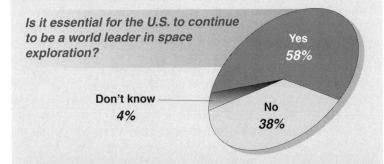

Is it essential for the U.S. to continue to be a world leader in space exploration?

Yes **58%**

Don't know **4%**

No **38%**

By family income			
Income level	Yes	No	Don't know
$75,000+	63%	35%	2%
$30,000-$75,000	55%	42%	4%
<$30,000	57%	37%	6%

By party affiliation			
Party	Yes	No	Don't know
Republican	67%	30%	3%
Democrat	54%	42%	4%
Independent	57%	40%	3%

* Figures may not total 100 because of rounding.

Source: "Majority Sees U.S. Leadership in Space as Essential," Pew Research Center, July 2011, www.people-press.org/2011/07/05/majority-sees-u-s-leadership-in-space-as-essential/

Is There Life on Mars?

NASA's mission to find out is nearing touchdown.

It's been called the "rover on steroids," a one-ton mobile geology lab bristling with instruments that will help determine whether conditions on Mars have ever been favorable for life.[1]

The rover — named *Curiosity* — is the heart of NASA's Mars Science Laboratory, a $2.5 billion mission that is the most sophisticated effort to date to look for signs of microbial life — past or present — on the so-called "red planet."

Launched last Nov. 26, a spacecraft carrying *Curiosity* will land on Mars Aug. 6 if all goes according to plan. The craft will descend in a series of S-curves through the Martian atmosphere, and three minutes before touchdown a parachute will slow it down. Then, retro rockets attached to an upper stage will fire, and in the final seconds the upper stage will act as a sky crane, gently lowering *Curiosity* on a tether to the ground.[2]

The Mars Science Laboratory is the latest in a long line of U.S. scientific missions to Mars dating back to 1965, when Mariner 4 flew past the planet and transmitted 21 images back to Earth.[3]

One of NASA's greatest achievements so far has been the mission of the twin Mars rovers *Opportunity* and *Spirit* that began in January 2004. Both about the size of golf carts, the solar-powered vehicles were scheduled to roam just a few miles of the Martian surface, examining soil and rocks, for only 90 days. But they kept going, and NASA repeatedly extended their missions based on the enormous quantity of information they sent back to Earth about Mars' geology.

Spirit drove 4.8 miles before ceasing communications in 2010. *Opportunity* is still at work, eight years after landing, having driven more than 21 miles — it was built to drive less than one mile. *Opportunity* has examined four craters, including one 14 miles in diameter known as Endeavour, where it has been positioned since last fall.[4]

Curiosity, which is about five times the size of *Spirit* and *Opportunity*, will use its instruments, including a rock-vaporizing laser, to collect and examine rock and soil, then send technical information back to Earth.[5] Among other things, it will look for evidence of methane gas, which might suggest Mars has some form of life.[6]

Despite its eight years on the job, *Opportunity* is not the longest-serving spacecraft to visit Mars. That distinction is held by *Mars Odyssey*, which has been in orbit around the "red planet" since 2001 and will continue for the indefinite future. In December 2010 *Odyssey* surpassed the previous record for Mars service held by the *Mars Global Surveyor*, which orbited the planet from 1997 to 2006. Among *Odyssey*'s achievements has been the detection of hydrogen beneath the Martian surface, leading scientists to believe water might also be present.[7]

Another major Mars program, planned by the United States in conjunction with the European Space Agency, may have fallen victim to budget cuts.[8] Known as ExoMars, it is supposed to have two components: the Trace Gas Orbiter, to be launched in 2016, with a mission of examining the Martian atmosphere in greater detail than previous orbiters could; and two rovers, to be launched in 2018, which would dig up soil samples to be retrieved by later missions. The goal is to learn much more than is currently possible about the planet's geological history.[9]

However, the proposed NASA budget issued Feb. 13 by the Obama administration eliminated funding for U.S. participation in ExoMars. Administration officials for months had signaled that such a cut was likely, leading the European and Russian space agencies in late 2011 to begin discussions about a joint program without U.S. participation.[10]

The proposed withdrawal from the mission has angered Mars exploration advocates, including Robert Zubrin, founder and president of the Mars Society. Zubrin says the Obama administration "is reneging on a deal we had with the Europeans. Not only are they wrecking our own program, but they are wrecking the European program as well."

Unless reversed by Congress, the U.S. withdrawal likely will affect a subsequent mission to retrieve the soil samples. Known as the Mars Astrobiology Explorer-Cacher (MAX-C), it was the highest-priority project in a NASA-sponsored survey of planetary science projects for the coming decade, according to the independent National Research Council. Cost estimates for the project have ranged from $2.2 billion to $4.7 billion. However, the council suggested deferring or even canceling the project if it could not be done for under $2.5 billion.[11]

NASA said last June that it concurred with that recommendation and was examining "a significant cost reduction" to enable the project to proceed.[12]

While most of the past and current U.S. explorations of Mars have been successful, the same cannot be said for the other great space power of the past 50 years. Since the 1960s, Russia (and its predecessor, the Soviet Union) have enjoyed partial successes in only two of 19 attempts to send spacecraft to Mars.[13] Moscow's best result came in 1971, when its *Mars 3* orbiter collected data for eight months, and a related lander got safely to the Martian surface but sent back only 20 seconds of data, according to NASA.[14]

Russia's latest stumble came in November, when the ambitious Phobos-Grunt mission failed to get out of Earth orbit. Russian engineers tried unsuccessfully for weeks to save the spacecraft, which eventually plunged into the Pacific Ocean on Jan. 15. Russian officials initially were quoted as suggesting that a U.S. military radar installation in Alaska might have damaged Phobos-Grunt, but subsequent reports said cosmic radiation damaged the spacecraft's software.[15]

The spacecraft included a probe that was supposed to land on the small Martian moon Phobos, scoop up soil, and then return it to Earth. If successful, the mission would have marked the first time that any object from Mars had been returned to Earth for scientific examination.[16]

— John Felton

A sky crane lowers the Curiosity rover to the surface of Mars in this artist's rendering.

[1]"NASA Launches Sophisticated Rover on Journey to Mars," The Associated Press, *The New York Times*, Nov. 26, 2011, www.nytimes.com/2011/11/27/science/ space/nasas-curiosity-rover-sets-off-for-mars-mission.html?scp=1&sq=nasa%20 launches%20sophisticated%20 rover% 20on%20journey%20to%20mars&st=cse. See also, "Mars Science Laboratory," NASA, www.jpl.nasa.gov/news/fact_ sheets/mars-science-laboratory.pdf.

[2]"Mars Science Laboratory," *ibid*. See also "Rover Mission," NASA, http://mars. jpl.nasa.gov/msl/mission/rover/.

[3]Mars Exploration Program, "Historical Log," Jet Propulsion Laboratory, http:// mars.jpl.nasa.gov/programmissions/ missions/log/.

[4]Chris Gebhardt, "Opportunity's eight years on Mars: A story of science and endurance," NASASpaceflight.com, Jan. 25, 2012, www.nasaspaceflight.com/ 2012/01/opportunitys-eight-years-mars-story-science-endurance/.

[5]"Mars Science Laboratory Overview," Jet Propulsion Laboratory, http://mars program.jpl.nasa.gov/msl/mission/overview/.

[6]Kenneth Chang, "On Mars Rover, Tools to Plumb a Methane Mystery," *The New York Times*, Nov. 22, 2011, www.nytimes.com/2011/11/23/science/space/ aboard-mars-curiosity-rover-tools-to-plumb-a-methane-mystery.html?ref=mars planet.

[7]"NASA's Odyssey Spacecraft Sets Exploration Record on Mars," Jet Propulsion Laboratory, Dec. 15, 2010, http://mars.jpl.nasa.gov/ odyssey/news/whatsnew/ index.cfm?FuseAction=ShowNews&NewsID=1091.

[8]Jeff Foust, "Tough decisions ahead for planetary exploration," *The Space Review*, April 4, 2011.

[9]"The ESA-NASA ExoMars Program 2016-2018," European Space Agency, http://exploration.esa.int/science-e/www/object/index .cfm?fobjectid=46048.

[10]Amy Svitak, "ESA, Roscosmos See ExoMars Without NASA," *Aviation Week*, Feb. 10, 2012, www.aviationweek.com/aw/generic/ story_channel.jsp?channel= space&id=news/awx/2012/02/10/awx_ 02_10_2012_p0-423750.xml&headline= ESA,%20Roscosmos%20 See%20ExoMars%20Without%20NASA.

[11]"Vision and Voyages for Planetary Science in the Decade 2013-2022," Committee on the Planetary Science Decadal Survey; National Research Council, The National Academies Press, pp. 9-15. www.nap .edu/catalog.php?record_ id=13117.

[12]Letter from Edward J. Weiler, NASA associate administrator for science mission directorate, to Dr. Charles F. Kennel, chair, Space Studies Board of the National Research Council, July 29, 2011, p. 6.

[13]Dwayne A. Day, "Red Planet blues," *The Space Review*, Nov. 28, 2011, www.thespacereview.com/article/1980/1.

[14]"Mars Exploration Program: Historical Log," *op. cit.*

[15]"Russia blames Phobos-Grunt failure on cosmic radiation," spacetoday .net, Feb. 1, 2012, www.spacetoday.net/getsummary.php?id=55170.

[16]Jonathan Amos, "Phobos-Grunt: Failed Probe 'Falls Over Pacific,' " BBC News, Jan. 15, 2012, www.bbc.co.uk/news/science-environment-16491457.

Mars Missions Date Back Nearly 50 Years

The launch of the sophisticated rover *Curiosity* last November was the latest of more than a dozen successful U.S. scientific missions to Mars dating back to *Mariner 4* in 1964. The *Odyssey* and *Opportunity* rovers and *Mars Reconnaissance Orbiter* continue to explore the planet.

Successful U.S. Mars Missions, 1964-present

Mission	Launch date	Purpose	Results
Mariner 4	Nov. 28, 1964	First Mars flyby	The first successful flight past Mars, on July 14, 1965, returned 21 photos
Mariner 6	Feb. 24, 1969	Mars flyby	Returned 75 photos on July 31, 1969
Mariner 7	March 27, 1969	Mars flyby	Returned 126 photos on Aug. 5, 1969
Mariner 9	May 30, 1971	Orbiter mission	Orbited Nov. 13, 1971-Oct. 27, 1972; returned 7,329 photos
Viking 1	Aug. 20, 1975	Orbiter/lander mission	Orbiter operated June 19, 1976-1980; lander in operation July 20, 1976-1982
Viking 2	Sept. 9, 1975	Orbiter/lander mission	Orbiter operated Aug. 7, 1976-1987; lander in operation Sept. 3, 1976- and 1980; more than 50,000 photos returned
Mars Global Surveyor	Nov. 7, 1996	Orbiter mission	Arrived Sept. 12, 1997; detailed mapping through January 2000; third extended mission completed Sept. 2006; last communication Nov. 2, 2006
Mars Pathfinder	Dec. 4, 1996	Lander/rover mission	Landed July 4, 1997; completed prime mission and began extended mission Aug. 3, 1997; last transmission Sept. 27, 1997
Mars Odyssey	March 7, 2001	Orbiter mission	Arrived Oct. 24, 2001; completed prime mission Aug. 25, 2004; currently conducting extended science and communication relay mission
Mars Exploration Rover Spirit	June 10, 2003	Rover mission	Landed Jan. 4, 2004, for three-month prime mission inside Gusev crater; completed several extended missions; last communication March 22, 2010
Mars Exploration Rover Opportunity	July 7, 2003	Rover mission	Landed Jan. 25, 2004, for three-month prime mission on Meridiani Planum plain region; currently conducting extended mission
Mars Reconnaissance Orbiter	Aug. 12, 2005	Orbiter mission	Arrived March 12, 2006; completed prime mission Sept. 26, 2010; currently conducting extended mission of science and communication relay
Phoenix Mars Lander	Aug. 4, 2007	Lander mission	Landed May 25, 2008; completed prime mission and began extended mission Aug. 26, 2008; last communication Nov. 2, 2008
Mars Science Laboratory	Nov. 26, 2011	Rover mission with analytical laboratory	Curiosity rover scheduled to arrive August 2012

Sources: "Mars Science Laboratory Launch," National Aeronautics and Space Administration, November 2011, pp. 60-61, www.jpl.nasa.gov/news/press_kits/MSLLaunch.pdf; Mars Science Laboratory Mission, Jet Propulsion Laboratory

Introducing the New and Improved Mars Rover

The new Mars mission rover Curiosity is a one-ton mobile geology lab bristling with cameras and instruments designed to determine whether climate and other conditions on Mars are, or ever have been, capable of supporting life. Using cameras, lasers, a spectroscope and other instruments, Curiosity will chemically analyze rock, soil and other samples. The dynamic albedo of neutrons, at right, analyzes minerals under the rover for possible water content. Actions by the rover will be controlled by scientists and technicians on Earth. Previous Mars rovers have sent back strong evidence that the planet has water and thus could host some form of life. The rover is powered by a multimission radioisotope thermoelectric generator (top right), a nuclear battery that converts heat into electricity.

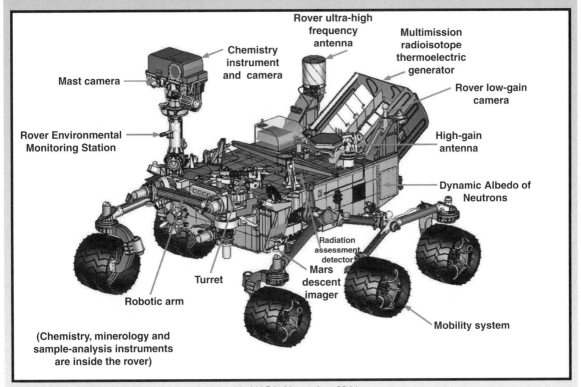

Source: Mars Science Laboratory Launch press kit, NASA, November 2011

sample back to Earth. Russian officials at first suggested a U.S. military radar might have damaged the spacecraft but later said it suffered a software malfunction.[14]

China put its first astronaut into space in 2003 and last year launched the first element of what it says will be a space station, possibly manned, by 2020.[15] A five-year plan issued in Beijing last December repeated talk of preliminary planning for a "human lunar landing" — an event most U.S. experts say is at least a decade off.[16]

Another opportunity that was nearly inconceivable at the dawn of the space age but is now nearing reality is

private space travel. At least three companies are building spacecraft to take paying customers for suborbital flights (about 60 miles in space) lasting about three to six minutes. Several hundred people already have put down deposits of up to $200,000 for a flight.[17] But the companies — all U.S.-based — have experienced repeated delays, and predictions of a booming private space business have yet to pan out.

The two companies with the most advanced programs are hoping to launch their first test flights (without paying customers) late in 2012.[18]

As debate continues over the direction and funding of the U.S. space program, here are some of the questions being asked:

Is the space program justified?

When the Pew Research Center asked Americans in a poll last June whether it was essential "that the United States continue to be a world leader in space exploration," most said yes, but more than a third said no. Republicans and people with family incomes above $75,000 were somewhat more likely to answer yes than Democrats, independents, and people with lower family incomes.[19]

The survey points up a huge divide in American society over whether space exploration is worth the cost, particularly during a time of staggering federal deficits.

NASA spends $5 billion to $8 billion of its annual $17.8 billion budget on programs related to human spaceflight. The biggest chunk, about $3 billion in fiscal 2012, is earmarked for a new rocket — or "space launch system" — to carry humans deep into space and a multi-purpose crew capsule.[20]

The U.S. space community, ranging from scientists to technicians to business people with a commercial interest in the space program, is more uniformly positive than Americans in general about the merits of the space program. But it is divided over two basic issues: how to justify human spaceflight and what the next destination for manned missions, if any, should be. Helping to drive that debate are worries about how mission costs can be explained to taxpayers.

"Money is the root of the problem," says Jeffrey A. Hoffman, a five-time shuttle astronaut and now a professor of aeronautics and astronautics at MIT. He adds that concerns about money come at a time when "clearly, there is a lack of consensus about what we should be doing" with the space program.

Historically, political leaders and space advocates have cited numerous reasons why the United States should lead the world in human spaceflight — everything from asserting global power, inspiring new generations of scientists and satisfying the human yearning for exploration to providing high-skill, high-paying jobs for tens of thousands of aerospace workers.[21]

Yet, while these justifications remain valid, space enthusiasts say, there seems to be little agreement on which are the most compelling in today's political and budgetary environment.

In 2010 Congress ordered NASA to contract with the independent National Research Council to review "the goals, core capabilities, and direction of human spaceflight" through 2023.[22] The study is unlikely to be finished until next year, says analyst Marcia Smith, founder and editor of *Space Policy Online*, which tracks space programs and spending. It could "profoundly" influence the direction of U.S. space policy, according to University of Texas astronomer Dan Lester.

Paul Spudis, senior staff scientist at the NASA-funded Lunar and Planetary Institute in Houston, says demonstrating global leadership is justification enough for the U.S. human spaceflight program. "One aspect of being a great power is the obligation to behave as one, to possess the ability to freely come and go and project power anywhere it might be challenged," he says. "If we abandon space, we will no longer possess that ability and, hence, our global stature will decline."

But Lester says that while human spaceflight has a role in future mission, using robots and other scientific instruments to explore space might be the better approach in some cases.

In the past, he notes, NASA and others compared human spaceflight to such great historical explorations as Columbus's journeys to the New World and the Lewis and Clark expedition to the uncharted American West in the early 1800s. "We're trying to be modern-day versions of all these guys who did noble things by going places that were off the map," says Lester. "But that historical template doesn't work that well anymore because we are in an era with sophisticated communications and robotic systems. We send rovers to drive around on Mars, and they send back thousands of pictures, so how can we say we don't know what is there and we have to go find out for ourselves? It's a harder case to make."

Roland, the former NASA historian, says robotic capabilities have reduced the need to send humans deep into space. "Virtually anything we can identify to do in space, we can do more economically, more safely, and more reliably with automated spacecraft controlled by human operators," he says. "This does not mean, however, that humans will not or should not fly in space. It means simply that with our existing technology, sending humans into space is more expensive, more dangerous and more unreliable than it is worth."

Many advocates of human spaceflight disagree that robots can always be as effective as humans in space. "Robots can be incredibly valuable, but if you are talking about really exploring the moon or Mars, both of which are so complex, that is where the value of humans as observers and scientists becomes so much greater," former astronaut Hoffman says.

But even the most avid supporters of human spaceflight say they are frustrated with the lack of a concrete plan for where astronauts will go once the next generation of rockets and space capsules is ready. "NASA literally has no goal," charges Robert Zubrin, president of the Mars Society, a group in Lakewood, Colo., that advocates human exploration and settlement of Mars. "They are spending $10 billion a year on human space flight and have no idea where they are going with it."

NASA says it is following Obama's space policy released in June 2010. That policy calls for a mission to an asteroid by 2025 and to Mars in the 2030s.[23] NASA administrator Bolden insisted to reporters on Feb. 13 that "we have a solid plan, a sustainable plan, and we're moving out to implement it . . . opening the next great chapter of American exploration."[24]

Edward Hudgins, advocacy director for the Atlas Society, a libertarian think tank in Washington, argues that the government should get out of the space business as much as possible and leave it to private enterprise. "The answer is to wait for costs to come down and allow natural market process to come into play," he says. It might be years before entrepreneurs can develop the necessary technology to send humans deep into space, even as far as the moon or Mars, he acknowledges. "But why the rush? Mars will still be there."

Should a human mission to Mars be the next big objective?

For more than a century, Mars has been the focal point for speculation about other life forms in the solar system.[25] U.S. orbiting observatories and rovers on the surface of Mars have sent back strong evidence that the planet has water and thus could host some form of life.[26]

For many space enthusiasts, the ultimate goal is sending humans to Mars, initially to explore it in greater depth than has been possible with machines and

AFP/Getty Images

A Chinese *AsiaSat 7* communications satellite sits atop a Russian *Proton-M* rocket on a launch pad at the Baikonur cosmodrome in Kazakhstan. With the retirement of the U.S. space shuttle system last year, China and Russia are now the only countries capable of putting humans into Earth orbit.

eventually to settle humans there. Some advocates argue that a Mars outpost could preserve the human species if it were destroyed on Earth.

The Mars Society's Zubrin, a former aerospace engineer for Martin-Marietta Corp., is among the most avid proponents of human missions to Mars. He insists that sending humans to the "red planet" need not be a massive, decades-long undertaking. Several years ago Zubrin developed his own plan for a relatively low-cost mission, called Mars Direct, which involves three successive flights to Mars, the third of which would carry astronauts who would spend up to 18 months on the planet before returning home.[27]

The International Space Station — the biggest and most expensive space endeavor ever — is still operating. The $100 billion project by the United States, Russia, Europe, Japan and others has been occupied by astronauts since 2000 and finally was completed last year. It will continue operating at least until 2020 and possibly as late as 2028, according to current plans. Companies operating under NASA contracts might begin taking cargo to the space station this year, but commercial flights to ferry astronauts to the station are several years away.

The most recent version of Zubrin's plan envisions using a launch rocket (the *Falcon-9 Heavy*) and crew capsule (*Dragon*) being developed by the private company SpaceX, led by PayPal co-founder Elon Musk. A decision to use these systems could put humans on Mars by 2020 or even earlier, Zubrin says, at a possible cost of about $50 billion — about the same amount, he says, that NASA plans to spend over that period on systems that will not be ready to launch until billions more have been spent many years later.[28]

NASA is "designing a completely fancy spaceship, like *Battlestar Galactica*, which is absolutely not needed," Zubrin says. "They have gone from the realm of, 'let's set a goal and then go do it,' into the realm of, 'let's dream about it, and maybe some time in the future we might get around to doing it.' It's not a mission. It's just being used as propaganda to justify a technology program."

Zubrin also advocates a much more ambitious concept than just one or two exploratory missions to Mars. He believes humans eventually can settle on Mars, assuming the planet actually has the buried frozen water that NASA orbiters suggest is there. "I believe that if we

can establish the first human foothold on a new world, 200 years from now there will be branches of human civilization on Mars, with their own dialects, their own cultures. If you have it within your power to do something grand like this, why not do it?"

Former astronaut Buzz Aldrin, one of the first two humans to walk on the moon in July 1969 as part of *Apollo 11*, also backs settlements on Mars, saying the idea "seems central to the vision many Americans have for the country." Moreover, he said it "uniquely protects U.S. leadership in space exploration, provides insurance for our national security, uniquely presses the envelope of science and is certain to trigger a fusillade of economic opportunities here on Earth."[29]

But others disagree that a human expedition to Mars makes sense. "A human mission to Mars would no doubt make some people feel good and inspire some people to bold or creative ventures," says Duke University's Roland. "It would not, however, improve upon the scientific research that could be done more economically, safely and effectively with automated spacecraft. And it would alienate and discourage those who think that the hundreds of billions of dollars could be better invested in economic development on Earth." In short, he says, "going to Mars, like going to the moon, would be a stunt with no payoff and no potential for further use."

Scott Pace, director of the Space Policy Institute at George Washington University and a former NASA executive, says going to Mars might be worthwhile in the future, but not anytime soon. The technical and budgetary challenges posed by a Mars mission actually are incentives, he says, because "it's in working on things that are hard that one learns new skills, discovers new things and builds relationships." However, he adds, "I wouldn't make a near-term national commitment to go to Mars. I would focus more on returning to the moon."

Pace says the moon should be the priority because it "is already challenging enough since it's been more than a generation since we left low-Earth orbit." Moreover, he says, the moon "is a subject of interest to many non-traditional, potential partners, particularly in Asia, and thus the moon is likely to be the most acceptable common goal for international cooperation."

Lester, the University of Texas astronomer, suggests a compromise between a full-scale human mission to Mars

C H R O N O L O G Y

1950s-1960s *Space race with Soviet Union yields huge gains for NASA.*

1957 Soviet Union launches *Sputnik* satellites.

1958 NASA formed.

1961 Soviet cosmonaut becomes first human in space; U.S. astronaut Alan B. Shepard Jr. takes suborbital flight. . . . President John F. Kennedy sets landing an astronaut on the moon as a national goal.

1962 John Glenn becomes first American to orbit Earth.

1964 U.S. launches *Mariner 4*; returns 21 photos of Mars.

1969 *Mariner 6* and *7* Mars missions launched. . . . *Apollo 11* astronauts Neil Armstrong and Buzz Aldrin land on moon.

1970s-1980s *Apollo moon missions end; space shuttle program begins.*

1971 *Mariner 9* launched; returns 7,329 photos of Mars.

1972 Final U.S. moon landing occurs as NASA budget shrinks. . . . President Richard M. Nixon agrees to reusable space shuttle system. . . . *Landsat*, first Earth-observing satellite, launched.

1973 *Skylab* space station launched; three crews occupy it for 171 days and perform 300 experiments before it is allowed to disintegrate.

1975 *Viking 1* and *2* Mars orbiters and landers launched; together they return m ore than 50,000 photos of the planet.

1981 Space shuttle begins flying.

1984 President Ronald Reagan calls for a "permanently manned space station . . . within a decade."

1986 Shuttle *Challenger* explodes during liftoff, killing all seven astronauts, including teacher Christa McAuliffe.

1990s-Present *Private space industry emerges as shuttle program ends.*

1996 *Mars Global Surveyor* launched. . . . *Mars Pathfinder* lander and rover launched; they return more than 17,000 images, plus scientific information on Mars.

1998 Space station assembly begins.

2001 *Mars Odyssey* orbiter launched; conducts extended scientific mission.

2003 Space shuttle *Columbia* disintegrates during re-entry, killing all seven astronauts. . . . NASA launches Mars rovers *Spirit* and *Opportunity.*

2004 President George W. Bush proposes Mars mission. . . . Privately financed SpaceShipOne claims $10 million Ansari X Prize by making two successful trips into space.

2005 NASA establishes Constellation program. . . . NASA launches Mars reconnaissance orbiter.

2007 *Mars Phoenix* lander launched.

2009 President Obama orders review of human spaceflight program; panel says Constellation program is "not viable" because of budget restraints.

2010 Obama announces decision to cancel Constellation, use private industry to ferry U.S. crews to the space station after shuttle is retired. . . . Obama also says he wants to send astronauts to an asteroid by 2025 and Mars by 2030. . . . Congress opposes Constellation cancellation.

2011 Space shuttle ends. . . . Congress allows Obama administration to cancel Constellation except for Orion program to build craft to ferry astronauts into Earth and lunar orbit and possibly deep space. . . . NASA announces plan for new launch vehicle but destination remains uncertain. . . . China launches what it says is first component of an eventual space station, reaffirms plan for a manned lunar mission.

2012 Obama's $17.8 billion 2013 budget request for NASA would shift more funding to the new Webb Space Telescope, eliminate U.S. participation in two unmanned missions to Mars. . . . First commercial cargo flight to space station delayed until April.

Webb Telescope Reaches Uncertainly for the Heavens

Delays and funding fights cloud its development.

For nearly two decades, the Hubble Space Telescope has opened a window on the universe, providing startling images of planets, galaxies, quasars, and nebulae. Now, a far more powerful celestial observatory — the $12 billion James Webb Space Telescope — is in development. But whether, literally, it gets off the ground depends on a very down-to-Earth issue: money.

The telescope, named for a former NASA administrator and under development for most of the past decade, has encountered more than its share of problems. Work has taken much longer than expected because of technical problems, repeatedly delaying the launch date from the original 2014 to 2018, at the earliest. Moreover, the costs have skyrocketed, from an original budget of about $2.4 billion.[1]

The project, in development since 2004 with financial or technical support from 14 other countries, went through a near-death experience in 2011, after the powerful House Appropriations Committee voted in July to stop funding it.[2] The vote deeply distressed space scientists, who launched a broad campaign to save the Webb, including a letter to *The New York Times* signed by 32 Nobel laureates. They argued that canceling the program "would deal a fatal blow to large and ambitious space science missions for the foreseeable future and would deny the public access to new and exciting images of the type that have captured the imagination of people of all ages."[3]

The Webb had more support in the Senate, which voted $529.6 million for it in fiscal 2012 — about 42 percent more than President Obama had requested in his budget. The final NASA budget, approved by Congress in November, included the Senate-approved amount, thus guaranteeing at least another year for construction of the Webb.[4] Obama's fiscal 2013 budget requested $627 million and projected comparable funding for the following four years.[5]

Unlike Hubble, which has both optical and infrared cameras, the Webb will be an all-infrared telescope that will see even deeper and more sharply into the universe. Also important, according to its advocates, the Webb will cut through the clouds of dust that sometimes obscure Hubble's vision.[6]

While the Webb's development has been rocky, it doesn't compare — at least so far — with the Hubble Space Telescope's long road to celestial superstardom. When it was launched from the space shuttle *Discovery* in April 1990, Hubble was supposed to be a miracle instrument for astronomers: capable of peering deep into the universe where the vision of Earth-bound telescopes was distorted by gases and atmospheric particles.

The miracle quickly evaporated, however, because Hubble's 94.5-inch mirror turned out to be distorted and incapable of producing crisp images. Space shuttle astronauts began repairing the Hubble in 1993 and eventually fixed or replaced most of its equipment.[7]

The renovated Hubble has been even more productive than astronomers had hoped, generating thousands of images and other observations about the deep recesses of

and not going at all. Lester notes that robots and rovers have become increasingly sophisticated, but their movements still need to be controlled by scientists and technicians on Earth. In the case of rovers, it takes as long as 40 minutes between the time a human gives a command and it arrives at the equipment on Mars — a lag that reduces the amount of work both the human researcher and the rover can accomplish. "If I want to turn over a rock, it can take an hour. That is a major impediment to research," he says.

On the other hand, sending humans to the surface of Mars "would be really cruel," Lester says, because it would expose them to intense cosmic radiation and other danger. In addition, landing astronauts on a planetary object and getting them back to the spacecraft for the return trip constitute a significant share of the cost

the universe. Hubble has collected information about planets orbiting other stars and light that originated some 13 billion years ago, not long after what scientists believe was the genesis of the universe, the so-called Big Bang.[8]

The Hubble's original lifespan, planned to last 20 years, was extended by its many replacement parts. Even so, NASA says the Hubble will need to be replaced soon. Its technology is dated, and its parts are wearing out. That means an opening for the more powerful Webb — if, that is, it makes it into the heavens.

Jeff Foust, publisher of *The Space Review*, an online publication that covers space exploration, wrote in January that the budget battle over the Webb "may be one sign of a much bigger issue: that government willingness to fund big science projects may be waning."

Although top NASA officials have said they are committed to the Webb and other space science research, they have acknowledged that budget pressures will cause some cutbacks, Foust noted. For example, officials have said NASA will have to cut from other planetary science programs to provide enough money for Webb. Foust quoted Steven Weinberg, a Nobel laureate physicist at the University of Texas, as saying, "We may see in the next decade or so an end to the search for the laws of nature which will not be resumed again in our own lifetimes."[9]

— John Felton

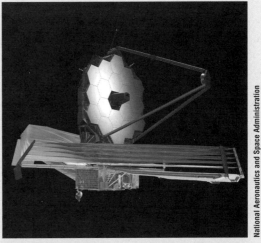

Launch of the $12 billion James Webb Space Telescope, shown in an artist's rendering, has been postponed from 2014 to 2018. It will replace the Hubble Space Telescope.

National Aeronautics and Space Administration

---

[1]Brian Verstag, "Budget fight rages over James Webb Space Telescope," *The Washington Post*, Oct. 26, 2011, www.washingtonpost.com/national/ health-science/budget-fight-rages-over-james-webb-space-telescope/2011/10/ 13/gIQALjYLKM_story.html.

[2]Dennis Overbye, "Panel Proposes Killing Webb Space Telescope," *The New York Times*, July 6, 2011, www.ny times.com/2011/07/07/science/07webb. html?_r=1&ref=hubblespacetelescope.

[3]"Keep the Webb Telescope, 32 Nobel Laureates Say," *The New York Times*, Aug. 26, 2011, www.nytimes.com/2011/08/27/opinion/

keep-the-webb-telescope-32-nobel-laureates-say.html?_r=1&ref=space&pagewanted=print.

[4]Denise Chow, "NASA's Webb Survives Funding Battle, But Challenges Remain," *Space News*, Jan. 23, 2012, www.spacenews.com/civil/nasa-webb-survives-funding-battle-but-challenges-remain.html.

[5]"Fiscal 2013 Budget Estimates," NASA, p. 12, www.nasa.gov/pdf/622655main_ FY13_NASA_Budget_Estimates.pdf.

[6]"Science on the Edge," WebbTelescope.org, http://webbtelescope.org/webb_ telescope/science_on_the_edge/.

[7]"Hubble Space Telescope," *The New York Times*, http://topics.nytimes.com/top/ news/science/topics/hubble_space_telescope/index.html.

[8]"Hubble Discoveries," Hubblesite, http://hubblesite.org/hubble_discoveries/.

[9]Jeff Foust, "Big science in an era of tight budgets," *The Space Review*, Jan. 16, 2012, www.thespacereview.com/article/2007/1.

(up to one-half by some estimates) and technical challenge of any human mission, he says.

As an alternative, Lester proposes that astronauts fly to Mars but only robots and rovers land on the surface. From orbit, the astronauts would control the machines, cutting to a minimum the lag time for sending and receiving instructions. "This would be the equivalent of putting human cognition on another world, but

without having humans actually being there and being in danger," Lester argues.

Is the space station worth the cost?

Over nearly 30 years, the United States, Russia, European Union, Japan and 10 other countries worked on the largest-ever global collaborative project in space: the International Space Station (ISS). At an estimated cost of

$100 billion (about half for modules and related equipment and half for travel to and from the orbiting station), the ISS has been both costly and controversial.

Supporters argue that the station is worth its cost because it promotes international collaboration, hosts sustained scientific research in a zero-gravity environment and allows scientists to examine the human-health effects of living for months in space.[30] But critics argue that these benefits are not worth the cost and that the money spent on the space station would be better spent on other space programs.

The ISS is the third long-term facility in space. U.S. *Skylab* was in service from 1973 until it was allowed to fall into the Indian Ocean in July 1979.[31] Russia's *Mir*, completed in 1996, remained in service until 2001 despite numerous problems. It was allowed to fall back into the atmosphere, where most of it disintegrated.[32]

The space station remains one of the single most costly items in NASA's budget: Congress appropriated $2.8 billion in the current fiscal year, about $500 million more than two years earlier.[33] Obama has proposed an increase to $3 billion for fiscal 2013. In addition, NASA is spending $406 million this fiscal year to help private companies develop systems to take cargo, and eventually human crews, to the space station, ending U.S. reliance on Russian spacecraft.[34]

The George W. Bush administration proposed to stop funding the station in 2016, just a few years after its completion. However, the Obama administration has called for keeping it in service at least until 2020 and possibly 2028.[35] Some components probably would need to be updated or replaced for the station to operate into the 2020s, MIT's Hoffman says.

The beginnings of a second space station already are in Earth orbit. Last Sept. 29, China launched the first module, known as *Tiangong-1*, for what it has said will be an unmanned space laboratory by "around" 2016 and a full-scale station "around" 2020. The Chinese government has offered few details about its plans, however.[36]

Glenn, the first American to orbit the Earth and the oldest person to fly in space — he flew on a shuttle mission at age 77 in 1998 — is an avid space station supporter.[37] "One of the things our country needs most is more innovation, more research, more of the new that has been the hallmark of this country," says Glenn, who served four terms as a Democratic U.S. senator from Ohio. "That's where the station fits in. It's the most unique laboratory ever put together, and I think we need that kind of research. We should be leading the world in that."

However, some space scientists are not convinced of the space station's research capabilities. The University of Texas' Lester lauds the "enormous success" of international collaboration that resulted in assembly of a large structure in space. But he says the station has been a disappointment in terms of scientific research. "We have never gotten enough science out of the space station, and it appears likely we never will," he says.

An even harsher assessment came from Nobel Prize-winning physicist Steven Weinberg, a university colleague of Lester. He told an American Astronomical Society conference in January that "the International Space Station was sold as a scientific laboratory, but nothing interesting has come from it."[38]

One of the primary justifications for the space station is its role as a platform for conducting research into the effects of long-term weightlessness on humans. Handberg, at the University of Central Florida, says "data on long-term endurance in space is absolutely necessary before we even think of going to places like Mars. We don't have that data yet."

But Zubrin of the Mars Society dismisses that role for the space station. "This idea of sending people to space to study the health effects of zero gravity is absurd," he says, comparing it to laboratory experiments on animals. "It would not pass a medical ethics test if someone proposed it here on Earth."

BACKGROUND

Obama's Course Change

The current — if highly uncertain — status of the U.S. human spaceflight program results from decisions made in the past eight years by President Obama and his predecessor, George W. Bush.

In 2004 Bush laid out what he called a "vision" for long-term human exploration of space, beginning with a return to the moon by 2020 and use of the moon as a base for a human expedition to Mars about a decade later.[39]

If Bush hoped his vision would capture the nation's imagination — as had President John F. Kennedy's ringing

1961 call to land a man on the moon and return him safely — he must have been disappointed, because neither the public nor Congress seemed overly excited by his pronouncement. Bush himself rarely mentioned his space vision afterward.[40]

Even so, NASA incorporated Bush's idea into a program called Project Constellation. The plan: build two new rockets to ferry astronauts to and from the space station following the end of the space shuttle, then use the technology to take humans well beyond Earth orbit. Congress endorsed Constellation in 2005 and 2008.[41]

But after taking office in 2009, Obama asked senior aerospace industry executives and space specialists to evaluate the Bush plan. In October 2009 they determined that it was "not viable" under the pared-back budget Obama had proposed.[42] With their conclusion in hand, Obama said in his fiscal 2011 budget, released in February 2010, that he had decided to cancel Constellation. Instead, he said NASA would contract with private industry to build new spacecraft to take astronauts and cargo to the space station after the shuttle program ended.[43]

In June 2010, Obama issued a new National Space Policy calling for the United States to build a new rocket and spacecraft that could take astronauts to a near-Earth asteroid by 2025 and then to Mars by the mid 2030s — skipping the moon altogether.[44]

Obama's decisions sparked huge controversy in Congress and among enthusiasts of human spaceflight, partly because of the shift from Bush's plan and partly because NASA already had spent billions of dollars on Constellation. Spudis, of the Lunar and Planetary Institute, charges that Obama "discarded the existing strategic direction, for which we had a hard-won bipartisan consensus, and replaced it with, literally, nothing."

Some in Congress also said private industry was not ready to build spacecraft that could substitute for the shuttle on missions to the ISS, as Obama proposed, and that relying on Russia to get to the space station was a mistake.

"Not only would we be turning our backs on 40 years of American space superiority, we would be giving up vital national security and economic interests to other nations that are eager to exploit this situation," Sen. Kay Bailey Hutchison, R-Texas, whose state includes the Johnson Space Center in Houston, told NASA officials in a February 2009 hearing.[45]

As a compromise, Congress in October 2010 passed a new authorization act that, in essence, told NASA to continue work on Constellation while adding the new elements Obama had proposed, including commercial flights to the space station. But the new law did not propose additional money.[46]

Finally, in one of a series of "continuing resolutions" that kept government appropriations flowing while Congress worked on regular spending bills, Congress in April 2011 allowed Obama to cancel Constellation, more than a year after he had proposed doing so.[47] In subsequent action, congressional committees have settled on an annual budget for new human spaceflight programs of about $3.7 billion — not enough for NASA to do all it wants to do, says Smith of *Space Policy Online*, which tracks NASA programs and spending. Obama's proposed budget for fiscal 2013 would continue about the same level of funding.

"Congress and the administration have reached an accommodation with each other on their different approaches," Smith says.

But that does not mean that congressional supporters of the space program, and of NASA in particular, are happy. Hutchison, for one, immediately denounced Obama's fiscal 2013 budget plan, saying it cut by "hundreds of millions of dollars" NASA's new rocket system and crew capsule.[48] The result of these proposals and congressional legislation is that NASA has moved on two tracks for human spaceflight, one intended to continue U.S. participation in the space station at least through 2020 and the other to build new systems to take humans deeper into space, including eventually to Mars and possibly even beyond.[49]

New Approaches

On the final space shuttle mission last July, the *Atlantis* delivered the last set of materials needed to finish construction of the space station, which had been under way since 1998. The $100 billion orbiting base has hosted human crews since November 2000 and has three major scientific laboratories, run by the United States, Japan and the European Space Agency.[50]

In addition to deliveries by the shuttles and European and Japanese cargo craft early in 2011, much of the space station's components, supplies and astronauts have been ferried by Russian *Soyuz* rockets, workhorses dating to the late 1960s.

Obama Seeks to Shift Funds to Webb Telescope

The Obama administration has requested a fiscal 2013 NASA budget of $17.71 billion, slightly less than the 2012 level. Obama proposes to spend about $5 billion on science missions, with an increase of more than $100 million on the James Webb Space Telescope, being built to replace the Hubble observatory, but less on planetary science projects. Spending would also increase for the International Space Station.

National Aeronautics and Space Administration Budget, FY2012-FY2013
(in $ millions)

	FY2012*	FY2013 (requested)
Science	**$5,073.7**	**$4,911.2**
Earth science	$1,760.5	$1,784.8
Planetary science	1,501.4	1,192.3
Astrophysics	672.7	659.4
James Webb Space Telescope	518.6	627.6
Heliophysics	620.5	647.0
Aeronautics	**569.4**	**551.5**
Space technology	**573.7**	**699.0**
Exploration	**3,712.8**	**3,932.8**
Exploration systems development	3,007.1	2,769.4
Commercial spaceflight	406.0	829.7
Exploration research and development	299.7	333.7
Space operations	**4,187.0**	**4,013.2**
Space shuttle	556.2	70.6
International Space Station	2,829.9	3,007.6
Space and flight support	800.9	935.0
Other	**3,653.4**	**3,603.7**
Total NASA Budget	**$17,770.0**	**$17,711.4**

* Figures for fiscal 2012 are estimates and may vary slightly from actual spending.
Source: "FY 2013 President's Budget Request Summary," National Aeronautics and Space Administration, 2012, www.nasa.gov/pdf/622655main_FY13_NASA_Budget_Estimates.pdf

The Obama administration's plan to continue relying on Russia for the next few years has been thrown into question in recent months, however. Concerns were raised last August when a *Soyuz* rocket carrying an unmanned cargo ship (called *Progress*) with three tons of food and fuel for the space station failed to achieve orbit and crashed in a Siberian forest.[51] Two *Soyuz* missions did reach the space station in September and December 2011, but a failed test of a *Soyuz* descent capsule in late January could delay the next cargo shipment to the station.[52]

Over the longer term, NASA plans for deliveries of supplies and humans to the space station to be handled by vehicles designed and built by private companies, under NASA contracts. The first commercial cargo deliveries, which have been postponed repeatedly, are expected to take place this year.

The other major part of the current U.S. plan for human spaceflight is development of a new launch vehicle and a spacecraft capable of carrying humans and cargo much deeper into space than ever before: to a near-Earth asteroid by 2025 and then Mars by 2030. This incorporates some aspects of Bush's Project Constellation and thus represents another part of a compromise between Obama (who wanted to cancel that project entirely) and Congress (which wanted to keep it going).

The launch vehicle, which NASA calls a Space Launch System, is intended to be the largest rocket built since the *Saturn V*, which delivered *Apollo* astronauts to the moon in the late 1960s and early '70s. Under pressure from Congress to move ahead with the program, NASA on Sept. 14 announced that it had selected a design for the booster rocket, which initially would be capable of lifting 70 to 100 metric tons into space. Eventually the rocket could handle 130 metric tons — the weight expected to be needed for a flight to and from Mars. NASA said the rocket's first test flight could be in 2017.[53]

Technical challenges aside, the biggest hurdle facing the new launch vehicle might be its price: A top NASA official estimated the initial development and construction cost at $3 billion a year for six years.[54]

Sitting atop that new rocket will be a new spacecraft, the *Orion Multi-Purpose Crew Vehicle*. The *Orion* will be similar to the *Apollo* spacecraft that took three astronauts into lunar orbit but will carry four crew members. The *Orion* is the one major component of Constellation that has survived relatively intact, although its mission has changed from Bush's plan for it to take crews to the space station and then to the moon; under Obama's plan, the *Orion* will ferry astronauts to an asteroid, which could be a launching pad for a later trip to Mars.[55]

However, some space advocates are unenthused by the prospect of a trip to an asteroid. "There are few to no asteroid targets that are both reachable and scientifically attractive," says Pace, at the Space Policy Institute at George Washington University.

"Mission Complete"

At dawn on July 21, 2011, the space shuttle *Atlantis* rolled to a stop at the Kennedy Space Center in Florida, and Capt. Christopher J. Ferguson, the shuttle's commander, immediately radioed to the Johnson Space Center halfway across the country: "Mission complete, Houston." It was the final mission, not just for *Atlantis* but for the famed, and often trouble-plagued, shuttle program, which for 30 years had represented America's once-vaunted commitment to sending humans into space but which Presidents Bush and Obama had both decided to end.[56]

The shuttle program was the compromise result of competing visions for U.S. space efforts after the end of the *Apollo* program in the early 1970s. Eventually, the shuttle ended up being a cargo workhorse with two main missions: taking into space the major components, and later the supplies for and occupants of, the space station; and repairing the Hubble telescope four times after design and production flaws hampered its usefulness.

The shuttles flew 135 missions, two of which remain seared into the nation's collective memory: the 1986 explosion of the *Challenger* shortly after liftoff, killing all seven astronauts on board, including school teacher Christa McAuliffe; and the 2003 break-up of the *Columbia* as it returned to Earth, also killing its seven astronauts.

Aside from those two tragedies and high-profile missions to repair the Hubble, most of the shuttle flights took place in relative obscurity. Shuttle astronauts, unlike their famed predecessors, were little-known to the public.

The space shuttle Enterprise served as the prototype for future shuttles. Though it never flew in space, it proved shuttles could fly in the atmosphere and land like a glider — without power. Now at the Smithsonian Institution's Udvar-Hazy Center in Northern Virginia, Enterprise will be moved to the Intrepid Sea, Air and Space Museum in New York City; another shuttle will take its place. Other shuttles are at space museums around the country.

The Economist magazine observed last summer that the shuttle eventually "made space travel seem routine, almost mundane — which helped to dampen public interest" in the space program.[57]

The shutdown of the shuttle program already has put about 7,000 people out of work, notably at the Kennedy Space Center in Florida.[58] Some advocates say they wish some way could have been found to keep the shuttles flying, if only as the one means for the United States to keep putting people into space until the next spacecraft are ready. "The shuttles were expensive, but I think that it was a mistake to not keep the shuttles going," says former astronaut Glenn.

The remaining space shuttles are being readied for their final resting places: not in space, but in museums. NASA administrator Bolden announced last April that the *Atlantis* would be displayed at the Kennedy Space Center in Florida; *Discovery* at the National Air and Space Museum's Steven F. Udvar-Hazy Center in Northern Virginia; the *Endeavor* at the California Science Center in Los Angeles; and a shuttle prototype, *Enterprise*, would be moved from the Udvar-Hazy Center (where it has been on display since 2003) to the Intrepid Sea, Air and Space Museum in New York City.[59]

Countdown for Private Spaceflight Has Begun

Space entrepreneurs include Virgin Galactic's Richard Branson.

Ever since the privately financed SpaceShipOne claimed the $10 million Ansari X Prize in 2004 by making two successful trips into space (but not into orbit) within two weeks, the once far-fetched idea of private space travel has seemed closer to reality than ever.[1]

Two companies claim to be almost ready to put rockets with passengers into space, possibly by the end of 2012. They would be the first private space flights since the prize-winning flights almost eight years earlier.

But private enterprise is not a new thing in space. Most of NASA's spacecraft have been built by commercial companies or, at least, assembled from parts produced commercially. Moreover, private companies have operated all of the U.S.-based commercial satellites that beam to Earth everything from weather observations to most of what appears on the Internet.

Now NASA and a handful of space entrepreneurs are betting that commercial uses of space are about to take off in much bigger ways — possibly just as government-run programs diminish because of budget cuts in Washington. In addition to satellites, two other private space enterprises are poised for launch. One is funded entirely by private investors and aimed at promoting travel to low-Earth orbit for those with Jupiter-size bank accounts; the other is more of a joint venture between NASA and private companies to promote the government's space endeavors.

Virgin Galactic, the brainchild of British entrepreneur Richard Branson, is using an updated version of *SpaceShipOne* (dubbed *SpaceShipTwo*). Branson plans to charge $200,000 for a flight 60 miles above the Earth that includes about three minutes of weightlessness. Also competing for space-tourism business are XCOR Aerospace of

Mojave, Calif., which hopes to begin flights with two customers each in 2013, and Space Adventures Ltd. of Vienna, Va., which is working with a Texas company to develop a pilotless spacecraft that can carry two passengers into space, briefly.[2]

Much more extensive involvement in space by private companies is likely to happen as a result of collaboration with NASA. The space agency already is working with private firms under two major programs intended to take supplies, and later, astronauts, to the International Space Station.

During the George W. Bush administration, in 2008, NASA awarded contracts, in a program called Commercial Orbital Transportation System, to two companies to deliver cargo to the space station after the shuttle program ended: Space Exploration Technologies (SpaceX) of Hawthorne, Calif., received a $1.6 billion contract for 12 cargo flights through 2016, and Orbital Sciences of Dulles, Va., won a $1.9 billion contract for eight supply flights.

Both companies have experienced repeated delays. The first commercial cargo flight to the space station by SpaceX's *Dragon* unmanned cargo capsule — originally scheduled for December 2011 — was first pushed back until February 2012, then in mid-January was delayed again until April for "additional work," according to a company spokeswoman.[3] Until SpaceX and Orbital can make regular cargo runs, NASA will continue using Russian *Soyuz* spacecraft to transport cargo and U.S. astronauts to the station.[4]

The Obama administration also has developed a separate program of paying private companies to develop new launch vehicles and spacecraft to deliver humans, as well as cargo, to the space station and into low-Earth orbit. NASA calls the program "commercial crew" and says the goal is to

Some museums that lost bids for the shuttles — and members of Congress and other politicians representing those locations — complained about Bolden's selections. But NASA's inspector general concluded last August that NASA followed proper procedures and had not been unduly influenced by political or other considerations.[60]

CURRENT SITUATION

Private Sector's New Role

The Obama administration plans to rely on private companies to handle routine missions, such as trips to the space station, leaving NASA to concentrate on more

have the spacecraft ready for flight by the middle of the decade. NASA's stated rationale for relying on commercial contractors is that spacecraft development will be cheaper if the government and private companies split the costs.[5]

Commercial crew has generated widespread opposition in Congress, where members in both parties worry about relying too much on profit-driven contractors. Appropriations committees in the House and Senate substantially trimmed the administration's $850 million request for the program in fiscal 2012, and in the end Congress approved only $406 million.[6] Eventually, says Marcia Smith, editor of *Space Policy Online*, which tracks space programs and spending, "If push comes to shove, Congress would probably keep money for NASA programs and drop the commercial crew component."

The commercial crew program also has generated controversy outside Congress, including from what might seem an unlikely source: Christopher Caldwell, a senior editor of the conservative *Weekly Standard*. Caldwell wrote in *The Financial Times* recently that private investors "need to be watched like hawks" when it comes to the use of tax dollars. "The public should remain vigilant . . . that these space entrepreneurs do not come to resemble the railroad-building industry in the time of the robber barons," he wrote.[7]

Meanwhile the first privately funded space station might also reach orbit in the next few years, according to American entrepreneur Robert Bigelow. He is developing lightweight components for an inflatable structure he says can be built in space at a fraction of the cost of the $100 billion International Space Station. The company's *Genesis I* and *Genesis II* spacecraft have been orbiting Earth since 2006 and 2007, giving Bigelow the data he says he needs to prove that a full-scale station is possible.[8]

Some supporters say Bigelow and other commercial entrepreneurs, rather than governments, might represent the best chance for the United States to return to and remain active in space — if not in the next few years, then in the decades to come. But other space enthusiasts are skeptical that private companies will ever represent more than a part of the nation's future in space.

PayPal co-founder Elon Musk unveils the *Falcon-9 Heavy* launch rocket developed by his firm, SpaceX.

Says Paul Spudis, senior staff scientist at the NASA-funded Lunar and Planetary Institute in Houston, "None of them have a positive cash flow from commercial customers yet, and it remains to be seen whether their markets develop or not."

— *John Felton*

[1]"Ansari X Prize," http://space.xprize.org/ansari-x-prize.

[2]Kenneth Chang, "Booking a Flight to Space With Travel Insurance," *The New York Times*, Jan. 3, 2012, www.nytimes.com/2012/01/04/science/space/spaceflights-prepare-to-expand-customer-base.html?ref=space.

[3]"SpaceX Postpones Station-bound Dragon Launch," *SpaceNews*, Jan. 16, 2012, www.spacenews.com/venture_space/011612-spacex-postpones-station-bound-dragon-launch.html.

[4]"NASA Commercial Partners: Cargo," www.nasa.gov/exploration/commercial/ cargo/index.html.

[5]"NASA Commercial Partners: Crew," www.nasa.gov/exploration/commercial/ crew/index.html.

[6]"NASA's FY2012 Budget Request and Final Action," *SpacePolicyOnline.com*, Jan. 11, 2012, Table 1, p. 2, www.spacepolicyonline.com/pages/images/stories/ NASA's%20FY2012%20Budget%20Request.pdf.

[7]Christopher Caldwell, "The folly of private space travel," *Financial Times*, Dec. 16, 2011, www.ft.com/cms/s/0/15aede0e-2713-11e1-b9ec-00144feabdc0. html#axzz1isZhCSIo.

[8]"Genesis I," Bigelow Aerospace, www.bigelowaerospace.com/genesis-1.php.

ambitious goals, such as manned and unmanned scientific missions to Mars and other deep-space destinations.

Private companies have long been significant actors in all aspects of the U.S. space program. Working under NASA contracts, hundreds of private firms have built launch vehicles and spacecraft and performed much of the necessary logistical work to put, and keep, objects and people in space.

The Obama administration has extended this traditional relationship between government and private industry to a new level. Building on a program started by the previous Bush administration, NASA under Obama

AFP/Getty Images

John Glenn, the first American to orbit Earth, receives a Congressional Gold Medal at the Capitol Rotunda on Nov. 16. The crew of the first moon landing, Neil Armstrong, Buzz Aldrin and Michael Collins, also were honored. "They will tell you that they are not heroes. Don't listen to them," said Senate Republican Leader Mitch McConnell. "America is only as strong as the citizens we produce, and here are four of the best."

is paying private companies — some with little experience — not only to build but also to operate vehicles that will carry cargo and, eventually, human crews to the ISS. Besides freeing up NASA for more ambitious projects, the administration hopes to reduce dependence on Russia for trips to the space station.

NASA's new relationship with private industry has two components:

• Under a program initiated by the Bush administration and known as the Commercial Orbital Transportation System, NASA has contracted with two companies to build rockets and spacecraft that will take food, fuel, scientific equipment and other supplies (but not people) to the space station. Space Exploration Technologies (SpaceX) of Hawthorne, Calif., has a $1.6 billion contract for 12 cargo flights through 2016;

Orbital Sciences of Dulles, Va. has a $1.9 billion contract for eight supply flights.[61] Both companies have experienced repeated delays, the most recent in January, when SpaceX postponed its first cargo flight to the space station. It also had postponed the flight from 2011 until Feb. 7, 2012. The company did not explain the delays but did set a new schedule of late April.[62]

• A program initiated by the Obama administration in 2010 called "commercial crew" will use private companies to send cargo and astronauts to the space station. NASA and the companies will share the cost of developing launch vehicles and spacecraft, and the companies will operate the flights under NASA contracts. The companies also can use the technologies they create for private commercial purposes.

Four companies are developing systems under the second of two rounds of NASA grants: the Boeing Corp., SpaceX, Sierra Nevada Corp. and Blue Origin (headed by Amazon.com founder Jeff Bezos). Representatives of the first three companies told a House subcommittee last October that they would be ready to launch their vehicles by 2015, but only if they receive what they called "adequate" funding from NASA. NASA's plan has been to pick two winners from among the four companies.[63]

Commercial crew has been highly controversial in Congress. Obama requested $850 million for the program in fiscal 2012, but lawmakers slashed that to $406 million. It remains uncertain how that cut will affect the program.[64] Obama has asked for $830 million for the program in fiscal 2013.[65]

"The irony is that you have a Democratic administration that wants to rely on private industry for a key element of the space program, while members of Congress, Republicans included, very much want this to be a government program," says Smith of *Space Policy Online*. She and others say most of the resistance has come from members of both parties who represent districts in states such as Alabama, Florida and Texas with large NASA installations or the facilities of other private contractors. "This about jobs and money, not about ideology," Smith says. Despite the congressional opposition, the administration's plan has won substantial support from within the space community. Last November, 23 retired astronauts asked Congress and the administration for full funding of Obama's request.[66] Among them was MIT's

Is the United States in danger of losing a space race to China?

YES
Paul D. Spudis
*Senior Staff Scientist, Lunar and
Planetary Institute*

Written for *CQ Researcher,* February 2012

Are we in a race back to the moon? Should we be? The Apollo program achieved not only its literal objective of landing a man on the moon (propaganda, soft power) but also its more abstract objective of intimidating our Soviet adversary (technical surprise, hard power) and thus played a key role in the end of the Cold War.

Its two follow-on programs, the space shuttle and space station, although fraught with technical issues, had significant success in pointing the way toward a new paradigm for space. That new path involves getting people and machines to satellite assets in space for construction, servicing, extension and repair.

We cannot access satellites now with people and machines because we do not have a transportation system that allows us freedom of movement in the space between Earth and the moon. Recent data from the moon show that it has not only near-permanent sunlight near the poles but also abundant water. This water would allow us to make fuel on the moon to power rockets. Such a system is the logical next step in both space security and commerce. A return to the moon for resource utilization thus contributes to national security and economic interests as well as scientific ones.

What societal paradigm shall prevail in the new space economy? What shall the organizing principle of society be in the new commerce of space resources: the rule of law or authoritarian oligarchy? An American win in this new race for space does not guarantee that free markets will prevail, but an American loss could ensure that free markets would never emerge on this new frontier.

In one of his early speeches defending the Apollo program, President John F. Kennedy laid out the reasons that America had to go the moon. Among the many ideas he articulated, one stood out. He said, "Whatever men shall undertake, free men must fully share."

We explore new frontiers not to establish an empire but to ensure that our political and economic worldview prevails — the system that has created the most freedom and the largest amount of new wealth in the hands of the greatest number of people in the history of the world.

By leading the world into space, we guarantee that space does not become the private domain of powers who view humanity as cogs in their ideological machine rather than as individuals to be valued and protected.

NO
Roger B. Handberg
*Professor of political science, University of
Central Florida*

Written for *CQ Researcher,* February 2012

China's ongoing advances in its space program have raised the question of whether the United States will become engaged in a space race similar to that which occurred in the 1960s.

That race began in 1961 when President John F. Kennedy announced that the United States would reach the lunar surface and return to Earth within the decade. The Apollo program was one fruit of that challenge, which the United States won in July 1969 when the Eagle landed on the moon with two crew members. To achieve that goal, the United States spent billions of dollars in a field of competition that had only come into existence in 1957 when the Soviet Union launched *Sputnik 1* into orbit.

Now, some say that China poses an equivalent challenge to the United States, meaning that a space race will be the logical outcome. I would suggest that the calls for a space race are overinflated because the conditions for such an endeavor do not presently exist.

First, China's rise to prominence has not been cast as a prelude to a weapons race in space; that occurred in the late 1950s when Nikita Khrushchev announced the Soviets would "bury" the United States. That threat was based on the Soviets' possession of nuclear weapons to which were added missiles to reach the United States. China's space program has been cast as a peaceful analogue to earlier American, European, Japanese and Russian/Soviet programs after the successful conclusion to the Apollo program. Weapons in outer space are often cited as a reason for a space race, but such weapons are not as useful as many think.

Second, China's space activities are tracking the earlier U.S.-Soviet space programs with no direct security threats. The Chinese, like the Americans, have a military space program, but that alone does not generate the political support for a space race. Instead, the Chinese are catching up because the United States finds manned space exploration a desired goal but not an overwhelming one into which billions must be poured in order to be first.

Third, human space-exploration efforts are becoming more international — an endeavor the Chinese at some point will join as full members based on their technological achievements and capabilities.

Putting humans in outer space remains a long-term process that crash projects do not in the end advance as readily as systematic efforts incorporating the world's talents most efficiently.

Hoffman, who says he sees the commercial crew concept as "one of the potentially most exciting things going. It might be a real game changer" for the space program. "If NASA could buy those services at a marginal cost, it would save a lot of money and allow NASA to concentrate its resources on exploration, where the private sector is not going to be involved."

NASA Budget

Except for politically sensitive items such as the commercial crew program, NASA escaped the 2011 congressional budget wars relatively unharmed. Of Obama's overall $18.5 billion request for the space agency, Congress approved $17.8 billion, with nearly all the $700 million cutback the result of resistance from the House of Representatives, where budget-cutting demands were most intense.

Two big hurdles face NASA in the near future, however. The first is Obama's fiscal 2013 budget, which proposed a small overall reduction to about $17.8 billion but kept most programs — except for the future Mars exploration missions that were to be conducted with the Europeans — relatively intact. Once again, the big battle in Congress could be over the "commercial crew" budget, which Congress has cut in each of the past two years, and the space launch vehicle and *Orion* crew capsule, both of which many in Congress want to fund at a higher level than Obama has proposed.

NASA also faces possible automatic budget cuts stemming from Congress's failure to deal effectively with budget issues in 2011. Up to $1.2 trillion in cuts in "discretionary" programs (which would include NASA) are to take effect in January 2013 unless Congress takes action this year to avert them.[67] NASA administrator Bolden told space advocates in December he was confident Congress would act.[68]

Scientific Missions

NASA currently has 94 active missions in space, and only one — the space station — is manned.[69] All the others are scientific endeavors using telescopes, X-ray observatories, robotic rovers and other pieces of scientific equipment.

Many of these missions orbit the Earth, sending back information intended to increase understanding of climate change, the oceans and other natural features. Most missions are exploring the solar system, from the moon

to Pluto, whose planetary status is still being debated. Other missions are focused on deep space well beyond the solar system, looking for information about how the universe was formed and whether other Earth-like planets might exist.

Among NASA's most notable current missions:

• In March 2011, NASA's *MESSENGER* (short for MErcury, Surface, Space ENvironment, GEochemistry and Ranging) became the first spacecraft to orbit Mercury, after a trip of more than six-and-a-half years covering 4.9 billion miles. The probe was scheduled to continue for one year, but in November NASA announced an extension until March 2013. *MESSENGER* is supposed to answer six questions about the smallest planet, including why it appears to be at least twice as dense as Earth and how it formed geologically.[70]

• The *New Horizons* spacecraft was launched in 2006 and will fly past Pluto and its moon, Charon, in July 2015. Last year the spacecraft sped by Uranus. It will be only the fifth spacecraft to travel so far from the sun and, NASA says, the first to come so close to a planet-like body at that distance. Its mission is to map and determine the composition of Pluto and Charon. After passing Pluto, the spacecraft will continue to the Kuiper Belt, the enormous collection of icy bodies (some nearly half the size of Earth's moon) that orbit just beyond Neptune, the most distant planet.[71]

• The *Cassini* spacecraft continues its observations of Saturn and its moons. It has sent back startling information that has altered much of what scientists thought they knew about the Saturnian system. Among *Cassini's* recent discoveries are the potential existence of an underground saltwater ocean on the moon Enceladus (suggesting that some form of life might be possible there) and seasonal "rain showers" of liquid methane that change the surface of the large moon Titan. *Cassini* was launched in 1997 and reached Saturn in 2004.[72]

• The mission known as GRAIL consists of twin spacecraft that were launched last September and reached lunar orbit Dec. 31, 2011, and Jan. 1 this year. During their planned 82-day mission, they are intended to conduct the most detailed study ever of the moon's surface and inner core. NASA scientists have said that understanding the makeup of the moon will provide information about how the Earth and other solid planets in the solar system were formed.[73] The spacecraft are named *Ebb* and *Flow*, based on entries from fourth-grade students in Bozeman, Mont.[74]

- *Juno*, launched last August, is scheduled to arrive at Jupiter in July 2016. The craft will orbit for 14 months, examining the giant planet's magnetic field, electrical and gas emissions and other features, including determining how much water is in the atmosphere. It is the most ambitious scientific mission to Jupiter since the highly successful *Galileo* probe, which orbited for nearly eight years, until September 2003.[75]

OUTLOOK

Leadership in Space

In the 1960s and '70s, the U.S. space program was driven as much by the Cold War rivalry with the Soviet Union as by the traditional American ambition to explore new frontiers. The Cold War ended two decades ago, however, eliminating that driving force and leading space advocates to search for new justifications for their ambitions. Into the foreseeable future, the nation's budget and long-term deficit problems could pose even greater hurdles to the space program than the technical obstacles that the Americans and Russians raced each other to overcome a half-century ago.

"Can this democracy continue to fly in space? I don't know that we can," says Handberg of the University of Central Florida. "It requires a long-term funding commitment, and there is no payoff except to say that we've been there, and given our budget problems the political support is not there for that type of commitment."

Some other observers are not quite so pessimistic. Smith of *Space Policy Online* notes that the space program faces little outright opposition on Capitol Hill or among the public at large. But even the optimists acknowledge that the space program will struggle to compete for increasingly scarce public dollars.

Smith recalls that the space program has gone through periods of retrenchment in the past, including after the end of the *Apollo* flights to the moon in the early 1970s, and managed to survive. Former NASA executive Pace and many of his counterparts point out that NASA's entire budget represents less than 0.5 percent of federal spending.

Spudis of the Lunar and Planetary Institute says "the idea that we cannot afford space is ludicrous. We could triple the NASA budget with no significant impact on the overall federal budget." Even so, the space program is one of the "discretionary" budget items that could be easier for Congress to cut than entitlement programs such as Medicare and Social Security. NASA's public support, Handberg says, "is a mile wide and an inch deep."

Privately funded spaceflight could represent at least part of the future in space, although few experts seem to believe it can take the place of government programs anytime soon. Even Hudgins, of the libertarian Atlas Society, acknowledges that without government contracts, space entrepreneurs Elon Musk, Jeff Bezos and others, for all their billions, will have trouble doing more than "tourism and honeymoon suites in space until they can figure out a way to make the economics work."

Many space advocates in the United States are paying attention to China, the up-and-coming superpower that is developing an ambitious program of space exploration — including the possibility of landing humans on the moon in the 2020s.[76] Spudis says China's ambitions should spur the United States not just to return to the moon but also to establish "the permanent presence of people on the moon."

Former astronaut Hoffman of MIT says he is not particularly concerned about China's space plans. "By the time China is ready to go to the moon," he says, "hopefully we will be doing more interesting things, and we can look back and say, 'Congratulations, and welcome to the moon.'"

Hoffman, however, says there is more reason to worry about what the Chinese military might be doing in space.[77] "China has clearly demonstrated that it will become a full space power, just like the United States and Russia, and that will include a military component. That has a lot of our military people concerned, as they should be."

NOTES

1. For background, see the following *CQ Researcher* reports: Thomas J. Billitteri, "Human Spaceflight," Oct. 16, 2009, pp. 861-884; David Masci, NASA's Future, May 23, 2003, pp. 473-496; Mary H. Cooper, "Space Program's Future," April 25, 1997,

pp. 361-384; and Richard L. Worsnop, "Mission to Mars: Benefits Vs. Costs," Oct. 1, 1969.

2. John Noble Wilford, "50 Years Later, Celebrating John Glenn's Feat," *The New York Times*, Feb. 13, 2012, www.nytimes.com/2012/ 02/14/science/ space/50-years-later-celebrating-john-glenns-great-feat.html?hpw. Glenn orbited the Earth three times on Feb. 20, 1962.

3. Kenneth Chang, "The Shuttle Ends Its Final Voyage and an Era in Space," *The New York Times*, July 21, 2011, www.nytimes.com/2011/ 07/22/science/space/ 22space-shuttle-atlantis. html?_r=1&ref=atlantis.

4. Marcia Smith, "Gingrich Wants Moon Base by 2020, Mars Colony, New Propulsion, Prizes-UPDATE," *SpacePolicyOnline*, Jan. 25, 2012, www .spacepolicyonline.com/news/gingrich-wants-moon-base-by-2020-mars-colony-new-propulsion-private-investment-UPDATE.

5. Charles Bolden, NASA administrator, Air Force Association Air & Space Conference and Tech Exposition, Washington, DC, Sept. 19, 2011, www .nasa.gov/pdf/593460main_Bolden_IAC.pdf.

6. "NASA's Odyssey Spacecraft Sets Exploration Record on Mars," Jet Propulsion Laboratory, Dec. 15, 2011, http://mars.jpl.nasa.gov/odyssey/ news/whatsnew/ index.cfm?FuseAction=Show News&NewsID=1091.

7. "NASA Launches Most Capable and Robust Rover To Mars," Jet Propulsion Laboratory, Nov. 26, 2011, http://mars.jpl.nasa.gov/news/ whatsnew/index.cfm? FuseAction=ShowNews&NewsID=1189.

8. Charles Bolden, Remarks at NASA fiscal 2013 budget presentation, Feb. 13, 2012, www.nasa. gov/ pdf/622812main_12_0213_Final_Bolden_ FY13_ Budget.pdf.

9. Sindya N. Bhanoo, "Kepler Finds More Planets Orbiting Two Stars," *The New York Times*, Jan. 11, 2012, www.nytimes.com/2012/01/17/ science/ scientists-find-more-planets-orbiting-two-stars .html?ref=space.

10. Dennis Overbye, "Astronomers Find Biggest Black Holes Yet," *The New York Times*, Dec. 5, 2011, www.nytimes.com/2011/12/06/ science/space/ astronomers-find-biggest-black-holes-yet.html?_ r=1&ref=hubblespacetelescope.

11. William H. Gerstenmaier, NASA associate administrator for human exploration and operations, statement to the House Subcommittee on Space and Aeronautics, Oct. 12, 2011.

12. Mars Exploration Program, Historical Log, Jet Propulsion Laboratory, http://mars.jpl.nasa. gov/ programmissions/missions/log/.

13. "Russia's Failed Mars Probe Crashes Into Pacific," *The New York Times*, Jan. 15, 2012, www. nytimes .com/2012/01/16/science/space/russias-phobos-grunt-mars-probe-crashes-into-pacific. html.

14. "Software glitch likely cause of Phobos-Grunt failure," *SpaceToday.net*, Jan. 20, 2012, www.spacetoday .net/Summary/5504.

15. Andrew Jacobs, "China's Space Program Bolstered by First Docking," *The New York Times*, Nov. 3, 2011, www.nytimes.com/2011/ 11/04/world/asia/ chinas-space-program-boosted-by-first-docking .html?ref=space&pagewanted= print.

16. "China's Space Activities in 2011, State Council Information Office of the People's Republic of China, December 2011, www.scio. gov.cn/zxbd/wz/201112/ t1073727.htm.

17. David Warmflash, "About Those Space Joyrides," *Air and Space*, Jan. 6, 2012, www.air spacemag.com/ space-exploration/About-Those-Space-Joyrides.html.

18. Jeff Foust, "Caution and optimism about the future of human spaceflight," *The Space Review.com*, Jan. 23, 2012, www.thespace review.com/article/2011/1.

19. "Majority Sees U.S. Leadership in Space as Essential," Pew Research Center, July 5, 2011, www.people-press.org/2011/07/05/majority-sees-u-s-leadership-in-space-as-essential/.

20. "NASA's FY2012 Budget Request and Final Action," *SpacePolicyOnline.com*, Jan. 11, 2012, Table 1, p. 2, www.spacepolicyonline.com/pages/ images/stories/ NASA's%20FY2012%20Budget %20Request.pdf.

21. "The Future of Human Spaceflight," Massachusetts Institute of Technology, Space, Policy, and Society Research Group, December 2008, http://web.mit .edu/mitsps.

22. NASA Authorization, fiscal years 2011-13 (PL 111-267), section 204.

23. "National Space Policy of the United States," The White House, June 28, 2010, p. 11, www. whitehouse .gov/sites/default/files/national_space_policy_6-28-10 .pdf.

24. Charles Bolden, "Remarks at NASA fiscal 2013 budget presentation," Feb. 13, 2012, www.nasa.gov/ pdf/622812main_12_0213_Final_Bolden_FY13_ Budget.pdf.

25. Pat Duggins, *Trailblazing Mars: Nasa's Next Giant Leap* (2010), p. 1.

26. "NASA Spacecraft Data Suggest Water Flowing on Mars," Mars Reconnaissance Orbiter, www.nasa.gov/ mission_pages/MRO/news/mro 20110804.html.

27. Robert Zubrin, *The Case for Mars* (2011).

28. Robert Zubin, "How We Can Fly to Mars in this Decade — And on the Cheap," *The Wall Street Journal*, May 14, 2011, http://online. wsj.com/article/SB1000 1424052748703730804576317493923993056 .html.

29. Buzz Aldrin, American Space Exploration Leadership — Why and How," *The Huffington Post*, Jan. 5, 2012, www.huffingtonpost.com/buzz-aldrin/american-space-exploration_b_118455 4.html.

30. Roger Handberg, "ISS Next: chasing humanity's future in space and the "next logical step," *The Space Review*, Dec. 19, 2011, www. thespacereview.com/ article/1993/1.

31. "Skylab Operations Summary, Kennedy Space Center, www-pao.ksc.nasa.gov/history/skylab/skylab-operations.htm.

32. Mir Space Station, NASA History, http://history .nasa.gov/SP-4225/mir/mir.htm.

33. "NASA's FY2012 Budget Request and Final Action," *op. cit.*

34. Marcia S. Smith, "Adequate Funding Key to Commercial Crew Timing," *Space Policy Online*, Oct. 27, 2011, www.spacepolicyonline. com/news/ adequate-funding-key-to-commercial-crew-timing.

35. Statement of William H. Gerstenmaier, *op. cit.*

36. "Tiangong-1 orbiter enters long-term operation management," Xinhua News, Nov. 19, 2011, http:// news.xinhuanet.com/english 2010/china/2011-11/19/c_131257600.htm.

37. STS 95, NASA, http://spaceflight.nasa.gov/ shuttle/ archives/sts-95/.

38. Jeff Foust, "Tough decisions ahead for planetary exploration," *The Space Review*, April 4, 2011.

39. President George W. Bush, "Remarks at the National Aeronautics and Space Administration," Jan. 14, 2004, www.gpo.gov:80/ fdsys/pkg/PPP-2004-book1/ pdf/PPP-2004-book1-doc-pg56.pdf.

40. Zachary Coile, "Bush's space vision finds few boosters: Costly proposal faces rebuff from GOP, Democrats," *San Francisco Chronicle*, Jan. 22, 2004, www.sfgate .com/cgi-bin/ article.cgi?f=/c/a/2004/01/22/MNGD64 F5M71.DTL.

41. "NASA's Project Constellation And The Future Of Human Spaceflight," *Space Policy Online*, May 24, 2011, www.spacepolicyonline. com/images/stories/ Constellation_Fact_Sheet_May_2011.pdf.

42. "Seeking a Human Spaceflight Program Worthy of a Great Nation," Review of Human Spaceflight Plans committee, Oct. 8, 2009, www1.nasa.gov/ pdf/396093main_HSF_Cmte_FinalReport.pdf.

43. "Launching a New Era in Space Exploration," Feb. 2, 2010, www.nasa.gov/pdf/421 063main_Joint_ Statement-2-1.pdf.

44. "National Space Policy," June 28, 2010, www .whitehouse.gov/sites/default/files/national_space_ policy_6-28-10.pdf.

45. Senator Kay Bailey Hutchison, "Challenges and Opportunities in the NASA FY 2011 Budget Proposal," Feb. 24, 1010, http://commerce.senate .gov/public/index.cfm?p=Hearings&Content Record_id=1fe8aef1-3b71-4380-921f-8283 11451d7e&Statement_id=f0457665-7571-4d01-977e-ad3367ce7d05&ContentType_id=14f995b9-dfa5-407a-9d35-56cc7152a7ed&Group_id=b06c 39af-e033-4cba-9221-de668ca1978a&Month Display=2&YearDisplay=2010.

46. Marcia S. Smith, "NASA's Project Constellation And The Future Of Human Spaceflight," *Space Policy Online*, May 24, 2011, www.spacepolicy online.com/free-fact-sheets-and-reports/nasas-project-constellation-and-the-future-of-human-spaceflight-a-spacepolicy online-com-fact-sheet.

47. "NASA's FY2012 Budget Request and Final Action," *op. cit.*

48. "Senator Hutchison To Work with Colleagues to Restore NASA Human Exploration Funding," Office of Senator Kay Bailey Hutchison, Feb. 13, 2012, http://hutchison. senate.gov/?p=press_release&id=975.

49. Doug Cooke, "Plans for Human Exploration Beyond Low Earth Orbit," NASA, March 4, 2011, www.nasa.gov/pdf/524774main_COOKE.pdf.

50. "NASA International Space Station Facts and Figures," www.nasa.gov/mission_pages/station/main/onthestation/facts_and_figures.html.

51. "Russian Rocket Set for Space Falls in Woods," *The New York Times*, Aug. 24, 2011, www.nytimes .com/2011/08/25/science/space/25space.html?_r=1&ref=space.

52. "Soyuz problem may delay next ISS mission," *Spacetoday.net*, Jan. 28, 2012, www.space today.net/.

53. "NASA Announces Design For New Deep Space Exploration System," NASA, Sept. 14, 2011, www .nasa.gov/exploration/systems/sls/sls1. html.

54. "NASA Unveils New Rocket Design," *The New York Times*, Sept. 13, 2011, www.nytimes. com/2011/09/15/science/space/15nasa.html?ref=nationalaeronauticsand spaceadministration& pagewanted=all.

55. "Orion MPCV," www.nasa.gov/exploration/ systems/mpcv/index.html.

56. "The Shuttle Ends Its Final Voyage and an Era in Space," *The New York Times*, July 21, 2011, www .nytimes.com/2011/07/22/science/ space/22space-shuttle-atlantis.html?ref=space.

57. "Into the Sunset," *The Economist*, July 2, 2011, p. 67.

58. Mike Schneider, "Space Coast feels ripple effect as 7,000 jobs are lost to the canceled space shuttle program," Associated Press, July 10, 2011, www.theday .com/article/20110710/OP03/307109983.

59. "NASA Announces New Homes For Shuttle Orbiters After Retirement," April 12, 2001, www. nasa.gov/home/hqnews/2011/apr/HQ_11-107_ Orbiter_Disposition.html.

60. "NASA Chose the Right Museums for Retired Space Shuttles, Report Finds," Space.com, Aug. 27, 2011, www.collectspace.com/news/ news-082711a.html.

61. "NASA Commercial Partners: Cargo," www. nasa .gov/exploration/commercial/cargo/index.html.

62. "SpaceX COTS launch delayed to late April," *Spacetoday.net*, Feb. 11, 2012, www. spacetoday.net/Summary/5529.

63. Marcia Smith, "Congressional Hearing Notes: NASA's Commercial Crew Development Program: Accomplishments and Challenges," *Space Policy Online*, Oct. 26, 2011, www.spacepolicy online.com/images/stories/Commercial_Crew_Hrg_Oct_26_2011.pdf.

64. "NASA's FY2012 Budget Request and Final Action," *op. cit.*

65. "Fiscal 2013 Budget Estimates," NASA, p. 19, www .nasa.gov/pdf/622655main_FY13_NASA_Budget_Estimates.pdf.

66. Group Letter To Congress and the Obama Administration Regarding NASA's Commercial Crew Program, SpaceRef.com, Nov. 8, 2011, www .spaceref.com/news/viewnews.html?id=1585.

67. Jennifer Steinhauer And Robert Pear, "The Deficit Deal That Wasn't: Hopes Are Dashed," *The New York Times*, Nov. 20 2011, www.ny times .com/2011/11/21/us/politics/deficit-deal-fell-apart-after-seeming-agreement.html?ref= politics#.

68. Marcia S. Smith, "Bolden: NASA Not Budgeting for Sequestration," *Space Policy Online*, Dec. 5, 2011, www.spacepolicyonline.com/news/ bolden-nasa-not-budgeting-for-sequestration.

69. Current Missions, NASA, www.nasa.gov/missions/current/index.html.

70. Mercury: the Key to Terrestrial Planet Evolution, NASA, http://messenger.jhuapl.edu/ why_mercury/index.html.

71. New Horizons: Mission to Pluto and the Kuiper Belt, NASA, http://pluto.jhuapl.edu/ mission/whereis_nh.php.

72. Cassini: Unlocking Saturn's Secrets, NASA, www .nasa.gov/mission_pages/cassini/main/ index.html.

73. GRAIL: Gravity Recovery and Interior Laboratory, NASA, www.nasa.gov/mission_pages/ grail/overview/index.html.

74. Montana Students Pick Winning Names for Moon Craft, NASA, www.nasa.gov/mission_ pages/grail/news/grail20120117.html.

75. Juno: Unlocking Jupiter's Mysteries, Jet Propulsion Laboratory, www.nasa.gov/mission_ pages/juno/main/index.html.

76. Edward Wong and Kenneth Chang, "Space Plan From China Broadens Challenge to U.S., *The New York Times*, Dec. 29, 2011, www.nytimes.com/2011/12/30/world/asia/china-unveils-ambitious-plan-to-explore-space.html?ref= space&pagewanted=all.

77. For background, see Konstantin Kakaes, "Weapons in Space," *CQ Global Researcher*, Aug. 16, 2011, pp. 395-420.

BIBLIOGRAPHY

Selected Sources

Books

Duggins, Pat, *Trailblazing Mars: NASA's Next Giant Leap*, University Press of Florida, 2010.
A veteran space journalist covers the history and potential of Mars missions.

Moltz, James Clay, *Asia's Space Race: National Motivations, Regional Rivalries and International Risks*, Columbia University Press, 2011.
An associate professor at the Naval Postgraduate School analyzes the forces driving space developments in China and other Asian nations.

Pelton, Joseph N., and Angelia P. Bukley (eds.), *The Farthest Shore: A 21st Century Guide to Space*, Collector's Guide Publishing, 2010.
The detailed reference work features essays by scientists, astronauts and other experts on topics dealing with space and spaceflight.

Seedhouse, Erik, *The New Space Race: China vs. USA*, Springer Praxis Books, 2010.
An aerospace scientist examines China's intentions in space.

Zubrin, Robert, *The Case for Mars: The Plan to Settle the Red Planet and Why We Must*, Free Press, 2011 (2nd ed.).
The founder of the Mars Society advocates an all-out U.S. effort to put humans on Mars.

Articles

"Into the sunset: The final launch of the space shuttle brings to an end the dreams of the Apollo era," *The Economist*, July 2, 2011, pp. 66-68.
The British journal insightfully analyzes what the end of the shuttle program means for the U.S. space program.

"Space 2012: What's Ahead," *The Daily Planet blog, Air & Space*, Dec. 29, 2011, http://blogs.airspacemag.com/daily-planet/2011/12/space-2012-what's-ahead/.
The list of likely or possible space events in 2012 includes the reassuring news that "the world won't end" during the year.

Broad, William J., "With the Shuttle Program Ending, Fears of Decline at NASA," *The New York Times*, July 3, 2011, www.nytimes.com/2011/07/04/science/space/04nasa.html?_r=1&ref=space.
The report details concerns about the future of spaceflight.

Foust, Jeff, "Caution and optimism about human spaceflight?," *The Space Review*, Jan. 23, 2012, www.thespacereview.com/article/2011/1.
An aerospace analyst examines the challenges facing the U.S. human spaceflight program.

Handberg, Roger, "American human spaceflight and future options, short- and long-term," *The Space Review*, Nov. 21, 2011, www.thespacereview.com/article/1974/1.
A longtime observer of the space program puts NASA's current challenges into historical and political context.

Reports and Studies

"America's Future in Space: Aligning the Civil Space Program with National Needs," National Research Council, 2009, www.nap.edu/catalog.php?record_id=12701.
Experts on space conclude that the U.S. civilian space program is "a national imperative today, and will continue to grow in importance in the future."

"Recapturing a Future for Space Exploration: Life and Physical Sciences Research for a New Era," National Research Council, 2011, www.nap.edu/catalog.php?record_id=13048.
Scientists in biology and other life sciences set out their priorities for space exploration in the coming decade.

"The Scientific Context for Exploration of the Moon: Final Report," National Research Council, 2007, www.nap.edu/cata log/11954.html.
Top lunar scientists analyzes what can be learned, and what might not be, from more extensive exploration of the Moon.

Ansdell, M., L. Delgado, and D. Hendrickson, "Analyzing the Development Paths of Emerging Spacefaring Nations," Capstone Research, April 2011, www.gwu.edu/~spi/assets/ docs/Ansdell_Delgado_Hendrickson.pdf.
Researchers examine the opportunities and challenges facing a wide variety of nations that are developing space programs.

Pace, Scott, and Giuseppe Reibaldi, eds., "Future Human Spaceflight: The Need for International Cooperation," International Academy of Astronautics, 2010.
"Human space exploration can and should be guided by questions that promote international collaboration and cooperation," the editors write.

For More Information

Mars Society, 11111 West 8th Ave., Unit A, Lakewood, CO 80215; 303-980-0890; www.marssociety.org/home. Advocates human and robotic exploration of the red planet.

NASA, Public Communications Office, NASA Headquarters, Suite 5K39, Washington, DC 20546-0001; 202-358-0001; www.nasa.gov. Conducts human and scientific exploration and aeronautical research.

National Space Society, 1155 15th St., N.W., Suite 500, Washington, DC 20005; 202-429-1600; www.nss.org/. Advocacy group that promotes the United States as a "space-faring civilization."

The Planetary Society, 65 N. Catalina Ave., Pasadena, CA 91106-2301; 626-793-5100; www.planetary.org. Advocacy group for space exploration.

Space and Technology Policy Group, LLC, 2503D N. Harrison St., Arlington, VA 22207; 571-286-9168; www .spacepolicyonline.com. Provides news, information and analysis about space program policy, international space activities and space law.

The Space Review, www.thespacereview.com. Website that publishes analysis and commentary pieces about space and space programs globally.

6

Financial Misconduct

Kenneth Jost

Angelo Mozilo, founder of Countrywide Financial Corp., testifies before a congressional committee in 2008. The next year the Securities and Exchange Commission charged Mozilo with securities fraud and insider trading for selling off his Countrywide stock despite his worries about the quality of subprime loans Countrywide had helped create and popularize. In 2010, Mozilo agreed to pay a $67.5 million fine and never again serve as a director or officer of a publicly traded company.

From *CQ Researcher*,
Jan. 20, 2012

The Securities and Exchange Commission (SEC) exuded confidence last fall when it announced a $285 million settlement with the financial conglomerate Citigroup for misleading investors about a $1 billion package of toxic mortgages sold in early 2007.

In its 25-page complaint filed Oct. 19, the federal agency depicted Citigroup as hatching a devious scheme to offload around $500 million of subprime mortgages to institutional investors without disclosing that Citi would be betting that the package would go bust.

Which it did. The investors — hedge funds and others — lost "several hundred millions of dollars" when the package defaulted in November 2007, according to the SEC. But Citigroup pocketed $160 million in profits by selling the mortgages with the expectation they would plunge in value — along with the original $34 million management fee for structuring and marketing the package.

The SEC had successfully brought similar securities-fraud complaints within the past 15 months against two other Wall Street giants: Goldman Sachs and JP Morgan Chase. The allegations underscored one dark side of the housing-market bust that led to the financial crisis of 2008. Big financial firms trading in securitized mortgages tried to profit or shield themselves from losses by concealing their own fears that many of the mortgages were likely to default.

Some news accounts, however, noted one potential stumbling block for the SEC's enforcement action against Citigroup. The case had been assigned to a federal judge in New York, Jed Rakoff, who — *The New York Times* pointed out — had previously "taken a hard line on SEC settlements." In February 2010, Rakoff had approved a $150 million settlement the agency negotiated with

AFP/Getty Images/Tim Sloan

SEC Targets Insider Trading

The Securities and Exchange Commission has brought more than 500 insider-trading cases against individuals and entities over the past 10 years, including 57 in fiscal 2011. Defendants include hedge fund managers, corporate insiders, attorneys and government employees who allegedly traded securities on nonpublic information.

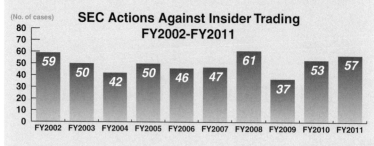

(No. of cases)
SEC Actions Against Insider Trading FY2002-FY2011

FY2002: 59, FY2003: 50, FY2004: 42, FY2005: 50, FY2006: 46, FY2007: 47, FY2008: 61, FY2009: 37, FY2010: 53, FY2011: 57

Source: "Year-by-Year SEC Enforcement Actions," Securities and Exchange Commission, www.sec.gov/news/newsroom/images/enfstats.pdf

Bank of America for inadequate disclosure about the details of its acquisition of the former investment firm Merrill Lynch, but only after criticizing the deal as "half-baked justice at best."

The caveat proved to be prophetic. On Nov. 28, Rakoff stunned the SEC and Citigroup alike by refusing to sign off on the accord. In a 15-page decision, Rakoff blasted the agency for allowing Citigroup to resolve the complaint without admitting allegations that, the judge added, had been inadequately laid out. The settlement was "pocket change" for Citigroup, Rakoff said, while the agency was seeking only "a quick headline" instead of fulfilling its "statutory mission to see that the truth emerges."[1]

Rakoff's rebuff to one of the key federal agencies charged with protecting the public from financial misconduct came just six days before a nationally televised news program blasted the U.S. Justice Department for failing to prosecute high-level executives responsible for the financial crisis. The CBS program "60 Minutes" showcased would-be whistleblowers from Citigroup and Countrywide Financial, the nation's largest mortgage lender until its collapse in 2008. Former Countrywide executive Eileen Foster and former Citigroup vice president Richard Bowen told correspondent Steve Kroft that the Justice Department had shown no interest in hearing their accusations.[2]

The unrelated episodes exemplify a sentiment widely shared by the public that the financial crisis stemmed at least in part from violations of the law and that the government has failed to bring the wrongdoers to justice. "We know there are insiders within the companies who say there is strong evidence that the companies committed criminal wrongdoing that should have warranted prolonged investigations and that should have resulted in actions by now," says Russell Mokhiber, editor of *Corporate Crime Reporter*, a Washington, D.C.-based newsweekly founded in 1987. "And we have no actions."

The SEC and Justice Department both reject the criticism. The SEC has brought charges against 87 companies and individuals stemming from the financial crisis, including 39 CEOs, chief financial officers or other senior officers. The agency, which can bring civil but not criminal charges, said financial penalties and "other monetary recovery" in the actions total nearly $2 billion.[3]

In the "60 Minutes" program, Assistant Attorney General Lanny Breuer, who heads the department's Criminal Division, insisted the government was pursuing investigations without any outside interference, but noted the difficulties of making a criminal case.

"I find the excessive risk-taking to be offensive," Breuer said. "I find the greed that was manifested by certain people to be very upsetting. But because I may have an emotional reaction and I may personally share the same frustration that American people all over the country are feeling, that in and of itself doesn't mean we bring a criminal case."[4]

Legal experts acknowledge some of the difficulties of bringing criminal prosecutions in cases based on complex and arcane financial transactions. Indeed, the government suffered a black eye in its most high-level prosecution when a federal jury acquitted two hedge fund managers at the defunct investment firm Bear Stearns of obstructing justice in November 2009.

Still, many experts agree with the public perception that the government could and should do more. "They aren't bringing as many cases against public firms for [misleading] financial statements as they could," says Jennifer Arlen, a securities law expert at New York University Law

School. "And they haven't been as aggressive in going against senior individuals as they could."

William Black, an associate professor of economics and law at the University of Missouri-Kansas City and a former federal regulator, strongly seconds Rakoff's criticism of the SEC practice of allowing defendants to settle complaints without admitting wrongdoing. "When something doesn't work and doesn't work profoundly, you really should reconsider," says Black, who worked with the former Office of Thrift Supervision in cleaning up the savings and loan crisis of the 1980s. "And the SEC hasn't worked for a very long time."

Some experts, however, dispute the widespread assumption that criminal conduct was at the heart of the financial crisis. "People think that because there's a scandal that people ought to go to jail," says Thomas Gorman, a Washington lawyer who publishes a blog on SEC litigation. "That's not necessarily true."

The SEC has helped win prison sentences for some Wall Street figures by referring insider-trading cases to the Justice Department for prosecution. Most notably, Raj Rajaratnam, the head of the Galleon Group hedge fund, was sentenced to 11 years in prison in October for orchestrating a large insider-trading scheme at Galleon over a six-year period. Rajat Gupta, a prominent Wall Streeter formerly at Goldman Sachs, was indicted later that month for tipping off Rajaratnam to valuable inside information about corporate deals.

In the latest insider-trading case, the U.S. attorney's office in Manhattan announced charges on Jan. 18 against a prominent hedge fund manager and six others in a scheme that allegedly netted nearly $62 million in illicit profits in 2008 and 2009 — rivaling the $70 million-plus in illicit gains that Rajaratnam was alleged to have realized. Anthony Chiason, co-founder of Level Global Investors LP, was charged along with others in a plot that allegedly used inside information from a paid tipster at Dell, the big computer maker, to trade in Dell stock. The tipster and two others pleaded guilty and were cooperating with authorities, the U.S. attorney's office said.[5]

Financial Crisis Sparks SEC Charges

The Securities and Exchange Commission has charged 87 entities and individuals — including 45 CEOs or other senior corporate officers — with financial misconduct in connection with the financial crisis that began in 2008. Penalties and other monetary relief total nearly $2 billion.

SEC Enforcement Actions Related to Financial Crisis*	
Number of entities and individuals charged	87
Number of CEOs, CFOs and other senior corporate officers charged	45
Total penalties, disgorgement and other monetary relief	$1.97 billion

* As of Dec. 16, 2011

Source: "SEC Enforcement Actions Addressing Misconduct That Led to or Arose From the Financial Crisis," Securities and Exchange Commission, December 2011, www.sec.gov/spotlight/enf-actions-fc.shtml

Apart from the insider-trading cases, however, the only prominent Wall Street figure to be prosecuted successfully since the financial crisis hit is Bernard Madoff, who is now serving a 150-year prison sentence for turning his wealth-management business into a Ponzi scheme that cost investors $18 billion or more. Madoff's prosecution brought no kudos to the SEC, however. A report by the SEC's inspector general showed the agency failed to detect Madoff's crimes despite a succession of ever-more-detailed tips going as far back as 1992.

Madoff's offenses were tangential, however, to the financial crisis. To date, no prominent executive who played a central role in the events leading up to the crisis has been prosecuted. The SEC did file civil complaints in December, however, against the former chief executives and four other top managers of the two government-sponsored mortgage lenders: Fannie Mae and Freddie Mac. The complaint, announced on Dec. 17, charges the executives with misleading investors about the extent of subprime mortgages in their portfolios.

The SEC is appealing Rakoff's rejection of its proposed Citigroup settlement, but at the same time somewhat revising its policy of allowing defendants to avoid admitting wrongdoing in resolving civil complaints. Under a new policy announced Jan. 6, the SEC will not allow a defendant to stand mute on the substance of a

Madoff Eluded SEC for 16 Years

Despite tips, agency failed to halt $18 billion Ponzi scheme.

The Securities and Exchange Commission (SEC) got its first tip about something fishy in Bernard Madoff's investment operations in 1992. The next, very detailed tip came in 2000, followed by four more reports before Madoff sons' accusations against their father in December 2008 finally got the agency to stop what appears to have been the largest Ponzi scheme in U.S. history.*

The missed opportunities to stop a scheme that bilked investors out of $18 billion in cash — and higher amounts in claimed but nonexistent profits — are catalogued in a damning report issued in late August 2009 by the SEC's inspector general. SEC investigators repeatedly failed to grasp the significance of tipsters' information, according to the 450-page report, and never took some rudimentary steps that could have verified the suspicions.[1]

Two years later, the agency confirmed on Nov. 11 that it had disciplined eight employees for mishandling the investigation, but fired no one. A ninth employee resigned before disciplinary action could be taken, according to *The Washington Post*'s account. Victims of Madoff's fraud denounced the disciplinary steps as inadequate.[2]

Madoff, now 73, is serving a 150-year sentence in a federal prison in North Carolina even as a court-appointed trustee seeks to recover and return to victims some of the misappropriated funds. As of December, an estimated $11 billion had been recovered.[3]

The inspector general's report clears the SEC of any conflicts of interest or inappropriate interference in the investigations but ends with an understated critique of the agency's thoroughly botched response to tips it received.

"The SEC never properly examined or investigated Madoff's trading and never took the necessary, but basic,

steps to determine if Madoff was operating a Ponzi scheme," the report states. "Had these efforts been made with appropriate follow-up at any time beginning in June 1992 until December 2008, the SEC could have uncovered the Ponzi scheme well before Madoff confessed."

The report prompted sharp criticism of the agency from members of Congress from both parties. Sen. Charles E. Schumer, D-N.Y., said the report showed "a level of incompetence unseen since [the Federal Emergency Management Agency's] handling of Hurricane Katrina." Sen. Charles Grassley, R-Iowa, said the agency's "utter failure" to follow up on the tips was "further evidence of a culture of deference toward the Wall Street elite."[4]

"The SEC was properly chastised," says Thomas Gorman, a Washington lawyer who publishes a blog on SEC litigation. "They had multiple opportunities to find that case. They simply failed to analyze the information."

Jennifer Arlen, a securities law professor at New York University, is more sympathetic to the agency's investigators' difficulties in dealing with what she calls "huge numbers" of tips" of varying quality and credibility. "They're making tradeoffs between, 'Here are these things that I know something wrong's going on,' and 'Here's something big but it could be something or it could be nothing.' "

The first of the tips against Madoff came in June 1992 from customers of an investment firm suspicious that the firm was claiming "100%" safe investments with "extremely high and consistent" rates of return. The firm's investments, it turned out, were managed exclusively by Madoff. "Inexperienced" investigators suspected a Ponzi scheme, the inspector general's report states, but failed to conduct a thorough investigation.

Eight years later, the SEC received the first of three detailed complaints about Madoff from Harvey Markopolos, a securities executive-turned-independent financial fraud investigator in Boston. Markopolos' reports grew from an eight-page complaint in May 2000 to a longer version in October 2005 with the headline, "The World's Largest Hedge Fund Is a Fraud."

---

* A Ponzi scheme, named after the early 20th-century swindler Charles Ponzi, is a fraudulent investment operation in which investors are paid gains from money deposited by new investors. The schemes typically collapse when new investors cannot be recruited or a large number of investors try to cash out all at once.

civil complaint if it already has admitted wrongdoing in a related criminal case.[6]

Meanwhile, the nation's biggest banks are squared off with attorneys general from all 50 states over legal

remedies for allegedly having used improper procedures to evict delinquent borrowers from their homes as the financial crisis deepened. The banks had been close to an agreement last summer, calling for a $20 billion

In each report, Markopolos said he had attempted but failed to replicate Madoff's claimed returns based on Madoff's reports of his investment strategy. Markopolos has forcefully criticized the agency in interviews and in his first-person account, *No One Would Listen*, published in 2010.[5]

By the third of his reports, Markopolos was being taken seriously by SEC investigators, according to the inspector general's report. They focused, however, more on the question of whether Madoff needed to register as an investment adviser than on whether he was operating a Ponzi scheme as Markopolos believed.

In addition, the report states, SEC investigators failed to take the basic step of attempting to verify through third parties whether Madoff actually was making the trades that he said he was making. "A simple inquiry . . . could have immediately revealed the fact that Madoff was not trading in the volume he was claiming," the report states.

Other complaints came to the SEC from "a respected hedge fund manager," an anonymous informant and a "concerned citizen," who first contacted the agency in December 2006 and again in March 2008. The last communication included the damning detail — later confirmed — that Madoff kept two sets of records, "the most interesting of which is on his computer which is always on his person."

Even when SEC investigators began probing his operations, Madoff, the one-time chairman of the NASDAQ stock exchange, fended them off in an interview, according to the report, by lording his credentials and knowledge over the less experienced agency personnel. Supervisors closed the investigation in January 2008 and declined to reopen it after receiving the report about double sets of books two months later.

Madoff's scheme finally unraveled when he confessed in December 2008 to his sons, Andrew and Mark, who reported him to federal authorities. Madoff was arrested on Dec. 10; he pleaded guilty on March 12, 2009, to 14 federal felonies, including securities fraud. In court, Madoff said he began his Ponzi scheme in 1991. Judge Denny Chin sentenced him three months later.

Madoff has apologized for his conduct, but his son Andrew has said he will never forgive his father. Mark

Bernard Madoff, once a prince of Wall Street, pleaded guilty to running a Ponzi scheme that bilked investors out of $18 billion. He is serving a 150-year prison sentence.

Madoff committed suicide by hanging himself in his Manhattan apartment. He was found dead on Dec. 11, 2010, two years to the day after his father's arrest.

— *Kenneth Jost*

[1]"Investigation of Failure of SEC to Uncover Bernard Madoff's Ponzi Scheme — Public Version," U.S. Securities and Exchange Commission's Office of Investigations, Aug. 31, 2009, www.sec.gov/news/studies/2009/oig-509.pdf. The executive summary is found at pp. 20-41. For coverage, see David Stout, "Report Details How Madoff's Web Ensnared S.E.C.," *The New York Times*, Sept. 3, 2009, p. B1; Zachary A. Goldfarb, "The Madoff Files: A Chronicle of SEC Failure," *The Washington Post*, Sept. 3, 2009, p. A1.

[2]See David S. Hilzenrath, "SEC disciplines 8 employees for Madoff failures," *The Washington Post*, Nov. 12, 2011, p. A1; "SEC's disciplinary steps in Madoff case enrage fraud victims," *The Washington Post*, Nov. 17, 2011, p. A17.

[3]See Diana B. Henriques, "A Lasting Shadow," *The New York Times*, Dec. 12, 2011, Business, p. 1.

[4]See Sean Lengell, "Schumer: Boost SEC's budget to fight fraud," *The Washington Times*, Sept. 4, 2009, p. 9; Marcy Gordon, "SEC bungled Madoff probes, agency watchdog says," The Associated Press, Sept. 3, 2009.

[5]Harry Markopolos with Frank Case, Neil Chelo, Gaytri Kachroo, and Michael Ocrant, *No One Would Listen: A True Financial Thriller* (2010).

settlement, but some states balked at their demand to be shielded from any further liability.

Another federal agency also is entering the field of policing financial misconduct with President Obama's appointment of a director for the newly established Consumer Financial Protection Board (CFPB). Obama named former Ohio Attorney General Richard Cordray to head the new agency on Jan. 4, using his power to make a recess appointment after Senate Republicans had stalled action on the nomination. GOP senators disputed the move, saying the Senate was technically in session. The legal wrangling masks a bigger issue, however, about whether the agency's powers to regulate non-bank financial institutions — such as payday lenders — will actually benefit consumers.

As the various legal proceedings continue, here are some of the questions being debated:

Was illegal conduct a major cause of the financial crisis?

Ralph Cioffi and Matthew Tannin were pulling down seven-figure salaries for managing hedge funds for the Wall Street firm Bear Stearns until the funds, heavily invested in mortgage securities, went belly up in July 2007. Federal prosecutors charged the two with securities fraud in June 2008, alleging that they knowingly misled investors about the funds' exposure to potentially toxic assets.

Cioffi and Tannin defended themselves in a three-week trial in fall 2009 by contending that they and their funds were victims of an unforeseeable market meltdown. Federal court jurors apparently agreed, finding the pair not guilty after barely six hours' deliberation. Columbia University securities law expert John Coffee called the result "a total rebuff to the prosecution."[7]

The too-clever-by-half financial deals that came crashing down in the summer and fall of 2008 naturally led many of the victims — investors left holding the bag, homeowners stuck with underwater mortgages — to assume that laws had been violated. But experts and financial-crisis watchers from President Obama down caution that illegal conduct was not necessarily to blame.

Answering a question at a press conference on Oct. 6 about the lack of major prosecutions, Obama replied: "One of the biggest problems about the collapse of Lehmans" —a reference to the investment bank Lehman Brothers, which declared bankruptcy in September 2008 —"and the subsequent financial crisis and the whole subprime lending fiasco is that a lot of that stuff wasn't necessarily illegal, it was just immoral or inappropriate or reckless."[8]

Assessing the verdict in the Bear Stearns case, financial journalists Bethany McLean and Joe Nocera voiced a similar view. "Much of what took place during the crisis was immoral, unjust, craven, delusional behavior—but

it wasn't criminal," McLean and Nocera write in their book, *All the Devils Are Here.*[9]

Other experts, however, are less inclined to give a legal pass to the companies and individuals whose actions helped topple respected Wall Street firms, forced the government to bail out the nation's biggest banks, caused millions of homeowners to lose their homes and left hundreds of thousands of others owing more than their homes were worth.

"Accounting-control frauds drove this financial crisis, as they did the two prior financial crises: the Enron era fraud [of the early 2000s] and the S&L debacle," says Black, the former regulator from the S&L crisis. "What caused the crisis was overwhelmingly garden-variety fraud, which can and should be prosecuted."

Fraud was widely seen as a major factor in the 1980s S&L crisis, but the extent to which fraud caused the collapse of so many thrift institutions defies simple calculation. Early on, the government suggested that fraud was a factor in 70 to 80 percent of the thrift failures. But a study by the Resolution Trust Corporation, the government-owned company organized to manage the assets of the failed thrifts, estimated more conservatively that fraud played a significant role in the failure of about a third of the institutions. Officials estimated that fraud was to blame for about 10 percent to 15 percent of net losses from the crisis.[10]

Any firm conclusion about how much fraud or other illegal conduct was to blame for the latest financial crisis is years away. For now, Arlen, the New York University professor, acknowledges uncertainty. "It does seem to me clear that there were disclosure problems," Arlen says, "but I'm not yet in a position to know whether the problems relate to judgment calls that are inherently part of the accounting profession or to actual fudging."

Lawyers who defend white-collar-crime cases voice doubts about the extent of fraud in the recent events. "In most of these cases, I don't see fraud," says David Douglass, a Washington lawyer and chair of the government enforcement and compliance committee of the defense bar organization DRI. "In most of these cases, I see why people would be unhappy with the results, but it's not fraud."

"You're talking about companies taking huge risks, companies being hugely leveraged," says Gorman, the lawyer with the securities litigation blog. "You might categorize that as reckless mismanagement or breach of fiduciary duty, but it's not criminal."

Even years from now, any assessment of the issue may be elusive, in part because of the difficulties of proving fraud or financial wrongdoing in court. "It is enormously problematic for prosecutors to prove beyond a reasonable doubt that the executives of a company acted with fraudulent intent," says Michael Perino, a professor at St. John's University School of Law in Jamaica, N.Y., and a former Wall Street litigator. "That is what you need to show a criminal prosecution under the federal security law."

But Black points out that federal regulatory agencies have referred far fewer cases for possible prosecution in the current scandal than the 10,000-plus criminal referrals that were made during the S&L crisis. As of November 2011, Black counted no referrals from the Office of Thrift Supervision, three from the Office of the Comptroller of the Currency and three from the Federal Reserve.[11]

"Yes, these are difficult cases," Black says. But, he adds, "Without criminal referrals there are no police on elite white-collar criminals."

Have federal agencies been tough enough in prosecuting financial wrongdoing?

Angelo Mozilo helped found Countrywide Financial in 1969 and built it over the next three decades into the largest lender of single-family home loans in the country. By 2006, however, Mozilo was worrying about a possible decline in home prices and the quality of some of the subprime loans his company had helped create and popularize.

Publicly, however, Mozilo voiced confidence in his company right up to its collapse in late 2007 and acquisition in January 2008 by Bank of America at the fire-sale price of $4 billion. As the storm clouds grew, the SEC in June 2009 charged Mozilo in a civil suit with securities fraud and insider trading for selling off his stock in Countrywide.

Financial Fraud Prosecutions on the Decline

Federal prosecutions for financial institution fraud have declined sharply over the past 20 years. They totaled 1,251 in the first 11 months of fiscal 2011 and were projected to reach 1,365 for the full year if trends continued. That would be 29 percent fewer than in 2006 and 58 percent fewer than a decade ago.

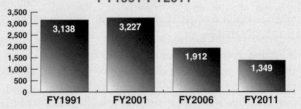

Criminal Fraud Prosecutions of Financial Institutions FY1991-FY2011

FY1991	FY2001	FY2006	FY2011
3,138	3,227	1,912	1,349

Source: Transactional Records Access Clearinghouse, Syracuse University, November 2011, trac.syr.edu/tracreports/crim/267/

In October 2010, the SEC negotiated a settlement with Mozilo that included a $67.5 million fine and a permanent ban on his serving as a director or officer in a publicly traded company. Robert Khuzami, director of the SEC's Division of Enforcement, said the "record penalty" was a "fitting outcome" in the case. But observers noted that the agreement allowed Mozilo to avoid any admission of wrongdoing. And the government's criminal investigation was quietly shelved a few months later.[12]

The decision to bring no criminal charges against Mozilo exemplifies what *The New York Times* called in a 4,000-word overview last spring the "dearth of prosecutions" in connection with the financial crisis.[13] The story by two of the *Times'* veteran financial reporters, Gretchen Morgenson and Louise Story, noted that under President George W. Bush, Attorney General Michael Mukasey declined to create a nationwide task force on financial crimes — as was done during the S&L crisis. A task force created by Obama's attorney general, Eric Holder, was given a broad mandate but no additional resources.

Black, who was prominently quoted in the story, continues to speak out about the lack of prosecutions. "There has been no prosecution of an elite Wall Street figure who played a major role" in the crisis, Black says today. "That's an astonishing fact."

Statistics compiled by the private Transactional Records Access Clearinghouse at Syracuse University show an uninterrupted, decade-long decline in the number of federal prosecutions for financial institution fraud. In a report in late 2011, the clearinghouse showed more than 3,000 such prosecutions per year in the 1990s but only 1,349 for fiscal 2011.[14]

In the "60 Minutes" segment, former Countrywide vice president for fraud investigations Eileen Foster said there was "systemic" fraud at the company — specifically, loan officers approving mortgages based on forged or manipulated statements of borrowers' incomes and assets. However, she told correspondent Kroft, she was never interviewed by the Justice Department.

In the second part of the segment, Richard Bowen, a former senior vice president in Citigroup's consumer-lending division, said he warned Citi's top executives in November 2007 that a high percentage of mortgages in its portfolio were "defective" and that the company was understating its financial risks. Kroft went on to suggest that Citi's CEO Vikrim Pandit and Chief Financial Officer Gary Crittenden may have violated a central provision of the post-Enron Sarbanes-Oxley Act by certifying inaccurate financial statements to the SEC. Kroft quoted the company as defending the statements.

Commenting generally, New York University's Arlen sharply criticizes the failure to bring legal actions against individual executives. "You can't safeguard the market unless securities fraud doesn't pay, and it has to not pay for the individuals who do it," Arlen says. "You need people to be personally afraid of the consequences of lying."

SEC officials insist the agency is not shying away from going after individual executives. In announcing the civil suit against the former Fannie Mae and Freddie Mac executives, enforcement chief Khuzami promised that "all individuals" would be held accountable for financial misrepresentations "regardless of their rank or position."[15]

The SEC also is touting its recent crackdown on insider-trading cases. In testimony to congressional committees in December, Khuzami described insider trading as "one of the Division of Enforcement's highest priorities" and listed several initiatives aimed at spotting suspicious trading patterns and abusive market practices.[16]

Private lawyers Douglass and Gorman both give the SEC credit for its insider-trading initiatives. "It's aggressive and innovative," says Douglass. "It captured the attention of the business community." Overall, however,

Douglass, an assistant U.S. attorney before going into private practice, calls the government's prosecution policies in the financial crisis "feckless."

"Insider trading should be prosecuted, but I don't think you can link insider-trading cases to these other kinds of fraud," Douglass says. "It undermines people's faith in the legal system when prosecutors say they're going to hold people accountable and they fail to do so."

Should mortgage lenders be punished for their role in improper foreclosures?

Among the more than 5 million home foreclosures since the financial crisis, banks and other mortgage lenders are now known to have completed a substantial number with procedures more akin to a factory assembly line than to a court of law. Banks, lenders and mortgage-servicing companies acknowledge the practice — dubbed "robo-signing" when first disclosed in October 2010 — where loan officers routinely signed foreclosure papers en masse without having read them.

Consumer advocates and some state attorneys general say the procedures amounted to "foreclosure fraud." Major banks admitted but somewhat minimized the problems even as they halted foreclosures for a while in order to clean up procedures. Investigations by news organizations and others, however, indicate that robo-signing and other documentation discrepancies continue.[17]

Banks hoping to put the issue behind them have been negotiating with representatives of state attorney general offices since spring 2011, looking to a multibillion-dollar settlement that would also limit their liability in further investigations. An accord looked close last fall, but the likelihood of agreement dimmed as some state attorneys general split off from the talks to take a tougher line.

In the most significant development, Massachusetts Attorney General Martha Coakley sued the nation's five largest mortgage lenders in state court on Dec. 1. The 57-page complaint charges the banks — Bank of America, Citigroup, GMAC Mortgage and its parent company Ally Financial, JP Morgan Chase and Wells Fargo — with having seized properties unlawfully. It asks for a court order that they change their practices and correct defects in previous foreclosures.[18]

In announcing the suit, Coakley said she pulled out of the settlement talks because the banks had failed to take responsibility for what she called "the devastation" on individual homeowners and communities. Critics of the lenders' practices similarly say the proposed settlement — which is being pushed by the Obama administration — would allow the banks to escape accountability for throwing people out of their homes without proper procedures.

"We should have prosecutions," says Yves Smith, who writes critically about financial industry news on the popular blog *Naked Capitalism.* "You don't settle unless you know what the crime was," she continues. "The attorneys general don't know what they're settling for, so they don't have any bargaining leverage."

Smith sharply criticizes the banks' effort to limit further legal exposure. "The banks have continued to ask for more and more and more," she says. Black, the law professor and former S&L regulator, agrees. "I would not have believed it possible in the United States that we would actually immunize them," Black says.

Banks involved in the negotiations have generally declined to comment about the talks. Spokesmen for three of the banks — Bank of America, JP Morgan Chase and Wells Fargo — all expressed disappointment with the filing of the Massachusetts suit. "We continue to believe that the collaborative resolution rather than continued litigation will most quickly heal the housing market and help drive economic recovery," BofA spokesman Lawrence Grayson said.

GMAC was more combative. "GMAC Mortgage believes it has strong legal and factual defenses," the company said in a statement, "and "will vigorously defend its position in court."[19]

The value of the proposed settlement as reported could reach $25 billion if all 50 states participate, most of it apparently in the form of principal write-downs, interest-rate reductions and other benefits to homeowners. Some cash penalties could be imposed on the banks. The settlement would be reduced if some states — most notably, California — balk at the accord.[20]

California is one of five states — all with Democratic attorneys general — that have pulled out of the talks to pursue separate legal actions. Besides Massachusetts, the others are Delaware, Nevada and New York.

Obama administration officials, including Treasury Secretary Timothy Geithner and Housing and Urban Development Secretary Shaun Donovan, have been pushing the settlement in the interest of stabilizing the banks and the housing market. Without commenting on the specifics of the proposed settlement, Christopher Mayer, a real estate finance expert at Columbia Business School, agrees on the importance of resolving the issues.

"Settling this is incredibly important because there's an enormous backlog of delinquent mortgages," Mayer says. "The process of doing nothing is a loser for everybody. We need to reduce uncertainty."

Mayer says most of the foreclosures are justified in economic terms. "The vast, vast majority of people who are involved are people who are not paying their mortgages," he says.

But Smith insists that the banks' actions are more than "innocent" mistakes. "These are not mistakes," she says. "They happened on too large a scale to be mistakes."

BACKGROUND
Policing the Markets
Federal regulation of the banking, housing and securities industries dates from the Great Depression, the economic calamity touched off by the stock market crash of 1929 that cost millions of Americans their homes, farms, jobs or life savings. The legislative and regulatory regimes set up to insure bank deposits, protect investors and support home mortgages appeared to serve the country's financial system well for half a century. By the 1970s, however, the Supreme Court began to balk at some of the SEC's expansive applications of anti-fraud rules. Since then, marketplace changes have combined with deregulatory initiatives and out-and-out dishonesty to jolt the financial system, first in the 1980s and twice already in the 21st century.[21]

The stock market crash of October 1929 — a 25 percent drop in two days — came unexpectedly after a decade of boom times. The subsequent congressional investigation documented abuses that, if known, might have foretold the collapse — in particular, risky investments in securities by banks. Over a four-year period, 43 percent of the 24,970 U.S. banks failed or were merged out of existence.[22]

The investigation by the so-called Pecora Commission — named after its lead investigator, Ferdinand Pecora — helped build support for new laws regulating banking and securities. The Glass-Steagall Act, passed in

1933, separated commercial from investment banking and also established the Federal Deposit Insurance Corporation (FDIC) to insure individual depositors' accounts. In the same year, Congress passed the Securities Act, which required disclosure of financial information by companies issuing stock or other securities. A year later, the Securities Exchange Act created the SEC, regulated securities trading and gave the SEC power to write anti-fraud rules.

Congress also sought to bolster home mortgages. The Federal Home Owners' Loan Corporation was created in 1933 to repurchase foreclosed homes and reinstate former mortgages; the Federal Housing Administration was established in 1934 to insure those mortgages. Meanwhile, deposit insurance was extended in 1934 to savings and loan associations, the main source of mortgage funds. Then in 1938, the Federal National Mortgage Association — dubbed "Fannie Mae" — was founded as a government-sponsored enterprise to invest in mortgages. Fannie Mae was transformed into a private corporation in 1968; that change prompted Congress two years later to create a competitor: the Federal Home Loan Mortgage Corporation, dubbed "Freddie Mac."

Despite congressional and law enforcement investigations, the Depression-era financial turmoil spawned only a "small handful" of criminal prosecutions, according to St. Johns professor Perino. "The point of the Pecora Commission was to show that the laws and regulations were inadequate," he explains. The highest profile prosecutions failed. Bank executive Charles Mitchell of National City Bank was found not guilty of tax evasion; utility tycoon Samuel Insull of Commonwealth Edison was acquitted of mail fraud and antitrust charges. The only big name to go to prison was Richard Whitney, president of the New York Stock Exchange from 1930 to 1935, who embezzled money from the exchange's gratuity fund to cover heavy investment losses. He pleaded guilty to state charges in 1938 and served three years in prison.

The banking and securities regulations remained controversial through the 1930s. In a memoir, Pecora warned in 1939 against allowing Wall Street to go back to the time "before Uncle Sam stationed a policeman at its corner."[23] Over the next several decades, however, the regulatory regimes appeared to gain general acceptance. With FDIC insurance, runs on banks by worried depositors became a relic of history. Investors grew accustomed to the financial disclosures required from companies issuing securities. By the 1950s and '60s, the SEC was being criticized not for over- but for under-regulating. President John F. Kennedy responded to a report by former SEC Chairman James Landis that called for strengthening regulatory agencies by increasing the SEC staff and appointing an activist-minded corporate law expert, William Cary, as chairman.

Cary laid the basis for the SEC's insider-trading enforcement with an administrative ruling in November 1961 sanctioning a broker who sold a company's stock based on advance word of a dividend cut that he learned from a partner who was on the company's board of directors. The ruling in *In re Cady, Roberts & Co.* established a so-called "disclose or abstain" rule: insiders had to disclose material information about a company's finances or abstain from trading on the basis of the information. In 1968 the rule gained judicial endorsement from the New York-based Second U.S. Circuit Court of Appeals in a case, *SEC v. Texas Gulf Sulphur Co.*, where company insiders had bought up stock and stock options in advance of an announcement of a major discovery of copper and zinc deposits. The appeals court interpreted the anti-fraud Rule 10b-5 to require that all investors have "relatively equal access to material information."[24]

The Supreme Court, which left the Texas Gulf Sulphur ruling in place by rejecting the company's appeal, had been generally supportive of SEC authority since the 1930s but began to shift in the 1970s. In a succession of rulings, the court cut back on SEC litigating positions. In 1976, for example, the court ruled 6-2 that the SEC's anti-fraud rule required proof of an intent to deceive, not mere negligence. A 1980 ruling rejected the SEC's attempt to expand the definition of insider to include people with no fiduciary relationship to the company.[25] Despite the adverse court rulings, however, the SEC increased its insider-trading enforcement, thanks in part to the creation of a computerized tracking system to monitor stock trading, corporate filings and news items.[26]

Losing Control

Twice over the next quarter century, the United States experienced seeming epidemics of financial misconduct, followed each time by strengthened federal regulation

CHRONOLOGY

Before 1960 *Federal regulation of banks, securities established.*

1933, 1934 Financial disclosure required to offer stock, other securities (Securities Act). . . . Commercial, investment banking separated; federal deposit insurance instituted (Glass-Steagall Act). . . . Securities and Exchange Commission (SEC) established.

1938 Federal National Mortgage Association ("Fannie Mae") created by Congress; becomes private company in 1968; Federal Home Loan Mortgage Corporation ("Freddie Mac") established as competitor in 1970.

1960s-1970s *SEC becomes more aggressive, meets Supreme Court resistance.*

1961 SEC prescribes "disclose or abstain rule" to bar insider trading.

1976 Supreme Court rules that securities fraud requires intent to deceive, not mere negligence.

1980s-1990s *Savings and loan crisis: government bailout, tightened rules.*

1980, 1982 Congress passes, two presidents sign legislation to deregulate thrift industry to aid competition with commercial banks.

Mid-1980s Hundreds of S&Ls fail; speculative loans, looting by executives blamed.

1989 Congress reregulates thrift industry, approves bailout of failed S&Ls (Financial Institutions Reform, Recovery and Enforcement Act). . . . Bailout cost later put at $88 billion; more than 1,800 S&L officials prosecuted, more than 1,000 sent to prison.

1996, 1998 Congress limits private securities-fraud suits in federal, state courts.

1999 Congress repeals Glass-Steagall; allows banks, securities firms to merge (Gramm-Leach-Bliley).

Early 2000s *Enron, accounting scandals followed by reforms.*

2001 Enron forced into bankruptcy after accounting frauds; top executives later prosecuted, convicted.

2002 Congress requires top executives to personally certify financial statements, creates agency to oversee accounting profession (Sarbanes Oxley).

2008-Present *Financial crisis freezes markets, brings financial overhaul, calls for tougher government action.*

2008 Government forces Bear Stearns fire-sale to JP Morgan Chase (March 16). . . . Government takes over Fannie Mae, Freddie Mac (Sept. 7). . . . Lehman Brothers declares bankruptcy (Sept. 15). . . . Treasury Secretary Henry Paulson strong-arms major banks to agree to bailout; Congress OKs plan (Emergency Economic Stabilization Act) (September/October). . . . Bernard Madoff charged with Ponzi scheme (Dec. 10).

2009 Madoff pleads guilty (March 12); later sentenced to 150 years in prison. . . . SEC Office of Inspector General says investigators could have stopped Madoff after first tip in 1992 (Aug. 31). . . . Bear Stearns hedge fund managers acquitted (Nov. 9).

2010 Goldman Sachs agrees to $550 million penalty in marketing subprime mortgages (July 15). . . . Dodd-Frank Act gives government more power to seize failing banks; creates Consumer Financial Protection Bureau (July 21). . . . Countrywide founder Angelo Mozilo settles with SEC for $67.5 million (Oct. 15).

2011 Meltdown could have been avoided, Financial Crisis Inquiry Commission says; Republican members file dissent (Jan. 27). . . . Hedge fund manager Raj Rajaratnam convicted in insider-trading case (May 11); later draws 11-year sentence; two dozen others convicted. . . . JP Morgan Chase agrees to $154 million penalty for rigged subprime mortgage package (June 21). . . . Citigroup agrees to $285 million settlement in toxic mortgage deal (Oct. 19), but judge balks at deal (Nov. 28).

2012 President Obama uses recess appointment to name Richard Cordray to head Consumer Financial Protection Bureau; Republican senators object (Jan. 4).

'Test Drive' for Wiretaps in Insider-Trading Case

Galleon hedge fund founder made more than $70 billion in illegal gains.

Federal prosecutors in New York City have used wiretaps and a wired informant to help win more than two dozen convictions in a sprawling insider-trading investigation, including a record-setting prison term against the billionaire hedge-fund founder at the center of the case.

Dozens of recorded telephone calls provided the critical evidence that netted Raj Rajaratnam an 11-year prison sentence after his May 11 conviction in federal court in New York on nine counts of insider trading and five counts of conspiracy.

Rajaratnam, founder of the now defunct Galleon Group, made more than $70 million in illegal profits over a six-year period, according to prosecutors, by trading on inside information gathered from multiple contacts in Wall Street and corporate circles.[1]

One of Rajaratnam's major sources is alleged to have been Rajat Gupta, a friend and former head of the giant consulting firm McKinsey & Co. Gupta was charged in a six-count indictment unsealed on Oct. 26 with passing valuable inside information to Rajaratnam from his position as a director with Goldman Sachs, a big investment firm constantly involved in potential corporate mergers and acquisitions.

Among the lesser figures in the investigation was Brien Santarlas, formerly a patent attorney with a New York law firm, whose secretly recorded conversations with other conspirators helped win convictions in June of a key stock trader linked to Rajaratnam and two other defendants. Santarlas, who pleaded guilty to securities fraud charges in November 2009, was given a reduced, six-month sentence on Nov. 30, 2011, based on his cooperation with the prosecution.[2]

The government's first extensive use of wiretaps in an insider trading case — a tactic usually associated with organized crime and public corruption investigations — is one of the issues being raised on appeal by lawyers for Rajaratnam. Patricia Millett, a Washington lawyer and veteran appellate litigator, previewed her argument in an unsuccessful attempt in late November to win bail for Rajaratnam pending appeal.

Millett told a panel of the Second U.S. Circuit Court of Appeals on Nov. 30 that the government had not filed a proper request for the taps. Assistant U.S. Attorney Jonathan Streeter said the requests had been proper and noted that the trial judge had considered the issue before admitting the tapes at the start of Rajaratnam's seven-week trial. The appeals court denied bail for Rajaratnam the next day without comment.[3]

The prosecution made the most of the tapes during the trial. "You heard the defendant commit his crimes time and time again in his own words," Assistant U.S. Attorney Reed Brodsky said in closing arguments. Former

and criminal prosecutions of prominent corporate executives. The savings and loan crisis of the 1980s required a $100 billion federal bailout to stabilize the thrift industry. By one count, more than 100 executives were prosecuted for various offenses. The accounting scandals of the early 2000s forced thousands of companies to revise their financial statements and led to prison terms for several top corporate managers. Meanwhile, Congress and the Supreme Court significantly tightened the rules governing civil suits for securities fraud while Congress also approved legislation to loosen regulation of abstruse financial instruments known as derivatives.

The S&L crisis stemmed from the competitive pressure on the thrifts created by the rise in interest rates in the late 1970s and a regulatory cap on interest they could pay on deposits. To aid the thrifts, Congress in 1980 and 1982 passed deregulatory legislation that, among other provisions, uncapped interest rates for most deposits, permitted adjustable-rate mortgages and allowed more speculative investments. Initially, the thrifts seemed to fare well, but many investments went bad as the real estate boom subsided. The thrifts also fell prey to high-flying entrepreneurs, some of whom simply looted the funds for personal benefit. By

government lawyers had praise after the verdict for the tactic. Prosecutors "took wiretaps for a test drive, and I'd say it was a resounding success," Stephen Miller, a former federal prosecutor in private practice in Philadelphia, told The Associated Press.[4]

Santarlas, who got into the insider-trading racket in October 2007 as a young associate at the New York office of the Boston-based firm Ropes & Gray, agreed to cooperate with the government in his first meeting with FBI agents in November 2009. He admitted being paid for tips about pending corporate deals gathered from confidential information at his firm. In the later trial, Santarlas testified that he was instructed to use a prepaid cell phone to relay information and then to cut the phone into pieces and throw the pieces into the river.

Santarlas testified, along with fellow lawyer-turned-tipster Arthur Cutillo, in the trial of stock trader Zvi Goffer, who had worked for Rajaratnam before starting his own firm. Goffer and two others who worked for him — his brother Emanuel and lawyer Michael Kimelman — were convicted on June 13 on multiple counts of securities fraud and conspiracy. Zvi Goffer later received a 10-year prison sentence, Emmanuel Goffer a three-year term, and Kimelman a 30-month sentence.

Cutillo, who like Santarlas pleaded guilty to a single count of conspiracy, was sentenced on June 30 to 30 months in prison. Both lawyers apologized at sentencing for their offenses. "I know what I did was terribly wrong," Cutillo said in the June 30 hearing. Five months later, Santarlas said he was "ashamed," "embarrassed" and "humiliated" about what he had done. "It's something I'll never forgive myself for," he said.

— *Kenneth Jost*

Former Goldman Sachs director Rajat Gupta is facing charges of passing inside information to hedge fund founder Raj Rajaratnam, who was convicted on fraud and conspiracy charges in connection with his making $70 million in illegal profits.

[1]Press releases on individual developments in the case can be found by date on the website of the U.S. attorney for the Southern District of New York: www.justice.gov/usao/nys/pressreleases/. Details on Rajaratnam's trial and conviction taken from Tom Hays and Larry Neumeister, "Hedge fund founder convicted in inside-trade case," The Associated Press, May 11, 2011.

[2]See Larry Neumeister and Tom Hays, "NY jury convicts 3 in NYC hedge fund trial," *ibid.*, June, 13, 2011; Tom Hays, "Tipster sentenced in NYC insider trading case," *ibid.*, Nov. 30, 2011.

[3]Larry Neumeister, "Fund boss loses bid to stay free during appeal," *ibid.*, Dec. 1, 2011.

[4]Quoted in Larry Neumeister and Tom Hays, "Wiretaps key in conviction of ex-hedge fund giant," *ibid.*, May 11, 2011.

the end of the decade, more than 1,000 had failed, sticking the government with a $100 billion bailout bill. By 1995, the Justice Department had conducted 1,852 prosecutions of S&L officials, with 1,072 sentenced to prison.[27]

Congress and President George H. W. Bush responded to the S&L crisis by enacting the Financial Institutions Reform, Recovery and Enforcement Act of 1989. In addition to authorizing the $100 billion bailout by the newly established Resolution Trust Corporation, the law revamped deposit insurance, raised capital requirements for thrifts and placed them under the authority of the newly established Office of Thrift Supervision within the Treasury Department.

In contrast to the heightened regulation of the thrift industry, Congress and the Supreme Court were erecting barriers in the 1990s to private lawsuits aimed at enforcing federal securities laws. Congress responded to business-community complaints about supposedly baseless securities class action suits by enacting, over President Bill Clinton's veto, the Private Securities Litigation Reform Act of 1996. The act raised the initial burden of proof for private securities-fraud suits to proceed and tightened various rules governing federal class action suits. When plaintiffs' lawyers tried to circumvent the law by bringing suits in state courts, Congress responded with a second law, the Securities Litigation Uniform Standards Act, effectively preempting state court jurisdiction over securities cases.

Earlier, the Supreme Court in 1994 had issued a closely divided ruling that barred extending civil liability for aiding and abetting securities fraud to outsiders, such as accountants, attorneys or other professionals.[28] In 1997, however, the court boosted both private and criminal enforcement against insider trading by endorsing the SEC's so-called misappropriation theory, which barred anyone — not just corporate insiders — from trading on confidential company information. The ruling in *United States v. O'Hagan* upheld the 57-count conviction of a Minneapolis lawyer who made $4.3 million in profits while trading in Pillsbury stock in advance of a planned tender offer by a corporate client of his firm.[29]

As the decade ended, Congress approved two additional deregulatory initiatives that helped set the stage for the later financial crisis. The Gramm-Leach-Bliley Act of 1999 effectively repealed the Glass-Steagall Act by allowing banks and financial holding companies to own both commercial banking and securities firms as well as insurance companies. A year later, the Commodity Futures Modernization Act blocked the Commodity Futures Trading Commission from asserting regulatory authority over the complex financial instruments known as over-the-counter derivatives. Clinton signed both measures after they had won bipartisan support in Congress.

The financial scandals of the early 2000s were embodied most dramatically in the story of Enron, a Houston-based energy trading company that used creative accounting tricks to conceal shaky finances until being forced late in 2001 to issue financial restatements and then seek bankruptcy protection. Top Enron executives were prosecuted, along with the company's outside accounting firm Arthur Andersen. Similar accounting scandals forced a succession of other companies to issue restatements, and a few other top executives faced criminal charges. The image of a corporate crime wave was heightened by a spike in unrelated cases of garden-variety insider trading and misappropriation of corporate funds.[30]

Even as criminal prosecutions were getting under way, Congress and President George W. Bush responded by overhauling corporate accounting practices. The bipartisan Sarbanes-Oxley Act — named after its principal Senate and House sponsors — included provisions to strengthen auditors' independence from corporate boards and to require top executives to take individual responsibility for the accuracy of financial statements. It also established a new, quasi-independent agency, the Public Company Accounting Oversight Board, to oversee accounting firms' compliance with the act. In signing the bill, Bush called it "the most far-reaching reforms of American business practices since the time of Franklin D. Roosevelt."

Digging Out

The financial crisis of 2008 formed under the surface for several years before emerging into public view in March when the government forced the sale of cash-strapped Bear Stearns to JP Morgan Chase for a paltry $2 a share. By year's end, Lehman Brothers had collapsed, Fannie Mae and Freddie Mac had been nationalized and the nation's nine biggest banks had been ordered to take billions in bailouts in exchange for a commitment to unfreeze the frozen credit markets. Government regulators and federal prosecutors then went to work, looking for culpability. The government won some significant victories but endured constant second-guessing from critics about the pace of investigations and the penalties imposed.[31]

Meanwhile, Congress was working on legislation aimed at preventing another financial meltdown. As signed into law by President Obama on July 21, 2010, the Wall Street Reform and Consumer Protection Act — more commonly, the Dodd-Frank Act after its principal Senate and House sponsors — gives the government more power to seize and wind down big financial firms. It also requires companies that sell mortgage-backed securities generally to retain at least 5 percent of the risk of the products. The bill also mandates regulation of over-the-counter derivatives and requires hedge funds to register with the SEC. And it established the Consumer Financial Protection Bureau as an independent agency within the Federal Reserve to enforce consumer-protection laws against not only banks and mortgage lenders but also credit card issuers, payday lenders and other financial-service companies.[32]

The charges against the ex-Bear Stearns hedge fund managers Cioffi and Tannin in June 2008 marked the first financial crisis-related prosecution to hit Wall Street directly. The pair were arrested June 19 on a fraud and conspiracy indictment based largely on e-mails showing undisclosed doubts about their funds' strength. Mark Mehrson, head of the FBI's New York office, told reporters the case was about "premeditated lies to investors and lenders." Lawyers for Cioffi and Tannin foreshadowed their successful defense by insisting their clients were victims of an unexpected crisis in financial markets. After the acquittals, a former Enron fraud prosecutor told *The New York Times* that the verdict showed the weakness of relying on " 'smoking gun' e-mails" to make a white-collar crime case.[33]

Once in office, the Obama administration made a public show of going after financial misconduct with the creation of an interagency task force on financial fraud in November 2009. Holder, accompanied by SEC Chairwoman Mary Schapiro and Cabinet colleagues Geithner from Treasury and Donovan from HUD, promised that the task force would be "relentless" in investigating and prosecuting corporate and financial wrongdoing. But Black, the Missouri law professor, notes that in addition to the task force getting no additional resources, its mission was extended beyond Wall Street. In April 2011, for example, a task force working group was formed to study the causes of rising oil and gas prices.[34]

The SEC, meanwhile, was achieving some success with civil actions carrying nine-figure settlements in cases against Goldman Sachs and JP Morgan Chase. Both companies were charged with securities fraud by misleading investors in subprime mortgage packages. The $550 million settlement that Goldman agreed to in July 2010 was described as one of the biggest penalties in SEC history. The agency charged Goldman with marketing a package of mortgages picked by the prominent hedge fund manager, John Paulson, who later bet against the bonds. News reports after the settlement disclosed that the five-member agency had split along party lines in initiating the complaint and approving the settlement, with three Democrats in favor and two Republicans against. Almost a year later, the agency won a $154 million settlement against Morgan in a similar case. In both cases, the firms neither admitted nor denied wrongdoing.[35]

Despite complaints in the press and from observers about the lack of prosecutions, the government was

With Richard Cordray at his side, President Obama addresses staffers at the new Consumer Financial Protection Bureau on Jan. 6, 2012. Obama used a recess appointment to install the former Ohio attorney general as the agency's head after Republicans blocked action on the nomination. Cordray is laying out an aggressive initiative for the agency despite potential legal challenges to his appointment.

Getty Images/Michael Reynolds-Pool

winning some significant convictions. It won a big case in April 2011 when a federal jury in Alexandria, Va., convicted Lee Farkas, the former majority owner of the big mortgage company Taylor, Bean & Whitaker, in a $3 billion fraud that toppled the Florida-based firm as well as the Alabama-based Colonial Bank. Farkas was sentenced on June 30 to 30 years in prison.[36]

In May 2011, the government notched a higher-profile victory with the conviction of prominent hedge fund manager Rajaratnam on 14 counts of securities fraud and conspiracy. Rajaratnam received an 11-year prison sentence in October — said to be the longest ever for insider trading — even as Gupta, one of his sources, a former chief executive of the giant consulting firm McKinsey & Co., was awaiting trial himself for insider trading.[37]

The SEC was still basking in the publicity glow from the Rajaratnam and Gupta cases when Judge Rakoff caught the agency by surprise by rejecting the proposed settlement with Citigroup. Two weeks later, on Dec. 15, the SEC announced that it would ask the Second U.S. Circuit Court of Appeals to overturn Rakoff's decision. "We believe the district court committed legal error by announcing a new and unprecedented standard that inadvertently harms investors by depriving them of substantial, certain and immediate benefits," enforcement chief Khuzami said in a statement accompanying the court filing.[38]

The next day, the agency shifted from defense to offense with its civil complaint charging the former Fannie and Freddie executives with fraud. The executives misled investors by understating their exposure to subprime mortgages, Khuzami said. In a briefing, Khuzami said the case was the 38th action brought by the commission in connection with the financial crisis.[39]

CURRENT SITUATION

Blaming Fannie, Freddie?

The SEC's fraud complaint against the former Fannie Mae and Freddie Mac executives is renewing the debate over the government-sponsored mortgage companies' responsibility for the subprime mortgage crisis, even as lawyers for the defendants call the charges baseless.

The parallel complaints, filed in federal district court in New York City, charge the former chief executives and two other ranking executives at each of the companies with making "materially false and misleading public disclosures" by understating the companies' exposure to subprime mortgage loans.

Named in the 59-page complaint against Fannie Mae executives are former CEO Daniel Mudd; Enrico Dallavecchia, former chief risk officer; and Thomas Lund, former executive vice president of Fannie's single-family mortgage business. The 49-page complaint against Freddie Mac executives names former CEO Richard Syron; Patricia Cook, former executive vice president and chief business officer; and Donald Bisenius, executive vice president for its single-family business.

The suits both seek disgorgement of profits, unspecified civil penalties and "other necessary and appropriate relief," which could include bans on their serving as officers or directors of publicly traded companies. The Fannie Mae case was assigned to Judge Robert Carter, the Freddie Mac case to Judge Richard Sullivan.[40]

None of the defendants has filed any response to the complaints, but Mudd and lawyers for Syron denied the allegations after the SEC announcement. "The SEC is wrong, and I look forward to a court where fairness and reason — not politics — is the standard for justice,"

Mudd said. Representing Syron, attorneys Thomas Green and Mark Hopson contended Freddie's filings had "no shortage of meaningful disclosures." They called the SEC's case "fatally flawed" and "without merit."[41]

The cases apparently will turn on how broadly to define the risks of unconventional loans offered by the two mortgage companies during the two-year period covered in the complaints up to their takeover by the government in August 2008. A chart accompanying the SEC's news release depicts Fannie as reporting $8 billion and Freddie $6 billion in subprime exposure as of second-quarter 2008, when their actual exposure to risky loans was $110 billion and $250 billion, respectively.

In the Fannie Mae complaint, the agency elaborates that its disclosures did not include so-called Alt-A reduced-documentation mortgages and loan products targeted to borrowers with weaker credit histories — also known as Expanded Approval or EA loans. Such loans, the complaint states, "were exactly the type of loans that investors would reasonably believe Fannie Mae included when calculating its exposure to subprime loans." Similarly, the Freddie Mac complaint says the company failed to include loans referred to internally as "subprime," "otherwise subprime" or "subprime-like."

The role played by the two mortgage giants — sometimes referred to as "government-sponsored enterprises" or GSEs — had been a partisan issue on Capitol Hill and elsewhere since the financial crisis emerged. Republicans and conservative experts argued that Fannie and Freddie led mortgage lenders into the subprime swamp in order to satisfy 1990s-era statutory and regulatory mandates to provide access to affordable housing. Democrats generally defended the affordable-housing mandates and depicted the mortgage companies' problems as due to profit-driven recklessness. Days after the SEC filing, Peter Wallison, a longtime critic of the GSEs and a senior fellow at the conservative American Enterprise Institute (AEI), wrote in an op-ed in *The Wall Street Journal* that the legal actions vindicated his critique. "For the first time in a government report, the complaint has made it clear that the two government-sponsored enterprises (GSEs) played a major role in creating the demand for low-quality mortgages before the 2008 financial crisis," Wallison wrote.[42]

In a sharp reply to Wallison's argument even before the op-ed appeared, *New York Times* columnist Joe

Will the Financial Protection Bureau benefit consumers?

YES
Robert L. Borosage
Co-director, Campaign for America's Future

Written for *CQ Researcher*, January 2012

The best tribute to the potential of the Consumer Financial Protection Bureau (CFPB) is the millions the banking lobby expended in an unrelenting campaign to block its creation and cripple it once it was established. The reason for the resistance is simple. The CFPB has one mission: to protect consumers against abuse by large banks and other previously unregulated nonbank financial institutions.

The CFPB consolidates consumer protections previously scattered across the federal government into one agency devoted to their enforcement. Every other financial regulatory agency gives priority to protecting the "safety and soundness" of the banks they supervise. The result, witnessed to catastrophic effect in the housing bubble, has been an utter failure to protect consumers, allowing what the FBI called an unchecked "epidemic of fraud" in subprime mortgages that cost consumers trillions and drove the economy into recession.

One of CFPB's priorities will be to police nonbanking institutions, particularly the payday lenders that levy obscene charges — effective interest rates of 400 percent or more and onerous penalties and fees — on the most vulnerable workers who live paycheck to paycheck. If it simply exposes the big banks engaged in these practices, while requiring and enforcing clear notice of costs, the CFPB can make a dramatic difference.

Already the CFPB is stepping up scrutiny of lenders peddling loans to students at profit-making colleges, many of which project 50 percent default rates. The CFPB also has set up special sections to monitor abuses of seniors and active-duty military personnel who are often targeted by predatory lenders.

The CFPB already has begun to develop clear "know before you owe" notifications of terms for mortgages, credit cards and student loans. Currently consumers sign forms that are purposefully too long, detailed and arcane to be read or understood. By forcing simplification, the CFPB will allow consumers to police the tricks and traps now used on unwary borrowers.

Despite the claims of the bank lobby and Republicans, the concern about the CFPB isn't that it is unaccountable, but that it will be constrained by budgetary limits and unique oversight requirements. Its rule-making can be overturned by a Financial Oversight Council, made up of traditional banking regulators, all more concerned about protecting the solvency of banks than fairness to consumers.

But an active CFPB will garner immense public support as it cracks down on financial predators. No wonder the banking lobby continues to try to weaken it.

NO
Diane Katz
Research Fellow in Regulatory Policy, Heritage Foundation

Written for *CQ Researcher*, January 2012

Some unknown number of individuals may benefit from the Consumer Financial Protection Bureau (CFPB). But the new agency's unparalleled powers — magnified by an absence of accountability — bodes ill for most consumers.

President Obama's recess appointment of Richard Cordray to direct the bureau demonstrates the indiscretion to which the CFPB is prone. To the extent its regulations unduly restrict the availability of financing, economic growth will be constricted. And when unnecessarily stringent regulation raises the cost of credit, consumers are forced to find alternatives that entail greater cost and risk than conventional sources.

Researchers have long documented these dynamics, which are also inherent in other provisions of the Dodd-Frank regulatory statute. For example, the so-called Durbin amendment, which imposed price controls on the fees that banks charge retailers to process debit card transactions, has led to higher fees for checking accounts and other bank services. Higher fees, in turn, force low-income Americans from banks and to less conventional lenders of the very sort regulatory advocates warn against.

Imbued with ill-defined powers and unparalleled independence, the bureau is the epitome of regulatory excess. Well-intended or otherwise, its proponents are wholly invested in saving us from ourselves, and thus disposed to overreach. That increases the likelihood that consumers will be lulled into a false sense of security and makes the absence of bureau oversight all the more problematic.

The CFPB is ensconced within the Federal Reserve, its funding set by statute. Therefore, its budget is not subject to the same congressional control as most other federal agencies. And the bureau's status within the Fed also effectively precludes presidential oversight.

Its accountability is also minimized by the vague language of its statutory mandate. It is empowered to punish "unfair, deceptive and abusive" business practices. While *unfair* and *deceptive* have been defined in other regulatory contexts, the term *abusive* is largely undefined, granting the CFPB officials inordinate discretion.

The financial crisis did not result from any lack of regulation over consumer financial products. Therefore, creation of the CFPB will not help to prevent a future crisis. But it will limit consumer choices. Congress should abolish the CFPB's funding mechanism and subject it instead to congressional control, strike the undefined term *abusive* from the list of practices under CFPB purview, and require the bureau to apply definitions of *unfair* and *deceptive* practices in a manner consistent with consumer choice.

Nocera argued that Wallison was wrong in blaming the two GSEs for what he called "imagined" mistakes. "Fannie and Freddie got into subprime mortgages, with great trepidation, only in 2005 and 2006, and only because they were losing so much market share to Wall Street," Nocera wrote. He went on to call the SEC's case "extraordinarily weak," insisting that the agency was exaggerating the amount of risky loans and ignoring the companies' relatively low default rates.[43]

As part of the legal action, the SEC agreed not to prosecute the two companies, and both agreed to cooperate with the agency in pursuing the case. The filing appeared to be drawing generally positive reaction. Appearing on the PBS "NewsHour," Lynn Turner, a former SEC chief accountant, called the complaints "a very positive development" that showed the government "is willing to go after and hold accountable the people at the very top."[44]

Less approvingly, Black, the former regulator from the S&L crisis, acknowledges that the agency has a lower burden of proof in a civil case than the government would have in a criminal case. But he still complains about the lack of criminal prosecutions. "The Department of Justice still has failed to prosecute any of the elite accounting-control frauds that drove this crisis," he says.

New Agency Under Way

The head of the new Consumer Financial Protection Bureau is promising to make full use of the agency's regulatory and enforcement powers even as Republicans and industry groups challenge his recess appointment to the post.

"It's a valid appointment," Richard Cordray said in remarks to the Brookings Institution on Jan. 5, the day after President Obama named him to the position. "I'm now director of the bureau."[45]

Cordray, a former Ohio attorney general, is signaling an initial priority to extend federal regulation to what he calls in a press release the "thousands" of so-called nonbanks. The non-depository financial businesses include mortgage lenders, mortgage servicers, payday lenders, consumer reporting agencies, debt collectors and money-services companies such as currency exchanges and traveler's check and money order issuers.

"This is an important step forward for protecting consumers," Cordray said in a Jan. 5 release. "Holding both banks and nonbanks accountable to consumer

financial laws will help create a fairer, more transparent market for consumers. It will create a better environment for the honest businesses that serve them. And it will help the overall economic stability of our country."[46]

The debate over Obama's invocation of his recess-appointment power adds to the controversies surrounding the new agency, created as part of the Dodd-Frank Act passed by the Democratic-controlled Congress and signed by the president in 2010. Senate Republicans had blocked action on Cordray's nomination and Obama's previous selection of Harvard law professor Elizabeth Warren in an effort to change the structure and powers of the agency as provided in the law. Warren, now running as a Democrat for the U.S. Senate seat from Massachusetts, was a prime architect of the new agency.

Obama named Cordray the day after the Senate formally convened on Jan. 3 (as required by law) and then resumed a long holiday break. But the Senate had been conducting pro forma sessions every two to three days during the interval. Minority Leader Mitch McConnell of Kentucky and other GOP senators say the Senate's pro forma sessions during the period barred the president from invoking his power under the Constitution to fill positions while the chamber is in recess.

A week after the appointment, the Justice Department released a memorandum from the Office of Legal Counsel supporting Obama's action. "[T]he convening of periodic pro forma sessions in which no business is to be conducted does not have the legal effect of interrupting an intrasession recess," assistant attorney general Virginia Seitz wrote in the 23-page opinion. Administration officials said Seitz had summarized her conclusion to Obama before his appointment.

Seitz acknowledged "substantial arguments" on the opposite side and possible "litigation risks" to the action. Sen. Charles Grassley of Iowa, ranking Republican on the Judiciary Committee, called the memorandum "unconvincing."[47]

The law establishes the CFPB as an independent agency within the Federal Reserve to be headed by a single director. Senate Republicans want to provide instead for a multimember board, comparable to other regulatory agencies. They also criticize the agency's independent budget authority. Democrats counter that Republicans should have tried to amend the law instead of blocking action on the nomination. If valid, Obama's recess appointment would allow Cordray to stay in the post through the remainder of the year.

In assuming the office, Cordray is making special efforts to solicit input from consumers and whistleblowers. In a two-minute video posted on the CPFB web site (www.consumerfinance. gov), Cordray personally invites consumer complaints. "Tell us your story today," he says in closing. In his remarks at Brookings, Cordray said the agency "will make clear that there are real consequences to breaking the law."

A week later, Cordray briefed reporters on plans to scrutinize the student loan business, particularly nontraditional lenders to students at for-profit and trade schools. Cordray said the bureau has seen evidence of loans made by lenders even though they knew borrowers would be unlikely to be able to pay off the loans.[48]

OUTLOOK

No Way to Know?

Ben Bernanke wrapped up his first meeting as chairman of the Federal Reserve Board of Governors in March 2006 with cautious optimism about what he described as the "cooling" in the housing market. Transcripts of the March 27-28 meeting — released in accord with the Fed's practice five years afterward — show Bernanke expected the economy's "strong fundamentals" to offset any reduced spending from homeowners as house prices sagged. "I think it would take a very strong decline in the housing market to substantially derail the strong momentum for growth that we are currently seeing in the economy," Bernanke concluded.[49]

Instead of the "soft landing" that Bernanke predicted, the United States' decades-long housing bubble burst dramatically and plunged the nation into recession by the end of 2007. Four years later, the economy has yet to recover. Many victims of the recession — those who lost their jobs, homes or both — naturally blame mortgage lenders and other financial institutions for driving the market catastrophically to unsustainable levels.

The financial industry has responded in general by insisting that it did not know — and could not have known — that the bubble would burst as it did. In the industry's view, all of the people at banks and investment firms who sliced and diced mortgages into marketable investment packages hardly could have known that they were selling what turned out to be "toxic assets."

The law enforcement agencies going through the wreckage — chiefly, the SEC and Justice Department at the federal level — have found plenty of cases of unmistakable financial misconduct, such as Bernard Madoff's giant Ponzi scheme or the flurry of insider-trading cases. In one of the most recent cases, the government is trying to determine what happened to $1.2 billion in customer money when the New York-based brokerage firm MF Global headed into bankruptcy in October 2011.[50]

The SEC also has found evidence of deception at some of the nation's banks in marketing securitized mortgages — deception that could amount to fraud under federal securities law. Two banks, Goldman Sachs and JP Morgan Chase, agreed to nine-figure payments to resolve such charges, and Citigroup was prepared to do the same until Judge Rakoff balked at the settlement. But the SEC may face an uphill fight in making a similar case against the former Fannie Mae and Freddie Mac executives if they contend that they cannot be held responsible for failing to spot the housing market crash that Bernanke and his Federal Reserve colleagues did not see coming.

Based on his experience in the S&L crisis, Black thinks the evidence of prosecutable "garden-variety fraud" is there for the looking. He sees a lack of political will to pursue cases. "It's the Wall Street folks who were the frauds, and nowadays they are the leading contributors to both parties," he says.

At the Justice Department, Breuer denies any political interference. "This Department of Justice is acting absolutely independently," he told correspondent Kroft in the "60 Minutes" interview. "Every decision that's being made by our prosecutors around the country is being made 100 percent based on the facts of that particular case and the law that we can apply."[51]

Gorman, the Washington lawyer and SEC litigation blogger, thinks the critics are exaggerating the extent of criminal activity involved. "It's one thing to run your business in a reckless way," Gorman says. "It's another thing to actually violate the law."

Washington defense lawyer Douglass thinks the government itself is to blame for feeding the public perception of serious wrongdoing. "If they think there's fraud, they should go out and build those cases," he says. "It's not that hard. It's just a heavy lift."

The government has been "pretty ineffective," says David Skeel, a professor of corporate law at the University of Pennsylvania in Philadelphia. "The pattern of enforcement and nonenforcement has been depressing, to put it mildly."

When Skeel was interviewed for *The New York Times* overview in March 2011, he said the lack of prosecutions led to "the whole perception that Wall Street was taken care of, and Main Street was not." Today, he says he is "hopeful but pessimistic" that the government will improve on its record.

"My fear is that two years from now the 2007-2008 crisis will seem to have been a long time ago," Skeel says. "The sense of urgency that regulators ought to have about stepping in will have dissipated."

NOTES

1. The decision is *U.S. Securities and Exchange Commission v. Citigroup Global Markets, Inc.*, 11 Civ. 7387 (JSR), U.S. Dist. Ct., S.D.N.Y., Nov. 28, 2011, www.scribd.com/doc/74040 599/Rakoff-Citigroup. For coverage, see Edward Wyatt, "Judge Rejects an S.E.C. Deal With Citigroup," *The New York Times*, Nov. 29, 2011, p. A1; David S. Hilzenrath, "Judge rebukes SEC on Citigroup deal," *The Washington Post*, Nov. 29, 2011, p. A1. For the SEC press release, and links to the complaint, see "Citigroup to Pay $285 Million to Settle SEC Charges for Misleading Investors About CDO [Collateralized Debt Obligation] Tied to Housing Market," Oct. 19, 2011, www.sec.gov/news/press/2011/2011-214.htm. For coverage, see Edward Wyatt, "Citigroup to Pay Millions to End Fraud Complaint," *The New York Times*, Oct. 20, 2011, p. B1. For coverage of the Bank of America case, see Louise Story, "Bank's Deal With S.E.C. Is Approved," *The New York Times*, Feb. 23, 2010, p. B1.

2. "Prosecuting Wall Street," "60 Minutes," Dec. 4, 2011, www.cbsnews.com/8301-18560_162-57336 042/prosecuting-wall-street/?tag=contentMain; cbsCarousel (video, script, and 'Web extras').

3. "SEC Charges Stemming From Financial Crisis," Oct. 19, 2011, www.sec.gov/news/press/2011/

2011-214-chart-stats.pdf. For background on the financial crisis, see these *CQ Researcher* reports: Marcia Clemmitt, "Financial Industry Overhaul," July 30, 2010, pp. 629-652; Thomas J. Billitteri, "Financial Bailout," Oct. 24, 2008, pp. 865-888, updated July 30, 2010; Kenneth Jost, "Financial Crisis," May 9, 2008, pp. 409-432.

4. "Prosecuting Wall Street," *op. cit.* The interview with Breuer ends the segment.

5. "Manhattan U.S. Attorney and FBI Assistant Director-in-Charge Announce Charges Against Seven Investment Professionals for Insider Trading Scheme That Allegedly Netted more than $61.8 Million in Illegal Profits," U.S. Attorney, Southern District of New York, Jan. 18, 2012, www.justice .gov/usao/nys/pressreleases/Janu ary12/newmantod detalchargespr.pdf; Jenny Strasburg, Michael Rothfeld and Susan Pulliam, "Federal Officials Charge Seven in Insider Probe," *The Wall Street Journal*, Jan. 18, 2012, http://online.wsj.com/article/SB10001424052970204468004577168450 897919374.html?mod=WSJ_hp_LEFTTopStories.

6. See Edward Wyatt, "S.E.C. Changes Policy on Firms' Admissions of Guilt," *The New York Times*, Jan. 7, 2012, p. B1.

7. Quoted in E. Scott Reckard, "Pair are cleared of fraud charges," *Los Angeles Times*, Nov. 11, 2009, p. B1; see also Zachery Kouwe and Dan Slater, "2 Bear Stearns Funds Leaders Are Acquitted," *The New York Times*, Nov. 11, 2009, p. A1. For an account of the rise and fall of the funds, see Bethany McLean and Joe Nocera, *All the Devils Are Here: The Hidden History of the Financial Crisis* (2010), pp. 285-295.

8. "News Conference by the President," Oct. 6, 2011, www.whitehouse.gov/the-press-office/2011/10/06/news-conference-president.

9. McLean and Nocera, *op. cit.*, p. 362. McLean is a contributing editor at *Vanity Fair*, Nocera a columnist with *The New York Times.*

10. See Kitty Calavita, Henry N. Pontell, and Robert H. Tillman, *Big Money Crime: Fraud and Politics in the Savings and Loan Crisis* (1997), p. 29.

11. Quoted in Bruce Maiman, "Occupy protest should focus on the bank," *Sacramento* (Calif.) *Bee*, Nov. 8, 2011.

12. For coverage, see Gretchen Morgenson, "Leading Magnate Settles Charges for $67 Million," *The New York Times*, Oct. 16, 2010, p. A1; Walter Hamilton and E. Scott Reckard, "Countrywide execs settle fraud charges," *Los Angeles Times*, Oct. 16, 2010, p. A1. Under an indemnification agreement, Bank of America will pay $20 million of Mozilo's fine. Background drawn from McLean and Nocera, *op. cit.*, *passim*, esp. pp. 219-221, 230-31.

13. Gretchen Morgenson and Louise Story, "A Financial Crisis With Little Guilt," *The New York Times*, April 14, 2011, p. A1.

14. "Criminal Prosecutions for Financial Institution Fraud Continue to Fall," Transactional Records Access Clearinghouse, Nov. 15, 2011, http://trac.syr.edu/tracreports/crim/267/. The report showed 1,251 prosecutions for the first 11 months of fiscal 2011; a separate update for the final month (September 2011) showed 98 more, for a total of 1,349. The pictured chart projected 1,365 cases.

15. "SEC Charges Former Fannie Mae and Freddie Mac Executives With Securities Fraud," Dec. 16, 2011, www.sec.gov/news/press/2011/ 2011-267.htm. For coverage, see David S. Hilzenrath and Zachary Goldfarb, "SEC charges ex-Fannie, Freddie chiefs," *The Washington Post*, Dec. 17, 2011, p. A1; Azam Ahmed and Ben Protess, "Ex-Fannie, Freddie Chiefs Accused of Deception," *The New York Times*, Dec. 17, 2011, p. A1.

16. "Statement on the Application of Insider Trading Law to Trading by Members of Congress and Their Staffs," testimony to Senate Committee on Homeland Security and Government Affairs, Dec. 1, 2011, www.sec.gov/ news/testimony/2011/ts120111rsk.htm. Khuzami delivered similar testimony to the House Committee on Financial Services on Dec. 6.

17. Background drawn in part from " 'Robo-Signing' Paperwork Breakdown Leaves Many Houses in Foreclosure Limbo," PBS "NewsHour," Oct. 6, 2010, www.pbs.org/newshour/bb/busi ness/july-dec10/foreclosures_10-06.html; Scot J. Paltrow, "Banks Continue 'Robo-Signing' Foreclosure Practices In Spite Of Promises to the Contrary: Investigation," Reuters Thomson, July 18, 2011, updated Sept. 17, 2011, published in *Huffington Post*, www.huffington post.com/2011/07/18/robo-signing-foreclosure-banks_n_902140.html?page=1/.

18. The lawsuit is *Commonwealth v. Bank of America et al.*, Suffolk County Superior Court, B.L.S. 1-4363, www.mass.gov/ago/docs/press/ag-complaint-national-banks.pdf. The suit is also against Mortgage Electronic Registration System Inc., a widely used mortgage recording firm, and its parent company. For coverage, see Jenifer B. McKim, "State sues big US lenders," *Boston Globe*, Dec. 2, 2011, p. 1; Gretchen Morgenson, "Massachusetts Sues 5 Major Banks Over Foreclosure Practices," *The New York Times*, Dec. 2, 2011, p. B1.

19. Reactions from McKim, *op. cit.*, and Morgenson, *op. cit.* (Dec. 2, 2011).

20. See Ruth Simon, Nick Timiraos and Dan Fitzpatrick, "Banks in Push for Pact," *The Wall Street Journal*, Dec. 13, 2011, p. C1.

21. Some background drawn from "Fair to All People: The SEC and the Regulation of Insider Trading," Nov. 1, 2006, www.sechistorical.org/museum/galleries/it/.

22. Cited in Robert J. Samuelson, "Fed bashing slander," *The Washington Post*, Dec. 12, 2011, p. A21. For background, see Hoyt Gimlin, "Wall Street: 40 Years After the Crash," *Editorial Research Reports*, Oct. 8, 1969, and Richard Boeckel, "Stock Exchanges and Security Speculation," *Editorial Research Reports*, Feb. 1, 1930; both available in *CQ Researcher Plus Archive*.

23. Ferdinand Pecora, *Wall Street Under Oath: The Story of Our Modern Money Changers* (1939), p. xi. For Perino's account of the commission's investigation, see *The Hellhound of Wall Street: How Ferdinand Pecora's Investigation of the Great Crash Forever Changed American Finance* (2010).

24. The citation is 401 F.2d 833 (2nd Cir. 1968). The Supreme Court declined to hear the company's appeal.

25. The cases are *Ernst & Ernst v. Hochfelder*, 425 U.S. 185 (1976); *Chiarella v. United States* — 445 U.S. 222 (1980).

26. See story by Judith Miller, no headline available, *The New York Times*, March 7, 1980, sec. 4, p. 1 (SEC begins crackdown on 'insiders').

27. U.S. Department of Justice, "Attacking Financial Institution Fraud: A Report to the Congress of the United States," June 30, 1995, June 30, 1995, cited by incomplete name in Gillian Tett, "Insight: A Matter of Retribution," *Financial Times*, Sept. 30, 2009.

28. The decision is *Central Bank of Denver v. First Interstate Bank of Denver*, 511 U.S. 164 (1994). For coverage, see Kenneth Jost, *Supreme Court Yearbook*, 1993-1994.

29. The citation is 521 U.S. 642 (1997). For coverage, see Jost, *Supreme Court Yearbook, 1996-1997*.

30. For background, see "Corporate Crime," *op. cit.* For a later listing of some companies implicated, see Perry E. Wallace, "Accounting, Audit and Audit Committees After Enron, *et al.*: Governing Outside the Box Without Stepping Off the Edge in the Modern Economy," *Washburn Law Review*, Vol. 94 (January 2004), pp. 102-103 & accompanying notes.

31. For a dramatized overview of the events of 2008, see Frontline, "Inside the Meltdown," PBS, originally aired Feb. 17, 2009, www.pbs.org/wgbh/pages/frontline/meltdown/.

32. See Brady Dennis, "Obama ushers in new financial era," *The Washington Post*, July 22, 2010, p. A13; "Historic Financial Overhaul Creates Bureau, Expands Oversight of Banks," *2010 CQ Almanac*, pp. 3-3 to 3-9.

33. Mehrson, defense lawyers Edward Little (Cioffi) and Susan Brune (Tannin) quoted in Tom Hays, "2 Former Bear Stearns Hedge Fund Managers Charged," The Associated Press, June 20, 2008; ex-Enron prosecutor John Hueston quoted in Kouwe and Slater, *op. cit.*

34. Government releases: SEC, www.sec.gov/news/press/2009/2009-249.htm; Justice Department: www.justice.gov/opa/pr/2011/April/11-ag-500.html.

35. See Sewell Chan and Louise Story, "S.E.C. Settling Its Complaints With Goldman," *The New York Times*, July 16, 2010, p. A1; David S. Hilzenrath, "J.P. Morgan to pay $153.6 million to settle fraud suit," *The Washington Post*, June 22, 2011, p. A14.

36. For the trial, see Matthew Barakat, "Jury convicts exec in $3B mortgage fraud case," The Associated Press, April 19, 2011.

37. For the trial, see Tom Hays and Larry Neumeister, "Hedge-fund founder convicted in inside-trade case," The Associated Press, May 11, 2011.

38. See Edward Wyatt, "Citing 'Legal Error,' S.E.C. Says It Will Appeal Rejection of Citigroup Settlement," *The New York Times*, Dec. 16, 2011, p. B3.

39. Quoted in Ahmed and Protess, *op. cit.*

40. The cases are *SEC v. Mudd et al.*, Case No. 11 CIV 9202 (S.D.N.Y., Dec. 18, 2011), www.sec.gov/litigation/complaints/2011/comp-pr2011-267-fanniemae.pdf; *SEC v. Syron et al.*, Case No. CIV 9201 (S.D.N.Y., Dec. 18, 2011), www.sec.gov/litigation/complaints/2011/comp-pr2011-267-freddiemac.pdf.

41. Mudd quoted in Andrew Strickler and Josh Bernstein, "FBI Launches Probe of Fannie, Freddie," *The Daily*, Dec. 17, 2011, www.thedaily.com/page/2011/12/17/121711-news-fannie-fredie-1-2/; Syron's lawyers quoted in Ahmed and Protess, *op. cit.*

42. Peter J. Wallison, "The Financial Crisis on Trial," *The Wall Street Journal*, Dec. 21, 2011, p. A19. Wallison served under President Ronald Reagan as general counsel for the Treasury Department and White House counsel and played a significant role in the administration's unenacted proposals to deregulate the financial services industry. As a member of the Financial Crisis Inquiry Commission, he joined with other Republican appointees in dissenting from the majority report.

43. Joe Nocera, "An Inconvenient Truth," *The New York Times*, Dec. 20, 2011, p. A33. See also Joe Nocera, "The Big Lie," *ibid.*, Dec. 24, 2011, p. A21.

44. "Former Fannie, Freddie Officials Face 'Significant' Fraud, Lying Charges," PBS "NewsHour," Dec. 16, 2011 (interview by Judy Woodruff), www.pbs.org/newshour/bb/business/july-dec 11/fanniefreddie_12-16.html.

45. See Edward Wyatt, "New Consumer Chief Promises Strong Agenda," *The New York Times*, Jan. 6, 2012, p. B3; Suzh Khimm, "Cordray Proceeds Despite Appointment Challenges," *The Washington Post*, Jan. 6, 2012, p. A16. See also Edward Wyatt, "Appointment Clears the Way for Agency to Act," *The New York Times*, Jan. 5, 2012, p. A16.

46. "Consumer Financial Protection Bureau launches nonbank supervision program," Jan. 5, 2012, www.consumerfinance.gov/press release/consumer-financial-protection-bureau-launches-nonbank-supervision-program/. See also Peggy Twohig and Steve Antonakes, "The CFPB launches its nonbank supervision program," Jan. 5, 2012 (blog), www.consumer finance.gov/the-cfpb-launches-its-non bank-supervision-program/.

47. The memorandum is entitled "Lawfulness of Recess Appointments During a Recess of the Senate Notwithstanding Periodic Pro Forma Sessions," Jan. 6, 2012, www.justice.gov/olc/ 2012/pro-forma-sessions-opinion.pdf. Grassley is quoted in Charlie Savage, "Justice Dept. Defends Obama Recess Appointments," *The New York Times*, Jan. 13, 2012, p. A19. See Lyle Denniston, "First challenge on new Obama appointees," SCOTUSBlog, Jan. 13, 2012, www. scotusblog.com/2012/01/first-challenge-on-new-appointees/.

48. See Edward Wyatt, "Some Lenders to Students to Face Greater Scrutiny," *The New York Times*, Jan. 13, 2012, p. B3. For background, see Marcia Clemmitt, "Student Debt," *CQ Researcher*, Oct. 21, 2011, pp. 877-900; and Barbara Mantel, "Career Colleges," *CQ Researcher*, Jan. 7, 2011, pp. 1-24.

49. "Meeting of the Federal Open Market Committee, March 27-28, 2006, www.federalreserve. gov/monetary policy/files/FOMC20060328meet ing.pdf. Bernanke's concluding comments begin at p. 95. For coverage, see Zachary A. Goldfarb, "As financial crisis brewed, Fed appeared unconcerned," *The Washington Post*, Jan. 13, 2012, p. A1; Binyamin Appelbaum, "Inside the Fed in '06: Coming Crisis, and Banter," *The New York Times*, Jan. 13, 2012, p. A1.

50. See Ben Protess and Azam Ahmed, "U.S. Inquiry of MF Global Gains Speed," *The New York Times*, Jan. 10, 2012, p. B1.

51. "Prosecuting Wall Street," *op. cit.*

BIBLIOGRAPHY

Selected Sources

Books

McLean, Bethany, and Joe Nocera, *All the Devils Are Here: The Hidden History of the Financial Crisis*, Portfolio/Penguin, 2010.

Veteran business journalists trace the origins and course of the financial crisis of 2008 from the invention of securitized mortgages through the proliferation of subprime mortgages and their dispersal to financial institutions and investors with limited disclosure of the financial risks. McLean is a contributor editor to *Vanity Fair*, Nocera a columnist for *The New York Times*. No notes or bibliography.

Morgenson, Gretchen, and Joshua Rosner, *Reckless Endangerment: How Outsized Ambition, Greed, and Corruption Led to Economic Armageddon*, Times Books, 2011.

The book focuses critically on the role played by Fannie Mae, the giant, government-sponsored mortgage company, in marketing subprime mortgages, especially loans written by its primary partner, Countrywide Financial. Morgenson is a Pulitzer Prize-winning reporter and columnist for *The New York Times*; Rosner is a consultant and early critic of the role of Fannie Mae and the other government-sponsored mortgage company, Freddie Mac. No notes or bibliography.

Articles

"Prosecuting Wall Street," 60 Minutes (Steve Kroft, correspondent; James Jacoby, producer), CBS News, Dec. 4, 2011, www.cbsnews.com/8301-18560_162-57336042/prose cuting-wall-street/?tag=contentMai n;cbsCarousel.

Two whistleblowers — former executives with Countrywide Financial and Citigroup — tell Kroft that they know of financial misconduct at their former companies but have not been questioned by government investigators.

Morgenson, Gretchen, and Louise Story, "A Financial Crisis With Little Guilt," *The New York Times*, April 14, 2011, p. A1.

The 4,000-word story details, in text and informative graphics, the lack of criminal prosecutions against companies or individuals involved in the financial crisis.

Reports and Studies

"The Financial Crisis Inquiry Report: Final Report of the National Commission on the Causes of the Financial and Economic Crisis in the United States," January 2011, www.gpoaccess.gov/fcic/fcic.pdf.
The congressionally appointed panel concluded that the financial crisis could have been avoided if the financial industry and public officials had heeded warnings and properly understood and managed evolving risks in the financial system. Republican members of the commission did not support the conclusions.

On the Web

"Chasing the Devil Around the Stump: Securities Regulation, the SEC, and the Courts," SEC Historical Society, Dec. 1, 2011, www.sechistorical.org/museum/galleries/ctd/.
The "gallery" in the SEC Historical Society's virtual museum and archive provides a compact, up-to-date overview of the Securities and Exchange Commission's regulatory activities and philosophy in the context of court decisions that alternately approve or disapprove of the agency's efforts at expansive enforcement. For a longer historical account, see the earlier gallery, "Fair to All People: The SEC and the Regulation of Insider Trading," Nov. 1, 2006, www.sechistorical. org/museum/galleries/it/.

Books on the Financial Crisis

The financial crisis of 2008 and the developments that led up to it have been chronicled and analyzed in a veritable flood of books. Here is a list of some that have drawn the most attention, with brief notations of the topics covered; all have been republished in paperback.

Cohan, William E., *House of Cards: A Tale of Hubris and Wretched Excess on Wall Street*, Doubleday, 2009. [Bear Stearns]

—, *Money and Power: How Goldman Sachs Came to Rule the World*, Anchor, 2011.

Lewis, Michael, *The Big Short: Inside the Doomsday Machine*, W.W. Norton, 2010. [bond and real estate derivative markets]

Lowenstein, Roger, *The End of Wall Street*, Reed Elsevier, 2010. [2008 financial collapse]

Sorkin, Andrew Ross, *Too Big to Fail: The Inside Story of How Wall Street and Washington Fought to Save the Financial System — and Themselves*, Viking, 2009. [2008 financial collapse]

Tett, Gillian, *Fool's Gold: How the Bold Dream of a Small Tribe at J.P. Morgan Was Corrupted by Wall Street Greed and Unleashed a Catastrophe*, Free Press, 2009.

Wessel, David, *In Fed We Trust: Ben Bernanke's War on the Great Panic*, Crown Business, 2009. [Federal Reserve]

Zuckerman, Gregory, *The Greatest Trade Ever: The Behind-the-Scenes Story of How John Paulson Defied Wall Street and Made Financial History*, Broadway Books, 2009. [hedge fund manager Paulson].

For More Information

American Bankers Association, 1120 Connecticut Ave., N.W., Washington, DC 20036; 1-800-226-5377; www.aba .com. Nation's largest banking trade association.

Campaign for America's Future, 1825 K St., N.W., Suite 400, Washington, DC 20006; 202-955-5665; www.ourfuture .org. Progressive political organization that opposes the influence of financial institutions in politics.

Consumer Financial Protection Bureau, 1500 Pennsylvania Ave., N.W., Washington, DC 20220; 202-435-7000; www.consumerfinance.gov. Independent agency within Federal Reserve that enforces consumer-protection laws against banks, mortgage lenders, credit card issuers, payday lenders and others.

Department of Justice, 950 Pennsylvania Ave., N.W., Washington, DC 20530; 202-514-2000; www.justice.gov. Federal executive department responsible for enforcing laws against financial misconduct.

Heritage Foundation, 214 Massachusetts Ave., N.E., Washington, DC 20002; 202-546-4400; www.heritage.org. Conservative think tank working to repeal financial reforms it says interfere with free enterprise.

Mortgage Bankers Association, 1919 Pennsylvania Ave., N.W., Washington, DC 20006; 202-557-2700; www.mbaa.org. National association promoting residential and commercial real estate markets and increased homeownership.

Securities and Exchange Commission, 100 F St., N.E., Washington, DC 20549; 202-942-8088; www.sec.gov. Federal agency that oversees publicly traded companies and enforces securities laws.

U.S. Chamber of Commerce, 1615 H St., N.W., Washington, DC 20062; 202-659-6000; www.uschamber.com. Lobbying group for businesses and trade associations.

7

Reviving Manufacturing

Peter Katel

Workers produce electronic components at the Mansfield Manufacturing plant in Dongguan, in southern China. Efforts to provide jobs for China's estimated 983 million working-age population could make it the world's No. 1 manufacturer as early as 2013. China exported an estimated $366 billion in goods of all kinds to the United States in 2010.

From *CQ Researcher*,
July 22, 2011

Gearing up for the 2012 election at a time when millions are jobless, President Obama is envisioning a tomorrow that looks like yesterday — when manufacturing jobs were plentiful. "I see a future where we train workers who make things here in the United States . . . working with their hands, creating value, not just shuffling paper," he told Northern Virginia Community College students in early June.[1]

The students are learning skills needed in today's computer-controlled factories, which have replaced the labor-intensive plants of the past. But critics on all sides fault Obama for not doing more to spur American manufacturing. Labor unions and small manufacturers want the government to take a more active role in boosting factory jobs, and big-business groups want less government regulation and more free-trade deals with other countries.

Other politicians besides Obama sense that voters are zeroing in on the issue. "They will say that we need . . . to be a center for making things, not just a service-sector, financial-sector economy," House Minority Whip Steny Hoyer, D-Md., said at a late-May forum sponsored by the Center for American Progress, a liberal think tank.[2]

The reason couldn't be simpler, said economist Jared Bernstein, who recently left the administration for the liberal Center on Budget and Policy Priorities. Manufacturing workers earn about 20 percent more than service-sector employees, he told NPR. "A stronger manufacturing sector with more employment opportunities is really important for loosening the middle class squeeze and providing people with better access to better jobs."[3]

Factory Jobs Have Plummeted

The number of U.S. factory workers rose dramatically in the industrial boom after World War II, but manufacturing employment began dropping in the late 1990s in the face of foreign competition, overseas production of U.S. goods (offshoring) and the recession.

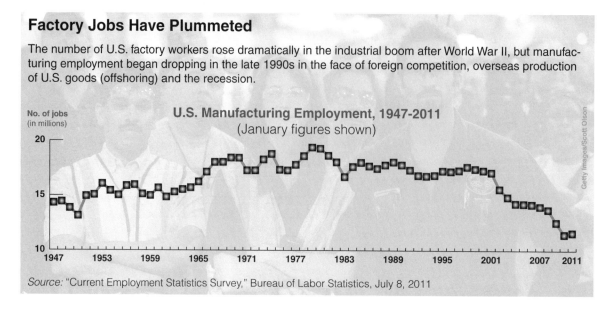

No. of jobs (in millions)

U.S. Manufacturing Employment, 1947-2011
(January figures shown)

Getty Images/Scott Olson

Source: "Current Employment Statistics Survey," Bureau of Labor Statistics, July 8, 2011

The growing attention to manufacturing comes amid persistently high unemployment, with a national joblessness rate of 9.2 percent. In numbers, 14.1 million people — out of 153.4 million working-age adults — are jobless, and another 8.6 million can find only part-time work.[4]

Manufacturing employment showed slight improvement from December 2009 to last April, adding 243,000 jobs. But the gain hardly compensated for the loss of more than 2 million jobs during the 2007-2009 recession — or of more than 5 million manufacturing jobs lost overall since 2001.[5]

And manufacturing itself, once the American economic dynamo, accounted for only 11.7 percent of gross domestic product (GDP) last year. In 1947 (as far back as official statistics go), the total of "value added" by industry — as manufacturing is formally defined — represented slightly more than 25 percent of the economy.[6]

The decline involves far more than the ups and downs of the business cycle, some experts say. "A number of global and domestic factors have contributed to a steady decline of U.S. manufacturing competitiveness, impacting the country's ability to produce . . . leading innovations," the Council on Competitiveness said in June, in a report endorsed by 32 university presidents and directors of national research centers, including Los Alamos National Laboratory. Above all, the group said, the educational

system, from elementary schools to universities, should raise standards and emphasize math, science and engineering. The council is a nonpartisan group of union, business and academic leaders "working to ensure U.S. prosperity."[7]

But some experts warn that a vast effort would be needed to bring new workers up to technological speed.

"Precision manufacturing, such as Germany specializes in, could potentially be a source of good jobs here," says Robert Reich, Labor secretary in the Clinton administration and now a public policy professor at the University of California, Berkeley, "but we'd have to redesign our educational system to prepare many more young people for these sorts of jobs."

Concern about education is shared across the ideological spectrum. But divisions run deep on matters as basic as the seriousness of the decline in manufacturing employment. Mark Perry, a visiting scholar at the American Enterprise Institute, a conservative think tank, notes that the automation of assembly lines and the growth of service sectors are global phenomena that have affected manufacturing sectors in all the long-industrialized countries, such as the nations of Western Europe. "Manufacturing as a share of GDP is declining here — but it's also declining for the whole world," says Perry. "Manufactured goods are falling as a share of overall income partly because the success of manufacturing has been huge increases in productivity." He acknowledges that the trend doesn't extend to the world's most rapidly industrializing country, China.

Economists at the Center for American Progress, which has close ties to the Obama administration, note that American manufacturing is underperforming its global competitors, with the U.S. share of world manufacturing down from about 28 percent in 1970 to about 18 percent in 2008.[8]

And Andrew N. Liveris, chairman and CEO of Dow Chemical Co., argues in a new book that productivity — the result of machines replacing people — didn't kill off manufacturing jobs in the 2000s. "These job losses" he writes, "are primarily the result of other countries attracting American business to their shores."[9] The post-2001 period coincides with China's full-scale entry into the global trading system.

Labor union activists, along with some small-scale manufacturers and academic economists and engineers, argue that other countries take an activist approach to manufacturing policy, including by training engineers to the same skill level as their U.S. counterparts on the high-end side of manufacturing. "If you're setting up an R&D facility in China or India," says T. Christopher Hill, retired vice provost for research at George Mason University in Fairfax, Va., and a longtime science and technology policy expert, "you're going to be hiring cosmopolitan, highly educated people just like you."

China figures in all (and India in many) discussions of U.S. manufacturing. Just as the United States became the world's top manufacturing power by mid-20th century, China seems to be on the way to achieving the same status in the 21st century. "The World's Factory," the Deloitte consulting firm dubbed China in a 2003 report. By 2007, another consultant, IHS Global Insight, forecast that China could become the world's No. 1 manufacturer as soon as 2013. The reasons include the Chinese government's relentless push to provide jobs for its huge working-age population, now estimated at 983 million.

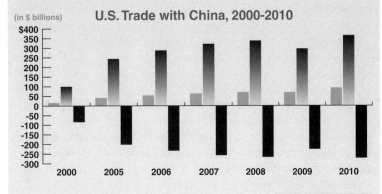

U.S.-China Trade Remains Unbalanced

The value of U.S. imports from China in 2010 exceeded U.S. exports by nearly $100 billion. The United States has had a negative trade balance with China since 2000.

U.S. Trade with China, 2000-2010
(in $ billions)

Source: Wayne M. Morrison, "China-U.S. Trade Issues," Congressional Research Service, June 2011, www.fas.org/sgp/crs/row/RL33536.pdf

- U.S. exports
- U.S. imports
- U.S. trade balance

Whether China breaks world trade rules in the process — by keeping its currency artificially low, for example — is a matter of fierce debate.[10]

China's exports to the United States in 2009 ran the gamut from sophisticated goods such as computer equipment (which tops the list), to relatively low-tech products such as clothing and toys. All told, China exported $296 billion in goods of all kinds to the United States (including food and lumber) in 2009. The estimate for 2010 was $366 billion.[11]

Meanwhile, U.S. exports to the enormous Chinese market consist overwhelmingly of agricultural products and raw materials — soybeans, scrap and waste products and resins and fibers. These categories accounted for $20.5 billion of the total $69.6 billion in U.S. exports to China in 2009. Manufactured U.S. goods shipped to China came to $11.3 billion.[12]

The predominance of manufactured goods — as opposed to agricultural and industrial raw materials — should be a matter of national concern, says Scott Paul, executive director of the Alliance for American Manufacturing, an advocacy organization formed by the United Steelworkers union and some manufacturers. "Our exports reflect very little value added by the U.S. economy," he says. "In essence we are fueling the Chinese industrial machine."

Business officials argue that American companies would have been irresponsible to stay out of one of the world's most rapidly expanding markets. "Sometimes it makes sense for a factory to locate in China," says Chad Moutray, chief economist for the National Association of Manufacturers. "In other cases, it can locate here. That is a company-by-company decision."

Those decisions may be starting to incline now in favor of American locations, the Boston Consulting Group reported last May. "Wages are rising in China, and it's far more advantageous to make things in the United States for U.S. consumption," says the report's author, senior vice president Harold Sirkin.

But one American with an eye on his future employment at the White House is still watching China and other foreign competitors nervously. "I don't want the new breakthrough technologies and the new manufacturing taking place in China and India," President Obama told workers at the Allison Transmission Corp. factory in Indianapolis last May. "I want all those new jobs right here in Indiana, right here in the United States of America, with American workers, American know-how, American ingenuity."[13]

As politicians and business and industry leaders confront the future of U.S. manufacturing, here are some of the questions being debated:

Is U.S. manufacturing reviving?

Since the late 1990s, growing numbers of U.S. firms and multinational corporations have set up factories in China, and billions of dollars' worth of China-manufactured goods line American store shelves.

Consequently, when the Boston Consulting Group (BCG) reported that some U.S. and multinational manufacturers, including Caterpillar and Ford, were planning to shift some jobs back to the United States, in part because of generous incentives offered by states and counties, the conclusion attracted considerable attention.[14]

"Higher wages in China may cause some firms that were going to scale back in the U.S. to keep their options open by continuing to operate a plant in America," Gary Pisano, a professor of business administration at Harvard Business School, told *The Economist* in a dispatch on the BCG report. Months earlier, *Wired*, which is widely read in technology-business circles, had chronicled smaller U.S. companies' growing disillusion with Chinese manufacturing.[15]

No one involved in debates over the state of U.S. manufacturing disputes the reports.

Nevertheless, Alan Tonelson, a research fellow at the U.S. Business & Industry Council Educational Foundation, an advocacy think tank promoting expansion of U.S.-based manufacturing, argues that examples of companies moving jobs back to the United States are "anecdotal" episodes that don't counter a more powerful offshoring trend. "From the late '90s through 2008, multinationals hired more people overseas," he says, citing data from the U.S. Bureau of Economic Analysis. The agency reported that corporations reduced U.S. workforces by 2.9 million during the past decade, while adding 2.4 million workers in foreign operations.[16]

Tonelson adds that rising labor costs in China may simply push corporations out of that country into other low-wage nations. "It just makes good business sense," he says. "When you're talking about very labor-intensive industries like garment making, there's no shortage of even worse-paid workers in places like Cambodia and Bangladesh."

Analysts from the big-business camp argue that labor-intensive industries are unlikely under any circumstances to remain in the United States, because companies looking to keep manufacturing costs down can easily find lower-wage countries. Moutray at the National Association of Manufacturers cites a U.S. Bureau of Labor Statistics report that U.S. manufacturing workers earned, on average, $26.19 an hour, including benefits, in 2009. "People have the perception that manufacturing is low-skilled," Moutray says, noting the relatively high pay scale. "The compensation continues to exceed that of nonfarm compensation in general. A large part of that is because of the high skills required."[17]

That pay advantage is likely to continue, Moutray says, because the American edge over global competitors lies in high-end production that demands skilled workers, who earn relatively high wages. "That's the kind of manufacturing we have to continue to emphasize," he says. "What is attractive about American manufacturing is its productivity." As these firms expand sales to the global market, they'll need to keep hiring Americans, he says.

But Reich, the former Labor secretary, argues that expanding U.S. manufacturing may have smaller effects than some hope, precisely because the U.S. manufacturing sector is so highly automated. "If the dollar continues to drop, and China's wages continue to rise, both absolutely and relative to the U.S. dollar," he says, "U.S.

manufacturing exports become more attractive, but that doesn't mean a lot more jobs."

Reich adds that the future of manufacturing wages isn't promising either. "Unionized wages in the auto industry are half for new workers relative to more senior workers," he says, citing an agreement between U.S. carmakers and the United Auto Workers (UAW) union under which new hires are paid about one-half the approximately $28-an-hour scale for current workers. "Even if some manufacturing jobs return, those jobs are not the same sort of high-wage, high-benefit jobs we used to have in manufacturing."[18]

Nevertheless, Perry of the American Enterprise Institute has a different take on lowered wages for manufacturing workers. "Maybe that is more realistic," he says, "and it makes companies more competitive, which makes it more likely that they expand operations here rather than in Mexico or other countries."

Perry, an economics professor at the University of Michigan, also argues that the declining role of manufacturing in the U.S. economy shouldn't be seen as an element of national weakness but as the inevitable result of technological advances. "It's not so much that manufacturing is getting outsourced but that the cost of manufactured goods is falling," he says. "Back in the late 1700s, something like 90 percent of people were employed in agriculture. Now, we only need less than 10 percent, but we spend less on food than at any time in history — but no one talks about agriculture being dead."

Do free-trade agreements with low-wage countries further weaken U.S. manufacturing?

The decline in U.S. manufacturing coincided with the rise of free-trade agreements between the United States

China and India Outpace U.S.

China and India are the world's two most competitive manufacturing nations, according to a study by the global consulting firm Deloitte. The United States ranks fourth. The assessment includes sales, service and distribution operations.

Manufacturing Competitiveness Rankings, 2010
(on a scale of 1 to 10)

1.	China	10.00
2.	India	8.15
3.	South Korea	6.79
4.	United States	5.84
5.	Brazil	5.41
6.	Japan	5.11
7.	Mexico	4.84
8.	Germany	4.80
9.	Singapore	4.69
10.	Poland	4.49

Source: "2010 Global Manufacturing Competitiveness Index," Deloitte, June 2010, www.deloitte.com/assets/Dcom-Global/Local Assets/Documents/Manufacturing/dtt_2010 Global Manufacturing Competitiveness Index_06_28_10.pdf

and a range of other countries, generally nations considered friendly to American interests. Pacts with 17 nations are now in effect. The agreements are designed to boost U.S. exports to partner countries — by allowing U.S. companies to bid for government contracts in free-trade partner nations, for example. Likewise, the United States agrees eventually to drop tariffs against imports from the partner countries.[19]

But ever since a long and intense debate leading up to the landmark 1994 North American Free Trade Agreement (NAFTA) between the United States, Mexico and Canada, critics have argued that the pacts serve above all to encourage U.S. companies to build factories abroad. Labor unions that portray free-trade agreements as vehicles for expanded offshoring are among the agreements' main critics. They are playing a major part in holding up congressional approval of pacts with Colombia, Panama and South Korea.

Defenders, including all recent Republican and Democratic presidents and their top officials, call the pacts essential to boosting U.S. job creation by expanding markets in which U.S. companies, including manufacturers, sell goods and services.

"We're in a global economy," says the National Association of Manufacturers' Moutray, noting the dynamism of the so-called BRIC nations — Brazil, Russia, India and China. "For multinationals, a lot of their growth in sales is coming from selling manufactured goods to the BRIC countries," he says, contrasting them to the "relatively mature" U.S. market.

Free-trade agreements, by that logic, play a key role in expanding opportunities for U.S. firms. "Where the growth is going to come from is in trade," Moutray says.

Manufacturing's Shrinking Share of U.S. Economy

Manufacturing accounts for only about 12 percent of the country's gross domestic product (GDP), or less than half of its share in 1953. Until 1969, manufacturing comprised at least 25 percent of the economy.

Manufacturing as a Share of GDP, 1947-2010

Percentage of GDP

Source: "Gross-Domestic-Product-by-Industry Accounts, 1947-2010," Bureau of Economic Analysis, April 2011, www.bea.gov/industry/gpotables/gpo_action.cfm

"When you lower barriers, you're going to see more trade going back and forth."

But the key to whether an agreement actually benefits the U.S. economy lies in the pact's details, says George Mason University's Hill. "When countries have highly asymmetric social and economic systems, with workplace standards, environmental standards and wage-and-hour standards that are very different," he says, "that's where problems can arise."

A deeper source of these problems, Hill argues, is that free-trade agreements often are proposed for political, rather than economic, reasons. He cites the proposed pact with Colombia, which has been awaiting congressional action for seven years. "Making an agreement with Colombia is a way of saying, in part, 'We appreciate the enormous effort you've made to bring drug cartels under control, and to open your markets,'" he says.

But Perry of the American Enterprise Institute argues that the proposed Colombia deal makes considerable economic sense. It would immediately eliminate Colombian tariffs on 80 percent of American consumer and industrial products exported to that country.[20] "If Caterpillar is selling to Colombia, the more they sell, the higher the profits," Perry says. The Illinois-based heavy-equipment maker strongly backs the proposed pact.

The need to step up exports makes trade deals essential, Perry says. "The more [trade agreements] we have, the easier it is for our manufacturers to export," he says. "That means more output and more jobs here."

Yet, argues economist Charles McMillion, the evidence is clear that free-trade pacts damage U.S. manufacturing. "After NAFTA, we've gone from a strong manufacturing surplus to a record manufacturing deficit," with Mexico, says McMillion, president of MBG Information Services, a Washington-based economic consulting firm. U.S. Commerce Department data he analyzed show trade surpluses in manufactured goods of $5.8 billion, $7.9 billion and $1.7 billion for the three years before NAFTA took effect — and deficits of $64.2 billion, $74.6 billion and $64.3 billion in 2006-2008.[21]

Should the government actively promote U.S. manufacturing and discourage further offshoring?

Debate on U.S. manufacturing reaches its sharpest point when the question is what, if anything, the federal government should do to ensure the viability of an important economic sector, such as auto manufacturing.

Big corporations and conservative economists argue that the best thing the government could do would be to lower and simplify corporate taxes.

Historically, the federal government didn't hesitate to protect developing industries from foreign competition. And free-trade pacts — strongly supported by export-oriented businesses — themselves represent a form of government action designed to boost business activity, hence profitability.

U.S. trading partners routinely make demands on U.S.-based multinationals who want to set up operations. James McGregor, an expert on foreigners doing business in China, told NPR that Chinese officials aren't hesitant to exact a price for access to their market. "The policy they've come up with is to force foreigners to hand over their technology if they want to do business here, he said, speaking from China. "In high-speed rail, in a lot of green energy, even in electric automobiles, they're telling companies, 'If you want to do business here, you come in, you take a minority share in a joint venture . . . and you hand over your technology.' What is worrisome for the companies is that they're creating their future global competitors."[22]

Nevertheless, McGregor also pointed out that the vast scale of the Chinese consumer market proves irresistible to U.S. and other foreign businesses. KFC, he said, is opening a restaurant in China every day, and Wal-Mart one store a week.[23]

Analysts whose perspectives tend to reflect corporate interests — and who dismiss the idea that U.S. manufacturing is eroding — reject what they view as heavy-handed federal

Union Members Earn More Than Non-Members

Union factory workers earn about 10 percent more than nonunion workers. Of the 13 million Americans employed in the manufacturing sector, only about 11 percent — 1.4 million — are union members.

Median Weekly Earnings of Full-time Manufacturing Workers, 2010

Manufacturing Workers in Unions

Sources: "Median Weekly Earnings of Full-Time Wage and Salary Workers by Union Affiliation, Occupation, and Industry," Bureau of Labor Statistics, January 2011, www.bls.gov/news.release/union2.t04.htm; "Union Affiliation of Employed Wage and Salary Workers by Occupation and Industry," Bureau of Labor Statistics, January 2011, www.bls.gov/news. release/union2.t03.htm

programs to spur American manufacturing growth. But they say they would welcome some government measures.

Daniel J. Ikenson, associate director of trade policy studies at the libertarian Cato Institute think tank, told a House panel last March that sweeping elimination of tariffs on imported materials and products used by U.S. manufacturers would keep U.S. goods competitive with those from Canada and Mexico. "Our bolder North American neighbors," he said, "have instituted permanent liberalization across the spectrum so as to afford their producers lower costs and an operational environment of greater business certainty," he said.[24]

Ikenson urged Congress to eliminate what he called "stifling" government regulations, echoing a longtime argument of business associations that complying with voluminous environmental and workplace-safety rules drives up costs and discourages manufacturing expansion. "Forward-looking governments around the world are wooing investment in R&D facilities [and] high-end manufacturing plants," he testified.[25]

Other experts argue, however, that the shrinking of American manufacturing capacity demands far more direct government measures. "Singapore, South Korea, Taiwan, Germany, Sweden all have pretty aggressive government engagement with their manufacturing firms," says Hill, the former George Mason University

AFP/Getty Images/Jim Watson

President Obama addresses workers at the Allison Transmission plant in Indianapolis, Ind., last May 6. "I don't want the new breakthrough technologies and the new manufacturing taking place in China and India," he said. "I want all those new jobs right here in Indiana, right here in the United States of America, with American workers, American know-how, American ingenuity."

would by definition be unfair. "Subsidies would have to come from someplace," he says. "And if we stimulate one sector, we have to de-stimulate another."

A better plan, Perry says, is to create a more "business-friendly environment" in general. Apart from free-trade agreements and immigration policies that encouraged foreign scientists and technology experts to work in the United States, he says, "One way would be to simplify taxes, either by reducing deductions and reducing the rate in larger tax brackets, or going to a flat tax." A flat tax is fixed, without going up or down according to the amount of money being taxed.

Advocates of government stimulus of manufacturing agree that at least one change in tax law would represent a crucial step in encouraging manufacturers to keep operations in the United States, or to move them back from overseas. "There is no tax benefit for making things in the United States and exporting them," says Paul of the Alliance for American Manufacturing. "The rest of the world has a value-added tax, which is rebatable for exports."

Paul argues that other sectors of the economy receive a variety of tax benefits designed to stimulate their businesses. "There are enormous advantages for oil and gas, which receive outsized benefits for exploration," he says, by way of example. "Manufacturing is almost unique in its lack of some sort of positive federal involvement. It is one sector of our economy that is mostly laissez-faire."

BACKGROUND

Giant in the Making

Recognition came early for American manufacturing prowess. At an international industrial exhibition in London in 1851, U.S. firearms makers showed off an innovative way to make guns from interchangeable parts shaped by machines.[27]

In the years that followed the London exhibition, British manufacturers trooped to the United States to learn how to use interchangeable parts to build consumer and industrial equipment, including clocks, watches and locks.

During the same period, one of the United States' most successful and celebrated manufacturers, Samuel

vice provost. "These governments provide R&D support, manufacturing demonstration centers and smarter kinds of education," Hill says. "A lot of that isn't being done in this country."

The reason for the lack of U.S. government support, Hill argues, is that the long-standing conservative view that the federal government should stay out of economic policy has proved more durable than programs that occasionally do get created.[26] "These things get adopted, usually by Democrats, get resisted in Congress, and as soon as the resisting power gets the upper hand, they reduce or kill them," Hill says.

But Perry of the American Enterprise Institute says policies specifically aimed at promoting manufacturing

Colt, built a factory in England to meet its demand for the revolver he had invented — the first firearm designed to fire several rounds in a row without reloading after each shot. The factory used machines made in Colt's home state of Connecticut.[28]

The New England origin of Colt and other innovators was no coincidence. In the pre-Civil War period, about half of the 143 important inventions patented in the United States were conceived in New England, writes Pulitzer Prize-winning historian James McPherson.[29] Yet the region accounted for less than 25 percent of the U.S. population.

Of all the factors behind New England's inventiveness, education was the indispensable ingredient. By 1850, McPherson writes, New England boasted a 95 percent adult literacy rate, extraordinarily high for the time. That background made them more adaptable to change, some historians reason, and more capable of devising new ways to produce goods.

In the South, by contrast, literacy levels were lower — 80 percent among white people and 10 percent among slaves. Eighty percent of the total labor force, slaves included, worked in agriculture — double the percentage in Northern states.

Manufacturing barely existed in the South, even when it came to making textiles from the region's No. 1 cash crop, cotton. Just before the war started in 1861, 97 percent of U.S. firearms, were manufactured in Northern states, along with 94 percent of the cloth, more than 90 percent of boots and shoes and 93 percent of the "pig iron" — the blast furnace-produced raw material of steel. The drastic imbalance in Northern and Southern manufacturing capacity played an enormous role in the North's victory in 1865.

A Giant Awakens

The 85 years following the end of the Civil War in 1865 saw the United States transformed into the world's manufacturing powerhouse.[30]

A crucial early event was the creation of "integrated" steel mills. Consolidating operations that had been carried out at separate plants, the integrated mills produced iron, refined it into steel and shaped it into parts needed for industry, such as railroad tracks.

The first integrated plant opened in 1875. Soon after, the growing supply of U.S. steel enabled speedy completion of a national railroad network, which made possible the wide distribution of manufactured goods and raw materials. A tariff of nearly 100 percent on imported British steel protected U.S. manufacturers.

Across industries, manufacturing became a massive, labor-intensive process starting in the 1880s. Factories, which had employed 200 workers at most, vastly expanded their workforces. By 1890, according to one count, the United States had 79 factories of at least 2,000 employees each.

As industrialization gathered strength, by 1900, 31 percent of the workforce was engaged in manufacturing, mining or construction. Over the course of the century, that share would decline, 100 years later, to 19 percent, as a consequence of automation.[31]

The big, new factories adopted the "continuous process" system that streamlined manufacturing into a single series of operations. Increasingly, machines at the heart of the process were powered by electricity. In 1890, 350 electricity generating stations were running across the country.

Another giant of industrial manufacturing took the continuous-process method further. In 1910, industrialist Henry Ford built an automobile factory in Highland Park, Mich., a Detroit suburb, that featured a major innovation — a moving assembly line that carried car frames past workers. By 1914, the factory was turning out 1,000 cars a day, and Ford was building 26 more assembly-line factories in other cities.

The Ford car itself represented another aspect of Ford's vision. Automobiles, in his view, should be a mass-consumption product instead of a custom-built luxury item. Automotive power got another boost from World War I, which the United States entered in 1917. Trucks proved crucial in the war. Afterwards, they played a growing role in civilian long-haul transportation. The war was also crucial to major advances in airplane technology, which helped lead to a postwar boom in the formation of airlines that transported mail and then passengers. Industry, in turn, kept on improving aircraft and engine design.[32]

The spread of electric power throughout cities meant the development of a vast, new market for manufactured consumer goods. By 1930, the overwhelming majority of dwellings in most major cities had electricity, and radios, irons, toasters, vacuum cleaners and washing machines were sold by the millions. Somewhat later, electric refrigerators also became a must-have in U.S. homes, replacing the old-fashioned ice-box.

The Great Depression, which began in 1929 and deepened through the 1930s, stifled manufacturing, but not permanently. Mass unemployment took a terrible human toll but also gave a powerful impulse to labor unions — seen as defenders of workers' rights. Unions had been steadily gaining strength since the late 19th century, as workers pushed back against unsafe and exploitative conditions. These included long hours — the average manufacturing workweek in 1900 was 53 hours — and factory work began at age 10. Data from the only two industries that kept safety statistics point to a high level of workplace dangers in the heyday of industrialization. Railroad accidents killed 2,550 workers in 1900, and almost 1,500 coal miners died in mining accidents.[33]

Manufacturing didn't recover from the Depression until World War II, which the United States entered in 1941 (two years after the conflict began). The war sparked a massive industrial revival. Airplanes, ships, tanks, transport vehicles, weapons and other war materiel poured out of American factories and shipyards. The vast output included 127,766 bombers, fighters and transport planes and 5,777 transport ships.[34]

Postwar Innovation

During the peacetime boom that followed the end of the war in 1945, the newly prosperous United States experienced huge demand for consumer goods of all kinds, from cars to television sets. In the late 1940s and the '50s, badly battered industrialized countries were still recovering from the war, leaving U.S. manufacturers with the American market, and much of the global market, to themselves.[35]

As late as 1963, U.S.-manufactured industrial products accounted for 40 percent of the world market — an extraordinary share for one country.

The postwar period of relative peace (numerous conflicts flared but not another major war) came at the price of the Cold War with the Soviet Union. From a manufacturing point of view, however, the nuclear-tinged hostility nourished America's military-industrial complex, which helped produce a series of world-changing technological innovations.

Starting in 1953, when IBM built the first electronic computer, big customers for the machines included the military, which used them in the fledgling space program and in designing ballistic missiles and nuclear submarines.

The early computers were huge, nearly room-sized affairs, and attention soon shifted to making them smaller and more powerful, but less power-hungry. The first solution lay in transistors, which replaced the larger, electricity-gobbling and burnout-prone glass vacuum tubes. In 1954, a design refinement allowed transistors to be made of cheaper and more plentiful silicon. Then, in a series of enormous advances in 1958, 1962 and 1965, engineers devised methods for etching integrated circuits — which combined the functions of transistors and other components — on silicon chips.[36]

The circuits were first used in computers for the military. Defense needs also played a part in the development of Arpanet, precursor of the Internet, created in 1969 to link computers used in government research projects. Nongovernment users gained access in the early 1970s.

The Cold War also helped propel the U.S.-led effort to rebuild the war-shattered economies of Western Europe and Japan. U.S. officials and their European counterparts wanted to rapidly create conditions for restoring prosperity and social tranquility, to ensure against discontent that the Soviet Union could exploit. In addition, postwar officials wanted to design a global trading system that would prevent the outbreak of the kinds of commercial rivalries that helped set the stage for both world wars.

Both efforts succeeded well enough that Western Europe and Japan would soon become major players in the global economy that began to emerge in the final decades of the 20th century. Competition from Asia extended all the way into the U.S. domestic market.

Asian Tigers

The first challenge came from Japan, which was developing its own steel industry. In the 1960s, American

C H R O N O L O G Y

1790s-1860s *Early Americans, especially New Englanders, show aptitude for manufacturing.*

1791 Eli Whitney invents cotton gin, revolutionizing U.S. agriculture.

1851 U.S. firearms maker Samuel Colt wows London industrial exhibition with guns made from identical, interchangeable parts.

1860 Almost all of the 143 inventions patented by Americans thus far came from non-slave states.

1865 Civil War ends with victory for Union, in part because of North's manufacturing power.

1870s-1945 *U.S. rapidly industrializes, becoming global manufacturing behemoth.*

1875 First steel plant opens with all manufacturing processes centralized under one roof.

1910 Henry Ford revolutionizes automobile manufacturing and marketing, with first moving assembly line and affordable prices.

1930 Electrification of U.S. cities spurs development of appliances.

1939-1945 Manufacturing expands during World War II.

1947-1970 *America reaches summit of global manufacturing power and innovation, but competition from abroad looms.*

1947 Invention of transistor is a milestone in early development of computers.

1955 U.S. carmakers supply 96 percent of domestic car market.

1965 Process for etching integrated circuits on silicon chips is perfected.

1969 Computer network created by researchers at national laboratories later becomes the Internet. . . . Japanese steelmakers acquire 15 percent of U.S. market share.

1970s-Present *Major new foreign competitors challenge signature U.S. manufacturing industries.*

1979 Japanese carmakers gain 13.1 percent of U.S. market as American-made gas guzzlers lose popularity.

1981 "Voluntary export agreement" with Japan temporarily reduces number of Japanese cars exported to U.S.

1990 Foreign-owned car factories in the United States produce 2 million vehicles for domestic market.

1994 After an intense, years-long political fight, Congress approves the North American Free Trade Agreement (NAFTA), lowering tariffs and other trade barriers between the United States, Canada and Mexico.

2001 China is admitted to World Trade Organization. . . . President George W. Bush grants China permanent normal trade status with U.S.

2002 U.S. trade deficit with China grows to $103 billion — up from $3.5 billion four years before.

2003 Asian carmakers supply 32.5 percent of U.S. car market.

2007 United States signs free-trade agreements with South Korea and Panama, which follow pact signed with Colombia one year earlier; congressional approval stalls after union-led political opposition.

2010 Manufacturing accounts for only 11.7 percent of U.S. gross domestic product.

2011 Manufacturing job losses since 2001 reach 5 million, including 2 million lost in 2007-2009 recession. . . . President Obama tours factories and community colleges to promote high-tech manufacturing, technical training. . . . Obama administration promises business community to eliminate burdensome and unneeded regulations. . . . Lawmakers from both parties in both chambers introduce legislation that would force U.S. action against China for allegedly manipulating its currency. . . . Obama urges Boeing Co. and International Association of Machinists to settle conflict over jobs relocated to a nonunion plant in South Carolina.

Where Have All the Skilled Workers Gone?

"The people out of work just don't match the types of jobs here."

If American manufacturing is eroding, as some experts say, Lee Combs says he knows one reason: Young people are ill-prepared to work in the field.

"The high schools, the colleges around here, they're just not training people for manufacturing," says Combs, who owns and runs SC Manufacturing Inc., a machine shop in Akron, Ohio, that produces parts for the steel, oil and gas and other industries. "Everybody has to be a lawyer; nobody wants to make things."

Four years ago Combs grew so concerned about the scarcity of qualified workers that he founded his own school. The Akron CNC Training Center offers a four-month course in operating the computer numerical control devices at the heart of modern manufacturing. Operators program and monitor CNC machines as they transform metal or other material into precisely shaped parts. Even furniture makers are now using CNC equipment.[1]

The center runs day and evening classes of 10 to 15 students each. The course costs $4,100. "Before graduation, each [student] had a job," Combs says. His daughter, Laurie Norval, runs the school. Most of the students, who include a small number of women, range in age from 30 to 45.

Typically, they found themselves jobless as the recession took its toll.

Combs' school operates as part of the state-licensed Cleveland Industrial Center, established by another machine shop in 1993 in response to the same manpower problem that Combs cites.[2] His frustration grew out of his steadily increasing need for skilled workers.

"There's so much work out there it's incredible," he says. "No one can find help. Wages are going up, companies are stealing workers from other companies."

Combs acknowledges that his experience is hard to reconcile with high levels of joblessness. But most people looking for work, he says, don't have the training or experience needed to do the skilled work his business requires.

Akron, historically a tire-manufacturing center, lies within an industrial zone centered in Cleveland. More than 40,000 manufacturing workers in the area lost their jobs in the recession. Manufacturers that survived, or are starting up, aren't looking to recreate the old days of assembly-line work. "We're not going to employ thousands of people in manual labor again," Combs says. "We'll never beat China for just labor."

---

steelmakers failed to invest in new technology. Consequently, by the late 1960s, imported Japanese steel supplied 15 percent of U.S. demand, a share that rose to about 20 percent by 1988.[37]

The U.S. steel industry's problems may have been invisible to most Americans outside of steel towns such as Pittsburgh and Youngstown, Ohio, which were directly affected. But no one could miss the transformation of the American auto market.

After major oil and gasoline price increases in the 1970s, a growing number of consumers opted for cars powered by four-cylinder engines — a Japanese specialty. Yet U.S. carmakers kept turning out roomy gas guzzlers powered by six- or eight-cylinder engines.

As early as 1979, Japanese imports accounted for 13.1 percent of U.S. motor vehicle sales (Volkswagen

and other German companies accounted for 3 percent). By 2003, Asian manufacturers, a group that now included Korean companies, accounted for 32.5 percent of the U.S. vehicle market.[38]

The trend so alarmed industry and government officials that the United States negotiated a "voluntary export agreement" with Japan. The four-year deal, signed in 1981, effectively cut back from 2 million to 1.68 million, initially, the number of fuel-efficient Japanese cars exported to the United States.

A similar deal in 1986 covered Japanese semiconductors and other key components of high-tech devices, which were becoming widely available.

Foreign carmakers, meanwhile, began setting up factories in the United States after the export agreement expired. By 1990, they were producing more

But Asian competitors who targeted his industry, Combs said, affected only a segment of it. "China manufacturing works if you're making a half-inch bolt that hasn't changed in years," he says. "But if you're upgrading, you can't get a response from the shops there, and the quality is not there on a consistent basis."

Combs is hardly a dispassionate observer on the issue of quality control in Chinese machine shops. But he's not the only machine-shop owner who has been lamenting a scarcity of workers. An executive of Astro Manufacturing and Design, in Eastlake, Ohio, outside Cleveland, told *The New York Times* last year that his firm was searching for six CNC machinists. But after combing through 50 resumes, the personnel office was still hunting.[3]

A pharmaceutical manufacturer that uses computer-controlled machines also found skills inadequate among the vast majority of job-seekers. "You would think in tough economic times that you would have your pick of people," said Thomas J. Murphy, CEO of Ben Venue Laboratories, a contract drug manufacturer for pharmaceutical companies. But the firm hired only 47 of 3,600 applicants for jobs that pay about $31,000 a year.[4]

And the chief executive of a nonprofit that is trying to promote the development of medical technology in the Cleveland area also noted the mismatch between jobs and job-seekers.

"The people that are out of work just don't match the types of jobs that are here, open and growing," Baiju R. Shah, told *The Times*.[5]

Still, in a labor climate afflicted simultaneously by unemployment and skill shortages, Combs says his small school has no trouble filling its classrooms. "We don't advertise," he says. "Word of mouth is the best."

Word of the school may travel especially quickly because — in another paradox — CNC training is scarce, despite the need. "Most of the high schools have gotten rid of machinist training," Combs says. "We've been talking about this in Akron in machine shop groups for years, and nobody listens. Everybody wants their little Johnny to go to college."

And yet, Combs says, a college graduate who finds work shouldn't count on it lasting. "Who gets laid off first? It's not the machinist, I guarantee you."

— Peter Katel

[1]David A. Keeps, "Shape of things to come," *Los Angeles Times*, Jan. 4, 2007, p. F1, http://articles.latimes.com/2007/jan/04/home/hm-future4.

[2]"About Us," Cleveland Industrial Training Center, undated, www.cleveland industrialtraining.com/aboutus.html.

[3]Quoted in Motoko Rich, "Jobs Go Begging As Gap Is Exposed In Worker Skills," *The New York Times*, July 2, 2010, p. A1, www.nytimes.com/2010/07/02/ business/economy/02manufacturing.html.

[4]Quoted in *ibid.*

[5]Quoted in *ibid.*

than 2 million vehicles a year. In 2000, foreign-owned factories produced more than 4 million vehicles.[39]

U.S. carmakers' foreign activities soon became a major focus of congressional debate over the proposed North American Free Trade Agreement (NAFTA), which sought to create a European Union-style continental trading partnership between the United States, Canada and Mexico. U.S. auto firms were already active in both neighboring countries and argued that expanding trade between the three nations would boost employment. Following a drawn-out political battle between unions and big-business interests in the late 1980s and early '90s during the George H. W. Bush administration, Congress approved the agreement in 1994 during the Clinton administration. Another major trade agreement came in November 2001, when China became a member of the World Trade Organization (WTO), a global system that lays out rules and standards of fair and unfair trading practices. A month later, President George W. Bush granted China permanent normal trade status, which he said would open China's vast market to American products.[40]

The new trade agreements capped China's opening to both domestic capitalism and to large-scale investment by foreign corporations, a process that began in 1978 and expanded in stages throughout the 1980s and '90s.

By 1988, American companies were exporting $5 billion worth of merchandise to China, while U.S. imports of Chinese products totaled $8.5 billion. As of 2002, the trade gap between the two nations had mushroomed from $3.5 billion to $103 billion.[41]

New Boeing Plant Tests South's Manufacturing Strategy

Federal government alleges effort to avoid paying union wages.

Southern states have been flying high as destinations for U.S. and foreign factories, but a conflict over a new Boeing Co. airplane plant in North Charleston, S.C., threatens to bring the South's manufacturing strategy back down to Earth.

The federal agency that polices unfair labor practices has charged that Boeing's opening of a production line for its new 787 Dreamliner passenger jet outside the company's unionized Pacific Northwest factories amounts to illegal retaliation against a labor union. The new $900 million, 1,200-employee South Carolina plant opened this year.[1]

The National Labor Relations Board (NLRB) alleged that Boeing was retaliating against the International Association of Machinists and Aerospace Workers (IAM) for past strikes at Boeing's main plant in Everett, Wash., and at plants in Oregon. Boeing denies the charge, arguing that it seeks to add jobs in South Carolina without eliminating any from its older manufacturing sites in the Pacific Northwest.

The politically charged case could have huge consequences for Southern states seeking to lure manufacturing jobs from labor-friendly localities in the North and West. South Carolina and seven other Southern states have union membership rates of less than 5 percent of their public- and private-sector workforces. In Washington state, by contrast, 19.4 percent of the workforce is unionized.[2]

The pay differential between union and nonunion labor forces is significant, too. Unionized fulltime workers in Washington state had median weekly pay of $917; the median rate for the non-unionized workers was $717.[3]

NLRB Acting General Counsel Lafe Solomon filed the allegation against Boeing last April after a complaint by the IAM. The action prompted a wave of criticism against Solomon and the Obama administration.

"I was a reluctant issuer of this complaint," Solomon told the House Oversight and Government Affairs Subcommittee. "I wanted it settled. I thought it was in everybody's best interest to be settled. The parties have a long-standing relationship with each other. . . . And I would have preferred them working this out."[4]

President Obama, whose chief of staff, William M. Daley, was a Boeing board member, as was Commerce secretary nominee John Bryson, made clear that he too would like the case settled without further litigation. "What defies common sense is the notion that we would be shutting down a plant or laying off workers because labor and management can't come to an agreement," Obama said at a June 29 press conference.[5]

The battle over Boeing is taking place as states and regions are competing ever more intensely for manufacturing jobs after U.S. companies "offshored" thousands of jobs to other countries. The competition often pits states with "right to work" laws that discourage unionization against those with laws that make it easier for unions to organize factories and other job sites. South Carolina and all other Southern states are in the "right to work" camp. Washington state and Oregon are union strongholds.[6]

The NLRB's Solomon said in the complaint that Boeing made the move because of five IAM strikes since 1977, the most recent in 2005 and 2008. He said the company was hitting back at workers who took part in the strikes and aimed to "discourage these and/or other employees from engaging in these or other union . . . activities." As evidence, Solomon cited statements by Boeing executives, including one in which President and CEO Jim McNerny said in a conference call that the South Carolina decision was due to "strikes happening every three or four years in Puget Sound."[7]

Boeing, in its official response, argues that the South Carolina operation would be an expansion that wouldn't cost any jobs in the unionized plants in the Pacific Northwest. And even if Boeing established the South Carolina operation to protect against future strikes, that action "would not be evidence that the decision to place the second assembly line in North Charleston was designed to retaliate against the IAM for past strikes," the company said.[8]

The NLRB began hearings in June in Seattle on its complaint.[9] Meanwhile, politicians and advocates on both sides of the business-labor divide were arguing over the case's possible effects on the South's manufacturing strategy.

"We should have another wave of suppliers headed to the Southeast," Republican Sen. Lamar Alexander of Tennessee said in response to the NLRB complaint, which he said would "freeze companies, such as these suppliers, who might be thinking about expanding into a right-to-work state."[10]

But Rep. Dennis Kucinich, a liberal Democrat from Ohio, argued that Boeing was trying to exploit economic anxieties in competing states. "It's Boeing that has pitted one state against the other," Kucinich said. "It's Boeing that's pitting one group of workers against another at a time of great economic uncertainty and at a time when corporate profits generally are rising during a jobless recovery."[11]

The South has been a manufacturing magnet long before Boeing arrived.[12] Nissan Motor Co. opened a Tennessee forklift distribution center in 1977, and a decade later Japanese automakers and other companies operated at least 56 factories in the state. In 1985, General Motors located its Saturn car factory in Spring Hill, Tenn. (The Saturn line was discontinued in 2009, but GM uses the factory for other products.) BMW opened a factory in Spartanburg, S.C., in 1993. The same year Mercedes-Benz picked Vance, Ala., as the site of an SUV factory.[13]

Kia, the Korean carmaker, opened a $1 billion factory in West Point, Ga., in 2009, hiring 2,500 workers. Chris Cummiskey, Georgia's economic development commissioner, said that with employment by supply firms added, the Kia plant was responsible for 20,000 jobs.[14]

Yet, some note that just because a manufacturer locates a plant in the South doesn't mean the jobs will be there forever. In West Point, some longtime residents remember when textile plants shut down and moved the jobs to Asia. "We've been there," said Jimmy Norred. "This place was almost desperate."[15]

— *Peter Katel*

Boeing will assemble its 787 Dreamliner passenger jet at this new $900 million plant in North Charleston, S.C.

[4]"House Oversight and Government Reform Committee Holds Field Hearing on Unionization and Regulation Issues . . . ," *CQ Congressional Transcripts*, June 17, 2011.

[5]Quoted in Michael D. Shear, "Obama: Republican Leaders Must Bend on Taxes," *The New York Times*, June 29, 2011, http://thecaucus.blogs.nytimes. com/2011/06/29/obama-republican-leaders-must-bend-on-taxes/?hp.

[6]National Right To Work Committee, (map), undated, www.nrtwc.org/.

[7]"Complaint and Notice of Hearing," before the National Labor Relations Board, Case 19-CA-32431, April 20, 2011, pp. 4-6, http://seattletimes. nwsource.com/ABPub/2011/04/20/2014824340.pdf.

[8]"Answer," before the National Labor Relations Board, May 4, 2011, www.deseret news.com/media/pdf/468907.pdf.

[9]Phuong Le, "Hearing begins in labor complaint against Boeing," The Associated Press, June 14, 2011.

[10]Quoted in Dave Flessner, "Lamar Alexander touts Tennessee," *Chattanooga Times Free Press* (Tennessee), May 24, 2011, p. C1.

[11]"House Oversight and Government Review Subcommittee," *op. cit.*

[12]John Holusha, "New G.M. Plant Site Linked to Shift in Population," *The New York Times*, July 31, 1985, p. A8.

[13]Doron P. Levin, "What BMW Sees In South Carolina," *The New York Times*, April 11, 1993, Sect. 3, p. 5; Donald W. Nauss, "Mercedes to Build Plant in Alabama," *Los Angeles Times*, Sept. 30, 1993, http://articles.latimes.com/1993-09-30/business/fi-40474_1_rural-alabama.

[14]"Job Creation and Economic Growth," Subcommittee on Commerce, Manufacturing and Trade, House Energy and Commerce Committee, written testimony, March 3, 2011.

[15]Quoted in Julia Bauer, "Georgia town knows Michigan pain," *Kalamazoo Gazette* (Michigan), Sept. 12, 2010, p. F1; Julia Bauer, "Union shops hindering job growth?," *Bay City Times* (Michigan), Sept. 5, 2010, p. A1.

[1]Steve Wilhelm, "Boeing's new Southern workplace gears up to show that it's the future," *Puget Sound Business Journal*, June 10, 2011, (no page number noted); Keith Laing, "Despite lawsuit, Boeing opens SC plant," *The Hill*, June 10, 2011, http://thehill.com/blogs/ transportation-report/aviation/165787-despite-lawsuit-boeing-opens-south-caro lina-787-plant.

[2]"Union affiliation of employed wage and salary workers by state," U.S. Bureau of Labor Statistics, updated Jan. 21, 2011, www.bls.gov/news.release/union2. t05.htm.

[3]"Union Members Summary," U.S. Bureau of Labor Statistics, Jan. 21, 2011, www.bls.gov/news.release/union2.nr0.htm.

CURRENT SITUATION

China's Currency

Proposals to boost U.S. manufacturing tend to fall into either the liberal Democratic or conservative Republican category. But one issue brings liberal Democrats together with some conservative Republicans, despite their disagreements about nearly everything else.

In the view of these unlikely allies, China keeps the value of its currency, known as the yuan, or renminbi, artificially low, measured against the dollar, so that Chinese exports will be cheaper, and hence sell better. Competing U.S. manufacturers, the argument goes, suffer as a result.

"China has been given free rein to manipulate its currency for far too long, with hundreds of thousands of American jobs lost and unsustainable global trade imbalances as a result," Rep. Sander Levin, D-Mich., said last February when he introduced the Currency Reform for Fair Trade Act of 2011. It would toughen existing law by requiring the federal government to impose duties — in effect, import taxes — on goods from countries that keep their currencies undervalued.[42]

The House bill has 110 Democratic and 46 Republican cosponsors. An identical Senate bill introduced by Sen. Sherrod Brown, D-Ohio, also has a bipartisan group of cosponsors, though an imbalanced one, with nine Democrats, two Republicans and one independent signed on.

Somewhat weaker Republican support for cracking down on China reflects a business community split. Small and medium-sized manufacturers back a hardline approach. Most large corporations, with big operations in China, shy away from tough action, fearing a trade conflict. They tend to support U.S. litigation against China in the World Trade Organization (WTO).[43]

That division was evident at a Joint Economic Committee hearing in June. One of two lawmaker witnesses, Democratic Sen. Debbie Stabenow of Michigan, condemned China for "breaking international trade rules." Republican Rep. Charles Bass of New Hampshire, on the other hand, argued against the view that manufacturing-sector problems grow out of "an unfair playing field with our trading partners."[44]

Of the other witnesses, Paul, of the Alliance for American Manufacturing, co-founded by the steelworkers union, devoted considerable attention to what he called China's "currency manipulation" and its effects on U.S. manufacturers. And economist Mark Zandi (a Democrat who advised Republican Sen. John McCain of Arizona in the 2008 presidential election) called China's currency policy the "most critical" barrier to free trade by a U.S. trading partner.[45]

But Alex Brill, a research fellow at the conservative American Enterprise Institute, made no mention of China's currency. Jay Timmons, president and CEO of the National Association of Manufacturers (NAM), whose board members include officials from major multinational corporations, referred briefly to the issue. The association's manufacturing strategy, which Timmons cited, does raise China's currency policy, but only in general terms: It calls for a trade policy that, among other things, "reduces distortions due to currency exchange rates."[46]

The Obama administration has also been handling the issue cautiously. In February, days before lawmakers introduced the crackdown bills, the administration declined to cite China as a currency manipulator. The Treasury Department, in a biannual report to Congress on China's currency, noted that the Chinese government had allowed the value of the yuan to rise 5 to 6 percent.[47]

That increase still left the Chinese currency "substantially undervalued," the department said. But the report concluded that the undervaluation wasn't extreme enough to be categorized as "manipulation," which could have triggered retaliation by the United States in the form of tariffs.[48]

An economist who follows the issue closely said the administration seemed to have calculated that quiet diplomacy would work better. "I smell a deal here," C. Fred Bergsten, director of the Peterson Institute for International Economics, told *The New York Times*, "deafening silence from the Americans in return for, maybe, some kind of commitment from the Chinese to let the rate move."[49]

Easing Regulations

The Obama administration is telling manufacturing executives that the White House feels their pain in dealing with federal regulations on environmental protection and consumer and workplace issues. President Obama directed his staff to identify regulations that are out-of-date, unnecessary, excessive or in conflict with other rules.[50]

"Sometimes you can't defend the indefensible," White House Chief of Staff William Daley said at a June meeting convened by the NAM.[51]

Doug Starrett, president and CEO of L.S. Starrett Co. of Athol, Mass., a precision toolmaker, had prompted Daley's comment, with an account of the firm's plans to upgrade a water-powered generator in Athol — plans that ran into a challenge from the U.S. Fish and Wildlife Service. Starrett characterized the conflict as one of thousands around the country in which the government "continues to throw sand into the gears of progress."[52]

Daley promised to look into the case. "We will . . . see," he said, "if there is any way to bring reason to what's happened."[53]

According to a First U.S. Circuit Court of Appeals decision on the case in June, the agency had concluded that expanding the generator could endanger migratory fish on the Millers River. The Federal Energy Regulatory Commission (FERC) then ruled that it would have to license the expansion, something Starrett had thought wasn't required.[54]

Judge Norman H. Stahl expressed sympathy for Starrett in terms that echo business executives' complaints. "Here we have the last full-line precision tool company producing its product within the United States," the judge wrote, in a concurring opinion endorsed by Judge Juan R. Torruella. "In order to remain competitive in the global marketplace, Starrett has aggressively sought to lower its cost structures and has instituted many energy conservation measures. . . . Our decision today, however, may well mean that this company loses the economic advantage it would have from its low-cost, nonpolluting power structure."[55]

Nevertheless, the law was clear that the Starrett project fell under FERC jurisdiction, the judges concluded. But they did hint that FERC might have handled the case differently. "It would seem," they wrote, "that Starrett's project is a prime example of efficient usage through a nonpolluting power source and is one that we should be encouraging, not stifling."[56]

But though excessive regulation is a long-standing complaint of manufacturers, and businesses in general, some accuse them of exaggerating the effects of red tape.

"If the problem was over-regulation, there wouldn't be manufacturing in Germany," says Paul of the Alliance for American Manufacturing. "Fundamentally, if you took

President Bill Clinton signs the North American Free Trade Agreement (NAFTA) between the United States, Mexico and Canada on Dec. 8, 1993. Critics, including labor unions, argue that such pacts encourage U.S. companies to build factories abroad. They are resisting congressional approval of U.S. pacts with Colombia, Panama and South Korea. Defenders, including all recent Republican and Democratic presidents, say trade agreements boost U.S. job creation by expanding markets in which American companies, including manufacturers, sell goods and services.

AFP/Getty Images/Paul J. Richards

that argument to the extreme, unless we had regulations as poor as China's we wouldn't be competing at all."

Free-Trade Agreements

Lawmakers are trying to reach a settlement seen by some as essential to approval of three pending free-trade agreements with potentially strong effects on U.S. manufacturers.

U.S. Chamber of Commerce President Thomas J. Donohue said in mid-June that lawmakers were "right on the doorstep" of a compromise on expanding some provisions of the Trade Assistance Act (TAA), a 1962 law that extends cash and other assistance to workers who lose their jobs as a result of foreign competition made possible by free-trade deals.[57]

Agreement on that assistance is considered crucial, in turn, for congressional approval of the free-trade agreements with South Korea, Colombia and Panama. The Colombia pact has been awaiting enactment since 2006, and the other two since 2007.[58]

The proposed expansions would increase a health care tax credit to 80 percent of medical costs and make service and public-sector employees, as well as workers who suffered when their jobs were outsourced to another

Do proposed free-trade agreements threaten U.S. manufacturing?

YES
Alan Tonelson
Research Fellow, U.S. Business and Industry Council

Written for *CQ Researcher*, July 2011

The economic acid test of any U.S. trade agreement is whether it promotes the nation's prosperity on net, or is likely to do so. According to this common-sense standard, the proposed U.S. free-trade agreements with Korea — an industrial powerhouse — and with Colombia and Panama look like clear losers, and doubly so when it comes to American domestic manufacturing. And since domestic manufacturing revival is central to America's recovery hopes — because of the sector's strong record of creating high-wage jobs and fostering innovation — any trade deals likely to weaken manufacturing should be rejected by Congress.

Quantifying the economic impact of individual trade agreements is difficult at best. But one set of conclusions seems reasonably uncontroversial. If trade deals result in U.S. trade deficits, or worsen America's trade balances, they detract from growth. If they result in trade surpluses or improve the nation's trade balances, they add to growth.

Further complicating analysis: Trade deals don't determine trade balances by themselves. Domestic conditions like growth rates and interest rates also matter. Because the agreements now before Congress are prospective, the evidentiary jury is still out. But Washington's trade diplomacy record over many decades, and long-standing approaches that shaped the Korea, Colombia and Panama agreements, are hardly encouraging.

America has reached several global free-trade deals since the end of World War II. Yet the nation has run large, growing trade deficits practically every year since 1970 — and the shortfalls have become especially big in manufacturing.

America's many bilateral trade deals have generated more mixed results, but major manufacturing deficits with leading manufacturing countries, like Korea, have proved remarkably persistent. In the case of China, these gaps have soared exponentially.

Korea also presents its own specific challenges. Its national business model emphasizes promoting manufacturing in Korea and shutting out foreign competition. Korea's main individual trade barriers are rarely written down in easily accessible regulatory and legal codes. Thus they're excruciatingly difficult for U.S. or any foreign officials or businesspeople even to identify, much less address.

Indeed, the proposed Korea trade deal is best seen as an agreement between a country determined to strengthen its manufacturing at all costs, and one content to leave the sector's fate to market forces — whether its trade partners take them seriously or not. As history teaches, such initiatives usually spell big trouble for U.S. domestic manufacturing.

NO
Jay Timmons
President and CEO, National Association of Manufacturers

From testimony before the Joint Economic Committee, June 22, 2011

Many policymakers oppose trade agreements in the mistaken belief that these agreements are the cause of the U.S. manufacturing job loss. The opposite is true. Trade agreements have never been a major factor in our manufactured goods deficit, and over the past three years we have had a manufactured goods trade surplus of $70 billion with our trade agreement partners. During that same period, our manufactured goods trade deficit with countries without trade agreements with us was $1.3 trillion.

The most important element of a progressive trade policy is a strategy that embraces market-opening bilateral and regional trade agreements.

A critical first step is to pass and implement immediately the pending trade agreements with Korea, Colombia, and Panama — agreements that are estimated to generate $13 billion of new exports and support 100,000 jobs.

These agreements have been pending in Congress for four years, and during this time our competitors have not been idle. There are hundreds of trade agreements, while the United States has free-trade agreements with only 17 countries. As our competitors race to negotiate barrier-reducing agreements for their companies, U.S. manufacturers are falling further and further behind in their ability to secure markets.

The United States also needs to keep pressing for meaningful multilateral agreements in the World Trade Organization (WTO) as well, but we must not let that delay us from obtaining the quicker and deeper liberalization that bilateral and regional agreements provide.

The U.S. domestic market for manufactured goods is not expected to grow more rapidly than it has in the past 20 years, when manufacturing productivity exceeded the growth of output. So if production is to outpace productivity and create new jobs, we will have to rely more on exporting to the more rapidly growing markets overseas, particularly in Latin America and Asia.

Even though the United States remains the world's largest manufacturer, producing one in every five dollars of all manufactured goods in the world, we steadily are losing ground in world markets. Manufacturers believe we need a trade policy that will strengthen manufacturing in America, improve our competitiveness and stimulate job creation at home.

There are 120 other free-trade agreements being negotiated around the world, but the U.S. is only party to one of those. Our competitors are looking for ways to take our mantle of economic leadership away from us, and we ought not to be unintentionally helping them do so.

country, eligible for the aid. Those assistance measures were included in the 2009 economic stimulus bill but lasted only two years.[59]

"Stimulus . . . wasn't meant to make permanent policy," Republican Sen. Charles E. Grassley of Iowa, an influential member of the Senate Finance Committee, told *CQ Weekly*.[60]

But Michigan's Rep. Levin, the top Democrat on the House Ways and Means Committee, countered, "In a period of high unemployment it is inexcusable, intolerable and unacceptable that the 2009 [Trade Assistance Act] provisions have not been extended."[61]

To be sure, even approval of the stepped-up assistance might not ensure passage of the trade deals. An AFL-CIO official criticized the TAA as an inadequate tradeoff for a free-trade agreement.[62]

However, the Chamber of Commerce, NAM and other major business federations that have been pushing hard for the trade deals told the White House in May that they considered the TAA "a central part of America's overall trade agenda."[63]

The set-to over the assistance bill raises the ideological issues that punctuate the entire question of U.S. manufacturing policy in the age of globalization. At the Puritan Products chemical firm in Bethlehem, Pa., in late June, Sen. Robert Casey, D-Pa., told workers in support of the TAA, "We have to compete every day of the week with countries that frankly cheat and make it much more difficult to have a level playing field for folks that are trying to manufacture a product in this difficult environment."[64]

OUTLOOK

Brain Drain?

For some of those most worried about America's manufacturing future, the looming danger isn't the loss of more factory smokestacks, it's brain drain. "The belief that we could invent stuff here and make stuff there is now, I think, under serious reconsideration," said Ron Bloom, the Obama administration's senior counselor for manufacturing policy.[65]

That belief, Bloom said, grew out of a thesis that America had evolved into a post-manufacturing era. "A lot of people in this town believed that manufacturing's decline was inevitable. . . . They actually thought it was a good thing," he said.[66]

But, said Bloom, a former special assistant to the president of the United Steelworkers union, the reality is that engineering and R&D can't be run separately from production, in the long run. "If you look at how companies are behaving . . . if they relocate their manufacturing operations, slowly over time, their R&D and their innovation will go with it."[67]

In a variation of that view, former Labor secretary Reich argues that the assembly phase of manufacturing can easily be carried out separately from the engineering and design functions. "It is important for designers and R&D people to be closely involved in making high-value-added components that find their way into manufactured items," he says.

Reich says the biggest American corporations are now multinational entities that don't necessarily have a vested interest in keeping their high-end operations in the United States, where higher wages and tougher regulations may make manufacturing costs higher for some products. And Reich argues that unions and smaller high-tech firms, which do have a stake in keeping the engineering side of manufacturing, at least, in the United States, don't pack much political punch. "It's an open question, where that lobbying for the high-value-added jobs of the future to be in the United States is going to come from," he says.

An even darker view comes from economist McMillion, who has been tracking indicators of shrinkage in U.S. manufacturing capacity. "We've sustained a massive shift out of production," he says. "In April, our total manufacturing output was 2.1 percent less than in April, 2000. That 11-year decline had not happened since 1927 to 1938."

Even more problematic, McMillion says, today's budget cuts at the federal and state levels further reduce physical and human resources on which manufacturers rely. "We don't build new roads, we close our schools, close our libraries." And, he adds, "I don't see the political will to fix this."

However, other tough critics of corporate and government policies argue that political and economic conditions are shifting in favor of a U.S. manufacturing revival. The value of the dollar on the world market seems likely to remain low in the foreseeable future, says Paul of the Alliance for American Manufacturing, a development that favors U.S. manufacturers that export products.

On a deeper level, "there is increasing awareness that we do need to have productive capacity in this country," Paul says. "And the underbelly of outsourcing is being exposed. It's quite possible that the economic fad of the next decade will be 'reshoring,' and I welcome it."

Perry of the American Enterprise Institute also sees reshoring as a trend with staying power. As manufacturers expand their stateside operations rather than send them abroad, even some manual workers — as opposed to engineers and designers — will benefit, he says. Nevertheless, they're not likely to earn as much as they used to. "U.S. manufacturing workers in the future are going to have to accept more realistic wages," he says.

Moutray of the NAM also argues that even though trends favor expansion of U.S. manufacturing, globalization is here to stay. "We were in a little bit of a bubble before," he says. "For a while, we were the only game in town. New opportunities for employment will come from finding markets and new opportunities overseas."

Editorial intern Daniel Bauer contributed research and reporting.

NOTES

1. "Remarks by the President at Skills for America's Future Manufacturing Event," The White House, June 8, 2011, www.whitehouse.gov/the-press-office/ 2011/06/08/remarks-president-skills-americas-future-manufacturing-event. For background see Peter Katel, "Vanishing Jobs," *CQ Researcher*, March 13, 2009, pp. 225-248.

2. "Future of U.S. Manufacturing," C-SPAN, May 31, 2011, www.c-spanarchives.org/program/29 9775-1.

3. Scott Horsley, "Obama: We Need More Manufacturing Jobs," NPR, June 24, 2011, www.npr. org/2011/06/ 24/137383302/obama-we-need-more-manufacturing-jobs.

4. "Employment Situation Summary Table," U.S. Bureau of Labor Statistics, updated July 8, 2011, http://bls.gov/news.release/empsit.a.htm.

5. Megan M. Barker, "Manufacturing employment hit hard during the 2007-2009 recession," *Monthly Labor Review*, U.S. Bureau of Labor Statistics, April 2011, www.bls.gov/opub/mlr/ 2011/04/art5full

.pdf; Mark Zandi, testimony to Joint Economic Committee, June 22, 2011, p. 4, http://jec.senate.gov/ public//index.cfm?a=Files.Serve&File_id=e922d094-bf87-47f2-9f5d-834ad cf16f7f.

6. "Value Added by Industry As a Percentage of Gross Domestic Product," U.S. Bureau of Economic Analysis, updated April 26, 2011, www. bea.gov/ industry/gpotables/gpo_action.cfm.

7. "Ignite 2.0: Voices of American University Presidents and National Lab Directors on Manufacturing Competitiveness," Council on Competitiveness, June 2011, p. 8, www.compete.org/ publications/ detail/1731/ignite-2.0/.

8. Michael Ettlinger and Kate Gordon, "The Importance and Promise of American Manufacturing," Center for American Progress, April 2011, p. 11, www.american progress.org/ issues/2011/04/pdf/manufacturing.pdf.

9. Andrew N. Liveris, *Make It In America* (2011), pp. 37-38.

10. "The World Factbook — China," CIA, updated weekly, www.cia.gov/library/publications/the-world-factbook/geos/ch.html; Judith Banister, *et al.*, "Population Aging and Economic Growth in China," Harvard School of Public Health, March 2010, www.hsph.harvard.edu/ pgda/WorkingPapers/2010/ PGDA_WP_53.pdf; "The World's Factory: China Enters the 20th Century," Deloitte Research, August 2003, www. deloitte.com/view/en_GX/global/ insights/de loitte-research/44c64d63e70fb110Vgn VCM100 000ba42f00aRCRD.htm; "China Set to Take the Lead in Global Manufacturing," HIS Global Insight, June 7, 2007, www.ihsglobalinsight .com/ Perspective/PerspectiveDetail9537.htm.

11. Wayne M. Morrison, "China-U.S. Trade Issues," Congressional Research Service, Jan. 7, 2011, p. 11, www.fas.org/sgp/crs/row/RL33536.pdf.

12. *Ibid.*, pp. 4-8.

13. "Remarks by the President to Workers at Allison Transmission Headquarters," The White House, May 6, 2011, www.whitehouse.gov/ the-press-office/2011/05/06/remarks-president-workers-allison-transmission-headquarters.

14. "The Return of U.S. Manufacturing: Current trends and implications," Boston Consulting Group, May

2011, p. 8, (report supplied by firm; not publicly available).

15. Quoted in "Moving back to America," *The Economist*, May 12, 2011, www.economist.com/ node/18682182? story_id=18682182&fsrc=rss; Brendan I. Koerner, "Made in America: Small Businesses Buck the Offshoring Trend," *Wired*, Feb. 28, 2011, www.wired .com/magazine/ 2011/02/ff_madeinamerica/all/1.

16. David Wessel, "Big U.S. Firms Shift Hiring Abroad," *The Wall Street Journal*, April 19, 2011, http://online .wsj.com/article/SB1000142405274870482170457 6270783611823972.html; "U.S. Direct Investment Abroad, U.S. Parent Companies," U.S. Bureau of Economic Analysis, http:// bea.gov/international/ ii_web/timeseries7-2.cfm? indtypeid=1,2&entitytyp eid=2&econtypeid=1& dirlevel1id=2&seriesid=8&r owtypeid= 99&step num=5&rowid=94&columnid= 47&tableid=205&yearid=28,29,30,31,32,33,34, 35,36,37 ,38,39&CFID=4869752&CFTOKEN=fa f4dcd 2bfcd5777-8F037 D72-9823-A0A0-6BB2AB 963DC4 D1A4&jsession id=a030616949a35efbe8 811cb791f1863146d5.

17. "Productivity and Related Measures: 1990 to 2009," U.S. Census Bureau, 2011, www. census.gov/compendia/ statab/2011/tables/11s 0642.pdf; "International Comparisons of Hourly "International Comparisons of Hourly Compensation Costs in Manufacturing," U.S. Bureau of Labor Statistics, updated March 8, 2011, http:// bls.gov/web/ichcc.supp.toc.htm#prod_worker.

18. Nick Bunkley, "U.A.W. Open to More Jobs At a Second-Tier Pay Level," *The New York Times*, March 30, 2011, p. B3, www.nytimes. com/2011/03/30/ business/30auto/html. For background see Pamela M. Prah, "Labor Unions' Future," *CQ Researcher*, Sept. 2, 2005, pp. 709-732.

19. The 17 free-trade partners are: Australia, Bahrain, Canada, Chile, Costa Rica, Dominican Republic, El Salvador, Guatemala, Honduras, Israel, Jordan, Mexico, Morocco, Nicaragua, Oman, Peru, Singapore. "Free Trade Agreements," Office of the United States Trade Representative, undated, www.ustr.gov/trade-agreements/free-trade-agreements.; "U.S. Free Trade Agreements," export.gov, updated April 26, 2011, www.export.gov/FTA/index.asp.

20. "Overview of the U.S.-Colombia Trade Agreement," undated, U.S. Trade Representative, www.ustr.gov/ uscolombiatpa/facts.

21. "U.S. Manufacturing Trade Surpluses With Mexico Plunged to Record Deficits Since Nafta," CW McMillion/MBG Information Services, undated.

22. "U.S. Companies target Chinese Consumers," NPR, "Morning Edition," June 16, 2011, www. npr.org/ 2011/06/16/137215569/u-s-companies-target-chinese-consumers.

23. *Ibid.*

24. Daniel J. Ikenson, written testimony, Subcommittee on Commerce, Manufacturing and Trade, House Committee on Energy and Commerce, March 16, 2011, http://democrats. energycommerce.house .gov/sites/default/files/ image_uploads/Ikenson .CATO%202011-3-16. pdf.

25. *Ibid.*

26. Gerald L. Epstein, "Restart the Congressional Office of Technology Assessment," *Science Progress*, March 31, 2009, www.scienceprogress. org/2009/03/ restart-ota/; Kenneth J. Cooper, "Lawmakers Ready to Shut Technology Office," *The Washington Post*, June 12, 1995, p. A17.

27. Except where otherwise indicated, this subsection is drawn from James McPherson, *Battle Cry of Freedom* (1988), pp. 15-40, 93-103, 318-320. For an extensive collection of more than 200 *CQ Researcher* reports on manufacturing dating back to 1926, see the *CQ Researcher Archive*.

28. "Samuel Colt," Who Made America?, pbs.org, undated, www.pbs.org/wgbh/theymadeamerica/ whomade/colt_hi.html.

29. McPherson, *op. cit.*, p. 19.

30. Except where otherwise indicated, this subsection is drawn from Ronald E. Seavoy, *An Economic History of the United States From 1607 to the Present* (2006).

31. Donald M. Fisk, "American Labor in the 20th Century," U.S. Bureau of Labor Statistics, Jan. 30, 2003, www.bls .gov/opub/cwc/cm2003 0124ar02p1.htm#3.

32. Glenn E. Bugos, "The History of the Aerospace Industry," Feb. 1, 2010, Economic History Association, http://eh.net/encyclopedia/ article/bugos.aerospace

.industry.history; Gene Smiley, "The U.S. Economy in the 1920s," Economic History Association, Feb. 1, 2010, http:// eh.net/encyclopedia/article/Smiley.1920s .final.

33. Fisk, *op. cit.*

34. Christopher J. Tassava, "The American Economy during World War II," Economic History Association, Feb. 5, 2010, http://eh.net/encyclo pedia/article/ tassava.WWII.

35. Except where otherwise indicated this subsection is drawn from Seavoy, *op. cit.*

36. "The History of the Integrated Circuit," No belprize. org, May 5, 2003, http://nobelprize. org/educational/ physics/integrated_circuit/his tory/index.html.

37. Except where otherwise indicated, this subsection is drawn from Seavoy, *op. cit.*

38. Stephen Cooney and Brent D. Yacobucci, "U.S. Automotive Industry: Policy Overview and Recent History," Congressional Research Service, April 25, 2005, p. 49, http://ncseonline. org/NLE/CRSreports/ 05Apr/RL32883.pdf.

39. *Ibid.*, pp. 24-25.

40. Scott Lindlaw, "Bush Grants China Normal Trade Status," *Los Angeles Times* (The Associated Press), Dec. 28, 2001, Part 3, p. 12.

41. Wayne M. Morrison, "China-U.S. Trade Issues," Congressional Research Service Aug. 4, 2003, pp. 2-4, http://fpc.state.gov/documents/ organization/23198 .pdf.

42. "Bipartisan, Bicameral Group of Lawmakers Call for Action on China Currency Manipulation," press release, House Ways and Means Committee Democrats, Feb. 10, 2011, http://democrats. waysandmeans.house.gov/ press/PRArticle.aspx?NewsID=11455.

43. Joseph J. Schatz, "Brown, Snowe Pushing for China Currency Vote," *CQ Today*, Nov. 29, 2010.

44. Testimony, Sen. Debbie Stabenow, Joint Economic Committee, June 22, 2011, http://jec. senate.gov/ public//index.cfm?a=Files.Serve&File_id=242f07e2-2de3-40c8-9c08-c83a179f8129; Testimony, Rep. Charles Bass, Joint Economic Committee, June 22, 2011, http://jec.senate.gov/ public//index.cfm?a=Files

.Serve&File_id=36eed0e8-10a4-4b44-82ff-1f38d 41889a6.

45. Testimony, Scott Paul, Joint Economic Committee, June 22, 2011, http://jec.senate.gov/ public//index .cfm?a=Files.Serve&File_id=19d9fe 8c-f7fb-437c-a7bf-97fb8c2e872d; Testimony, Mark Zandi, Joint Economic Committee, June 22, 2011, http://jec .senate.gov/public//index.cfm? a=Files.Serve&File_ id=e922d094-bf87-47f2-9f5 d-834adcf16f7f; Shailagh Murray, "Moody's Economist Has Become a Go-To Guy on Stimulus Plan," *The Washington Post*, Feb. 3, 2009, www.washingtonpost.com/ wp-dyn/con tent/article/2009/02/02/AR2009020 202971.html.

46. "Manufacturing Strategy for Jobs and a Competitive America," National Association of Manufacturers," January, 2011, www.nam.org/ System/Capture-Download.aspx?id=99977bfa-d78b-4da1-b812-c4dd3f3cc94f; Jay Timmons, testimony, Joint Economic Committee, June 22, 2011, http://jec .senate.gov/public//index.cfm? a=Files.Serve&File_ id=ef33d476-f29a-4798-92 b7-728638504efa; Alex Brill, testimony, Joint Economic Committee, June 22, 2011, http://jec. senate.gov/public//index.cfm?a=Files .Serve&File_id=41ca86df-a0c3-4621-bee2-5bcc 5307054b.

47. Sewell Chan, "China's Currency Avoids 'Manipulated' Ruling," *The New York Times*, Feb. 5, 2011, p. B3.

48. *Ibid.*; Jackie Calmes, "Geithner Hints At Harder Line on China Trade," *The New York Times*, Jan. 22, 2009, www.nytimes.com/2009/ 01/23/business/world business/23treasury.html.

49. Quoted in Chan, *op. cit.*

50. "2011 Manufacturing Summit," (video), *op. cit.*

51. *Ibid.*

52. *Ibid.*

53. *Ibid.*

54. *L.S. Starrett Company v. Federal Regulatory Energy Commission*, U.S. Court of Appeals for the First Circuit, No. 10-1470, June 15, 2011, www. ca1.uscourts .gov/pdf.opinions/10-1470P-01A.pdf.

55. *Ibid.*, p. 23.

56. *Ibid.*, pp. 24-25.

57. Quoted in Finlay Lewis, "Heat Rises on Hill Around Trade Program Extension," *CQ Weekly*, June 20, 2011, p. 1305.

58. Sarah Russell, "U.S. Chamber Launches Offensive to Push Free Trade Deals," *Market News International*, June 15, 2011.

59. Lewis, *op. cit.*

60. Quoted in *ibid.*

61. Quoted in *ibid.*

62. Quoted in *ibid.*

63. Quoted in *ibid.*

64. Quoted in Andrew George, "Senator urges renewed job aid," *Eastern Express Times* (Pennsylvania), June 21, 2011, p. A1.

65. "Future of U.S. Manufacturing," C-SPAN, *op. cit.*

66. *Ibid.*

67. *Ibid.*

BIBLIOGRAPHY

Selected Sources

Books

Karabell, Zachary, *Superfusion: How China and America Became One Economy and Why the World's Prosperity Depends on It*, Simon & Schuster, 2009.
A financial writer argues that the mutually dependent relationship between the United States and China has to be managed — but can't be reversed.

Liveris, Andrew N., *Make It In America: The Case for Re-Inventing the Economy*, John Wiley & Sons, 2011.
The chairman and CEO of Dow Chemical Co. raises an alarm over what he views as eroding U.S. manufacturing capability and government's responsibility to help reverse the trend.

Articles

Allen, Jodie, "America's Biggest Trade Export to China? Trash," *U.S. News & World Report*, March 3, 2010, www.us news.com/opinion/blogs/jodie-allen/2010/03/03/ameri cas-biggest-trade-export-to-china-trash.
A veteran business writer for the nonprofit Pew Research Center analyzes the growing volume of U.S. exports of "scraps and trash" to China, which sends back manufactured goods in return.

Bradsher, Keith, "As China's Workers Get a Raise, Companies Fret," *The New York Times*, May 31, 2011, www.ny times.com/2011/06/01/business/global/01wages.html.
The newspaper's Hong Kong bureau chief reports on rising factory pay in China and the resulting upward pressure on prices of Chinese exports.

Bunkley, Nick, "U.A.W. Open to More Jobs At a Second-Tier Pay Level," *The New York Times*, March 30, 2011, www.nytimes.com/2011/03/30/business/30auto.html.
The United Auto Workers union is showing willingness to extend an initial agreement under which newly hired workers are paid about one-half the $28 an hour earned by workers already on the payroll.

Fingleton, Eamonn, "Germany's Economic Engine," *The American Prospect*, Feb. 24, 2010, http://prospect.org/cs/ articles?article=germanys_economic_engine.
Many critics of the U.S. government's treatment of manufacturing point to Germany as an example of how to maintain a country's manufacturing sector and keep unemployment low. Writing for the liberal magazine, business writer Fingleton argues the case for the German example (a *Washington Post* editorial writer, takes the opposing view: Lane, Charles, "The U.S. does not need to copy Germany," *The Washington Post*, June 24, 2011, www.washingtonpost.com/blogs/post-partisan/ post/the-us-does-not-need-to-copy-germany/2011/03/04/AGRb 0XjH_blog.html).

Gavin, Robert, "Retooling an industry," *The Boston Globe*, Oct. 17, 2010, Business Sect., p. 1.
Massachusetts Institute of Technology's president, concerned at the state of U.S. manufacturing, has launched a university-wide initiative to re-energize the sector.

Hagerty, James R., "Industry Puts Heat on Schools to Teach Skills Employers Need," *The Wall Street Journal*, June 6, 2011, http://online.wsj.com/article/SB10001424 052702304563104576355230583773702.html.
Companies and trade associations, alarmed at high-schoolers' low levels of math and science achievement, are teaming up with community colleges to train prospective workers in the skills they'd need for specific jobs.

Rampell, Catherine, "Companies Spend on Equipment, Not Workers," *The New York Times*, June 9, 2011, www .nytimes.com/2011/06/10/business/10capital.html. Corporations are using their growing cash reserves to buy equipment, which allows them to produce goods with fewer people.

Wessel, David, "Big U.S. Firms Shift Hiring Abroad," *The Wall Street Journal*, April 11, 2011, http://online .wsj. com/article/SB1000142405274870482170457 6270783611823972.html. An analysis of government data shows that U.S. firms have been creating more jobs in other countries than at home.

Reports and Studies

Ezell, Stephen J., and Robert D. Atkinson, "The Case for a National Manufacturing Strategy," Information Technology and Innovation Foundation, April 2011, www.itif.org/ files/2011-national-manufacturing-strategy.pdf.

The United States should emulate foreign competitors who follow strategies designed to support their manufacturers, writers for a nonpartisan think tank argue.

Morrison, Wayne M., "China-U.S. Trade Issues," **Congressional Research Service, updated June 2, 2011, www.fas.org/ sgp/crs/row/RL33536.pdf.** An expert at Congress' nonpartisan research agency analyzes the debates that arise from the trade relationship that has had a major effect on U.S. manufacturing.

Popkin, Joel, and Kathryn Kobe, "Manufacturing Resurgence: A Must for U.S. Prosperity," National Association of Manufacturers, January 2010, www .nam.org/~/media/ F36EC9F57BFF4DA4AEBAFA AB4B009B92.ashx. Writing for the major manufacturers' trade group, two economists argue that tax reductions on manufacturers' U.S. operations, among other measures, are essential to strengthen U.S. manufacturing.

For More Information

Alliance for American Manufacturing, 727 15th St., N.W., Washington, DC 20005; (202) 393-3430; www.american manufacturing.org. Co-founded by the United Steelworkers union and some manufacturers, the group advocates tougher enforcement of trade rules against China and greater government efforts to strengthen U.S. manufacturing.

Bureau of Economic Analysis, 1441 L St., N.W., Washington, DC 20230; (202) 606-9900; www.bea.gov. The bureau's website is rich in data on U.S. manufacturing, including the foreign operations of U.S. corporations.

Bureau of Labor Statistics, Postal Square Building, 2 Massachusetts Ave., N.E., Washington, DC 20212-0001; (202) 691-5200; www.bls.gov. The principal federal agency responsible for measuring labor market activity, working conditions, and price changes in the economy. Its website contains data on a vast range of labor and business-related subjects.

Council on Competitiveness, 1500 K St., N.W., Washington, DC 20005; (202) 682-4292; www.compete.org. A

nonpartisan advocacy group with ties to business, labor and academia that is developing a national manufacturing strategy proposal.

National Association of Manufacturers, 1331 Pennsylvania Ave., N.W., Washington, DC 20004; (1-800) 814-8468; www.nam.org. Represents major manufacturers and calls for tax cuts and easing of government regulation to strengthen U.S. manufacturing.

U.S. Business and Industry Council, 512 C St., N.E., Washington, DC 20002; (202) 266-3980; http://american economicalert.org. A trade association that represents smaller manufacturers who advocate reshaping U.S. trade policy to provide more benefits to domestic companies and consumers.

The White House, whitehouse.gov. The administration's main website contains all of President Obama's speeches about manufacturing, as well as blog posts on the subject by White House staff.

8 Attracting Jobs

Marcia Clemmitt

Boeing's 2,160-worker plant in Wichita, Kan. — centerpiece of the local economy — is closing. Just two years after the state spent $43 million to build a training center for aerospace workers, Boeing announced the plant would shut down by year's end because of high operational costs. States and localities spend up to $70 billion annually on business subsidies. Proponents say they generate prosperity. Critics say they often fail to deliver promised jobs and end up losing money.

From *CQ Researcher*, March 2, 2012

AP Photo/The Wichita Eagle/Brian Corn

Shocking news greeted the 2,160 employees at Boeing's military aircraft plant in Wichita, Kan., in early January. After 80-plus years as a centerpiece of the city's economy — and two years after Kansas spent $43 million to build a training center for aerospace workers — Boeing announced it was shutting down the plant.

Republican Gov. Sam Brownback, a former U.S. senator, called Boeing's decision "very disappointing," noting that, "no one worked harder for the success of the Boeing Company than Team Kansas."[1]

But according to a company executive, "Business costs in Wichita are not competitive" for Boeing's operations.[2]

Kansas is far from alone in offering millions of dollars in tax breaks, plus millions more for training centers, roads and other incentives aimed at enticing companies to relocate to an area or keep jobs from moving elsewhere. Such tax-funded perks have proliferated over the past decade as the economy has cratered and unemployment has soared.

But serious questions are being raised about the effectiveness of incentives, which can put a big dent in state and local revenues. Economists say many companies that receive perks fail to deliver promised jobs. And many also question whether the intense rivalry for jobs among states leads to little more than an economic shell game, with jobs moving from one place to another without a significant net national gain in employment.

In the case of Boeing, it eliminated most of its jobs in Wichita and moved the rest to company operations in Oklahoma and Texas.

"In a given year, it is estimated that, on average, some 15,000 communities vie for roughly 1,500 major industrial projects available nationally," wrote Jonathan Q. Morgan and David M. Lawrence

'Right-to-Work' Laws Enacted in 23 States

Twenty-three states, mostly in the South and Midwest, have enacted laws that bar companies and unions from signing contracts requiring employees to join or pay fees to a union. Some industries, such as federally regulated airlines, are exempt. Proponents say the laws give states a business-friendly advantage in competing for jobs, but critics say they reduce wages and don't promote job growth.

Source: "Right to Work States," National Right to Work Legal Defense Foundation, 2012, www.nrtw.org/rtws.htm

at the University of North Carolina, Chapel Hill.[3] "This creates an intensely competitive and often costly situation in which the odds of success are low for many communities."[4]

Estimates of how much states and localities spend on location incentives annually range between $40 billion and $70 billion.[5] The amounts have skyrocketed nationwide. In Arizona, for example, businesses in 1994 claimed just $5 million in state tax credits, which reduce companies' state tax bill. By 2008 the credits had grown 17-fold, to $86 million.[6]

Proponents of business subsidies insist, however, that they generate jobs and help localities prosper.

Kentucky is seeing large effects from new tax breaks enacted in 2009, said Larry Hayes, who heads the Kentucky Cabinet for Economic Development, the state's main economic-development agency. Those breaks include a tax credit for filmmakers that shoot in the state and job-creation incentives for companies both existing and new to Kentucky. The more than 200 companies working their way through the new programs'

approval process could potentially generate more than 13,500 jobs and help retain 4,800 existing ones in Kentucky, he said.[7]

But Kentucky isn't the only state attracted by Hollywood's glitter. About 45 states offer tax credits to filmmakers. Rhode Island's filmmaker credits, which totaled $56.7 million between 2005 and 2009, created 4,184 full-time jobs in that period — including jobs directly connected to movie production and in other industries such as food and lodging that saw increased business while the movies were made, wrote Edward M. Mazze, a business professor at the University of Rhode Island.[8]

Although tax incentives can give an area an economic boost, focusing on a quick local hit misses some big-picture questions, says Joseph J. Seneca, a professor of economics at the Edward J. Bloustein School of Planning and Public Policy at Rutgers University in New Jersey. What's seldom asked — but probably should be — is "whether those jobs are taken away from, say, Brooklyn, or whether they're jobs the company would have created anyway," even if it hadn't received an incentive, he says.

Many communities, especially rural ones, have offered incentives to lure so-called "big box" retail stores such as Walmart and Home Depot. Those transactions can be as pricey — and as uncertain in their effects — as incentives to lure manufacturing companies.

Last year, towns that had provided significant incentives to lure Borders book stores were left high and dry when the retailer went bankrupt. Pico Rivera, an eastern suburb of Los Angeles, for example, had spent $1.6 million in federal grant money to get a Borders outlet, including helping to pay the store's rent for eight years. When the chain went bust, the town lost more than just jobs and a bookstore that was a center of economic activity. It also will be on the hook for rent until a new tenant is found for the vacated 18,100-square-foot site, plus for other costs, the *Whittier Daily News* reported.[9]

In 2009 alone, Walmart stores got $1.8 million in tax credits to build five stores in Louisiana. Bridgeton, Mo., approved a $7.2 million deal in 2010 to bring a single Walmart outlet to town.[10]

Businesses are growing accustomed to incentives and often tell states and localities to "fight amongst yourselves" to win our favor, says Katherine Chalmers, an assistant professor of economics at California State University, Sacramento.

Yet, the ammunition communities often use to outgun their rivals, including so-called business-climate rankings, can be suspect. Many such rankings give top billing to states that offer generous business tax breaks and go easy on environmental or workplace regulations. But some economists say a high ranking on such lists doesn't necessarily equate with a strong or competitive economy.

South Dakota, for example, ranks second in a 2012 index from the Tax Foundation, a business-oriented think tank in Washington, and 17th — comfortably in the top half of states — in a *Forbes* ranking.[11] The state's unemployment rate was 4.2 percent in December, compared to 8.2 percent nationally.[12]

But South Dakota contains four of the nation's 15 poorest counties, including the three poorest, according to the latest census data.[13] Moreover, South Dakota's economy rests largely on only two legs: agriculture and public employment at Ellsworth Air Force Base, the state's second-largest employer, near Rapid City.[14]

Robert W. Wassmer, a professor of economics also at Cal State, Sacramento, points to South Dakota as typical of many states that may rank high in some economic-climate measures but "don't have other things" that businesses need to thrive, such as access to markets and raw materials, good infrastructure and a skilled workforce. Rank, Wassmer says, doesn't necessarily translate to overall economic strength.

Development Subsidies Take Many Forms

States and local governments offer a variety of subsidies to attract businesses ranging from tax cuts to cash grants.

Common Types of Economic Development Subsidies

Tax abatements — Reduce or eliminate taxes paid to state and local governments. Often apply to property, inventory or sales taxes.

Tax credits — Reduce or eliminate corporate income taxes by allowing companies to deduct a percentage of certain expenses, such as research-and-development or new-equipment costs.

Industrial revenue bonds — Bonds with tax-free interest, giving companies what amounts to low-interest loans.

Infrastructure assistance — Reduces construction costs by giving local governments the responsibility for improving roads, sewers, water lines and other utilities.

Grants — Cash subsidies that companies may use for general or specific purposes.

Land-price write-downs — Reduce land-purchasing costs typically through third-party transfers. Local governments may also pay for such expenses as eminent domain or environmental cleanup.

Tax-increment financing — Uses property tax collected on the appreciation value of a new development to pay for infrastructure, land acquisition or other related costs.

Enterprise zones — Economically depressed areas in which companies are eligible for multiple subsidies.

Source: "Beginner's Guide," Good Jobs First, 2010, www.goodjobsfirst.org/accountable-development/beginners-guide

The disjoint exists because breaks on taxes and regulation have less influence on business-location decisions than many think, Wassmer argues. California, with relatively high business taxes and tough regulations, has a good record of retaining companies and jobs, he says. "Not that many businesses are being driven out," Wassmer asserts. Meanwhile, low-tax, lightly regulated Reno in neighboring Nevada "should be booming right now. Everybody should be flooding there, but they're not," Wassmer says.

"There's a consensus among economists that smokestack chasing is not effective," says Laura Kalambokidis, an associate professor of applied economics at the University of Minnesota, St. Paul. For one thing, "using tax incentives to chase employers is pretty much universal now, so they're not going to be effective" because businesses can get similar breaks from virtually any state, she says.

Rural Areas Find Barriers to Job Creation

"Before incentives can matter, fundamentals have to be strong."

Hard as it is to generate jobs in cities, it's even tougher in rural areas. An aging workforce and less easy access to markets and suppliers are among the barriers to expanding employment in rural counties. Even so, economic-development experts say some strategies show promise.

In North Carolina, for example, "metro areas are doing well income-wise, but the other 90 counties aren't," says Jason Jolley, senior research director of the Carolina Center for Competitive Economies at the University of North Carolina, Chapel Hill. North Carolina's core economy has shifted from tobacco, textiles and furniture to high-tech industries such as pharmaceuticals, but many jobs in new industries have gone to people moving into the state, Jolley says, while native rural residents lack access to similar opportunities.

In economists' perfect world, people would simply move where jobs are. "But people aren't as mobile as economic theory would argue" — especially since the housing crash left many with houses they can't sell, says Robert Greenbaum, professor of public policy at Ohio State University. That makes finding ways to develop rural jobs crucial, he and others say.

Rural areas lose young, educated workers at a high rate, another factor making those areas less attractive to employers, wrote Jonathan Q. Morgan, associate professor of public administration at the University of North Carolina (UNC), Chapel Hill, and colleagues. Nationwide, the median age in rural counties was 40.1 years in 2007, compared to 36.1 in metropolitan areas. Moreover, 16.3 percent of rural residents were 65 or older, compared to 11.9 percent in metro areas.[1]

Like most states that provide incentives to businesses, North Carolina gives larger ones to companies that put jobs in high-need areas, says Morgan. But if fundamentals such as adequate sewers and transportation infrastructure are lacking — often the case in rural areas — most businesses aren't interested, he says. "Before incentives can matter, fundamentals have to be strong."

"For the longest time, rural areas did what everybody else did — try to recruit big industry," says Morgan. "Some had success, but even they are realizing that they need a more diversified base so they are not dependent on one big company that might move offshore."

Options exist, though none is close to foolproof, and different areas need different approaches, economists say.

Localities shouldn't necessarily disdain retail and service jobs, despite their low wages and a prevailing view that only exporting industries can sustain an economy, says Katherine Chalmers, an assistant professor of economics at California State University, Sacramento. "With computer manufacturing, for example, you worry that it'll be outsourced, but it's hard to outsource your hairdresser."

In West Texas, where Chalmers grew up, retailing essentially is an export industry for towns where it's clustered, "because people drive long distances to shop there," she says.

Policymakers waste effort using strategies suited only for urban areas in rural places, says Thomas G. Johnson, a professor of development economics at the University of Missouri's

Policymakers who promote location incentives intend to boost job prospects for local residents, but the measures can fail on that score even when they bring jobs, says Robert Greenbaum, a professor of public policy at Ohio State University. If the targeted companies are suitable to a different — that is, a mobile or more educated — workforce than the local one, for instance, "people coming in from out of state take the jobs."

Nevertheless, lawmakers are very reluctant to give up the incentives because they "are good politics," wrote Terry F. Buss, a professor of public policy at Carnegie Mellon University's Heinz School of Business campus in Adelaide, Australia. "There is little risk to politicians when incentives fail because failure can be blamed on . . . market forces" or other hard-to-control factors. Then, when economic times are good, "policymakers can claim credit" — but only if they've enacted incentives, said Buss.[15]

Economists see things very differently. "I think the academic consensus would be, 'It would be best if we didn't have interstate competition' " to offer incentives,

Harry S Truman School of Public Affairs in Columbia. "Urban areas exist because there is value in clustering; rural areas exist because there's a value in space," he says.

For rural jobs, "you should look at sparsity-based businesses" such as forestry and tourism as well as manufacturing that doesn't depend on having complementary industries nearby.

In North Carolina, some coastal and mountain towns are trying to start clusters of heritage-based enterprises by helping artisans such as potters and woodworkers strengthen their businesses and enticing more artisans to the area. Morgan says those efforts often begin with "revitalizing Main Streets," which "are the heart and soul of towns," then using "quality of life to attract entrepreneurs who are located elsewhere," as well as tourists and, possibly, retirees looking for an interesting place to settle.

How well this approach works "is not fully documented," but there is evidence that it has encouraged some communities to pull together with a "can-do attitude" to try to revitalize themselves, says Morgan. "At issue is whether such approaches "can make a dent, when you realize how many jobs aren't coming back."

Nevertheless, "there's a lot of literature showing that small businesses are job creators if they can stay alive," says Karen Chapple, associate director of the Institute of Urban and Regional Development at the University of California, Berkeley. So providing help to local small businesses, such as assistance with tax analysis and preparation, might help sustain entrepreneurs, she says.

One oft-heralded economic-development tool is the cluster — a geographical concentration of companies that are interconnected by being in the same industry, being part of the same supply chain or using the same set of job skills, for example. But while clusters can work for rural areas, they're no silver bullet, economists say.

"If there is a misperception" about clusters "it's that these programs have the potential to be adopted almost everywhere," says David L. Barkley, professor emeritus of applied economics at South Carolina's Clemson University.

Existing businesses with solid growth potential to form the seed of the cluster are essential, Barkley says. Sometimes creativity is required to discover growth potential. For example, while American textile manufacturing has moved offshore, in South Carolina the industry has "spotted growth in the 'miracle fiber' sector," such as athletic apparel that wicks away moisture and extra-warm lightweight hikers' clothing, he says.

Even then, Barkley says, "you still have to be introspective and ask, 'Do we have the resources needed' " to compete with other places to attract companies, including areas that have a head start. In the current economy, especially, "many communities aren't likely to be able to do it."

Despite difficulties, however, "there are lots of interesting" small-scale clusters sustaining local economies, including rural ones, Barkley says. Montana sports a high-end custom log cabin industry, Kentucky has houseboat builders and an area in Mississippi manufactures custom upholstered furniture.

In North Carolina, a group of four distressed rural counties hopes to piggyback on an existing cluster in a nearby metropolitan area — the high-tech Research Triangle Park area, near Durham, just to their south, says Morgan. "They are trying to get economies of scale by collaborating on a large industrial park" that might attract complementary businesses "interested in the lower-cost" living of the rural counties.

— *Marcia Clemmitt*

[1] Jonathan Q. Morgan, William Lambe and Allan Freyer, "Homegrown Responses to Economic Uncertainty in Rural America," *Rural Realities*, Mid-year [Issue 2] 2009, http://ruralsociology.org/StaticContent/ Publications/Ruralrealities/ pubs/RuralRealities3-2.pdf.

says Seneca, at the Bloustein School of Planning and Public Policy. "The real things that incentivize [business] investment" are states' long-term commitment to providing good "infrastructure, effective and efficient regulation and taxation, research and development spending, education and quality of life" that apply to all residents and businesses, not specially targeted efforts.

"In a sense, you do want states to compete with one another — but to be able to say that 'we are the best-run state,' " says Kalambokidis, at the University of Minnesota.

As policymakers and taxpayers consider how best to bring jobs to their towns and cities, here are some of the questions being asked:

Do state and local tax incentives for businesses create jobs?

Over the past few decades, states and metropolitan areas have offered an increasing number of special tax breaks for businesses that pledge to bring new jobs to their areas. Economic-development officials say the incentives are effective in leading businesses to create local jobs. Most economists, however, argue that often the tax breaks don't create jobs but merely induce companies to move them from one place to another, often rewarding companies for location decisions that they would have made anyway.

"Incentives do work," said Alex Labeau, president of the Idaho Association of Commerce and Industry, a business lobby. Idaho recently learned a hard lesson when Boeing bypassed its capital, Boise, as the site for a new $750 million plant the state had hoped to snag thanks to its proximity to Boeing's Seattle headquarters. Instead, the plant went to South Carolina, which will pay Boeing approximately $3,100 in incentives per job created, said Labeau.[16]

The Charleston, S.C., *Post and Courier* reported that the total incentive package, which the state government did not officially announce, totaled more than $900 million, twice as much as state officials announced.[17] By contrast, Idaho, with its small population, offers companies that create jobs only a small tax credit, worth thousands, not millions, of dollars, a harsh economic reality that may have doomed Boise in this case, according to the *Idaho Statesman*.[18]

"When it comes down to two or more equally satisfactory sites, a superior incentive package and 'red carpet treatment' can clinch a deal," wrote Bill Schweke, who recently retired as a senior fellow at the Corporation for Enterprise Development, a group in Washington that focuses on low-income communities.[19]

Alabama, Louisiana and Texas, widely considered to be "leading in the economic recovery" from the recession, "excel in their incentive offerings" to business, according to *Area Development*, a magazine for corporate site-selection professionals. The Texas Development Fund, for example, offers cash grants and tax breaks to companies making a final location decision between Texas and another state.[20] (Many large and medium-sized Texas cities, along with some in Alabama and Louisiana, have repeatedly topped lists of cities showing strong recession recovery.)[21]

Timothy J. Bartik, senior economist at the W.E. Upjohn Institute for Employment Research, an independent group in Kalamazoo, Mich., acknowledged that some critics of incentives argue that they are "too small" compared to a company's total costs "to affect business location." But, he wrote, that argument is "unpersuasive." "Many states and metropolitan areas will be close

substitutes" as sites, "offering similar access to markets and suppliers," so that "even small . . . cost differentials" such as what might come from a tax credit "could prove decisive for a particular . . . decision," he said.[22]

Many economists who criticize location-based tax and cash incentives for businesses, however, argue that such incentives don't create jobs but simply cause them to shift from one place to another — and generally don't do that as efficiently as economic-development officials claim.

One of the oldest forms of tax incentive are so-called enterprise-zone programs, in which businesses get tax breaks for locating in distressed areas. "There is really no evidence that these zones boost employment," says David Neumark, a professor of economics at the University of California, Irvine. Research findings on enterprise zones are clear enough, he says, that policymakers have only two realistic choices —"either kill them, or scale them way back to test" whether some specific tweaks and applications may make them work better.

Shawn M. Rohlin, a University of Akron assistant professor of economics, says his research shows enterprise zones do attract some businesses, especially retail and service operations. "However," he adds in an email interview, "the overall effect is smaller than one would anticipate, making the program quite expensive per new firm/employee." Furthermore, areas neighboring enterprise zones "seem to have lost almost as many firms as the zone gained, indicating that the zones improved at the expense of the neighboring areas."

In a study of North Carolina's tax credits, "We found that slightly more than half of companies had more jobs" after receiving a credit, but "45 percent had fewer," says Jason Jolley, senior research director of the Carolina Center for Competitive Economies at the University of North Carolina, Chapel Hill. "Many companies told us that they didn't even know they were getting" some of the state credits, which seriously undercuts the argument that they are a vital factor in attracting and retaining companies, says Jolley.

"Firms that relocate are typically in declining industries" that must keep cutting costs to stay afloat, and this can mean successful job-luring efforts are short-lived victories, wrote Scott Loveridge, a professor of agricultural economics at Michigan State University.[23]

"For example, North Carolina gave away $240 million in tax credits to Dell in 2004 to lure them . . . while the closest competitor offered only $30 million," according to the Institute on Taxation and Economic Policy (ITEP) a Washington think tank that studies tax fairness. But six years later, as the market for personal computers became increasingly cost-focused, a struggling Dell announced that it would shut the North Carolina plant, "leaving at least 400 people without jobs," according to ITEP.[24]

"Several good studies . . . suggest that well-run, customized job training and manufacturing extension services" — government- or university-run initiatives that provide expertise to help local businesses improve their practices — "are far more cost-effective in creating jobs than is true of general business tax cuts or business tax incentives," wrote Bartik at the Upjohn Institute.[25]

More Companies Receiving Tax Breaks

Forty-two states offered companies multiyear property tax breaks known as abatements in 2007, a nearly threefold increase from four decades earlier. The incentives reduce or eliminate property taxes paid to state and local governments in exchange for doing business in the area.

States Offering Companies Multiyear Property Tax Abatements, 1964-2007

(No. of states)

Year	No. of states
1964	15
1979	31
1991	33
2004	35
2007	42

Source: Robert W. Wassmer, "The Increasing Use of Property Tax Abatement as a Means of Promoting Sub-National Economic Activity in the United States," Social Science Research Network, December 2007, papers.ssrn.com/sol3/papers.cfm? abstract_id=1088482

Are location-based business incentives good for communities?

Critics of incentives offered to attract businesses to new locations say that many of the tax breaks actually have a reverse effect, siphoning public funds needed to provide roads, airports and other infrastructure and services that businesses need to thrive. The effect, critics say, is that the incentives may actually discourage job growth in the long run.

Supporters of incentives argue, however, that even when companies don't quite meet job goals, bringing businesses to an area and helping them stay profitable improves communities in many ways.

After the Sears Holdings Corp., in Hoffman Estates, Ill., announced in December that it would close more than a 100 Sears and Kmart stores, officials in Jackson, Miss., and other towns said that tax breaks to keep their stores would be worth the cost. Should its Sears store close, Jackson stands to lose $129,000 annually in property taxes plus one of only two large "anchor" stores that bring in enough customers to a Jackson shopping mall to keep it alive for other businesses.[26]

Many businesses argue that a valid purpose for incentives is helping local companies stay competitive by lowering their costs, says UNC's Jolley.

In Tulsa, Okla., some taxpayers cried foul when McLean, Va.-based media giant Gannett Co. moved a 500-worker call center out of state last year after receiving $260,000 in tax breaks from the city. But the fact that Gannett had supplied 500 jobs at the center for four years means that "the state gave Gannett nothing" and has no spilt milk to cry over, said Mike Neal, president of the Tulsa Chamber of Commerce. Gannett supplied jobs, "paid taxes, and they, in return, have got a little bit of that tax returned to them," making the situation a win for Tulsa, despite the move, he said.[27]

Many economists call the relocation of jobs from state to state or city to city a "zero-sum" game with no net benefits for the national economy. But Upjohn's Bartik argues that "such reshuffling may benefit the nation," at least in some cases. If jobs move to a high-unemployment area — as they may under enterprise-zone programs, for example — those areas "will benefit more" from the jobs than the business' previous location would have, since "the social benefits from hiring the average unemployed person are higher" than the benefits derived from hiring a less needy person, Bartik wrote.[28]

Critics of incentive programs argue that the economic improvements they spur are often short-lived and benefit the wrong people while the tax breaks drain needed public funds.

Jennifer Lawrence waits for her cue during filming of "The Hunger Games" in North Carolina, one of more than 40 states offering tax subsidies and other inducements to filmmakers. Critics call for more transparency for incentives. Since they often come in the form of tax credits or other tax breaks that are not included in state budgets, they don't face the annual legislative reviews given to other government programs.

Incentives such as the tax credits that states often give to moviemakers filming on location are intended to produce only temporary jobs. Critics of the program say that this and other common features of incentives raise questions about their value.

Massachusetts' filmmaker credits allow moviemakers to take the credits in cash or sell them to others if their state tax bills aren't high enough to need the full credit as an offset, even though the movie jobs won't "even be there next year," said Peter Enrich, a professor at Northeastern University School of Law, in Boston. In 2008, the state issued $100 million in film credits, but only $100,000 was used to reduce filmmakers' own tax liabilities, while "the rest was paid out in cash or to reduce the taxes of insurance companies and banks" that bought the credits.[29] It's not clear that taxpayers would see that result as much of a boon to the community, Enrich says.

But taxpayers, and even lawmakers, often don't know the details of incentives that have been in place for years, says UNC's Jolley. Many incentives come in the form of tax credits or other tax breaks that are not included in state budgets, so they don't face annual legislative review as other government programs do, he says.

Some of North Carolina's filmmaker subsidy will go to the company that's filming the action movie "Iron Man 3"

in Wilmington this year, says Jolley. And because the state basically hands over the credit, with no say in how it's used, "for all we know we could be subsidizing [lead actor] Robert Downey Jr.'s salary for up to $1 million," he says. "This makes you say, 'Wait a minute. Shouldn't we consider whether this is what we really want to do?' "

Even when monetary caps and so-called "sunset" provisions — which require lawmakers to reauthorize credits periodically — are written into credit programs most lawmakers uncritically extend the credits and raise the caps when businesses ask them to, said Missouri state Sen. Jason Crowell, a Republican. "History has shown" that "we will just raise those caps in exchange for campaign contributions."[30]

Some analysts argue that incentives ostensibly designed to bring jobs to high-need areas can actually end up increasing inequality of opportunity.

A study of Ohio's enterprise zones, for example, found that "higher-income districts reap most of the jobs and investment," even though the program aims to improve economies in low-income areas.[31]

Another Ohio study, by Good Jobs First, a Washington, D.C.-based national policy resource center that seeks accountability in subsidies, found that many taxpayer-funded relocations in the Cleveland and Cincinnati areas moved jobs away from public-transit-accessible neighborhoods, potentially putting the jobs out of reach of residents who cannot afford cars.[32]

Some praise tax credits as a valuable counterbalance to high business tax rates, which they argue inhibit economic growth, but many economists disagree. "People say, 'Taxes distort markets,' and I agree. But then they say, 'Tax credits will offset that distortion,' and I say, 'No, it just gives you two distortions,' " says Thomas G. Johnson, a professor of development economics at the University of Missouri's Harry S Truman School of Public Affairs, in Columbia. "Unless tax credits are really well designed, they get people to do things they don't want to do," which promotes economic inefficiency, not improvement, he says.

Should states and localities compete for business locations?

Some analysts say interstate business-incentive competition has become a "race to the bottom" in which governments undermine their neighbors and even themselves by giving away more than they can afford. Others argue, however, that interstate competition has always been a valuable spur to improvement.

"Competition for economic growth is undeniably, irrevocably American — and therefore unavoidable. In some ways, the whole history of the United States is the history of communities competing with each other," wrote William Fulton, an economic-development expert and a former mayor of Ventura, Calif.[33]

Tax competition "is an effective restraint on state and local taxes," keeping them at business-friendly levels, says a 2012 study by the conservative The Tax Foundation.[34]

"There is a role for competition" when each state strives to create the best "general tax-and-spend policy," said Arthur J. Rolnick, a former research director of the Federal Reserve Bank of Minneapolis and now a senior fellow at the University of Minnesota's Humphrey School of Public Affairs. "Such competition leads states to provide a more efficient allocation of public and private goods."[35]

"I do believe that states and localities should compete but not in superficial ways," says the University of Missouri's Johnson. "They should compete to be better hosts to jobs," mainly using longer-term strategies such as beefing up transportation and other infrastructure and workforce training, and creating an efficient tax system.

Competition on infrastructure and education can constitute a race to the top, rather than to the bottom, says Ohio State's Greenbaum. "If a business you brought in leaves, tax breaks may be wasted, but human and infrastructure investments" remain.

But much interstate competition takes the form of location-based incentives and has grown so intense that "politicians aren't acting rationally, and they're giving away too much," says Wassmer at California State University.

Competition on giveaways — unlike competition to improve state systems and services — quickly becomes an inescapable trap, even for states that believe it may not be in their best interest, said Rolnick. "As long as a single state engages in this practice, others will feel compelled to compete."[36]

When state competition "takes the form of preferential treatment for specific businesses," it undercuts the goal of having a strong national economy by causing some businesses to locate in places that might not be the best sites for them in the long run and also may decrease tax revenues so that money can't go to transportation projects or schools, for example, said Rolnick.[37]

Borders stores in cities around the country, including this one in Washington, D.C., closed after the retailer declared bankruptcy last year. Many of the communities had provided incentives to lure the stores. Pico Rivera, a suburb of Los Angeles, for example, had spent $1.6 million, including helping to pay the store's rent for eight years.

"Ideally, you would expect a firm to locate where things are most efficient for it," not in the place that fought hardest to attract it, says Tonya Hansen, an assistant professor of economics at Minnesota State University Moorhead. "If a firm is only local because of an incentive," then it may not be operating in the most efficient business mode, she says.

Federal-level programs generally are more efficient than state competition because "they bring in more money, the money is more stable, and it blankets the 50 states" with similar incentives "so it's not pitting state against state," says Chalmers, at Cal State. In addition, the most blighted, neediest areas may have a better chance of capturing federal dollars because when decisions are made on the state level "the self-interest of politicians to get reelected" sometimes shifts dollars toward communities with more votes rather than high needs.

BACKGROUND

Early Competition

The first property-tax break for a North American business was awarded in 1640 — more than 125 years before the United States was founded. Given in the region that later became Connecticut, it started a persistent tradition. Along the way, doubts arose about whether interstate competition for business was an effective strategy.

But local self-interest has won the day, and competitive use of business incentives has steadily increased.[38]

In 1791, Treasury Secretary Alexander Hamilton and other investors persuaded the New Jersey Assembly to exempt from state and county taxes a group called the Society for Useful Manufactures. They argued that the tax break would provide, "by moderate calculation," jobs for "20,000 persons" in the state.[39]

Nearby states reacted with horror. The "powers, rights and privileges, given to this company would be . . . very injurious to this state as well as other states," complained a member of the Pennsylvania House of Representatives.[40]

As the country grew, competition for businesses spread. After the Civil War, Southern states excused some companies from property taxes in an attempt to get Eastern and Midwestern industries to relocate.

In the 1920s, a wealthy industrial real estate executive, Felix Fantus, founded the Fantus Corp., the first consultancy to specialize in helping companies find the most advantageous locations for facilities — a service that included analysis of tax breaks and other incentives. By the 1950s, the company advised businesses to encourage state competition for lucrative incentive packages.[41]

Beginning in 1975, Fantus published the first state "business climate" rankings, which helped drive interstate competition on incentives.[42]

In the 1980s, worries began about American industrial jobs "getting slashed" by automation and foreign, low-wage competition, says Ohio State's Greenbaum. In hopes of bringing jobs back to the United States and placing them in struggling neighborhoods, the states and later the federal government established enterprise-zone programs. The zones "had appeal in a time when government budgets were limited, since they targeted" high-need areas with the incentives, he says.

Economics vs. Politics

The University of North Carolina's Jolley says that while studies show that location-based tax incentives don't work well, researchers "have failed to convince policymakers" of that.

"Our political and government structure is not set up for the most efficient economic policies," says Kalambokidis, of the University of Minnesota. Business

supply chains and markets relate to geographic and demographic features that span regions rather than stop at city or state borders.

Most tax breaks decrease government revenues in later years — leaving "the cost to fall on future officeholders" — but demonstrate to voters that today's politicians are working to bring in jobs, says Greenbaum. As a result, he says, many lawmakers are reluctant to end them.

"One legislator told us, 'This is the best study we've ever ignored,' " says Jolley, whose legislature-requested 2008 study showed that North Carolina's incentives aren't effective.[43] "There was excitement" in the legislature when Jolley and colleagues said that scaling back the tax breaks would allow the state to lower corporate tax rates. But lawmakers so far have opted to keep the incentives. "They wouldn't be able to demonstrate" immediate budget savings if they traded the incentives for lower corporate tax breaks, and economic-development officials insist that "there's value in staying in the game," Jolley says.

Lawmakers and courts have long been ambivalent about location-based incentives.

Prior to 1789, when the Articles of Confederation governed the United States, "the states were very autonomous, and the standard was to impose tariffs" on out-of-state business to protect in-state companies, says Enrich, of Northeastern Law School. Part of the impetus to adopt the Constitution's stronger central government was to keep "interstate commerce" flowing, since "the Framers recognized that tariff competition between the states didn't make sense" for a country that needed to establish a strong national economy, he argues.

Under the Commerce Clause of the Constitution, Congress alone has the power to "regulate commerce . . . among the several states." The clause has been interpreted as banning states from regulating — including imposing taxes — in ways that interfere with interstate business dealings.[44]

The Supreme Court has repeatedly upheld states' right to discriminate between in-state and out-of-state businesses by actions such as buying services from local rather than out-of-state businesses, since those aren't regulatory acts, just market activity, Enrich says. Rulings in regulation- and tax-related cases have been mixed.

C H R O N O L O G Y

1960s-1970s *As the nation's hot economy slows, policymakers look for ways to create jobs.*

1967 Sen. Robert F. Kennedy, D-Mass., introduces a bill to award tax credits to businesses for bringing jobs to low-income urban "enterprise zones," but Congress doesn't act.

1975 Fantus Corp. publishes first rankings of advantageous locations for facilities, including analysis of tax breaks and other incentives.

1980s-1990s *As manufacturing jobs dwindle, lawmakers hope tax-advantaged "enterprise zones" in low-income areas can create jobs.*

1980 Prime Minister Margaret Thatcher's conservative government introduces enterprise zones in the United Kingdom. Presidential candidate Ronald Reagan and two New York representatives, Republican Jack Kemp and Democrat Robert Garcia, propose enterprise-zone bills, but they are not enacted. . . . Connecticut and Louisiana adopt enterprise-zone legislation in 1981.

1985 Early evidence that enterprise zones attract business to depressed areas — although sometimes only through relocation from nearby neighborhoods — spurs at least 40 states to enact enterprise-zone laws.

1993 First federal enterprise zones created in cities including Atlanta and Baltimore and rural areas including Mississippi's Delta region and Texas's Rio Grande Valley.

1997 Spurred by research showing that fierce state job competition doesn't create jobs but merely moves them, progressive lawmaker Rep. David Minge, D-Minn., proposes legislation to impose a heavy federal tax on states' location-based tax credits to business; Congress doesn't act on the measure.

2000s *State competition for business relocations heats up, but studies find most programs are ineffective.*

2005 Sen. George Voinovich, R-Ohio, and bipartisan list of cosponsors introduce a bill to guarantee states the right to compete for business sites using tax incentives. Congress doesn't act on the measure.

2007 U.S. cities have built 28 major-league stadiums and arenas since 2000, as teams encourage cities to compete for them using taxpayer-funded incentives.

2008 As recession begins, some states require businesses to forgo incentive funds if job-creation goals aren't met.

2009 Walmart gets $1.8 million in tax credits to build five stores in Louisiana. . . . South Carolina attracts new Boeing plant by offering financial incentives and a lower-wage workforce because the state's right-to-work law makes unionization less likely. . . . In fierce competition to attract conventioneers, American cities have spent $23 billion since 1993 to build convention centers; 320 cities now have them.

2010 Reflecting the growing trend of transparency for subsidies, 37 states post some information online about business-subsidy recipients, up from 23 states in 2007.

2011 Jackson, Miss., officials propose tax breaks to keep a Sears store open after Sears Holdings Corp. announces closures of about 100 Sears and Kmart stores. . . . Newspaper publisher Gannett moves a 4-year-old call center out of Oklahoma despite receiving $260,000 in tax credits. . . . North Carolina lures Chiquita Brands International's headquarters from Cincinnati to Charlotte with $22 million in incentives.

2012 Boeing closes Wichita military aircraft plant, moves jobs to Texas and Oklahoma, two years after Kansas built a $43 million aerospace training center. . . . Proposal for a new Minnesota Vikings football stadium, with about $700 million in taxpayer funding, may reach state lawmakers this spring. . . . Indiana becomes first Rust Belt state and 23rd nationwide to enact business-friendly "right-to-work" legislation banning contracts requiring workers to join or pay dues to a union. . . . Louisiana Republican Gov. Bobby Jindal proposes allowing localities to offer 10-year tax abatements for facilities such as corporate headquarters and data centers.

Subsidies Spark Debate — and New Ideas

"At least give them to companies that reflect your values."

Public officials aren't likely to stop using tax incentives and other benefits to lure businesses and jobs to their communities. But experts see ways to make such subsidies more effective.

"It's hard to end the incentives, but you can try to mend them," says economist Robert W. Wassmer, a professor at California State University, Sacramento.

Step one might be for policymakers to expand their vision of where jobs come from, says Jonathan Q. Morgan, associate professor of public administration at the University of North Carolina, Chapel Hill. Recruiting businesses to a location by offering subsidies and other inducements has been at the top of most states' agendas, he says.

But "business retention and expansion and figuring out how to help" businesses grow that are already in a community is "an important and under-appreciated tool of job creation." Finding ways to help residents who want to "create new businesses from scratch" is another, Morgan says.

Public officials should consider offering tax breaks to lure business relocations only under very specific circumstances, Wassmer says. "Do a benefit-cost assessment" for any incentive under consideration, he says: "Am I just being played by this plant?" Only a company known to face a real choice between very suitable, profit-making locations should be offered an incentive package, Wassmer wrote. Otherwise, he argued, taxpayer dollars will go to companies that would have moved in anyway.

Furthermore, Wassmer advised sober analysis to make sure businesses receiving incentives will generate enough tax revenues, jobs and other benefits to more than compensate for the cost of the inducements.[1]

But it's not always easy to persuade local politicians to cast a skeptical eye on business incentives, Wassmer says.

"Asking those questions goes against the whole political movement" that's driven increased state competition on subsidies for decades, he says. "If more politicians would do it, though, we'd see the end of those bidding wars" between states and cities that consume public money.

Some researchers note that emotions can get in the way of making realistic decisions about which job-building strategies to use.

It's "enormously difficult to do economic development" with analysis done just by local policymakers and officials, says David L. Barkley, professor emeritus of applied economics at South Carolina's Clemson University. A person has a tendency to "exaggerate both the good and the bad of one's own area, saying, 'We have great schools' or 'Woe is me, we have no possibilities here,'" he says. Bringing in outside analysts who can be objective and know what competing regions are doing is necessary, he says.

"A public-private partnership" that includes scholars who study the regional economy could "figure out what kinds of business could thrive in a region, and that, I think, could be beneficial," says Laura Kalambokidis, associate professor of applied economics at the University of Minnesota, St. Paul. "Pitfalls include the fact that every state wants to be the next 'green revolution' state or the next Silicon Valley, but that simply won't work everywhere."

"If you're going to use incentives, at least give them to companies that reflect your values," such as paying workers well and having environmentally sustainable practices, says Jason Jolley, senior research director of the Carolina Center for Competitive Economies at the University of North Carolina, Chapel Hill. To accomplish that, states are better off requiring the legislature or another official body to choose each incentive recipient, rather than automatically offering incentives to any company that meets statutory requirements, Jolley says.

Research shows that some types of incentives are simply more effective at expanding employment and strengthening economies, scholars say.

Tax credits that simply reward companies for hiring the unemployed are relatively efficient and effective, partly because they have relatively low administrative costs, says David Neumark, professor of economics at the University of California, Irvine.

Tax credits that go only to new companies or companies with definite plans to expand also have promise, says Jolley.

Building in accountability provisions also matters. A periodic vetting process involving both the legislature and a state bureaucracy should be part of all incentive programs, to ensure "that they're worth doing long term," Jolley says.

A strong requirement for firms to report their employment numbers is also vital, says Tonya Hansen, assistant professor of economics at Minnesota State University Moorhead. Accurate performance data can be a basis for awarding further incentives and studying program effectiveness, she says.

States are getting smarter, says the University of North Carolina's Morgan. Incentive agreements that impose performance standards and force companies to return incentive money to the government if they don't meet agreed-upon goals will grow more common, "slowly but surely," he says.

— *Marcia Clemmitt*

[1] For background, see Robert W. Wassmer, "The Increasing Use of Property Tax Abatement as a Means of Promoting State and Local Economic Activity in the United States," in *Erosion of the Property Tax Base: Trends, Causes, and Consequences*, Nancy Augustine, Michael Bell, David Brunori and Joan Youngman, eds., 2009, pp. 221-259.

In a case that reached the Supreme Court in 2006, Enrich and attorney Terry Lodge, working on behalf of some Michigan and Ohio residents, challenged tax incentives the city had offered to keep a DaimlerChrysler Jeep plant in town. They argued, among other things, that a property-tax exemption in the package interfered with interstate commerce because it favored the Ohio plant over other businesses, including out-of-state companies. The court didn't rule on the merits of the case, however, but dismissed the challenge on the grounds that the citizens who brought it had not suffered actual harm and therefore had no standing to sue.[45]

Congress should enact legislation clarifying which incentives are allowable and which are not, many say — and have said for decades.

"Congress alone can provide for a full and thorough canvassing of the multitudinous and intricate factors which compose the problem of the taxing freedom of the states and the needed limits on such state taxing power," Supreme Court Associate Justice Felix Frankfurter wrote in 1959.[46]

During the 1990s, Rep. David Minge, D-Minn., tried several times to blunt the effect of state incentives. His bills would have levied high federal taxes on any "preferential" state subsidies, thus making them worthless to businesses.[47]

Conversely, in 2005, two Ohio Republicans — U.S. Sen. George Voinovich and Rep. Patrick Tiberi — introduced legislation, with bipartisan support, to allow most subsidies. Their bill would have barred commerce clause-based legal challenges of "all state and local tax incentives," with seven narrow exceptions.[48]

No bill on incentives has made it out of committee.

Regional Cooperation and Accountability

Regional cooperation on economic development is still rare, but some states seek greater accountability for subsidies.

Some multistate economic-development programs do exist, says Rutgers' Seneca. For example, the New York/New Jersey Port Authority opened in 1921, with congressional authorization, to develop the harbor region the states share.[49] Since economic regions don't stop at state boundaries, "that's the kind of thing that gives a positive return on investment," Seneca said.

Two jurisdictions in the Columbus, Ohio, area recently "agreed to disarm from competition" after the

Many communities, especially rural ones, offer substantial incentives to lure "big box" retail stores such as Walmart. In 2009, Walmart got $1.8 million in tax credits to build five stores in Louisiana. Bridgeton, Mo., approved a $7.2 million deal in 2010 to bring a single Walmart outlet to town. Above, a Walmart store in Valley Stream, N.Y.

headquarters of the Bob Evans restaurant chain "got a lot of state incentives to move from a depressed area" in the region "to a higher-income area nearby," says Ohio State's Greenbaum. To avoid an escalating economic arms race — and to limit the harm to the lower-income area that lost the facility — the towns agreed to share tax revenues from the project, he says.

Regional agreements are tough to enforce, however, says Enrich. In the 1990s, Illinois, Indiana and Wisconsin agreed not to discriminate against employers based in any of the states, but after one state was suspected of doing so, the compact broke down, he says.

Some advocacy groups, such as Good Jobs First, are pushing for greater accountability for subsidies, such as requiring public disclosure and periodic legislative scrutiny of tax credits or other incentives.[50]

Some state programs have accountability features. New Jersey's Business Employment Incentive Program "has some very attractive elements that other states have emulated" such as paying companies only if they create a net number of new jobs, based on verifiable tax records, says Seneca.[51]

As of December 2010, 37 states posted online information about what companies received at least one major state subsidy, up from only 23 states that did so in 2007, according to Good Jobs First.[52]

If Cities Build Stadiums, Will Fans Come?

Critics view sports subsidies as waste of tax dollars.

The Minnesota Vikings ended the 2011 football season with three wins and 13 losses, but they could end the year victorious anyway. The Vikings may finally come out on top of a years-long battle to score a new, mostly public-funded stadium if state lawmakers approve a plan this spring supported by Democratic Gov. Mark Dayton.[1]

Minnesotans have wrangled for years over which jurisdiction should house the facility and how to cover two-thirds of the stadium's estimated $1 billion cost using public funds. Last fall, for example, Minneapolis and nearby Ramsey County both tried to sweeten their bids by proposing to levy new sales taxes without first getting voters' approval. But the legislature upheld a Minnesota law requiring a vote, and those plans, like earlier ones, went back to the drawing board.[2]

The push for tax-subsidized stadiums is happening not only in Minnesota. Professional sports teams and their supporters, who include some lawmakers, repeatedly argue that new arenas create jobs and spur economic activity. Regions from Los Angeles to Tampa Bay are locked in struggles over proposed facilities for both major- and minor-league teams.[3]

Between 2000 and 2007, 28 new arenas for Major League Baseball, basketball, football and hockey teams were built around the country at a total cost of about $9 billion, with at least $5 billion paid by taxpayers.[4]

"There is likely no major metropolitan area in this country that has not been held hostage at some point by the owner of a sports franchise" who threatened to move the team if taxpayers didn't ante up, Arthur J. Rolnick, former research director of the Federal Reserve Bank of

Minneapolis, told Congress in 2007, when the Vikings battle was already under way.

At the time, construction had just begun for a new Minnesota Twins baseball stadium after a 10-year fight in which the team finally secured "about $400 million in public financing" from "a previously reluctant state legislature," said Rolnick, now a senior fellow at the University of Minnesota's Humphrey School of Public Affairs.[5]

Proponents say the public funding has value for communities.

When jurisdictions in the Washington area vied for a Major League Baseball team that was set to come in 2005, supporters of a Northern Virginia site predicted their plan would give the state more than a $287 million annual boost. The National Football League urges cities to build large, updated stadiums partly to snag the annual Super Bowl, which the league claims brings about $400 million in business to the host city.[6]

Skeptics of taxpayer-funded business subsidies, along with many academic economists, disagree about the benefits, however.

The New York Yankees' stadium that opened in the Bronx in 2009 with substantial public funding created jobs, but most "are part time and low wage" and of little help to the neighborhood, argued Bettina Damiani, project director of Good Jobs New York, an advocacy group that seeks accountability in business subsidies.

"Few fields of empirical economic research offer virtual unanimity of findings. Yet independent work on the economic impact of stadiums and arenas has uniformly found there is no statistically positive correlation between sports facility construction and economic development," wrote

Yet, many politicians continue to resist transparency. In 2010, for example, Gov. Arnold Schwarzenegger, R-Calif., vetoed a bill that would have disclosed tax-credit recipients.[53]

"This is public money and there is a big accountability issue, but you can't make the negotiation public; your prospects" — businesses considering a move to one's state —"will walk away and just laugh at you," said Graham Toft, president of the Indiana Economic Development Council.[54]

CURRENT SITUATION

Tight Times

With jobs on voters' minds, many policymakers are pushing new incentive competition in 2012.

In February, Louisiana's Republican governor, Bobby Jindal, proposed allowing localities to offer up to 10 years of tax breaks to facilities such as corporate headquarters, data centers and research-and-development operations. The move would ultimately bring 10,000 jobs, Jindal said.[55]

Andrew Zimbalist, a professor of economics at Smith College, in Northampton, Mass.[7]

The controversy extends beyond sports. Many cities use public funds to build convention centers, museums and similar venues in hopes of attracting paying visitors to town.

U.S. cities have poured more than $23 billion into convention centers from 1993 to 2009, when there were 320 throughout the country, reported *Next American City* magazine.[8]

As with sports arenas, hopes that a business boom will follow can be misplaced. As the number of convention centers rose between 1996 and 2003, attendance at many declined, the magazine reported. In response, many cities actually undertook major facility expansions, competing to snag the very biggest conventions, which previously found only a few cities with facilities large enough to host them, such as Las Vegas.

But that strategy has proved disappointing in many cities. A 420,000-square-foot expansion of Houston's George R. Brown Center, for example, was expected to bring 600,000 single-night visits to Houston in 2005. But it yielded only 220,000 — just over a third of expectations.[9]

— *Marcia Clemmitt*

Getty Images/Hannah Foslien

The Minnesota Vikings and Denver Broncos play at the Hubert H. Humphrey Metrodome in Minneapolis on Dec. 4, 2011. Minnesota lawmakers are considering long-debated plans to build a new $1 billion stadium, mostly with public funds.

[1]Mike Kaszuba, "Vikings Stadium Plan East of Dome Now on Fast Track," *Star Tribune* [Minneapolis], Feb. 5, 2012, www.startribune.com/politics/stateloc al/138721284.html.

[2]Tom Scheck, "Dayton and Legislative Leaders Say Sales Tax Increase Won't Work for Stadium," MPR News, Minnesota Public Radio, Nov. 1, 2011, http://minnesota.publicradio.org/collec tions/special/columns/polinaut/archive/ 2011/11/dayton_and_legi.shtml.

[3]For background, see Michael Hunt, "NFL Teams Are Bold Because They Can Be," *Journal Sentinel* [Milwaukee], Feb. 9, 2012, www.jsonline.com/sports/nfl-teams-are-bold-because-they-can-be-iv44veu-139067354.html; Barry Wilner, "Goodell: 34 Teams Likely if LA Included," Associated Press/Globe [Boston], Feb. 3, 2012, http://articles.boston. com/2012-02-03/sports/31022006_1_concussion-research-la-stadium-brain-trauma.

[4]Sarah Wilhelm, "Public Funding of Sports Stadiums," Policy Perspectives, Center for Public Policy and Administration, University of Utah, April 30, 2008, www. imakenews.com/cppa/e_article001083889.cfm?x=b11,0,w.

[5]Arthur J. Rolnick, "Congress Should End the Economic War Among the States Testimony," The Federal Reserve Bank of Minneapolis website, Oct. 10, 2007, www.minneapolisfed.org/publications_papers/studies/econwar/rolnick_testi mony_2007.cfm.

[6]Robert A. Baade, Robert Baumann, and Victor A. Matheson, "Selling the Game: Estimating the Economic Impact of Professional Sports Through Taxable Sales," *Southern Economic Journal*, January 2008, pp. 794-810, www.all business.com/government/public-finance-taxes-taxation/7068215-1.html.

[7]Quoted in "Build It and They Will Come: Do Taxpayer-Financed Sports Stadiums, Convention Centers and Hotels Deliver as Promised For America's Cities?" Hearing transcript, House Oversight and Government Reform Domestic Policy Subcommittee, March 29, 2007, www.gpo.gov/fdsys/pkg/CHRG-110h hrg38037/html/CHRG-110hhrg38037.htm.

[8]Josh Stevens, "Unconventional Thinking," *Next American City*, Summer 2009, http://americancity.org/magazine/article/unconventional-thinking.

[9]*Ibid.*

Last December, the Illinois legislature and Democratic Gov. Pat Quinn approved at least $100 million in tax breaks to keep Sears Holdings Co. and the Chicago Mercantile Exchange, a financial and commodities trading market, in the state.[56] "If Ohio is offering $400 million to Sears . . . we will defend ourselves," said Quinn.[57]

States are adopting many kinds of tax incentives. "Tax stabilization agreements" — which guarantee a business's tax rates won't rise — are used in 12 states, says Hansen, of Minnesota State University. "Nearly everything else" in the way of tax incentives is used by at least 40 states today, she says.

Some states are courting not just employers but the site-location consultants who advise corporations about where to locate. Last spring, New Jersey economic-development officials entertained executives from the top 12 site-location firms. From the comfort of a hotel suite, they watched the NCAA basketball tournament and met with New Jersey's governor.[58]

An opponent of the proposed "right-to-work" law in Indiana demonstrates outside the State House on Jan. 23, 2012. On Feb. 1 Indiana became the 23rd state to enact such legislation, which bans workplace contracts requiring people to join or pay dues to a union. Republican governors and state legislators have pushed the laws, which they say give states a business-friendly edge in jobs competition.

Concerns are building about whether incentives deliver.

A group of local governments in the St. Louis area recently determined that more than $5.8 billion in public funds had gone to business incentives over the past 20 years, more than 80 percent of it to develop big-box stores and shopping centers. Despite the huge outlay, the number of retail jobs ticked up only slightly, "retail sales or per capita spending have not increased in years" and more than 600 small businesses closed, eliminating nearly as many jobs as the new stores brought in, said the group.[59]

Right to Work

Republican governors and state legislators have pushed to enact "right-to-work" laws that ban workplace contracts requiring people to join or pay dues to a union. Proponents argue that the laws give states a business-friendly edge in the jobs competition.

On Feb. 1, Indiana became the 23rd state to enact right-to-work legislation and the first in the once-vibrant Midwest and Northeastern industrial heartland to do so.[60] New Hampshire, Michigan, Wisconsin and Ohio also are considering such measures.[61]

Opponents see no relationship between right-to-work laws and job creation. "Both the highest and the lowest unemployment rates in the country are found in states" with right-to-work laws, wrote Gordon Lafer, an associate professor of political economics at the University of Oregon's Labor Education and Research Center. The auto industry's continued commitment to Michigan — traditionally a union bastion — shows that workforce skills and state technology-development projects are more important to at least some companies, he wrote.[62]

But James Hohman, assistant director of fiscal policy at the Mackinac Center for Public Policy, a free market-oriented think tank in Midland, Mich., argued that because Michigan has no right-to-work law, the state was forced to offer millions of dollars in incentives to retain the car companies. That would not have been necessary had the state had "an attractive business environment," with a right-to-work law, Hohman said.[63]

Tax incentives have made an appearance in the 2012 presidential race. In January, former House Speaker Newt Gingrich, R-Ga., blasted former Sen. Rick Santorum, R-Pa., for endorsing 1997 Pennsylvania legislation that gave the Pittsburgh Steelers football team and Pittsburgh Pirates baseball team taxpayer dollars for stadiums — often touted as job creators — without requiring repayment.[64]

Meanwhile, another contender for the Republican presidential nomination, former Massachusetts Gov. Mitt Romney, approved at least one location-based tax break for job creation as governor: a tax rebate for biotechnology companies.[65]

President Obama is proposing a new federal "growth zone" plan to replace the longstanding enterprise zone program. Under the new plan, which Congress so far has not approved, 20 rural and urban areas with economic-growth potential would get federal funds for business tax credits and other incentives for job creation.[66]

Some economists say such federally administered programs work better than state incentives in part because they're less politicized. However, any locality offering incentives, no matter how they're administered

Do "right-to-work" laws help states attract businesses?

YES   Paul Kersey
Director of Labor Policy, Mackinac Center for Public Policy

Written for *CQ Researcher*, March 2012

Under a state right-to-work law, an employee cannot be forced to pay union dues or fees as a condition of employment; individual workers can support a union or withhold their support. The law does not change the process for recognizing a union or lessen the obligation to bargain with a union once it has proved it has majority support in the workforce. Since the evidence indicates that most workers join the union in their workplace voluntarily in right-to-work states, right-to-work is actually a fairly modest change.

Yet unions treat right-to-work with alarm, while employers respond very positively to the provision of worker choice.

The attraction of right-to-work for employers is hard to deny. Between 2002 and 2010, employment was up 3 percent on average in right-to-work states and down 3 percent in non-right-to-work states. Union apologists have argued that the job gains in right-to-work states have been due to weather or other factors, but research into economic growth along the borders between right-to-work and non-right-to-work states shows that job growth is one-third higher in counties that have right-to-work than in neighboring counties that don't.

In a right-to-work state, employers know that unions will have the resources workers want them to have, no more and no less. Union officials must pay close attention to the desires of workers who can leave the union and keep their dues money if they are not happy.

Without that protection, unions are tempted to substitute their own ideological agenda for workers' real-world interests. Most employers accept the need for bargaining with employees and understand that over the long term they are better off if employees are happy with their wages and working conditions. If workers prefer to bargain collectively, so be it, but employers want to know that the union they bargain with will pursue the best interests of their employees, not the preferences of union officials.

But the real reason why states should pass right-to-work laws is because they respect the First Amendment right of workers to associate as they see fit, to join a union or not, to give or withhold support from an institution that they may or may not support. If political leaders really value workers, in terms of both recognizing their rights and respecting their judgment, they won't hesitate to give workers that choice. There is every reason to have confidence that workers will use that choice responsibly, to the benefit of both businesses and workers themselves.

NO   Gordon Lafer
Associate Professor, Labor Education and Research Center University of Oregon

Written for *CQ Researcher*, March 2012

In 2011-12, statehouses across the country saw renewed battles over so-called "right-to-work" (RTW) laws. Contrary to what the public might assume, right-to-work does not guarantee anyone a job. Rather, it makes it illegal for unions to require each employee who benefits from the terms of a contract to pay his or her fair share of the costs of administering it.

The aim of RTW — according to its backers — is to cut wages and benefits on the gamble that this will bring more jobs into a state. As the Indiana Chamber of Commerce explains, "unionization increases labor costs," and therefore "makes a given location a less attractive place to invest new capital." By giving up unions and lowering wages, workers are supposed to increase their desirability in the eyes of manufacturers.

Research shows that RTW cuts wages and benefits — but fails to promote job growth. According to multiple studies, RTW laws lower average income by about $1,500 a year and decrease the odds of getting health insurance or a pension through your job — for union and nonunion workers. But RTW does not boost job growth.

It may be that companies in the 1980s moved to RTW states in search of lower wages. But in the globalized economy, companies looking for cheap labor overwhelmingly look to China or Mexico.

In this sense, the most important case study for any state considering RTW in 2012 is that of Oklahoma, which adopted RTW in the post-NAFTA era.

When Oklahoma debated RTW in 2001, corporate location consultants told legislators that if the state adopted RTW, it would see "eight to 10 times as many prospects." What happened? The number of new companies coming into the state has fallen by one-third in the 10 years since RTW was adopted. Manufacturing employment has decreased 30 percent.

Surveys of manufacturers confirm that RTW is not a significant draw; in 2010 manufacturers ranked it 16th among factors affecting location decisions. For higher-tech, higher-wage employers, nine of the 10 most-favored states are non-RTW.

RTW is promoted as providing a competitive advantage to a state. But to the extent more states go RTW — or a national bill passes — wages will be lowered in all states, no one will have an advantage and the number of jobs in the country will be exactly the same as before. This is how RTW undermines the American middle class.

> *Even as some proponents of location-based incentives question their value, fierce struggles among states to lure employers are likely to continue. "It's like a nuclear-arms standstill. No one is willing to blink first."*
>
> **— Jon Shure Director, State Fiscal Strategies, Center on Budget and Policy Priorities**

and paid for, feeds the fevered competition, says Hansen at Minnesota State. "No state or locality will unilaterally disarm" unless federal policy simply eliminates the use of incentives altogether, she says.

OUTLOOK

Beyond Incentives

Even some incentive proponents now question whether interstate competition for jobs is the best strategy. Hanging over the whole enterprise, meanwhile, is the question of whether the United States can actually expand the number of good jobs.

Fierce struggles among states to lure employers are likely to remain the norm for some time, many say.

"It's like a nuclear-arms standstill. No one is willing to blink first," said Jon Shure, director of state fiscal strategies at the Center on Budget and Policy Priorities, a liberal think tank in Washington.[67]

Among state officials, "a few more are skeptical than 10 years ago, but an awful lot still say, 'We need this tool,' " says Enrich, of Northeastern University Law School.

Still, says the University of North Carolina's Morgan, incentive agreements that impose performance standards and force companies to return incentive money to the government if they don't meet agreed-upon goals will grow more common "slowly but surely," he says.

Congress has the constitutional right to either ban or authorize incentive competition, but while legislation giving a green light to it seemed a strong possibility several years ago, the current Senate's Democratic leadership reportedly wouldn't support such a move, says Enrich.

Even without location-based incentives, localities engaged in fierce competition for jobs can still spur employment in their areas, says Karen Chapple, associate director of the Institute of Urban and Regional Development at the University of California, Berkeley. For example, governments might offer various kinds of targeted assistance to businesses that try to create entirely new labor-intensive industries, she says.

Meanwhile, with the environment a growing concern, localities might offer expert assistance and even cash to business startups interested in "green retrofitting" of buildings or in recycling throwaway materials into new products such as carpets, she says. Recycling-based manufacture could be a net job creator because it would require more workers than the old throwaway economy, and "states and local economies can do something to help develop these new capacities and help develop markets" for new products, she says.

Offshore competition has made it more and more difficult to create jobs in America, "but energy and climate change could someday change that," bringing manufacturing and agriculture back to America so that states no longer have to engage in such bitter rivalries for a dwindling number of good jobs, adds California State's Wassmer. "Shipping all these containers from China" may become too costly and environmentally damaging, "and you might end up with more domestic goods production" — and the jobs that go with it.

NOTES

1. For background, see Aubrey Cohen, "Boeing Closing Wichita Plant," *Seattle Post-Intelligencer*, Jan. 4, 2012, www.seattlepi.com/business/ boeing/article/Boeing-closing-Wichita-plant-2440784.php; and Emily Knapp, "Governments Rob Taxpayers of Billions to Fund Ill-advised Incentive Programs," *Wall St. Cheat Sheet*, Jan. 19, 2012, http://wallstcheatsheet.com/stocks/gov ernments-rob-tax-payers-of-billions-to-fund-ill-advised-incentive-programs.html.

2. Cohen, *ibid.*

3. Jonathan Q. Morgan and David M. Lawrence, "Economic Development," County and Municipal Government in North Carolina, Chapel Hill School of Government, 2007, p. 2, http://sogpubs.unc.edu/

cmg/cmg26.pdf. Morgan is an associate professor of public administration; Lawrence is now retired as a professor of government.

4. *Ibid.*

5. For background, see "Boeing Tax Grab Shows Peril of Offering Tax Dollars for Growth," Bloomberg, Jan. 19, 2012, www.bloomberg. com/news/2012-01-19/ boeing-job-grab-shows-peril-of-offering-tax-dollars-for-growth.html, and "Money-Back Guarantees for Taxpayers," Good Jobs First, January 2012, www .goodjobs first.org/moneyback. Alan Peters and Peter Fisher, "The Failures of Economic Development Incentives," *Journal of the American Planning Association*, Issue 1, 2004, pp. 27-37.

6. Ronald J. Hansen, "Arizona Tax Credits Rising for Business," *The Arizona Republic*, Nov. 22, 2011, www.azcentral.com/news/articles/2011/ 11/21/2011 1121arizona-tax-credits-rising-for-business.html.

7. "Kentucky Business Climate Boosted by State Incentives," *BusinessClimate.com*, http://business climate.com/kentucky-economic-development/ kentucky-business-climate-boosted-state-incentives.

8. Edward M. Mazze, "The Economic Impact of the Motion Picture Production Tax Credit on the Rhode island Economy for the Years 2005-2009," www .film.ri.gov/MazzeStudy.pdf.

9. Ruby Gonzales, "Pico Rivera Faces Paying Rent Even With Borders Leaving," *Whittier Daily News* [Calif.], March 19, 2011, www.whittierdailynews .com/news/ci_17652157.

10. Stacy Mitchell, "Don't Subsidize Big Boxes at Local Shops' Expense," *Bloomberg BusinessWeek*, Sept. 9, 2011, www.businessweek.com/small-business/ dont-subsidize-big-boxes-at-local-shops-expense-09092011.html.

11. Mark Robyn, "2012 State Business Tax Climate Index," Jan. 25, 2012, www.taxfoundation.org/ news/show/22658.html; "The Best States for Business," *Forbes*, www.forbes.com/pictures/ mli45ggdd/17-south-dakota/#content.

12. "Unemployment Rates — Most Current Available," South Dakota Department of Labor and Regulation, http://dlr.sd.gov/unem ploymentrate.aspx; "Employment Situation Summary," U.S. Bureau of Labor Statistics news release, Feb. 3, 2012, www.bls .gov/news.release/ empsit.nr0.htm.

13. "The Poorest Counties in the America," MSN Money, http://money.msn.com/family-money/ the-poorest-counties-in-america.

14. Vincent Fernando and Betty Jin, "10 States With Ridiculously Low Unemployment," MSNBC/ Business Insider, www.msnbc.msn.com/id/38838429/ ns/business-us_business/t/states-ridiculously-low-unemployment/#.TzLAco H0izV.

15. Terry F. Buss, "The Effect of State Tax Incentives on Economic Growth and Firm Location Decisions: An Overview of the Literature," *Economic Development Quarterly*, February 2001, http://edq.sagepub.com/ content/15/1/90.abstract.

16. Quoted in Kiersten Valle Pittman and Tim Funk, "In Scramble for New Jobs, Incentives Play a Key Role," *Idaho Statesman*/McClatchy Newspapers, Dec. 13, 2011, www.idahostates man.com/2011/12/ 13/1914317/in-scramble-for-new-jobs-incentives .html.

17. David Stade and Katy Stech, "Boeing's Whopping Incentives," *The Post and Courier* [Charleston], Jan. 17, 2010, www.postandcour ier.com/news/2010/ jan/17/boeings-whopping-incentives.

18. Pittman and Funk, *op. cit.*

19. Bill Schweke, "Major Questions About Economic Development, Part V," CFED website, Dec. 2, 2009, http://cfed.org/blog/inclusive economy/major_ques tions_about_economic_ development_part_v.

20. Mali R. Schantz-Feld, "Top Site Selection Factors: Tax Rates, Exemptions, and Incentives — Keeping an Eye on the Competition," *Area Development*, November 2011, www.area development.com/laborEducation/ November 2011/site-selection-factors-skilled-labor-220743.shtml.

21. For background, see "2011 Best-performing Cities," Milken Institute, http://bestcities.milken institute.org.

22. Timothy J. Bartik, "Boon or Boondoggle? The Debate Over State and Local Economic Development Policies," in *Who Benefits from State and Local Economic Development Policies?* W.E. Upjohn Institute for Employment Research, pp. 1-16, http:// research.upjohn.org/up_ bookchapters/88.

23. Scott Loveridge, "Local Industrial Recruitment: Boondoggle or Boon?" May 1995, www.rri. wvu.edu/pdffiles/wp9510.pdf.

24. "Taxes and Economic Development 101," Institute on Taxation and Economic Policy, September 2011, www.itepnet.org/pdf/pb42.pdf.

25. Timothy J. Bartik, "State Economic Development Policies: What Works," presentation at the Center on Budget and Policy Priorities Annual State Fiscal Policy Conference, Washington, D.C., Nov. 30, 2011, http://research.upjohn. org/presentations/27.

26. Alice Hines, "As Sears Plans Closings, Cities Fight to Keep Stores," *Huffington Post*, Jan. 26, 2012, www .huffingtonpost.com/2012/01/26/ sears-closes-cities_n_1231326.html?ref=mostpopular.

27. Quoted in Ashli Sims, "Tulsa Taxpayers Upset After Company Receiving State Rebate Shuts Down," NewsOn6 website, April 11, 2011, www.newson6 .com/story/14426304/quality-jobs-program.

28. Bartik, "Boon or Boondoggle?" *op. cit.*

29. Quoted in Penelope Lemov, "Is the Hollywood Tax Credit Under Attack?" *Governing*, March 16, 2011, www.governing.com/ columns/public-finance/holly wood-tax-credit-under-attack.html; for background, see "Tax Credits for Filmmakers — By U.S. State and Canadian Province," Making the Movie website, http://makingthemovie.info/2006/07/tax-credits-for-filmmakers-state-by-state.html.

30. Quoted in Brian R. Hook, "Critics Blast Tax Credit Proposals by Missouri Review Panel," Missouri Watchdog website, Dec. 2, 2010, http://missouri .watchdog.org/7972/critics-blast-tax-credit-proposals-by-missouri-review-panel.

31. Mark Cassell, "Zoned Out; Distribution and Benefits in Ohio's Enterprise Zone Program," Policy Matters Ohio, October 2003, www.kent.edu/ cpapp/research/upload/eco-enterprise-zones.pdf.

32. Greg LeRoy and Leigh McIlvaine, "Paid to Sprawl: Subsidized Job Flight for Cleveland and Cincinnati," Good Jobs First, www.good jobsfirst.org/paidto-sprawl, July 2011.

33. William Fulton, *Romancing the Smokestack: How Cities and States Pursue Prosperity* (2010), p. 4.

34. Robyn, *op. cit.*

35. Arthur J. Rolnick, "Congress Should End the Economic War Among the States," The Federal Reserve Bank of Minneapolis website, Oct. 10, 2007, www.minneapolisfed.org/publications_ papers/studies/econwar/rolnick_testimony_ 2007.cfm.

36. Quoted in "Professional Sports Stadiums: Do They Divert Public Funds From Critical Public Infrastructure?" Hearing transcript, House Oversight and Government Reform Domestic Policy Subcommittee, Oct. 10, 2007.

37. *Ibid.*

38. For background, see Robert W. Wassmer, "The Increasing Use of Property Tax Abatement as a Means of Promoting State and Local Economic Activity in the United States," in Nancy Augustine, Michael Bell, David Brunori and Joan Youngman, eds., *Erosion of the Property Tax Base: Trends, Causes and Consequences* (2009), pp. 221-259, and P.G. Marshall, "Do Enterprise Zones Work?" *Editorial Research Reports*, 1989 (Vol. 1).

39. Joseph J. Seneca, James W. Hughes and George R. Nagle, "An Assessment of the New Jersey Business Employment Incentive Program," July 27, 2004, www.policy.rutgers.edu/reports/ beip/beip_report .pdf.

40. Quoted in *ibid*.

41. Ann R. Magnusen and Katherine Nesse, "Institutional and Political Determinants of Incentive Competition," in *Reining in the Competition for Capital*, W.E. Upjohn Institute for Employment Research, 2007, pp. 1-42, http://research.upjohn.org/up_bookchapters/237.

42. *Ibid.*

43. Brent Lane and G. Jason Jolley, "An Evaluation of North Carolina's Economic Development Incentive Programs: Summary of Analysis, Findings and Recommendations," University of North Carolina Center for Competitive Economies, Jan. 21, 2009, www.kenan- flagler.unc.edu/kenan-institute/about/organi zation/competitive-economies/~/media/Files/kenaninstitute/UNC_KenanInstitute_NCIncen tivesStudy.ashx.

44. For background, see David G. Savage, *Guide to the U.S. Supreme Court* (5th ed.) (2010), Vol. 1, p. 142.

45. The decision is *DaimlerChrysler v. Cuno*, 547 U.S. 332 (2006). For background, see Russell Mokhiber and Robert Weissman, "Corporate Shakedown in Toledo," *Common Dreams*, Feb. 8, 2000, www.commondreams .org/views/021000-105.htm, and Chris Atkins, *Cuno v. DaimlerChrysler: A Pyrrhic Victory for Economic Neutrality*, Fiscal Facts, Tax Foundation, April 18, 2005, www.taxfoundation.org/ publications/ show/344.html.

46. *Northwestern States Portland Cement Co. v. Minnesota*, 358 U.S. 450 (1959) (Frankfurter, J. dissenting). "Dissent of Justice Felix Frankfurter," http://caselaw.lp .findlaw.com/ scripts/getcase.pl?court=us&vol=358& invol=450.

47. Quoted in "Professional Sports Stadiums: Do They Divert Public Funds From Critical Public Infrastructure?" Hearing transcript, House Oversight and Government Reform Domestic Policy Subcommittee, Oct. 10, 2007, Government Printing Office, www.gpo.gov/ fdsys/pkg/CHRG-110hrg51756/html/CHRG-110hrg51756.htm; for background, see H.R. 3044.IH, Thomas, Library of Congress, http:// thomas.loc.gov/cgi-bin/query/ z?c105:H.R.30 44.IH:.

48. For background, see "S. 1066: Economic Development Act of 2005," govtrack.us, www. govtrack.us/congress/ bill.xpd?bill=s109-1066 &tab=summary; Michael Mazerov, "Should Congress Authorize States to Continue Giving Tax Breaks to Businesses?" Center on Budget and Policy Priorities, June 30, 2005, www .cbpp.org/files/2-18-05sfp.pdf; "Voinovich, Tiberi, Stabenow and Chandler Propose Bill to Protect Key Economic Development Tools," press release, website of Rep. Pat Tiberi, May 19, 2005, http://tiberi.house .gov/News/ DocumentSingle.aspx?DocumentID =32632.

49. For background, see "History of the Port Authority," The Port Authority of New York & New Jersey, www.panynj.gov/about/history-port-authority .html.

50. For background, see "Key Reforms: Overview," Good Jobs First website, www.good jobsfirst.org/ accountable-development/key-reforms-overview.

51. For background, Seneca, Hughes and Nagle, *op. cit.*

52. "Show Us the Subsidies," Good Jobs First, December 2010, www.goodjobsfirst.org/sites/ default/files/ docs/pdf/showusthesubsidiesrpt.pdf.

53. Ronald J. Hansen, "Ariz. Tax Credits Rising for Business," *Arizona Republic*, Nov. 22, 2011, www .azcentral.com/arizonarepublic/news/ articles/ 2011/11/21/20111121arizona-tax-credits-rising-for-business.html.

54. Quoted in David Fettig, "A Report from the Battlefield," *The Region*, Minneapolis Federal Reserve Bank, June 1, 1996, www.minneapolis fed .org/publications_papers/pub_display.cfm?id=3660.

55. Ed Anderson, "Proposed Business Tax Breaks Could Produce 10,000 Jobs, Gov. Bobby Jindal Says," *The Times Picayune* [New Orleans], Feb. 2, 2012, www .nola.com/business/ index.ssf/2012/02/proposed_ business_tax_breaks_c.html.

56. Christopher Wills and David Mercer, "In the Game of Tax Breaks, States Play at Their Own Risk," Associated Press/*Salt Lake Tribune*, Dec. 17, 2011, www.sltrib.com/sltrib/money/ 53126758-79/tax-illinois-state-companies.html.csp.

57. Quoted in Kathy Bergen, "Tax Breaks for Sears, CME Head to Governor," *Chicago Tribune*, Dec. 14, 2011, http://articles.chicagotribune. com/2011-12-14/business/ct-biz-1214-cme-sears-20111214_1_ corporate-income-tax-tax-rate-business-tax.

58. Alejandra Cancino and Julia Wernau, "States Go All Out With Tax Incentives, Deals to Hook Firms," *The Chicago Tribune*, May 15, 2011, http://articles .chicagotribune.com/2011-05-15/ business/ct-biz-0515-incentives-20110515_1_ tax-incentives-state-incentives-illinois-companies.

59. "An Assessment of the Effectiveness and Fiscal Impacts of the Use of Development Incentives in the St. Louis Region," East-West Gateway Council of Governments, January 2011, www.ewgateway.org/pdffiles/library/ dirr/TIFFinalRpt.pdf, and Stacy Mitchell, "Don't Subsidize Big Boxes at Local Shops' Expense," *Bloomberg Businessweek*, Sept. 9, 2011, www. business week.com/small-business/dont-subsi dize-big-boxes-at-local-shops-expense-0909 2011.html.

60. For background, see Mary Beth Schneider and Chris Sikich, "Indiana Becomes Rust Belt's First

Right-to-Work State," *The Indianapolis Star/USA Today*, Feb. 2, 2012, www.usa today.com/news/nation/story/2012-02-01/ indiana-right-to-work-bill/52916356/1.

61. For background, see Steven Greenhouse, "Strained States Turning to Laws to Curb Labor Unions," *The New York Times*, Jan. 3, 2011, www.nytimes.com/2011/01/04/business/04labor. html?pagewanted=all; Kyle Maichle, "Midwest States Are Focus of a New Push for Right-to-Work in 2011," Dec. 10, 2010, http://ballot pedia.org/wiki/index.php/Midwest_states_are_focus_of_a_new_push_for_Right-To-Work_in_ 2011.

62. Gordon Lafer, 'Right to Work': The Wrong Answer for Michigan's Economy, *EPI Briefing Paper*, Economic Policy Institute, Sept. 15, 2011, www.epi.org/publication/right-to-work-michigan-economy. Garry Rayno, "Hundreds Gather to Fight Right-to-work Bill," *UnionLeader.com*, Feb. 10, 2012, www.union-leader. com/article/20120210/NEWS06/702109989.

63. Quoted in Tom Gantert, "Debate: Could Union Costs Be Pricing Michigan Out of Auto Jobs?" CAPCON: Michigan Capitol Confidential, Mackinac Center for Public Policy, Oct. 13, 2011, www.michigancapitol confidential.com/15873.

64. Pema Levy, "Newt Goes Ballistic on Pretty Much Everyone," *Talking Points Memo*, Jan. 9, 2012, http://2012.talkingpointsmemo.com/ 2012/01/newt-is-not-here-to-make-friends.php; for background, see Kevin Clark Forsythe, "The Stadium Game Pittsburgh Style: Observations on the Latest Round of Publicly Financed Stadia in Steel Town, USA, and Comparisons With 28 Other Major League Teams," *Marquette Sports Law Review*, Spring 2000, http://scholarship.law.marquette.edu/cgi/viewcontent. cgi?article=1470&context=sportslaw.

65. Jeanne Sahadi, "Mitt Romney's Tax Record: Tax Cutter or Tax Hiker?" *CNNMoney*, Jan. 23, 2012, http://money.cnn.com/2012/01/23/news/economy/Romney_tax_record/index.htm.

66. For background, see "2012 Federal Budget Proposals," CCH Group, Feb. 17, 2011, http://tax .cchgroup.com/downloads/files/pdfs/legislation/treasury-greenbook.pdf.

67. Quoted in Cancino and Wernau, *op. cit.*

BIBLIOGRAPHY
Selected Sources
Books

Fulton, William, *Romancing the Smokestack: How Cities and States Pursue Prosperity*, Solimar Books, 2010.

In a collection of articles, a longtime economic-development analyst describes the many methods cities use to attract and retain jobs and businesses.

LeRoy, Greg, *The Great American Jobs Scam: Corporate Tax Dodging and the Myth of Job Creation*, Berrett-Koehler Publishers, 2005.

The head of the advocacy group Good Jobs First, which promotes accountability for tax subsidies, argues that case studies demonstrate community harm from interstate and inter-local subsidy competition, including deteriorating infrastructure and sprawl.

Articles

Johnston, David Cay, "On the Dole, Corporate Style," Tax.com, Jan. 4, 2011.

Tax breaks for business are increasing worldwide, but Canada and the European Union are trying to curb the trend. Some sought-after businesses, such as companies that store data for Internet giants Yahoo! and Google, produce few jobs and therefore may be particularly questionable recipients of subsidies.

Pittman, Kirsten Valle, and Tim Funk, "In Scramble for New Jobs, Incentives Play a Key Role," *Idaho Statesman/* McClatchy Newspapers, Dec. 13, 2011, www.idahostates man.com/2011/12/13/1914317/in-scramble-for-new-jobs-incentives.html.

Some Idaho economic-development officials say they lost a Boeing aircraft plant to South Carolina because their state wouldn't give the company a big enough financial incentive, but other analysts argue that states should be cautious about such interstate competition.

Schantz-Feld, Mali R., "Top Site Selection Factors: Tax Rates, Exemptions and Incentives — Keeping an Eye on the Competition," *Area Development Online*, November 2011, www.areadevelopment.com/taxes Incentives/November 2011/site-selection-factors-taxes-incentives-224443.shtml.

Some states that offer location incentives to meet specific companies' wish lists are emerging from the recession with stronger job growth than average, according to a magazine for business site-selection professionals.

Spathelf, Christof, "First Person: The Site Selection Process Behind VW's First U.S. Manufacturing Facility," *Area Development Online*, November 2011, www.areadevelopment. com/Automotive/November 2011/VW-Christof-Spathelf-Overseas-manufacturing-77780192.shtml.

A training partnership with a local university and community college played a role in bringing a Volkswagen plant to Chattanooga, Tenn.

Reports and Studies

"Money-Back Guarantees for Taxpayers," Good Jobs First, January 2012, www.goodjobsfirst.org/sites/default/ files/docs/pdf/moneyback.pdf.

With states and cities spending an estimated $70 billion annually on economic-development subsidies, governments are monitoring the outcomes of subsidy programs more closely but are far from requiring real accountability, says a subsidy watchdog group.

"Report of the Missouri Tax Credit Review Commission," Missouri Tax Credit Review Commission, Nov. 30, 2010, http://tcrc.mo.gov/pdf/TCRCFinal Report113010.pdf.

A panel of Missouri lawmakers and business and community representatives concludes that "there currently exists a problem in interstate competition where states manipulate the marketplace with incentives and cannibalize each other's industries."

"Show Us the Subsidies," Good Jobs First, December 2010, www.goodjobsfirst.org/showusthesubsidies.

Analysts for a nonprofit group that advocates for subsidy accountability finds that states are disclosing more information about who gets business incentives but that complete transparency is a long way off.

Bartik, Timothy J., "State Economic Development Policies: What Works?" Upjohn Institute, Nov. 30, 2011, http://re search.upjohn.org/presentations/27.

Research shows that well-administered customized job-training programs are much better than tax cuts and tax incentives at creating good-paying jobs in a state.

Coates, Dennis, and Brad R. Humphreys, "The Stadium Gambit and Local Economic Development," *Regulation,* Cato Institute, Summer 2000, www.cato .org/pubs/regu lation/regv23n2/coates.pdf.

In a report for a libertarian magazine, two University of Maryland economists say that evidence over the years demonstrates that bringing a professional sports team to a city doesn't increase residents' per capita income and isn't worth the taxpayer dollars spent.

Fisher, Peter S., "Corporate Taxes and State Economic Growth, Iowa Fiscal Partnership," February 2011, www.iowa fiscal.org/2011docs/110209-IFP-corptaxes .pdf.

A University of Iowa professor emeritus of urban and regional planning argues that because taxes make up a relatively small portion of business costs, tax breaks have much less effect than policymakers believe in influencing companies' location decisions.

For More Information

Area Development, www.areadevelopment.com. Advertising-supported magazine for the site-location industry.

Good Jobs First, 1616 P St., N.W., Suite 210, Washington, DC 20036; 202-232-1616; www.goodjobsfirst.org. Research and advocacy group that tracks accountability in economic-development subsidies.

HandMade in America, P.O. Box 2089, Asheville, NC 28802; 828-252-0121; www.handmadeinamerica.org. Group that works to revitalize small towns in North Carolina through small-scale economic development.

International Economic Development Council, 734 15th St., N.W., Suite 900, Washington, DC 20005; 202-223-7800; www.iedconline.org. Membership group for the economic-development profession.

New Carolina, 1411 Gervais St., Suite 315, Columbia, SC 29201; 803-760-1400; www.newcarolina.org. Group that works on public and private projects to strengthen industry clusters in South Carolina.

Site Selection, 6625 The Corners Parkway, Suite 200, Norcross, GA 30092-2901; 770-446-6996; www.siteselection.com. Magazine of the Industrial Asset Management Council; covers corporate real estate and economic development.

The Tax Foundation, National Press Building, 529 14th St., N.W., Suite 420, Washington, DC 20045-1000; 202-464-6200; http://taxfoundation.org. Research group that publishes state business-climate rankings.

W.E. Upjohn Institute for Employment Research, 300 S. Westnedge Ave., Kalamazoo, MI 49007-4686; 269-343-5541; www.upjohninst.org. Research group that studies ways to prevent unemployment.

9

Digital Education

Marcia Clemmitt

Corina Dill and other low-income middle-school students in San Angelo, Texas, participate in a new program on Oct. 8, 2011, that teaches them to use open-source software. The students can take the computers home after completing three Saturday workshops at Angelo State University. Debate is raging over whether digital technologies have proven their worth as learning tools.

From *CQ Researcher*, Dec. 2, 2011

S tudents learning to read have long followed a familiar routine: They read a passage of text aloud in class and wait for the teacher to correct their pronunciation.

But in the digitized world of 21st-century education, computers are increasingly taking on the teachers' role. Computers can now "hear" students speak, for example, correct their pronunciation and evaluate their progress over time, says Michael L. Kamil, a professor emeritus at the Stanford University School of Education. "Until recently, computers couldn't listen to oral reading and understand it," he says. But new programs make it possible.

Such advances are part of a much bigger movement to integrate technology into classrooms, creating what education scholars call a "blended learning environment." As computers increasingly dominate every realm of business and life, experts say schools must prepare young people not only to use digital technology but also to understand how to program it, how it shapes culture and behavior and how it can be harnessed to perform tasks once considered the sole realm of humans.

Yet, while digital devices have become ubiquitous worldwide, debate is raging over whether — and which — technologies have proved their worth as learning tools. Some school systems have fully embraced technology, for example by providing every student with a laptop computer. But critics argue that money for such programs would be better spent on teachers.

And in some localities, technology is threatening teachers' very jobs. In cash-strapped Ohio, for example, schools could attain a 50-1

Views Differ on Online Courses

Sixty percent of adults believe online courses do not offer the same educational value as a traditional classroom courses. More than half of college presidents say online courses are of equal value.

Does an online course provide an equal educational value compared with a course taken in person in a classroom?

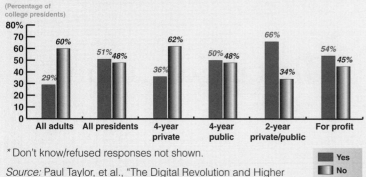

(Percentage of college presidents)

* Don't know/refused responses not shown.

Yes
No

Source: Paul Taylor, et al., "The Digital Revolution and Higher Education," Pew Internet & American Life Project, August 2011, pp. 11, 13, www.pewinternet.org/~/media//Files/Reports/2011/PIP-Online-Learning.pdf

student-teacher ratio — more than twice the conventional 20 or so pupils per teacher — by combining live teaching with large amounts of online study, Robert Sommers, director of the Office of 21st Century Education in the Ohio governor's office, told the state legislature last spring.[1] Similar proposals are surfacing in many other states.

"I teach a class for aspiring school administrators, and the first thing I tell them is that the schools you are in today are not the schools you are going to be leading," says James Lerman, director of the Progressive Science Initiative, a program at Kean University in Union, N.J., which helps experienced teachers become certified to teach math and science. "What happened to the music industry and the publishing industry" as the digital revolution turned their business models upside down "is just beginning to happen to schools."

Digital learning has been getting a boost in localities across the nation this year. For example, Idaho became the first state to require high-school students to complete two or more online courses to receive a diploma.[2] And a mere two years after spending $500 million to upgrade Internet access in its public schools, New York City announced it will spend the same amount in 2012 on more technical improvements.[3]

Many education specialists are somewhere in the middle on the issue of computerized education. Decades of experience make clear that computer software can effectively train people to perform certain complex tasks, says David Moursund, an emeritus professor of education at the University of Oregon, at Eugene. "We've known for a long time that computers could take on part of the task of the human teacher or tutor," notably by teaching basic skills such as multiplication or spelling, and do the job as well as the average teacher, says Moursund.

The military and the airline industry, he notes, both use computer simulations to train people for tough, high-stakes jobs such as distinguishing between incoming missiles and harmless radar-screen blips, and servicing jet aircraft. "With enough money, you can develop simulation that's quite good, nearly indistinguishable from the real thing," Moursund says. Similarly, software programs that tutor students in subjects such as arithmetic are customizable for any skill level and thus uniquely helpful in schools, said John Danner, co-founder of Palo Alto, Calif.-based Rocketship Education, which operates a network of well-regarded K-5 charter schools in low-income Northern California communities. "When students learn things that are developmentally appropriate for where each of them are, they learn things much faster than if you teach to the middle," as classroom teachers typically must do, he said.[4]

Nevertheless, computers can never replace the human touch in elementary and high school classrooms, experts say. Teachers do what technology can't, "such as being a live person who cares about you," says Grover J. Whitehurst, director of the Brown Center on Education Policy at the Brookings Institution, a centrist think tank in Washington.

"Blended models" of schooling that combine computer-based learning with live classes seem to be emerging as the most common model, Whitehurst says. In fact, as computers increasingly take over routine tasks and the Internet provides easy access to unlimited streams of information, demands for teachers to possess more sophisticated conceptual skills will increase, some analysts say. But education specialists worry that teachers aren't receiving adequate training to function in this new, digitally dominated world.

"The teacher of the future helps you navigate the ocean of information" that the online world provides, says Paulo Blikstein, an assistant professor of education at Stanford University and director of its Transformative Learning Technologies Lab. "I can go to Wikipedia to memorize historical figures' names, but I need somebody to talk with me about power relations" and other concepts, "to help me make sense" of the facts. Teachers will "need to know much more about learning how to learn, about how to help students make sense of these huge amounts of information, where you need to interpret what you see," Blikstein says. "But we're not training teachers to help with these things."[5]

Some digital-technology enthusiasts argue that computer games tailored for learning could be an education booster. But many education-technology scholars say that, so far, most games developed as teaching tools don't actually teach much.[6]

Learning claims for games such as the popular "Oregon Trail" — a simulation game developed in the 1970s to teach about pioneer life — are overblown and rest on the too-frequent misunderstanding that student motivation guarantees learning, says Kamil, at Stanford's School of Education. For players to learn from a game, winning and enjoying the game must both depend on whether the player learns something that the game intends to impart, he says. "If you watch a bunch of boys play "Oregon Trail" they spend all their time shooting deer," clearly enjoying themselves, but not accruing any history-related skills or knowledge.

Too many games can be won by using non-learning-related strategies such as repeated blind guessing, Kamil says. "They may get kids engaged, but they don't get them engaged in an actual learning task."

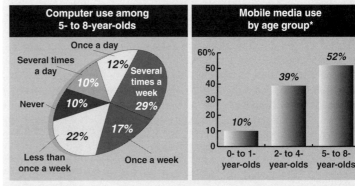

Digital-Media Use Common Among Young

Fifty-one percent of 5- to 8-year-olds use computers at least several times a week. Only 10 percent have never used a computer (left). More than half of children 5 to 8 years old have used a smartphone, iPad or other kind of mobile device at least once (right).

* Percentages do not add to 100 because of rounding.

Source: "Zero to Eight: Children's Media Use in America," Common Sense Media, Fall 2011, p. 9, www.commonsensemedia.org/sites/default/files/research/zerotoeightfinal2011.pdf

Nevertheless, some games do contain the seeds of very effective learning, but researchers are only just learning the principles that underlie such games, education-technology analysts say.

A game in which a player enters some virtual world and advances through it by solving challenges that involve uncovering the rules of the place offer the very highest form of learning, wrote James Gee, a professor of literacy studies at Arizona State University. A game in which a player solves a science mystery, for example, could be a much more fruitful learning experience than an ordinary biology course in which a student learns facts and repeats them on a test. In fact, "decades of research have shown that students taught under such a regime . . . cannot actually apply their knowledge to . . . understand the conceptual lay of the land in the area they are learning," said Gee.[7]

By contrast, a computer game can closely approximate an activity such as practicing biology in real life, Gee wrote. "Biology is not a set of facts but a 'game' certain types of people 'play' " by doing certain activities, using particular tools and languages, holding certain principles and playing "by a certain set of 'rules,' " all activities that games players do in virtual game worlds. "Keep in mind that . . . 'Full Spectrum Warrior' " — a

'Virtual' Public Schools Gaining Students

Students excel in some but struggle in others.

Online K-12 schools are spreading across the country, but controversy is simmering over how well they perform and whether all students should be eligible to "attend" them.

As of 2010, at least 27 states had at least one entirely full-time, publicly funded online school, including high schools and schools serving pre-kindergarteners through 12th grade. While enrollment numbers are hard to find, researchers estimate that more than 150,000 K-12 students nationwide attended virtual schools full time in the 2009-2010 school year.[1]

Online-only schools originally were set up to accommodate students facing illness, pregnancy, bullying or some other issue, but they have since begun to accommodate those who, for whatever reason, wish not to attend a brick-and-mortar institution.

But about two dozen states prohibit students whose schooling is tax-supported from taking all their courses online and insist that publicly funded schools include some live instruction, according to researchers at the National Education Policy Center at the University of Colorado in Boulder.

The number of students taking online courses has soared at many state-run virtual schools. At the Florida Virtual School, established in 1997, attendance rose 39 percent in the 2009-2010 school year and another 22 percent in 2010-11.

At New Mexico's IDEAL (Innovative Digital Education and Learning) school, established in 2008, the number of courses rose 37 percent in 2009-2010 and 85 percent in 2010-11.[2]

Some all-online schools are established by individual school districts and others by states. Some are available only to students living in certain school districts, while others are open to out-of-state students. Most, however, draw taxpayer funding according to much the same per-student formula used for traditional schools. Yet most virtual schools — though not all — are operated by private companies.[3]

While online schooling is a growing phenomenon, some researchers say it is not appropriate for students to attend virtual schools full time — that is, without taking at least some classes in a traditional classroom setting.

Online-only education provides a helpful haven for some, however, says James Lerman, director of the Progressive Science Initiative, a program at Kean University in Union, N.J., that helps experienced teachers become certified to teach math and science. For example, when the Florida Virtual School opened, "it was for kids who had problems going to regular school, such as being pregnant, having failed before, being disaffected or having to work," he says. For those students, he says, virtual schools may provide welcome shelter from a hostile climate they might face in a traditional school.

computer-simulation game about anti-guerrilla fighting — "is a game when I buy it off the rack but serious learning when a soldier 'plays' the professional training version," Gee wrote.[8]

As policymakers and schools struggle to keep up with ever-advancing digital technology, here are some of the questions that are being asked:

Are computers in schools improving education?

Hopes have been high for decades that computer games, tutoring software and other digital technologies could make students more engaged and effective learners. But with many schools now coming online with high-speed Internet connections, the evidence on learning outcomes remains mixed.

For elementary-school students, decades of research demonstrate that "we can develop computer programs that teach kids to do more mundane things" — such as add, subtract and multiply — better than the average classroom teacher can, says Moursund of the University of Oregon.

Computers' strength as skills instructors lies partly in data-gathering and data-analysis abilities that humans can't match, says Moursund. For example, to learn to type on a keyboard, "a program can time how long you touch a key, tally mistakes, note your fast and slow fingers" and adjust the task in real time to provide additional exercise for an individual's weak spots. "A human tutor can't possibly adjust so much" and thus is less efficient, he says.

But whether large numbers of students would benefit from all-virtual education and whether online schools produce academic-achievement results equal to those of traditional schools remain in hot dispute.

In a 2007 study of both full- and part-time online students, the nonpartisan Florida TaxWatch research group found that Florida Virtual School students "consistently outperformed their public school counterparts" on reading and math in state achievement tests. The school earned "high marks" for both student achievement and cost-effectiveness, said the group.[4]

Studies in some other states have found problems, though.

A 2011 study of Pennsylvania's virtual schools by Stanford University's Center for Research on Education Outcomes (CREDO) found that in both reading and math achievement students at all eight online schools performed "significantly worse" than their counterparts at brick-and-mortar institutions.[5]

In a 2006 audit of online schools in Colorado, state analysts found that "in the aggregate, online students performed poorly" on state achievement exams, were "about four to six times more likely to repeat a grade than students statewide" and had a dropout rate between three and six times higher than the statewide rate.[6]

High dropout rates — in the range of 50 percent or greater — are common among online schools, but that's not surprising, says Paul Kim, chief technology officer of Stanford University's School of Education. "Why? They joined the online school because they hated regular school, and the online school turned out to be just like it" in

stressing standardized testing and rote memorization, for example, he says.

In addition, while teachers in virtual schools communicate individually with students via email, chat programs and other Internet-based modes, in general "online schools don't give students the support they need" to learn from computer-based material on their own, Kim says. Unlike students in traditional schools, those who learn online must pace themselves through their studies. And to succeed, they need skills of "self-regulation and self-assessment," he says. "A lot of this is not supported in the online school."

— *Marcia Clemmitt*

[1]Gene V. Glass and Kevin G. Welner, "Online K-12 Schooling in the U.S.: Uncertain Private Ventures in Need of Public Regulation," National Education Policy Center, University of Colorado Boulder, October 2011, http://nepc.colo rado.edu/files/NEPC-VirtSchool-1-PB-Glass-Welner.pdf.

[2]"Keeping Pace with K-12 Online Learning: An Annual Review of Policy and Practice," Evergreen Education Group, 2011, p. 30, http://kpk12.com/ cms/wp-content/uploads/EEG_KeepingPace2011-lr.pdf.

[3]*Ibid*. See also Glass and Welner, *op. cit.*

[4]"Final Report: A Comprehensive Assessment of Florida Virtual School," Florida TaxWatch, www.inacol.org/research/docs/FLVS_Final_Final_Report% 2810-15-07%29.pdf.

[5]"Charter School Performance in Pennsylvania," CREDO, Stanford University, April 2011, http://credo.stanford.edu/reports/PA%20State%20Report_20110404_ FINAL.pdf.

[6]"Online Education/Department of Education Performance Audit," State Auditor, State of Colorado, November 2006, www.cde.state.co.us/onlinelearning/ download/2006%20Report%20of%20the%20State%20Auditor.pdf.

"If you asked me to bet" on whether "picking an elementary teacher at random or a million-dollar piece of software" would produce better learning outcomes for "30 young kids learning an essential" basic skill such as adding or recognizing how different combinations of letters sound, "I'd pick the software," says Brookings' Whitehurst.

But technology is often put into classrooms with little technical support and thus is seldom as effective as it might be, says Paul Resta, director of the Learning Technology Center at the University of Texas, Austin. "If a teacher has technical problems [with operating a software program] more than once" and can't get a quick remedy from an information-tech specialist, which many schools don't

have, "guess what's going to become of that software" after that? "I call it the dark-screen phenomenon."

Some research on computer-based learning initiatives shows small or no learning gains.

In a 2009 study for the Texas state government, analysts at a nonprofit research group found that a pilot project that "immersed" some high-need middle schools in technology by providing a wireless computer for every teacher and student increased participants' ability to use technology and modestly improved math scores, especially among higher-achieving students. But the technology didn't improve students' ability to direct their own learning, apparently worsened their school-attendance rates and had no apparent effect on reading-test scores.[9]

Selective Schools Offer Fewest Online Courses

Eighty-two percent of community college presidents say their institutions offer online courses, slightly more than their counterparts at research universities and noticeably more than presidents at liberal arts colleges. Similarly, 86 percent of presidents at the least selective schools say they have online classes, more than those at more selective institutions. Education experts say online offerings vary depending on the educational mission of each school.

Percentages of Colleges Offering Online Classes

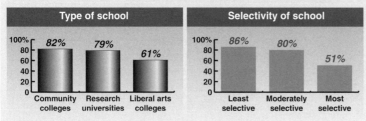

Source: Paul Taylor, et al., "The Digital Revolution and Higher Education," Pew Internet & American Life Project, August 2011, p. 6, www.pewinternet.org/~/media//Files/Reports/2011/PIP-Online-Learning.pdf

In the technology-intensive Kyrene School District in Chandler, Ariz., classrooms have numerous laptop computers with Internet access and interactive software that provide a wide variety of instructional opportunities: drills in every subject, individual-study programs and multimedia projects that help students create blogs and social-networking profiles for books they read in class. But according to one key benchmark — standardized test scores — the technology hasn't helped learning. Since 2005, the district's math and reading scores have remained stagnant, even as scores statewide have risen.[10]

The results baffle local school leaders. "My gut is telling me we've had growth. But we have to have some measure that is valid, and we don't have that," said Kyrene school Superintendent David K. Schauer.[11]

In a review of high school math programs that blend customized tutoring software with in-class lessons, both developed by researchers from Pittsburgh's Carnegie-Mellon University, the U.S. Department of Education found that the programs had "no discernible effect" on students' math-test scores.[12] The widely used and highly regarded "Cognitive Tutor" software, developed by Pittsburgh-based Carnegie Learning Inc., a startup created by cognitive and computer scientists, also came up short in

other federal analyses. Carnegie Learning was recently bought by Apollo Group Inc., the owners of the online, for-profit University of Phoenix.[13]

Can computers replace classroom teachers?

In search of budget savings, some public officials are touting online learning and so-called "blended" classes that use both computer-based and in-person instruction as potential means of saving money on teacher salaries. However, some technology experts say getting rid of teachers is a mistake. Instead, they say, school districts should be helping students navigate the digital world by searching out the best learning technology and hiring more teachers who are well trained in using it.

Still, financial strains and demands for better performance by schools mean that schools must — and ultimately will — replace some teaching slots with digital technologies, says Christopher Dede, a Harvard University professor of learning technologies. A "perfect storm" of trends is driving toward that outcome, he says.

Because of "permanent" financial problems in K-12 education, Dede wrote, "student-teacher ratios are climbing to levels unworkable for even the best conventional instruction. We cannot solve this problem by the personal heroism of individual teachers," on whom schools have largely relied up to now to succeed in difficult conditions. Instead, Dede added, administrators "must find technology-based strategies effective for classroom teaching and learning with large numbers of pupils."[14]

But, he adds, so far few technologies have been up to the task. While many computer-based learning programs require well-trained, intensely committed teachers to be effective, "large-scale educational improvement requires more," Dede wrote. He urged education researchers to double their efforts to create learning technologies that will work even in the worst of circumstances, including in schools with scant resources and many ill-prepared teachers, since those are conditions many students face.[15]

Experience outside of education proves this is achievable, Dede wrote. "All other professions are successfully transforming to affordable models that use technology to empower typical professionals to be effective," so there's no reason technology can't be developed to help average teachers spur strong student learning, too, he wrote.[16]

"We may be at a transition point" at which "we can offload some teachers' responsibilities" onto software, to free teachers to do other tasks, such as working with students on special projects, says Brookings' Whitehurst. At least a few college-level institutions, notably the private, nonprofit Salt Lake City-based Western Governors University, seem to have mastered the knack of delivering low-cost computer-based education that works, so there seems no reason that good technology-based approaches can't be developed for K-12 as well, he says.

Demands to improve student learning — perhaps using technology — fall heaviest on the lowest-performing schools, most of which enroll many disadvantaged students. Yet, in these schools it's particularly unlikely that technology could replace staff, says Stanford's Blikstein. "This is the critical part of the story. These kids need so much help to be brought up to speed. I don't think this kind of technology could replace a teacher."

At the college level, where computer-based courses have taken a stronger hold, nearly 64 percent of public-university faculty who have taught both online and traditional courses said in a 2009 survey that it took "somewhat more" or "a lot more" effort to teach online than in person. Nearly 85 percent said it takes more effort to develop online courses than regular ones.[17]

Making good use of digital technology requires substantial change in how teachers view their roles. "It comes back to authority and control," says Christine Greenhow, an assistant professor in the School of Education and Information Studies at the University of Maryland, College Park. "If you see your job as pouring knowledge into the minds of students who are empty vessels," that doesn't mesh with the technology revolution, she says. Today's students have cell phones, laptops and other devices on which they can research anything and everything on their own, she says.

Eventually, computer-teaching systems will diagnose students' learning problems on the spot, based on data collected from the students' interaction with the software, then design appropriate interventions. Those interventions might include calling for a live teacher, many of whom, in the future, may act more like "coaches" who address particular problems that learning software has identified, predicts Paul Kim, chief technology officer at Stanford's School of Education.

Tomorrow's teachers will have to both tailor instruction more individually and deal with deeper, more

Defining Online Learning

Traditional academic courses typically use no online technology and deliver content through face-to-face interactions between instructors and students. In contrast, online courses deliver at least 80 percent of content through the Internet. Other courses may use the Internet to complement traditional in-person meetings.

How Different Types of Courses Use Online Technology

Proportion of content delivered online	Course type	Description
0%	Traditional	No online technology used. Content is delivered orally or in writing.
1%-29%	Web facilitated	Uses Web-based technology to facilitate face-to-face interactions. Often uses coursemanagement system or Web pages to post syllabi and assignments.
30%-79%	Blended/ hybrid	Substantial portion of content delivered online. Typically uses online discussions and has a reduced number of in-person meetings.
80+%	Online	Most content is deliveredonline; course typically lacks face-to-face meetings.

Source: I. Elaine Allen and Jeff Seaman, "Class Differences: Online Education in the United States, 2010," Sloan Consortium, November 2010, p. 5, sloan consortium.org/publications/survey/pdf/class_differences.pdf

conceptual learning, many analysts say. For example, "one challenge, especially at upper grade levels, is to come up with questions for which Wikipedia won't supply good answers," says Stanford education Professor Daniel Schwartz.

Within a few decades, teachers may be sharply divided into an elite class of professionals who are savvy at both technology and teaching and a second, less-prestigious group who act more or less as babysitters, managing students in classrooms, wrote Whitehurst. A teacher will be "either . . . an expert on the design and delivery of instruction through technology or . . . the equivalent of a hall monitor or a tutor for struggling students, with commensurate salaries."[18]

Are computer games effective for learning?

From computer games' earliest development, in the 1950s and '60s, it was clear that they motivated players to commit time and energy to conquering their challenges to a degree that school lessons seldom do. This discovery, together with computers' ability to hold massive amounts of text, pictures and sound, encouraged development of games especially tailored for learning. However, not every game that has academic content and motivates students to play it actually provides a learning experience, some scholars say.

In many current games, players, alone or in groups, enter virtual worlds — such as Yellowstone National Park, in the game "WolfQuest" — or real-world sites that they visit while accessing added digital information about the place via technology such as smartphones. The idea is to explore the real or virtual place and solve problems there, explains a new report on games and learning by the National Research Council (NRC), a federal agency staffed by scholarly researchers.[19] In the well-regarded game "River City," developed by Harvard's Dede, for example, players explore a highly detailed simulation of a 19th-century American city to uncover and solve a public-health crisis.[20]

The NRC said games that challenge students to solve complicated problems in rule-based virtual worlds have the potential to kick-start the kind of inquiry- and project-based scientific learning that many education theorists have sought for decades. Such games can help students "visualize, explore and formulate scientific explanations for scientific phenomena" that they wouldn't otherwise be able to observe and manipulate, the NRC said. The games also tend to "spark high levels of engagement, encourage repetition and practice and motivate learners with challenges and rapid feedback," it said.[21]

Still, many researchers say they're less interested in figuring out how to increase the supply of educational computer games than in discovering the principles that fuel enthusiasm and hard work by students.

"I don't think we should make school into a game," says Barry Fishman, an associate professor of learning technologies at the University of Michigan. "My objective is to find out why people work so hard at games" and then figure out how the same principles might be applied to many kinds of learning situations.

Hoping to find out why his 6-year-old son enjoyed computer games so much, Gee says he "failed many times" at the first game he tried, one he picked randomly from a store shelf: "The New Adventures of the Time Machine." He says he "had to engage in a virtual research project via the Internet to learn some things I needed to know" to play. Gee grew amazed that "lots of young people pay lots of money" to get this difficult experience and "realized that this was just the problem our schools face: How do you get someone to learn something long, hard and complex and yet enjoy it?"[22]

Research is revealing underlying principles of effective learning games, says Eric Klopfer, an associate professor of education at the Massachusetts Institute of Technology (MIT). Such games allow for many different solutions to the problems and questions they pose; encourage both collaboration with other players and independent action on the part of players; set up novel problems for players to solve and provide feedback to help players advance, he says. A compelling narrative and characters to identify with also are important, he says.

But many games don't operate on those principles, and some don't teach much, or anything, of value, critics say.

"In trivial games, you solve a problem and then get a reward," but the learning and the other aspects of the game aren't connected, so that the game only provides some traditional drill-type instruction rather than deep learning, says Klopfer. In the popular "MathBlaster" game, for example, players earn opportunities to participate in an outer-space adventure video game by giving the right answers to math questions, but the questions aren't conceptually connected to the game's story.

Adding elements of play or contest to all learning activities, including rote memorization, is what some education theorists call for when they suggest "gamifying everything." But that's a shallow use of game principles and an approach that may even be inferior to more traditional educational methods, Klopfer suggests.

In fact, not all researchers find that games are useful at motivating and engaging students. In a 2007 study based on student surveys and interviews, Nicola Whitton, a research fellow in educational-games technology at Manchester Metropolitan University in England, found that "a large proportion" of students "do not find games motivational at all" and that "there is no evidence of a relationship between an individual's motivation to play games recreationally and his or her motivation to use games for learning."[23]

Serious attempts to develop highly effective learning games are in their infancy, experts say.

One barrier is that "gamers and educators are very different cultures, and you need to get them together" to have a real shot at figuring out how the principles of the two disciplines may intersect, says Stanford's Schwartz. The two sides often resist such cross-disciplinary discussions, he says.

Furthermore, the effectiveness of any education technology, including games, "depends on a combination of the technology and the context in which it's delivered," which includes school and classroom conditions, teacher skills and more, says MIT's Klopfer. Generally, for a game to succeed as a learning tool, a teacher or a community of people must be available to support and help players navigate it, he says.

Currently, teachers often don't use games to optimize learning and in many cases aren't equipped to do so, the NRC said. In the "River City" game, for example, players are supposed to explore the town, then formulate and test original hypotheses about what's causing disease there. But "some teachers have asked students to use the curriculum to simply confirm correct answers that the teachers provided in advance," essentially canceling out the opportunity for intellectual initiative, the NRC said. Behind teachers' misuse of the game lie lack of time, pressure to prepare for high-stakes standardized tests and

a lack of the "deep-content knowledge and effective teaching strategies" suitable for inquiry-based learning, the group said.[24]

BACKGROUND

A Digital World

The Information Age is only decades old. But many scholars argue that, eventually, digital technology will change everything, including concepts of learning, as surely as the greatest upheavals in history have done.[25]

"We can liken this age to the age of the invention of the printing press, and I don't think that's an exaggeration," says Kean University's Lerman. Especially in these early days, however, "there's more than one way things can change," he says.

Technology can be employed to "do old things in new ways," Lerman says. For example, he says, teachers can learn to give more effective lectures, and students can learn from master teachers they'll never meet if outstanding lectures are archived on YouTube. However, digital technology also can encourage "doing new things" to transform education into the student-driven, lifelong enterprise that many scholars see as the wave of the future, Lerman says.

Experts say that many characteristics of the Information Age will transform schools and learning, and each raises important questions about the future of education.

For example, "in the Age of Information, everything can be customized, and the last frontier is education," says Stanford's Blikstein. One need only pick up an American pre-calculus, biology or history textbook to see that the number of possible subjects of study is huge and beyond the ability of any one student or class to cover, even within a single discipline. Rather than trying to cram in as many as possible, as schools tend to do today, future schools with extensive access to online and other computer-learning technologies can allow students to pursue subjects of special interest. "Apart from the very basic things" — such as reading and basic math —"you should learn things that relate to your life and community," with one student studying trigonometry and another studying statistics, for example, Blikstein says.

Furthermore, with digital devices ubiquitous, "we're emerging into the era of student as content creator," says Lerman. "That has profound implications for almost

Getty Images/McClatchy Tribune/Jonathan Alcorn

Mike Kerr, principal of the KIPP Empower Academy in Los Angeles, said kindergarteners participated in an experiment last year with "blended learning," which uses both computers and classroom teachers. Results from the trial year were so promising that school administrators decided to continue using computers in kindergarten. The charter school serves minority and low-income students in impoverished south Los Angeles.

everything we do in schools." How, he asks, does one assess learning when students create their own projects? What, Lerman continues, is the role of a teacher, if not as the sole "expert dispenser of validated knowledge?"

As much of the world's information moves online, learning facts becomes less important than knowing how to find and use them. "Should we require students to regurgitate facts they've assimilated from classes, or should we allow students to access on a test any information they want" and use it to analyze a problem and propose a solution? asks Lerman. "In business, we'd call that collaboration. In school, we call it cheating."

Tutor, Tool, Tutee

Electronic computers were invented in the early 1940s and used as early as 1943 for a wartime educational purpose — as flight simulators whose mock aircraft "controls" responded to pilots' actions the same way controls on real planes did. In the 1960s computers entered K-12 classrooms after software was developed to lead students step-by-step through a process such as long division.

Soon the number of computers in schools began rising. In 1963, just 1 percent of high schools used computers for instruction. By 1975, 55 percent had computers, though only 23 percent used them primarily for learning. The rest used them for administrative purposes.[26]

Robert P. Taylor, a professor at Columbia University Teachers College in New York City, identified three ways computers can aid learning.[27]

First, step-by-step instructional software can "tutor" students in some subjects. In 1963, computer giant IBM partnered with Stanford's Institute for Mathematical Studies in the Social Sciences to develop programmed-learning software for elementary schools, jointly created by computer scientists and learning experts. In 1966, IBM introduced its Model 1500 computer, especially designed to run instructional programming. The computer had unusual-for-the-time features such as audio capability and a "light pen" that allowed users to write on the computer screen.

Second, Taylor wrote, a computer can serve as a tool, such as a calculator or word processor. In fact, he said, outside of schools, "tool-mode computing is popularly seen as synonymous with computer use, period."[28] (Nevertheless, schools often have ignored the potential usefulness of digital tools such as database and spreadsheet software for homework and vocational training, instead expecting students to learn such programs on their own, says Stanford's Kamil.)

Finally, Taylor wrote, a student can learn to program a computer to do new tasks, effectively acting as the machine's "tutor."

"Because you can't teach what you don't understand, the human tutor" — the programmer —"will learn what he or she is trying to teach the computer," wrote Taylor. Furthermore, "learners gain new insights into their own thinking through learning to program."[29]

This argument — that students should learn the inner workings of computers and learn to "teach," or program them — proved persuasive. In the 1970s and '80s, many schools installed computer labs and required every high school student to take a programming course,

C H R O N O L O G Y

1960s *More schools have computers, but most are used for record-keeping, other administrative purposes.*

1963 Vocational Education Act provides funds for school technology. . . . Two Dartmouth College scholars create the simple BASIC programming language, mainly for student use. . . . Scientists at IBM and Stanford University develop programmed-learning materials for grade-school math and reading.

1966 IBM introduces computer adapted to run instructional programs.

1967 MIT scientist Seymour Papert invents LOGO drawing language to expand programming and logic training in grade schools.

1970s-1980s *More schools adopt tutoring software and require programming classes; firms begin selling educational software.*

1974 "Oregon Trail" computer game, designed to teach about pioneer life, is introduced.

1975 Twenty-three percent of schools use computers in the classroom.

1984 Apple's Macintosh computer is introduced and quickly gains popularity, especially in elementary schools.

1987 Students in National Geographic's KidsNet program collect local data on acid rain and water pollution and email their findings to schools and scientists around the country.

1990s *Schools use CD-ROMs, videodiscs and the Web to provide multimedia materials.*

1991 Students in 72 countries participate in KidsNet.

1994 President Bill Clinton's Education secretary, Richard Riley, convenes first White House conference on expanding computer-based education.

1996 Telecommunications Act of 1996 requires telecom companies to discount their services for schools.

1997 Florida Virtual School, the first state online school, is founded.

2000s *Enrollment in computer-science and programming classes drops, but school social-media use expands.*

2000 Maine Gov. Angus King, an Independent, announces that the state will provide laptops to all middle-school students and for teacher training in computer-based education.

2005 MIT architecture Professor Nicholas Negroponte forms One Laptop Per Child program to develop low-cost computers for distribution to children in developing countries and other low-income areas.

2007 MIT developers introduce online Scratch community as an after-school hobby destination, where children and teens can create games and multimedia using the Scratch programming language. . . . First One Laptop Per Child computers go to children in Uruguay, Peru and Birmingham, Ala. . . . College computer-science enrollment drops to half its 2000 level.

2009 College Board drops one of its two Advanced Placement tests in computer science.

2010 With online-course enrollments reportedly growing 30 percent per year, Wyoming appoints its first state director of distance learning. . . . San Francisco Flex Schools open as California's first public schools to offer a blend of traditional and online courses. . . . Connecticut authorizes online courses to fulfill high school graduation requirements.

2011 New Florida law allows charter schools and individual school districts to offer online instruction and permits elementary-school students to study full time at Florida Virtual School. . . . Idaho becomes first state to require students to complete two or more online courses as a graduation requirement. . . . Computer Science Education Act introduced in the House and Senate to bring more programming and computer-problem-solving classes to K-12 schools. . . . New York City announces new investments in school technology while laying off teachers and canceling school construction projects. . . . Young Scratch hobbyists have posted more than 2 million media projects online.

Big Hurdles Confront Learning-Technology Developers

"You can't just have big companies, or you'll have no revolution."

Good digital tools can improve learning, but the system for developing them is riddled with pitfalls, technology analysts say.

For one thing, creating effective educational technology takes time, but software and hardware can become obsolete nearly overnight, says Michael L. Kamil, a professor emeritus at the Stanford University School of Education. Technology's short shelf life has doomed numerous projects, he says.

"We developed a game for Nintendo" that became useless when a new version of the popular device hit the market, Kamil says. Glitches in new technology often can be fixed, but that usually entails delays and more financing, which education researchers may not have, he says.

In some cases, fast-moving technology has doomed educational materials irrecoverably. In the mid-1990s, for example, many CD-ROMs were developed based on solid educational principles. But as content migrated to the Internet, CD-ROMs "were quickly left behind, and you couldn't fix them" for use as online media, Kamil says.

The size and clout of a developer also play a big role in a technology's success or failure. Digital technology developed by small companies and academic researchers may be suitable and effective in the classroom, but it can have a hard time competing with products offered by large companies.

Giants like Dell and Apple have successfully placed digital technologies in schools because they are adept at doing business in the fast-moving technology world and generally don't delay product rollout to test its educational effectiveness, says Barry Fishman, an associate professor of learning technologies at the University of Michigan.

"I don't fault Dell or Apple. Their job is to sell," he says. But "some things widely sold to schools are adapted from the [corporate] board room," and aren't necessarily very helpful to schools, he says.

A case in point is the expensive digital whiteboard that displays, records and stores information and graphics and has replaced traditional whiteboards in many schools, Fishman says. "Only about 5 percent of teachers are doing anything interesting with them," making their high cost largely a waste, he says.

Evaluation standards pose another challenge. The U.S. Department of Education analyzes learning technologies and posts on its "What Works" website conclusions about whether and how well they work. But the standards for evaluation, which are borrowed from medical research, don't give technologies a fair shake, many researchers say.

Steven M. Ross, director of Johns Hopkins University's Center for Research and Reform in Education, says the

the aim being to teach thinking skills and prepare young people for computer-science careers.

Special programming languages were developed for beginners. Many high school courses used BASIC, invented in 1964, which featured short programs and simple-to-understand error messages. In the early days, the classes seemed successful. Student programmers have "taught" computers to "tutor younger students in arithmetic operations, to drill students on French verb endings, to play Monopoly, to calculate loan interest, . . . draw maps" and "to generate animated pictures," Taylor wrote in 1980.[30]

LOGO, a language created in 1967 to extend the supposed benefits of programming to elementary-school students, allowed students to move a cursor — called a "Turtle" — around a screen to draw simple pictures.

A child gradually learns the different programming commands — expressed in words and numbers typed on a keyboard — that move the Turtle around the screen to draw a picture, wrote LOGO inventor Seymour Papert, an MIT mathematician. The challenge of drawing on the screen by typing out a series of programming commands "is engaging enough to carry children through" the lengthy process of ferreting out how

"clinical-trial" evaluation model, used to gauge whether a particular technology is effective in the classroom, is problematic. The model demands that a learning methodology produce better results than traditional instructional methods before it can be deemed a success. But that standard is unreasonable for computer-based learning tools, Ross says.

"If you use technology in a tutorial program and the kids do just as well" as they do with a live tutor or teacher, he says, "then the technology is freeing up a teacher" to undertake other teaching tasks that only a human can perform. That, he says, means the technology is a useful addition to a schools' repertoire of learning strategies.

Money is yet another challenge for educational-technology creators. The research and development needed to produce a good piece of educational software can cost millions of dollars, notes Grover J. Whitehurst, director of the Brown Center on Education Policy at the Brookings Institution, a centrist think tank in Washington. "Where do you get the venture capital" to support it? he asks. Would-be investors are hesitant because they know schools may not buy "if they have to spend $500 a student," Whitehurst says. The federal government could bolster technology development by "providing a guaranteed market," such as the worldwide network of schools that serve children of Defense Department personnel, for some products, he suggests.

Then there is a real, although largely unintended, bias toward big software developers. The Department of Education generally throws out the findings of small research studies on learning technologies on the grounds that they don't provide enough evidence to warrant a conclusion, says Daniel Schwartz, a Stanford University professor of education. But the only developers who can pay for "the big clinical trials" that the department considers gold-standard evidence are the "big, established, heavily capitalized companies," he says.

"The big question is, how do you make it possible to disseminate and test" educational technology so that small players with innovative ideas can gather sufficient data on their products, Schwartz says. "You can't just have big companies, or you'll have no revolution, just bookkeeping."

Schwartz envisions a "continual-improvement" system in which the government establishes an infrastructure to help academic researchers test their technologies-in-development in a few schools. Because digital products such as learning software can be continuously tinkered with, "I can put something out and keep collecting data over time about how it works" and mine user feedback for problems and suggested changes, Schwartz says. "Teachers could post commentaries on how things work" and how to use them, he says.

Perhaps the biggest barrier to developing innovative technology is the current student-assessment system, which relies on standardized tests that mainly gauge rote-memorization skills, many researchers say. "What gets tested is what gets taught," says James Lerman, director of the Progressive Science Initiative, a program at Kean University in Union, N.J., that helps experienced teachers become certified to teach math and science. With testing focused on old-fashioned rote learning and ignoring technology use altogether, Lerman and others say, the chances that innovative digital-learning tools will be developed and widely used are greatly diminished.

— *Marcia Clemmitt*

to write LOGO programs to create any design that they envision, said Papert.[31]

Ultimately, the process "can change the way they learn everything," by encouraging habits such as exploring new situations to figure out the rules by which they operate and accepting mistakes as inevitable consequences of exploration that are correctable with patience and logic, Papert said.[32]

Research has failed, however, to produce evidence that problem-solving skills used in programming classes transfer to other types of learning or even to later programming work, wrote Roy D. Pea, director of Stanford's Center for Innovations in Learning. Children who studied programming engaged in "very little preplanning" when they worked on new programs, he said. Rather than using logic to "debug" nonworking programs — as programming classes teach — they usually just erased them and started over from scratch, Pea reported. "Transfer of problem-solving strategies between dissimilar problems" proved "notoriously difficult . . . even for adults."[33]

By the 1990s, enthusiasm for teaching programming to students all but died out for a "whole host of reasons," says Yasmin B. Kafai, a professor of learning and technology at

Technology Opens New Doors to Learning

Scholars say "transformative ideas" could bolster student engagement.

The digital revolution, with its staggering number of inexpensive new tools and capabilities, eventually will change the way students learn, many education scholars say.

Handheld GPS-equipped cell phones can enhance science or history field trips and more, says Barry Fishman, an associate professor of learning technologies at the University of Michigan. Teachers can set up applications — or "apps" — that allow students' phones to point out interesting information or pose puzzles to be solved at certain locations. For example, University of Michigan undergraduates have been introduced to the school's complex library system via such interactive walk-throughs. "That's a possibly transformative idea" that could "lead to more student engagement," Fishman says.

Websites' multimedia features can help students travel virtually around the globe by posting live and archived videos, photographs, sound recordings, text, chat logs and more, and inviting visitors to interact with the material and each other, says Aaron Doering, an associate professor of curriculum and instruction at the University of Minnesota. Through his "adventure learning" website, Go North! (www.polarhusky.com), students can follow along as he and a team of environmental researchers explore oil drilling and global warming in the Canadian Arctic, in real time and in archives. "What brings people back is that there is a narrative" of the journey "that individuals can connect to. We feed the students all the media and interviews we do."

The Web allows everybody, including kids, to publish their work and find an audience, so students can share their own scientific adventures, says Doering. In a new project, he's encouraging classes to document local environmental conditions and share them in what could become a student-generated knowledge map of large geographical regions. Students in New Orleans, for example, document with photos and videos what's happening with frogs in the Mississippi River near their homes and share their observations with students 1,000 miles north in Minnesota who are studying their local stretch of the Mississippi, Doering says.

Digital devices drastically lower the cost of taking scientific measurements, and computers make once-formidable data analysis easy, says Paulo Blikstein, an assistant professor of education at Stanford University and director of its Transformative Learning Technologies Lab. Today, a $50 science-lab setup can include data loggers — digital devices that can record physical measurements such as temperature, humidity, light intensity or voltage and upload them to a computer, where the data can be put into visual form, graphed and analyzed mathematically. The low price and ability to analyze data without having advanced math skills put deep science concepts within reach of high-school-age and even younger students, Blikstein says.

By showing who's connected to whom, social media can give students a "sense of being connected to a larger network and to the world" and encourage them to link their learning with real-world action, says Christine Greenhow, an assistant professor in the Schools of Education and Information Studies at the University of Maryland, College Park. When studying a topic such as global warming, for example, Web-connected students find ways of connecting with stakeholders, policymakers and other interested citizens. Such work can increase students' engagement with their academic studies and also increase their civic engagement, she says.

Computer software that collects detailed information about exactly how a student behaves when taking a test or working math problems can help pinpoint the kind of help the student needs, says Daniel Schwartz, a Stanford education professor. It's always been one of the toughest nuts for schools to crack, Schwartz says.

"A kid's taking a test and fails. Now what? What do you do? There are a million possible reasons why he may be getting things wrong," each calling for a different remedial strategy, Schwartz says. "Does he have a misconception" about the subject? "Does he not persevere" in problem-solving? "If you can find out exactly what the student's process is" — when he hesitated, moved through a question too fast, changed an answer and so on — the information provides the clues to help him improve. Digital sensing, data collection and data analysis to reveal subtle behavior patterns are exactly what computers do well — and humans can't do at all, Schwartz says.

— Marcia Clemmitt

the University of Pennsylvania's Graduate School of Education.

For one thing, most schools "had not integrated programming into the rest of the curriculum," leaving it without obvious applications to other activities, Kafai says. Then, beginning around 1990, multimedia CD-ROMS provided a more immediately attractive use for computers, with games to play and videos to view.

Many teachers weren't up to the task of teaching programming adequately, says Oregon's Moursund. When training teachers to teach LOGO, Moursund says he found that "many had no insight into problem solving" and thus couldn't teach students the deeper thinking skills that programming could impart.

Proponents of getting students to program didn't give up, however. In the 1990s and 2000s, new languages for beginners emerged. Perhaps the most prominent is Scratch, a free online Web community designed to teach programming concepts by letting users create and post online videos, music, graphics and computer games. Scratch's developers, which include the National Science Foundation and MIT, aimed to make the language a favorite hobby rather than a school subject.[34]

"Kids only spend 18 percent of their waking hours in school, so there's lots of time outside that can be leveraged," says Kafai, a Scratch developer and researcher. In the past, students had no access to programming resources except through schools, "but now the situation has flipped. Every child has a smartphone" that can be used to program. As of October, the website had 921,785 registered members, 270,318 of whom had created more than 2.1 million projects.[35]

After enrollment surged in the 1980s and '90s, the percentage of high schools offering elective introductory courses in computer science dropped from 78 percent to 65 percent between 2005 and 2009. During the same period the percentage offering Advanced Placement (AP) courses also declined, from 40 to 27 percent.[36] The College Board, which had offered two levels of computer-science

exams, ended its more advanced AP exam after the May 2009 tests.[37]

College computer-science enrollment also fell, from a record per-department average of 100 newly enrolled students in 2000 to 50 by 2007.[38]

Enrollments have remained "in a trough" in recent years, says Joan Peckham, a professor of computer science at the University of Rhode Island, in Kingston. Part of the problem is image. "Research finds that students have a very poor image of computing" as "boring" and "full of these nerdy people facing a screen all day," she says. There's a lot to lose should interest remain low, Peckham says. "We have a technical and an interdisciplinary world" in which virtually every profession depends on sophisticated computer applications.

Connected Computers

Perhaps the heaviest blow to programming came from the Internet. As schools gained online access, networked computers' potential to serve as tools of hitherto unimagined power for accessing information and communicating quickly outpaced other computer uses. Internet-connected learning provides a tantalizing glimpse of the world of

---

Growth in Online Courses Predicted

The presidents of four-year public colleges expect nearly half of their undergraduate students to be taking an online course in 10 years, up from only 14 percent now. Two-thirds of presidents at two-year colleges and 54 percent at for-profit colleges predict that more than half their students will be taking online courses in 10 years.

Percent of College Presidents Saying Undergraduate Students Are Taking or Will Be Taking an Online Class

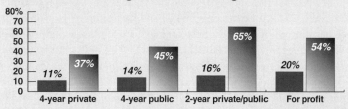

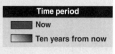

Source: Paul Taylor, et al., "The Digital Revolution and Higher Education," Pew Internet & American Life Project, August 2011, p. 10 www.pewinternet.org/~/media//Files/Reports/2011/PIP-Online-Learning.pdf

personalized study that many scholars say the Information Age will ultimately bring.

The Internet allows students and teachers to try out different ways of learning, something that was hard to do when every learning methodology was available only as a pricey textbook or software purchase, says Stanford's Schwartz. For example, the Kahn Academy offers a large number of short lectures posted on YouTube on such subjects as solving quadratic equations and learning the parts of a cell. MIT graduate Salman Kahn's videos are "a good example of stuff that's easy to use" and that multiplies learning options cheaply, Schwartz says.

Original documents, maps, archived film footage and interviews with people involved in historical events began appearing online in the past 15 years, providing opportunities for more in-depth, self-directed learning, says Resta of the University of Texas. For example, with primary sources online, "you can have kids actually practice historical thinking" by using original sources to construct their own versions of how and why some historical events happened, he says.

As the Internet has provided learning opportunities, it has increased pressure on schools to provide Internet-connected devices.

"An infrastructure for learning should support learning in and out of the classroom," and thus an effective, modern education system should find a way to supply students and educators with Internet-access devices for around-the-clock use, said the federal government's most recent national education-technology plan, issued in 2010.[39] Some school districts and one state, Maine, as well as countries such as Uruguay and Peru, have implemented one-digital-device-per-student programs, typically dispensing laptop computers to students in some grades.

Maine debuted the biggest U.S. program in 2002, placing a laptop into the hands of every middle-school student. The program didn't mandate specific uses but provided training for teachers to help them integrate the computers into the curriculum. "If you just drop the computers on the kids' desks, it won't work," said Gov. Angus King, an Independent. "It's a fundamentally different way of teaching. It's not standing up in front of the classroom lecturing."[40]

Research on one-child, one-device programs supports King's contention, scholars say.

Few studies show that laptop programs raise standardized-test scores significantly. However, "greater quantity and improved quality of writing; more teacher and peer feedback on student work; wider opportunities to access information from a wide variety of sources; and deeper exploration of topics through in-depth research" are demonstrated outcomes of programs that are integrated into the curriculum, according to Mark Warschauer, a professor of education and informatics at the University of California, Irvine.[41]

Some studies do show test-score improvement. For example, between 2000 and 2005 the percentage of Maine's eighth-graders who met the state's proficiency standard for writing rose from 29.1 percent to 41.4 percent, and classes that used laptops for drafting and editing outperformed those that didn't.[42]

Other one-child, one-device programs operate on the principle that ownership of computers is enough by itself to improve learning. "When every child has a connected laptop, limits are erased as they can learn to work with others around the world, to access high-quality, modern materials, to engage their passions and develop their expertise," according to the Cambridge, Mass.-based One Laptop Per Child Foundation, which distributes laptops free to children in developing countries.[43]

But research fails to back up that contention, some scholars contend.

In Birmingham, Ala., researchers found that two years into a program that gave students computers but didn't formally integrate them into curricula, only 20 percent used the laptops "a lot" in class, while 60 percent used them "a little" and 20 percent said they never used them.[44]

In Uruguay, which received laptops from the foundation in 2007, "only about 25 percent of the kids are bringing them to class," says Kim, at Stanford's School of Education. He cites the limited use as evidence that before students can be motivated to use free laptops in class, educators must actively engage them in projects that encourage them to do their own Internet research.

In the past few years, as cell phones have aqcuired as much memory as computers, some schools have been flirting with the notion of bring-your-own-technology programs. Such initiatives generally allow students to use their own devices — usually smartphones — in class while allowing students who don't own Internet technology to borrow devices that belong to the school. In a

Should schools use as much digital technology as they can afford?

YES

Curt Bonk
Professor, Instructional Systems Technology Department, Indiana University

Written for *CQ Researcher*, December 2011

Despite persistent budget dilemmas and constraints, this is no time to ban, control, limit or passively ignore possible uses of technology in teaching and learning. Instead, it should be an age filled with heavy doses of learning-technology experimentation and creative initiatives. With proper planning, discussion and evaluation, there is much that technology dollars can afford, even for the smallest or most impoverished school or district.

A couple of years ago, I authored the book *The World Is Open: How Web Technology Is Revolutionizing Education.* In it, I detailed many free and openly available resources for learning. With careful budgeting, laptops, tablet computers such as the iPad or other hardware can be acquired and embedded with a wide range of free tools and applications for learning basic mathematics, spelling, grammar and scientific concepts.

Is that not enough? Then have students explore learning portals containing the works of Shakespeare, Darwin, Einstein, Jane Austen, Jane Goodall, the Dalai Lama and other major historical figures. For those concerned about resource quality, such contents are often created by NASA, the U.S. government, the Smithsonian, National Geographic, the United Nations, MIT, Berkeley, and many other reputable sources.

Digital technologies offer much hope to learners and educators today. Students can be inspired by mentors and role models from all corners of the Earth. Feedback on one's ideas can be received in the early morning hours or late at night. E-books can be loaded into mobile devices that can represent events through simulations, animations, videos and hyperlinked text.

Web technology situates students in authentic contexts analyzing real world data and interacting with their global peers about the results of their investigations. If this requires a cheap $20 membership in some service that fosters such expert advice or interaction, that is $20 well spent. Ditto the tens of thousands of dollars many school districts are spending today on iPads and other learning technologies.

Effective learning requires an environment designed for multiple paths to success. In the 21st century, digital technologies — social networking, e-books, shared online video, mobile applications, virtual worlds, collaborative tools, etc. — enhance the learning opportunities for untold millions of learners. The maximization of technologies in the learning space, in effect, provides a distinct advantage for learning. Now is the time to move ahead, not retrench or retrace.

NO

Paul Thomas
Associate Professor of Education, Furman University

Written for *CQ Researcher*, December 2011

Technology represents the essence of American consumerism by feeding our popular clamor for acquiring the current hot thing. Yet the ever-increasing significance of technology in our daily lives and its contribution to powerful advances as well as a widening equity gap place education in a complex paradox.

Author Kurt Vonnegut quipped, "Novels that leave out technology misrepresent life as badly as Victorians misrepresented life by leaving out sex." As with novels, so with schools, I believe, but we must take one step beyond "whether schools should address technology" to "how."

Two experiences from my 18 years teaching high school English inform my belief that schools should not incorporate as much digital technology as finances allow. I began teaching in the 1980s during the rise of MTV and witnessed my field make a claim that text was dead, and thus English teaching had to shift to the brave new video world — failing to anticipate instant messaging, email, texting, blogging and the text-rich social-media boom.

The intersection of technology's unknowable future, its inflated costs, and its inevitable obsolescence must give us pause as we spend public funds. Let me suggest simply looking into the closets and storage facilities at schools across the United States, where cables, monitors and other artifacts costing millions of dollars lie useless, replaced by the next-best thing we then had to acquire. In fact, just think of one thing, the Laserdisc video player (soon to be joined by interactive "smart" whiteboards in those closets).

Chalkboard, marker board, interactive board — this sequence has not insured better teaching or learning, but has guaranteed greater costs for schools and profits for manufacturers.

In *Walden,* Henry David Thoreau offered two warnings that should guide how we approach technology: "We are in great haste to construct a magnetic telegraph from Maine to Texas; but Maine and Texas, it may be, have nothing important to communicate," and, "We do not ride on the railroad; it rides upon us."

The foundational principles of public education for democracy and human agency must not fall prey to preparing children for the future by perpetually acquiring new technology because we can never know that future. Thus, we must not squander public funds on ever-changing technology but instead focus on the human interaction that is teaching and learning as well as the critical literacy and numeracy every child needs. We can anticipate only one fact of our futures — change.

survey of school administrators in the fall of 2010, nearly two-thirds said they were unlikely to allow students to use their own mobile devices in class. However, just under a quarter said they were likely to do so.[45]

Using bring-your-own-technology programs to save schools money and encourage student engagement raises fears, however. Besides worrying about unfairness to students who don't own high-tech phones, administrators see murky areas of legal liability if students access inappropriate Web pages, cheat or disrupt classes using their own equipment.[46]

"You can see the tension as some schools say, 'We have to ban personal cell phones in class,' " says Kean University's Lerman. But many young phone owners are discovering phones' productive capabilities, doing "unbelievable things," he says. "Some have written novels." Schools should encourage such innovations, not ban them, he says.

CURRENT SITUATION

Digital Expansion

Tight school budgets and concerns about preparing students for technology-heavy workplaces are driving efforts to expand computer-based learning. But controversy continues over whether fast-changing digital technology is the best use of scarce funds.

The New York City Department of Education last spring announced it would boost technology spending by $542 million for the 2011-12 school year to pay for new wiring and other infrastructure upgrades, despite imposing major cuts elsewhere. Over the next three years, the city will cut $1.3 billion from planned school construction and eliminate 6,100 teachers — more than 6 percent of the city's workforce — 4,600 through layoffs. The new tech spending comes on top of an initiative, completed in 2009, that equipped every classroom with plug-in and wireless Internet connections.[47]

"If we want our kids to be prepared for life after school in the 21st century, we need to consider technology a basic element of public education," said New York's Deputy Chancellor of Education John White.[48]

But history shows it's all too easy to make flawed technology purchases, some analysts say. "We have seen circumstances where schools have overbought for bandwidth

that they didn't touch," said Douglas A. Levin, executive director of the State Educational Technology Directors Association, a national membership group.[49]

A growing number of states are expanding access to so-called "virtual" or online public schools, where students take all or some of their courses via the Internet using technologies such as tutoring software and webcasts and are assisted by teachers using email or chat software.[50]

And some states now require students to undertake online study. In November, Idaho became the first to require students to take at least two online courses to graduate. The state Board of Education approved the plan to begin in the 2012-2013 school year, though the legislature will review the decision in 2012.[51] After prolonged debate, the board substantially scaled back an original proposal by Idaho state School Superintendent Tom Luna to require eight online credits.[52]

"There is no magic bullet . . . that is going to meet every single need for every single student," but making online study mandatory "is saying that there is," said Sue Darden, a teacher in the Meridian School District, near Boise. "Those of us in education can tell you that that's just not going to work."[53]

But advocates of online courses say they aren't much different from courses in brick-and-mortar schools. "There is still a live teacher. It may be at a distance, but that teacher is still instructing and interacting with the student," said Susan Patrick, president of the International Association for K-12 Online Learning, a membership group for public and private entities involved in online education.[54]

Idaho joins three other states that already had approved online-study requirements. Alabama and Michigan require high-school students to complete some online learning as a prerequisite for graduation but not necessarily an entire course. In June, Republican Gov. Rick Scott of Florida signed legislation requiring students to complete one online course for graduation.[55]

As concerns grow that lack of computer-science education — mainly training in programming and the theory and methods of stating problems in a form computers can solve — may threaten economic competitiveness, bills were filed in both the House and the Senate this fall to beef up computer-science instruction in K-12 schools.

Sponsored by Sen. Robert Casey, D-Pa., and Rep. Jared Polis, D-Colo., the Computer Science Education Act would fund grants to states to improve computer-science education; pay for teacher training; appoint a national commission to coordinate state efforts; and develop a plan for independent evaluation of programs.[56]

Scaling Up

The number of digital devices in K-12 classrooms continues to climb. While computers proliferate, however, adequate support and appropriate curricula to ensure they're used productively are still lacking, and many classroom computers are still being used mainly by teachers, not students.

Use of digital technologies to improve learning "is working in pockets, but scaling up is very difficult," says the University of Maryland's Greenhow.

Many education schools include technology training in their curricula, but aspiring teachers still "often end up doing their student teaching in an environment where they don't have this stuff," says Steven M. Ross, director of the Johns Hopkins University's Center for Research and Reform in Education.

Several recent surveys put the percentage of K-12 classrooms with computers at more than 90 percent, says Karin S. Forssell, program director for Stanford's master's degree program in Learning, Design and Technology. However, says Forssell, while "a lot of stats we have say that there is a computer in nearly every classroom, they're not necessarily in the hands of the students." In an extensive survey Forssell conducted of California teachers at all grade levels who hold national board certifications, about 75 percent said their classrooms include work with computers. While one can't generalize too much from the limited survey, it suggests that the 90-plus percent estimates of classrooms with computers don't reflect student access, she says.

Schools sensibly start by giving the teacher a computer to serve as a grade book, communicate using websites and email and replace audio-visual aids such as overhead projectors, Forssell says. Helping teachers become comfortable with technology is an important first step toward helping them figure out how to use it productively for student learning, she says.

While many schools now have digital equipment, far fewer have overhauled curricula and teaching practices to facilitate productive use of it.

"We've got schools wired, and we have significant purchases of instructional software," says Brookings'

President Barack Obama visits Parkville Middle School and Center of Technology in Baltimore on Feb. 14, 2011, to promote his 2012 budget proposal, which calls for increasing investment in math, science and engineering education. Some public officials are promoting online learning and so-called "blended" classes that use both computer-based and in-person instruction.

Whitehurst. However, "it's at the back of the room," rather than in daily use by all students, and few schools have integrated computers into well-thought-out curriculum goals, he says.

OUTLOOK

Transformers?

A transformative shift in education to the personalized, student-focused, lifetime-learning model that the Information Age demands will happen, many scholars say. It's just a question of when.

"Years of budget cuts, with more to come," plus the need to train more math, science and engineering students, will help drive the shift to more computer-based learning, says Harvard's Dede. "If the United States doesn't fix its education, in 10 years we'll be like a developing country."

Change might come quickly, Dede suggests. "A century ago the United States reinvented its education system in a very short time, moving from one-room schoolhouses to the industrial model" of large classes of same-age students all studying the same thing at the same time, he says. That model was "based on best practices in industry at that time." Pushback from supporters of the current system may slow progress, though. "The one-room schoolhouse was not set up to defend itself," while today many people have a vested interest in keeping major change at bay, Dede says.

There are more barriers to a quick transformation than teacher resistance, however, say many experts.

"We haven't really solved" the problem of how to successfully teach "the reading and writing tool" to all students yet, "and now we've got a new tool" — the computer — for which successful learning methods must be developed, says the University of Oregon's Moursund. "We should do it systematically and put a lot of government effort into it, or we'll have a boondoggle."

Despite hopes by some that online courses can accommodate ever more students, brick-and-mortar "schools won't go away quickly," says the University of Michigan's Fishman. For one thing, "people need someone to watch the kids while they work," so switching to all-online education would require overhauling other major social structures as well.

Overhauling the curriculum to include digital technology will be contentious, says Stanford's Blikstein. "There's lots of legacy stuff in the curriculum, and there is lots of fighting if someone suggests" eliminating traditional subjects, he says. "But if we don't get rid of some of them, you can't move forward. Some will think that the basics are always the basics, but a lot of the math we teach," for example, "was originally included in textbooks because other subjects, such as physics, depended on it, he says. Today, when computers handle much of the physics computation, many traditional high school math topics could be dropped, he says.

Up to now, most research demonstrating the success of computer-based learning tools has carried the caveat that the technologies produced significant gains only in classrooms with well-trained teachers and a carefully designed curriculum.

But Dede says that to move forward as the nation's technological and economic future requires, learning-technology designers must develop computer-based educational products that work under challenging circumstances.

" 'Boutique' interventions that work only under ideal conditions for success (skilled teachers, motivated and well-prepared students, special resources) are useful for theoretical development," Dede wrote. "However, large-scale educational improvement requires . . . interventions that work at scale under a variety of adverse circumstances."[57]

NOTES

1. Quoted in "Student Teacher Ratios Could Go as High as 50/1, Says Top Ed Advisor," Ohio Budget Watch blog, March 25, 2011, http://ohiobudget watch.com/2011/03/student-teacher-ratios-could-go-as-high-as-501-says-top-ed-advisor.

2. Jessie L. Bonner, "Board Approves Idaho Online Class Requirement," The Associated Press/msnbc .com, Nov. 3, 2011, http://today. msnbc.msn.com/ id/45156135/ns/us_news-life/ #.Tr0_PFZho44.

3. Sharon Otterman, "In City Schools, Tech Spending to Rise Despite Cuts," *The New York Times*, March 29, 2011, www.nytimes.com/2011/ 03/30/nyregion/ 30schools.html?pagewanted=all.

4. Quoted in Julianne Hing, "News Corp. Will Save Our Schools, and Other Scarily Seductive Reforms," *Colorlines: New for Action*, Oct. 20, 2011, http://color lines.com/archives/2011/10/ the_seductive_appeal_ of_market-based_edu cation_reform.html.

5. For background, see Marcia Clemmitt, "Internet Accuracy," *CQ Researcher*, Aug. 1, 2008, pp. 625-648.

6. For background, see Sarah Glazer, "Video Games," *CQ Researcher*, Nov. 10, 2006, pp. 937-960.

7. James Paul Gee, "Good Video Games and Good Learning," www.academiccolab.org/resources/ documents/Good_Learning.pdf.

8. *Ibid.* For background see "Virtual Iraq," Virtually Better website, www.virtuallybetter.com/ IraqOverview .html.

9. "Evaluation of the Texas Technology Immersion Pilot: Final Outcomes of a Four-year Study," Texas Center for Educational Research, January 2009, www.tcer.org/research/etxtip/ documents/y4_etxtip_ final.pdf.

10. Matt Richtel, "In Classroom of Future, Stagnant Scores," *The New York Times*, Sept. 3, 2011, www .nytimes.com/2011/09/04/technology/technology-in-schools-faces-questions-on-value.html?page wanted=all.

11. Quoted in *ibid.*

12. "Carnegie Learning Curriculum and Cognitive Tutor Software," High School Math, Department of

Education What Works Clearinghouse, August 2010, http://ies.ed.gov/ncee/wwc/pdf/intervention_reports/wwc_cogtutor_083110.pdf.

13. For background, see Trip Gabriel and Matt Richtel, "Inflating the Software Report Card," *The New York Times*, Oct. 8, 2011, www.ny times.com/2011/10/09/technology/a-classroom-software-boom-but-mixed-results-despite-the-hype.html?page wanted=all; Angela Gonzales, "Apollo Group Buys Carnegie Learning for $75 Million," *Phoenix Business Journal*, Sept. 13, 2011, www.bizjournals.com/phoenix/news/2011/09/13/apollo-group-buys-carnegie-learning.html; and Barbara Mantel, "Career Colleges," *CQ Researcher*, Jan. 7, 2011, pp. 1-24.

14. Christopher Dede, "Reconceptualizing Technology Integration to Meet the Challenges of Educational Transformation," *Journal of Curriculum and Instruction 5*, May 2011, pp. 4-16, www.joci.ecu.edu/index.php/JoCI/article/down load/121/127.

15. *Ibid.*

16. *Ibid.*

17. "Online Learning as a Strategic Asset: Volume 1: A Resource for Campus Leaders," Association of Public and Land-Grant Universities/Sloan Foundation, p. 19, http://sloancon sortium.org/publications/survey/APLU_Reports.

18. Grover J. Whitehurst, "Curriculum Then and Now," American Education in 2030: An assessment by Hoover Institution's Koret Task Force on K-12 Education, 2010, http://media. hoover.org/sites/default/files/documents/Cur riculumThenAndNow_Whitehurst.pdf.

19. Margaret A. Honey and Margaret Hilton, eds., "Learning Science Through Computer Games and Simulations," Committee on Science Learning, National Research Council, 2011, www.nap.edu/catalog.php?record_id=13078.

20. For background, see Joseph Rosenbloom, "International Education: That's Not a Video Game, It's an Educational Tool," *The New York Times*, Feb. 17, 2004, www.nytimes.com/2004/ 02/17/news/17 iht-rvideo.html?pagewanted=all.

21. Honey and Hilton, *op. cit.*, p. 20.

22. Gee, *op. cit.*

23. Nicola Whitton, "Motivation and Computer Game Based Learning," *Proceedings of the Australian Society for Computers in Learning in Tertiary Education*, 2007 conference, Singapore, www.ascilite.org.au/conferences/singapore07/procs/whitton.pdf.

24. Honey and Hilton, *op. cit.*, p. 63.

25. For background, see Robert Taylor, *The Computer in the School: Tutor, Tool, Tutee* (1980); Andrew Molnar, "Computers in Education: A Brief History," *The Journal*, June 1, 1997, and Kathy Koch, "The Digital Divide," *CQ Researcher*, Jan. 28, 2000, pp. 41-64.

26. Molnar, *op. cit.*

27. Robert P. Taylor II, "The Computer in School: Tutor, Tool, Tutee," CITE, summer 2003, www.cite journal.org/vol3/iss2/seminal/article1.cfm.

28. *Ibid.*

29. *Ibid.*

30. *Ibid.*

31. Seymour Papert, *Mindstorms: Children, Computers, and Powerful Ideas* (1980), p. 11.

32. *Ibid.*, p. 8.

33. Roy D. Pea, "Logo Programming and Problem Solving," paper presented to American Educational Research Association Montreal symposium, April 1983, www.stanford.edu/~roypea/ RoyPDF%20folder/A39_Pea_87d_CCT_TR_MS.pdf.

34. For background, see John Maloney, *et al.*, "Scratch: A Sneak Preview," http://scratchfr. free.fr/beauvais262710/1Scratch_Articles_Videos/ ScratchSneakPreview.pdf.

35. Scratch website, http://scratch.mit.edu.

36. Michael Alison Chandler, "Fewer High School Students Taking Computer Science Classes," *The Washington Post*, Dec. 21, 2009, p. B1, www. washingtonpost.com/wp-dyn/content/article/ 2009/12/20/AR2009122002477.html.

37. Tim Finin, "College Board Eliminates AP Computer Science AB Test," University of Maryland, Baltimore County, ebiquity blog, April 4, 2008, http://ebiquity .umbc.edu/blogger/2008/ 04/04/college-board-eliminates-computer-science-ap-test, and "AP Computer Science AB Course Home Page," College

Board website, http://apcentral.collegeboard.com/apc/public/ courses/teachers_corner/8153.html.

38. Azad Ali and Charles Shubra, "Efforts to Reverse the Trend of Enrollment Decline in Computer Science Programs," *Issues in Informing Science and Information Technology*, 2010, http://iisit.org/Vol7/IISITv7 p209-224Ali825. pdf.

39. "Transforming American Education: Learning Powered by Technology," U.S. Department of Education Office of Educational Technology, 2010, p. 54, www.ed.gov/sites/default/files/NETP- 2010-final-report.pdf.

40. Quoted in Diane Curtis, "A Computer for Every Lap: The Maine Learning Technology Initiative," *Edutopia*, www.edutopia.org/stw-maine-project-based-learning-technology-ini tiative.

41. Mark Warschauer, "Netbooks and Open Source Software in One-to-One Programs," paper presented at annual meeting of American Educational Research Association in Denver, May 2010, http://olpcnews .com/images/warschauer-netbooks-aera2010-olpc news.pdf.

42. "Digital Education Revolution NSW: One-to-One Computers in Schools," *2010 Literature Review*, Education & Training, Government of New South Wales, Australia, www.project red.org/uploads/lit_ review10_TrMbcLRPRT.pdf.

43. "Education," *About the Project*, One Laptop Per Child website, http://one.laptop.org/about/education.

44. Marie Leech, "Most Birmingham Classrooms Not Using XOs Much, But Supporters Urge Not Giving Up on Them," *The Birmingham News*, July 25, 2010, http://blog.al.com/spotnews/2010/07/study_ shows_majority_of_birmin.html.

45. Quoted in Ian Quillen, "Districts Tackle Questions Surrounding BYOT Policy," *Education Week*, Oct. 17, 2011, www.edweek.org/dd/ articles/2011/10/ 19/01byot.h05.html.

46. *Ibid.*

47. Otterman, *op. cit.*

48. Quoted in *ibid.*

49. Quoted in *ibid.*

50. Lyndsey Layton and Emma Brown, "Virtual schools expand territory," *The Washington Post*, Nov. 27, 2011, p. A1, www.washingtonpost.com/ local/ education/virtual-schools-are-multiplying-but-some-question-their-educational-value/2011/ 11/22/gIQA-NUzkzN_story.html.

51. Bonner, *op. cit.*

52. John Funk, "Community Voices Concern Over Online Education Requirements," *Idaho Press-Tribune*, Aug. 19, 2011, www.idahopress. com/news/community-voices-concern-over-online-education-requirements/ article_9e77e6 2a-ca27-11e0-a5b5-001cc4c03286.html.

53. Quoted in *ibid.*

54. Quoted in Bonner, *op. cit.*

55. "Gov. Scott Signs Bill to Expand Digital Learning," Florida: Recent Developments, Liberating learning: technology, Politics and American Education, June 2, 2011, http://sites.google.com/site/ liberatelearn/ home/florida.

56. David B., "Computer Science Education Act Introduced in Both Houses," Public Policy blog, United States Association for Computational Mechanics website, Sept. 23, 2011, http://tech policy .acm.org/blog/?p=1796.

57. Dede, *op. cit.*, pp. 4-16.

BIBLIOGRAPHY
Selected Sources
Books

Bonk, Curtis, *The World Is Open: How Web Technology Is Revolutionizing Education*, **Jossey-Bass, 2011.**
An education professor at Indiana University, Bloomington, describes the rapidly expanding Web resources used for education around the world.

Collins, Allan, and Richard Halverson, *Rethinking Education in the Age of Technology: The Digital Revolution and Schooling in America*, **Teachers College Press, 2009.**
Collins, a professor emeritus of education at Northwestern University, and Halverson, an education professor at the University of Wisconsin, Madison, argue

that digital technologies are poised to transform education and learning into a much more personalized and customized enterprise that will extend far beyond the walls of traditional schools.

Cuban, Larry, *Oversold and Underused: Computers in the Classroom*, Harvard University Press, 2003.
A Stanford University education professor argues that, historically, computers have been placed in schools with little attention to providing technical or teacher support or consideration of how the technology can serve curriculum goals.

Articles

Barshay, Jill, "More Schools Trying Out Computers — on Kindergarteners," The Hechinger Report/McClatchy Washington Bureau, Oct. 11, 2011, www.mcclatchydc.com/2011/ 10/11/126891/more-schools-trying-out-computers.html.
Computer-based learning for the youngest students is spreading but remains controversial.

Fang, Lee, "How Online Learning Companies Bought America's Schools," *The Nation*, Dec. 5, 2011, www.the nation.com/article/164651/how-online-learning-companies-bought-americas-schools.
A writer for a liberal magazine's investigative unit finds that big education-technology companies, including media mogul Rupert Murdoch's News Corp., are using political influence to speed up school districts' shift to online education, mainly to boost their own bottom lines.

Mitchell, Nancy, and Burt Hubbard, "Investigation Finds Lax Oversight of Online Education," *Education Week*, Oct. 6, 2011, www.edweek.org/ew/articles/2011/10/06/ 07enc_virtualoversight.h31.html.
State auditors and independent investigators found that Colorado officials have been lax in overseeing online schooling and made policy decisions that unfairly favored online-school companies with political connections.

Richtel, Matt, "Children Fail to Recognize Online Ads, Study Says," "Bits" blog, *The New York Times*, April 21, 2011, http://bits.blogs.nytimes.com/2011/04/21/children-fail-to-recognize-online-ads-study-says.
Developing a critical stance toward media is necessary to figure out who is behind information encountered online, but a study demonstrates that children have trouble with the skill.

Richtel, Matt, "In Classroom of Future, Stagnant Scores," *The New York Times*, Sept. 3, 2011, www.nytimes.com/ 2011/09/04/technology/technology-in-schools-faces-ques tions-on-value.html?pagewanted=all.
An Arizona school district struggles to understand why its large supply of digital classroom technology hasn't raised standardized test scores, when scores elsewhere in the state have increased.

Trucano, Michael, "Worst Practice in ICT Use in Education," "EduTech" blog, World Bank, April 30, 2010, http://blogs. worldbank.org/edutech/worst-practice.
Many programs to beef up technology use in education simply "dump hardware in schools," then "hope for magic to happen," says a World Bank education-technology specialist.

Reports and Studies

"Transforming American Education: Learning Powered by Technology, National Education Technology Plan 2010," National Education Technology Plan Technical Working Group, U.S. Department of Education, November 2010, www. ed.gov/sites/default/files/NETP-2010-final-report.pdf.
An expert panel calls for aggressive transformation of the education system to fully integrate digital technology, such as by adding technology skills to student assessments.

Gee, James Paul, "Good Video Games and Good Learning," undated, www.academiccolab.org/resources/documents/ Good_Learning.pdf.
An Arizona State University professor of literacy studies says interactivity, opportunities for players to shape games to their own liking and incentives to try again after failures are qualities that make some games effective learning tools.

Honey, Margaret A., and Margaret Hilton, eds., "Learning Science Through Computer Games and Simulations," Committee on Science Learning, National Research Council, 2011, www.nap.edu/catalog.php?record_id=13078.
An expert panel finds that computer-simulation games can spark more inquiry-based, project-oriented science learning but that research on how games work is in very early stages.

For More Information

Classroom 2.0, www.classroom20.com. Social network for people interested in using social media and the Web for education.

Computer Science Teachers Association, 2 Penn Plaza, Suite 701, New York, N.Y. 10121-0701; 800-401-1799; http://csta.acm.org. Membership organization that promotes the teaching of computer science.

Edutopia, The George Lucas Educational Foundation, P.O. Box 3494, San Rafael, CA 94912-3494; www.edutopia.org. Website founded by "Star Wars" director George Lucas that disseminates information about and advocates for education techniques and technologies to refit schools for the digital age.

Information Age Education Preservice and Inservice K-12 Teachers and Other Educators, http://pages.uoregon.edu/moursund/dave/index.htm. Website of University of Oregon education Professor Emeritus David Moursund, founder of the International Council for Computers in Education (now the International Society for Technology in Education); offers information on computer computational thinking, a problem-solving approach that seeks to maximize the combined powers of computers and human brains.

ISTE (International Society for Technology in Education), 1710 Rhode Island Ave., N.W., Suite 900, Washington, DC 20036; 866-654-4777; www.iste.org. Membership and advocacy group for educators involved in advancing technology use in K-12 schools.

Liberating Learning, http://sites.google.com/site/liberatelearn. Website for the book *Liberating Learning: Technology, Politics and American Education* by scholars Terry M. Moe and John E. Chubb of the Hoover Institution, a conservative, Palo Alto, Calif.-based think tank; the website tracks state developments in online learning.

Scratch, http://scratch.mit.edu. Online community developed by the Massachusetts Institute of Technology Media Lab; helps users learn the Scratch programming language to create and publish online interactive stories, animations, games, music and art.

Thomas B. Fordham Institute, 1016 16th St., N.W., 8th Floor, Washington, DC 20036; 202-223-5452; www.edexcellence.net. Conservative research and advocacy group that explores the expansion of digital learning.

10

Student Debt

Marcia Clemmitt

University of California students in Los Angeles protest the UC Board of Regents' decision in November 2009 to raise undergraduate tuition 32 percent. More increases in the past 18 months have pushed up tuition by another 17.6 percent. For the first time in history, student debt for higher education is higher than the nation's credit-card debt. Congress has passed some reforms aimed at making the loan system fairer for lower-income students, but critics say lawmakers need to do more.

From *CQ Researcher*,
Oct. 21, 2011

New York City lawyer Robert Applebaum graduated from law school in 1998 with more than an impressive diploma. He also was saddled with $80,000 in student loans. Over the next five years, as Applebaum delayed repayment while working as an assistant district attorney, interest drove the balance to $100,000.

Still making payments 11 years after graduation, Applebaum had a brainstorm. Why, he wondered, shouldn't the federal government forgive student loans as a way to stimulate the economy?

"With the stroke of the President's pen, millions of Americans would suddenly have hundreds, or in some cases thousands, of extra dollars . . . every month . . . to spend," reads a petition Applebaum placed online at the liberal activist site Moveon.org.[1]

Applebaum's proposal may be quixotic, but his story points to what many experts see as a growing crisis in higher education: As college and university enrollments mushroom and tuition soars, they say, college is fast becoming unaffordable to tens of thousands of current and prospective students.

Student debt surpassed credit-card debt in June 2010 for the first time in history, rising to about $830 billion — or nearly 6 percent of the nation's annual economic output. Meanwhile, new student loans surpassed $100 billion for the first time in the 2010-2011 academic year.[2] As loans have rocketed, so has tuition: It exploded 375 percent — nearly four times the inflation rate — between 1982 and 2005 and has been climbing 4 percent to 8 percent annually since.[3]

"Student loans should help people," says Lauren Asher, president of the Institute for College Access and Success, a research and

Students at For-Profit Schools Have Most Debt

More than half of bachelor-degree recipients at four-year for-profit institutions carried education debt of $30,500 or more during the 2007-2008 academic year, compared with 24 percent of those at private four-year institutions and 12 percent at public four-year schools. Only 4 percent of degree recipients at the for-profit schools were debt-free, compared with 28 percent at the private schools and 38 percent at the public institutions.

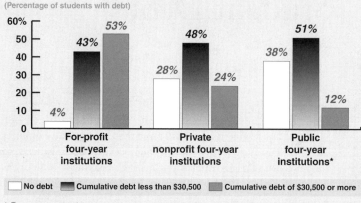

Education-Loan Debt for Bachelor's Degree Recipients, 2007-2008

(Percentage of students with debt)

□ No debt   ■ Cumulative debt less than $30,500   ■ Cumulative debt of $30,500 or more

* Percentages do not total 100 because of rounding.

Source: Sandy Baum and Patricia Steele, "Who Borrows Most?" College Board, 2010, advocacy.collegeboard.org/sites/default/files/Trends-Who-Borrows-Most- Brief.pdf

advocacy group in Oakland, Calif. That purpose is lost "when people face the prospect of debt they can never repay."

What's more, critics complain that many student borrowers face repayment requirements far more onerous than those for mortgage and car-loan borrowers. For example, it is exceedingly difficult, if not impossible, for students pleading hardship to delay repayment or have loans forgiven through bankruptcy — even though consumer borrowers can declare insolvency and wipe their debt slate clean.

And unlike consumer debtors who fall into arrears, college borrowers can have their Social Security and other federal benefits garnished — an especially frightening prospect for older students attending college to retrain for employment.

Some consumer advocates say recent legislative changes, such as easier payment options for lower-income students and loan forgiveness for those working in public-service jobs, should make borrowing less risky. However, college loans made by private lenders unaffiliated with federal loan programs lack such options. Thus, say critics, as tuitions continue rising, the sheer size of college debt, public and private, poses greater financial risk to students and their families.

Few argue that education borrowing is bad in itself. Indeed, boosting attendance and graduation have long been national goals. But college-loan experts debate whether students, on the whole, are borrowing too much.

Many students incur debt that will never pay dividends in higher wages or greater job satisfaction, argued Richard Vedder, an economics professor at Ohio University, in Athens, and director of the Center for College Affordability and Productivity, a think tank in Washington. About 45 percent of those who go to a four-year college don't complete a bachelor's degree in six years, so "their investment isn't particularly good" because they spend years earning less than college graduates, Vedder said.[4]

Ross Rubenstein, an associate professor of public administration at Syracuse University's Maxwell School, calls student loans "a human-capital investment" that, for most, will likely pay lifetime dividends of higher wages and better quality of life. Still, he says, "beyond the big-picture theoretical idea is the question of what's the appropriate level of debt."

Donald Heller, a professor of education at Pennsylvania State University, has a more optimistic view. He acknowledges "heightened concern" that high unemployment and lagging wages make it difficult for students to see a return on their education investment. "But," he says, "we have to remember that the vast majority of people getting bachelor's degrees are getting jobs" and have better employment odds than people without degrees.

"When people question whether degrees are worth their cost, I ask, what's the alternative?" Heller says. Furthermore, he says, earnings data "show that having some college is better than no college."

Government grants and other aid often can help low-income students reduce their borrowing. Families with annual earnings of about $75,000 typically are the first to seek loans because they aren't eligible for need-based aid. But it is not always the middle class that suffers most. In a bid to induce their best students to attend in-state schools, Georgia and Missouri, among others, handed out education grants based on good grades rather than student need.

And although the switch to merit-based state aid has slowed in the economic downturn, the trend has forced many low-income students — many of whom are the first in their families to attend college — to borrow more, divide their time between work and classes or quit school altogether when they run out of money.

Loans Make Up Half of Financial Aid

More than $129 billion in undergraduate financial aid was distributed in the 2007-2008 academic year, half in loans from the federal government and private sources. Grants, work-study payments and tax breaks that helped families pay for higher education made up the other half of the total.

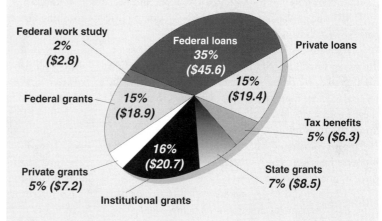

Sources of Financial Aid for U.S. Undergraduates
(in $ billions, 2007-2008)

Federal work study
2% ($2.8)

Federal loans
35% ($45.6)

Private loans
15% ($19.4)

Federal grants
15% ($18.9)

Tax benefits
5% ($6.3)

Private grants
5% ($7.2)

Institutional grants
16% ($20.7)

State grants
7% ($8.5)

Source: Donald E. Heller and Claire Callender, "Institutional Bursaries in England and the United States: A Comparative Analysis," Organization for Economic Cooperation and Development, September 2010, www.oecd.org/dataoecd/49/58/46130211.pdf

On balance, says Heller, lower-income students still "bear more of the brunt" of paying for school. And, he says, because "many of these students are reluctant to borrow," many of them "go part time and work while enrolled." But research shows that working beyond a minimal number of hours greatly increases the risk of dropping out.

Even when financially struggling students don't drop out, they often take far longer than four years to complete their degrees — adding to the cost of their education, experts note.

Sandy Baum, a professor emerita of economics at Skidmore College, in Saratoga Springs, N.Y., and a long-time college-funding analyst for the College Board, says that while declining four-year completion rates are a problem, "it's hard to know" whether they stem from rising tuition costs. But, she adds, "we know that we can't continue this trend of tuition increases that are

rapid and huge forever" because the steep increases make it impossible for families to plan and save for school.

While many economists say soaring tuition fuels college debt, some argue the opposite is true: that the growing availability of government-subsidized college loans has induced schools to hike tuition in a drive to increase revenue. That prospect "flows quite logically" from an understanding of how colleges operate, wrote Andrew Gillen, research director for the Center on College Affordability and Productivity.

"First," he wrote, "any additional resources obtained by a school will be spent" at least partly on services and amenities aimed at enhancing the school's reputation and competing for the best students. That might mean shelling out big money to attract famous professors or to build well-equipped gymnasiums for students' use, he wrote.

Then, Gillen argued, a vicious cycle begins. As improvements are added, tuition climbs, and the higher tuition qualifies students to obtain still larger subsidized loans to pay the growing bill. As the school rakes in more tuition dollars, it spends them the next year on more improvements. Ultimately, Gillen argued, this "arms race in spending . . . reduces access and affordability — the exact opposite of what [grant and loan programs] intend."[5]

But not all experts agree. The argument that college prices rise mainly in response to students' ability to pay is "way too simple-minded," says Robert B. Archibald, an economics professor at the College of William and Mary, in Williamsburg, Va. "I don't think the link between price and the availability of loans holds up at all."

Manufacturers have used technology to increase productivity, but industries like higher education rely on highly skilled workers — college professors — who can't be replaced by machines, Archibald says. No wonder, then, he says, that the cost of college has climbed at a far faster rate than for goods like clothing and cars.

"It's no coincidence that the price of services" such as higher education "has increased more rapidly than the price of goods," Archibald says.

As students and policymakers mull a future of rising debt, here are some of the questions being asked:

Are students incurring too much education debt?

Many analysts call current education-debt levels truly alarming, arguing that college loans saddle students with long-term burdens that can affect their choice of jobs and ability to shoulder other responsibilities such as mortgages. Others, however, contend that while total debt is high by historical standards, the average student's debt is reasonable in light of potential higher lifetime wages that education offers.

A growing number of students find their debt unmanageable, reported the finance website *Smart Money*. Nearly 10 percent of federal student-loan borrowers defaulted during the two years ending Sept. 30, 2010, "meaning they failed to make a payment on their loans for more than 270 days." That was a leap from a 7 percent default rate in 2008. Much of the increase came at for-profit colleges, where 15 percent of borrowers defaulted, up from 11.6 percent two years earlier.[6]

A substantial number of college graduates "end up taking jobs for which college education is not really a prerequisite," making any debt they incurred to get the education essentially a waste, argued Ohio University's

Vedder. "Twelve percent of the mail carriers in the United States today have college degrees."[7]

But others warn against dismissing the value of student loans.

"Lately, a lot of the public discussion is geared towards panic," some of which results from focusing on the wrong statistics about debt, says Baum of Skidmore College. Many recent news stories "have focused on the total amount of debt that's out there," but that number inevitably has risen steeply in recent years because of climbing enrollments, she says.

Furthermore, Baum says, while it makes sense to be concerned about the minority of students who rack up very high debts, "the typical bachelor's student is borrowing $25,000 or less" — about $5,000 less than the average car loan in 2009.[8]

Jennifer Delaney, an assistant professor of educational organization and leadership at the University of Illinois at Urbana-Champaign, argues that a shift has occurred in people's thinking about how college should be funded, with many now seeing students' future income as the most important funding source. "Our student-aid system is based on the idea that parents will help, but the volume of loans and the debt levels tell us that there's a greater and greater reliance on students and their future employment" to pay for school by borrowing against future income, she says.

That approach can make sense, although the size of the college "wage premium" is often overstated, especially by public officials, says Robert K. Toutkoushian, a University of Georgia professor of higher education.

"The returns of going to college are still high enough to justify" some debt, Toutkoushian says. But, he adds, an oft-cited statistic that puts the "wage premium" for a bachelor's degree at $1 million is too high. The $1 million figure compares bachelor's-degree holders with people who have a high-school diploma — leaving out those who have some college but no degree, he says. A more accurate number is about $500,000, still "worth the debt" most graduates incur, Toutkoushian says.

Two scholars at the Brookings Institution, a centrist think tank in Washington, compared the wage premium from a college degree to historical earnings on stocks and other investments. "On average, the benefits of a four-year college degree are equivalent to an investment that returns 15.2 percent per year" — more than double what stocks earned since 1950, and more than five times the returns on corporate bonds, gold, long-term government bonds and residential real estate, wrote Adam Looney and Michael Greenstone, of the Hamilton Project, a study group on economic development at Brookings.[9]

Still, while student loans may pay off in the long run, many analysts say the tandem trends of rising debt and rising tuitions are highly worrisome. "College sticker prices are too high, and debt will continue to rise," says Penn State's Heller.

"Borrowing really works for a lot of people, but there's a growing segment for whom it becomes problematic," especially those who don't obtain their degrees or certificates, adds Laura W. Perna, a professor at the University of Pennsylvania's Graduate School of Education, in Philadelphia.

Increasingly, student loans are the fallback source for college financing, as taxpayer dollars and parental contributions pay less of the bill, many say.

"The need-based aid available isn't keeping up with rising costs, and the country's anti-tax attitude" is limiting public subsidies at the same time that many government officials are demanding higher rates of college attendance and completion, says Edward St. John, a professor at the University of Michigan's School of Education, in Ann Arbor.

Furthermore, many families, by necessity or choice, are picking up a smaller portion of the tab. Says Baum, "When the grandparents of today's college students went to college, you just assumed that you worked hard and paid for it. In the interim, people started to assume that the government would pay for it."

Does rising college debt limit who attends and completes college?

Increasing the number of Americans who graduate from college or other post-secondary training programs has been deemed a national goal for decades, but many experts worry that rising college debt is undermining that aim.

History suggests that when people worry about their ability to pay for college, it deters them from applying, says Donald Hossler, a professor at Indiana University's School of Education, in Bloomington, and director of the research center at the National Student Clearinghouse, an organization founded by the nation's colleges and universities to collect national student data.

Sixteen-year-old Bianca Gutierrez and other Hispanic students from the New Design Charter School attend the Cash for College convention in Los Angeles on Dec. 8, 2010. The convention helps low-income students find funding for college. The College Board recently reported that only 19.2 percent of Latino college students ages 24-35 graduate, less than half the national average.

Hossler recalls that in the 1980s, when false rumors circulated that Congress was about to cut federal Pell Grants for low-income students, "some low-income people didn't even apply" for college.

Data from the 1970s through the 1990s show that financial concerns play a major role in college decisions, especially for students from low- and middle-income families earning less than about $70,000 a year, says Michael Lovenheim, an assistant professor of public finance at Cornell University in Ithaca, N.Y. Families' financial resources affect "where and whether" students attend college and "whether they complete" degrees, he says. What's more, evidence suggests that this effect "is growing over time," Lovenheim says.

Among the 2007-08 graduating class at four-year public colleges, about 62 percent of families carried loans, according to FinAid, a consumer-assistance website. The average cumulative debt per student, including so-called federal PLUS loans borrowed by parents to help foot their children's college costs, was $23,227.[10]

At a public four-year university today, students from low-income families typically face an annual net cost of $11,700 after need-based grants are factored in, according to the Advisory Committee on Student Financial Assistance, an independent panel jointly appointed by Congress and the secretary of Education. Students from

Debt Heaviest for Moderate-Income Students

Students and families with moderate incomes often incur the heaviest college debt. At a typical public university costing $80,000 for a four-year degree, a low-income student can expect to receive about $43,000 in aid, including need-based federal Pell grants, and to need an additional $37,000. But a student in a moderate-income family earning $50,000 to $60,000 per year can expect to receive only about $16,000 in aid, leaving a shortfall of about $64,000.

Typical Costs and Financing for a Four-year Public University

Low-income student	
Cost of four-year degree	$80,000
Grants and work-study available	$43,200
Amount remaining	$36,800
Moderate-income student	
Cost of four-year degree	$80,000
State and university need-based grants plus federal work-study grants	$16,200
Federal grants	$0
Amount remaining	$63,800

Source: "The Rising Price of Inequality," Advisory Committee on Student Financial Assistance, June 2010, chronicle.com/items/biz/pdf/acsfa_rpi.pdf

lower-middle-income families earning just above the federal Pell Grants cutoff incur annual net college costs of $18,450. As a result, families with moderate incomes, which don't qualify for need-based aid, typically borrow about 75 percent more than low-income families do, the panel calculated.[11]

The figures "are staggering and have a profound effect on the decision-making of qualified high-school graduates" as to whether and where to attend college, the panel said.[12]

Yet some analysts worry that an outsized focus on debt — not debt itself — will discourage some students from applying. News stories about student debt "often make it seem that borrowing for education ruins your life, as if it's the same as running up a big bill on a trip to the Caribbean," says Skidmore College's Baum.

Numerous studies have found that so-called debt aversion can push students to take on such excessive working hours that they drop out or avoid college altogether. The problem is especially acute in some minority communities.[13]

St. John at the University of Michigan says the picture is changing somewhat, so that debt aversion is "not quite the problem it used to be." By and large, African-American students are no longer as reluctant to borrow as in the past, he says. However, he adds, "Latinos still have more debt aversion" than others, with college-completion rates likely suffering for it.

A new report from the College Board finds that only 19.2 percent of Latino students ages 24-35 who begin college complete it, far below the national average of just over 40 percent.[14]

So far, however, researchers are still seeing a higher number of people going to college and finishing than in the past, says the University of Georgia's Toutkoushian.

Indeed, the number of bachelor's and associate's degrees and the proportion of the workforce that attains them both have risen continually, says Arthur M. Hauptman, an independent public-policy analyst in Arlington, Va., who has advised the World Bank, several federal agencies and more than two dozen national governments on higher-education finance. In 1970, about 10 percent of Americans over age 25 had attended four years of college, compared with about 30 percent today, he says.[15]

While debt may not deter many people from enrolling, it is subtly changing the way a college education is viewed, says Burton A. Weisbrod, an economics professor at Northwestern University in Evanston, Ill. "It was always true there were college majors that were not going to open doors to high incomes," he says, pointing as examples to sociology and art history. Yet, in the past, such studies were widely viewed as worthwhile because they were seen as vital to American culture and helped create "better voters," he says.

As education debt rises, however, students who are struggling financially will increasingly seek to major in subjects that lead to high-wage professions, Weisbrod argues. "That'll work against" the humanities, potentially putting them out of reach for many, he says. "We need to have a discussion about that."

Has the increasing availability of education loans driven up college costs?

In 1987, William J. Bennett, President Ronald Reagan's Education secretary, wrote that while making federal college grants and subsidized loans more available did "not cause college price inflation, . . . there is little doubt" that it helps "make it possible."[16] Today, as college costs and student debt rise, debate over that proposition grows louder.

Some economists argue that increasing access to college funding — especially loans, which are available to rich and poor students alike — creates a vicious cycle: As more money flows to students, colleges are induced to raise their prices, which in turn causes the government to increase its limits on subsidized loans, and so on.

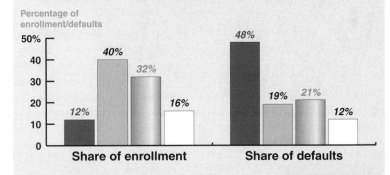

Default Rates Highest at For-Profit Colleges

For-profit colleges accounted for 12 percent of college enrollment but 48 percent of student-loan defaults in the 2008-2009 academic year. By contrast, students at two-year public colleges accounted for 40 percent of college enrollment but less than 20 percent of defaults.

College Enrollment and Three-year Default Rates*

Percentage of enrollment/defaults

* Percentage of student borrowers who began repaying loans in 2008 and had defaulted within three years. Enrollment was in 2008-2009.

Source: "For-Profit College Student Loan Default Rates Soar," Project on Student Debt, February 2011, project onstudentdebt.org/files/pub/TICAS_3YR_CDR_NR.pdf

Type of School
- For-profit
- Public two-year
- Public four-year
- Private nonprofit

"Without anybody intending this, the subsidized student-loan programs actually incentivize states to raise tuition," says Northwestern's Weisbrod. "Anything that makes it less expensive for a student to attend makes it easier for a school to raise the tuition."

When Bennett's piece was published, "I disagreed with it, but I changed my mind," says Hauptman, the policy consultant. "I don't see grants" pushing school-spending increases "because they aren't big enough," but "there is a correlation between loans and pricing." Just as the increased availability of mortgage loans helped drive up home prices in recent years, Hauptman argues, increased availability of subsidized loans can help boost college prices.

Early results of a study of for-profit schools suggest that institutions with students eligible for federal grants and subsidized loans have higher tuition than comparable schools where students aren't eligible, says Stephanie R. Cellini, an assistant professor of public policy and public administration at George Washington University in Washington. However, the research, which she is conducting with Claudia Goldin, a Harvard University economics professor, doesn't reveal whether the pricier institutions are "just better schools" using the funds to provide students with superior training or are simply "capturing more money for themselves," Cellini says.

While some economists see a connection between loan and grant availability and rising tuition, others debunk the idea of a link. All high-skill service industries — including not only higher education but also health care and legal services — have raised their prices in recent decades for reasons that have little or nothing to do with rising demand or availability of funds, they argue.

"When you purchase a personal service like a haircut, you are purchasing the time of the barber, and there are limited things he or she can do to shorten the experience that will not be perceived as a reduction in the quality of the haircut," wrote William and Mary's Archibald and fellow economics professor David H. Feldman. The same is true of college teaching and other professions with highly educated workforces, such as law, they argued.[17]

The University of Phoenix, an online, for-profit institution, maintains a satellite office in Raleigh, N.C., above. Nearly 10 percent of federal student-loan borrowers defaulted during the two years ending Sept. 30, 2010, up from 7 percent in 2008. Much of the increase came at for-profit colleges, where 15 percent of borrowers defaulted during the same two-year period.

In addition, says Archibald, colleges must constantly upgrade expensive technology to prepare students adequately for tomorrow's workplaces. "Take chemistry, for example," he says. "These students are going to go to [the pharmaceutical giant] Pfizer and try to get a job," but they won't get the work "if to save money the college said, 'We'll do chemistry using nothing but [old-fashioned] beakers and test tubes.' "

The unpredictability of technology trends also is driving up costs, Archibald says. At William and Mary, for example, "we spent a whole lot of money wiring every dorm room" to link to the Internet just before technological change meant "we had to put wireless hubs everywhere" instead. While that double spending could be perceived as wasteful, it's not clear how schools could avoid it, he says.

Still, Archibald says, while loans aren't driving up costs, "a financial-aid arms race" among some colleges might be.

"If you're a school that's not Ivy League but close, you offer big financial aid to nab a potential Yalie who may end up being a Rhodes Scholar" and boost your school's reputation, he says. To lure students from more prestigious schools, a college will raise its own stated "full sticker price," then offer prized students discounts that appear to be deals too good to pass up. These new,

inflated sticker prices are then published as the schools' base tuition rates, even though only a handful of people actually pay them, he says.

BACKGROUND

Private System

Unlike most other countries, the United States built a higher-education system that is supported more by private money — much of it in the form of tuition — than public dollars. But as more and more low-income students enroll, efforts to maintain that private support have made education loans increasingly prevalent in the college-finance equation.[18]

U.S. "colleges started out as private entities," says William and Mary's Archibald. Indeed, William and Mary, founded in 1693 and now part of Virginia's system of state colleges and universities, "was private until 1906," he says, and just before World War II half of U.S. students attended private colleges.

A century or more ago, when college attendance was confined mainly to the very well-off, reliance on private tuition rather than tax-supported loans and grants may have been the world's fairest system, Archibald suggests. England, by contrast, required taxpayers to subsidize university costs for a tiny elite — mostly students from upper-class families, he notes.

In the United States, tax-supported efforts to expand the college system — and therefore the number of graduates — began, albeit slowly, in the mid-19th century. In 1862, for example, the federal government granted states federal land to establish technical colleges, forerunners of many of today's state colleges and universities.

Public support for college attendance expanded sharply after U.S. involvement in World War II (1941-1945). The so-called G.I. Bill, which provided tuition subsidies to military veterans, was the largest public initiative to date.

Beginning in the late 1950s, other tax-funded higher education initiatives burgeoned.

In 1957, the Soviet Union launched *Sputnik*, the first manmade Earth-orbiting satellite, and the following year Congress passed and President Dwight D. Eisenhower signed into law the National Defense Education Act. It contained programs to improve math, science and language training and post-secondary education, plus the National Defense Student Loan Program for low-income students.

The program, precursor of today's low-interest Perkins loans through which post-secondary institutions disburse federal loans to needy students, was the first explicitly aimed at helping students from poor families attend college. It provided for direct loans from a designated tax-supported fund.

Lawmakers expanded college lending in 1965 with a new program under which private banks made loans that were guaranteed by the federal Treasury.

Robert Shireman, chief consultant for California Competes, a group in San Francisco that advocates for increased public support for higher education, says one reason for enlisting banks was to help keep student loans off the government's books. Under federal budget rules, a direct loan counted as "a total loss" to the Treasury "in the year it was made, even though most of it would be paid back with interest," Shireman wrote. By contrast, so-called guaranteed loans from private banks, which the government agreed to reimburse if students defaulted, did not count as immediate government costs.[19]

In 1965, Congress established the Guaranteed Student Loan Program, which subsidized low-income students by paying the interest on their loans from government funds while they were attending school or otherwise deferring repayment. Moderate-income students also could get loans, but without the interest subsidies. In 1978 students at all income levels became eligible for nonsubsidized loans, and in 1980 the government agreed to guarantee private lenders against borrower defaults in a new loan program — PLUS, Parent Loans for Undergraduates.

The programs came to represent an attempt to leverage both public and private funding to expand post-secondary education, says Baum of Skidmore College. The principle behind this split responsibility, in which the government pays upfront and students pay more down the road, is that college-educated adults "will make more money than others, so you can argue that they should pay for [their education] rather than taxpayers."

Several federal need-based college-grant programs also target lower-income students. They include the Educational Opportunity Grant, enacted in 1965, and the Basic Educational Opportunity Grant — forerunner of today's Pell Grants — in 1972.

But with college costs and enrollments rising steeply, loans have gained ground on grants as the main source of funding. And that, says St. John of the University of Michigan, gradually has turned a college education into an individual "debt burden for average Americans" rather than a shared public responsibility. That's emblematic of "how the conception of the public role in education has changed" over the six-plus decades since the federal government began subsidizing college attendance, he says.

Both the percentage of students borrowing and the amounts they borrow have swollen recently. At for-profit colleges, for example, 92 percent of students borrowed in the 2007-2008 academic year, up from 61.3 percent in 1995-1996.[20] In 1996, 23,000 students owed at least $40,000 in college loans, but by 2008, more than 200,000 did.[21]

The United States, Canada and South Korea are the only countries that commit 2 percent or more of annual gross domestic product to higher education. The United States tops the list, at 2.9 percent, of which 1.9 percent consists of private resources, including tuition payments and charitable donations, a higher private share than any other country.[22]

The bulk of enrollment, however, has shifted from private to public colleges and universities in recent decades, says Hauptman, the policy consultant. In 1950, half of college students attended private colleges, while only a fifth do today.

The growth of tuition and fees as a proportion of total revenues at public colleges and universities is "one of the most marked trends in post-secondary finance in recent decades in the U.S. as well as in many other countries," Hauptman wrote. Tuition payments now fund more than a third of the educational activities of public institutions in the United States, up from a tenth 30 years ago, he said. Proportions vary widely among states, from 13 percent in New Mexico to 77 percent in Vermont, Hauptman wrote.[23]

A state-university president is said to have quipped that "once we were a state university, then we were a state-supported university, now we're state-located," observes Philip G. Altbach, director of the Center for International Higher Education at Boston College.

Nevertheless, "I don't think the public side is quite as privatized as some say," says Hauptman. The University of Virginia, for example, claims that only about 8 percent of its funding comes from the state. But when funding for educational activities only — rather than research and a UVA-affiliated hospital — is counted, "a third to a half" consists of state dollars, he estimates.

Borrower, Beware?

Even as the students' loan burden grew, consumer protections for education loans shrank.

The strict repayment conditions facing today's student borrowers are a far cry from the gentler atmosphere previous generations remember, wrote *New York Times* business columnist Joe Nocera.

Nocera graduated in 1974 with about $8,000 in debt and a journalism degree, and in 2007 he recalled "constantly falling behind on my payments. The bank . . . would send a stern notice whenever I got too far behind, which would prompt me to cobble together a few payments by skipping some other bill." However, "it never raised my interest rate as punishment, nor did I ever have to pay any late fees. My chronic tardiness didn't even affect my credit rating. And had I defaulted, I would not have had my wages garnished, or been stuck with the debt if I had filed for bankruptcy. All of which can happen today."[24]

To keep private lenders' cash flowing and to reimburse the Treasury in cases when the government must pay a bank after a borrower defaults on a guaranteed loan, Congress has enacted stricter rules for education loans than for most other lending.

In 1976, Congress barred writing off education loans through bankruptcy for five years following graduation. Lawmakers extended that period to seven years in the 1990s, and in 2005 they made it nearly impossible to use bankruptcy to discharge any college loans, including bank loans not guaranteed by the federal government. Other lender protections include guaranteeing "that banks . . . get back not just the principal but the interest" should a student default. "It took all the risk out of lending," wrote Nocera.[25]

The tough rules are justified, said J. Douglas Cuthbertson, a McLean, Va., lawyer who represents the National Council of Higher Education Loan Programs, a trade group for financial institutions that make student loans. He told a House Judiciary subcommittee in 2009 that if hardship exemptions were easy to get, student borrowers could "enjoy the benefits of their education," then seek "bankruptcy without ever attempting to repay." That would convert "a student loan . . . into a scholarship" and cause banks to stop lending for education, Cuthbertson said.[26]

John A. Hupalo, managing director of Boston-based Ramirez Capital Managers and an adviser to banks and other groups on setting up student-loan programs, told the Judiciary panel last year that, in fact, college loans "are the most consumer friendly products in the marketplace." Features include the absence of prepayment penalties "for borrowers who wish to pay ahead of schedule, and . . . opportunities for borrowers to stop making payments for a period of time," he said.[27]

Other experts disagree. Deanne Loonin, a staff attorney at the Student Loan Borrower Assistance Project at the National Consumer Law Center in Boston, acknowledges that in the past 10 to 15 years, loan policies have "become much more liberal at the front end about who can get how much money" as loan limits and eligibility restrictions have been lifted. "But at the same time," she says, "we've steadily increased the government's collection power."

Loonin points out that the government can even seize money from a low-income student borrower's Social Security benefits and Earned Income Tax Credit, a federal program designed to help needy families. Garnishing that money "contradicts another policy goal" — reducing poverty, she says.

"There should also be more due process, to give people the opportunity to challenge" rulings about their qualification for hardship exemptions, Loonin says. And she wants "more relief for people affected by abusive practices such as fraud" by schools that, for example, make false claims about the value of their degrees.

Alan Collinge became a student-loan reform advocate after penalties and interest pushed $38,000 in college debt to $50,000 and then $95,000 following temporary payment deferments while he finished degree requirements in aerospace engineering and then was unemployed, he said in a 2010 book, *The Student Loan Scam.*

A bureaucracy that seemed hostile to borrowers compounded his difficulties, he wrote. The big loan-originating and collections company Sallie Mae mistakenly billed him multiple times for what should have been a one-time late-payment fee and apparently lost his request for an economic-hardship suspension, Collinge wrote.[28]

CHRONOLOGY

1940s-1970s *Federal-aid programs improve access to higher education, which previously has been funded mainly by private dollars.*

1944 First major federal college-aid program, the G.I. Bill, offers tuition payment to veterans.

1950 Fifty percent of students attend private colleges.

1958 National Defense Education Act creates the first federal college-loan program, for low-income students.

1965 Expanded federal loan program provides nonsubsidized loans to middle-income students and covers some interest payments for low-income student borrowers. New private-lender college loans are launched, with banks protected by the government from losses if students default.

1970 About 10 percent of Americans over age 25 have attended four years of college.

1972 Student Loan Marketing Association (Salle Mae) established as a government-sponsored enterprise to buy student loans from private lenders to free up banks to make more loans.

1976 Congress bars student loans from being written off through bankruptcy for five years after graduation.

1978 Congress makes students of any income eligible for federal loans.

1980s-1990s *Controversies grow over whether federal loan programs harm students while enriching lenders and driving up college costs. New for-profit colleges spring up.*

1980 Government protects private lenders against loss in new Parent Loans for Undergraduate Students program.

1986 Federal Loan Consolidation Program permits consolidation of college loans into one debt with lower monthly payments, longer repayment period.

1987 Reagan administration Secretary of Education William J. Bennett argues in *The New York Times* that federally subsidized loans help drive college-price inflation.

1993 New direct government-loan program to compete with federally guaranteed bank loans. . . . Income-contingent repayment option for direct loans introduced.

1996 Congress permits Sallie Mae to become a private company.

1998 Colleges with high default rates are barred from federal loan programs.

2000s *College debt and tuition soar.*

2005 Tough, new law bans virtually all discharge of college debt through bankruptcy proceedings.

2007 New York Attorney General Andrew Cuomo alleges private-lender kickbacks to universities and financial-aid officers; accused universities and banks reach financial settlement, agree to new conduct code. . . . Congress adds new income-based repayment option for direct loans. . . . More than 61 percent of students at four-year public colleges carry education debt (including borrowing by parents).

2010 Total college debt rises to $830 billion, surpasses total credit-card debt. . . . Volume of new federal college loans tops $100 billion for first time in 2010-2011 school year. . . . Congress replaces federally guaranteed private-lender loan program with direct federal loans, effective July 1, 2010, and, starting in July 2014, eases terms of income-based repayment. . . . Twenty percent of nation's students attend private colleges. . . . Loan defaults by students who attended for-profit colleges soar 30 percent over previous two-year period.

2011 To free up money for Pell grants for low-income students, congressional and White House debt-ceiling negotiators end loan-interest subsidies for graduate- and professional-school students and eliminate incentives for on-time repayment. . . . About 30 percent of Americans over age 25 have attended four years of college. . . . Tuition for 2011-2012 in the University of California system is 18 percent higher than in previous year and 80 percent higher than in 2007-2008. . . . Beginning this month, all college websites must post net-price calculators for prospective students.

Colleges Challenged to Give Students More Value

Rising student debt fuels call for tuition cuts, better education.

With a growing number of students facing big debts when they leave college, calls are increasing for educational institutions to do more to provide value for tuition dollars.

"Public-college tuitions just can't keep going up at the rate they have," even though "the net prices that people actually pay haven't gone up as rapidly," says Sandy Baum, a professor emerita of economics at Skidmore College, in Saratoga Springs, N.Y., and a longtime college-funding analyst for the College Board.

There's little doubt that many colleges are overspending and could cut costs, say many education-policy experts.

"When some people on a faculty are teaching only one course a semester, one obvious answer is to get them teaching more," says Arthur M. Hauptman, an independent public-policy consultant in Arlington, Va.

Others argue, however, that cutting costs can be easier said than done.

"I'm skeptical about ideas for things that can reduce costs dramatically," such as increasing online education, says Donald Hossler, a professor at the Indiana University School of Education, in Bloomington. For one thing, much online instruction would likely take place in introductory courses and at community colleges, where lower-income, less-prepared and younger students likely need "more personal intervention" to succeed, not less, Hossler says. "I think we will see pretty high dropout rates if that's all we can offer them."

Recently, institutional spending has risen faster in a relatively small cost category dubbed "student services" than for the biggest-ticket spending items, such as teaching, says Douglas A. Webber, a doctoral student in economics at Cornell University and a researcher at Cornell's Higher Education Research Institute. Webber defines student services as "anything outside of the classroom that encourages student engagement" with school, such as counseling, tutoring, clubs and student publications.

While many see such services as potential sources of cost cuts, Webber says a solution that looks good in theory may be more complicated in practice. At current spending levels, extra dollars spent on student services pay off better in improved student retention and achievement than equivalent investments in teaching, especially at schools with many lower-income students, he says.

In the current system, states award funding to public colleges and universities based on cost lists that schools submit. But with prices skyrocketing, more discriminating judgment is required, says Hauptman. Lawmakers themselves wouldn't necessarily make the judgment calls but might instead assemble panels of academic experts to set reasonable compensation for different sorts of college investments, he suggests.

The rates would be based on how much those investments furthered such public goals as increasing the proportion of entering freshmen who complete their degrees, Hauptman says. Expensive institutions should also be required to make financial contributions, given the fact that taxpayers must pony up money in advance for loans and students must pay back those debts for years afterward, Hauptman argues.

Under current rules, a school's "sticker price," which only a handful of the very richest students actually pay, determines how big a federal loan students may obtain, Hauptman says.

"The analogy to subprime [mortgage] loans is a good one" for student loans, Collinge says. Just as easy-seeming mortgage terms drove up home prices, he said, the availability of education loans fuels consumer demand that helps drive up the price of college. And in both situations, Collinge says, "people got involved in a form of debt that they don't understand," with multiple loan provisions "that run up the total that must be paid." College loans don't represent a price bubble that can pop, but borrowers "experience a complete loss of faith in a government lending system" supposedly intended to help people, he said.

Basically, a loan is capped at the difference between the school's sticker price and a student's estimated family contribution, calculated according to the government's Free Application for Student Aid (FAFSA).

A student with $30,000 in resources who attends a school with a $50,000 sticker price is authorized to borrow $20,000 from the government, for example. To pressure colleges to think twice before pushing sticker prices sky high, students might instead be permitted to borrow half the difference — $10,000 — with the school required to discount its sticker price by the other $10,000, Hauptman suggests.

Furthermore, when colleges see the need to spend more to provide their services, "Why do they raise tuitions rather than increasing enrollments" to pay for it? Hauptman asks. Adding more tuition-paying students is just as valid a means to increase revenue as increasing individual tuitions, he says. But while community colleges and some other lower-tier public colleges are required to follow that course, higher-priced schools seldom do, he says. "The focus of faculty members is to keep enrollment down, but I think we need a more fundamental discussion" of how rising costs are funded.

School accountability "is really important," says Deanne Loonin, staff attorney at the Student Loan Borrower Assistance Project at the National Consumer Law Center in Boston. With students accumulating ever-greater debt to attend college, "schools should care about their completion rates" and take more responsibility for ensuring that students who enter get what they're paying for, she says.

Higher-education groups say that figuring out exactly what colleges should be held accountable for, and how to measure that performance, isn't easy. "Effective assessment of student learning is complex and multifaceted," said Christine M. Keller, executive director of Voluntary System of Accountability, a membership group of public colleges and universities. "A top-down approach that imposes a one-size-fits-all . . . method" of judging schools' educational accomplishments would be "counterproductive."[1]

And while colleges are accused of engaging in a pricey institutional "arms race" in their quest for prestige and better students, more than just the institutions may be to blame.

An Iowa State University student reads the student paper. Institutional spending has risen faster for student services, such as clubs and student publications, than for big-ticket items such as teaching.

"It would be nice to think that students are making their decisions about school on the basis of pedagogy," but, in fact, many are not, says Robert K. Toutkoushian, an education professor at the University of Georgia. Instead, decisions about which school to attend often are influenced by factors that are costly for schools to accommodate. For students, it may be, "I have my own bathroom," he says. And for parents: "The grounds are kept well."

— *Marcia Clemmitt*

[1]Christine M. Keller, statement to the National Advisory Committee on Institutional Quality and Integrity, June 8, 2011, www.voluntarysystem.org/docs/news/Keller-VSA_NACIQI_comments_060911.pdf.

Furthermore, Collinge complained that when a student defaults and the Department of Education must reimburse the lending bank, the government can easily recoup the money and then some by pursuing the student all the way into retirement. The government has no incentive to help students and lenders work out a payment plan, he argues.

Consumer Protections

Education lending has "been an extraordinarily profitable business," wrote *Fortune* magazine reporter Bethany McLean in 2007. Sallie Mae, for example, had had one of the highest rates of return on shareholder investments of any American company and compensated its executives

Getty Images/Michael Nagle

In 2007 New York Attorney General Andrew Cuomo revealed what he called an "unholy alliance" in which colleges and college officials accepted kickbacks for naming certain banks "preferred lenders" for student loans. Financial-aid officers at several universities, including Columbia and Johns Hopkins, resigned. Some universities and lenders, including Citibank, agreed to settlements that included financial penalties and pledges to submit to a new industry conduct code.

handsomely, paying CEO Albert Lord more than $200 million between 1999 and 2004, McLean wrote.[29]

But consumer concerns that the loan industry put profits above students have led to several changes over the past 20 years, notably instituting income-related repayment plans and limiting private banks' role in college lending.

In the early 1990s the Clinton administration argued that direct loans from the federal government, rather than banks, were safer for students and cheaper for taxpayers because they eliminated subsidies to commercial lenders. That view prevailed, and in 1993 Congress passed the Student Loan Reform Act, giving universities the option of offering direct federal loans rather than loans offered through banks. The law also introduced a program for lower-wage borrowers that pegged payments on direct loans to income.

But many in the financial industry, along with many political conservatives, opposed direct loans. The government is not as well positioned as banks to "manage risk, market student loans or service ongoing lending," wrote Douglas Holtz-Eakin, a former chief of the Congressional Budget Office who served as economic adviser to

Presidents George H. W. and George W. Bush and to the Consumer Bankers Association. Budget estimates pegging direct government loans as cheaper for taxpayers failed to capture their true costs, including lost income-tax revenues from private lenders, he wrote.[30]

For more than a decade, the student-loan industry fought hard to induce colleges to stick with federally guaranteed bank loans. But those efforts backfired in 2007, when then-New York Attorney General Andrew Cuomo revealed what he called an "unholy alliance" in which colleges and college officials accepted kickbacks for naming "preferred lenders."

Financial-aid officers at universities including Columbia, in New York City, Johns Hopkins, in Baltimore, and the University of Texas, at Austin, resigned. Some universities and lenders, including banking giant Citibank, agreed to settlements that included financial penalties and pledges to submit to a new industry conduct code.[31]

Over the past few years, Congress has changed the federal education-loan programs in ways that many analysts say should make them less onerous, at least for future borrowers and some past ones eligible to opt into the new repayment plans.

In 2007, Congress created a loan-forgiveness program for some student debtors who go into public-service jobs and added an income-based repayment option for direct loans to the one it had passed in 1993. It allowed borrowers to opt into a repayment plan that caps payments at 15 percent of discretionary income and forgives any remaining debt after 25 years. Then last year Congress lowered the cap to 10 percent of income and shortened the pay period to 20 years, beginning July 1, 2014.[32]

Many higher-education analysts welcome the plans that offer lower-income people smaller monthly payments but say they wish they covered more people. "It's good, but not as good as it could be," says Skidmore's Baum.

Delaney of the University of Illinois complains that the programs require students to opt in rather than being automatically enrolled — a problem she says guarantees that relatively few students will be covered.

Another 2010 provision fulfilled a longtime Democratic goal — replacing federally guaranteed bank loans with direct federal loans. The provision, which applies to loans made in July 2010 or later, will work better for consumers and taxpayers because it cuts out fees charged by private institutions acting as middlemen,

Tips on Taming the College-Debt Monster

Track costs and pay high-interest loans first, experts say.

Soaring college tuition is translating into bigger education loans, so college-bound students must mull their higher-education choices more carefully than ever. Here are some tips from experts:

- **Consider alternatives.** Deciding between a four-year college and a cheaper two-year community college should be based on more than just money. If you know you're going for a bachelor's degree, starting at a four-year school may be the better choice, says Douglas A. Webber, a doctoral student in economics at Cornell University and a researcher at Cornell's Higher Education Research Institute. But for professional fields that don't necessarily require four years, such as nursing, he says, community college certificate programs are "often undervalued." They cost less than comparable programs at four-year schools, "so they're well worth considering," Webber says.

Shopping around among two-year colleges also is important, says Stephanie R. Cellini, an assistant professor of public policy at George Washington University in Washington. For example, if a for-profit college in your area advertises a certificate you want, such as in auto mechanics, it's worth checking to see if a community college near you offers it, too, because community colleges are the lowest-cost option, Cellini says.

- **Find out whether you qualify for aid**, such as need-based federal Pell grants, so you don't foreclose the option of attending a favorite school too early. "Students simply don't know what aid is available" and may simply write off the possibility of attending some schools because they don't think they can afford their advertised "sticker prices," says Donald Heller, an education professor at Pennsylvania State University in State College.

Very few students pay those sticker prices, however, and low-income students never do because need-based grants are available, Heller says. Starting this October, all colleges must post so-called "net-price calculators" on their websites to help students figure out their bottom-line cost. The calculators factor in grants, loans and upfront costs, and the figures are adjusted to reflect discounts based on the financial status of students' families. Although the calculators aren't perfect, they can provide a much better sense of actual costs than the estimates available in the past.[1]

Too often overlooked in the financial-planning stage is the question of "how are you going to live?" says Sandy Baum, a Chicago-based independent education consultant and longtime College Board analyst. Living expenses run about $12,000 to $15,000 a year, "which can give you a lot of added debt," she says.

- **Borrow your permitted maximum through federal loan programs before considering private loans**, which have much higher interest rates and don't allow the deferred or income-related payments or loan-forgiveness programs that apply to most federal loans.
- **Keep careful records of your borrowing.** "People are making these huge financial decisions, and a lot of times they don't even realize how big, because loans are so easy to get," says Webber.

Track the lender, balance and repayment status of each loan. These details will determine your options for repayment schedules and loan forgiveness down the line, advises the Oakland, Calif.-based Project on Student Debt. Details matter. For example, different loans have different "grace periods" — the amount of time you can wait after leaving school before you must make your first payment. The federal website http://studentaid.ed.gov/PORTALSWebApp/students/english/index.jsp provides information about federal aid and loan programs and allows you to manage and track your personal financial-aid application process, loans and more.

- **Make savvy choices about repayment**, suggests financial analyst Mark Kantrowitz, publisher of the college-aid website FinAid. Paying off your debt as soon as possible will save on interest, and the best way to cut interest costs is to pay off the loan with the highest after-tax interest rate first. If you have both federally guaranteed and private loans or have used a credit card to pay some college expenses, the highest-interest loan — and thus your first target for repayment — should be the credit-card or private-lender loan, Kantrowitz said.

— Marcia Clemmitt

---

[1] For background on net price calculators, see Daniel de Vise, "Calculating the Net Price of College," *Washington Post blogs*, March 17, 2010, http://voices. washingtonpost.com/college-inc/2010/03/more_on_the_net_price_of_colle. html, and Tim Johnson, "Colleges Unveiling 'Net Price Calculators,' " *Burlington Free Press* [Vermont] blogs, Sept. 27, 2011, http://blogs.burlingtonfreepress. com/highered/2011/09/27/colleges-unveiling-net-price-calculators.

[2] Mark Kantrowitz, "Best Strategies for Paying Off Debt Quicker," *Fastweb. com*, Oct. 11, 2010, www.fastweb.com/financial-aid/articles/2747-best-strategies-for-paying-off-debt-quicker.

Getty Images/Steven Vlasic

New York University graduates celebrate commencement at Yankee Stadium on May 18, 2011. Education experts generally agree that while the cost of obtaining a college degree may pay off in the long run, the dual trends of rising debt and rising tuition are becoming increasingly problematic, especially for low-income students who rack up large debt and those who don't obtain degrees or certificates.

supporters argue. Private lenders can still make college loans, but no new education loans made by banks will be affiliated with any federal loan-guarantee program.

The 2010 changes are "hugely significant," says Delaney. "I'm not sure we'll fully understand their significance for a long time, but it's the biggest thing that's happened in student aid for 30 years."

CURRENT SITUATION

Debt and Deficits

Student-loan programs continue to play a role in heated debates over federal spending. In negotiations between Congress and the White House this summer over raising the federal debt ceiling — the amount Congress authorizes the government to borrow — college-loan programs took a hit as negotiators struggled to find money to shore up the Pell Grant program for low-income students.

On Aug. 2, lawmakers passed and President Obama signed the Budget Control Act of 2011, raising the debt ceiling to forestall a government default.[33] Negotiators authorized a temporary $17 billion boost in Pell Grant funds for 2012 and 2013, in part to replace expiring increases passed in 2009 and 2010 as part of economic-stimulus and health-care reform bills.

The Pell increase isn't a done deal, however. Congress ultimately must make additional spending cuts elsewhere before it can appropriate the funds. An appropriations bill recently approved in the Republican-led House, for example, would trim $44 billion from Pell over 10 years by limiting eligibility, according to the advocacy group Institute for College Access and Success.[34]

What's more, in passing the Budget Control Act, Congress eliminated programs offering loan-interest subsidies for graduate- and professional-school enrollees and interest reductions on loans that students pay on time.[35]

Student-loan programs have long been part of Washington debt-reduction debates, but with new loans all using government rather than private funds, many may see the matter in a new light.

In the past, observed the online magazine *Inside Higher Ed*, "because significant proportions of the programs' profits flowed to banks and other lenders, slashing [the programs] — to increase spending on grants to students or even to pay down the federal deficit — was often portrayed as taking money from 'fat cat' companies" and using it for students or other public purposes. Today, however, with commercial lenders removed from the picture, "it is clearer than ever before" that cutting loan programs actually means taking money from cash-strapped "borrowers themselves."[36]

Meanwhile, taxpayer funding for public colleges in at least some states is drying up. And as the economic downturn lingers and federal stimulus funds wind down, state lawmakers are resisting tax hikes to shore up higher education.[37] That means tuitions at public colleges will likely rise, fueling further increases in student debt.

In the University of California system, for example, 2011-2012 tuition will rise 18 percent from 2010-2011 and more than 80 percent from 2007-2008, according to Equal Justice Works, a Washington-based advocacy group that promotes access to education.[38]

More Students, More Loans

The biggest higher-education trend, in the United States and elsewhere, is the ever-growing number of students who get post-secondary training. But as costs outpace public funding, the trend sets education debt on a permanent upward path, worldwide.

Are students borrowing more than their educations are worth?

YES
Alan Collinge
Founder, StudentLoanJustice.org

Written for *CQ Researcher*, October 2011

President Obama made it clear in his State of the Union address that two areas of focus going forward will be education and "fixing what is broken" in the federal government. The most meaningful way for the president to demonstrate this — on both fronts — lies in the federal student-loan system.

Like subprime lending, the student-lending system has been corrupted deeply, enabling college prices to rise faster than both housing and health care over the past three decades. Today, we owe an astounding $1 trillion in student debt, and instead of decreasing in the slow economy, borrowing has accelerated massively to keep pace with record-breaking tuition increases.

Unlike loans for housing, student loans were stripped of bankruptcy protections and nearly every other consumer protection Americans assume is there when they borrow. At the same, time, Congress gave the student-lending system collection powers so draconian that big lenders, guarantors and likely even the Department of Education have made far more money on defaults than healthy loans. This is not tolerable in this or any other country. On this there is no debate.

As Harvard Law Professor Elizabeth Warren, who established the government's new Consumer Finance Protection Bureau, put it: It's impossible to buy a toaster that has a one-in-five chance of exploding, but similar standards aren't imposed on financial products. Indeed, education-loan defaults have been greater than one in four for many years and are probably between 30 percent and 40 percent today, yet the Department of Education has not warned the public. Congress, too, needed to know this as they debated whether to raise loan limits time and again. But they were shown only misleading cohort rates that reflected a small fraction of the true default rate. As a result, students now borrow far more than their educations are worth, and they (and often their co-signing relatives) are being decimated financially.

Ultimately, the removal of bankruptcy protections is the root of this mess, and their immediate return is the solution to both the exploitation of borrowers and the prices being charged to all students, rich and poor. Economists and true conservatives everywhere should agree with this assertion. Student debt is a top issue in the protests going on around the country this fall, demonstrating that the public is unlikely to tolerate for much longer the political and administrative games that perpetuate this harm.

NO
Neal McCluskey
Associate Director, Center for Educational Freedom, Cato Institute

Written for *CQ Researcher*, October 2011

Looking at the basic facts, college students are not absorbing more debt than their educations are worth. But that doesn't mean debt shouldn't be much smaller.

While methodologies for calculating it are hotly debated, the college-earnings premium is generally considered to be substantial. On the high end, the Census Bureau estimates expected lifetime earnings to be $1.1 million greater with a bachelor's degree than just a high-school diploma. Low-end estimates — between $100,000 and $300,000 — also suggest that debt pays off. Why? Because the average debt for graduates is only $24,000, so most are paying only a modest price for the return in additional wages — at least $100,000, even by the most conservative estimates. Those, though, are just basic averages. There is much that they miss.

First, many students enroll in college, incur debt, but never finish their studies, failing to obtain the degree that is crucial to increased earnings. Indeed, the six-year graduation rate for first-time, full-time students enrolled in four-year institutions is just around 57 percent, and most who do not finish in six years probably never will.

Then there's what a degree does. Rather than indicating mastery of valuable skills, it often signals to employers only that the possessor has some basic positive traits, such as threshold levels of intelligence or perseverance. The extent to which that is the case varies greatly by major — as do earnings — but generally speaking, paying for college is a very expensive way just to indicate that you'll show up at work on time.

Proving this, to be fair, is tough, because we have no comprehensive measures of what students actually learn in college. What we do have, though, is discouraging. The National Assessment of Adult Literacy shows markedly decreasing literacy rates for college grads between 1992 and 2003. Meanwhile, research by academics Richard Arum and Josipa Roksa, authors of *Academically Adrift: Limited Learning on College Campuses*, suggests that 45 percent of four-year college students learn little in their first two years, and 36 percent nearly nothing in four years.

Finally, there's price inflation: Going into debt might be worthwhile, but the levels shouldn't be nearly as high as they are. College prices have inflated at astronomical rates over the last several decades, at least in part because student aid, including grants and cheap federal loans, enable it. Give students an extra dollar, and schools raise tuition by a buck.

So does a degree pay off handsomely? Generally, yes. Does that mean debt levels are just right? No way.

"We are in a new era where resources don't seem endless, and nobody's found a cheap way to pay for a college education," says Indiana University's Hossler.

As a result, "lots of countries," both developing and industrialized, "are looking into loans," including countries such as the United Kingdom that formerly relied on tax revenues rather than students' tuition loans, says Boston College's Altbach.

Countries looking to expand the use of student debt are unlikely to use the U.S. system as a model, though, says independent analyst Hauptman. More likely models are Australia and New Zealand, where student borrowers are automatically enrolled in plans that are administered through the tax system and base repayment amounts on students' post-graduate incomes. While those nations face their own struggles over how heavily government should subsidize higher education and how much individual debt is acceptable, their systems are far preferable to the U.S. approach, Hauptman contends.

But others criticize schemes that base loan repayment on income, arguing that they are merely stealth methods of shifting more college costs from society at large to individual students. Low earners end up paying more in interest than high earners who can pay off their loan relatively quickly, said the Canadian Federation of Students, a student-advocacy group in Ottawa that has opposed income-contingent repayment plans in Canada. Many women, in particular, might end up with a "lifelong debt sentence" because women earn less on average than men, the group said.[39]

OUTLOOK

Explosive Debt?

Even as college costs rise, many policymakers are calling for expansion of post-secondary schooling to create a better-prepared pool of workers to build tomorrow's economy. But college-price increases, coupled with policies encouraging more people to complete post-secondary training, will continue to raise questions about how heavily taxpayers are willing to subsidize higher education and how much debt students can be expected to shoulder.

The nation faces a huge dilemma, says the University of Pennsylvania's Perna. "How do we balance these budgets and achieve our goals" for improving college-completion rates "in the face of declining revenues? You can become paralyzed by the magnitude of the problem."

Experts say some states that have been basing student aid on recipients' grades rather than financial need may be starting to back away from that policy, concerned that it isn't expanding access to college. But, says Penn State's Heller, "in the nation as a whole I don't expect to see merit-based aid back off" — a trend that could continue to bode ill for cash-strapped students lacking top-tier grades but who nonetheless seek a college degree.

Even as students pay more to attend college, look for the nature of higher education to change. Huge class sizes, reflecting colleges' struggles to accommodate enrollment surges, will be one manifestation, says Northwestern's Weisbrod. "In a class with 500 students rather than a class of 20, you'll be less likely to assign papers," for example, "so there is a quality issue," he says. "The nature of education is changing as we try to make it available to everybody."

In such a climate, requiring individuals to take on more and more debt for schooling will eventually lose political support, Weisbrod argues. "Leaders will come to realize that you can't have a successful program" of encouraging college graduation "if you are saddling people with unworkable debt" to do it.

St. John of the University of Michigan says "loans have become very important" because "they enable the working class" to get post-secondary training. Still, he says, "there are ways to work within a problematic system to move toward something that's fairer."

But student debtor and activist Collinge thinks it may take a near-revolution to get there. Congress seems unlikely to take a serious step, such as restoring bankruptcy protection, he says. On Capitol Hill, "they're scared of the power" of the higher-education establishment, including colleges, private lenders and even the Department of Education, Collinge asserts. All have vested interests in opposing such large-scale changes, he says.

As debt burdens become untenable for more students, the federal programs supposedly intended to help people pay for college "will become a national joke," Collinge predicts. "Nobody will pay. There could be a national strike. It could get very dodgy at that point," as Americans suffer "a loss of faith in a major government-lending system."

NOTES

1. For background, see "MoveOn.org, U.S. Rep. Promoting Student Loan Debt Forgiveness," *The Daily Caller*, Sept. 15, 2011,http://daily caller.com/2011/09/15/moveon-org-u-s-rep-promoting-student-loan-debt-forgiveness; Carolyn Elefant, "Law Student Organizing Loan Forgiveness Drive," Legal Blog Watch, March 26, 2009, http://legalblog watch.typepad.com/ legal_blog_watch/2009/03/law-student-orga nizing-loan-forgiveness-drive.html; "Robert Applebaum's Bio," Robert Applebaum.com, www. robertapplebaum.com/content/robert-apple baums-bio.

2. Mark Kantrowitz, "Total College Debt Now Exceeds Total Credit Card Debt," *Fastweb*, Aug. 11, 2010, www.fastweb.com/financial-aid/ articles/2589-total-college-debt-now-exceeds-total-credit-card-debt.

3. The 1982-2005 data are from Patrick M. Callan, "College Affordability: Colleges, States Increase Financial Burdens on Student and Families," Measuring Up 2006: The National Report Card on Higher Education," National Center for Public Policy and Higher Education, http://measuringup. highereducation.org; more recent figures are from "Trends in College Pricing," College Board, p. 3.

4. Quoted in Korva Coleman, "Is a College Education Worth the Debt?" NPR, Sept. 1, 2009, www.npr. org/templates/story/story.php?story Id=112432364.

5. Andrew Gillen, "Financial Aid in Theory and Practice: Why It Is Ineffective and What Can Be Done About It," Center for College Affordability and Productivity, April 2009, www. centerforcollege affordability.org/uploads/Finan cial_Aid_in_Theory_and_Practice%281%29.pdf.

6. Annamaria Andriotis, "For Student Borrowers, a Hard Truth," *SmartMoney*, Sept. 16, 2011, www .smartmoney.com/borrow/student-loans/ for-student-borrowers-a-hard-truth-131611895 5339/?link=SM_hp_ls4e. For background, see Barbara Mantel, "Career Colleges," *CQ Researcher*, Jan. 7, 2011, pp. 1-24.

7. Quoted in Coleman, *op. cit.*

8. "Car-Financing Basics," *Money-Zine.com*, www .money-zine.com/Financial-Planning/Leasing-or-Buying-a-Car/Car-Financing-Basics.

9. Michael Greenstone and Adam Looney, "Where Is the Best Place to Invest $102,000 — In Stocks, Bonds, or a College Degree?" Brookings Institution website, June 25, 2011, www.brookings.edu/papers/2011/0625_edu cation_greenstone_looney.aspx.

10. "Student Loans," FinAid, www.finaid.org/loans.

11. "The Rising Price of Inequality: How Inadequate Grant Aid Limits College Access and Persistence," Advisory Committee on Student Financial Assistance, June 2010, http://chronicle. com/items/biz/pdf/acsfa_rpi.pdf.

12. *Ibid.*

13. For background, see "Paving the Way: How Financial Aid Awareness Affects College Access and Success," The Institute for College Access & Success, October 2008, http://project onstudentdebt.org/fckfiles/Paving_the_Way.pdf, p. 7.

14. "The College Completion Agenda: 2011 Progress Report, Latino Edition," The College Board, October 2011, http://completionagenda.college board.org/sites/default/files/latino_pdf/progress_report_latino_2011.pdf.

15. For background, see David Moltz, "Is Completion the Right Goal?" *Inside Higher Ed*, Feb. 16, 2011, www.insidehighered.com/news/ 2011/02/16/scholars_debate_merits_of_com pletion_agenda.

16. William J. Bennett, "Our Greedy Colleges," *The New York Times*, Feb. 18, 1987, www.ny times.com/1987/02/18/opinion/our-greedy- colleges.html.

17. Robert B. Archibald and David H. Feldman, "Avoiding Tunnel Vision in the Study of Higher Education Costs," College of William and Marry Department of Economics Working Paper Number 53, June 2007, http://ideas.repec.org/p/cwm/wpaper/53.html.

18. For background, see Charlene Wear Simmons, "Student Loans and Higher Education," California Research Bureau, January 2008, www.library.ca.gov/crb/08/08-002.pdf; "History of Student Financial Aid," FinAid, www.finaid. org/educators/history .phtml; and the following *CQ Researcher* reports: Thomas J. Billitteri, "The Value of a College Education," Nov. 20, 2009, pp. 981-1004; Marcia Clemmitt, "Student Aid," Jan. 25, 2008, pp. 73-96;

and Tom Price, "Rising College Costs," Dec. 5, 2003, pp. 1013-1044.

19. Robert Shireman, 'Straight Talk on Student Loans," University of California, Berkeley, Occasional Paper Series, 2004, http://cshe.berkeley. edu/publications/publications.php?id=66.

20. "Web Tables" for "Trends in Student Financing of Undergraduate Education: Selected years, 1995-96 to 2007-08," National Center for Education Statistics, U.S. Department of Education, January 2011, http://nces.ed.gov/ pubs2011/2011218.pdf.

21. Lisa Wade, "Number of College Students Owing $40,000+ in Loans, 1996-2008," *Sociological Images*, May 23, 2010, http://thesociety pages.org/socimages/2010/05/23/number-of-college-students-owing-40000-in-school-loans-1996-2008.

22. Arthur M. Hauptman and Young Kim, "Cost, Commitment and Attainment in Higher Education: An International Comparison," *Jobs for the Future*, May 2009, www.jff.org/publications/ education/cost-commitment-and-attainment-higher-ed/836.

23. Arthur M. Hauptman, "Thirty Per Cent Hold Bachelor's Degrees," *Federations Magazine*, Forum of Federations, June/July 2007, www.forumfed.org/en/products/magazine/vol6_num2/ special_us.php.

24. Joe Nocera, "The Profit and the Pauper," *The New York Times*, July 29, 2007, www.ny times.com/2007/07/29/education/edlife/nocera. html?pagewanted=all.

25. *Ibid.*

26. J. Douglas Cuthbertson, testimony before the House Judiciary Subcommittee on Commercial and Administrative Law, Sept. 23, 2009, http://judiciary.house.gov/hearings/pdf/Cuth bertson090923.pdf.

27. John A. Hupalo, testimony before the House Judiciary Subcommittee on Commercial and Administrative Law, April 22, 2010, http://judiciary.house.gov/hearings/pdf/Hupalo100 422.pdf.

28. Alan Collinge, *The Student Loan Scam: The Most Oppressive Debt in U.S. History — and How We Can Fight Back* (2010), pp. vii-ix.

29. Bethany McLean, "The Surprising Profits of Student Loans," CNN Money, April 16, 2007, http://money.cnn.com/2007/04/16/news/com panies/pluggedin_mclean_sallie.fortune/index.htm.

30. Douglas Holtz-Eakin, "Budget-Scoring Barriers to Efficient Student Loan Policy," paper prepared for Consumer Bankers Association, *et al.*, December 2006, www.studentloanfacts.org/NR/rdonlyres/65 DDECF9-3020-4C6A-8C8F-B568556FEA64/7398/BudgetScoringBarrierstoEfficientStudentLoanPolicy.pdf.

31. For background, see Karen W. Arenson and Diana Jean Schemo, "Report Details Deals in Student Loan Industry," *The New York Times*, June 15, 2007, www.nytimes.com/2007/ 06/15/washington/15 loans.html.

32. For background, see Mark Kantrowitz, "President Obama Proposes Capping Student Loan Payments at 10 Percent of Discretionary Income," *Fastweb*, Jan. 25, 2010, www.fastweb.com/financial-aid/articles/2057-president-obama-proposes-capping-student-loan-payments-at-10-of-discretionary-income.

33. For background, see Stephen Burd and Jason Delisle, "A Temporary, Albeit Tenuous, Reprieve for Pell Grants," *Higher Ed Watch*, New American Foundation, July 28, 2011, http://higheredwatch.newamerica.net/blogposts/2011/a_temporary_albeit_tenuous_reprieve_for_pell_grants-55499.

34. "House FY12 Appropriations Bill Cuts Pell Grants by $44 Billion: Reduces College Access, Penalizes Work and Hurts the Neediest Students," The Institute for College Access and Success, Oct. 11, 2011, http://ticas.org/files/pub/House_FY12_Approps_Bill_one-pager.pdf.

35. Isaac Bowers, "Make Sense of the Debt Ceiling Jabberwocky," *U.S. News & World Report blogs*, Aug. 10, 2011, www.usnews.com/ education/blogs/student-loan-ranger/2011/08/10/make-sense-of-the-debt-ceiling-jabberwocky.

36. Libby A. Nelson and Doug Lederman, "Loans and the Deficit," *Inside Higher Ed*, July 18, 2011, www.insidehighered.com/news/2011/ 07/18/increased_student_loan_interest_rates_to_reduce_deficit_and_probably_not_expand_grants.

37. For background, see Erica Williams, Michael Leachman and Nicholas Johnson, "State Budget Cuts in the New Fiscal Year Are Unnecessarily Harmful," Center on Budget and Policy Priorities,

July 28, 2011, www.cbpp.org/ cms/index.cfm?fa=view&id=3550.

38. Bowers, *op. cit.*

39. "Study Now, Pay Forever: Income Contingent Repayment Loan Schemes," Canadian Federation of Students, Winter 2007, www.cfs-fcee.ca/html/english/research/factsheets/fact sheet-icr.pdf.

BIBLIOGRAPHY

Selected Sources

Books

Cohen, Arthur M., and Carrie B. Kisker, *The Shaping of American Higher Education: Emergence and Growth of the Contemporary System*, **2nd Edition, Jossey-Bass, 2009.**
Cohen, a professor emeritus of higher education at the University of California, Los Angeles, and education-policy consultant Kisker put the development of the U.S. higher-education system from the early 1600s to the 21st century into its social and economic context, focusing on the continued push to expand access and examining the recent privatization trend.

Collinge, Alan, *The Student Loan Scam: The Most Oppressive Debt in U.S. History and How We Can Fight Back*, **Beacon Press, 2010.**
A student-debt activist chronicles the growth of the education-loan business and accompanying federal bureaucracy, which he argues have profited on the backs of student debtors.

Weisbrod, Burton A., Jeffrey P. Ballou and Evelyn D. Asch, *Mission and Money: Understanding the University*, **Cambridge University Press, 2008.**
Weisbrod, a professor of economics at Northwestern University, and his coauthors describe how colleges fund their academic activities with a complicated revenue mix that includes tuition, private donations, taxpayer dollars and proceeds from commercial-type activities, such as research and intercollegiate sports.

Articles

Byrne, John A., "Wharton MBA 2013: The Class the Loans Fell On," *CNN Money*, **Aug. 22, 2011, http:// management. fortune.cnn.com/tag/tuition-payments.**
At the University of Pennsylvania's Wharton School, members of the MBA class of 2013 will be the first to owe more than $100 million in education debt, including interest, when they complete their degrees.

Chavkin, Sasha, "Education Department Backs Away From Fix to Help Disabled Student Borrowers," *Pro Publica*, **August 2011, www.propublica.org/article/education-department-backs-away-from-fix-to-help-disabled-student-borrowers/single.**
Students who become disabled after taking out loans can be excused from repayment, but the Education Department hesitates to adopt a simplified disability-certification process.

Nelson, Libby A., and Doug Lederman, "Loans and the Deficit," *Inside Higher Ed*, **July 18, 2011, www .inside highered.com/news/2011/07/18/increased_student_loan_interest_rates_to_reduce_deficit_and_probably_not_expand_ grants.**
The revenues flowing to banks and the Department of Education as students repay their loans far exceed the loans' cost, making student-loan programs a hot business.

Reports and Studies

The Rising Price of Inequality: How Inadequate Grant Aid Limits College Access and Persistence, **Advisory Committee on Student Financial Assistance, June 2010, www.im magic.com/eLibrary/FIN_AID/US_ED/A100630R.pdf.**
Too few need-based grants are available to ensure that qualified low- and moderate-income students can complete college, says a federal advisory panel.

Abernathy, Pauline, "Drowning in Debt: Financial Outcomes of Students at For-Profit Colleges," Institute for College Access, June 7, 2011, http://projecton studentdebt. org/files/pub/Abernathy_testimony_June_7_2011.pdf.
For-profit career colleges have the highest proportion of students with debt, says the vice president of a student-debt research and advocacy group.

Carey, Kevin, and Erin Dillon, *Drowning in Debt: The Emerging Student Loan Crisis*, **Education Sector, July 2009, www.educationsector.org/sites/default/files/publications/ CYCT_Drowning_In_Debt.pdf.**

As tuitions soar, more students are taking on the riskiest kind of education debt — non-federally guaranteed private-lender loans, write analysts at an independent think tank.

Cunningham, Alisa F., and Gregory S. Kienzl, *Delinquency: The Untold Story of Student Loan Borrowing,* **Institute for Higher Education Policy, March 2011, www.ihep.org/assets/files/publications/a-f/Delinquency-The_Untold_Story_FINAL_March_2011.pdf.**
Analysts for a nonprofit group say policymakers remain unaware of the seriousness of student-debt problems because federal statistics don't reveal that many borrowers temporarily fall behind in their payments.

Vedder, Richard, *The Coming Revolution in Higher Education,* **Center for College Affordability and Productivity, October 2010, www.centerforcollegeaffordability.org/ uploads/Revolution_in_Higher_Ed.pdf.**
The combination of rising tuitions, rising debt and pressure for more Americans to complete college may soon force colleges to demonstrate that they provide value for the dollar, says the founder of a nonprofit group that advocates for accountability in higher education.

From the CQ Researcher Archive:
"Financial Support for Higher Education," May 5, 1948; "Costs of Education," May 25, 1959; "College Financing," Feb. 24, 1971; "What's Behind High College Price Tags," May 19, 1989.

For More Information

Advisory Committee on Student Financial Assistance, 80 F St., N.W., Suite 413, Washington, DC 20202-7582; 202-219-2099; www2.ed.gov/about/bdscomm/list/acsfa/edlite-index.html. Independent expert panel that issues in-depth analyses of and advises the federal government on financial aid for higher education.

The Center for College Affordability and Productivity, 1150 17th St., N.W., Suite 910, Washington, DC 20036; 202-375-7831; http://centerforcollegeaffordability.org. Independent, nonprofit think tank that analyzes college finances and spending.

Delta Project on Postsecondary Education Costs, Productivity and Accountability, 1250 H St., N.W., Suite 700, Washington, DC 20005; 202-349-4143; www.deltacostproject.org. Research group studying ways to hold down college costs and improve productivity in higher education.

FinAid, www.finaid.org. Independent, advertising-supported news and information website about loans and other college-finance issues, run by financial analyst Mark Kantrowitz.

Project on Student Debt, Institute for College Access and Success, 405 14th St., 11th Floor, Oakland, CA 94612; 510-318-7900; http://projectonstudentdebt.org. Independent research and education group.

Sallie Mae, 888-272-5543 and 317-570-7397; www.salliemae.com. Publicly traded corporation, no longer government-chartered, that provides, manages and services education loans and education-savings plans.

Student Loan Borrower Assistance Project, National Consumer Law Center, 7 Winthrop Square, Boston, MA 02110-1245; 617-542-8010; www.studentloanborrowerassistance.org. Foundation-supported information and education center on student loans.

StudentLoanJustice.org, http://studentloanjustice.org. Grassroots group that advocates greater consumer protections for student borrowers, including the right to discharge student loans in bankruptcy.

StudentLoans.gov, https://studentloans.gov. Government information portal about federal education loans.

11

Youth Volunteerism

Marcia Clemmitt

Students from Tulane University in New Orleans volunteer at City Park as part of efforts to restore the devastated city following Hurricane Katrina in 2005. Tulane made community service a graduation requirement after the disaster and saw applications to the school shoot up. Nearly 90 percent of the nation's colleges provide service-learning opportunities.

Tulane University Center for Public Service

From *CQ Researcher*,
Jan. 27, 2012

After Hurricane Katrina devastated New Orleans in 2005, Tulane University began requiring students to work on community projects closely tied to their coursework as a condition of graduation. Education majors might tutor elementary students, for instance, and architecture students could help restore parks.

The aim, says Vincent Ilustre, executive director of the university's Center for Public Service, is "to engage our students in rebuilding New Orleans."

Some worried the graduation requirement would send applications to Tulane into a nose dive. Instead, it has been a huge hit, Ilustre says. Before it was added in 2006, "we had about 18,000 applications for 1,500 slots" in the freshman class, he says. "Last year we had 44,000 applications for the same 1,500 places." Anecdotal evidence suggests the remarkable increase is closely related to the school's new mandate.

Tulane is far from alone in requiring — or at least encouraging — public service. *

Over the past two decades, schools and colleges nationwide have increased the number of volunteer opportunities they provide for students. Today, 89 percent of colleges sponsor some form of service

---

*Campuswide service requirements at the college level are rare. Some schools have them, however, including Catholic-affiliated Belmont Abbey College, in Belmont, N.C.; Methodist-affiliated Centenary College, in Hackettstown, N.J.; historically black Benedict College, in Columbia, S.C.; and at least one public university, California State University at Monterey Bay.

Where College Students Volunteer

Educational or youth service organizations attract the most college student volunteers, followed by religious programs.

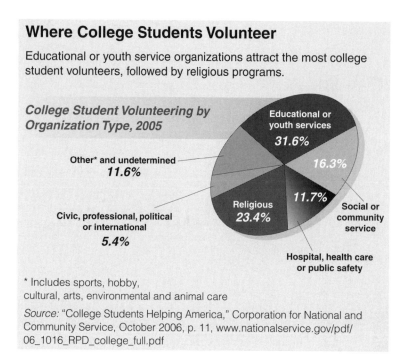

College Student Volunteering by Organization Type, 2005

Educational or youth services
31.6%

16.3%

11.7%

Other* and undetermined
11.6%

Religious
23.4%

Social or community service

Civic, professional, political or international
5.4%

Hospital, health care or public safety

* Includes sports, hobby, cultural, arts, environmental and animal care

Source: "College Students Helping America," Corporation for National and Community Service, October 2006, p. 11, www.nationalservice.gov/pdf/06_1016_RPD_college_full.pdf

learning, in which volunteer work such as helping at a homeless shelter, is linked to studies in, for example, urban policy, says Andrew Furco, associate vice president for public engagement at the University of Minnesota. Meanwhile, volunteer rates among youths ages 16 to 19 soared from 13.4 percent to 24.5 percent between 1989 and 2007, largely because a rising number of high schools sponsor or require service.[1]

Still in question, however, is how many programs are of high enough quality to improve students' learning, help communities and encourage greater civic and social commitment as students grow into adulthood.

Researchers see ample evidence that at least some service programs encourage students to participate in their communities later. "I'm working on a paper right now about whether willingness to serve on a jury" relates to an earlier history of volunteerism, and data suggest that "yes, it does," says sociology professor Marc A. Musick, associate dean for student affairs in the College of Liberal Arts at the University of Texas (UT), Austin. Volunteering makes people more civic minded," says Musick, coauthor of the 2008 book *Volunteers: A Social Profile.* For example, he says, young people who have volunteered are likely "to look at government organizations in a different

way because they've done some of the same kinds of service" for the community.

Students who do community-service projects "meet people unlike those they know" and "learn to know them as individuals," says Steven Meyers, a professor of psychology and social justice at Roosevelt University, in Chicago. That, he says, "can lead to a much more informed worldview" that encourages engagement in civic and community life later on.

But Leslie Lenkowsky, a clinical professor of public affairs and philanthropic studies at Indiana University, in Bloomington, argues that it's not so much service experiences as education that spurs civic engagement. "People don't just wake up one morning and say, 'How can I get engaged in something today?'" says Lenkowsky, who during the George W. Bush administration headed the Corporation for National and Community Service, a federal agency that runs AmeriCorps and other programs that place volunteers in nonprofit organizations and help support their service with stipends and other assistance.

Lenkowsky says people pursue volunteer opportunities mainly "because they're concerned about something" — such as abortion, taxation or homelessness. "And how do people get involved in issues? It depends on the quality of education," he says. "The ability of young people to see public issues as important to their own concerns" — and thus worth committing themselves to through voting, volunteering or the like —"is less than it used to be," he says.

In the 1990s, some high schools began adding community service to their graduation requirements, but the practice remains controversial. Skeptics argue that so many students already have the motivation to volunteer that requirements are overkill.

"I don't see the necessity for a mandate," said Brett Fortin, a senior at Mansfield High School, in Mansfield, Mass., where instituting a requirement was discussed last fall. "I do believe that most of the student body is actively involved," said Fortin, president of the student-run

Student Service Corps, which has researched and helped organize voluntary student participation in more than 50 projects in the Mansfield area, including helping out at Special Olympics events and joining a community leaf-raking effort.[2]

Some researchers say the opinions about service that students draw from school programs depend almost entirely on how well the programs are structured and managed, not on whether the service is required or not. After decades of research on the mandate question, "the data's clear on this, although people haven't really listened," says James Youniss, a research professor of psychology at Catholic University, in Washington. Numerous studies demonstrate that student attitudes after they'd performed service depended on the structure and quality of the programs they participated in, not on whether they'd chosen to volunteer or been required to do so, he says.[3]

Youniss and other researchers caution that unless volunteer programs actively promote thoughtful analysis of students' experiences and issues involved in their service, the programs' effects on students' attitudes and behavior will be nil.

"We studied one Catholic school where kids went to a soup kitchen" and through observation and discussion worked out theories for themselves about how homelessness originates and what things might help it, Youniss says. Data show that only programs that include such follow-up work affect student attitudes and behavior in the long term, he says.

Effective service experiences can be integrated into all kinds of subject matter, Youniss says. In two public schools in Iowa, he says, "kids looked at the disposal of oil filters from cars" in a science class, collected data, analyzed it in light of the science they learned, and ultimately "got a bill passed" directing proper disposal methods.

Community-service participation is particularly high among students at selective colleges and among college-bound high school students, a trend that reveals

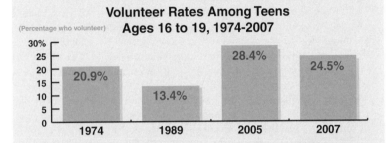

Teen Volunteerism Declined

Teen volunteerism rates have fluctuated drastically in the nearly four decades beginning in 1974. After declining to a low of 13.4 percent, volunteering more than doubled, to 28.4 percent in 2005, but then dropped nearly 4 percentage points in the next two years.

Volunteer Rates Among Teens Ages 16 to 19, 1974-2007
(Percentage who volunteer)

1974: 20.9%
1989: 13.4%
2005: 28.4%
2007: 24.5%

Sources: "Reaching Our Goals: An Overview of Research in Support of the Strategic Initiatives," Corporation for National and Community Service, March 2009, p. 3, www.nationalservice.gov/pdf/08_1113_rpd_reachingourgoals.pdf; "Volunteer Growth in America: A Review of Trends Since 1974," Corporation for National and Community Service, December 2006, p. 2, www.nationalservice.gov/pdf/06_1203_volunteer_growth.pdf

a troubling socioeconomic divide in who gets access to volunteer opportunities. Critics worry that volunteer opportunities are more prevalent among wealthier students and that those facing financial challenges often lack the time for public service because they are working to pay for school.

"There is a huge socioeconomic gap" for the poor in service opportunities, as there is for most other educational opportunities, says Youniss. "If a school has low-income students [or] many immigrants," for example, "it's less likely to have" programs known to improve students' civic involvement, including volunteer-service programs and even student government, he says.

The socioeconomic gap not only deprives young people of community-engagement opportunities but also likely discourages activities such as voting, Youniss says. He notes that people with high school diplomas or less, and especially poor people, vote at much lower rates than college graduates. "You might want to trace that back to poor civics" education and fewer opportunities to build engagement among youth, at least partially, he says.

As lawmakers, colleges and school districts mull whether to expand or limit community-service programs, here are some of the questions that are being asked:

'Voluntourists' Mix Pleasure and Altruism

Doing good in exotic lands has an allure — but also a downside.

In an era of easy worldwide travel and the ubiquitous, information-packed Internet, new kinds of volunteering have grown quickly over the past decade. There's voluntourism — in which travel is combined with service work — and computer-based volunteering initiatives that invite Internet users to participate in social-issues campaigns. Reactions to both are mixed, however.

Combining volunteering with travel as an alternative to traditional vacations is growing in popularity, partly because of some other trends in volunteer behavior, wrote Beth Gazley, an associate professor in the School of Public and Environmental Affairs at Indiana University. More people are volunteering today, including more young people, "but for fewer average hours" than the typical volunteer committed in the past, she wrote.

Spending a week's vacation performing service in a potentially exotic location — such as a wild-elephant preserve or a remote village abroad — fits in well with the shrinking time frame of modern volunteering, Gazley said. Furthermore, "potential volunteers often cite lack of available leisure time as one barrier to service," so "volunteer vacations neatly circumvent this problem."[1]

Volunteer vacations also can last from a few days to months, most involve hands-on helping, such as building a trail or helping conduct research, and tourist volunteers pay their own way and, in some cases, also make additional financial contributions.[2]

Earthwatch, one of the oldest voluntourism organizations, began sponsoring environmental voluntourism in 1973. "We began with rocks and stars, where amateurs couldn't hurt anything," said founder Brian Rosborough.[3] Now Earthwatch projects enable volunteers to help conduct scientific research and protect endangered animals and fragile habitats, Rosborough said.[4]

Nevertheless, since many, if not most, "voluntourists" are attracted more by the exotic travel than by the service itself, there's a danger that trips will be created "just for the travelers," and that is "usually a waste of money and not a lasting solution to any problem," said Daniela Papi, founder of PEPY Tours, which arranges voluntourism in Cambodia. "The hardest part is finding projects that both make the volunteers feel 'needed' and really ARE needed," said Papi. A good project, for example, would be to have volunteers clear land for a new school in a community "already organized in a way that will take care" of the land when the tourists depart, she said.[5]

While some web-based volunteerism initiatives draw criticism as promoting a dangerously shallow view of what constitutes useful service, others provide substantive help to those in need.

In the Thurston school district of Lacey, Wash., the Intergenerational Grandfriend Project helped students, including those with special needs, link online with older people in nursing homes or retirement communities. The elders mentored the teens, while the teens provided stimulating youthful companionship. "Silver [Web] surfers and high-school students exchanged e-mails," and most were extremely enthusiastic about the project, wrote teacher Martin Kimeldorf, who directed the project.[6]

Some websites link volunteers with service projects that need help. At San Francisco-based Sparked.com, for example, nonprofit service organizations post "challenges," or projects where added assistance and expertise are needed. For example, Cincinnati's Ronald McDonald House — which houses families of sick children during hospitalizations — used the site to find Arabic translators for its written materials, while Chimpanzee Sanctuary Northwest found computer experts to help figure out how to prevent hacks of its website.[7]

For volunteers who can't travel, some websites post do-at-home opportunities. The Extraordinaries, another San Francisco-based website, developed a mobile phone app

Does community service lead to greater civic engagement?

Supporters of volunteerism argue that community work encourages people to become more willing to help others and to fulfill civic duties such as voting later in life. The jury is out on how effectively service programs accomplish those goals, however. Researchers report that some programs appear very effective while others don't lead to long-term improvement in community engagement.

that alerts users to small volunteer tasks that can be "completed in small snatches of time," wrote Mike Bright, founder of a British microvolunteering site, Help from Home. Microvolunteering "invites quick actions" such as signing up to donate your hair for wigs for sick children suffering from hair loss, making a "micro loan" to someone in a developing country, signing an online petition, or counting plants or birds in your back yard for a biodiversity project. Evidence is accumulating that microvolunteers can make "meaningful contributions," Bright wrote.[8]

Others aren't so sure. "My favorite pet peeve at the moment is . . . the notion that you can volunteer spontaneously via your cell phone for tiny periods of time — saving the world in 10-second intervals," wrote Steve McCurley, editor of the online journal *e-Volunteerism*. "It's an idea that is emotionally endearing and intellectually absurd."[9]

Other trends attract similar criticism. For example, some analysts worry that a shallow view of service may arise from high-profile volunteerism-related activities such as "sporting colorful empathy ribbons" or forwarding social-media messages — such as Twitter posts calling attention to a dangerous disease or environmental threat. "It's legitimate to worry that public displays of emotion run the danger of diverting people from a more complex message . . . or course of action," wrote *e-Volunteerism* Editor-in-Chief Susan J. Ellis.[10]

Nevertheless, wrote Ellis, even such shallow service participation presents an opportunity. "Public outpourings of emotion imply reservoirs of desire to affiliate and make a difference," and service organizations and longtime volunteers could help to turn ribbon-wearers and message-forwarders into active volunteers, said Ellis.[11]

— *Marcia Clemmitt*

Teenagers Cranston Mitchell and Amelia Hampton assemble parts for a water filtration system for use in Senegal last June. Eight students from Kalamazoo, Mich., spent 15 days in the West African nation last year doing community service as part of the Urban Youth for Africa program sponsored by the Kalamazoo Deacon's Conference.

[4]For background, see Earthwatch Institute, www.earthwatch.org.

[5]Quoted in "The Growth of Voluntourism," *op. cit.*

[6]Martin Kimeldorf, "Wiring Friendships Across Time, Space, and Age: An Evaluation of Intergenerational Friendships Created Online," *e-Volunteerism*, October 2001, www.e-volunteerism.com/quarterly/01fall/kimmeldorf.

[7]Kivi Leroux Miller, "Microvolunteering: Small Jobs on Your Own Time," *Kivi's Nonprofit Marketing Guide blog*, June 22, 2011, www.nonprofitmarketingguide.com/blog/2011/06/22/microvolunteering-small-jobs-on-your-own-time-mds11.

[8]Mike Bright, "Micro-Volunteering: Quickies, Quandaries and Questions," *e-Volunteerism*, October 2010, www.e-volunteerism.com/volume-xi-issue-1-october-2010/feature-articles/812.

[9]Steve McCurley, "Reflections on a Decade of e-Volunteerism," *e-Volunteerism*, October 2009, www.e-volunteerism.com/quarterly/09oct/09oct-points.

[10]Susan J. Ellis and Steve McCurley, "Public vs. Private Compassion: Colored Ribbons, T-shirts and SUVs," *e-Volunteerism*, April 2004, www.e-volunteerism.com/quarterly/04apr/04apr-points.

[11]*Ibid.*

[1]Beth Gazley, "Volunteer Vacationers and What Research Can Tell Us About Them," *e-Volunteerism*, January 2001, www.e-volunteerism.com/quarterly/01win/facintro.

[2]*Ibid.*

[3]Quoted in "The Growth of Voluntourism," *e-Volunteerism*, July 2007.

History provides strong evidence that at least some volunteer experiences — notably on behalf of a political cause, such as civil rights — can spur young people to remain socially engaged, says Youniss of Catholic University. "Young people who were involved in the civil rights movement" as well as Vietnam-era anti-war activities are "still very much engaged" in community life today, and even their children show high degrees of civic engagement, he says. "It's very clear that activism on behalf of these justice causes remains" with people throughout life.

Youniss sees two main reasons for the long-lasting effects. Civil rights and anti-war activists "were very effective" and thus saw the fruits of their labors in society, which likely encouraged them to remain engaged, he says. Furthermore, young civil rights volunteers saw themselves as part of a historical tradition stretching back centuries. This gave them a sense of belonging and a feeling that their work had meaning beyond themselves, both factors that encourage continued involvement in community causes, Youniss says. Civil rights volunteers "saw themselves as jumping into history to participate in the abolition movement" against slavery that dated back 200 years.

In fact, simply belonging to any group in which service is the norm can lead to a longer-term interest in volunteering, even when the group's main function isn't service, says Musick. For example, at UT, Austin, and on other campuses where "students volunteer in groups," often through fraternities and sororities, the phenomenon "creates a little culture of volunteering that's self-reinforcing" and encourages future involvement, he says.

Similarly, church-related service is fostered not just by religious principles but by the notion of "fellowship — getting together with other believers" to serve, Musick says. "To get civic engagement, you need structures like this — situations where, if you're not volunteering, you're left out," he says.

Many advocates of service-learning courses argue that volunteering frequently brings students into contact with people from very different backgrounds and circumstances than their own, which can spur civic engagement by broadening students' understanding of the world and its problems.

"Our students are more privileged, and when they go into inner-city schools and students begin to talk to them, the takeaway is, 'Those kids have the same dreams I did, but they have challenges in their lives that I hadn't even imagined,' " says Sandra Enos, an associate professor of sociology at Bryant University, in Smithfield, R.I. "They get into conversations that disrupt their thinking" and, usually for the first time, learn things from experience without the learning being "mediated" by parents, teachers or textbooks, she says. Students regularly report that "their parents kept them in a bubble" that a service experience has broken.

However, many scholars say that while there's good evidence that some volunteer programs increase the likelihood of long-term civic engagement, others don't.

"There's no evidence that anything happens, that anything takes" when students participate in volunteer programs that don't help them think about the underlying causes of community problems they observe or don't encourage them to see themselves as part of a solution, says Youniss.

"There's nothing wrong with going to a soup kitchen to help out, but it won't have a long-lasting effect on you" if "you just end up thinking of yourself as a sweet, little individual do-gooder," Youniss says. Only students who actively think about the issues their service raises and see those issues in a historical and philosophical perspective are likely to parlay service into long-term community engagement, he says. Often, that deeper perspective grows out of volunteering with a group that holds certain beliefs about social problems, such as a church or environmental organization, Youniss notes.

"People think of service as an individual action that by itself can somehow modify something inside a kid's head" to increase his or her civic-mindedness, says Youniss. "But that's not it." Change in future behavior comes only when a young volunteer is induced to consider volunteering as part of some larger vision of society and one's place in it, he says.

For example, if a young person in the mid-Atlantic region gets involved with one of the "hundreds of local and regional conservation organizations that have strong philosophies of protecting the environment" of the Chesapeake Bay, volunteering with the group "provides values education" and makes the student see himself or herself "as an actor in a larger story," he says. It's by "working your way into some civic tradition" rather than just engaging in individual "character-building activities" that long-term civic commitment is fostered, says Youniss.

"Focusing on trying to solve a particular problem, seeing that problem in a historical perspective" and, often, working with long-standing, service-oriented groups "who have a ready-made identity and offer a part that the kid can play" are the key elements of programs that change behavior in the long run, he says.

Should students be required to perform community service?

Over the past two decades, school districts around the country — including the entire Maryland system — have added community service as a high school graduation requirement. Critics argue that the requirements are a burden and disliked by so many students that they may decrease interest in volunteering later in life. Some studies find, however, that similarly structured service programs — whether voluntary or required — have basically the same effect on most students.

Students who face service requirements often approach the jobs halfheartedly and may become turned off to service altogether, some college students told University of Maryland researchers in a 2008 study. The "bad side" of a requirement is that it "reduces feelings of being altruistic, kind and loving, because it is seen as just a mandate that I'll just get done and it will be over with," said one. "This cuts down motivation to want to go out and help others."[4]

Requirement supporters argue that "everyone born owes a debt to society," said Barbara Moralis, a librarian whose son attended high school in Bethlehem, Pa., which instituted a requirement in 1990. But "I don't think it's up to government to decide who owes a debt and how it should be paid." Mandates are "spreading like a cancer. Someone has to stand up for an American's right to freedom," Moralis said.[5]

Requirements sour some but not all students on service, according to a study by scholars from the University of Northern Colorado and two other colleges. Specifically, students who were inclined to volunteer before they faced a requirement still said, after completing the service, that they were open to volunteering in the future. Students who originally were "less inclined to volunteer of their own free will" and who felt they were "being controlled" by the requirement, however, told researchers that the mandate made them even less likely to volunteer in the future.[6]

"I'm not in favor of community service for everyone," says Tulane's Ilustre. When schools require a certain number of service hours for graduation, "I think it's too easy for volunteering to lose its flavor and turn people off against service" and, potentially, against community engagement generally, he says. "I don't like it when

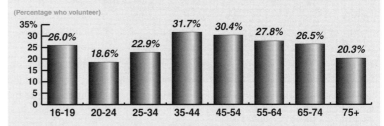

Older Americans Volunteer Most

Nearly one-third of Americans between ages 35 and 54 — the highest rate — participate in volunteer activities. Youths ages 16-19 are in the next-highest participation bracket, along with people from 54 to 74. Young adults ages 20-24 have the lowest volunteerism rate.

Volunteer Rates by Age Group, 2008-2010

(Percentage who volunteer)

Age group	Percentage
16-19	26.0%
20-24	18.6%
25-34	22.9%
35-44	31.7%
45-54	30.4%
55-64	27.8%
65-74	26.5%
75+	20.3%

Source: "Volunteering in the U.S.," Corporation for National and Community Service, August 2011, www.volunteeringinamerica.gov/national

universities penalize students with service hours," for example. "That's penalizing the community as well by sending them students who don't want to be there." Volunteering "should be done by those who want to do it," Ilustre says.

Even though Ilustre runs the office that manages student placements under Tulane's mandatory service program, he says he sees no conflict between his job and his opposition to requirements elsewhere. For one thing, he says, many if not most Tulane students actually choose the school because of its commitment to community involvement. And, most important, service to fulfill requirements is always tightly linked to students' own curricular interests. For example, a Tulane student taking pre-med courses to prepare for a career in cancer medicine will get a volunteer placement in a hospital oncology department, doing work that's closely tied to classwork.

Some researchers find that required or voluntary service can turn students into more engaged citizens.

In research comparing two groups of college-bound high school students in Ontario, Canada — one that attended before service was required for graduation and one afterward — scholars at Wilfrid Laurier University, in Waterloo, Ontario, found that mandating service is beneficial for the community because it "draws students into the volunteer sector who probably would not go there if not required to do so." Furthermore, the

Student volunteers clear debris around a tornado-damaged apartment complex in Joplin, Mo., on July 30, 2011. A twister that hit the city on May 22 killed more than 150 people and destroyed some 7,500 homes. Nationwide, volunteer rates among youths ages 16 to 19 soared from 13.4 percent to 24.5 percent between 1989 and 2007, largely because a rising number of high schools sponsor or require service.

study of more than 1,200 students concluded that even those who said their personal experience wasn't very rewarding still ended up holding "mandatory volunteering in high regard" as a way to create more "engaged citizens."[7]

Another study by the Wilfrid Laurier researchers found that, at least in the short term, most "students who were mandated to perform community service exhibit the same attitudes and perspectives about community engagement as those who" didn't face a requirement. "Requiring community service . . . does not detract from" young people's "motivation to volunteer in the future," and the quality of the service experience is likely a much more important determinant of young people's attitudes toward volunteering than is the mandated or non-mandated nature of the experience," the Canadian analysts said.[8]

Are more young people volunteering today?

School and government programs have led to steep increases over the past two decades in the number of young people who volunteer. But there is a significant socioeconomic divide in volunteering, with high rates concentrated among certain groups, such as college-bound high school students. Community-service participation remains low among people in their early 20s.

The volunteer rate among people ages 16 to 19 soared from 13.4 percent to 24.5 percent between 1989 and 2007, according to the Corporation for National and Community Service.[9]

Service learning — courses that require students to do a service project and analyze the experience in the light of ideas studied in class — continues to rise around the country. Between 2008 and 2010, for example, the average number of service-learning courses offered per campus rose from 43 to 64 among colleges that responded to a survey by the college service consortium Campus Compact.[10]

Furthermore, more young people heading for college and graduate school are adding volunteer activities to their résumés, says Musick of UT. Many more people attend college today than in past decades, but because selective schools aren't significantly expanding their enrollments applicants must try harder than ever to gain an edge over the competition, he points out. Volunteering is one way to do that, he says.

But Musick cautions that the way colleges count volunteerism in admission decisions can lead to inequities between wealthy and low-income students.

"I look at these kids' résumés and see that some are doing an enormous amount of volunteering," he says. "But colleges have to be very careful" about how they compare students' records in this regard because many impressive-sounding volunteer opportunities are available for students who don't have to help out at home or take paying jobs to cover their school costs, says Musick. "If a kid lists going abroad to build clinics, it's likely that his or her family has paid for this," making it unfair to count it much in the student's favor because it's an opportunity that isn't available to most applicants, he says.

While volunteering rates among older teens have soared over the past two decades, a longer historical look reveals that recent rates, hovering around 24 percent, aren't much higher than they were decades ago. That's because between the mid-1970s and late 1980s teen community-service rates dropped substantially, from 20.9 percent in 1974 to 13.4 percent in 1989. That decline helped spur the recent rise in school community-service programs.[11]

The dropoff raised concerns that schools were not turning out graduates who were likely to be involved in their communities or fulfill civic responsibilities, such as voting, when they became adults. What's more, Lenkowsky of Indiana University says concerns grew that laissez-faire policies promulgated during the administration of President Ronald Reagan (1981-89) "were causing people to grow too self-interested." Those worries fueled establishment of programs to build a new spirit of service among American students, he says.

And while young volunteers showed the greatest percentage gain since 1989, young people still lag behind their parents when it comes to volunteering. The proportion of 16- to 19-year-olds performing service remained lower in 2007 than among the baby-boom generation born between 1946 and 1964, whose volunteer rates grew from 24.1 percent in 1989 to 29.9 percent in 2007. Among those over 65, the volunteering rate rose from 16.9 percent to 23.8 percent from 1989 to 2007.[12]

In 2010, people in their early 20s volunteered at the lowest rate — 18.4 percent — while 35- to 44-year-olds volunteered at the highest rate — 32.2 percent — according to the U.S. Bureau of Labor Statistics.[13] The rate for people ages 16 to 24 hovered around 22 percent between 2006 and 2010, the lowest of any age group and well below the average volunteer rate for all people age 16 and over, which was about 27 percent.[14]

Low volunteering rates among the older part of the 16-24 age group account for the low overall rate in that segment of the population, says Lenkowsky. "We have data showing that over 90 percent of college-bound high school students" perform some kind of service, but the 18- to 24-year-old contingent "has the lowest rates of any age group" for several reasons, Lenkowsky says.

Students in that age group who are enrolled in selective colleges have high service rates, around 50 percent in some cases, he says. But very low rates of volunteering prevail among "many who aren't going to college and thus are less engaged" in the community. Meanwhile, 20-somethings who are just out of college or who didn't attend are busy with the "Sex and the City" scene — socializing and looking for jobs and careers — and thus have very low community-service rates, Lenkowsky says. Beginning around age 25, volunteer rates increase as people settle into jobs, have families and become more settled members of their communities, he says.

Furthermore, the country "is very stratified" when it comes to volunteerism opportunities for young people, says UT's Musick. Volunteering among college students and college-bound high school students is at high levels, but "there's too much tendency to focus on these populations," which inflates the overall picture of whether volunteering is actually becoming more prevalent in our society, Musick says.

Based on his extensive study of factors that lead to volunteering, Musick says, even though rates have risen at selective colleges and among college-bound high-school students, "in the rest of the population, I'll bet it hasn't changed very much." Churches are the main center of American volunteering, "and are they fundamentally changing in ways that would lead to more volunteering? No."

BACKGROUND
Volunteers of America

From volunteer firefighting to street-cleaning brigades, grassroots voluntary efforts to serve and improve communities date back to America's earliest history. Starting in the mid-20th century, however, the federal government, schools and colleges began establishing formal volunteerism programs, sometimes integrated into class work, as education theorists found that real-life work enhanced learning.[15]

In 1736, young men in Philadelphia signed up for the first American volunteer firefighting company, founded by Benjamin Franklin. In the early 1800s, a Protestant religious revival in the United States known as the Second Great Awakening spurred many young people to work for the abolition of slavery and for the temperance movement to discourage drunkenness. In the early 19th century, juvenile anti-slavery societies collected signatures of teens and children on petitions they forwarded to Congress, urging lawmakers to abolish slavery.

In New York City in 1915, 25,000 children in neighborhood groups picked up litter, reported overflowing trash cans and urged adults to keep communities tidy. In the 1920s, the National Safety Council — a nonprofit group founded by volunteers in 1915 to tackle safety issues — helped students form school-based committees to study safety hazards and propose solutions.[16]

Beginning in the 1920s, volunteers conceived of and built the Appalachian Trail — the wilderness pathway for hikers that spans the mountain ranges of the East Coast. And in 1954, Philadelphia volunteers opened the first U.S. Meals on Wheels programs — begun in Britain in 1939 — to deliver food to homebound people; the initiative soon spread nationwide, with high school and college students making many of the deliveries.

During emergencies such as wars and natural disasters, many children and teens helped out because adults were busy elsewhere. During the Civil War, child volunteers sewed bandages and bedding for soldiers and collected money to buy them food. During World War II, the city of Chicago established 30,000 small plots in parks where fifth- through eighth-graders cultivated "victory gardens" to boost the nation's food supply. Communities around the country followed suit.[17]

American membership organizations, such as the business-networking group Kiwanis, founded in 1915 in Detroit, routinely included volunteer service as a top activity, "and many had youth auxiliaries," says Catholic University's Youniss.

The Great Depression of the 1930s saw students as well as adults volunteer in soup kitchens and breadlines for the jobless and homeless, says Youniss. "The thought was that if you were well enough off to be in school, then you should help" those in greater need.

The 1930s Civilian Conservation Corps (CCC), established by President Franklin D. Roosevelt, provided work and a small stipend for young men who couldn't find other jobs. The program was the first in a long line of government service projects for young people that have offered stipends. Others include today's AmeriCorps and Teach for America programs. Despite its modest pay, mainly sent home to the young men's families, the CCC was widely viewed as a volunteer program because the work benefited the community rather than private interests.

Beginning in the 1960s, some policymakers' interest grew in government-sponsored volunteerism. Government service programs have had two main goals, says Indiana University's Lenkowsky. "One is to get more people involved in working on society's problems," and the other "to encourage a lifetime of civic engagement."

In 1961 President John F. Kennedy proposed and Congress approved establishment of the Peace Corps. The goal was to place volunteers of all ages — although mainly young adults — in less industrialized countries, to help with community-development projects and spread goodwill for the United States; volunteers received modest stipends.[18]

In 1964, as part of his War on Poverty, President Lyndon B. Johnson created VISTA — Volunteers in Service to America — which placed volunteers in community organizations to help educate and train low-income people. VISTA workers got a modest living stipend and either a small cash payment or an education grant after a year's service.

Individual programs came and went, but presidents Richard M. Nixon (Republican, 1969-1974), Jimmy Carter (Democrat, 1977-1981) and George H. W. Bush (Republican, 1989-1993) all supported and worked to maintain at least some federal role in youth volunteerism.

In 1993, Democratic President Bill Clinton created AmeriCorps — which places young people in community-based nonprofit organizations to help with education, health, environmental and other projects — and the Corporation for National and Community Service to manage government volunteerism efforts.

During the Clinton years, however, Republican lawmakers increasingly argued that public-sector activity was damaging in arenas where private-sector initiatives existed.

"The program distorts the true sense of volunteerism and perpetuates the notion that the solution to every problem is just one big-government program away," said Rep. Todd Tiahrt, R-Kan., pitching repeal of AmeriCorps in 1997.[19]

AmeriCorps won more Republican friends in the late 1990s and 2000s, however. Sen. John McCain, R-Ariz., who had voted against establishing the program in 1993, said in January 2000 that "overall, the program has been a success. And it was a failure on my part not to recognize that earlier."[20]

To the surprise of some, when Republican President George W. Bush took office in 2001, he urged every American to devote 4,000 hours over a lifetime to community service and won substantial conservative backing for doubling Peace Corps membership and increasing AmeriCorps membership by 50 percent. At Bush's urging, Congress increased funding for both programs, although Peace Corps funds fell short of Bush's goal.[21]

C H R O N O L O G Y

1700s-1910s *Americans form volunteer groups to tackle social problems from disease to drunkenness.*

1736 Benjamin Franklin enlists young Philadelphia men as the first American volunteer firefighters.

1835 In his classic book *Democracy in America*, French historian Alexis de Tocqueville reports on Americans' many voluntary groups promoting "public safety, commerce, industry, morality and religion."

1916 In *Democracy and Education*, American philosopher John Dewey argues that children's minds are formed only in the context of their experiences in society.

1930s-1970s *Beginning in the Great Depression, the federal government creates community-service programs.*

1933 President Franklin D. Roosevelt creates the Civilian Conservation Corps, in which young unemployed men get modest stipends to restore public lands.

1961 President John F. Kennedy establishes the Peace Corps.

1964 President Lyndon B. Johnson establishes domestic volunteer programs, including VISTA, Job Corps, Neighborhood Youth Corps and the Teacher Corps.

1971 White House Conference on Youth calls for schools to link studies to community service.

1979 Volunteer rate among 16- to 19-year-olds is 20.9 percent.

1980s-1990s *As young people's volunteering rates drop, colleges, schools and the federal government seek ways to encourage community service.*

1985 The presidents of Brown, Georgetown and Stanford universities promote community service.

1989 Volunteer rate for 16- to 19-year-olds hits a low of 13.4 percent.

1990 National Service Act authorizes funds for independent Points of Lights Foundation, proposed by President George H. W. Bush, to encourage volunteerism.

1992 Democratic presidential candidate Bill Clinton promises to create a young people's service corps and give college aid to anyone serving for at least a year.

1993 Congress enacts AmeriCorps, as proposed by President Clinton. . . . Federal appeals court declares that schools may require community service for graduation (*Steirer v. Bethlehem Area School District*).

1994 Led by House Speaker Newt Gingrich, R-Ga., congressional Republicans begin an unsuccessful multiyear campaign to end AmeriCorps.

1996 Two more federal appeals courts rule that service requirements don't violate students' constitutional rights.

2000s *Volunteer service becomes a standard feature of high school and college life.*

2005 After Hurricane Katrina, volunteers clear debris and begin rebuilding New Orleans.

2007 Volunteer rate for 16- to 19-year-olds rises to 24.5 percent.

2009 President Barack Obama signs a law to triple AmeriCorps in eight years.

2010 People ages 20 to 24 continue to have the lowest volunteer rate.

2011 Congressional Republicans vote to phase out AmeriCorps, but Senate Democrats block the move. . . . House Education and the Workforce Committee warns AmeriCorps against politicization after some volunteers are found to have worked in advocacy positions for Planned Parenthood. . . . AmeriCorps volunteers perform energy audits to aid conservation in Iowa and help police in Albany, N.Y., collect information from neighbors about a crime wave.

2012 White House says summer jobs program for disadvantaged youth will include 4,000 AmeriCorps positions.

Volunteer Programs Lacking for Low-Income Kids

"It's not because adolescents aren't interested."

Volunteer opportunities are much scarcer for students from low-income families than for those from wealthy backgrounds — a problem that can have life-long impacts, including low participation in voting and other civic engagement, scholars say.

"There is a huge socioeconomic gap" in service opportunities, as there is for most other educational opportunities, says James Youniss, a research professor of psychology at Catholic University, in Washington.

"If a school has low-income students or many immigrants," for example, "it's less likely to have" programs known to improve students' civic involvement, including service-learning programs that link classroom work with volunteer opportunities, Youniss says. It's well known — and often lamented — that poor people generally vote at lower rates than better-off people, and fewer opportunities to build civic engagement during youth are partly to blame, he says.

Robert Atkins, an associate professor of nursing and childhood studies at Rutgers University, runs STARR, a multi-faceted youth-development program for teens in Camden, N.J., which consistently ranks among the nation's poorest cities. In 2009, for example, 36 percent of residents lived below the poverty level and 18 percent of those had incomes 50 percent or more below the poverty threshold.[1]

The gulf between volunteerism opportunities for low-income and middle- and upper-income students mirrors many other socioeconomic gaps in society, such as health-care access, Atkins says.

Volunteerism among low-income young people isn't rare "because adolescents aren't interested," Atkins says. His program, which he launched in 1995, includes various service opportunities that "the kids love," he says.

For example, "we deliver turkey baskets" each Thanksgiving to needy families, Atkins continues. A church donates a room, "and the adolescents put the baskets together," then "we sit in the car while they go to the door and say, 'Happy Thanksgiving.' It's great for them, and they love doing the turkey baskets. They're often the recipients of giving, so the opportunity to give themselves" is rare.

Other activities have included tree planting, voter-registration drives and walkathons for causes such as the immune-system disease lupus. "They don't know in advance that they're going to love doing these things," Atkins says. "But once they do it, they volunteer to do it again. And it's very good for the communities they're part of" because it gives everyone a different view of the teens, he says.

A low ratio of adults to young people in low-income areas is one of the biggest obstacles to improving the rate of

University Service

Around the turn of the 20th century, some American philosophers theorized that real-world experience integrated into schooling would improve learning and society. John Dewey (1859-1952), a professor of psychology and philosophy at the University of Chicago and Columbia University, developed the theory that lies behind many of today's university programs. "All genuine education comes about through experience" that the learner then reflects on, Dewey wrote.[22] When education fosters "membership within . . . a little community, saturating" students "with the spirit of service, . . . we shall have the deepest and best

guarantee of a larger society which is worthy, lovely and harmonious."[23]

These ideas percolated in the education community throughout the 20th century. A follow-up report to a 1971 White House Conference on Youth, for example, recommended that schools and colleges utilize the service-learning link to improve education.

But the movement among campuses to foster student service really took off in the 1980s, says Enos, of Bryant University. At the time, social analysts had christened the current generation of students the "Me Generation," focused on furthering careers and making money and unconcerned with being good citizens and youth volunteering in poverty-stricken neighborhoods, Atkins says. "There are just simply fewer adults to pitch in and help" kids get involved, he says.

Atkins says low-income urban communities tend to be "child-saturated," with 30 to 40 percent of the population under age 18, making a ratio of only about two adults per child, compared to three in middle-income towns such as nearby Cherry Hill, where Atkins lives.

The high ratio of children to adults also "makes the kids seem more like a problem to be dealt with and kept out of trouble," not "a resource that could do some service," he adds. As a result, communities are more likely to organize activities they hope will keep teens off the street, such as "midnight basketball leagues," and less likely to come up with ideas for adolescents to perform community service.

"There's been a national effort to get kids more engaged, but I'm not sure if that can trickle down to Camden," says Atkins. "Instead of helping these kids get involved in actively doing things, people are more likely to talk to them about what not to do, such as avoiding pregnancy."

Adults in low-income neighborhoods generally "are less educated, and they're working a lot. And . . . many don't have any volunteering experience of their own" to draw on, he says.

Urban adults also tend to be younger, and many have young children of their own. Older adults are more likely to have the time and ability to engage in volunteer work and help out youngsters, Atkins says. Younger adults also "have less confidence in their ability to structure these opportunities," and if adults aren't there to provide the foundation, "it's not surprising that it doesn't happen."

Atkins is pushing one potential solution: "micro" projects serving perhaps a dozen kids rather than hundreds.

Tree planting draws eager volunteers from the STARR program at Rutgers University's campus in Camden, N.J. STARR President Robert Atkins is at right.

"You don't need to build a big community center but just get individuals who are interested in something" — participating in the arts or fixing up a local park, for example — and encourage adults "to find a way to share that interest with some kids," he says.

— *Marcia Clemmitt*

---

[1] "Camden, New Jersey, Poverty Rate Data — Information About Poor and Low-Income Residents," City-Data website, www.city-data.com/poverty/poverty-Camden-New-Jersey.html.

---

neighbors. In response, new organizations emerged to promote service.[24]

Notably, in 1985, the presidents of Stanford, Brown and Georgetown universities joined the president of the Education Commission of the States — an information-exchange forum consisting of the governments of 49 states, three territories and the District of Columbia — to form Campus Compact, a group that would help colleges develop systems to foster student service. As of 2011, more than 1,100 colleges and universities are members.[25]

"The most important thing an institution does is not to prepare a student for a career but for life as a citizen,"

said Campus Compact co-founder Frank Newman, former president of the University of Rhode Island.[26]

Initially, Campus Compact mainly helped schools establish extracurricular service programs, but around 1990 the group began to focus on integrating volunteer work into academic courses —"service learning," wrote Enos.[27] Also in 1990, President George H. W. Bush signed into law Serve America — now called Learn and Serve America, a federal grant program to establish service learning on campuses.

As usually defined, "service learning" means incorporating service, such as working in a homeless shelter, into a class in a subject such as urban policy. But service done without a class tie-in also may fall under the definition if

Habitat for Humanity/Stefan Hacker

Students from the Habitat for Humanity campus chapter at the University of Wisconsin, Madison, spent their week-long spring break building houses in Miami as part of Habitat's Collegiate Challenge program for high school and college volunteers.

students are required to analyze the service by, for example, writing about it. Some schools, such as Kentucky's Berea College, have decades-long service-learning traditions, and in the 1990s the idea spread nationwide.

Today, 89 percent of colleges and universities sponsor service learning, says the University of Minnesota's Furco. Key to successful programs is integrating service into academic goals, he says. For example, tutoring might be good service experience in a math class if "one of a professor's learning objectives for students is how to communicate technical information so that it can be understood by lay people."

"The knowledge from the class informs what students do in the community, and what they do in the community makes information come alive in class," providing specific examples "to illuminate general concepts being studied," says Roosevelt University's Meyers.

But creating service-learning experiences that benefit both students and the community is difficult, many analysts say.

Some programs mainly provide good publicity for the school and résumé padding for students without meeting community needs, charged John W. Eby, a professor of sociology at Messiah College in Grantham, Pa.[28] For example, a semester's worth of course-related service may encourage a potentially harmful habit among young volunteers: pursuing service on a given issue only briefly, wrote Eby. Short-term service "has potential to do actual

harm to individuals," especially children who become attached to a young volunteer who disappears a few months later, he wrote.

Schools and Service

Beginning in the late 1980s, interest in service learning, along with general volunteerism, increased in high schools and even in some middle and elementary schools. A sharp drop-off in teen volunteering between the early 1970s and the late 1980s sparked the interest.

In 1979, 92 percent of high schools reported making some extracurricular community-service options available to students, mostly informally, but only 15 percent offered service learning. By 1999, though, 83 percent of high schools offered service opportunities, many actually required it, and 46 percent offered some service learning.[29]

In the 2000s, volunteer programs, including requirements, persist in schools but service learning has been decreasing. In the 2003-04 school year, 44 percent of high schools offered service learning, but by 2008 only 35 percent did. Budget cuts and the need to prepare students for high-stakes standardized tests may explain the decrease. In a 1999 government study, almost all principals whose schools offered service learning said the programs helped the community and promoted altruism, but only 12 percent said they helped with academics and only 19 percent said they taught critical thinking.[30]

California, Vermont and Wisconsin no longer put many resources into what were strong public school service-learning programs several years ago, and Florida's may be the only remaining volunteerism effort that truly weaves service and learning goals together, says the University of Minnesota's Furco.

In the 1990s, students brought three major lawsuits claiming that service requirements are unconstitutional. Federal courts decided all three in the schools' favor.

In a 1993 decision in *Steirer v. Bethlehem Area* [Pennsylvania] *School District*, the Third U.S. Circuit Court of Appeals rejected the argument that a district's 60-hour service requirement amounted to "involuntary servitude," banned under the 13th Amendment outlawing slavery. The amendment bans "forced labor through physical coercion," not service that is "primarily designed for the students' own benefit and education"

Service-Learning Programs Aid Students, Nonprofits

Linking schoolwork and volunteerism is biggest challenge.

Service-learning programs, which tie students' volunteer work to their academic studies, are growing in popularity on college campuses, but they can be challenging to set up and administer effectively.

Schools must help both the students and the service organizations where they volunteer to understand what to expect from one another, says Vincent Ilustre, executive director of the Center for Public Service at Tulane University, in New Orleans.

On the volunteer end, "we encourage students to find something they love and stick to it, because we don't want the nonprofits to have to keep training new people," Ilustre says. Then "we need to educate the community about what these students can do," a challenge that generally requires a dedicated campus office, Ilustre and other experts say.

At Tulane, "I look at our community partners not just in terms of placement but as partners in educating our students," Ilustre says. "We run workshops that allow the community to understand the students, the university calendar" and so on.

Tulane has 420 nonprofits in its database, but with 1,200 to 1,500 students participating per semester, about two-thirds of the organizations won't get a placement at any given time, says Ilustre. To keep local organizations involved, the university provides workshops on topics such as nonprofit fundraising and budgeting.

Steven Meyers, a professor of psychology and social justice at Roosevelt University, in Chicago, says service-learning programs are most successful when they are "promoted by a university office that supports them" using "an up-to-date, well-vetted database of suitable programs for professors to use."

"It's unreasonable to expect" individual professors to delve into the community to find service-learning opportunities unaided, Meyers says.

Developing service projects that both serve the community and advance learning goals is a challenge for nonprofits as well as faculty.

Different schools and courses can take different approaches to doing this, says Sandra Enos, an associate professor of sociology at Bryant University, in Smithfield, R.I. Bryant, which began as a business school but recently added liberal-arts majors, generally favors projects in which students make specific, practical use of their class work, Enos says. For example, students might work with a community "client" to make the organization's marketing message more effective. Or students might help a school enhance the math-readiness of its kindergarteners.

For service learning to be effective, students must analyze their experiences and tie them to material they learn in class, says James Youniss, a research professor of psychology at Catholic University, in Washington.

"Discussions are a very effective tool" for fostering such learning, he says. For example, high-school students who volunteer in a daycare center should afterward be encouraged to discuss such issues as whether a pregnant 16-year-old should get a job, be allowed to go on welfare or be given an incentive to finish her education, he says.

Course-based service learning can work across the curriculum, says Meyers. For example, he describes an English composition course in which students worked with an anti-domestic-violence group, interviewed workers and then developed an effective way to write and post a blog to help inform people how to cope with domestic violence.

— Marcia Clemmitt

---

by teaching them about the value of community work, said the court.[31]

While battles over service requirements grab headlines, researchers say the more important question is whether programs are well managed.

For example, "the state of Maryland has this crazy 74-hour requirement" of service for graduation, "but they don't want to put resources into it," so that the quality of individual programs is all over the map, says Catholic University's Youniss. Furthermore, it's not even

City Year volunteer Daniel Curme clears brush on a trail in Seattle on Oct. 7, 2011. The education-focused organization partners with public schools to provide full-time intervention for at-risk students.

clear that such large programs are feasible, Youniss says. If every Maryland senior were to participate even in the most well-structured service programs, "organizations in the state couldn't absorb them all," he says.

AmeriCorps Questioned

Soon after Barack Obama took office in 2009, conservative opposition to AmeriCorps began building again.

Midway through 2009, his first year in office, Obama raised congressional eyebrows when he abruptly fired AmeriCorps' Inspector General Gerald Walpin. Inspectors general are government officials appointed to be independent watchdogs over federal programs. The administration said that the then-77-year-old Walpin had been "confused, disoriented" and "unable to answer questions" at a Corporation for National and Community Service board meeting, raising doubts about "his capacity to serve."[32]

Walpin argued that he was fired because he'd stated that an Obama supporter, Kevin Johnson, now mayor of

Sacramento, Calif., had misused AmeriCorps grants at his nonprofit community-development agency, St. HOPE.[33]

"While firing an investigator who uncovered the abuse of funds by a political ally might be considered an act of 'political courage' in Chicago politics, for most Americans it raises troubling questions," said Rep. Darrell Issa, R-Calif., chairman of the House Committee on Oversight and Government Reform.[34] (In November 2009, however, a Republican inquiry failed to find evidence that Walpin's dismissal was politically motivated.[35] In January 2011, a federal appeals court ruled against Walpin in a lawsuit he filed claiming wrongful firing.)[36]

Also in 2009, Obama signed a bill passed by the Democratic-led Congress to triple AmeriCorps' size in eight years.[37]

But AmeriCorps remains controversial, especially among staunch conservatives. As AmeriCorps expands, "there is a very strong chance that we will see that young people will be put into mandatory service," said Rep. Michele Bachmann, R-Minn., who campaigned unsuccessfully for the Republican presidential nomination. "There are provisions for what I would call re-education camps . . . where young people have to go and get trained in a philosophy that the government puts forward," she said.[38]

CURRENT SITUATION
Federal Phaseout?

The Republican-led House of Representatives is pushing to phase out AmeriCorps, arguing that the program wastes public money to accomplish community service that the private sector would effectively and willingly handle on its own.

In 2011 the House Appropriations Committee proposed cutting funding by about 70 percent, leaving money to support the National Senior Volunteer Program but gradually eliminating young-adult programs. Appropriators in the Democratic-led Senate, however, forced a compromise that resulted in only a minimal funding cut — about 2 percent — for the Corporation for National and Community Service.[39]

Allegations continue to surface of left-wing politicization of AmeriCorps and were the subject of a June 2011 hearing in the House. Lawmakers queried Robert

Should AmeriCorps be eliminated?

YES
Doug Bandow
Senior Fellow, Cato Institute

NO
Shirley Sagawa
Visiting Fellow, Center for American Progress; founding managing director, Corporation for National and Community Service

Written for *CQ Researcher*, January 2012

Americans always have organized to help their neighbors. The government should stop paying for service through AmeriCorps. The budget crisis is reason enough to terminate AmeriCorps — and even the Corporation for National and Community Service, which oversees AmeriCorps.

Washington has funded many service, training and "volunteer" initiatives, which usually achieve some good but also plenty of bad. Journalist Jim Bovard has documented political abuse, waste and low priority work at AmeriCorps. Inexplicably, the Obama administration fired the corporation's inspector general while Congress cut funding for his office.

Waste and inefficiency are inevitable because free labor will be treated like a free good. But even seemingly productive jobs won't necessarily produce significant social benefits.

The critical question is not the cost-benefit ratio but the opportunity cost of AmeriCorps funding. Could the resources be better spent elsewhere? There is no reason to believe that a dollar for "national service" yields more good than an additional dollar spent on medical research or business investment.

Indeed, service comes in many forms. Being paid by Uncle Sam to shelve books in a library or teach in a public school is no more laudable than being paid by the local used book store or private school. Moreover, who should do the giving? It might be simpler if Washington empties pockets nationwide, giving either grants or labor to charity. But the right way is for individuals to directly aid deserving groups.

Nor is dependence on government healthy for private charities. Although charities get to train publicly funded volunteers, government inevitably will favor some activities. Such preferences subtly pressure organizations to adjust their mission to ensure eligibility for funding. An early review by Public/Private Ventures, a nonprofit that seeks to improve the effectiveness of anti-poverty programs, noted that the corporation aggressively shaped service programs. An assessment in the *Journal of Public Administration Research and Theory* found that those involved sought to "influence the type of implementation process that fits their own political interests."

Moreover, AmeriCorps is likely to encourage people to further abdicate their civic responsibilities. Federally funded service makes it less necessary for people to contribute and volunteer. People won't do more if they perceive no need to do so, and they will see less need if Washington provides charities with "volunteers."

Never content to wait for government to act, Americans always have worked with families, friends and neighbors to help those around them. Uncle Sam should stop paying them to help today.

Written for *CQ Researcher*, January 2012

The vast majority of volunteers act without support from government, and that's the way it should be. Every year, 63 million Americans strengthen their communities by leading scout troops or coaching soccer, raising money for band uniforms or leading museum tours. These are good things, and government doesn't need to interfere.

On the other hand, many functions widely understood to be public priorities are in desperate need of an affordable source of dedicated human capital. For example, providing a quality education is labor intensive, particularly in high-poverty schools where many children need extra supports. National service can be a key part of a strategy to turn around failing schools. That's why the widely acclaimed Diplomas Now initiative deploys City Year corps members to take action when middle school students exhibit early warning signs of dropping out.

In other cases, national service members play a critical role organizing community volunteers. For example, in Madison, Wis., the Schools of Hope initiative has wiped out racial disparities in reading with community and college volunteer tutors recruited and supervised by national service members. This kind of low-cost intervention saves significant public funding down the road.

AmeriCorps funding is key to both City Year and Schools of Hope. AmeriCorps members serve full time (or make a substantial part-time commitment) and receive a modest stipend and education award in return. In addition to serving in schools, AmeriCorps members address a wide range of locally determined needs, including community health centers, early-childhood programs and college access initiatives. In fact, AmeriCorps figures prominently in a Joplin, Mo., monument to the volunteers who helped its post-tornado recovery.

Not only is AmeriCorps a low-cost way to direct human resources to public problems but it also creates badly needed entry jobs for priority populations. Most AmeriCorps positions are filled by young adults — a group facing the highest rates of unemployment. Older adults who have more to give after retirement also serve — and by so doing, stay healthy and independent. A new priority for AmeriCorps is to engage veterans, a population suffering from high rates of unemployment and a strong desire to serve their communities.

At a time when nonprofit organizations are stretched thin with the weak economy, too many schools are struggling and millions of Americans are out of work and ready to serve, we should be expanding AmeriCorps, not eliminating it.

Velasco, the corporation's acting CEO, about two incidents, in New York City and Tacoma, Wash., in which AmeriCorps apparently violated laws against the use of federal funds to place volunteers in positions related to "advocacy, lobbying, protesting, union organizing" or "partisan political activity." In both incidents, volunteers' work was related to the advocacy functions of Planned Parenthood, the reproductive-health provider and advocacy organization.[40]

How the placements "could possibly abide by the spirit of volunteerism is beyond me," said Rep. Virginia Foxx, R-N.C., chairman of the Education and the Workforce Subcommittee on Higher Education. "I appreciate that once notified of these situations, the corporation acted swiftly to stop the prohibited activities," said Foxx. "However, our goal should be to prevent these kinds of activities before they take place."[41]

Both the corporation and AmeriCorps actively monitor local organizations that host volunteers for compliance with laws, but the large number of volunteers and organizations makes it difficult to spot all problems before they start, Velasco said.[42] From now on, he said, the corporation would require organizations that host volunteers to reaffirm each year that they're following regulations.[43]

Changing Landscape

The nature of volunteerism may be changing.

The worker pool has declined for some services traditionally provided by volunteers. Volunteer fire and emergency personnel, long a rural mainstay, have become harder and harder to find, for example.

Thomas F. O'Hara, coordinator of the Firemen's Association of the State of New York volunteer programs, noted last summer that the number of volunteer firefighters in New York "has declined over the past two decades — from nearly 100,000 in the 1990s to a little over 88,000 today," even as the population needing service has increased.[44]

Largely thanks to school and university programs, young people volunteer more today than in the past. Studies also report, however, that young people tend to perform their service with less regularity than adult volunteers and don't volunteer for the same causes for years, as adults often do, so organizations and causes may benefit less, long term, from youth service.[45]

"Religion is the best predictor we have of both giving and volunteering, including for non-religious causes," and religious affiliation is in a long decline, says Lenkowsky of Indiana University. Alongside the long, slow drop in religious affiliation, "we see giving and volunteering declining too."[46]

Participation is sharply up for some community-service programs. Applications for AmeriCorps rose from 360,000 for 80,000 available slots in 2008-2009 to 536,000 applications for 2009-2010. Teach for America, which places graduates of selective colleges in high-need schools for two-year teaching stints, received 25,000 applications in 2008 and 48,000 in 2011.[47]

The recession and resulting bad job market cloud the meaning of these statistics, however. The federal programs offer modest payment, a possible draw in a tough job market. In addition, volunteer service offers a chance to network and learn new skills, and "people might recognize this more in the recession . . . because they don't have a job and they are looking for ways to build their résumés," said Peter Levine, director of CIRCLE —The Center for Information on Research Learning and Engagement, a research group based at Tufts University, in Medford, Mass.[48]

But Teach for America Executive Vice President Elissa Kim is skeptical of that analysis. "I don't think people are just jumping on the bandwagon . . . because the economy is shaky." Teach for America applicants make the choice based on whether "this is the right thing for them," she says.[49]

OUTLOOK

Good Citizenship

Schools and colleges have built volunteer programs partly in hopes of creating a more involved citizenry. Research suggests that participating in thoughtfully structured service makes people more likely to participate in activities such as voting, which is traditionally seen as the key responsibility of citizenship.

Recently, however, some scholars have spotted an unforeseen trend that may change that equation. Young people, especially, say some researchers, have begun to view volunteer service itself as a far more important part of being a good citizen than political activities such as staying informed on public issues and voting.

"In the 1960s and '70s, young people's involvement [in society] tended to be political," as when they fueled the civil-rights and anti-war movements, says Catholic University's Youniss, "but now when kids think of doing service to society, they think of doing good deeds" — acts of charity, essentially — "not any kind of political acts."

Over the past three decades, numerous political analysts have raised alarms about Americans becoming too disconnected from society. They have pointed to evidence such as low voting rates, especially among younger people, and surveys showing that many people have lost faith in government's ability to tackle important problems, wrote Russell J. Dalton, a political science professor at the University of California, Irvine. But alongside the drop in some traditional measures of active citizenship has come a rise in young people's affinity for volunteer service as a primary form of social engagement, wrote Dalton, one of the main researchers following that trend.[50]

Despite the alarms of some, the new view of citizenship is not necessarily something to fear, since it replaces interest in politics with more concern about "the welfare of others," Dalton said. He describes a conversation he had with a college student who helped out in New Orleans in 2005, after Hurricane Katrina. While the young man "was active on a variety of social and political causes," including poverty in Africa and the Iraq War, he had "a stark lack of interest" in political parties and voting. That's typical of the "many Americans" who now "believe they are fully engaged in society even if they do not vote," Dalton said. Still, he argues, the rise in volunteerism can be used to turn young people on to voting as well.[51]

It's unclear whether the new trend relates to schools' emphasis on volunteer work or exactly how it will affect political and social life. However, the trend does mean that traditional groups such as political parties will have to retool their messages to appeal to young nonvoters who are nevertheless interested in public service, Dalton wrote. For example, a political campaign could explain "how elections can have an even greater impact on the issues for which youth now volunteer" than volunteering itself can have, he said.

Many experts on volunteerism would like to see it continue to rise among young people but wonder how to accomplish that. "We don't call on young people enough," says Indiana University's Lenkowsky. Rebranding might help, according to some social-marketing experts, he says.

"The word 'volunteer' sounds like something your grandmother would do. You need to make it cool" to continue to entice a new generation.[52]

NOTES

1. "Reaching Our Goals: An Overview of Research in Support of the Strategic Initiatives," Corporation for National and Community Service, March 2009, p. 3, www.nationalservice.gov/ pdf/08_1113_rpd_reach ingourgoals.pdf.

2. Quoted in Heather Harris, "Community Service Requirement Mulled for MHS," *Wicked Local Mansfield*, Nov. 16, 2011, www.wickedlocal .com/mansfield/features/x1821246343/Com munity-service-requirement-mulled-for-MHS# axzz1g3WqP0n8. Jeff Sullivan, "Mansfield School Committee Discusses Mandated Community Service," *Mansfield* [Mass.] *Patch*, Nov. 18, 2011, http://mansfield-ma.patch.com/articles/mans field-school-committee-mulls-madated-commu nity-service.

3. For background, see Jeffrey A. McLellan and James Youniss, "Two Systems of Youth Service: Determinants of Voluntary and Required Youth Community Service," *Journals of Youth and Adolescence*, February 2003, pp. 47-58.

4. Quoted in Susan R. Jones, Thomas C. Segar and Anna L. Gasiorski, " 'A Double-Edged Sword'; College Student Perceptions of Required High School Service-Learning," *Michigan Journal of Community Service Learning*, Fall 2008, pp. 5-17, http://quod.lib.umich.edu/cgi/t/text/text-idx? c=mj csl;view=toc;idno=3239521.0015.101.

5. Quoted in Michael Winerip, "Required Volunteerism: School Programs Tested," *The New York Times*, Sept. 23, 1993, www.nytimes.com/1993/09/23/us/ required-volunteerism-school-programs-test ed.html?pagewanted=all&src=pm.

6. Arthur A. Stukas, Mark Snyder and E. Gil Clary, "The Effects of 'Mandatory Volunteerism' on Intentions to Volunteer," *Psychological Science*, Jan. 1, 1999, p. 59.

7. Marlene Ritchie, "Volunteering Trends Including Required Volunteer Experience for Ontario High School Students," Child Research Net website, www.childresearch.net/RESOURCE/ RESEARCH/ 2010/RITCHIE2.HTM; Steven Brown, S. Mark Pancer, Alisa Henderson and Kimberly Ellis-Hale, "The Impact of High School Mandatory Community Service Programs on Subsequent Volunteering and Community Engagement," Draft Research Report to the Knowledge Development Centre, Imagine Canada, January 2007, www.lispop.ca/PDF%20 working%20paper/WPS6.pdf.

8. Alisa Henderson, Steven Brown, S. Mark Pancer and Kimberly Ellis-Hale, "Mandated Community Service in High School and Subsequent Civic Engagement: The Case of the 'Double Cohort' in Ontario, Canada," Working Paper, Laurier Institute for the Study of Public Opinion and Public Policy, www.lispop.ca/PDF %20working%20paper/WPS3 .pdf.

9. Reaching Our Goals: An Overview of Research in Support of the Strategic Initiatives, Corporation for National and Community Service, March 2009, p. 3, www.nationalservice. gov/pdf/08_1113_rpd_reach ingourgoals.pdf.

10. "Annual Membership Survey Results: Executive Summary 2010," Campus Compact, 2011, p. 3, www.compact.org/wp-content/uploads/ 2008/11/2010_Annual-Survey_Exec_Summary-4-8 .pdf.

11. "Volunteer Growth in America: A Review of Trends Since 1974," Corporation for National and Community Service, December 2006, p. 2, www .ideaencore.com/item/volunteer-growth-america-review-trends-1974-1.

12. "Reaching Our Goals," op. cit., p. 3.

13. "Volunteering in the United States — 2010," news release, U.S. Bureau of Labor Statistics, Jan. 26, 2011, www.bls.gov/news.release/volun.nr0.htm.

14. Ibid.

15. For background, see Susan J. Ellis and Katherine H. Campbell, By the People: A History of Americans as Volunteers (2006).

16. Susan J. Ellis, "The Legacy of Volunteering by Children," e-Volunteerism, January 2008, www .e-volunteerism.com/quarterly/08jan/08jan-voices.

17. Ibid.

18. For background, see John Greenya, "National Service," CQ Researcher, June 30, 2006, pp. 577-600; H. B. Shaffer, "Voluntary Action: People and Programs," Editorial Research Reports, 1969, Vol. 1; H.B. Shaffer, "Domestic Peace Corps," Editorial Research Reports, 1963, Vol. 1; "National Service Timeline," AmeriCorps website, www.nationalser vice.gov/about/role_ impact/history_timeline.asp; Harris Wofford, "The Politics of Service: How a Nation Got Behind AmeriCorps," Brookings Institution, Fall 2002, www.brookings.edu/arti cles/2002/ fall_civilsociety_wofford.aspx.

19. "H.R. 993, 'The AmeriCorps Program Elimination Act: What It Does," National Center for Public Policy Research, www.nationalcenter.org/ AmeriCorps597.html.

20. Quoted in "AmeriCorps Is Changing the Minds of Congressional Republicans," press release, Clinton White House, Jan. 15, 2001, http://clinton5.nara .gov/library/hot_releases/ January_15_2001_7 .html.

21. Wofford, op. cit.

22. Quoted in Dwight E. Giles, Jr., and Janet Eyler, "The Theoretical Roots of Service Learning in John Dewey: Toward a Theory of Service Learning," Michigan Journal of Community Service-Learning, 1994, p. 79, http://quod.lib. umich.edu/m/mjcsl/32 39521.0001.109/1?page=root;rgn=full+text;size=10 0;view=image.

23. Quoted in ibid., p. 82.

24. For background, see Sandra Enos, "Service-Learning on American Campuses: Challenges for Pedagogy and Practice," Issues in Teaching and Learning, 2003, www.ric.edu/itl/volume_ 02_enos.php.

25. "Who We Are," Campus Compact website, www .compact.org/about/history-mission-vision.

26. "Quotes to Use," Campus Compact website, www .compact.org/resources-for-presidents/ quotes-to-use.

27. Enos, op. cit.

28. John W. Eby, *Why Service-Learning Is Bad*, March 1998, www.messiah.edu/external_programs/agape/servicelearning/articles/wrongsvc.pdf.

29. "Community Service and Service-Learning in America's Schools," Corporation for National and Community Service, November 2008, www.nationalservice.gov/pdf/08_1112_lsa_prevalence.pdf.

30. *Ibid.*

31. For background, see *Steirer v. Bethlehem Area School District*, 987 F. 989 (3rd Cir. 1993), http://openjurist.org/987/f2d/989/steirer-steirer-v-bethlehem-area-school-district; *Immediato v. Rye Neck School District*, 873 F. Supp. 846 (2nd. Cir. 1996), Jan. 2, 1996, http://caselaw.lp.find law.com/scripts/getcase. pl?navby=search&case=/data2/circs/2nd/957237.html; *Herndon v. Chapel Hill School District*, 89 F.3d 174 (4th Cir. 1996), http://caselaw.findlaw.

32. Quoted in Josh Gerstein, "W.H.: Fired IG 'Confused, Disoriented,' " *Politico*, June 16, 2009, www.politico.com/news/stories/0609/23831. html.

33. *Ibid.*; for background, see "Kevin Johnson (Politician)," Times Topics, *The New York Times*, April 10, 2009, http://topics.nytimes.com/topics/reference/timestopics/people/j/kevin_johnson/index.html.

34. Quoted in "Republicans not Satisfied With White House Explanation for Walpin Firing," Fox News.com, June 18, 2009,www.foxnews.com/politics/2009/06/18/republicans-satisfied-white-house-explanation-walpin-firing.

35. Justin Elliott, "GOP Inquiry Fails to Show Obama's Firing of AmeriCorps IG Was Politicized," *Talking Points Memo*, Nov. 20, 2009, http://tpmmuckraker.talkingpointsmemo.com/2009/11/issa_grassley_inquiry_hits_white_house_on_walpin.php.

36. "Ex-AmeriCorps IG Loses Appeal in Wrongful Firing Suit," *Talking Points Memo*, Jan. 5, 2011, http://tpmmuckraker.talkingpointsmemo.com/gerald_walpin.

37. For background, see Justin Ewers, "Congress Sends Obama a Bill to Boost Community Service," *U.S. News & World Report*, April 8, 2009, www.usnews.com/news/obama/articles/2009/04/08/congress-sends-obama-a-bill-to-boost-community-service, and "Money for College for Volunteers Under New Obama Service Bill," *Edu in Review*, April 21, 2009, www.eduin review.com/blog/2009/04/obama-to-triple-size-of-americorps-by-signing-national-service-bill/.

38. Quoted in Chris Steller, "Bachmann Fears 'Politically Correct Re-education Camps for Young People,' " *The Minnesota Independent*, April 6, 2009, http://minnesotaindependent.com/ 31237/bachmann-reeducation-camps.

39. For background, see "Legislative Update," Save Service in America website, www.saveservice.org/pages/legislative-update, and FY 2012 Appropriations Update: "House Appropriations Committee Releases Draft Labor, Health and Human Services, Education, and Related Agencies Bill," Lewis-Burke Associates LLC, Sept. 29, 2011, http://research.brown.edu/ovpr/HouseAppropriationsBill_092911.pdf; *Policy News*, Afterschool Alliance, Jan. 11, 2012, www.afterschoolalliance.org/PolicyFedNewsArchive.cfm.

40. For background, see "Demanding Accountability in National Service Programs," hearing transcript and report, House Committee on Education and the Workforce, 2011, http://fr webgate.access.gpo.gov/cgi-bin/getdoc.cgi?db name=112_house_hearings&docid=f:66967.pdf.

41. Quoted in *ibid.*, p. 2.

42. *Ibid.*, p. 15.

43. *Ibid.*

44. Jaegun Lee, "Ohio Fire Chief Addresses Shortage of Volunteers," *Watertown Daily Times* [NY], Aug. 19, 2011, www.watertowndailytimes.com/article/20110819/NEWS03/708199918.

45. Mark Hugo Lopez and Karlo Barrios Marcelo, "Volunteering Among Young People," The Center for Information & Research on Civic Learning and Engagement, April 2007, p. 2, www.civicyouth.org/PopUps/FactSheets/FS07_Volunteering.pdf.

46. For background, see Marcia Clemmitt, "Protestants Today," *CQ Researcher*, Dec. 7, 2007, pp. 1009-1032.

47. Natalie DiBlasio, "College Students and Graduates Volunteering for Longer Terms," *USA Today*, Nov. 28, 2011, www.usatoday.com/ news/nation/story/2011-11-23/sharing-college-students-volunteering/51447910/1.

48. Quoted in *ibid.*

49. Quoted in *ibid.*

50. Russell J. Dalton, *The Good Citizen: How a Younger Generation Is Reshaping American Politics* (2008), p. 2-3.

51. *Ibid.*, p. 1.

52. *Ibid.*, p. 173.

BIBLIOGRAPHY

Selected Sources

Books

Butin, Dan W., *Service Learning in Theory and Practice: The Future of Community Engagement in Higher Education*, Palgrave Macmillan, 2010.
An associate professor of education at Merrimack College, in North Andover, Mass., argues for focusing more on service learning's intellectual content and embedding it more formally into school curricula.

Ellis, Susan J., and Katherine H. Campbell, *By the People: A History of Americans as Volunteers*, Energize Inc., 2006.
Ellis, the editor of a journal on volunteerism, and Campbell, a consultant, chronicle the service projects and organizations that American volunteers have participated in throughout the nation's history.

Youniss, James, and Miranda Yates, *Community Service and Social Responsibility in Youth*, University of Chicago Press, 1997.
A psychology professor at the Catholic University of America (Youniss) and a psychology and public-health researcher describe how a social-justice class that included work in a soup kitchen led urban high school students to examine their political and moral convictions and develop a sense of themselves as participants in the community.

Articles

Giegerich, Elizabeth, "A Look at Tulane's Service-Learning Post-Katrina," *The Nation*, Aug. 25, 2008, www.thenation. com/article/look-tulane-universitys-service-learning-post-katrina.
The process was difficult, but after a 2005 hurricane devastated its home city of New Orleans, Tulane University transformed its curriculum to include a strong emphasis on social service for all students.

Tugend, Alina, "The Benefits of Volunteerism, if the Service Is Real," *The New York Times*, July 30, 2010, www.nytimes.com/2010/07/31/your-money/31shortcuts.html?pagewant ed=all.
Researchers find that high school students who perform community service and have a chance to analyze and discuss their experiences are more likely to remain civically involved and think in terms of larger-scale solutions to social problems.

Reports and Studies

***Community Service and Service-Learning in America's Schools, Corporation for National and Community Service*, November 2008, www.aces4kids.org/public/uploads/research-news/service_learning_corporation_for_national_and_com munity_service_.pdf.**
Elementary, middle and high schools continue to offer students volunteer opportunities. But interest by school leaders in establishing service-learning programs dropped off during the 2000s, and schools in low-income communities are especially unlikely to offer service learning.

***Serving Communities: How Four Organizations Are Using National Service to Solve Community Problems*, Abt Associates/Corporation for National and Community Service, December 2011, www.national service.gov/pdf/serv ingcommunities_11_30.pdf.**
Based on interviews at service organizations that employ federally sponsored youth and senior volunteers from the AmeriCorps and Senior Corps programs, the report explains how four such groups manage their volunteers and the benefits and challenges they see in the programs.

Enos, Sandra, "Service-learning on American Campuses: Challenges for Pedagogy and Practice," *Issues in Teaching and Learning*, Rhode Island College, 2003, www.ric.edu/ itl/volume_02_enos.php.
An associate professor of sociology at Bryant University, in Smithfield, R.I., explains what's led to a recent increase in service learning.

Hart, Daniel, Thomas M. Donnelly, James Youniss and Robert Atkins, "High School Community Service as a Predictor of Adult Voting and Volunteering," *American Educational Research Journal*, March 2007, pp. 197-219, http://aer.sagepub.com/content/44/1/197.full.

Researchers find that high school students who perform community service during high school, whether the service is freely chosen or mandatory, are more likely to vote and do volunteer work as young adults.

Jones, Susan R., Thomas C. Segar and Anna L. Gasiorski, " 'A Double-Edged Sword': College Student Perceptions of Required High School Service-Learning," *Michigan Journal of Community Service Learning*, Fall 2008, pp. 5-17, http://quod.lib.umich.edu/cgi/p/pod/dod-idx?c=mjcsl;idno=3239521.0015.101.

Researchers from the University of Maryland find that many Maryland high school students consider their state's community-service requirement burdensome but often develop a more positive opinion of the experience once they enter college.

For More Information

AmeriCorps, 1201 New York Ave., N.W., Washington, DC 20525; 202-606-5000; www.americorps.gov. Federal program that places volunteers in community-service organizations around the country.

Bureau of Labor Statistics, Volunteering in the United States, www.bls.gov/news.release/volun.toc.htm. Federal agency that tracks volunteering rates.

Campus Compact, 45 Temple Place, Boston, MA 02111; 617-357-1881; www. compact.org. National coalition of 1,100 colleges that promote community service by students.

CIRCLE (The Center for Information and Research on Civic Learning and Engagement), Jonathan M. Tisch College of Citizenship and Public Service, Lincoln Filene Hall, Tufts University, Medford, MA 02155; 617-627-4710; www.civicyouth.org. Conducts research on civic education in schools, colleges and community settings and on young Americans' voting habits and political and civic involvement.

Corporation for National and Community Service, 1201 New York Ave., N.W., Washington, DC 20525; 202-606-5000; www.nationalservice.gov. Agency that manages all federal domestic community-service programs, including AmeriCorps and the service-learning program Learn and Service America.

International Association for Research on Service-Learning and Community Engagement, Tulane University Center for Public Service, Alcee Fortier Hall, 6823 St. Charles Ave., New Orleans, LA 70118; 504-862-3366. Nonprofit association of service-learning and community-engagement researchers.

National Service Learning Clearinghouse, 866-245-7378; www.servicelearning.org. Website operated by a federal contractor that provides information for schools, colleges and others running service-learning programs.

Voluntourism.org, www.voluntourism.org/index.html. Private group that provides information on how the tourism industry and nonprofit service organizations can coordinate volunteer activity.

12

Occupy Movement

Peter Katel

An Occupy protester in Los Angeles on Nov. 5, 2011, urges people to move their money from large banks into small banks or credit unions. "I believe that I am not represented by the big interest groups and the big-money corporations, which have increasing control of our money and our politics," said an activist.

From *CQ Researcher*, Jan. 13, 2012

W hen hundreds of demonstrators suddenly appeared in New York's Financial District last September — along with their tents, sleeping bags and drums — their "1 percent v. 99 percent" buzz-phrase decrying economic inequality caught on immediately.

But sympathizers and critics did have some questions: What did the protesters want to happen? What did they want government to do? Some thought the campers would quickly give up and disperse.

The Occupy Wall Street activists held their ground, however, and the movement grew in strength. And its objectives became a little clearer.

"People are coming out here to voice, you know, their disapproval with the system and to voice themselves in a direct, democratic fashion," said Patrick Bruner, a 23-year-old from Brooklyn. "It's really refreshing for people to think that they can effect change in this system that has essentially made it so that only 1 percent of the population are citizens."[1]

The New York encampment in Zuccotti Park was the seed from which hundreds of Occupy movements sprouted in cities, towns and college campuses across the country. From one coast to the other, activists spoke in similar tones, often with drum circles pounding in the background. "I believe that I am not represented by the big interest groups and the big money corporations, which have increasing control of our money and our politics," Elise Whitaker, 21, a freelance script editor and film director, said at the Occupy Los Angeles site at City Hall Park. Demonstrators want "a more equal economy," she said.[2]

Public Backs Occupy's Concerns, Rejects Tactics

Forty-four percent of Americans support the Occupy Wall Street movement while about half agree with the concerns the protests have raised. A similar percentage, however, disapproves of the movement's tactics, such as staging sit-ins in public places.

Public Views of Occupy Wall Street

The Occupy Wall Street movement

Other/don't know 22%
Support 44%
Oppose 35%

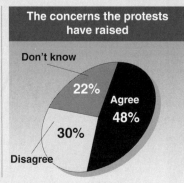

The concerns the protests have raised

Don't know 22%
Agree 48%
Disagree 30%

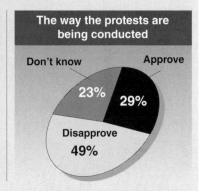

The way the protests are being conducted

Don't know 23%
Approve 29%
Disapprove 49%

* Percentages may not total 100 because of rounding.

Source: "Frustration With Congress Could Hurt Republican Incumbents," Pew Research Center, December 2011, p. 3, www.people-press.org/files/legacy-pdf/12-15-11 Congress and Economy release.pdf

Mayors of Los Angeles, New York and other cities sent police to break up encampments. Winter weather or declining political momentum did in some others, though Occupy Washington was still going in early 2012. And other Occupy groups, including the original New York movement, were still holding meetings as well, though not in a round-the-clock encampment.[3] In addition, the most engaged activists are meeting face-to-face and on the Web, and a major revival of a street presence in the spring seems virtually certain.[4] Already, the movement's image of a country divided between the "1 percent" and the "99 percent" has forced politicians from President Obama on down to confront economic inequality.

"For years, people were saying, 'When are the pitchforks going to come out? When are people are going to get mad?' But no one was doing anything," says Ken Margolies, director of organizing programs at Cornell University's Industrial Labor Relations School. "The Occupy movement caught the imagination of the country."

The occupiers' message was soon buttressed by studies charting substantial income growth for Americans at the top, and relatively meager growth for everyone else.[5]

Weeks after the Occupy movement took off, the nonpartisan Congressional Budget Office (CBO) reported that from 1979 to 2007 the highest-income 1 percent of the population saw after-tax household income grow 277 percent. By contrast, for the 60 percent of the population in the middle, incomes grew less than 40 percent.[6]

The Organisation for Economic Co-operation and Development (OECD), a policy think tank for industrialized nations, reported that the richest 1 percent of Americans took in 20 percent of national income — a bigger share than in any other industrialized country examined.[7]

Meanwhile, according to a survey released Jan. 11, 2012, by the Pew Research Center, about two-thirds of Americans see "strong conflicts" between rich and poor in the United States, indicating the income inequality message from Democrats and the Occupy movement is seeping into the national consciousness.[8]

The Occupy movement signifies refusal to accept more of the same. Until it appeared, says Rory McVeigh, director of the Center for the Study of Social Movements at the University of Notre Dame, "The conservative side has been pretty effective in managing public opinion in a way that gets people worried about debt reduction and not really thinking about consequences of joblessness and inequality and stimulating the economy."

Left-wing activists have driven the movement from the beginning, marking the first time since the days of the anti-Vietnam War movement that ideas from the left have helped set the national agenda. "It took three years from the start of the anti-Vietnam War movement to the point when the popularity of the war sank below 50 percent," Todd Gitlin, a professor at the Columbia University journalism school and a participant in and chronicler of the 1960s radical movement, told *New York* magazine in November. "Here, achieving the equivalent took three minutes."[9]

A closer precedent to Occupy arguably lies not in the 1960s but in the 1930s, when the left and unions made common cause — including in the organization of factory occupations. Nevertheless, notes historian Michael Kazin of Georgetown University, "The union movement had no problem with leaders."

The Occupy movement, inspired by anarchist principles, rejects hierarchy in favor of direction by consensus — in other words, "pure" democracy. What's more, the movement lacks a clear-cut program and has little to point to in the way of measurable results. "The Occupy movement is rooted in the idea that the political system is broken to such a degree that we can no longer work through the Republican or Democratic parties," Tim Franzen, an Occupy Atlanta activist, told The Associated Press.[10]

To be sure, Democratic Gov. Andrew Cuomo of New York in December suddenly reversed his avowedly unbending opposition to a so-called "millionaires' tax" on the earnings of high-income New Yorkers. Occupy activists had dubbed Cuomo "Governor 1 Percent."[11]

Survey data make clear that discontent over inequality isn't limited to New York. A substantial majority — 77 percent — of respondents to a November survey by the nonpartisan Pew Research Center agreed that corporations and a small number of rich people wield too much

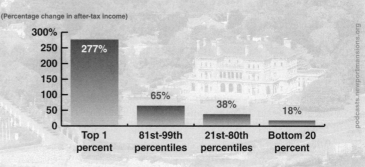

Top 1 Percent Has Biggest Income Gain

The after-tax income of the top 1 percent of American households rose nearly 300 percent between 1979 and 2007, while that of other groups grew at much slower rates. The bottom 20 percent saw only an 18 percent rise over the period.

Income Gains, by Income Group, 1979 to 2007

(Percentage change in after-tax income)

- Top 1 percent: 277%
- 81st-99th percentiles: 65%
- 21st-80th percentiles: 38%
- Bottom 20 percent: 18%

Source: Chad Stone, et al., "A Guide to Statistics on Historical Trends in Income Inequality," Center on Budget and Policy Priorities, November 2011, www.cbpp.org/cms/?fa=view&id=3629; Congressional Budget Office.

power. And — in a remarkable loss of faith in a bedrock tenet of the American Dream — 40 percent said hard work and determination don't guarantee success.[12]

However, agreeing with some of Occupy activists' points doesn't automatically mean supporting the movement. In December, Pew found that 49 percent of respondents disapproved of the way demonstrations were conducted — almost the exact share that registered agreement with the movement on issues.

By then, coverage of the movement had included news accounts of November street clashes in Oakland, Calif. Some featured ultra-radical activists who saw breaking store windows as a form of political action. Others featured aggressive police who in one instance fired a tear gas canister that fractured the skull of an Iraq War veteran.[13]

"Americans usually like the idea of rebellion more than rebellion itself," says Kazin, "not people fighting with cops, even if it's not the fault of the demonstrators. They like protest as long as it's orderly."

Still, for Democrats, the Occupy movement has opened a window of political opportunity. In early December, Obama traveled to historic Osawatomie, Kan., to deliver a major speech on economic inequality. "The typical CEO who used to earn about 30 times more than his or her worker now earns 110 times more," he said. "And yet, over the last decade the incomes of most Americans have actually fallen by about 6 percent. . . . Today, thanks to loopholes and shelters, a quarter of all millionaires now pay lower tax rates than millions of you, millions of middle-class families. Some billionaires have a tax rate as low as 1 percent."[14]

Osawatomie is a political landmark — the site of a 1910 speech by President Theodore Roosevelt urging that corporate power be reined in. "The great special business interests too often control and corrupt the men and methods of government for their own profit," declared Roosevelt, who would soon run again for president as Progressive Party candidate.[15] The White House republished Roosevelt's address simultaneously with the text of Obama's speech. As for the Occupy movement, the president mentioned it only once, and briefly.

Republican primary candidates' responses to Occupy, meanwhile, have ranged from equivocal to hostile. Former Massachusetts Gov. Mitt Romney, who became a multimillionaire in the corporate takeover business, defended Wall Street financiers in October against what he called attempts at "finding a scapegoat, finding someone to blame."[16] But a more recent campaign commercial used hand-written signs bearing gloomy economic statistics, seeming to mimic a well-known Occupy technique.[17]

Meanwhile, former House Speaker Newt Gingrich, R-Ga., offered some mocking advice to demonstrators: "Go get a job, right after you take a bath," he said in November. He went on to disparage them as non-tax-paying freeloaders.[18]

As the Republicans spoke out, the Tea Party faction of their party, which helped the GOP regain control of the House in 2011, was heading downward in public opinion. The trend held true both nationally and in congressional districts represented by lawmakers identified with the faction, the Pew Center reported in November. In those districts, 48 percent of respondents said they viewed the Tea Party unfavorably, and 41 percent favorably — a sharp shift from last March, when the favorability rate was 55 percent.[19]

The Occupy movement could face its own decline — but not for some time, say many observers. "Just when you thought demonstrations and people putting bodies on the line was over," says former Democratic Gov. Madeleine Kunin of Vermont, "it re-emerges."

As debate continues over the impact and future of the Occupy movement, here are some questions being asked:

Can the Occupy movement reduce inequality?

After reading some of the hundreds of stark, personal accounts offered on "We Are the 99 Percent" — a website that offers stories behind the statistics, charts and slogans about economic inequality — Rich Lowry, a prominent Republican commentator and Occupy opponent, acknowledged that the protest movement had raised some legitimate questions.[20]

"There are tales of men losing decent-paying jobs and finding nothing comparable," wrote Lowry, editor of *National Review* magazine, the flagship of Republican conservatism since 1955. "Such downward mobility is a dismaying constant. . . . The recession has added a layer of joblessness on top of punishingly dysfunctional and expensive health-care and higher-education systems."[21]

The accounts on the website are by low-paid workers, unemployed people with experience but no job prospects, students accumulating debt and sufferers of chronic illness with inadequate health insurance — or none at all.

Lowry's take on the issue animating the movement may be a minority view among conservatives. But his commentary — though critical of the Occupy movement's politics — illustrated a point made by reporter Dylan Byers of *Politico*, an influential Washington newspaper. He noted that the term "income inequality" had soared in frequency in news stories, from 91 appearances before the demonstrations began to 500 a week in early November.[22]

Occupiers "already can take credit for starting a national conversation about the increasingly inequitable distribution of growth that stands as a profound economic problem in our country," wrote Jared Bernstein, a senior fellow at the liberal Center on Budget and Policy Priorities and former chief economist for Vice President Joseph Biden.[23]

Generating attention and debate, though an important achievement, might mark the limit of what the Occupy movement can do, some sympathizers acknowledge.

"We've had a wave of columns and news stories based on inequality," says Dean Baker, an economist and co-founder and co-director of the Center for Economic and Policy Research. "But I don't think anyone is going to say that he changed his position based on the movement."

The very nature of the Occupy movement may limit its direct political effects, Baker says. "It's an amorphous group; it doesn't want to embrace politicians," he says. "One can argue about whether that is the most effective way to proceed."

However, activists can point to one example of a politician who appears to have responded to the Occupy message by reversing himself on an important piece of legislation with a direct effect on income inequality.

Cuomo, the New York governor, in early December suddenly embraced and pushed to legislative approval a so-called "millionaires' tax" on individuals who earn more than $200,000 a year.

In the weeks leading up to his move, Cuomo had declared unbendable opposition to the tax. Said Tim Dubnau, an organizer for the Communication Workers of America (CWA) who has been working closely with Occupy Wall Street, "There is no doubt in anyone's mind that that is a result of the Occupy Wall Street movement educating people" about tax policy.

And Dubnau noted that the tax debate that Occupy amplified is being echoed in the nationwide focus on equality. "In every single paper in the country almost every single day for months there have been stories about how we have an unequal society," he says. "I can't see that as a bad thing."

Nevertheless, New York, where labor unions still carry political weight and leftwing activism is deeply embedded in the state's history and political culture, may not be a national indicator of Occupy influence. "A movement is likely to get concessions in a sympathetic environment," says McVeigh of Notre Dame.

From a national perspective, "The polls are showing a fair number of people are fairly sympathetic to what Occupy Wall Street is putting forward, but without an intense commitment," McVeigh says. "So it's risky for anybody in power to completely embrace the movement and call it his or her own."

Even so, says Cornell University's Margolies, congressional Republicans' internal disagreement over Obama's efforts to extend the payroll tax cut may reflect confusion over how to deal with the inequality issue that Occupy activists have emphasized. "The movement has certainly changed the debate," Margolies says. "The Republicans realized they're getting caught by their own rhetoric; they finally found a tax cut they don't like." (He spoke before

Occupy Wall Street activists gather in New York City's Duarte Square on Nov. 15, 2011, after police removed them from Zuccotti Park. The police action, endorsed by Mayor Michael Bloomberg, followed similar moves in Oakland, Calif., and Portland, Ore.

House Republicans caved to pressure from the White House and their own Senate partners, backing a two-month extension of the tax cut.)

But Margolies qualifies his favorable reading of the movement's effects. "A real test would be if it helps a union win a major strike or get a contract in a tough situation, or helps change labor law, or helps a group of workers organize."

Is Occupy good for the Democratic Party?

In his Kansas speech in December, President Obama drew on themes sounded by Occupy members, connecting them to longstanding political traditions that energized the early 20th-century wave of political and financial regulation known as the Progressive Era.

Obama made much of the fact that the politician who laid the groundwork for those changes, President Theodore Roosevelt, had been a Republican.

But the president went on to underline the difference between Roosevelt and his party descendants of today. "Thanks to some of the same folks who are now running Congress, we had weak regulation, we had little oversight, and what did it get us?" he asked rhetorically.

Whether Obama can draw on the anger that has fed the Occupy movement remains unclear, however. A cautionary example comes from the recent experience of the

Republican Party with its Tea Party faction. The Tea Party propelled a number of Republican congressional candidates to victory in 2010, giving the GOP the House majority. But in the GOP presidential primaries, many candidates arguably have tacked so far to the right to appeal to the Tea Party that they may have alienated mainstream Republican voters.

"Republicans now are growing very nervous" because Tea Party freshman in the House have been so adamant against compromise, Norman Ornstein, a resident scholar at the American Enterprise Institute (AEI), a conservative think tank, said in December. "By standing so firm against taxing the rich . . . they lost sight of where the zeitgeist was, and it hurt them."[24]

But Obama faces problems within his own party, most notably disillusion among many Democrats over what they see as a lack of progress on social and economic reforms. That disillusion has helped animate the Occupy movement. "People went through the experience of 2008 and had their hopes raised significantly by Obama in a way we haven't seen in this generation," says Amy Muldoon, a CWA union member participating in an Occupy Wall Street working group on organized labor. "And now the Occupy movement in part is people who went through that experience and said, 'it didn't deliver for me.' "

Muldoon, speaking for herself and not the union, says a significant number of the most engaged Occupy activists are "looking past elections as a way of changing society." Democrats' attempts to "utilize what Occupy has exposed — with rhetoric about a candidate for the 99 percent, meaning Obama — I don't think will fly with the people who are most involved with Occupy."

To voters at large, however, argues Georgetown's Kazin, the Occupy movement has provided an appealing narrative "as long as people see the economy in serious trouble and are worried about their futures."

Moreover, the electoral alienation of the most committed Occupy activists doesn't pose an active threat to Democratic prospects, Kazin says. In the 1960s, "The antiwar movement saw Democrats and [President Lyndon B. Johnson, a Democrat who escalated the Vietnam War] as prime villains," he says. "I haven't seen that same hostility and hatred for Obama. A lot of core activists clearly think there is no difference between Republicans and Democrats, but that's not the same as

saying that it's the Democrats' fault that we have economic inequality and a financial crisis."

But Nick Schulz, a fellow at AEI and editor of its online magazine, argues that the nature of the Occupy movement itself poses a potential problem for Democrats in general and Obama in particular. "I come from the school that says that being positive in your politics is a winning formula," he says. "That's not what emerged from Occupy. I understand why people in Occupy are angry, but if the negative animating spirit of Occupy comes to dominate the Democratic Party, that's a political loser."

Obama owes much of his success to his ability to convey optimism, Schulz says. But in the coming election, he argues, if voters see the president's message as intertwined with Occupy grievances, "The moderately conservative, college-educated cohort that went in large numbers for Obama because they liked his upbeat, aspirational message. If it becomes a negative —'we're going after the rich and the top 1 percent' — that will turn them off."

Baker of the Center for Economic and Policy Research suggests that Occupy likely will benefit some Democrats and hurt others. "It's bad news for the more business-oriented Democrats," he argues, pointing to Robert Rubin — a Wall Street financier, former director of Citigroup and former Treasury secretary in the Clinton administration who still wields considerable influence on administration economic policy. "Their room to maneuver has been sharply reduced by the Occupy movement; they certainly don't see it as good news."[25]

On the other hand, Baker says, "The labor-progressive wing of the Democratic Party certainly does see it as good news." Even so, adds Baker, repercussions from Occupy attacks on business-oriented Democrats could hurt the movement's liberal allies. "The Rubin types provide money for campaigns," Baker says. "Do you run the risk that you're going to so antagonize the business wing of the party that you won't be able to run effective campaigns?"

Is the Occupy movement over?

The onset of winter, and police evictions, have deprived the Occupy name of its emotional punch — the occupations themselves — lending new strength to questions about the movement's goals. Those questions have been circulating virtually ever since it began: What exactly does the movement want to achieve? And does it have staying power?

Some observers see change within the political system as a waste of time. Many call themselves disenchanted after investing their political energies. "Obama syndrome: lost hope," says Sri Louise, who is active in Occupy Oakland. "I feel like I've been there and done that. I have no interest in the electoral process."

Others argue that improving that process is the movement's natural goal.

"If you want to get at the root of what's wrong with this system, in my opinion the way we fund and run elections has become skewed in the direction of powerful money interests," says Kunin, the former Vermont governor, summarizing a column she wrote for *The Huffington Post* website.[26] "If we're going to have the voice of the 99 percent back, we have to change that system and find a way to do public financing or limit contributions."

The tension between reformers and revolutionaries — a natural condition in all social movements — remains unresolved. "At some point, movements must take on some form, some identifiable agenda," the Rev. Jesse Jackson, a veteran of the 1960s civil rights movement, told *New York* magazine. "At some point, water must become ice."[27]

Whether many people like camping in city parks when water turns to ice is another question. Nevertheless, some argue that the loss of New York's Zuccotti Park did take a toll on Occupy Wall Street — the national movement's starter motor. "The fact that people were willing to sleep out in the cold rain and snow was inspiring," says the CWA's Dubnau. "There are some signs the movement is fizzling with the physical space of Zuccotti Park lost."

Activists reoccupied the park in early January after city authorities removed barricades and checkpoints that had limited the number of people allowed in; but a ban on tents and sleeping bags remained in force.

But Dubnau, like many others, expects open-air demonstrations to revive with the coming of warm weather. The movement has struck a chord, he says. "Everyone is anxious about jobs in America; everyone knows what the occupiers are talking about."

Nevertheless, Artur Davis, a former Democratic congressman from Alabama and now a Washington lawyer who writes political commentary for *Politico*, argues that

Getty Images/Win McNamee

Occupy activists demonstrate as Republican presidential candidate Newt Gingrich and his wife Callista, both at right, arrive at a town hall meeting in Littleton, N.H., on Jan. 5, 2012. In November, he told Occupy demonstrators: "Go get a job, right after you take a bath." He went on to disparage them as non-taxpaying freeloaders.

maintaining a physical presence "is a low bar to meet." The real test of lasting influence, he says, will be the Occupy movement's ability to accomplish political goals.

One obstacle so far, Davis says, is that the "99 percent" versus "1 percent" paradigm is too broad and vague. "It equates the interests of a hungry child in the Mississippi Delta with a stockbroker who makes six figures but whose mortgage is underwater," he says. "It's as if the civil rights movement had said in the 1960s, 'We're not going to make this about African-Americans, we're going to make it about people who are struggling all over the country; we're going to equate our interests with those of white suburbanites who are paying too much property tax.' "

From within the movement, though, some lifelong activists who've seen other political waves rise and fall argue that skeptics are thinking too small. Adam Hochschild, a journalist and author who co-founded the left-wing *Mother Jones* magazine in 1976 and who has written on the 18th- and 19th-century campaign to abolish slavery in the British Empire, likened that effort to Occupy. "By 1792 at least 400,000 people in the British Isles were refusing to eat slave-grown sugar," Hochschild wrote in the "Occupied Wall Street Journal," published by New York activists.[28]

"In combating entrenched power of a different sort — a system with obscene profits for the 1 percent and hardship and a downward slide for many of the rest — I think we're now at about 1792 in this process," Hochschild wrote.[29]

Hochschild and others who see the movement reaching for changes in how wealth and power are distributed agree — in a sense — with some of their most fervent foes. "The philosophical political movement that these extreme leftists have decided to participate in will try to continue," says David Bossie, president and board chairman of Citizens United, a conservative advocacy group that specializes in producing politically charged documentary-style movies.*

The encampments reflected the movement's philosophical underpinnings, Bossie says. "It's the closest form of communal living," he says, tracing the tent cities to "socialism, communism — you name the institutions by which they believe. They believe in taking from everyone and giving it to them."

BACKGROUND

Rising Militancy

Economic transformation capped by major depression marked the late 19th century, prompting a wave of activism among farmers and factory workers. Wall Street financiers, industrialists and politicians who served business interests were their common targets.[30]

In the 1880s, a wave of labor organizing spread across manufacturing, shipping and mining centers throughout the country. Twelve-hour work days, paltry pay, child labor, the right to collectively bargain and the often hazardous nature of the work spurred workers to demand change. Many went further, demanding that society be reordered so that the fruits of labor were distributed more equitably.

Workers had been forming and joining unions for decades, but they were made up of craftspeople whose skills gave them considerable power in dealing with employers. As industrialization advanced in the latter decades of the 1800s, a new kind of union arose.

The Knights of Labor, founded in secret in 1869, grew into an open organization for all skilled and unskilled members of the "producing classes." (Members included African-Americans and, eventually,

women — revolutionary policies at the time.) "We declare an inevitable and irresistible conflict between the wage system of labor and republican system of government," the Knights said, vowing to fight big-business domination of government.[31]

In 1885, the Knights led a successful strike against one of the country's leading corporations, the Southwestern Railroad, whose majority owner was fabled Wall Street financier Jay Gould. By 1886, as many as 1 million members, about 10 percent of the country's nonagricultural workforce, had joined the union.

A five-year depression that began in 1893 saw labor-business conflicts escalate into armed confrontations between workers and police and military forces deployed against them. President Grover Cleveland sent 10,000 Army troops to Chicago to quell a nationwide strike against the Pullman Palace Car Co., which manufactured sleeping cars for railroads. Thirteen strike supporters were killed in clashes with anti-union forces.[32]

Newly unemployed workers mounted campaigns of their own. The most well-known centered on a march from Ohio to Washington led by evangelical businessman Jacob S. Coxey, who advocated a major road-building program to put jobless men to work. "Coxey's Army" was met in Washington by U.S. marshals, who arrested Coxey and other leaders, snuffing out the effort.[33]

Shortly before the 1893 depression struck, a mass movement arose featuring rural Americans demanding better prices from companies that bought their crops, as well as a host of other improvements in conditions in the countryside. The movement evolved quickly into a political organization — from the Farmers' Alliance to the People's Party, founded in 1892, and soon dubbed "Populists."

In 1892, populist candidates around the country earned more than 1 million votes. Colorado and Kansas elected Populist governors, and Populist presidential candidate James Weaver captured three states, thus winning electoral votes. But ultimately, the third-party effort benefited the Republicans. In the 1896 presidential election, Republican William McKinley defeated William Jennings Bryan, who ran as both Democrat and Populist. And in 1912, Woodrow Wilson beat William Howard Taft, thanks partly to Theodore Roosevelt's third-party candidacy.

The labor movement divided as well, with more radical unionists (including anarchists) forming the

CHRONOLOGY

1880s-1920s *Organizing drives and strikes by industrial workers provoke repression.*

1885 Knights of Labor leads successful strike against Southwestern Railroad.

1894 Workers strike at Pullman Palace Car Co. in Chicago; President Grover Cleveland sends troops to break the labor action. . . . Men demanding jobs march on Washington.

1905 Left-wing unionists found anti-capitalism Industrial Workers of the World.

1910 President Theodore Roosevelt denounces corporate power in speech in Osawatomie, Kan.

1929 Wall Street crash marks beginning of Great Depression.

1930s *Nation's worst depression sparks massive discontent, rise of new unions.*

1932 "Bonus Army" of 20,000 jobless World War I veterans sets up camp in Washington but is eventually routed by Army troops and police.

1934 Wagner Act restricts employer interference in union activities.

1936 "Sitdown" tactic spreads to General Motors factories; company recognizes the United Automobile Workers union.

1950s-1960s *Civil rights and anti-Vietnam War movements make mass protest a major political force.*

1955 The Rev. Martin Luther King Jr. leads bus boycott in Montgomery, Ala.

1956 Montgomery desegregates buses.

1957 President Dwight D. Eisenhower orders Army troops to enforce desegregation in Little Rock, Ark.

1960 Black students sit in at Greensboro, N.C., lunch counter to challenge segregated seating; tactic spreads.

1961 "Freedom Riders" defy segregation in interstate buses and terminals.

1964 Civil Rights Act prohibits racial discrimination in public accommodations, public education and most employment.

1965 Voting Rights Act outlaws racial discrimination in election process.

1967 Tens of thousands march in Washington to protest Vietnam War.

1968 The Rev. King is assassinated in Memphis.

1970 As demonstrations against U.S. invasion of Cambodia sweep campuses and cities, National Guard troops kill four students at Ohio's Kent State University, and police kill two students at Jackson State College in Mississippi.

1990s-Present *Left-wing activism targets liberalized trade rules, job outsourcing and Iraq War.*

1993 Over strong opposition from unions and the left, President Bill Clinton pushes North American Free Trade Agreement (NAFTA) through Congress.

1997 College students organize boycott to protest athletic-wear companies using sweatshops.

1999 Anti-globalization protesters in Seattle battle with police at World Trade Organization meeting.

2003 Iraq War sparks a new anti-war movement.

2007 Richest 1 percent of population sees after-tax income grow by about 275 percent since 1979 while middle-income sector sees modest growth. . . . Recession begins.

2008 Obama presidential campaign awakens hope for rebirth of left-Democratic Party alliance that collapsed during Vietnam War.

2010 Energized by Tea Party faction, Republican candidates sweep House elections, gaining majority. . . . Left-wing Obama supporters grow disillusioned with economic policies seen as too timid.

2011 "Arab spring" in Tunisia, Egypt and elsewhere, and protests against austerity programs and inequality in Spain and Israel prompt U.S. activists to consider similar efforts.

Tracking Occupy's Evolution

The Occupy movement began in September in New York City to protest economic inequality and corporate greed. Since then the movement has spread across the U.S. Here is a timeline of its evolution:

2011

July 13 — Canadian anti-consumerist magazine *Adbusters* calls for a Sept. 17 protest on Wall Street demanding "democracy not corporatocracy."

Zuccotti Park

Sept. 17 — Protests begin as about 1,000 participants walk up and down Wall Street. Protesters settle into Zuccotti Park.

Sept. 20 — Police arrest mask-wearing protesters under state law banning non-entertainment masked gatherings.

Sept. 24 — About 80 arrested in Manhattan after marching without permit. The use of pepper spray against women earns Occupy movement its first major media coverage. Occupy protests begin in Chicago.

Moore

Sept. 26 — Filmmaker and activist Michael Moore addresses crowd at Zuccotti Park.

Sept. 28 — Transport Workers Union Local 100 in New York City becomes first large union to support Occupy protest.

Oct. 1 — Nearly 700 protesters arrested in march across Brooklyn Bridge. Protests begin in Los Angeles, Washington, D.C.

Oct. 3 — Protests begin in Boston, Memphis, Minneapolis, St. Louis, Hawaii and Maine.

Oct. 5 — New York labor unions join march through N.Y. Financial District.

Obama

Oct. 6 — Protests begin in Austin, Houston, San Francisco and Tampa. President Obama says the movement "expresses the frustrations the American people feel."

Oct. 7 — New York Mayor Michael Bloomberg says protesters are taking jobs from people and discouraging tourism.

Oct. 10 — Bloomberg softens criticism, saying protesters can stay if they obey the law.

Oct. 25 — Oakland police clear about 170 protesters from a City Hall encampment, use tear gas when protesters return.

Nov. 5 — "Bank Transfer Day" protesters encourage Americans to move their money out of big banks.

Nov. 15 — Police evict protesters from Zuccotti Park under orders from Bloomberg. A judge rules protesters do not have a First Amendment right to camp in the park, but can return without tents.

Cuomo

Nov. 17 — Protesters march in front of the New York Stock Exchange to mark movement's two-month anniversary.

Dec. 17 — Protesters mark three-month anniversary of Occupy Wall Street by marching across the city.

Dec. 20 — Hacker group Anonymous exposes personal information of police officers who have arrested protesters.

2012

Jan. 1 — Nearly 70 protesters arrested after attempt to resettle into Zuccotti Park. Protesters march at the end of Rose Bowl parade in Pasadena, Calif., on float made of plastic bags.

Romney

Jan. 2 — Protesters interrupt speech by Republican presidential candidate Mitt Romney in Des Moines, Iowa.

Jan. 4 — Protesters attend New Hampshire town hall meeting with Romney prior to state's primary Jan. 10. Organizers say they plan protests at future primaries, caucuses.

Jan. 10 — Protesters are permitted back into Zuccotti Park.

All photos/Getty Images

Industrial Workers of the World (IWW), in 1905, to fight for the overthrow of capitalism.

The years of union and populist activism, as well as the depression of 1893, presaged the early-20th-century "progressive" era, embodied by Presidents Theodore Roosevelt and Wilson. The period was marked by federal and state moves to improve working conditions. By 1912, 38 states prohibited or limited child labor, and the federal government had imposed regulations on the banking industry.

Often forgotten today is the extent of death and destruction — some of from the radical side — that accompanied the rise of the labor movement and the enactment of laws that granted legal protection to unions. "For more than half a century, between the 1870s and the 1930s," writes historian Beverly Gage of Yale University, "labor organizers and strikers regularly faced levels of violence all but unimaginable to modern-day activists."[34]

Marching and Occupying

The Great Depression that began in 1929 brought massive unemployment and widespread misery. In 1932, as the administration of Republican President Herbert Hoover drew to a close, following years in which he minimized the Depression's effects and refused to mount a major government response, thousands of jobless World War I veterans demanded assistance. Specifically, they wanted the government to immediately pay a cash bonus they had been promised. When no help was offered, a group of vets began marching on Washington from Portland, Ore. As the idea caught on, "bonus marchers" from across the country headed for the capital. Their encampments eventually housed about 20,000 people, including some vets' families.

After Congress — with Hoover's support — defeated resolutions to make early payments of the bonus, Washington police and then the U.S. Army heavy-handedly destroyed the bonus marchers' camps. Most notoriously, Army Chief of Staff Douglas A. MacArthur ignored orders to the contrary and sent troops across the Anacostia River to break up the vets' biggest tent city.[35]

Occupation tactics proved far more successful in the workplace. Following a wave of strikes in 1934 that descended into armed conflict in several cities, Congress passed the landmark Wagner Act, endorsed by President

Franklin D. Roosevelt. The law authorized unions to organize and to strike. With factory production resuming as the economy slowly revived, workers at the Firestone tire factory in Akron, Ohio, hit on a new tactic in response to the company's suspension of a union activist.[36]

Instead of leaving the factory and mounting a picket line, the workers stopped working but stayed in place. The union won: The suspended worker was reinstated, and the occupiers were paid (though at a lower rate) for the time they'd spent on strike.

The occupation — or "sitdown" — tactic spread rapidly through the entire automobile industry (and even to department stores and smaller shops in Detroit and Chicago). It generally was designed to pressure companies into recognizing and negotiating with unions. Factory takeovers were marked by workers' discipline in preventing damage to machinery.

Factory takeovers reached their peak in 1936. The standout was the occupation of General Motors factories in Flint, Mich., where GM employed about 80 percent of the workforce. The company fought back, on at least one occasion sending police to try to retake a Chevrolet plant. That move failed. And after sitdown strikes spread to GM factories elsewhere, the company gave in, formally recognizing the United Automobile Workers (UAW) as bargaining agent for workers in the occupied factories.

By late 1937, the union's victory against the world's major carmaker brought an influx of members that swelled UAW rolls to nearly 400,000, from 30,000 the previous year. And the union's example encouraged workers in other industries: 4.7 million took part in strikes in 1937, including 400,000 who joined sitdowns. That same year, total union strength reached 7 million.

Businesspeople and politicians who saw the hand of the Communist Party in the labor upsurge weren't entirely wrong, although major sectors of the movement were led by strongly anti-communist socialists. Communist Party members occupied important positions in the Congress of Industrial Organizations (CIO), the labor federation to which the new breed of more militant unions belonged, as well as in steel, automobile, maritime and electrical unions.[37]

Civil Rights and Vietnam

The movement for black equality, which had been building steadily throughout the 20th century, grew into an

Surprising Alliance: Activists and Union Members

"We are united in the belief that our country needs a change."

As he marched through Lower Manhattan last October leading telephone workers side by side with Occupy Wall Street activists, Tim Dubnau, a union organizer for the Communications Workers of America (CWA), could tell that the OWS movement's message was reaching beyond its natural leftwing constituency.

"When we passed the World Trade Center, "I chanted, 'Every job a union job,' and the hard-hat people [working on the site] were giving us the thumbs up," says Dubnau, one of a number of unionists across the country building ties with the movement.

A salute from New York City "hard-hats" carries special significance for left-wing activists. Ever since a contingent of construction workers beat up anti-Vietnam War protesters (only blocks from the eventual World Trade Center site) in 1970, the building trades have been considered a bastion of working-class patriotism and contempt for the left and the counterculture.[1]

But the hardhat reception witnessed by Dubnau during the march to the headquarters of communications giant Verizon — which is locked in a contract fight with the CWA — was only one sign of a budding Occupy-union alliance.

CWA donated thousands of dollars' worth of walkie-talkies and air mattresses to occupiers and also provided meeting rooms. Other unions have supplied ponchos and storage space. Unions elsewhere have been generous as well.[2]

Top union leaders have been showering the movement with praise since shortly after the first OWS encampment, at Manhattan's Zuccotti Park, went up. "Across America, working people are turning out with their friends and neighbors in parks, congregations and union halls to express their frustration — and anger — about our country's staggering wealth gap," Richard Trumka, president of the AFL-CIO,

declared in October, vowing continued union support for the Occupy movement.[3]

Mary Kay Henry, president of the Service Employees International Union (SEIU) declared her solidarity in *The Wall Street Journal.* "While unions cannot claim credit for Occupy Wall Street," she wrote, "SEIU members are joining the protesters in the streets because we are united in the belief that our country needs a change."[4]

Amy Muldoon, a phone worker who also works part time with the Occupy movement for the CWA, says activism focused on social and economic inequality creates a political climate favorable to organized labor.

"The unions recognize," she says, "that it's beneficial to negotiate contracts at a time when people are saying the rich and banks and corporations get away with whatever they want, and politicians are bought and sold by them."

Nevertheless, union-Occupy ties could fray when the presidential race intensifies. Already, some Occupy activists have made plain their distance from unions' long and close ties to the Democratic Party.

"There will be debates in the movement about whether people should put their energy into supporting Democrats," says Jackie Smith, a University of Pittsburgh sociology professor and Occupy activist. In that atmosphere, she says, "It will be difficult to maintain coalitions with labor."

Relations were tested on the West Coast by Occupy-initiated attempts to shut down two ports on Dec. 12. "U.S. ports have become economic engines for the elite; the 1 percent these trade hubs serve are free to rip the shirts off the backs of the 99 percent who turn their profits," the organizers of the West Coast Port Blockade announced online.[5]

In addition to the port of Oakland, Calif., the shutdowns targeted SSA Marine, a West Coast port operator, and EGT, which runs a grain shipping terminal in Longview, Wash., that is in a contract dispute with the International Longshore and Warehouse Union (ILWU). SSA is also partly owned by Goldman Sachs, a major Wall Street firm, making it an even more tempting target for Occupy activists.[6]

But union leadership opposed the Longview shutdown. "Support is one thing, organization from outside groups attempting to co-opt our struggle in order to advance a broader agenda is quite another," ILWU President Robert McEllrath said in a letter to local unions a week before the shutdown attempts, "and one that is destructive to our democratic process and jeopardizes our over-two-year struggle."[7]

In the end, port shutdowns in Longview, Oakland and Portland, Ore., cost union longshoremen all or most of their day's pay. Non-unionized truck drivers weren't paid at all. "This is a joke," driver Christian Vega told The Associated Press. "What are they protesting? It only hurts me and the other drivers."[8]

Some union longshoremen were happy with the protests. The website of the Southern California ILWU local carried a video in which Anthony, a shutdown-supporting longshoreman in Oakland, says that members were split 50-50 on the matter. "Some are upset because they lost a day's pay," he said.[9]

Anthony supported the shutdown as a "warning that the working class is serious." But, he added, the Occupy movement "probably has to get away from that 99 percent slogan, because then a lot of people say, 'You're hurt by the 99 percent not letting you go to work.' "[10]

Even some leftwing union activists found the shutdown troubling in ways that suggest that maintaining union-Occupy relations may take some work. "The ILWU is not a corrupt, stodgy union," says Dubnau of CWA. "If they're saying this is not a good tactic, you don't from the outside say this is a good tactic; you can't disrespect them," he says. "Yeah, it feels good to shut down ports; it's relatively easy to do — that doesn't mean it's a good strategy. You can't do it just because it's militant."

— *Peter Katel*

Long Beach police arrest an Occupy protester on Dec. 12, 2011, for blocking the road leading to SSA Marine, a shipping company partially owned by investment bank Goldman Sachs.

Getty Images/Kevork Djansezian

[1]For newspaper articles and other documentary material on the event, see "The HardHat Riots, an Online History Project," George Mason University, http://chnm.gmu.edu/hardhats/ homepage.html.

[2]Quoted in David B. Caruso, "Occupy movement accepts modest help from the left," The Associated Press, Nov. 1, 2011.

[3]"Statement by AFL-CIO President Richard Trumka on Occupy Wall Street," AFL-CIO, press release, Oct. 5, 2011, www.aflcio.org/media center/prsptm/pr 10052011.cfm.

[4]Mary Kay Henry, "Why Labor Backs 'Occupy Wall Street,' " *The Wall Street Journal*, Oct. 8, 2011, http://online.wsj.com/article/SB10001424052970203 47680457661520093812005 0.html.

[5]"Wall Street On the Waterfront?" West Coast Port Blockade, undated, http://westcoastportshutdown.org/content/wall-street-waterfront.

[6]"Occupy protesters seek to shut West Coast ports," The Associated Press, Dec. 12, 2011; Terry Collins, "Protesters halt operations at some western ports," The Associated Press, Dec. 13, 2011.

[7]"Message from Pres. McEllrath: We share Occupy's concerns about America, but EGG battle is complicated," ILWU Local 13, Dec. 6, 2011, www.ilwu13. com/message-from-pres.-mcellrath-we-share-occupy's-concerns-about-america-but-egt-battle-is-complicated-4580.html.

[8]Quoted in Collins, *op. cit.*

[9]"Anthony from ILWU on OccupyOakland.TV," OccupyOaklandTV, Dec. 12, 2011, www.ilwu13.com/dec.-12th — -anthony-from-ilwu-on-occupyoakland.tv-4800.html.

[10]*Ibid.*

Time Life Pictures/Getty Images/Francis Miller

Arkansas National Guard troops block Minnijean Brown, center, and other black students from entering Central High School in Little Rock on Sept. 4, 1957. After President Dwight D. Eisenhower sent U.S. Army troops to enforce desegregation at the school, a white mob resisted, unsuccessfully. Arkansas Gov. Orval Faubus charged the troop deployment had turned Little Rock into "an occupied territory."

irrepressible force in the 1950s as it adopted the tactic of mass defiance of segregation.

In 1954, the U.S. Supreme Court outlawed school segregation. The following year, the Rev. Martin Luther King Jr. led a boycott of city buses in Montgomery, Ala., in response to the arrest of NAACP activist Rosa Parks for defying the back-of-the bus law and occupying a "white" seat. The boycotters won their demand to abolish segregated seating on the buses.

In 1957, President Dwight D. Eisenhower sent Army troops to enforce the desegregation of Central High School in Little Rock, Ark. — a move that a mob of white residents resisted, unsuccessfully. Arkansas Gov. Orval Faubus charged that after the troop deployment, all of Little Rock was "an occupied territory."[38]

These dramatic events set the stage for the politically and socially tumultuous 1960s. The decade was only a month old when 20 black students from North Carolina Agricultural & Technical College in Greensboro challenged segregation in public places with a new tactic aimed at lunch counters.

After lunch counter sit-ins spread throughout the South — soon forcing stores to desegregate — activists refusing to obey state "Jim Crow" laws in buses and bus stations in the South began mounting "freedom rides" in 1961. By year's end, after the Freedom Riders had braved

mob violence, the federal Interstate Commerce Commission issued a categorical ban on racial segregation in interstate trains, buses and terminals.[39]

The next major civil rights campaign — challenging exclusion of black people from voting in southern states — followed demonstrations throughout the South that sparked police violence and killings and bombings by hardcore segregationists. The campaign resulted in the Civil Rights Act of 1964 and the Voting Rights Act of 1965, which outlawed racial discrimination in public accommodations, public education and most jobs, as well as voting procedures.[40]

King and some other civil rights leaders followed those victories by shifting their focus to poverty, including in northern cities. King was assassinated in Memphis in 1968 as he lent support to sanitation workers, all of them black, striking over discriminatory pay and working conditions. A more radical wing of the civil rights movement embraced a black nationalist doctrine in which economic goals were subordinated to political objectives, especially a rejection of racial integration.[41]

As debate raged over the civil rights movement's future, opposition to the Vietnam War was expanding, especially on college campuses. Tens of thousands of male students were becoming eligible for the draft upon graduation (or dropping out), ensuring that the escalating war commanded their attention.

By the late 1960s, the anti-war movement became polarized between ultra-leftist radicals and traditionally minded leftist activists who wanted to focus on electoral politics.

On the radical left, the only antiwar mass organization — Students for a Democratic Society (SDS) — imploded in 1969 after a bitter conflict between the "Weatherman" faction,* which preached immediate armed struggle, and a Maoist group, the Progressive Labor Party, which advocated organizing workers. Less fanatical activists fell away and SDS vanished.

At the peak of anti-war activism, news in May 1970 of a U.S. military invasion into Cambodia brought millions of war opponents into the streets throughout the country. Student demonstrations at some 1,350 colleges and universities involved an estimated 4.3 million people — 60 percent of the country's total student population. Four students at Kent State University in Kent, Ohio, were shot and killed by National Guard troops during a demonstration; and two students at predominantly African-American Jackson State College in Mississippi were shot to death by police.[42]

The anti-war movement faded away with the U.S. military withdrawal from Vietnam in 1973. Many members whose goals transcended an end to the war — that is, they sought a more equitable society — continued their activism. (An SDS founder, Tom Hayden, was a California legislator from 1982-2000.) But since the draft ended in 1973, America's military campaigns haven't mobilized an opposition even close to the size and intensity of the anti-Vietnam War movement.[43]

Globalization

Issues that aroused the left in the post-Vietnam years included nuclear power (opposed), U.S. policy in Central America (opposed) and environmental protection (supported). In the 1990s, these concerns largely gave way to opposition to the package of liberalized foreign trade rules and job outsourcing known as "globalization."

Opposition had been building for years among unions and residents of industrial areas in the Northeast and Midwest, which were losing jobs to foreign factories. When the North American Free Trade Agreement (NAFTA) came before Congress for approval in the early 1990s, the globalization question went national.[44]

At first, the NAFTA debate took place almost entirely in the political arena, not the streets. Both the Democratic and Republican parties backed NAFTA; Democratic President Bill Clinton pushed it through Congress in 1993 after his Republican predecessor, George H. W. Bush, tried but failed to do so.[45]

Opposition to globalization simmered through the 1990s, drawing much of its inspiration from movements in more politicized societies in Latin America, Asia and Africa. In the United States, one major form of activism, starting on campuses in 1997, centered on boycotts of firms whose running shoes, sweatshirts and other apparel were made in foreign and domestic sweatshops. Garment-workers unions played a major role as well, an early sign that unions and the left were rebuilding their historic alliance.[46]

A more significant sign of that convergence came in 1999 during street demonstrations in Seattle that disrupted a meeting of the World Trade Organization (WTO) convened to negotiate international commerce rules. The demonstrations, which attracted as many 50,000 globalization opponents, included a small contingent of self-styled anarchists who smashed windows in chain stores and committed other acts of vandalism.

Seattle police were by their own accounts unprepared and overwhelmed. They responded by declaring a 50-block area of the city a "no-protest" zone, at one point declaring an all-night curfew in the area and deploying massive amounts of tear gas. Police Chief Norm Stamper, who resigned following the event, said recently that he unwittingly escalated conflict by using tear gas. Police who have recently used pepper spray against Occupy demonstrators are repeating his error, he told the BBC. "Today it is being used indiscriminately," he said, "and that is really appalling."[47]

The Seattle demonstrations were a forerunner of the Occupy movement in other respects as well. Activists used email, Web chat rooms and cell phones — all in their infancy at the time — to mobilize and strategize. And they welcomed the participation of labor unions, which saw globalization as a job-killer. "We told people, if you pick up a CD or a paper cup or a stereo, under this [WTO] system, this product has more protections than the workers producing it," Ron Judd, executive secretary of the King County Labor Council in Washington state, told the *Los Angeles Times*, describing outreach to union members.[48]

In 2001, the Sept. 11 terrorist attacks transformed the political landscape. Left-liberal activists — those not transformed into hawks by the attacks — threw themselves into anti-Iraq War organizing, as well as civil liberties work and opposition to the George W. Bush administration.

Many commentators saw the 2008 Obama presidential campaign and the early phase of his administration as the rebirth of a liberal movement in sync with the Democratic Party — an alliance not seen since before the Vietnam War. "President Obama has a historic opportunity to restore an alliance that was crucial to the success of twentieth-century liberalism," Julian Zelizer, a Princeton historian, wrote in the liberal *Dissent* magazine in 2010. "The 2008 election depended on a broad Democratic coalition that bridged left and center."[49]

But the consensus is that the coalition is, at best, badly frayed. "For two years," wrote Columbia University's Gitlin after Occupy Wall Street began,

Movement Mixes Anarchy and "Pure" Democracy

Everybody gets to talk . . . and talk . . . and talk.

What's the difference between pure democracy and anarchy? The Occupy movement's decision-making process offers some answers. But one thing is certain: The process isn't neat and tidy. And sometimes it can be pretty raw.

At each occupation site, a General Assembly (G.A.) of all the activists present makes decisions through a process of "direct" democracy: Everyone votes on everything, everyone gets to speak. And speak. And speak. . . .

Some of them shout as well. At a December meeting of Occupy Oakland, one G.A. attendee periodically yelled four-letter obscenities during the assembly.

But occasional shouts are a price that the anarchist-inspired activists behind Occupy have been willing to pay. They launched Occupy Wall Street as a deliberately anti-hierarchical movement, providing a model for the entire nationwide movement and its sometimes chaotic decision-making process.

During preparations for a G.A. meeting in Manhattan in late October, a man approach the Facilitation Working Group, which would run the meeting, and proposed that the G.A. demand jobs for everyone. "The G.A. already said this is a movement without demands," another man said. "So how can there be a working group on demands?"[1]

In reality, the entire Occupy movement embodies a demand for change in an economic and political system that activists view as deeply unequal. "We come to you at a time when corporations, which place profit over people, self-interest over justice and oppression over equality run our governments," says the "Declaration of the Occupation of New York City," adopted by the Occupy Wall Street G.A. last Sept. 29.[2]

How to change the system? The declaration isn't specific: "Create a process to address the problems we face, and generate solutions accessible to everyone."[3]

That hard-to-disagree-with goal reflects organizers' initial vision of a movement that welcomed all comers and gave them all equal voice. But anarchists, while opposed to hierarchy and political domination, don't necessarily oppose leadership and structure.

"The G.A. is beautiful, but it's not an effective decision-making body," an Occupy Wall Street organizer, filmmaker Marisa Holmes, told *The New Yorker.*[4] She developed a proposal for a "Spokes Council" that would run the encampment's day-to-day affairs. In late October, the G.A. approved the plan. (Though the 24-hour Wall Street camp no longer exists, the G.A. and the Spokes Council are still meeting.)[5]

Anarchism is popularly linked with wild-eyed bomb-throwers, who were indeed a presence in the late 19th and early 20th centuries. But anarchism as a political philosophy that traced social ills to hierarchical control had a deep influence on the early labor and radical movements, including the militant Industrial Workers of the World (IWW). Its accomplishments included a landmark victory in a textile workers' strike in Lawrence, Mass., in 1912, led in part by anarchists.[6]

Later, the antifascist side in the Spanish Civil War — which inspired generations of U.S. leftwingers — had a major anarchist presence. Though anarchism in theory rejects state power, four Spanish anarchist leaders became ministers in the Republican government that was under attack by right-wing military forces.[7]

Many European anarchists had become convinced years before, says Stephen Schwartz, a historian of the Spanish conflict, that their movement needed strong leaderships because "the anarchist workers could not attain on their own the necessary quality of leadership they needed to prevail in a major political conflict."[8]

Among U.S. radicals, anarchist influence has more recent roots as well. "There were strong anarchist streaks in the New Left of the 1960s," wrote Todd Gitlin, a professor at the Columbia University School of Journalism who was president of the radical Students for a Democratic Society (SDS) in 1963-64.[9]

An SDS slogan, "Let the people decide," Gitlin added, "meant in practice, 'Let's have long meetings where everyone gets to talk.' " The eventual effect, he adds, was that "tiny hierarchies" of highly ideological Marxist-Leninists were able to take over the organization, which eventually splintered and fell apart.[10]

But that outcome only encouraged even deeper suspicion of hierarchies in later radical movements. And when the collapse of the Soviet Union seemed to spell the end of Marxism-Leninism as a viable model, and Western European socialist governments failed as well, Gitlin wrote, "Anarchism's major competitors for a theory of organization imploded."[11]

But none of that makes running a non-hierarchical organization any easier. One question already prompting debate is whether Occupy activists will work in the 2012 presidential campaign — conducted within a hierarchical, centralized, corporate-influenced political system. Many, anarchists or not, are disinclined. "A lot of activists, myself included, we vote, but we don't necessarily put much energy into the electoral process," says Jackie Smith, a University of Pittsburgh sociology professor who is working with the Occupy movement in her city.

Some activists, members of small groups formed under the Occupy umbrella, are more interested in what anarchist theoreticians call "direct action" — the other side of the sometimes cumbersome G.A. process.

In Oakland, one young group of activists who constituted Occupy Oakland's Tactical Action Committee took over a foreclosed house in a tough section of West Oakland, intending to use it as a base to organize resistance to foreclosures (as Occupy activists have done in Brooklyn, Chicago and Atlanta).[12]

Occupying homes to prevent foreclosure reflects a classically anarchist approach — the opposite of, say, asking a bank not to foreclose, or a sheriff not to evict occupants.

"The reason anarchists like direct action is because it means refusing to recognize the legitimacy of structures of power," David Graeber, an American professor of anthropology at the University of London and a Wall Street occupation planner, said before the movement began. "Nothing annoys forces of authority more than trying to bow out of the disciplinary game entirely and saying that we could just do things on our own. Direct action is a matter of acting as if you were already free."[13]

— *Peter Katel, with reporting in*
Oakland by Daniel McGlynn

OFF/AFP/Getty Images

Vladimir Lenin, main founder of the Soviet state, clashed with anarchists. In the 1960s, young American radicals inspired by Lenin clashed with anarchist-inspired counterparts, hastening the eventual collapse of Students for a Democratic Society.

[4]Schwartz, *op. cit.*

[5]New York City General Assembly, /www.nycga. net/events/event/general-assembly-2012-01-05/.

[6]Dorothy Gallagher, *All the Right Enemies: The Life and Murder of Carlo Tresca* (1988), pp. 35-40; Michael Kazin, *American Dreamers: How the Left Changed America* (2011), pp. 127-129.

[7]Hugh Thomas, *The Spanish Civil War* (1961), pp. 44, 318.

[8]For background see Victor Alba and Stephen Schwartz, *Spanish Marxism Versus Soviet Communism: A History of the P.O.U.M. in the Spanish Civil War* (2009).

[9]Todd Gitlin, "The Left Declares Its Independence," *The New York Times*, Oct. 9, 2011, Section SR, p. 4.

[10]*Ibid.*

[11]*Ibid.*

[12]Jason Cherkis, "Occupy Atlanta Helps Save Iraq War Veteran's Home From Foreclosure," *Huffington Post*, Dec. 19, 2011, www.huffingtonpost.com/2011/12/ 19/occupy-atlanta-saves-iraq-veterans-home-from-foreclosure_n_1158097.html; Adam Martin, "Occupy Our Homes Takes Over Properties in New York and Chicago," *The Atlantic Wire*, Dec. 6, 2011, www.theatlanticwire.com/national/ 2011/12/occupy-our-homes-occupies-its-first-home/45832/.

[13]Ellen Evans and Jon Moses, "Interview With David Graeber," *The White Review*, 2011, www.thewhitereview.org/interviews/interview-with-david-graeber.

[1]Quoted in Mattathias Schwartz, "Pre-Occupied," *The New Yorker*, Nov. 28, 2011, www.newyorker. com/reporting/2011/11/28/111128fa_fact_schwartz.

[2]"Declaration of the Occupation of New York City," New York City General Assembly, www.nycga.net/ resources/declaration.

[3]*Ibid.*

"Barack Obama got the benefit of the doubt from fervent supporters — I'd bet that many of those in Lower Manhattan during these weeks went door-to-door for him in 2008 — and that support explains why no one occupied Wall Street in 2009."[50]

CURRENT SITUATION

Occupy Caucuses

As the 2012 presidential race moves into full swing, Occupy demonstrators are trying to turn the primary-election process for evaluating presidential candidates into the latest theater of action.

The Iowa caucuses, held Jan. 3 and narrowly won by Romney by just eight votes over former Pennsylvania Sen. Rick Santorum, provided a preview of the Occupy efforts. Activists who organized "Occupy Iowa Caucuses" vowed to confront both Republican contenders and supporters of President Obama. "President Obama and the other bought-and-paid-for candidates who give us the brush-off when we try to ask real questions will be forced to hear us as we converge upon their campaign headquarters," organizers said on a website set up for the occasion. "We will chase the candidates and their Wall Street cronies around the state of Iowa. . . . We are taking American democracy back!"[51]

When the Republican primary road show moved to New Hampshire in early January, Occupy activists followed. Their numbers were not large, though Occupy New Hampshire members did manage to draw attention by attending GOP candidates' campaign events, sometimes chanting slogans. One of their targets, Romney, won the primary with 39.3 percent of the vote. Rep. Ron Paul, R-Tex., came in second, with 22.9 percent, followed by former Utah Gov. Jon Huntsman, 16.9 percent; Gingrich, 9.4 percent; and former Sen. Rick Santorum, 2.2 percent. All vowed to pursue their candidacies in the South Carolina Republican primary.[52]

In Iowa, activists' main targets were Republican candidates for the presidential nomination. For them, the Iowa caucuses — that state's more complicated version of a primary election — were a critical step in the process by which the list of contenders gets narrowed down.

On the last day of 2011, 18 Occupy protesters were arrested in separate episodes outside the Iowa headquarters of Republican candidates Michele Bachmann, a Minnesota representative who subsequently dropped out of the presidential race after finishing sixth in the state's caucuses; and former House speaker Gingrich, who finished fourth, and Santorum.[53]

Most of those arrested — members of a contingent small enough to fit in three rented buses — were arrest-hardened veterans of previous Occupy demonstrations. One of them, 16-year-old Heaven Chamberlain, had been arrested at an Occupy demonstration at the Iowa state capitol in October. She professed pride in her record. "It shows that I'm active with the community," she told *The New York Times*, "and that I care about people's opinions."[54]

Her mother and fellow Occupy activist shares that view of the teenager's rap sheet. "For her record I don't worry, because she's standing up for what's right," Heather Ryan told *The Times*.[55]

Iowa is not the only place in which the movement has been trying to demonstrate a 2012 presence. "Whose year? Our year!," chanted several hundred people gathered in New York's Zuccotti Park on New Year's Eve.[56] Their attempt to reclaim the park ended as did several of the Occupy events of 2011 in New York — with arrests, including at least one police use of pepper spray.[57]

Activists reoccupied the park in early January after city authorities removed barricades and checkpoints that had limited the number of people allowed in; but a ban on tents and sleeping bags remained in force.

But while the New York events resembled past confrontations between Occupy and the New York Police Department, the attempt to bring the movement to the caucuses apparently represented the first collision between Occupy and the electoral process.

Occupy activists aren't neglecting events that may enjoy higher visibility than primary elections. On New Year's Day, several thousand Occupy marchers followed the Rose Bowl parade in Pasadena, Calif., with a parade of their own. Their props included a 250-foot banner that said "We the People," and a 70-foot plastic octopus intended to represent the tentacles of corporate greed.[58]

Occupy Elections

One political campaign stands out as the best test case so far of the Occupy movement's effect on voters and candidates.

AT ISSUE

Will the Occupy movement continue to affect American politics?

YES
Dean Baker
Co-director, Center for Economic and Policy Research

Written for *CQ Researcher*, January 2012

The Super Committee, the big topic of conversation in Washington in early October, was the longstanding dream of many D.C. deficit hawks. It had the power to produce a deficit-reduction plan that would be fast-tracked through Congress.

But as it turned out, the Super Committee produced no plan to send to Congress for a vote. Its deadline passed, and the committee became just another deficit-reduction plan to be tossed into history's dustbin.

Part of the committee's story was undoubtedly the intransigence of Republican members who refused to go along with anything that could raise taxes. However, part of the story was the constraints perceived by Democrats who were openly willing to include cuts to Social Security and Medicare as part of a deal.

As the Occupy Wall Street movement spread across the country, the obsession with deficit reduction dwindled. Almost every major news outlet ran one or more major stories on the rise in income inequality over the past three decades. The distinction between the "1 percent" who were the big gainers in the economy over the last three decades and the "99 percent" who had almost nothing to show became a standard feature of political debate.

In this context, it became almost inconceivable for the Democrats on the Super Committee to "reward" the 99 percent with big cuts in Social Security and Medicare. The party that has pretenses of protecting working people and the poor could not be seen slashing these two essential programs at a time when the country is still suffering from the recession.

President Obama's December speech in Osawatomie, Kan., which focused on inequality and helping ordinary workers get ahead, should also be seen in this context. There is a renewed commitment — at least in rhetoric — to pursue an economic agenda that advances the interest of the vast majority.

In this context it is striking to see the surge in interest in a financial-speculation tax. This is the sort of measure that gets to the heart of the Occupy agenda. It would strike a big blow directly against the financial speculation that has dominated Wall Street in the last few decades, while raising hundreds of billions of dollars over the next decade. The fact that this tax and other comparable measures are now part of the national debate is directly attributable to the Occupy movement.

NO
Nick Schulz
DeWitt Wallace Fellow, American Enterprise Institute

Written for *CQ Researcher*, January 2012

The current movement protesting income inequality aims its guns at the wrong targets. As long as that is so, it will not have much of an effect on American politics.

Most Americans aren't interested in redistributing income from the rich to the poor as a way of addressing inequality. They are more interested in living in a society with adequate social mobility — where a person can climb the socioeconomic ladder through talent and hard work. To the extent that envy animates today's anti-inequality movement, it will fail to gain sufficient political traction.

Upward mobility in America today requires an individual to possess adequate amounts of human, social and cultural capital. In order to address the obstacles to upward mobility, we could start by thinking about what I call a different kind of "home economics": the economic consequences of America's changing family structure. The collapse of intact families over the last half-century, manifest in rising numbers of single-parent homes and rising out-of-wedlock birthrates, has eroded vital human and social capital, and it has had baleful economic consequences as a result. This is a problem for which there is no easy solution, but it is a mistake to ignore it as a driver of economic outcomes.

We could also think creatively about another critical institution for inculcating and developing essential human and social capital — schools. There are good ideas across the ideological spectrum for reforming and strengthening schools. But genuine reform will require a period of messy experimentation and trial and error. As a nation we must be open to radical ways of thinking about education as entrepreneurs find new ways of educating students; develop new business, academic and management models; and build new technology.

To the extent that today's movement to protest inequality is comfortable with the educational status quo, it will fail to make a genuine difference.

While relative income and living standards matter, absolute living standards matter most of all. Ask yourself if you'd prefer to live in an unequal country with the living standards of the United States or an equal country with the living standards of Congo. The point is that snapshots of a nation's income inequality matter less over time to a nation's welfare than economic growth and increases in productivity. It's not that income inequality doesn't matter; it's just that many things matter a great deal more.

Elizabeth Warren, front-runner for the Democratic nomination for the 2012 Senate election in Massachusetts, is a favorite of the Occupy movement. The Harvard Law School professor gained national attention as a fierce critic of the financial industry. She launched her candidacy after President Obama bowed to massive opposition from Republicans and backed off nominating her to head the new Consumer Financial Protection Bureau, which she largely created.

Elizabeth Warren, the front-runner for the Democratic nomination for the 2012 Senate election in Massachusetts, is the closest thing to an Occupy candidate within the two-party system.

A Harvard Law School professor of commercial law who gained national attention as a fierce critic of the financial industry, Warren launched her candidacy after President Obama backed off nominating her to head the new Consumer Financial Protection Bureau. He bowed to massive opposition from Republicans, echoing the position of industries the bureau is charged with overseeing. Warren, a specialist in consumer debt, largely wrote the legislation that created the bureau.[59]

The Oklahoma-born Warren's advocacy on behalf of ordinary consumers who sign up for credit cards and take out mortgages has done wonders for the campaign treasury of her possible general-election opponent. Finance-industry executives are pouring money into the campaign of Sen. Scott Brown, R-Mass., whom Warren would oppose in the November election if she wins the primary race in September.[60]

"Elizabeth is about 99-1-99," a Wall Street executive, Anthony Scaramucci, managing partner of Skybridge Capital, told *The New York Times*, referring to former Republican presidential primary candidate Herman Cain's "9-9-9" tax plan. "She thinks the 99 percent want to tax the 1 percent 99 percent. It is a failed strategy."[61]

The Center for Responsive Politics reports that the securities and investment, law and real-estate industries are among the top five sectors of Brown's campaign contributors. They account for about $3.2 million of $5.3 million in donations Brown has received since he began his national political career, winning a special election in January 2010 for the Senate seat vacated by the death of Democratic Sen. Edward M. (Ted) Kennedy.[62]

If her Wall Street enemies didn't suffice to link Warren with the Occupy movement, she herself drew the connection in late October soon after entering the primary race. "I created much of the intellectual foundation for what they do," she said of the movement, then in its second month.[63]

Republicans leapt to attack. A National Republican Senatorial Campaign Committee spokesman, Brian Walsh, noted that two Occupy Boston demonstrators had been arrested for allegedly selling heroin. "Professor Warren has yet to comment on whether these were also some of the individuals that she's now claiming to have provided the 'intellectual foundation' for as well," Walsh said in a press release.[64]

Warren then followed up her remark by drawing a line between her campaign and the Occupy movement. "What I meant to say was I've been protesting Wall Street for a long time," she told The Associated Press. "The Occupy Wall Street [Movement] is organic, it is independent, and that's how it should be." And she pointedly opposed law-breaking by demonstrators.[65]

But Republicans kept up their strategy of portraying Warren as comrade-in-arms of radical demonstrators. One TV ad produced by an affiliate of American Crossroads, a so-called "super PAC" not subject to funding or spending restrictions for its political advocacy, juxtaposed images of

Warren with those of demonstrators, to illustrate that she "sides with extreme left" demonstrators who "attack police, do drugs and trash public parks."[66]

Strikingly, the next ad in the Crossroads campaign took an entirely different tack. Apparently responding to poll data showing voter discontent with banks and big business, the follow-up commercial depicted Warren as overly friendly to Wall Street. The ad focused on Warren's role as staff director of a congressional investigation of Treasury Department administration of the $700 billion financial industry bailout. "Congress had Warren oversee how your tax dollars were spent, bailing out the same banks that helped cause the financial meltdown," Crossroads declared.[67]

Warren shot back, calling the charge "ridiculous" in an ad of her own.[68]

Occupy and Anti-Semitism

Of all the accusations hurled at the Occupy movement, the potentially most damaging is that it's become an outlet for haters who follow a classic anti-Semitic script by arguing that Jews pull the strings on Wall Street.

Jewish supporters of Occupy responded immediately, noting that an author of the accusation is a Republican strategist. But that conflict has morphed into a debate within the amorphous movement itself over what role it should take, if any, on the conflict between Israel and Palestinians.

The anti-Semitism charge surfaced almost as soon as the movement began. A Web-broadcast video featured clips of anti-Jewish statements and placards from people at Occupy Wall Street.[69]

The video — which also featured cautious expressions of sympathy for the demonstrators by President Obama, former House Speaker Nancy Pelosi, D-Calif., and former New York Attorney General Eliot Spitzer — was produced by the Emergency Committee for Israel (ECI), whose chairman, William Kristol, editor of the *Weekly Standard*, is a prominent Republican of the hawkish neoconservative school.[70]

Aimed at rallying opposition to the movement, the video prompted immediate counterattacks from within the Jewish community.

"It's an old, discredited tactic: find a couple of unrepresentative people in a large movement and then conflate the oddity with the cause," said a statement signed by 15 prominent liberal Jewish Occupy supporters. "Occupy Wall Street is a mass protest against rising inequality in America."[71]

The nonpartisan Anti-Defamation League, a nearly century-old organization that fights anti-Semitism, declared in October that "anti-Semitism has not gained traction more broadly with the protesters, nor is it representative of the larger movement at this time."[72]

Before long, however, the issue of Occupy and anti-Semitism shifted from an argument between politically opposed foes and supporters of the movement. Activists began arguing over whether the Occupy movement should involve itself in the fight between Israel and the Palestinians. That debate reawakened the original conflict over Occupy as a refuge for anti-Jewish sentiment, given the long-running debate over when anti-Israel, pro-Palestinian politics cross the line into anti-Semitism. That highly charged issue runs through all debate over Israel, especially on the left and most especially among Jews.

One of the events that prompted the conflict was a Nov. 4 sit-in at the Israeli consulate in Boston by about 20 Occupy members who had marched from a downtown encampment in Dewey Square.[73]

The action was intended to support a failed attempt to bring supplies by ship to Gaza, a Palestinian enclave under Israeli military control, in defiance of an Israeli maritime blockade. In New York, Occupy Wall Street issued a Nov. 3 tweet of support for the blockade-running effort. But the tweet was deleted, on the grounds that the entire Occupy Wall Street movement hadn't taken a position on the matter, the nonpartisan JTA news service on Jewish affairs reported.[74]

Some in the movement were demanding that it oppose Israeli policies. But Daniel Sieradski, an Occupy activist who organized Occupy Judaism, which held Jewish services at Zuccotti Park, has been working to keep Occupy open to supporters as well as foes of Israeli policy by keeping the movement out of Middle Eastern matters. "We are being sidetracked by some in our community and some outside our community who are insisting on integrating this into the Occupy Wall Street platform," Sieradski told JTA.[75]

A long piece in the neoconservative monthly *Commentary* criticized that approach as a dodge to avoid grappling with the challenges posed by anti-Israel sentiment on the left — often, the Jewish left. "The blind quest for 'social justice' in its left-wing understanding, despite the onslaught of leftist hatred for the Jewish people and the Jewish state, demonstrates the degree to which too many Jews overlook or excuse the indefensible," wrote Jonathan Neumann, a fellow at the magazine who specializes in the Middle East.[76]

One of the targets of Neumann's criticism, staff writer Marc Tracy of *Tablet*, an online magazine on Jewish affairs, responded: "The main reason I did not enjoy seeing certain OWS [Occupy Wall Street] protests adopting an anti-Zionist agenda is because I saw neither the relevance nor the connection between anti-Zionism and OWS's '1 percent' message, and I didn't see the connection because I am in fact a Zionist who also supports OWS's economic message."[77]

OUTLOOK

New Progressive Era?

Of all the forecasts about the possible future of the Occupy movement, one of the most far-reaching comes from Jeffrey D. Sachs, an influential economist who directs the Earth Institute at Columbia University.

"A third progressive era is likely to be in the making," Sachs wrote in *The New York Times* in November. The Occupy movement, he argued, is harbinger and engine of a 21st-century version of the periods of the late 1800s and early 1900s and the 1930s characterized by sweeping social and regulatory legislation.[78]

"Twice before in American history, powerful corporate interests dominated Washington and brought America to a state of unacceptable inequality, instability and corruption," Sachs wrote. "Both times a social and political movement arose to restore democracy and shared prosperity."[79]

Kazin, the Georgetown University historian and veteran of the 1960s anti-war movement, offers a more cautious assessment. "Movements of this kind," he says, "especially ones that are this fluid and rise quickly, may also fragment quickly." He adds, however, that the large community of activist young people suddenly made visible by Occupy is likely to remain engaged, given the persistence of the economic conditions underlying the movement.

If Kazin is wary of declaring the dawn of a new age, he has the experience of having written in 1999 that

the anti-globalization demonstrations in Seattle likely represented the birth of a new populist movement.[80] Yet Kazin in that piece may simply have been ahead of his time. "Something like Occupy would have come much sooner if not for 9/11," says Muldoon, the CWA union member working with the Occupy movement in New York. "It was like someone threw the emergency brake."

As for the future, Muldoon says, "I think you'll be able to look back and say that things shifted." She adds, "Some of this is up to us about how significant a shift."

Also up to the movement and its tentative allies in the Democratic Party is whether and how to bridge the profound differences between believers and nonbelievers in the two-party system.

Columbia University's Gitlin acknowledged: "Of course, it's also conceivable that the structural divergences are so great that they can't be bridged. Sometimes these things blow up and leave everything in ruins."[81]

Among Occupy opponents, Bossie of Citizens United, the producer of conservative videos, describes in a tone of deep satisfaction what he says will be the short and unremembered life of Occupy. "I don't think the movement had any effect except to tell the American people just what they don't want America to become," he says.

Alliances with conventional politicos are doomed, Bossie says. "The leftist politicians are now trying to distance themselves from it, because they understand the American people are so turned off by this really sick movement."

Davis, the former Democratic congressman, who describes himself as a centrist, argues that the movement's future depends on whether activists decide to remain outside the conventional political system. "You can influence society simply by making a point over and over again, which is relatively easy to do," he says. "Influencing politics is much harder. It requires mobilizing people, keeping them energized, raising money, building a structure."

Moreover, he says, the movement will have to develop a clearer analysis of America's ills — moving beyond frequently voiced complaints about the burdens of college loans. "I haven't heard Occupy Wall Street spend any time talking about 35 million children being income-insecure," he says, "Those children have a higher moral priority than people paying student loans."

Occupy's future also depends on the nature of authorities' response, argues the CWA's Dubnau. Repression, he notes, has been known to radicalize its targets.

Dubnau cites widely circulated video footage of a University of California, Davis, police officer squirting pepper spray into the faces of students conducting a peaceful sit-in on campus.[82] "You get pepper-sprayed," he says, "you're going to come out a different person."

* Freelance writer Daniel McGlynn contributed reporting from Oakland.

NOTES

1. Quoted in "Inside Occupy Wall Street: A Tour of Activist Encampment at the heart of Growing Protest," "Democracy Now," Sept. 30, 2011, www .democracynow.org/2011/9/30/inside_ occupy_ wall_st_a_tour.

2. Quoted in Erik Eckholm and Timothy Williams, "Anti-Wall Street Protests Spreading to Cities Large and Small," *The New York Times*, Oct. 4, 2011, p. A18.

3. Paul Courson, "Occupy DC demonstrators bolstered by migrating NYC Occupiers," CNN, Jan. 3, 2012, www.cnn.com/2012/01/02/us/occupy-migration/?hpt=us_c2; New York City General Assembly, www.nycga.net/events/event/ general-assembly-2012-01-05/.

4. John Heilemann, "2012=1968," *New York* magazine, Nov. 27, 2011, http://nymag.com/ news/politics/occupy-wall-street-2011-12; Sean Captain, "Occupy Geeks Are Building a Facebook for the 99%," *Wired* (Threat Level blog), Dec. 27, 2011, www.wired.com/ threatlevel/ 2011/12/occupy-facebook.

5. For background, see the following *CQ Researcher* reports: Peter Katel, "Child Poverty," Oct. 28, 2011, pp. 901-928; Maryann Hagerty, "Business Ethics," March 6, 2011, pp. 409-432; Marcia Clemmitt, "Income Inequality," Dec. 3, 2010, pp. 989-1012; Marcia Clemmitt, "Financial Industry Overhaul," July 30, 2010, pp. 629-652; Peter Behr, "Fixing Capitalism" (*CQ Global Researcher*), July 1, 2009, pp. 177-204; and Thomas J. Billitteri, "Middle Class Squeeze," March 6, 2009, pp. 201-224.

6. "Trends in the Distribution of Household Income Between 1979 and 2007," Congressional Budget Office, October 2011, p. ix, www.cbo. gov/ftpdocs/124xx/doc12485/10-25-Household Income.pdf.

7. "Divided We Stand: Why Inequality Keeps Rising — An Overview of Growing Inequalities in OECD Countries," OECD, 2011, p. 38, www.oecd.org/ dataoecd/40/12/49170449.pdf.

8. Sabrina Tavernise, "Survey Finds Rising Perception of Class Tension," *The New York Times*, Jan. 11, 2012.

9. Heilemann, *op. cit.*

10. Quoted in Beth Fouhy, "Democrats see minefield in Occupy protests," The Associated Press, Nov. 17, 2011; Michael Kazin, "Anarchism Now: Occupy Wall Street Revives an Ideology," *The New Republic*, Nov. 7, 2011, www.tnr.com/ article/politics/97114/ anarchy-occupy-wall-street-throwback.

11. Thomas Kaplan, "Albany Tax Deal To Increase Rate For Top Earners," *The New York Times*, Dec. 7, 2011, p. A1; Andrew Rosenthal, "Fighting the 'Governor One Percent' Label," The Loyal Opposition blog, *The New York Times*, Nov. 30, 2011.

12. "Frustration with Congress Could Hurt Republican Incumbents," Pew Research Center, Dec. 15, 2011, pp. 3-4, www.people-press.org/ files/legacy-pdf/ 12-15-11%20Congress%20and %20Economy%20 release.pdf.

13. Adam Gabbatt, "Scott Olsen injuries prompt review as Occupy Oakland protests continue," *The Guardian*, Oct. 26, 2011, www.guardian. co.uk/world/2011/ oct/26/scott-olsen-occupy-oakland-review; Joshua Holland, "Who's Behind the Mayhem at the Occupy Oakland Protests?," *AlterNet*, Nov. 11, 2011, www .alternet.org/ media/153053/who's_behind_the_mayhem_at_the_occupy_oakland_protests/?page=entire.

14. "Remarks by the President on the Economy in Osawatomie, Kansas," The White House, Dec. 6, 2011, www.whitehouse.gov/the-press-office/2011/ 12/06/remarks-president-economy-osawatomie-kansas.

15. "From the Archives: President Teddy Roosevelt's New Nationalism Speech," The White House Blog, Dec. 6, 2011, www.whitehouse. gov/blog/2011/12/

06/archives-president-teddy-roosevelts-new-nation alism-speech.

16. Nicholas Confessore, Christopher Drew and Julie Creswell, "Buyout Profits Keep Flowing to Romney," *The New York Times*, Dec. 18, 2011, www.nytimes .com/2011/12/19/us/politics/ retirement-deal-keeps-bain-money-flowing-to-romney.html?page wanted=all. See also Sarah B. Boxer, "Mitt Romney zings 'Occupy Wall Street' and praises Herman Cain in N.H.," CBS News, Oct. 11, 2011, www.cbsnews .com/8301-5035 44_162-20118511-503544.html.

17. Meg Handley, "Romney Conjures Occupy Wall Street in New Campaign Video," *U.S. News & World Report*, Dec. 28, 2011, www.us news.com/news/blogs/ballot-2012/2011/12/28/ romney-conjures-occupy-wall-street-in-new-campaign-video; "We Are the 99 Percent," http://wearethe99percent.tumblr.com.

18. Quoted in "Newt Gingrich on Occupy Wall Street: Protesters Should 'Get a Job' and 'Take a Bath,' " *Huffington Post*, Nov. 19, 2011, www.huffingtonpost .com/2011/11/19/newt-gingrich-occupy-wall-street-job-bath_n_1103172.html.

19. "More Now Disagree With Tea Party — Even in Tea Party Districts," Pew Research Center, Nov. 29, 2011, www.people-press.org/2011/11/29/more-now-disagree-with-tea-party---even-in-tea-party-districts.

20. "We Are the 99 Percent," http://wearethe 99percent .tumblr.com.

21. Rich Lowry, "Heed the 99 Percent," *National Review*, Oct. 14, 2011, www.nationalreview.com/ articles/280104/heed-99-percent-rich-lowry.

22. Dylan Byers, "Occupy Wall Street is winning," *Politico*, Nov. 11, 2011, www.politico.com/blogs/bensmith/ 1111/Occupy_Wall_Street_is_winning.html#.

23. Jared Bernstein, "On Inequality: Why Now?," *On the Economy* (blog), Dec. 6, 2011, http:// jaredbernstein blog.com/on-inequality-why-now/.

24. "A Report Card for the Tea Party," "Weekend Edition Sunday," NPR, Dec. 25, 2011, www.npr .org/2011/12/25/144248297/a-report-card-for-the-tea-party-2011.

25. Neil Irwin, "Hamilton Project relaunches in a more friendly environment," *The Washington Post*, April 22, 2010, p. A17.

26. Madeleine Kunin, "Occupy Congress," *The Huffington Post*, Dec. 9, 2011, www.huffington post.com/madeleine-m-kunin/occupy-congress_ b_1138870.html.

27. Heilemann, *op. cit.*

28. Adam Hochschild, "Common Threads: We Are Not Alone," *Occupied Wall Street Journal*, Nov. 18, 2011, http://occupiedmedia.us/2011/ 11/wearenotalone.

29. *Ibid.*

30. Stephen Brier, *et al.*, *Who Built America?: Working People & the Nation's Economy, Politics, Culture & Society* (1992), pp. 68-154.

31. *Ibid.*, pp. 111-112.

32. Richard Schneirov, "The Pullman Strike and Boycott," *Illinois During the Gilded Age* (2007), http://dig.lib .niu.edu/gildedage/pullman/events3.html.

33. Amanda Wisner, " 'General' Jacob S. Coxey," Massillon (Ohio) Museum, 2006, www.massillon museum.org/research_massillonhistory_coxey.html.

34. Beverly Gage, "Lessons for Occupy Wall Street," *Slate*, Nov. 2, 2011, /www.slate.com/articles/business/ moneybox/2011/11/occupy_ wall_street_how_how_ the_protesters_should_respond_to_esca.single.html.

35. "The Bonus March," "American Experience," PBS, undated, www.pbs.org/wgbh/amex/macarthur/people events/pandeAMEX89.html.

36. Jim Pope, "Worker Lawmaking, Sit-Down Strikes, and the Shaping of American Industrial Relations, 1935-1958," *Law and History Review*, Spring 2006, www.historycooperative.org/journals/lhr/24.1/ pope.html.

37. *Ibid.*

38. Quoted in "Desegregation of Central High School," National Park Service in *Encyclopedia of Arkansas History and Culture*, updated Sept. 28, 2011, http:// encyclopediaofarkansas.net/encyclopedia/entry-detail.aspx?entryID=718.

39. "Freedom to Travel," in "Freedom Riders," PBS, 2011, www.pbs.org/wgbh/americanexperience/ freedomriders/issues/freedom-to-travel.

40. "Major Features of the Civil Rights Act of 1964," Dirksen Congressional Center, undated, www.con gresslink.org/print_basics_histmats_civilrights

64text.htm; "The Voting Rights Act of 1965," U.S. Justice Department, undated, www. justice.gov/crt/about/vot/intro/intro_b.php.

41. "1968 AFSCME Memphis Sanitation Workers' Strike Chronology," AFSCME, undated, www .afscme.org/union/history/mlk/1968-afscme-memphis-sanitation-workers-strike-chronology; Daniel Levine, *Bayard Rustin and the Civil Rights Movement* (2000), pp. 191-192.

42. Jerry M. Lewis and Thomas R. Hensley, "The May 4 Shootings at Kent State University: The Search for Historical Accuracy," Prof. Jerry M. Lewis website, http://dept.kent.edu/sociology/lewis/lewihen.htm; Kirkpatrick Sale, *SDS* (1974), pp. 635-636.

43. Drummond Ayres Jr., "Political Briefing; System Catches Up With Tom Hayden," *The New York Times*, Aug. 27, 2000, www.nytimes.com/2000/08/27/us/political-briefing-system-catches-up-with-tom-hayden.html?src=pm.

44. For background, see Peter Katel, "Reviving Manufacturing," *CQ Researcher*, July 22, 2011, pp. 601-624.

45. "NAFTA and Democracy," Public Citizen, undated, /www.citizen.org/trade/nafta/votes; "NAFTA," *Duke Law Library & Technology*, updated January 2011, www.law.duke.edu/lib/ researchguides/nafta.

46. Liz Featherstone, "Students Against Sweatshops: A History," in Daniel E. Bender and Richard A. Greenwald, eds., *Sweatshop USA: The American Sweatshop in Historical and Global Perspective* (2003), pp. 247-264.

47. Quoted in Chloe Hadjimatheou, "Ex-Seattle chief: 'Occupy' police used 'failed' tactics," BBC News, Nov. 28, 2011, www.bbc.co.uk/news/magazine-15929017.

48. Quoted in Kim Murphy and Nancy Cleeland, "Labor Unions Revive Powerful Past as WTO March Looks to New Future," *Los Angeles Times*, Dec. 4, 1999, p. A18.

49. Julian E. Zelizer, "Carter, Obama, and the Left-Center Divide," *Dissent*, June 9, 2010, www.dissent magazine.org/online.php?id=361.

50. Todd Gitlin, "The Left Declares Its Independence," *The New York Times*, Oct. 9, 2011, Opinion Section, p. 4.

51. "First in the Nation Caucus Occupation," Occupy Iowa Caucuses, undated, www.occupyiowacaucuses .org.

52. "New Hampshire Primary Results," *The New York Times*, Jan. 10, 2012, http://elections.nytimes. com/2012/primaries/results/live/2012-01-10.

53. Brian Bakst, "Occupy Protesters Arrested Outside Republican Presidential Candidates' Iowa Campaign Headquarters," The Associated Press (*Huffington Post*), Dec. 31, 2011, www. huffingtonpost.com/2011/12/31/occupy-protests-iowa-caucuses-2012_n_1177997 .html?ref= occupy-wall-street.

54. Quoted in Will Storey, "For 'Occupy the Caucus' Protesters, a Successful Day of Arrests," *The New York Times* (The Caucus blog), Dec. 31, 2011, http://the caucus.blogs.nytimes.com/2011/12/31/for-occupy-the-caucus-pro testers-a-successful-day-of-arrests.

55. Quoted in *ibid.*

56. Quoted in Colin Moynihan and Elizabeth A. Harris, "Surging Back Into Zuccotti Park, Protesters Are Cleared by Police," *The New York Times* (City Room blog), updated Jan. 1, 2012, http://cityroom.blogs .nytimes.com/2011/12/31/protesters-surge-back-into-zuccotti-park.

57. *Ibid.*

58. "Rose Bowl parade gets occupied," The Associated Press (CBS News), Jan. 2, 2012, www.cbsnews .com/8301-201_162-57350999/rose-bowl-parade-gets-occupied.

59. Samuel P. Jacobs, "Warren Takes Credit for Occupy Wall Street," *Daily Beast*, Oct. 24, 2011, www.the dailybeast.com/articles/2011/10/24/ elizabeth-warren-i-created-occupy-wall-street. html; Jim Puzzanghera "U.S. Senate race puts spotlight on Wall St.," *Orlando Sentinel*, Dec. 30, 2011, p. A13.

60. Quoted in Nicholas Confessore, "Vilifying Rival, Wall St. Rallies for Senate Ally," *The New York Times*, Nov. 18, 2011, www.nytimes.com/ 2011/11/19/us/politics/wall-street-rallies-around-scott-brown-for-senate-race.html?pagewanted =all.

61. Quoted in *ibid.*

62. "Total Raised and Spent, 2012 Race: Massachusetts Senate," Center for Responsive Politics, updated

Dec. 30, 2011, www.opensecrets.org/races/summary .php?cycle=2012&id=MAS1.

63. Quoted in Jacobs, *op. cit.*

64. Quoted in Andrew Miga, "Warren claims credit for Occupy Wall St. protests," The Associated Press, Oct. 25, 2011.

65. Quoted in Bob Salsberg, "US Senate hopeful Warren clarifies protest remark," The Associated Press, Oct. 27, 2011.

66. Quoted in Andrew Miga, "Outside groups air barrage of ads in Mass. Race," The Associated Press, Dec. 27, 2011.

67. Quoted in Puzzanghera, *op. cit.*

68. Miga, *op. cit.*, "Outside groups."

69. "Hate at Occupy Wall Street," Emergency Committee for Israel, Oct. 13, 2011, www.you tube.com/watch? feature=player_embedded& v=NIlRQCPJcew#!.

70. "Emergency Committee for Israel," www. committee forisrael.com.

71. "Jewish Leaders Denounce Right-Wing Smears of Occupy Wall Street," Jewish Leaders Against Smears, Nov. 1, 2011, http://jewish leadersagainstsmears .wordpress.com.

72. " 'Occupy Wall Street' Demonstrations: Anti-Semitic Incidents Surface," Anti-Defamation League, updated Nov. 1, 2011, www.adl.org/main_Extremism/ occupy_wall_street.htm.

73. Dennis Trainor Jr., "Occupy Boston Occupies Israeli Consulate," ncftv, YouTube, Nov. 4, 2011, www .youtube.com/watch?v=xd1uO29UwzY.

74. Dan Klein, "Pro-Palestinian activists push cause within Occupy Wall Street movement," JTA, Nov. 15, 2011, www.jta.org/news/article-print/2011/11/15/3090241/ pro-palestinian-activists-face-pushback-within-occupy-wall-street-movement?TB_iframe=true& width=750& height=500.

75. Quoted in *ibid.*

76. Jonathan Neumann, "Occupy Wall Street and the Jews," *Commentary*, January 2012, www.commen tarymagazine.com/article/occupy-wall-street-and-the-jews.

77. Marc Tracy, "How Jewish is Occupy Wall Street?," *Tablet*, Dec. 29, 2011, www.tabletmag.com/ scroll/87123/how-jewish-is-occupy-wall-street/.

78. Jeffrey D. Sachs, "The New Progressive Movement," *The New York Times*, Nov. 12, 2011, www. nytimes .com/2011/11/13/opinion/sunday/the-new-progressive-movement.html.

79. *Ibid.*

80. Michael Kazin, "Saying No to W.T.O.," *The New York Times*, Dec. 5, 1999, Sec. 4, p. 17.

81. Heilemann, *op. cit.*

82. "UC Davis Protesters Pepper Sprayed," Aggie TV, Nov. 18, 2011, www.youtube.com/watch?v= 6AdDLhPwpp4.

BIBLIOGRAPHY

Selected Sources
Books

Flank, Lenny, ed., *Voices From the 99 Percent: An Oral History of the Occupy Wall Street Movement*, Red and Black, 2011.
Participants tell the movement's brief story thus far.

Gessen, Keith, et al., eds., *Occupy: Scenes from Occupied America*, n+1, 2011.
A series of reports and essays by sympathetic observers chronicle the movement and examine its possibilities.

Kazin, Michael, *American Dreamers: How the Left Changed a Nation*, Knopf, 2011.
A Georgetown University historian, sympathetic but not naive, examines the role of the left in U.S. history.

Articles

Abelson, Max, "Bankers Join Billionaires to Debunk 'Imbecile' Attack on Top 1%," Bloomberg, http:// mobile.bloom berg.com/news/2011-12-20/bankers-join-billionaires-to-debunk-imbecile-attack-on-top-1-.html.
Wealthy Americans explain their anger at, in their view, being vilified for their success.

Colin, Chris, "A teepee grows in Oakland," *Salon*, Nov. 30, 2011, www.salon.com/2011/11/30/a_tee pee_grows_in_oak land/.

A writer chronicles Occupy Oakland activists' search for direction after the forcible closing of their encampment.

Dupuy, Tina, "The Occupy Movement's Woman Problem," *The Atlantic*, Nov. 21, 2011, www.theatlantic.com/politics/archive/2011/11/the-occupy-movements-woman-problem/248831/.
A journalist sympathetic to the Occupy movement reports on gender imbalance in the encampments.

Gage, Beverly, "Occupy Wall Street: How the protesters should respond to escalating violence," *Slate*, Nov. 2, 2011, www.slate.com/articles/business/moneybox/2011/11/occu py_wall_street_how_how_the_protesters_should_respond_ to_esca.html.
A Yale historian puts repression of Occupy demonstrations in the context the violent birth of the labor movement.

Lowry, Rich, "Heed the 99 Percent," *National Review Online*, Oct. 14, 2011, www.nationalreview .com/articles/280 104/heed-99-percent-rich-lowry.
Though critical of the Occupy movement, a conservative magazine editor acknowledges the economic and social distress that prompted its rise.

Meighan, Patrick, "My Occupy LA Arrest," myoccupyla arrest.blogspot.com/2011_12_01_archive.html.
An Occupy LA demonstrator gives a long, angry account of his arrest and contrasts the gratuitous brutality he says he and others suffered with the non-prosecution of bankers.

Packer, George, "All the Angry People," *The New Yorker*, Dec. 5, 2011, www.newyorker.com/reporting/2011/12/05/ 111205fa_fact_packer.
A writer specializing in political movements covers Occupy New York through the experience of a previously apolitical participant, a high-tech specialist who lost his job in the recession.

Wallsten, Peter, "Lending a little organized labor to Occupy Wall Street," *The Washington Post*, Oct. 21, 2011, p. A1.
Ties are growing between Occupy and unions.

Whoriskey, Peter, "Growing wealth widens distance between lawmakers and constituents," *The Washington Post*, Dec. 26, 2011; and Lichtblau, Eric, "Economic Downturn Took a Detour at Capitol Hill," *The New York Times*, Dec. 26, 2011.
In two major and similar reports, reporters detail lawmakers' increasing affluence.

Reports and studies

"Trends in the Distribution of Household Income Between 1979 and 2007," Congressional Budget Office, October 2011, www.cbo.gov/ftpdocs/124xx/doc12485/10-25-HouseholdIncome.pdf.
In painstaking detail, the nonpartisan congressional agency documents the growth and extent of the wealth gap.

"Frustration with Congress Could Hurt Republican Incumbents," Pew Research Center, Dec. 15, 2011, www.people-press.org/files/legacy-pdf/12-15-11%20 Congress%20and%20 Economy%20release.pdf.
One section of the nonpartisan center's report analyzes survey responses on the Occupy movement and inequality.

On the Web

Occupy Wall Street page, Huffington Post, www.huff ing tonpost.com/news/occupy-wall-street.
Daily coverage by the liberal-leaning news site.

Occupy Videos, http://occupyvideos.org.
Videos sympathetically documenting Occupy activities.

We Are the 99 Percent, http://wearethe99percent .tumblr.com.
Individual accounts by those who call themselves part of the "99 percent."

For More Information

Center for the Study of Social Movements, University of Notre Dame, Notre Dame, IN 46556; http://nd.edu/~cssm. The center's blog includes discussion and analysis of developments in the Occupy movement.

Center on Budget and Policy Priorities, 820 First St., N.E., Washington DC 20002; 202-408-1056; www.cbpp.org. Liberal think tank and major center of research on inequality, unemployment, and policies to counteract them.

Citizens United, 1006 Pennsylvania Ave., S.E., Washington, DC 20003; 202-547-5420; www.citizensunited.org. The conservative media-production and advocacy group is preparing a movie on the Occupy movement.

Congressional Budget Office, Ford House Office Building, 2nd and D Streets, S.W., Washington DC 20515; 202-226-2602; www.cbo.gov. Nonpartisan agency that has conducted research on inequality and other issues raised by the Occupy movement.

New York City General Assembly, www.nycga.net. Website has information on meetings of the Occupy Wall Street General Assembly and of many single-topic working groups.

13

Child Poverty

Peter Katel

Impoverished Los Angeles residents queue up for free food, household items and toys at the Miracle in South Central event on Dec. 13, 2008. The national poverty rate is 15.1 percent — the highest in 28 years. More than a third of the 46.2 million people living below the poverty line are children.

From *CQ Researcher*,
Oct 28, 2011

J ason Barnett and his two brothers have better reason than many kids to welcome Friday afternoons. That's when they open a special backpack full of donated food that Jason brings home from his elementary school in Belen, N.M.

Inside are plastic-wrapped single servings of peanut butter and jelly, crackers, raisins, milk, juice and other healthy items. "You should see their eyes," says the boys' mother, Shannon Barnett. "There's usually cereal in it, which helps with breakfast over the weekend. If they're still hungry, I'm able to give them another bowl."

The Roadrunner Food Bank, New Mexico's major food charity, started the program 11 years ago after school officials in Albuquerque said some students went hungry on weekends. Now, demand is booming throughout the state, where 40 percent of New Mexicans — 806,000 out of a total population of 2 million — missed meals last year, according to a Roadrunner study.[1]

How many children went hungry isn't known. But children make up one-fourth of the population of New Mexico, which has a child-poverty rate of 30 percent, second only to Mississippi's (33 percent).[2]

Jason, 7, and his brothers — Andrew, 5, and Elias, 11 — weren't in danger of missing meals until about three years ago, their mother says. The family lives on about $15,000 a year that Paul Barnett earns at a building-supply company. That's well below the government's poverty threshold of $26,023 for a family of five with three children.[3]

The Barnetts had managed to scrape by with the help of food stamps, a federal housing subsidy and a federal income-tax credit for low-income families. But about three years ago, when gas and food

Parental Unemployment Fuels Child Poverty

More than 12 percent of children in 14 states — including two of the biggest, California and Florida — have at least one unemployed parent, a factor that experts say contributes significantly to child poverty. In another dozen states, including New York and Texas, between 8 and 9 percent of children have at least one jobless parent. The national poverty rate has risen to 15.1 percent as unemployment hovers above 9 percent because of the recent recession.

Percentage of Children With At Least One Unemployed Parent, 2010

Percentage of children
- ☐ 5%-7%
- ☐ 8%-9%
- ▨ 10%-11%
- ■ 12%-16%

Source: "America's Children, America's Challenge," Annie E. Casey Foundation, 2011, www.aecf.org/~/media/Pubs/Initiatives/KIDS COUNT/ 123/2011KIDSCOUNT DataBook/2011KCDB_FINAL_essay.pdf

1959, the rate hit 22.4 percent, concentrated among whites in isolated Appalachian mountain hollows and blacks in squalid urban ghettos and the rural South. The era spawned a spate of reform efforts, culminating in President Lyndon B. Johnson's War on Poverty program, which centered on providing welfare benefits to low-income families with children.

But by the mid-1990s, conservatives and some liberals alike were arguing that many of the Johnson-era reforms had created a culture of dependency on government aid. In 1996 Congress overhauled the welfare system, imposing work requirements and putting time limits on cash payments to the needy.

Welfare rolls plunged in the aftermath of the reforms. But the economic crisis, which began in 2007 and has pushed the national unemployment rate above 9 percent, has forced millions of families to seek government or private aid, or both. In response, Congress has expanded the welfare caseload, but only by 13 percent — not enough, advocates argue, to keep millions of children out of poverty. They are urging renewal of an emergency fund that Congress created in 2009 through the so-called economic stimulus bill — with an expiration date of Sept. 30, 2010.[7]

Child poverty arouses special concern because its effects can last a lifetime. "Children who are reared in poor families are more likely to fail in school, drop out of school, get arrested," says Ron Haskins, co-director of the Center on Children and Families at the Brookings Institution, a centrist think tank in Washington. "And the earlier the poverty starts, and the more years that a kid is reared in a household in poverty, the more likely those bad things are to happen."

Experts on both sides of the liberal-conservative divide agree that child poverty is causing the gap between rich and poor to widen. But they disagree on why more

prices rose sharply, the family sought help: monthly baskets from the food bank, and the backpack for the boys.[4]

"I just kind of suck in my pride and just get help," Paul Barnett says. "I was kind of embarrassed at first. But a lot of my friends are in a lot worse shape."

Indeed, millions of Americans are in dire financial straits. The national poverty rate, 15.1 percent, is the highest in 28 years. In 1983 it hit 15.2 percent.[5]

The picture is even bleaker for children, who make up a fourth of the U.S. population and more than a third of the 46.2 million people living below the poverty threshold. Over all, one in five U.S. children lives below the poverty line, a far higher rate than adults (13.7 percent) and the elderly (9 percent).[6]

It has been 52 years since the United States suffered a sustained bout of poverty as bad as the current one. In

than 16 million Americans under age 18 live below the poverty line — and on how to improve the situation.

For conservatives skeptical of government anti-poverty projects, child poverty above all is a behavioral issue — a reflection of the growing tendency to have children out of wedlock. A report last year by the National Center for Health Statistics shows that unwed mothers — a growing number of them in their 20s — accounted for 40 percent of U.S. births in 2008, the most recent year for which data are available. That rate has risen steadily over two decades. It was 26 percent in 1988 and 33 percent in 1998.[8]

And last year, children below the poverty line in single-mother households outnumbered poor children in married-couple families, by 8.6 million to 5.8 million.[9]

"Our society is bifurcating into one of upper-middle-class children raised by college-educated couples who are married and children born out of marriage to . . . women who have an overwhelming probability of being poor and remaining poor," says Robert Rector, a senior research fellow at the Heritage Foundation, a conservative think tank in Washington.

But liberal poverty experts, while acknowledging a link between single motherhood and poverty, reject the notion that out-of-wedlock child-bearing is either the main cause of child poverty or the key to its solution. "People are poor because they don't have enough income," says LaDonna Pavetti, vice president for family-income support policy at the liberal Center on Budget and Policy Priorities. "There is also a problem of people not having the skills to qualify for jobs that will move them out of poverty."

That problem is especially acute among Hispanics, who account for the single biggest number of children in poverty of any ethnic or racial group — 6.1 million.

Poverty Most Prevalent in Single-Parent Families

More than half of poor children in the U.S. come from households with single mothers — whether divorced, separated, widowed or never having married — compared with one-fourth for all children. Two-thirds of all children live in families headed by married couples. Only about one-third of children in poverty come from such families.

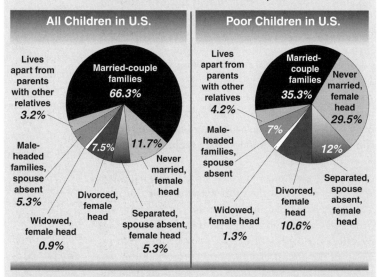

Family Living Arrangements for All Children and Poor Children, 2009

* Poverty measures are based on families' annual pre-tax income. In 2009, the threshold for a family consisting of a single mother with one child was $14,787; with two children it was $17,285. The poverty line for a married couple with one child was $17,268; with two children it was $21,756.

** Percentages do not total 100 because of rounding.

Source: Thomas Gabe, "Welfare, Work, and Poverty Status of Female-Headed Families With Children: 1987-2009," Congressional Research Service, July 2011, digitalcommons.ilr.cornell.edu/cgi/viewcontent.cgi?article=1852&context=key_workplace

Non-Hispanic whites account for 5 million poor children and African-Americans for 4.4 million.[10]

Educational achievement — closely tied to employment skills — traditionally has lagged among Hispanics. And that deficiency is greatest among immigrants, many without legal status. About 68 percent of poor Hispanic children have at least one immigrant parent. And though a relatively small proportion of poor Latino children have unemployed parents — about 19 percent — that proportion has risen significantly, from about 12 percent, in 2007.[11]

Anti-poverty activists want the federal government to boost spending on programs aimed at helping millions of people climb the socioeconomic ladder. Conservatives, on the other hand, contend that Washington already spends billions on such programs.

"I have no doubt that we have more people in poverty," says Michael Tanner, a senior fellow at the Cato Institute, a libertarian think tank in Washington. "But we're spending more money fighting poverty than ever before."

Conservatives also complain that in calculating the poverty rate, the government doesn't count food stamps, medical care, housing subsidies and other benefits for the poor. (The Census Bureau is studying how to devise a new poverty-calculation method that would include the value of benefits.)[12]

But anti-poverty advocates argue that including the benefits would simply show that while the government safety net is keeping some people from the severest levels of need, many more Americans are sliding beneath the poverty threshold.

"If you try various ways of correcting the data, you find fewer people in the most extreme forms of poverty," says Arloc Sherman, a senior researcher at the Center on Budget and Policy Priorities. "That has a bigger effect on counts of deeply poor people than on counts of the poor overall."

Such policy debates can seem far removed from the everyday lives of children living in poverty, but they ultimately shape the economic trajectory of families struggling to make ends meet.

Jane Trujillo and her husband, both deaf, have been unable to find jobs in Belen and can't afford to commute 60 miles roundtrip to Albuquerque.

Speaking by phone through a sign-language interpreter, Mrs. Trujillo says the backpack-food program has become essential to ensuring that her 6-year-old son and 9-year-old daughter don't go to bed hungry on weekends. "I have had to restrict the amount of milk," she says. "The backpack really helps, particularly toward the end of the month. We get $300 a month in food stamps, but $300 is not enough. Toward the end of the month, when food is tight, the kids eat first. They're more important than we are."

As policy advocates, lawmakers and anti-poverty groups seek solutions to the nation's child-poverty problem, here are some of the issues they are discussing:

Should Congress expand welfare funding?

When Congress overhauled the welfare system in 1996, it made a major change in the way Washington disburses welfare funds to the states. Under the old system, the government made annual appropriations that Congress adjusted according to need, as reflected in the number of eligible applicants in each state. Under the new system, states receive fixed amounts in the form of "block grants" that they then use to make monthly payments to the poor.[13]

Conservatives hail block-grant funding because it limits the expansion of a program that many of them distrust. But liberals complain that it leaves states with little or no flexibility to expand welfare rolls when economic disaster hits and poverty rises.

Total outlays to the states under the block-grant program — called Temporary Assistance to Needy Families (TANF) — have remained unchanged since 1996, at $16.5 billion per year. In addition, states contribute a total of $10.4 billion to TANF and related programs for the needy. That amount also has remained the same since 1996.[14]

But inflation eroded the value of the federal block grants by 28 percent from 1997 through last January, the nonpartisan Congressional Research Service calculated.[15]

A safety mechanism created by Congress when it switched to the block-grant approach provided $63 million, divided among 16 of the hardest-hit states, in fiscal 2010.[16] A separate "emergency contingency fund" created by the American Recovery and Reinvestment Act of 2009 — the "stimulus" law — gave states another $5 billion for TANF programs, including job-subsidy payments to employers, in fiscal 2009 and 2010.[17]

But critics say those measures haven't done nearly enough to keep millions of Americans from falling out of the middle class or sliding deeper into poverty.

"It used to be the case that TANF and its predecessor" — Aid to Families with Dependent Children (AFDC), the old welfare program Congress eliminated in 1996 —"kept millions of people above the poverty line and responded during recessions," says Sherman of the Center on Budget and Policy Priorities. "Now, having dwindled to a fraction of the previous real [inflation-adjusted] funding level, it is protecting many fewer people from recession and bouts of joblessness."

Indeed, argue Sherman and other critics, the TANF caseload has grown only modestly compared with the scale of the recession and what they see as the true level of need. In September 2010, the caseload stood at 1.9 million families — representing 4.4 million people, three-fourths of them children. That was only 200,000 more families than in July 2008, when the worst of the economic crisis began to grip the nation.[18] Yet, between 2009 and 2010, the number of people below the poverty line rose by 2.6 million — including 900,000 more children.[19]

Critics such as Sherman look to another program for needy families — food stamps — as a better approach than TANF for adjusting benefits during hard times. Unlike TANF, food-stamp allocations rise and fall according to need. "When the unemployment rate soared, the food stamp program responded," Sherman says.

The number of food-stamp recipients increased by nearly 82 percent, from 24.9 million to 45.3 million people, from July 2006 to July of this year, according to the nonprofit Food Research and Action Center, an advocacy organization. During that period, the nation's unemployment rate rose from 4.7 percent to 9.1 percent.[20]

But conservative policy analysts cite the food-stamp increase for a different reason than proof of flexibility. They point to it as evidence that the welfare system as a whole has been steadily expanding, not contracting. Along with TANF cash payments and food stamps, they also cite continuing funding increases in medical assistance for the poor, child development programs such as Head Start, subsidized housing and other programs.[21] In this context, says the Heritage Foundation's Rector, TANF "only supplies 10 percent of assistance given to families with children."

As for expanding TANF funding, Rector argues, "I can't think of anything more foolish to do, and I can't think of anything more unpopular with the public than resurrecting an entitlement program for single parents. It would put a Band-Aid on the problem of single parenthood while ignoring the causes of poverty and the ever-increasing problem of dependency and poverty."

Some liberal poverty experts acknowledge that TANF is no panacea. "No one gets out of poverty by receiving cash assistance," says Elizabeth Lower-Basch, senior policy analyst for the Center for Law and Social Policy (CLASP), an advocacy organization in Washington. But, she says, welfare payments have been effective at lifting or keeping people out of extreme poverty. "One of the

Children of homeowners facing eviction in Long Beach, Calif., eat Thanksgiving dinner on Nov. 24, 2010, during a protest outside a bank. The economic crisis has forced millions of families to seek government or private aid, or both. Congress has expanded welfare benefits, but not enough, advocates argue, to keep millions of children out of poverty.

AFP/Getty Images/Mark Ralston

places where you see the weakness of TANF showing up is the growth of extreme child poverty."

Lower-Basch argues that the TANF emergency fund of 2009 provides a worthy model of how to extend the program's reach. But she acknowledges that the outlook for increasing anti-poverty funding in general is poor. "Not having things become worse feels like an accomplishment," she says.

The views expressed in September by Rep. Geoff Davis, R-Ky., chairman of the House Ways and Means Committee's Subcommittee on Human Resources, suggest that the priority of the House Republican majority, at least, is to tighten work requirements and curb reported abuses by recipients rather than expand funding.

"Not enough adults on welfare are working or preparing for work today," Davis said at a hearing he called on welfare-to-work rules and enforcement. He cited a July report by the Department of Health and Human Services that said only about one-fourth of "work-eligible adults" were meeting work requirements under TANF.[22]

Davis did say that "TANF can and should be strengthened to help more low-income families support themselves." But his remarks focused on what he said are abuses by state administrators. "Instead of the state helping more adults prepare for and begin work," he said, "they scour their books to uncover more spending they can credit to the TANF program and thereby reduce the number of people they have to engage in work activities."[23]

Are poor children now in elementary school a lost generation?

Experts of all political orientations agree that the longer children spend in poverty, the less their chances for bettering themselves as they grow up.

Researchers for Child Trends, a nonpartisan Washington think tank, wrote in 2009 that 10 studies found strong links between child poverty and poor academic performance, especially during early childhood. A host of social, emotional and behavioral problems are associated with child poverty as well, the researchers noted. One possible cause, they said, is that poor families are more likely to live in single-parent households, often under less supervision and amid more turmoil.[24]

"Studies find that those who experienced persistent poverty as children are much more likely to be poor as adults than those who were not poor during childhood," the researchers wrote. That trend runs more strongly in the black than the white population, they added, with 33 percent of African-Americans who were poor as children remaining in poverty as young adults. Among their white counterparts, only 7 percent were poor in their mid-20s.[25]

Haskins, the Brookings Institution scholar, disputes the notion that a generation of young people living through today's economic woes has, on the whole, lost its chance at advancement. But he says their circumstances are cause for "great concern."

Poverty Highest Among Minorities

Some 46 million Americans — 15.1 percent of the U.S. population — lived below the poverty line in 2010, including more than one-fourth of blacks and Hispanics. About one-fifth of those younger than 18 and a third of families headed by a single mother lived below the poverty threshold.

Percentage of People and Families in Poverty, 2010

Race	
White	22.9%
Black	27.4%
Asian	12.1%
Hispanic (any race)	26.6%
Age	
Under 18	22.0%
18 to 64	13.7%
65 and older	9.0%
Family type	
Married couple	6.2%
Female head, no husband present	31.6%
Male head, no wife present	15.8%
Total	**15.1%**

Source: "People and Families in Poverty By Selected Characteristics: 2009 and 2010," U.S. Census Bureau, March 2011, www.census.gov/hhes/www/poverty/data/incpovhlth/2010/ table4.pdf

"We want people to have an equal chance," he said. "That's been the whole idea of the country — and they don't."

Nevertheless, the possibility of upward mobility still exists, Haskins says. "If kids from the bottom get to college, they increase their odds of making it to the top by a factor of four."

Yet, college is not a sure ticket to stability or upward mobility. Linda Gonzales, 63, of Corrales, N.M., who helps take care of her 4- and 12-year-old grandchildren, is questioning her son's decision to pursue a college degree in civil engineering. "A lot of people are wanting to go back to school because they'll get better jobs, but I don't think the jobs are there," says Gonzales, who lost her nursing-care business last year. Gonzales says her son's part-time job selling hot tubs may not have much of a future either.

Joseph T. Jones, president and CEO of the Center for Urban Families, a Baltimore nonprofit that runs job-training and "responsible fatherhood" projects, argues that very young poor children may have better prospects than present conditions indicate. "Elementary-school students have a better shot at the economy turning around" by the time they are in their teens, he says.

But teenagers in poverty are in danger, Jones says. Speaking after meeting with African-American high-school students in Louisville, Ky., he says, "We are really at risk of saying to them, 'We don't care how much effort you put into education, once you graduate we don't have a darn thing for you.' "

Sherman of the Center on Budget and Policy Priorities argues strongly against the idea that poverty is an immovable obstacle to poor children's futures.

Early-childhood education programs alone, he says, "deliver huge impacts on academic achievement and behavior even decades later."

In general, Sherman says, disadvantages that come with poverty are not immutable. "Successful interventions enable children to get the stimulation they need to grow," he says. At the same time, policies such as the Earned Income Tax Credit for poor families, or employment opportunities for struggling parents, can go a long way toward "removing the strains of poverty on the rest of the family, which might otherwise interfere with a child having a nurturing home environment," he says.

But analysts who contend that poverty is a cultural phenomenon more than an economic one offer a grimmer prognosis for today's poor young people. "Certainly a generation of kids who are going to struggle through a host of social problems — very poor school performance, marginal work ethic when they get out of school, drugs, a lot of criminal behavior — they're likely to repeat those problems when they become adults," says Rector of the Heritage Foundation.

He argues that government programs, especially those that involve boosting income, miss the point. "We clearly are not going to make any progress until we deal with the real causes of why families are poor," he says. Chief among them, he says, is the growing number of single-mother families.

Is single motherhood a bigger cause of child poverty than the low-wage economy?

A striking increase in out-of-wedlock births is adding fuel to a debate that's been running for decades — or, by some lights, for more than a century: To what extent does single motherhood lead to child poverty?

The two trends clearly are connected. The latest U.S. Census report on poverty notes that the poverty rate for children in single-mother households was 47 percent, but 11.6 percent in married-couple households. Overall, 31.6

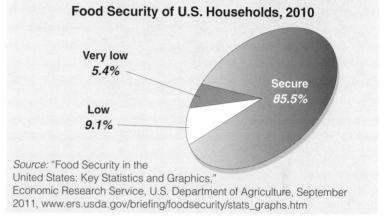

One in Seven Households Is Short of Food

Nearly 15 percent of U.S. households lack enough food to meet their needs. Those with low food security have enough to avoid disrupting eating patterns if they turn to such strategies as dieting, using food stamps or visiting food pantries. Households with very low food security lack adequate income or other resources to obtain food and must periodically reduce their food intake.

Food Security of U.S. Households, 2010

Very low
5.4%

Low
9.1%

Secure
85.5%

Source: "Food Security in the United States: Key Statistics and Graphics," Economic Research Service, U.S. Department of Agriculture, September 2011, www.ers.usda.gov/briefing/foodsecurity/stats_graphs.htm

percent of single-mother households were below the poverty line, compared with only 6.2 percent of married-couple families.[26]

In Mississippi, 48 percent of children lived in single-parent families.[27]

Academics and advocates have been studying links between single motherhood and child poverty for decades. James Heckman, a Nobel laureate economist at the University of Chicago who specializes in social inequality, has written that the consequences of growing up in poverty can be deep and far-reaching. "There are large gaps in cognitive stimulation and emotional support at early ages," between children in two-parent and those in single-parent households, he wrote this year. But he went on to argue that early-childhood programs can compensate for some of the disadvantages.[28]

As Heckman noted, the issue has taken on greater urgency because childbirth by married women is on the decline. Among African-Americans, 72 percent of births are to single women. The statistic stands out given the disproportionate extent of poverty in the black population: 27.4 percent of African-Americans live below the poverty line. In the white, non-Hispanic population, the rate is about 10 percent.[29]

Reuters/Lucy Nicholson

Children from homeless shelters walk to an after-school program at the South Los Angeles Learning Center on March 16, 2011. School on Wheels runs the program, which uses volunteers to tutor children in shelters, parks and motels around the city, as well as at two centers.

For conservative poverty experts, the trends indicate that unmarried motherhood is by far the greatest cause of child poverty. "Those women have an overwhelming probability of being poor and remaining poor," says the Heritage Foundation's Rector. "In general, being married reduces the probability of poverty by about 80 percent."

Rector acknowledges that joblessness caused by the recession has put more families below the poverty line. "But when the recession goes away," he says, "we'll have the same child poverty we had before it began. The reality of this debate is that it is politically incorrect to ever discuss why people are actually poor. This factor — marriage — is more important than dropping out of high school, but we never tell anyone."

Nevertheless, few dispute that households headed by married couples are less vulnerable to poverty. Jones, of the Center for Urban Families, says, "We shouldn't be shy about talking about the institution of marriage. It's pretty clear that children who are raised in two-parent households, particularly if they are married households, fare better than their counterparts in single-parent families."

But Jones — who fathered a son out of wedlock before settling down to married life, and another son, with another woman — warns that single-minded focus on marriage as the cure for poverty is potentially dangerous. Single parenthood should not be a reason for excluding people from benefits, he argues. "We should not be so rigid as to say you are not worthy of support if you are not on a path to marriage," Jones says.

Yet no other way to significantly reduce single parenthood may exist other than curtailing benefits, says Tanner of the Cato Institute. "You can't go on just giving people money for having kids," he says. Such a move undoubtedly would cause personal crises for any number of women — and their children — he acknowledges, adding that private charities could soften some of the blows. But, he says, "Without crises you're not going to get behavioral changes."

Unlike Rector, Tanner says he doesn't believe that single parenthood outranks all other poverty-generating factors. But, he says, it's important enough for policy-makers to zero in on. "Having a child out of wedlock is a pretty good guarantee of being in poverty," he says.

Haskins of Brookings argues that unemployment out-ranks unmarried motherhood on the list of poverty's causes. In a recent paper, he cited a 30 percent decrease in poverty among single mothers and their children, from 47 percent in 1991 to 33 percent in 2000.[30] During that period — just before and after the 1996 welfare overhaul — "we saw a 40 percent increase in work rates of never-married mothers," he says. "Poverty fell like a rock for single-parent families to its lowest level ever."

Nevertheless, Haskins says, marriage — along with education — is almost as important as work in reducing child poverty. "If we don't do something about reducing the proportion of kids in female-headed families and don't do something about getting kids through at least two years of post-secondary school or vocational training," he says, "we are not going to have an impact on poverty."

BACKGROUND

Focus on Children

Children have been the main concern of U.S. anti-poverty efforts since such endeavors began in systematic fashion in the early 1900s. Until the last years of the 20th century, government's emphasis was on ensuring that mothers raising children on their own wouldn't have to enter the workplace.[31]

Likewise, officials wanted to ensure that orphans and poverty-stricken children could be raised in families rather than institutions. In 1909, the White House Conference on the Care of Dependent Children, presided over by President Theodore Roosevelt, led to establishment of a federal Children's Bureau and a foster-care system designed to place children in homes rather than orphanages.[32]

State governments, meanwhile, were making their own efforts to keep needy children at home. At a time when nearly all families depended on a father's paycheck, a movement to establish widows' pensions scored its first victory when Missouri enacted a pension law in 1911.

In reality, the promise of subsidized child care was not always kept, historians write. Payments were small enough that widows and divorced or abandoned women had to supplement them with paid work. In Philadelphia, 84 percent of pension recipients held jobs. In Chicago the rate was 66 percent and in Los Angeles 57 percent. County pension administrators worried that more substantial payments would encourage wives to walk out on their husbands, or husbands to desert their families.[33]

An even greater weakness of the state pension laws was that counties didn't have to participate. In 1931, the Children's Bureau reported that half of the nation's counties had not established pension systems.

At that point, the widespread misery of the Great Depression had created enormous demand for a comprehensive nationwide system of providing for children whose families had fallen on hard times. Part of the New Deal package of social legislation pushed through Congress by President Franklin D. Roosevelt's administration was the Aid to Dependent Children (ADC) program, created by the Social Security Act of 1935.

Under ADC, the federal government contributed to states' pension programs. Payments to families, which by the law's language were intended to help provide a "reasonable subsistence compatible with decency and health," were capped at $18 a month for the first child and $12 monthly for subsequent children.[34]

Nearly all the child beneficiaries lived with widowed mothers. Women who had been abandoned, or were divorced, accounted for most of the remaining pensioners.

President Lyndon B. Johnson greets a resident during a tour of the impoverished Appalachia region in June 1964. Widespread poverty in Appalachian mountain hollows, urban ghettos and the rural South spawned a spate of reform efforts, culminating in Johnson's War on Poverty program, which targeted low-income families with children.

Lyndon Baines Johnson Library & Museum

Only 2 percent of the children in the program lived with mothers who had given birth out of wedlock.

The overall population of households headed by unwed mothers was greater than the number who received government assistance. State ADC administrators tended to bar support to families of unmarried women, who were considered far outside the bounds of respectability and traditional morality. During the 1950s, at least 19 states adopted policies that prohibited aid to children who were born to unwed mothers after they had begun receiving welfare.[35]

ADC gave state officials considerable power in setting eligibility standards. Under rules that were struck down by courts in 1960, states could require that aid go only to children living in so-called "suitable homes." In practice, that provision was used to block aid to unmarried mothers as well as many black mothers.[36]

Distinctions between categories of single mothers were reinforced by a change to the Social Security law in 1939. A separate Social Security benefit was created for widows and their surviving children. The effect was to divide beneficiaries of government support between the children of women whose husbands had died and the offspring of mothers who had divorced, been abandoned or had never married.

CHRONOLOGY

1909-1935 *Early welfare goals include keeping widowed mothers from having to join the workforce.*

1909 President Theodore Roosevelt calls first White House Conference on Care of Dependent Children.

1911 Missouri passes nation's first pension for widows, to free them from working.

1931 Nearly all states have widows' pensions, but half the counties don't participate.

1935 New Deal's Social Security Act includes first federal welfare system, Aid to Dependent Children.

1960s *Democratic president launches biggest package of domestic social programs since New Deal.*

1962 President John F. Kennedy praises new book, *The Other America*, documenting widespread poverty. . . . Aid to Dependent Children is renamed Aid to Families with Dependent Children (AFDC).

1964 Democratic President Lyndon B. Johnson declares War on Poverty, which sparks a number of federal initiatives, including Head Start.

1965 *The Negro Family: A Case for National Action*, by Labor Department staffer Daniel Patrick Moynihan, argues for jobs for men over welfare, expresses concern at the growth in single-mother black households.

1967 In an early effort to link welfare to work, Congress establishes voluntary Work Incentive (WIN) program to encourage AFDC recipients to obtain job training and jobs.

1971-1987 *Welfare opponents argue AFDC fosters dependency.*

1971 Congress makes WIN mandatory but doesn't fully fund revamped program.

1972 Children in single-mother families account for 50 percent of all children below poverty line.

1981 Congress lets states use welfare funds to subsidize job training.

1986 President Ronald Reagan decries "welfare culture" marked by family breakdown.

1988 Family Support Act requires AFDC recipients to log 20 hours a week of job training or employment.

1992-2010 *Democratic president oversees major transformation of welfare system.*

1992 Vowing to "end welfare as we know it," Democratic presidential candidate Bill Clinton promises to revamp the system into a "second chance, not a way of life."

1995 New Republican House majority introduces welfare-revamping Work Opportunity Act, which passes both houses.

1996 President Clinton vetoes the bill. . . . White House negotiations with both parties produce Personal Responsibility and Work Opportunity Reconciliation Act, with stiff work requirements for welfare recipients.

1999 Work rate of never-married mothers on welfare rises to 66 percent, up from 46.5 percent in 1995.

2000 Poverty among single mothers and their children falls to all-time low of 33 percent of population.

2008 Forty percent of U.S. births are to unmarried mothers.

2009 "Stimulus" law creates $5 billion emergency fund for national welfare system.

2010 Poverty rate grows to 15.1 percent, with population below poverty line growing by 2.6 million to 46.2 million in one year.

2011 Agriculture Department reports nearly 15 percent of population, including 16.2 million children, lives in "food-insecure" households. . . . Florida and three other states require drug tests for welfare applicants.

By 1961 nearly all families headed by widowed mothers were receiving Society Security benefits, while only 7.7 percent of families receiving ADC funds were headed by widows.

War on Poverty

President John F. Kennedy's inauguration in 1961 followed a campaign in which poverty surfaced as a national issue for the first time since the 1930s.

Kennedy's campaign visit to impoverished Appalachian communities in West Virginia made an obvious impression on the candidate and received wide media coverage. One year after becoming president, Kennedy praised a new book, *The Other America*, by writer and political activist Michael Harrington, who reported on and denounced the extent of poverty in a rich nation.[37]

Harrington's book also influenced Kennedy's successor, Lyndon Johnson.

Providing children the opportunity to rise from poverty was one of the threads running through Johnson entire War on Poverty — the name he gave to a collection of social programs passed during his administration — and the main idea animating Head Start, an early-childhood education program still operating today.

Specifically, Head Start owed its existence to data presented to Johnson's poverty czar, Sargent Shriver. Shriver's researchers told him that half of the nation's 30 million poor were children, most of them under age 12. "It was clear that it was foolish to talk about a 'total war against poverty,' the phraseology the president was using, if you were doing nothing about children," Shriver told associates.[38]

The "war," in combination with the social and political changes that rocked the country during the 1960s, helped shape welfare policy and law during the decades that followed.

Child Poverty Most Prevalent in South

Mississippi has the nation's highest child-poverty rate, with one in three residents under age 18 below the poverty threshold. Three other Southern states — Alabama, Arkansas and Louisiana — are in the top five. New Mexico ranks second, with 30 percent of children in poverty. California far outpaces other states in the total number of children in poverty, at slightly more than 2 million.

Percentage and Number of Children Under 18 in Poverty
(by state, 2010)

State	Percent	Number	State	Percent	Number
United States	**22%**	**15,749,000**	Illinois	19%	600,000
Mississippi	33%	242,000	Pennsylvania	19%	522,000
New Mexico	30%	154,000	Rhode Island	19%	42,000
Alabama	28%	311,000	Wisconsin	19%	250,000
Arkansas	28%	193,000	Delaware	18%	37,000
Louisiana	27%	300,000	Kansas	18%	131,000
Kentucky	26%	263,000	Maine	18%	48,000
South Carolina	26%	278,000	Nebraska	18%	82,000
Tennessee	26%	377,000	South Dakota	18%	36,000
Texas	26%	1,751,000	Washington	18%	284,000
Georgia	25%	611,000	Colorado	17%	211,000
North Carolina	25%	560,000	Vermont	17%	21,000
Oklahoma	25%	227,000	Iowa	16%	115,000
West Virginia	25%	96,000	North Dakota	16%	24,000
Arizona	24%	392,000	Utah	16%	136,000
Florida	23%	924,000	Minnesota	15%	192,000
Michigan	23%	539,000	Hawaii	14%	41,000
Ohio	23%	624,000	Massachusetts	14%	201,000
California	22%	2,013,000	New Jersey	14%	295,000
Indiana	22%	342,000	Virginia	14%	265,000
Nevada	22%	144,000	Wyoming	14%	19,000
Oregon	22%	184,000	Alaska	13%	24,000
Missouri	21%	291,000	Connecticut	13%	103,000
New York	21%	901,000	Maryland	13%	173,000
Montana	20%	44,000	New Hampshire	10%	28,000
Idaho	19%	80,000			

Source: "Data Across States," Annie E. Casey Foundation, 2011, datacenter. kids count.org/data/acrossstates/Default.aspx

One way it did so was by spurring a notable expansion in welfare rolls. The federal family-support program — renamed Aid to Families with Dependent Children (AFDC) in 1962 — saw beneficiaries more than double, from 3.5 million in 1962 to 7.4 million in 1970.[39]

Poverty itself didn't double in that period. But, encouraged by a welfare-recipients movement that

States to Welfare Seekers: Drug Test Comes First

"Taxpayers deserve to know money is being used for its intended purpose."

As the bad economy drives up demand for welfare and employment aid, some state governments are imposing a controversial new condition for assistance: drug screening.

This year alone:

- Florida required welfare applicants to pay for — and pass — a drug test. They are reimbursed the $25 to $35 fee unless they fail. However, a federal judge in late October temporarily blocked enforcement of the new law on constitutional grounds.
- Missouri authorized drug testing of welfare recipients suspected of drug use — a step Arizona took two years ago. Those who test positive lose benefits unless they sign up for treatment.
- Indiana required aid recipients applying for job training to be tested for drugs. A positive result for drug use bars an applicant from training for 90 days, or for one year after a second positive result.

And legislators in some 35 other states have introduced similar drug-testing measures.[1]

"The taxpayers deserve to know that the money they are spending is being used for its intended purpose," said Joe Follick, a spokesman for the Florida Department of Children and Families. "If a family receiving [cash assistance] includes someone who has a substance-abuse problem, the odds of that money being used for purposes other than helping that family increases."[2]

But the American Civil Liberties Union (ACLU) won the first round in a legal challenge to the lawsuit when U.S. District Judge Mary Scriven of Orlando ruled that the new law was unlikely to survive a lawsuit that claims the law violates the Fourth Amendment's protection against unreasonable search and seizure. Scriven was appointed by President George W. Bush.

The judge said the state had failed to show a "special need" warranting exemption from the requirement to show probable cause or reasonable suspicion. "If invoking an interest in preventing public funds from potentially being used to fund drug use were the only requirement to establish a special need," she wrote, "the state could impose drug testing as an eligibility requirement for every beneficiary of every government program." The injunction she granted suspending the law remains in effect pending a full hearing, not yet scheduled.[3]

The ACLU sued on behalf of Luis Lebron, a 35-year-old Navy veteran who is caring for his 4-year-old son and disabled mother while studying accounting at the University of Central Florida. Responding to Scriven's order, he said he was "happy that the judge stood up for me and my rights and said the state can't act without a reason or suspicion."[4]

The lawsuit's Fourth Amendment argument echoed a federal court decision in 2000 that threw out a similar drug-test law in Michigan.

Drug testing of individuals not suspected of a crime is constitutionally permissible only where public safety is concerned, the court said, citing testing of people whose work requires them to carry a gun. "In this instance, there is no indication of a concrete danger to public safety which demands departure from the Fourth Amendment's main rule and normal requirement of individualized suspicion," the ruling said.[5]

Despite the resistance from civil-liberties advocates, however, conservative politicians and lawmakers see drug testing as a way to avoid channeling welfare money to people they view as undeserving of it.

In advocating for Florida's law, Republican Gov. Rick Scott asserted that drug abuse is more common among welfare recipients. "Studies show that people that are on welfare are higher users of drugs than people not on welfare," Scott said in a CNN interview in June. "Our taxpayers don't want to subsidize somebody else's drug addiction."[6]

The results from the first batch of about 1,000 tests didn't bear out Scott's impression, however. About 2 percent of applicants tested positive for drug use, the state's Department of Children and Families announced. Another 2 percent did not complete the application process, including the drug test for unspecified reasons. Test supporters said the abstainers knew they would fail the drug exam. Opponents said the walkaways couldn't afford to advance the drug test fee or couldn't reach a testing facility.[7]

By comparison, in 2010 just under 9 percent of the population age 12 and above reported using illicit drugs in the preceding month, according to the Department of Health and Human Services.[8]

Like Florida's governor, Rep. Geoff Davis, R-Ky., chairman of the House Ways and Means Human Resources Subcommittee, has spoken approvingly of drug tests for welfare applicants.

"In a world where many employers require drug testing to ensure workers are clean and sober, neither taxpayers nor welfare recipients are helped if we have a lower standard for those collecting welfare benefits designed to help them enter work," Davis said.

He spoke at a recent hearing on the federal welfare law, Temporary Assistance for Needy Families (TANF). Passed in 1996 with bipartisan support, the law imposed work requirements, put time limits on cash payments to the needy and authorized drug tests as a condition of aid.

But others in Congress are questioning whether money spent on drug testing might divert funds from the poor.

"Do you think it's a better investment, given the limited nature of the resources that we have, to drug test everyone?" Rep. Joseph Crowley, D-N.Y., asked Scott Wetzler, chief of psychology at New York's Montefiore Hospital, who runs a treatment program for welfare recipients with histories of drug abuse.[9]

"It would be a huge, huge, practical problem to actually drug test everybody," said Wetzler, whose program tests only people in drug treatment. "And it's not clear that you actually would be able to have the treatment capacity to receive all those people into treatment. So it's not clear what you even do with that information if you had it."[10]

— *Peter Katel*

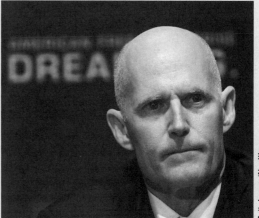

Getty Images/Alex Wong

Republican Gov. Rick Scott of Florida contends that drug abuse is more common among welfare recipients and that "our taxpayers don't want to subsidize somebody else's addiction."

Post-Dispatch, May 11, 2011, www.stltoday.com/news/local/ govt-and-politics/article_953196cf-8104-5758-8198-60e151debe90.html; Amy B. Wang, "Welfare recipients face drug tests," *Arizona Republic*, Nov. 25, 2009, www.azcentral.com/arizonarepublic/local/articles/2009/ 11/25/20091125urinetesting1125.html.

[2] Quoted in Catherine Whittenburg, "Welfare drug-testing yields 2% positive results," *Tampa Bay Online*, Aug. 24, 2011, www.tbo.com/news/ politics/2011/aug/ 24/3/welfare-drug-testing-yields-2-percent-positive-res-ar-252458/.

[3] Quoted in Rebecca Catalenello, "Florida's welfare drug testing halted by federal judge," *The Miami Herald*, Oct. 25, 2011, www.miami herald.com/2011/ 10/24/2470519/florida-welfare-drug-testing-halted .html.

[4] Quoted in Schneider and Kennedy, *op. cit.*

[5] *Marchwinski v. Howard*, 113 F.Supp.2d 1134, www.aclufl.org/pdfs/ March winski.pdf.

[6] Aaron Sharockman, "Rick Scott Says Welfare Recipients Are More Likely to Use Illicit Drugs," *St. Petersburg Times*, June 9, 2011.

[7] Whittenburg, *op. cit.*; Kelli Kennedy, "Nearly 1,600 welfare applicants decline drug test," The Associated Press, Oct. 11, 2011.

[8] "Results from the 2010 National Survey on Drug Use and Health: Summary of National Findings," Health and Human Services Department, September 2011, http://oas.samhsa.gov/NSDUH/2k10NSDUH/2k10Results .htm#Fig7-1.

[9] "Hearing of the House Ways and Means Committee, 'Improving Work and Other Welfare Reform Goals, Focusing on Reauthorization of the Temporary Assistance for Needy Families Program," Federal News Service, Sept. 8, 2011.

[10] *Ibid.*

[1] A.G. Sulzberger, "States Adding Drug Test as Hurdle for Welfare," *The New York Times*, Oct. 11, 2011, www. nytimes.com/2011/10/11/ us/states-add ing-drug-test-as-hurdle-for-welfare.html? ref=us; Mike Schneider and Kelli Kennedy, "Florida Welfare Drug Testing Law Blocked by Federal Judge," The Associated Press, Oct. 24, 2011, www .huffingtonpost.com/2011/10/24/ rick-scott-drug-testing-welfare-florida_ n_1029332.html; Tom Coyne, "Indiana the first state to require drug tests for job training," The Associated Press, *Chesterton Tribune* (Indiana), July 11, 2011, http://chestertontribune.com/ Business/indiana_the_first_state_to_requi. htm; Rebecca Berg, "Missouri Legislature approves drug tests for welfare recipients," *St. Louis*

considered benefits a right, not a privilege, low-income citizens became more likely to apply for welfare. During the 1960s, an estimated 33 percent of eligible families received assistance. By 1971, more than 90 percent of eligible households were on the welfare rolls.

Also promoting welfare expansion were U.S. Supreme Court decisions that overturned state welfare rules limiting eligibility. They included so-called "man in the house" policies that barred or stopped payments when adult males were found in recipients' or applicants' homes. Another court decision eliminated long-term residency requirements for recipients.

By 1971, a backlash was already under way. *U.S. News & World Report*, the most conservative of the three national newsweeklies, published a piece reporting that welfare spending threatened to "bankrupt the States and cities, and to drain the U.S. Treasury with chronic federal deficits."[40]

The magazine pointed to one development in particular: the growth in mother-headed households. AFDC child recipients whose fathers had deserted or whose mothers had never wed accounted for 80 percent of young beneficiaries, up from 60 percent a few years earlier, the magazine reported (without specifying the number of years).[41]

While some may have viewed *U.S. News*'s take on the issue as political spin, there was no question that female-headed households were becoming more common, especially in the poor population. In 1960, children in such households accounted for 9.2 percent of all children and 23.7 percent of all poor children. By 1972, children in single-mother families represented 14.2 percent of all children and more than 50 percent of poor children.[42]

Families in Crisis

Single motherhood was especially prevalent among African-Americans, who were also disproportionately represented on welfare rolls. As early as 1965, Daniel Patrick Moynihan, a liberal New Deal-style Democrat who was then a staff member of the Labor Department's Office of Policy Planning and Research, zeroed in on that trend. In a report titled, "The Negro Family: The Case for National Action," he argued that employment of fathers was far more valuable than welfare payments in lifting families out of poverty.[43]

"In the beginning, the number of AFDC families in which the father was absent because of desertion was less than a third of the total," Moynihan wrote. "Today it is two-thirds." He linked paternal abandonment to persistent joblessness for black men. "Negro unemployment, with the exception of a few years during World War II and the Korean War, has continued at disaster levels for 35 years."[44]

Initially, Moynihan's report was greeted positively by African-American leaders, including the Rev. Martin Luther King Jr., many of whom had also expressed alarm at a growing number of black households headed by single mothers. They were echoing concerns of earlier generations of black leaders. W. E. B. DuBois, the most prominent African-American scholar and intellectual activist of the 20th century, had condemned the single-motherhood trend as far back as 1899.[45]

Nevertheless, applause for Moynihan's report faded quickly. Reactions among black leaders and white liberals turned hostile, guided by the view that Moynihan was holding African-Americans entirely responsible for black poverty.

To some extent, that response may have been inspired less by Moynihan's paper than by the favorable reception that the report got from conservatives. They took it, wrote John McWhorter, a present-day analyst of race-related issues, "as a statement rather than as a 'case for action.' "

Nonetheless, McWhorter argued that the decades that followed provided evidence that Moynihan had focused accurately on one element of the poverty equation in the country's most disproportionately poverty-stricken population: "Multigenerational welfare dependency and all-but-fatherless neighborhoods became a norm in poor black communities," McWhorter wrote. "Surely the burden of proof is upon those who would argue that this was unconnected with the relaxation of eligibility rules for AFDC benefits in the 1960s."[46]

Other scholars argue from a more liberal perspective that Moynihan's emphasis on male employment discouraged efforts to raise AFDC payments or provide well-paying jobs for welfare mothers. At the same time, liberals contend, the report strengthened efforts to require AFDC mothers to get jobs. "Requiring welfare recipients to work, the argument went, might put pressure on mothers and fathers to stay together or not have children in the first place," three historians wrote in a history of welfare.[47] As debate swirled over the Moynihan report, its examination of the links between family structure, economics and poverty may have influenced the first War on Poverty-era congressional efforts to promote employment for welfare recipients.

In 1967, Congress established the Work Incentive (WIN) program, which required states to provide training and employment programs for "appropriate" AFDC beneficiaries. And to encourage recipients to work, some of what they earned — the first $30, plus one-third of the remaining amount — wouldn't be counted against their welfare payments. (A similar, smaller program set up in 1961 had stricter incentives for recipients to find employment.)[48]

Overall, the welfare-law amendment that created WIN marked a shift in attitude, notes Thomas Gabe, a social policy analyst for the Congressional Research Service. The law replaced requirements that services to recipients be "rehabilitative" and "competence-enhancing." Instead, the law now emphasized practical, job-finding assistance, such as job and training referral.[49]

Requiring Work

The WIN program only hinted at the transformation ahead. Discontent with the idea of paying people who didn't work, even if they were single mothers, was increasing both in Washington policy circles and in the states.[50]

In 1971, Congress changed WIN from a voluntary program to one in which welfare recipients were required to participate if they had no preschool-age children at home or other special circumstances. However, the practical effects of the new requirement were limited because the program wasn't fully funded.

Similarly, in 1971, California's Republican governor, Ronald W. Reagan, promoted a new approach to welfare that he dubbed "workfare." The legislature authorized a pilot program that required welfare recipients to get jobs. The program never got fully off the ground, however. A 1976 study by the state Employment Development Department concluded that it was badly designed, but a legislative sponsor said that counties ignored the project.[51]

Still, the appeal of requiring welfare recipients to work continued to grow. In 1981, during the first year of Reagan's presidency, Congress granted states the power

Seven-year-old Jayla gets ready for her weekly tutoring session last March 16 at the shelter in Los Angles where she lives with her mother. One in five U.S. children lives below the poverty line, a far higher rate than adults (13.7 percent) and the elderly (9 percent).

Reuters/Lucy Nicholson

to tailor WIN programs as they saw fit. States also gained authority to use federal welfare funds to subsidize on-the-job training.

States got further encouragement to step up work requirements from a 1986 report by the private, non-profit Manpower Demonstration Research Corp. (MDRC), a think tank on poverty-related issues. After studying reorganized welfare-to-work programs in eight states, Manpower concluded that they could increase employment and be cost-effective — though not to an extraordinary extent.

In his 1986 State of the Union address, Reagan called for changing the welfare system, arguing that it should be judged by how many recipients left the program because they no longer needed support. "In the welfare culture, the breakdown of the family, the most basic support system, has reached crisis proportions — in female and child poverty, child abandonment, horrible crimes and deteriorating schools," Reagan declared. He announced that his domestic-policy council would develop a new approach to aiding the poor.[52]

By the following year, Congress took another step toward making work a condition of welfare. The Family Support Act of 1988 obliged AFDC recipients, unless specifically exempted, to enroll in job training or find employment. That goal was reflected in the name given

Food Banks Support Many in New Mexico

"We always ate, but sometimes just a little."

On a sunny morning in late September, 75 mothers and children, mostly Spanish-speaking Mexican immigrants, lined up in the parking lot of a mobile home community in the dusty South Valley of Albuquerque, N.M.

The crowd waited in line to fill baskets with cucumbers, onions, jalapeño chilies, cartons of long-life milk, dry pasta and other supplies from the Roadrunner Food Bank.

In the days before the monthly food deliveries started, "We always ate," says Laura Sánchez, the mother of a 4-month-old girl and two older children, "but sometimes just a little." Her husband works construction, earning about $350 a week when there's work, but often there is none.

"We started to see this two years ago," says Guillermo Yelo, pastor of Camino de Vida (Pathway of Life) church, who organized the food distribution. "A lot of people here don't have jobs. It made me realize the need for help."

A few hours later and about 10 miles north, another group gathered in a school gym in Corrales, a village that began as an 18th-century land grant by the Spanish crown.[1]

Among them was Lynette Bratvold, a homeowner who works two clerical jobs to support her husband and 3-year-old son. "My husband stays home with our child so that we don't have to pay outrageous child-care costs," she says. "So we need assistance with food."

Her husband, a high-school graduate, worked as a security guard when he was employed — earning at most $10 an hour. "I'm working 50-60 hours a week, and it's still not enough," she says.

As more people, even those working full time, needed assistance, the food bank, the state's main food charity, saw its distribution rise to about 24 million pounds in fiscal 2010-11 — a 10 percent increase over the previous year, says spokeswoman Sonya Warwick.

Nationally, food banks served 5.7 million a week in 2009 (the latest numbers available), a 27 percent increase since 2005, according to Feed America, a national alliance of food charities.[2]

Now, Feed America is warning Roadrunner and other food operations in New Mexico of a looming cutback in the free food it receives from the U.S. Department of Agriculture, which contributes about 20 percent of Roadrunner's stock. "We've been told to expect a reduction of 40 percent to 50 percent of that food," Warwick says. "We are trying to make sure we have various food sources so that when the cuts hit we don't have a crisis."

In fact, New Mexico is a state with two distinct populations, and one already is in crisis. Affluent New Mexicans, those who support the state's international reputation as an artists' haven, skiing destination and nuclear research center, are doing just fine, on the whole.

But the other New Mexico has been suffering a slow-motion crisis for several years. The state's 30 percent child-poverty rate is exceeded only by Mississippi's 33 percent.[3] And while the unemployment rate of 6.6 percent is lower than the national average of 9.1 percent, the state's 18.2 percent poverty rate in 2009 is significantly higher than the latest national rate of 15.1 percent. A longtime prevalence of low-wage work, compounded by the scarcity of regular employment in parts of the state, including the New

to related state programs, Job Opportunities and Basic Skills Training (JOBS). Because recipients who could not obtain child care were exempt from the new standard, Congress stepped up funding for that service. JOBS participants were required to work or train for 20 hours a week.

But by the standards of those who hoped that the 1988 law would transform the welfare system, actual changes were modest. The General Accounting Office (now the Government Accountability Office) reported in 1995 that about 20 percent of eligible AFDC recipients participated in some JOBS activity each month, though not all of them for the mandated 20 hours a week.

But the law set a new tone concerning welfare recipients and what was expected of them. Politicians took

Mexico portion of the Navajo Nation (most of which is in Arizona), explain the disparity between relatively low joblessness and high poverty.

"We have chunks of counties where people just aren't in the formal economy," says Gerry Bradley, research director at New Mexico Voices for Children, a nonprofit advocacy group.

"We're sort of bouncing along the bottom," Bradley says. He adds, citing 0.9 percent employment growth during the 12 months ending last August, "Maybe we're starting to turn around."[4]

New Mexico is a so-called "majority minority" state, with a population that's 46 percent Hispanic (both citizens and immigrants) and 9 percent Native American, a white, non-Hispanic population of 40 percent, plus small percentages of black, Asian and multi-racial people. The state ranks fourth from the bottom nationwide in a composite score of child-development indicators assembled by Voices for Children that includes the percentages of low-birth-weight babies and households with no stable employment.[5]

Hispanic New Mexicans tend to be concentrated in occupations that require less education — construction, above all. And construction, Bradley says, was "hammered by the recession."

Echoing Bradley's conclusion are the mothers gathered for food in South Valley.

"My husband works sometimes for two days, sometimes for a couple of weeks," says Soledad Murillo, a 47-year-old grandmother of six and mother of three daughters, none married. A 15-year New Mexico resident who comes from Durango, Mexico, Murillo says that jobs used to be far easier to find.

Linda Aguayo, who fled the ultraviolent Mexican border town of Ciudad Juárez three years ago, then returned, then fled again five months ago, says her husband fixes refrigerator cases and other store appliances.

Roadrunner Food Bank

The Roadrunner Food Bank's Mobile Food Pantry helps struggling families throughout New Mexico. The program served 85,000 children and 127,500 adults last year.

"But it's not stable work," she says. "Whatever he makes just pays the rent."

Without the donated food, she says, "We'd be eating less."

— *Peter Katel*

[1] "Brief History of Corrales," Corrales Historical Society, 2004, www.corrales history.com/html/morehistory.html.

[2] "Hunger in America: Key Findings," 2010, http://feedingamerica.org/hunger-in-america/hunger-studies/hunger-study-2010/key-findings.aspx.

[3] "Children in Poverty (Percent) — 2010," Kids Count Data Center, Annie E. Casey Foundation, undated, http://datacenter.kidscount.org/data/acrossstates/ Rankings.aspx?ind=43.

[4] *Ibid.*

[5] "Early Childhood Supports in New Mexico," New Mexico Voices for Children, updated 2010, www.nmvoices.org/attachments/ece-supports-2010-update.pdf.

note that those expectations reflected attitudes among a broad swath of voters in both parties.

Accordingly, Democratic presidential candidate Bill Clinton vowed during his 1992 campaign to "end welfare as we know it." Elaborating, Clinton said in a campaign commercial: "Those who are able must go to work. . . . It's time to make welfare what it should be — a second chance, not a way of life."[53]

Slightly more than two years later, newly triumphant Republicans who had overturned longtime Democratic control of the House introduced the Work Opportunity Act of 1995. The bill reflected Republicans' campaign pledge, laid out in their "Contract With America" political platform, to "achieve what some 30 years of massive welfare spending has not been able to accomplish: reduce illegitimacy, require work and save taxpayers money."[54]

As debate over welfare intensified, Clinton vetoed two Republican-crafted bills that he said were too harsh in their treatment of welfare mothers. He pointed to their failure to provide adequately for child care and medical care for AFDC recipients entering the job market.[55]

For a Democratic president, welfare was politically tricky. Clinton's party was divided between so-called "neo-liberals" (like himself), who strongly supported replacing the old welfare system, and traditional Democrats, who found more to support than to oppose in AFDC.[56]

In 1996, intense negotiations between Clinton and Republican leaders, and between Clinton and his fellow Democrats, produced the Personal Responsibility and Work Opportunity Reconciliation Act of 1996.

Hailed as the most significant piece of social legislation since the War on Poverty, the law required that recipients of what had become TANF go to work within two years of receiving aid and that aid be limited to five years. Moreover, the welfare-funding system was changed to fixed "block grants," replacing need-gauged appropriations.[57]

In the context of the economic boom of the late 1990s, the new law showed some remarkable results. The work rate of never-married mothers shot up from 46.5 percent of their total population in 1995 to 66 percent in 1999, an increase of about 40 percent in four years.[58]

As a result, Haskins of Brookings reported in a study last summer that poverty among single mothers and their children decreased from a 1991 peak of 47.1 percent to 33 percent in 2000 — the lowest level ever for that group.[59]

When the full force of the recession hit in 2009, however, another feature of the new welfare system became apparent. The block-grant funding scheme had the effect of limiting expansion of welfare rolls, the Congressional Research Service reported. "The fixed nature of TANF funding imposes some financial risk on states," it said. "Generally states bear the risk of increased costs from a cash welfare-caseload rise."[60]

CURRENT SITUATION

Budget Worries

Poverty experts worry that deficit-reduction efforts could shortchange funding for medical care for poor children and their families. Up to now, they say, the medical system for the poor has been responding effectively to the nation's worsening economic conditions.

While the number of poor children has grown in recent years, the population of those not covered by medical insurance declined — from 7.9 million in 2007 to 7.3 million in 2010, the Census Bureau reported. During that period, the number of children covered by Medicaid — the state- and federally funded medical-care system for the poor — grew from 20.9 million to 26 million.[61]

Medicaid and the Children's Health Insurance Program (CHIP) "stepped into the void," says Bruce Lesley, president of First Focus, a child-policy advocacy organization in Washington. CHIP provides low-cost medical care to children whose family incomes are low but above the poverty line.

But advocates have grounds for concern. Decisions by the Joint Committee on Deficit Reduction — the so-called congressional "super committee" charged this fall with proposing measures to reduce federal deficits by $1.5 trillion over 10 years — could lead to an erosion of medical care for the poor.[62]

And the Obama administration, as part of its own deficit-reduction proposal, has recommended cutting $72 million from Medicaid. "The Medicaid cuts in the president's proposal shift the burden to states and ultimately onto the shoulders of seniors, people with disabilities and low-income families who depend on the program as their lifeline," Ronald F. Pollack, executive director of Families USA, an organization that advocates for expanded health-care coverage, told *The New York Times*.[63]

As evidence of subsidized health care's vulnerability, Lower-Basch of the Center for Law and Social Policy (CLASP) cites lawmakers' reluctance to make sharp cuts in Social Security and Medicare, plus Obama's aim of raising $1.5 trillion over 10 years largely by raising taxes on high earners and cutting subsidized health programs.

"The president commented that 'it's not class warfare, it's math,'" Lower-Basch says. "At some point there are, mathematically, only a certain number of things to cut. Particularly if you take Social Security and Medicare off the table, that doesn't leave a lot of targets" besides food stamps and Medicaid, she says.

The political mechanics of deficit reduction also work in favor of cutting Medicaid funding because most Americans don't understand the technical language surrounding entitlements, Lower-Basch says.

Should mothers who have children out of wedlock be denied welfare?

YES
Michael D. Tanner
Senior Fellow, Cato Institute

Written for *CQ Researcher*, October 2011

Since Lyndon Johnson declared a War on Poverty in 1965, the federal government has spent roughly $18 trillion fighting poverty, almost $700 billion this year alone, on some 107 separate programs. Yet, the poverty rate stands at 15.1 percent. While this number may be partially inflated because of the poor economy, it is important to realize that, despite trillions in spending, we have never gotten the poverty rate below 11 percent. Clearly we are doing some things wrong.

One is perpetuating government programs that create an incentive for behavior that is likely to lead to poverty. In particular, our welfare programs continue to provide benefits to women who give birth out of wedlock.

The concern over this trend is not about personal morality. Having a child out of wedlock often means a lifetime of poverty. Children living with single mothers are almost six times more likely to be poor than those living with two parents. More than 20 percent of welfare recipients start on welfare because they have an out-of-wedlock birth. They also tend to stay on welfare longer than other recipients.

The trend is even worse among unwed teenage mothers. Half go on welfare within one year of the birth of their first child; 75 percent are on welfare within five years of the child's birth. Women who started on welfare because of an out-of-wedlock birth average more than nine years on welfare and make up roughly 40 percent of all recipients who are on welfare for 10 years or longer.

While there are many factors behind the rise in out-of-wedlock births, the availability of welfare is one. Of the more than 20 major studies of the issue, more than three-quarters show a significant link between benefit levels and out-of-wedlock childbearing.

Obviously no one gets pregnant to get welfare. But by softening the immediate as opposed to the long-term economic consequences of out-of-wedlock births, welfare has removed a major incentive to avoid them. As Charles Murray, a political scientist at the American Enterprise Institute, put it, "The evil of the modern welfare state is not that it bribes women to have babies — wanting to have babies is natural — but that it enables women to bear children without the natural social restraints."

A good start to a welfare policy that might actually reduce poverty would be to set a date — say nine months from today — after which an out-of-wedlock birth would no longer make one eligible for welfare.

NO
LaDonna A. Pavetti
Vice President for Family Income-Support Policy, Center on Budget and Policy Priorities

Written for *CQ Researcher*, October 2011

The case for rejecting a policy that would deny cash assistance to mothers who have children out of wedlock was compelling in 1996, when Congress created Temporary Assistance for Needy Families (TANF) — the current welfare law — and it's even more compelling now.

For starters, such a policy would deny support to children who bear no responsibility for their parents' actions. With growing evidence that poverty among young children reduces their chances of success throughout their lives, we should do everything we can to make sure that all children have the support they need to become productive adults.

A recent article by University of California, Irvine, education professor Greg J. Duncan and University of Wisconsin, Madison, professor of social work Katherine Magnuson provides all the evidence we need. Duncan is one of the most respected academic researchers on the consequences of childhood poverty, and he has always been particularly cautious in drawing policy conclusions from academic research. Two key points from the article stand out:

- Income matters for young, low-income children's learning;
- Poverty in early childhood may reduce earnings much later in life.

The authors recommend that states avoid TANF policy changes that threaten the well-being of young children. Indeed, we should be seeking more ways to remediate deep and persistent poverty in early childhood — not fewer.

Besides, although TANF provides an important safety net for single-parent families, it is not the main source of support for families with out-of-wedlock children. So, denying them these benefits will play no role in changing societal behavior. In the late 1990s, when the economy was strong, record numbers of single parents entered the labor force, reaching a high of 83 percent by 2000. Even in the current economy, 74 percent of them still work. In contrast, only 27 families for every 100 in poverty receive TANF benefits. And, TANF benefits are meager: In the median state in 2011, a family of three received $429 per month; in 14 states, such a family received less than $300.

In 1968, the Supreme Court ruled that children born to unmarried parents could not be punished for their parents' actions. The question we should be answering is: How can we make investments in our children that guarantee bright and productive futures for all of them? The answers matter not only for our children, but for all of us.

Eight-year-old Briana, left, and her sister, Daneen, 9, watch as their mother asks for a Thanksgiving turkey at the "banquet in a box" food-distribution event held by the Denver Rescue Mission in Colorado on Nov. 23, 2010. In 2009 food banks served 5.7 million people a week in the United States (the latest figure available), according to Feed America, a national alliance of food charities.

"Part of what we worry about is the process of getting to these very high-level procedural issues that are abstract," she says. "People don't know what they mean, and what they mean is cuts in critical programs for low-income families."

Alarm among liberal advocates has stepped down a notch since earlier in the year, when Rep. Paul Ryan, R-Wis., a top Republican deficit hawk, proposed a federal budget in which Medicaid would be funded by fixed block grants to the states. The Center on Budget and Policy Priorities calculated that the proposal would have reduced Medicaid funding by at least 25 percent, based on 2009 budget figures.[64]

Obama and congressional Democrats would firmly oppose any such move, advocates say. But Haskins of the Brookings Institution suggests that the logic behind the block-grant idea remains plausible. He says, in fact, that he would support a Medicaid block grant if it came with annual funding increases.

Citing the growing costs of Medicaid and Medicare, Haskins says, "We've got to get hold of that or it's going to bankrupt us."

But Haskins adds, "If you gave a block grant with no mechanism for increasing funding, or just an increase

with the rate of inflation, states would either have to cut services or spend more, and they can't spend more."

Child Support

For some poverty experts, enforcement of child-support payments is an anti-poverty tool that gets too little attention.

"We've actually reduced our investment in child-support enforcement," says Lesley of First Focus. "If we think that fathers should have responsibility for their kids, one way to address that is enforcement."

Federal "incentive" grants had been awarded to states that showed enforcement results, but those grants were eliminated by deficit-reduction legislation in 2005. The grants, which supplied from 6 percent to 39 percent of state enforcement budgets, were restored for 2009 and 2010 by the "stimulus" bill at the beginning of the Obama administration.[65]

"In 2008, 625,000 children would have been poor if they had not received child support, increasing child poverty by 4.4 percent," Elaine Sorensen of the Urban Institute, a centrist think tank in Washington, wrote last year in laying out the case for strengthening enforcement efforts. In that year, by her calculation, child-support payments aided 17 million children, ranking second to Medicaid, whose child caseload was 22.8 million — in the number of young people who received support.[66]

Sorensen also noted that among poor families with children, child support represents an average of 10 percent of family income — marginally more than the 9 percent that welfare payments represented.[67]

Nevertheless, the high and persistent joblessness that dominates the economy is having an effect on child support. The Government Accountability Office (GAO), Congress's nonpartisan investigative arm, reported in a study early this year that child-support collections had decreased for the first time in 2009, by $641 million.[68]

"Obtaining collections from a noncustodial parent with a limited ability to pay, such as those whose employment or earnings have been affected by the economic recession, is more difficult," the GAO noted.[69]

Some anti-poverty advocates point to a finding in the GAO study that they believe supports their view that enforcement is useful to only a minority of poor families, at least in present economic circumstances. The GAO found that only a third of families eligible for child-support and welfare payments actually received child-support money.[70]

Child-support payments "make a huge difference to families that receive it," says Lower-Basch of CLASP. But, she adds, most fathers of children who live under the poverty line with their mothers aren't in any position to provide significant support. "People talk about deadbeat dads, then figured out that many of them are dead broke, not deadbeat. They have minimal incomes themselves."

Jones of the Center for Urban Families warns that child-support enforcement laws, if not written with an eye to the realities that dominate families who live in poverty, can end up making matters worse. Maryland law authorizes the state to claim 65 percent of a worker's take-home pay for child support, he notes.[71]

"You take 65 percent from somebody who makes less than $10,000 a year," Jones says, and "you're setting someone up to live in the underground economy: 'I'm not going to take a legal job because I can't afford to have my money taken.' And when I become a senior citizen, I have no Social Security to draw on."

Cartoon Debate

The increase in child poverty may not have gotten much notice from politicians. Over on "Sesame Street," though, the development has prompted a new Muppet to join the cast for a special program. Lily, a purple-faced girl in a denim jumper, was created to represent the 16.2 million children who live in what the U.S. Agriculture Department calls "food-insecure" households.[72]

These are families who don't have guaranteed access at all times to nutritious food — a condition affecting nearly 15 percent of the U.S. population, according to the Agriculture Department.[73]

Lily appeared on a one-hour Public Broadcasting System special in early October, "Growing Hope Against Hunger." "While collecting foods at a food drive and from a community garden, the Sesame friends meet Lily, a new character whose family has an ongoing struggle with hunger," the show's production company, "Sesame Workshop," said in a press release. "The Sesame characters learn how their simple actions, such as planting a seed, can make a world of difference to others. . . . The special reassures children that they are not alone: There are people who care and can help."[74]

At a time when poverty and related issues have generated little political debate, the addition of Lily to the "Sesame Street" cast prompted sniping in some conservative media.

"I just don't understand why this Muppet is hungry," Andrea Tantaros, co-host of a Fox News talk show, "The Five," said on her Oct. 7 show. "Obama has expanded Medicaid by $60 billion, he's expanded food stamps, he's expanded WIC — Women's, Infants and Children (nutrition). . . . Why is Lily hungry? Bob, should Lily be taken away from her parents? . . . There's so much money out there to feed these kids."[75]

Tantaros was echoing a theme sounded by conservative analysts, who point to the expanded food-stamp program and other anti-poverty programs as evidence of liberal mischaracterization of U.S. poverty as severe deprivation.

Nevertheless, another school of conservative commentary takes poverty indicators at face value to criticize Obama's presidency. "With a record number of Americans on food stamps, increased debt and record poverty, Sesame Street will introduce a poor, starving muppet to educate on the growing number of starving children in Obama's America," Jim Hoft, a conservative blogger, wrote at his site, "Gateway Pundit."[76]

Hoft's comment was circulated on the left side of the blogosphere by "Media Matters for America," which monitors conservative media for a liberal audience. In the same way, another liberal site, *Crooks and Liars*, posted a clip of the Fox News discussion.[77]

Liberals, for their part, have been applauding "Sesame Street" for tackling the hunger issue. "Good they're doing it, sad it's necessary," wrote Laura Clawson, a contributor to the *Daily Kos*.[78]

OUTLOOK

Needed: Poverty Target

If the poor and the well-off occupy different spheres of reality, so do poverty policy experts of opposing political views. Their differences run far deeper than disagreements over specific policies.

Lesley of First Focus, for instance, insists that the political establishment — Democrats and Republicans alike — is neglecting the issue of poverty. "What we really need in this country is something like a poverty-reduction target," he says. "Every year you would have the target, and the administration would be required to come up with its agenda on how to address the problem. If we had a conversation among Republicans and Democrats about who is not doing enough about child poverty, I would retire."

For now, despite the Census Bureau poverty statistics that got policy experts talking, politicians have taken a pass, Lesley says. "The conversations are among advocates and think tanks. There's 22 percent of children in poverty — where's Barack Obama? [House Speaker John] Boehner, where's his agenda?"

Rector of the Heritage Foundation dismisses the idea that poverty is being ignored. "That's just a ploy," he says. "Programs are growing like crazy. The sky is always falling from their perspective. There's been a gargantuan expansion of welfare spending that's not going to go down when the recession ends," he says.

Rector and two colleagues wrote in 2009 that welfare spending aimed at poor and low-income people had grown thirteen-fold, after adjusting for inflation, to more than $700 billion, since President Johnson launched the War on Poverty in 1964.[79]

At the same time, Rector sees no end to the growth in out-of-wedlock births — the major source, in his view, of poverty. "We're on a trajectory where the working-class white family is slowly disintegrating. That creates an automatic poverty population."

Liberal analysts raise their own fear about changes in the social structure. "It's widely thought in the United States that we're the land of opportunity," says Gerry Bradley, research director at New Mexico Voices for Children, an Albuquerque-based advocacy group. "But we're getting to the point where it's more difficult for people to move out of their income group than it is in European countries that are thought to be more stratified."

The likelihood of Congress cutting benefit programs that help lower-income people afford higher education will worsen the picture, Bradley argues. "Cutting these programs is going to ensure that we have a more rigid class structure than we already do."[80]

Jones of the Center for Urban Families sounds a guardedly optimistic note. "I have to believe that in 10 years the economy will be better," he says. But he's less certain about the level of national leadership.

"Our democracy depends on our political system to make the necessary recalibration to respond to circumstances," he says. "Unless the people in control change, or our system changes, we will be worse off than we are now. I think the American people are going to have rise up and say to policy makers, 'You've got to stop the ideological warfare.' "

On another note of tempered optimism, Jane Trujillo and Shannon Barnett of Belen, N.M., are both counting the value of education. Trujillo is studying for an associate's degree in nursing. Barnett vows to do likewise.

"I didn't finish school, so I've now started classes for my GED," Barnett says. "As soon as I'm done with that I'm going to try to get into nursing school. I'm hoping that once that happens we won't be struggling so much. I am just focusing on my education."

NOTES

1. "Missing Meals in New Mexico," Roadrunner Food Bank, December 2010, www.rrfb.org/wp-content/uploads/2011/02/Executive-Summary-Version-2.pdf; "New Mexico QuickFacts," U.S. Census Bureau, updated June 3, 2011, http://quickfacts.census.gov/qfd/states/35000.html.

2. "Children in Poverty (Percent) — 2010," Kids Count Data Center, Annie E. Casey Foundation, undated, http://datacenter.kidscount.org/ data/acrossstates/Rankings.aspx?ind=43.

3. "Poverty thresholds," U.S. Census Bureau, updated Sept. 13, 2011, www.census.gov/hhes/ www/poverty/data/threshld/index.html.

4. Increases in food and gasoline prices in 2009-2011 are major reasons that U.S. incomes have fallen in value, a study by two former Census Bureau professionals concluded. See Robert Pear, "Recession Officially Over, U.S. Incomes Kept Falling," *The New York Times*, Oct. 10, 2011, www.nytimes.com/2011/10/10/us/recession-officially-over-us-incomes-kept-falling.html?_r=1&hp.

5. Carmen DeNavas-Walt, *et al.*, "Poverty Status of People by Family Relationship, Race, and Hispanic Origin: 1959 to 2010," U.S. Census Bureau, updated Sept. 13, 2011, p. 62, www.census.gov/

hhes/www/poverty/data/historical/ people.html. For background, see Thomas J. Billitteri, "Domestic Poverty," *CQ Researcher*, Sept. 7, 2007, pp. 721-744, updated April 27, 2011.

6. "Income, Poverty, and Health Insurance Coverage in the United States: 2010," U.S. Census Bureau, September 2011, p. 17, www.census.gov/ prod/2011pubs/p60-239.pdf.

7. Gene Falk, "The TANF Emergency Contingency Fund," Congressional Research Service, Dec. 22, 2010, Summary page, www.fas.org/sgp/crs/misc/ R41078.pdf.

8. Joyce A. Martin, *et al.*, "Births: Final Data for 2008," National Vital Statistics Reports, National Center for Health Statistics, Dec. 8, 2010, p. 44, www.cdc .gov/nchs/data/nvsr/nvsr59/nv sr59_01.pdf; "U.S. Births Rise for First Time in Eight Years," Family Planning Perspectives, Guttmacher Institute, September-October 2000, www.guttmacher.org/ pubs/journals/3226300. html; Current Trends in Fertility and Infant and Maternal Health — United States, 1980-1988," Centers for Disease Control, June 14, 1991, www.cdc.gov/mmwr/preview/ mmwrhtml/00014440.htm; Stephanie J. Ventura, "Changing Patterns of Nonmarital Childbearing in the United States," National Center for Health Statistics, May 2009, www.cdc.gov/nchs/data/data-briefs/ db18.pdf.

9. "Related Children Under 18 by Householder's Work Experience and Family Structure: 2010," Current Population Survey, U.S. Census Bureau, Labor Department, updated Sept. 13, 2011, www.census .gov/hhes/www/cpstables/032011/pov/new21_ 100_01.htm.

10. Mark Hugo Lopez and Gabriel Velasco, "Childhood Poverty Among Hispanics Sets Record, Leads Nation," Pew Hispanic Center, Sept. 28, 2011, p. 4, http://pewhispanic.org/ files/reports/147.pdf.

11. *Ibid.*, pp. 11-14; "Educational Attainment: Better Than Meets the Eye, But Large Challenges Remain," Pew Hispanic Center, January 2002, http://pew hispanic.org/files/factsheets/ 3.pdf.

12. See Kathleen S. Short, "The Supplemental Poverty Measure: Examining the Incidence and Depth of Poverty in the U.S. Taking Account of Taxes and Transfers," U.S. Census Bureau, June 30, 2011, www.census.gov/hhes/pov meas/methodology/ supplemental/research.html.

13. "A Brief History of the AFDC Program," Health and Human Services Department, June 1998, http://aspe.hhs.gov/hsp/afdc/afdc base98.htm.

14. Gene Falk, The Temporary Assistance for Needy Families (TANF) Block Grant: Responses to Frequently Asked Questions," Congressional Research Service, May 4, 2011, www.work forceatm .org/assets/utilities/serve.cfm?path=/sections/pdf/ 2011/TheTemporaryAssistancefor NeedyFamilies TANFBlockGrantResponsesto FrequentlyAsked Questions3.pdf.

15. *Ibid.*, p. 6.

16. *Ibid.*, pp. 1, 3, 7.

17. *Ibid.*, p. 2.

18. *Ibid.*, p. 9; "Caseload Data 2011," Administration for Children and Families, Health and Human Services Department, updated July 25, 2011, www .acf.hhs.gov/programs/ofa/ data-reports/caseload/ caseload_current.htm# 2011.

19. Sabrina Tavernise, "Soaring Poverty Casts Spotlight on 'Lost Decade,' " *The New York Times*, Sept. 13, 2011, www.nytimes.com/ 2011/09/14/us/14census .html?pagewanted=1&_r=1&sq=census%20 2010%20poverty&st=cse&scp=2; DeNavas-Walt, *op. cit.*, pp. 14, 17.

20. "Supplemental Nutrition Assistance Program: Number of Persons Participating," Food Research and Action Center, updated monthly, http://frac .org/wp-content/uploads/2011/03/ snapdata2011_ july.pdf; "Labor Force Statistics from the Current Population Survey," U.S. Bureau of Labor Statistics, updated regularly, http://data.bls.gov/timeseries/ LNS14000000.

21. Robert Rector, *et al.*, "Obama to Spend $10.3 Trillion on Welfare," Heritage Foundation, Sept. 16, 2009, www.heritage.org/Research/ Reports/2009/09/ Obama-to-Spend-103-Trillion-on-Welfare-Uncovering-the-Full-Cost-of-Means-Tested-Welfare-or-Aid-to-the-Poor.

22. "Hearing of the House Ways and Means Committee, 'Improving Work and Other Welfare Reform Goals, Focusing on Reauthorization of the Temporary Assistance for Needy Families Program," Federal News Service, Sept. 8, 2011; "Engagement in Additional Work Activities and Expenditures for Other Benefits and Services, a TANF Report to Congress," March 2011, (no page numbers), www.acf.hhs.gov/ programs/ofa/data-reports/cra-report-to-congress/ cra_report-to-congress.html#_Toc29 8161525.

23. Hearing, *ibid.*

24. Kristin Anderson Moore, *et al.*, "Children in Poverty: Trends, Consequences, and Policy Options," Child Trends, April 2009, www.child trends.org/files/child_ trends-2009_04_07_rb_ childreninpoverty.pdf.

25. *Ibid.*

26. DeNavas-Walt, *et al.*, *op. cit.*, pp. 17-18, 74.

27. "2011 Kids Count Data Book," Annie E. Casey Foundation, 2011, p. 62, http://datacenter.kids count.org/databook/2011/OnlineBooks/2011 KCDB_FINAL.pdf; Vanessa R. Wight, *et al.*, "Who are America's Poor Children?," National Center for Children in Poverty, Columbia University, March 2011, www.nccp.org/publications/ pub_1001.html.

28. James J. Heckman, "The Economics of Inequality," *American Educator*, Spring 2011, p. 33, www.aft.org/ pdfs/americaneducator/ spring2011/Heckman.pdf.

29. "Income, Poverty, and Health Insurance Coverage," *op. cit.*, p. 15.

30. Ron Haskins, "Fighting Poverty the American Way," Brookings Institution, June 20, 2011, p. 32, www .brookings.edu/~/media/Files/rc/ papers/2011/0620_ fighting_poverty_haskins/ 0620_fighting_poverty_ haskins.pdf.

31. Except where otherwise indicated, this subsection is drawn from Premilla Nadasen, *et al.*, *Welfare in the United States: A History With Documents 1935-1996* (2009); Thomas Gabe, "Welfare, Work and Poverty Status of Female-Headed Families With Children: 1987-2009, Congressional Research Service, July 15, 2011, http://digitalcommons.ilr.cornell.edu/cgi/ view content.cgi?article=1852&context=key_work place; for background, see Kathy Koch, "Child Poverty," *CQ Researcher*, April 7, 2000, pp. 281-304.

32. Jennifer Michael and Madeleine Goldstein, "Reviving the White House Conference on Children," Children's Voice, Child Welfare League of America, January-February 2008, www.cwla.org/voice/0801whconf .htm.

33. Nadasen, *et al.*, *op. cit.*, pp. 15-16.

34. Quoted in Susan W. Blank and Barbara B. Blum, "A Brief History of Work Expectations for Welfare Mothers," *Future of Children* (Journal), Spring 1997, p. 30, www.princeton.edu/futureofchildren/publi cations/docs/07_01_02.pdf.

35. *Ibid.*, p. 30.

36. Blank and Blum, *op. cit.*, p. 30.

37. Richard B. Drake, *A History of Appalachia* (2001), p. 173; Maurice Isserman, "Michael Harrington: Warrior on Poverty," *The New York Times*, June 19, 2009, www.nytimes.com/2009/ 06/21/books/review/ Isserman-t.html. Except where otherwise indicated, this subsection is drawn from Gabe, *op. cit.*

38. Quoted in Edward Zigler and Susan Muenchow, *Head Start: The Inside Story of America's Most Successful Educational Experiment* (1992), p. 3.

39. "Trends in the AFDC Caseload since 1962," U.S. Health and Human Services Department, undated, p. 15, http://aspe.hhs.gov/hsp/afdc/ baseline/2case load.pdf.

40. Report included in Nadasen, *et al.*, p. 169.

41. *Ibid.*

42. Gabe, *op. cit.*, p. 69.

43. Daniel Patrick Moynihan, "The Negro Family: The Case for National Action," U.S. Department of Labor, March 1965, www.dol.gov/ oasam/programs/ history/webid-meynihan.htm.

44. *Ibid.*

45. Nadasen, *et al.*, *op. cit.*, pp. 45-46; John McWhorter, "Legitimacy at Last," *The New Republic*, April 16, 2010, www.tnr.com/book/ review/legitimacy-last.

46. *Ibid.*

47. Nadasen, *et al.*, *op. cit.*, p. 47.

48. Gabe, *op. cit.*, pp. 59-60.

49. *Ibid.*, p. 60.

50. For background, see Peter Katel, "Straining the Safety Net," *CQ Researcher*, July 31, 2009, pp. 645-668. Except where otherwise stated, this subsection draws on Blank and Blum, *op. cit.*

51. Katel, *ibid.*

52. "Address Before a Joint Session of the Congress Reporting on the State of the Union," Feb. 4, 1986, http://reagan2020.us/speeches/ state_of_the_union_1986.asp.

53. Quoted in Richard L. Berke, "Clinton: Getting People Off Welfare," *The New York Times*, Sept. 10, 1992, www.nytimes.com/1992/09/10/ us/the-1992-campaign-the-ad-campaign-clinton-getting-people-off-welfare.html.

54. Quoted in Gabe, *op. cit.*, p. 8.

55. "Fact Sheet, The Personal Responsibility and Work Opportunity Reconciliation Act of 1996," Health and Human Services Dept., September 1996, http://aspe.hhs.gov/hsp/abbrev/prwora96.htm; "Interview: Welfare reform, 10 years later (with Ron Haskins)," Brookings Institution, Aug. 24, 2006, www.brookings.edu/ interviews/2006/0824welfare_haskins.aspx.

56. *Ibid.*, Haskins; Ronald Brownstein, "A Stormy Debate Is Brewing Within GOP Over Clinton's Big Lead in Polls," *Los Angeles Times*, Sept. 9, 1996, p. A5.

57. *Ibid.*

58. Ron Haskins, "Fighting Poverty the American Way," Brookings Institution, June 20, 2011, pp. 4, 32, www.brookings.edu/~/media/Files/ rc/papers/2011/0620_fighting_poverty_haskins/ 0620_fighting_poverty_haskins.pdf.

59. *Ibid.*

60. Gene Falk, "The Temporary Assistance for Needy Families (TANF) Block Grant: Responses to Frequently Asked Questions," Congressional Research Service, Jan. 21, 2009, p. 1, http:// stuff.mit.edu/afs/sipb/contrib/wikileaks-crs/wikileaks-crs-reports/RL32760.pdf.

61. "Income, Poverty, and Health Insurance . . .," *op. cit.*, p. 82.

62. "Joint Select Committee on Deficit Reduction," undated, www.deficitreduction.gov/public.

63. Quoted in Robert Pear, "In Cuts to Health Programs, Experts See Difficult Task in Protecting Patients," *The New York Times*, Sept. 20, 2011, www.nytimes.com/2011/09/21/us/politics/ wielding-the-ax-on-medicaid-and-medicare-without-wounding-the-patient.html.

64. Edwin Park and Matt Broaddus, "What if Ryan's Medicaid Block Grant Had Taken Effect in 2000," Center on Budget and Policy Priorities, April 12, 2011, www.cbpp.org/cms/ index.cfm?fa=view&id=3466.

65. "Child Support Enforcement," Government Accountability Office, January,www.gao.gov/new .items/d11196.pdf.

66. Elaine Sorensen, "Child Support Plays an Increasingly Important Role for Poor Custodial Families," Urban Institute, December 2010, p. 1, www.urban.org/publications/412272.html.

67. *Ibid.*, p. 3.

68. "Child Support Enforcement," *op. cit.*, p. 11.

69. *Ibid.*, p. 14.

70. *Ibid.*, p. 14.

71. "Department of Human Resources, Child Support," Maryland state government, undated, www.dhr.state .md.us/csea/download/EMPLOY ERJOBAID.doc.

72. Dave Itzkoff, " 'Sesame Street' Special on Hunger Introduces New Muppet Character," *The New York Times*, ArtsBeat blog, Oct. 3, 2011, http://artsbeat .blogs.nytimes.com/2011/10/03/ sesame-street-special-on-hunger-introduces-new-muppet-character; "Food Security in the United States," U.S. Agriculture Department, updated Sept. 7, 2011, www.ers.usda .gov/Brief ing/FoodSecurity/stats_graphs.htm.

73. *Ibid.*

74. "Project Overview, growing hope against hunger," Sesame Workshop, Oct. 4, 2011, www. s2.cine magnetics.com/press-release/english.html.

75. "Sign of the Times: Poverty-Stricken Muppet," "The Five" transcript, Oct. 7, 2011, www.fox news.com/ on-air/the-five/transcript/sign-times-poverty-stricken-muppet.

76. Melody Johnson, "Strings Attached: Right-Wing Media Take Shots At New Poverty-Stricken Sesame

Street Character," Media Matters for America, Oct. 6, 2011, http://mediamatters.org/blog/ 201110060010.

77. "Fox Panel Attacks Sesame Street for Wanting to Educate Children About Poverty," *Crooks and Liars*, Oct. 8, 2011, http://videocafe.crooks andliars.com/heather/fox-panel-attacks-sesame-street-wanting-ed.

78. Laura Clawson, "This week in the War on Workers: The hungry Muppet," *Daily Kos*, Oct. 8, 2011, http://labor.dailykos.com.

79. Robert Rector, Katherine Bradley, Rachel Sheffield, "Obama to Spend $10 trillion on Welfare," Heritage Foundation, Sept. 16, 2009, p. 1, www.heritage.org/research/reports/2009/09/obama-to-spend-103-trillion-on-welfare-un covering-the-full-cost-of-means-tested-welfare-or-aid-to-the-poor.

80. For background, see Marcia Clemmitt, "Student Debt," *CQ Researcher*, Oct. 21, 2011, pp. 877-900.

BIBLIOGRAPHY

Selected Sources

Books

Mead, Lawrence M., *Expanding Work Programs for Poor Men*, AEI Press, 2011.
A leading conservative poverty-policy expert lays out a case for requiring low-income men to work, following the example of the 1996 welfare law and its demands on largely female welfare recipients. Poor children would benefit, he writes, as child-support payments increased.

Nadasen, Premilla, Jennifer Mittelstadt and Marisa Chappell, *Welfare in the United States: A History With Documents, 1935-1996*, Routledge, 2009.
Three historians chronicle and analyze welfare history from a pro-welfare recipients' perspective.

Articles

Alderman, Lesley, "Government Helps to Insure Children, Even Above the Poverty Line," *The New York Times*, Oct. 9, 2010, p. B6, www.nytimes.com/2010/10/09/health/ 09patient.html.
Successful results are reported for the federal-state health coverage program for low-income children.

Crary, David, *et al.*, "Behind the poverty numbers: real lives, real pain," *The Associated Press*, Sept. 19, 2011.
In a series of profiles from across the country, AP correspondents report on the hardships faced by growing numbers of families.

D'Innocenzio, Anne, and Dena Potter, "Food-stamp shoppers buy at midnight across the country," *The Washington Post*, Oct. 24, 2010, p. A8, www.washington post.com/wp-dyn/content/article/2010/10/23/AR2010 102300179.html.
The Post uncovers a nationwide trend of families racing to stock up on food as soon as their electronic food-stamp cards are recharged once a month at midnight.

Davey, Monica, "Families Feel Sharp Edge of State Budget Cuts," *The New York Times*, Sept. 7, 2011, p. A22, www.ny times.com/2011/09/07/us/07states .html?pagewanted=all.
Hard-pressed states are reducing aid to poor families, a correspondent reports from the Midwest.

Egger, Robert, "5 Myths about hunger in America," *The Washington Post*, Nov. 21, 2010, p. B2, www .washington post.com/wp-dyn/content/article/2010/11/19/AR2010111 906872.html.
The founder of a Washington food-preparation business argues that hunger and poor nutrition are far bigger problems than generally recognized.

Gordey, Cynthia, "Welfare, Fathers and Those Persistent Myths," *The Root*, June 17, 2011, www.theroot.com/views/ welfare-fathers-and-those-persistent-myths.
A writer for an online magazine on African-American issues reports on the growing recognition of fathers' importance for children growing up in mother-headed households.

Reports and Studies

Falk, Gene, "The Temporary Assistance for Needy Families (TANF) Block Grant: Responses to Frequently Asked Questions," Congressional Research Service, Feb. 16, 2011, www.naswa.org/assets/utilities/serve.cfm? gid=231C9E08-41AA-4283-9E35-7625F0575B4E.
A social-policy expert for Congress' nonpartisan research arm provides a wealth of basic information on the welfare system.

Gabe, Thomas, "Welfare, Work, and Poverty Status of Female-Headed Families with Children: 1987-2009," Congressional Research Service, July 15, 2011, http://digitalcommons.ilr. cornell.edu/cgi/viewcontent .cgi?article=1852&context=key_workplace.
Another CRS specialist provides a detailed, data-rich analysis of one of the most long-running issues in anti-poverty policy.

Haskins, Ron, "Fighting Poverty the American Way," Brookings Institution, June 2011, www.brookings.edu/papers/2011/0620_fighting_poverty_haskins.aspx.
A key figure in the 1996 welfare overhaul examines welfare policy against the backdrop of American political culture.

DeNavas-Walt, Carmen, *et al.*, "Income, Poverty, and Health Insurance Coverage in the United States: 2010," U.S. Census Bureau, September 2011, www .census.gov/ prod/2011pubs/p60-239.pdf.
Census Bureau experts marshal enormous quantities of data to illustrate ongoing trends in income and well-being.

Rector, Robert, *et al.*, "Obama to Spend $10.3 Trillion on Welfare," Heritage Foundation, Sept. 16, 2009, www.heritage.org/research/reports/2009/09/obama-to-spend-103-trillion-on-welfare-uncovering-the-full-cost-of-means-tested-welfare-or-aid-to-the-poor.
Analysts for a leading conservative think tank present a case for extreme skepticism about government anti-poverty programs.

Seith, David, and Courtney Kalof, "Who Are America's Poor Children?" National Center for Children in Poverty, Columbia University, July 2011, www.nccp.org/publications/ pdf/text_1032.pdf.
Researchers for a leading child-poverty think tank analyze the defining characteristics of children in poverty.

For More Information

Center for Urban Families, 2201 North Monroe St., Baltimore, MD 21217; 410-367-5691; http://cfuf.org/index. Develops and runs training programs in job skills and fatherhood.

Center on Budget and Policy Priorities, 820 First St., N.E., Suite 510, Washington, DC 20002; 202-408-1080; www.cbpp.org. Research and advocacy organization specializing in legislative and policy analysis.

CLASP, 1200 18th St., N.W., Washington, DC 20036; 202-906-8000; www.clasp.org. Advocacy organization focusing on children and family law and policy.

Feeding America, 35 East Wacker Drive, Chicago, IL 60601; 800-771-2303; http:// feedingamerica.org. National alliance of food banks that provides information on hunger, nutrition conditions and relevant laws and policies.

Heritage Foundation, 214 Massachusetts Ave., N.E., Washington, DC 20002-4999; 202-546-4400; www.heritage.org/Issues/Poverty-and-Inequality. Conservative think tank that conducts research on poverty and related issues.

National Center for Children in Poverty, 215 W. 125th St., 3rd Floor, New York, NY 10027; 646-284-9600; www .nccp.org. Columbia University think tank providing data-analysis tools on poverty and health.

U.S. Census Bureau, 4600 Silver Hill Road, S.E., Washington, DC 20233; 301-763-4636; www.census.gov/hhes/www/poverty/poverty.html. Federal agency providing a vast amount of current and historical information on poverty.

14

Immigration Conflict

Kenneth Jost

Arizona residents rally in Phoenix on July 31, 2010, in support of the state's hard-hitting immigration law, which gives police new responsibilities to look for immigration law violators. Five states last year followed Arizona's lead. The U.S. Supreme Court will hear arguments on the disputed Arizona measure on April 25.

Getty Images/John Moore

Micky Hammon minced no words when he urged his fellow Alabama legislators to enact what would become the toughest of a batch of new state laws cracking down on illegal immigrants. "This bill is designed to make it difficult for them to live here so they will deport themselves," Hammon, leader of the Alabama House of Representatives' Republican majority, said during the April 5, 2011, debate on the bill.[1]

Immigrant-rights groups say the law, which took effect Sept. 28 after partly surviving a court challenge, is as tough as Hammon hoped — and more. "It's been pretty devastating," says Mary Bauer, legal director of the Southern Poverty Law Center in Montgomery, Alabama's capital. "Tens of thousands of people have left, and the people who remain are completely terrorized by this law."

Among other provisions, Alabama's law requires state and local law enforcement officers to determine the immigration status of anyone arrested, detained or stopped if there is a "reasonable suspicion" that the person is an alien "unlawfully present" in the United States. Failure to carry alien-registration papers is made a state crime, punishable by up to 30 days in jail for a first offense.

Alabama, with an estimated 120,000 unlawful aliens living within its borders as of 2010, was one of five states that last year followed Arizona's lead a year earlier in giving police new responsibilities to look for immigration law violators.* Republican-controlled legislatures in each of the states said they were forced to

From *CQ Researcher*,
March 9, 2012

---

* The others were Utah, Indiana, Georgia and South Carolina.

West Has Highest Share of Unlawful Aliens

Undocumented immigrants comprise at least 6 percent of the population of Arizona, California, Nevada and Texas and at least 3.8 percent of the population of New Mexico, Oregon and Utah. Unlawful immigrants also make up sizable percentages of several other states' populations, including New Jersey and Florida. The nationwide average is 3.7 percent.

Unauthorized Immigrants as a Share of State Population, 2010

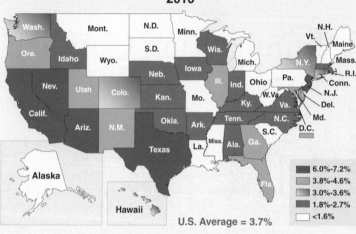

6.0%-7.2%
3.8%-4.6%
3.0%-3.6%
1.8%-2.7%
<1.6%

U.S. Average = 3.7%

Source: Jeffrey Passel and D'Vera Cohn, "Unauthorized Immigrant Population: National and State Trends, 2010," Pew Research Center, February 2011, p. 29, www.pewhispanic.org/files/reports/133.pdf

act because the federal government was not doing enough to control illegal immigration at the border or in U.S. workplaces. Opponents warned the laws risked profiling Latinos, including U.S. citizens and aliens with legal status.

All six of the laws are being challenged in federal court, with the "stop and check" provisions blocked except in Alabama's case. In the most important case, the Arizona measure is scheduled to be argued before the U.S. Supreme Court on April 25 after a federal appeals court struck some of the law enforcement provisions as interfering with federal immigration policy.[2]

Alabama's law includes a unique provision that prohibits unlawful aliens from entering into any "business transaction" with state or local governments. Some public utilities in the state interpreted the provision to require proof of immigration status for water or electricity service. Until a federal judge's injunction on Nov. 23,

some counties were applying the law to prevent unlawful immigrants from renewing permits for mobile homes.[3]

Once the law went into effect, school attendance by Latino youngsters dropped measurably in response to a provision — later blocked — requiring school officials to ascertain families' immigration status. The fear of deportation also led many immigrants in Alabama to seek help in preparing power-of-attorney documents to make sure their children would be taken care of in case the parents were deported, according to Isabel Rubio, executive director of the Hispanic Interest Coalition of Alabama. "You have to understand the sheer terror that people fear," Rubio says.

The law is having a palpable effect on the state's economy as well, according to agriculture and business groups. With fewer migrant workers, "some farmers have planted not as much or not planted at all," says Jeff Helms, spokesman for the Alabama Farmers Federation. Jay Reed, president of Associated Builders and Contractors of Alabama, says it has been harder to find construction workers as well.

Reed, co-chair of the multi-industry coalition Alabama Employers for Immigration Reform, wants to soften provisions that threaten employers with severe penalties, including the loss of operating licenses, for hiring undocumented workers. He and other business leaders also worry about the perception of the law outside the state's borders. "Some of our board members have expressed concern about our state's image and the effect on economic-development legislation," Reed says.

Reed says the state's Republican governor, Robert Bentley, and leaders in the GOP-controlled legislature are open to some changes in the law. But the two chief sponsors, Hammon and state Sen. Scott Beason, are both batting down any suggestions that the law will be repealed or its law enforcement measures softened.

"We are not going to weaken the law," Hammon told reporters on Feb. 14 as hundreds of opponents of the measure demonstrated outside the State House in Montgomery. "We are not going to repeal any section of the law."[4]

On the surface, Alabama seems an improbable state to take a leading role in the newest outbreak of nativist concern about immigration and immigrants. Alabama's unauthorized immigrant population has increased nearly fivefold since 2000, but the state still ranks relatively low in the proportion of unauthorized immigrants in the population and in the state's workforce.

Alabama's estimated 120,000 unauthorized immigrants comprise about 2.5 percent of the state's total population. Nationwide, the estimated 11.8 million unauthorized immigrants represent about 3.7 percent of the population. Alabama's estimated 95,000 unauthorized immigrants with jobs represent about 4.2 percent of the workforce. Nationwide, 8 million undocumented workers account for about 5.2 percent of the national workforce.[5]

Nationwide, the spike in anti-immigrant sentiment is also somewhat out of synch with current conditions. Experts and advocates on both sides of the immigration issues agree that the total unauthorized immigrant population has fallen somewhat from its peak in 2007, mainly because the struggling U.S. economy offers fewer jobs to lure incoming migrant workers.

"The inflow of illegals has slowed somewhat," says Mark Krikorian, executive director of the Center for Immigration Studies (CIS) in Washington. The center describes its stance as "low-immigration, pro-immigrant."[6]

Jobs were a major focus of the debate that led to Alabama's passage of the new law. "This is a jobs bill," Beason said as the measure, known as HB 56, reached final passage in June. "We have a problem with an illegal workforce that displaces Alabama workers. We need to put those people back to work."[7]

Today, Beason, running against an incumbent congressman for the U.S. House seat in the Birmingham

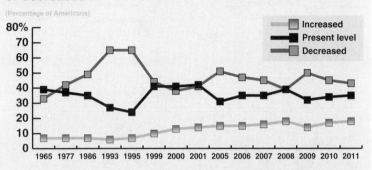

Americans Want Less Immigration

More than 40 percent of Americans say they favor a lower level of immigration, reflecting a view that has prevailed over most of the past half-century. About one in six want immigration to increase, while about one-third favor the current level.

Should immigration be kept at its present level, increased or decreased?

Sources: Jeffrey M. Jones, "Americans' Views on Immigration Holding Steady," Gallup, June 2011, www.gallup.com/poll/148154/americans-views-immigration-holding-steady.aspx; Roger Daniels, *Guarding the Golden Door,* Hill and Wang Press, December 2004, p. 233

area, credits the law with helping Alabama lower its unemployment rate from 9.8 percent in September to 8.1 percent in December. "I promised that the anti-illegal immigration law would open up thousands of jobs for Alabamians, and it has done that," Beason said in a Jan. 26 statement.

A University of Alabama economist, however, doubts the law's claimed effect on unemployment. Samuel Addy, director of the university's Center for Business and Economic Research in Tuscaloosa, notes that unemployment actually has increased, rather than declined, in the four sectors in the state viewed as most dependent on immigrant labor: agriculture, construction, accommodation and food and drinking places.[8]

In a nine-page study released in January, Addy contends instead that the immigration law is likely to hurt the state's economy overall. After assuming that 40,000 to 80,000 workers leave the state, Addy calculated that the law could reduce the state's gross domestic product by $2.3 billion to $10.8 billion. State income and sales taxes could take a $56.7 million to $265.4 million hit, Addy projected, while local sales tax revenue could

Immigration Law Basics

Even experts find it confusing.

Immigrating legally to the United States is difficult at best for those who fit into categories defined in mind-numbing detail by federal law and impossible for those who do not. Here is a primer on a body of law that is complex and confusing even to immigration experts, and all the more so for would-be Americans.

The Immigration and Nationality Act — sets an overall limit of 675,000 permanent immigrants each year. The limit does not apply to spouses, unmarried minor children or parents of U.S. citizens, but the sponsoring U.S. citizen must have an income above the U.S. poverty level and promise to support family members brought to the United States.

Who gets visas — Out of the 675,000 quota, 480,000 visas are made available under family-preference rules, and up to 140,000 are allocated for employment-related preferences. Unused employment-related visas may be reallocated to the family-preference system.

The family-sponsored visas are allocated according to a preference system with numerical limits for each category. Unmarried adult children of U.S. citizens are in the first category, followed, in this order, by spouses and minor children of lawful permanent residents; unmarried adult children of lawful permanent residents; married adult children of U.S. citizens; and brothers and sisters of U.S. citizens. No other relatives qualify for a family preference. Again, the sponsor must meet financial and support requirements.

Visa categories — The employment-based preference system also sets up ranked, capped categories for would-be immigrants. The highest preference is given to "persons of extraordinary ability" in the arts, science, education, business or athletics; professors and researchers; and some multinational executives. Other categories follow in this order: persons with professional degrees or "exceptional" abilities in arts, science or business;

workers with skills that are in short supply and some "unskilled" workers for jobs not temporary or seasonal; certain "special immigrants," including religious workers; and, finally, persons who will invest at least $500,000 in a job-creating enterprise that employs at least 10 full-time workers.

In addition to the numerical limits, the law sets a cap of 7 percent of the quota for immigrants from any single country. The limit in effect prevents any immigrant group from dominating immigration patterns.

Refugees — Separately, Congress and the president each year set an annual limit for the number of refugees who can be admitted based on an inability to return to their home country because of a fear of persecution. Currently, the overall ceiling is 76,000. The law also allows an unlimited number of persons already in the United States, or at a port of entry, to apply for asylum if they were persecuted or fear persecution in their home country. A total of 21,113 persons were granted asylum in fiscal 2010. Refugees and asylees are eligible to become lawful permanent residents after one year.

Debate over the rules — An immigrant who gets through this maze and gains the coveted "green card" for lawful permanent residents is eligible to apply for U.S. citizenship after five years (three years for the spouse of a U.S. citizen). An applicant must be age 18 or over and meet other requirements, including passing English and U.S. history and civics exams. About 675,000 new citizens were naturalized in 2010, down from the peak of slightly more than 1 million in the pre-recession year of 2008.

Applying for citizenship — Immigration advocates say the quotas are too low, the rules too restrictive and the waiting periods for qualified applicants too long. Low-immigration groups say the record level of legal and illegal immigration over the past decade shows the need to lower the quotas and limit the family-reunification rules.

— *Kenneth Jost*

decline by $20.0 million to $93.1 million. Hammon dismissed the report as "baloney."[9]

Five months after it took effect, however, the law's impact may be ebbing. Police appear not to have enforced

the law vigorously, perhaps stung by the nationwide embarrassment when a visiting Mercedes-Benz executive from Germany carrying only a German identification card was held after a traffic stop until he could retrieve his passport. With police enforcement lagging, some of the immigrants who left appear to be coming back. "Some people have returned," Rubio says.[10]

Meanwhile, attorneys for the Obama administration and the state were preparing for arguments on March 1 before the federal appeals court in Atlanta in the government's suit challenging the state law on grounds of federal pre-emption, the doctrine used to nullify state laws that conflict with U.S. laws and policies. The Hispanic Interest Coalition had challenged the law on broader grounds in an earlier suit, represented by the American Civil Liberties Union and other national groups.

In a massive, 115-page ruling, U.S. District Court Judge Sharon Blackburn upheld major parts of the law on Sept. 28 and then allowed the upheld parts to go into effect even as the government and civil rights groups appealed. Blackburn blocked half a dozen provisions on pre-emption grounds but found no congressional intent to prevent states from checking the immigration status of suspected unlawful aliens.[11]

With the legal challenges continuing, the political debates over immigration are intensifying. Republican presidential candidates generally agree on criticizing the Obama administration for failing to control illegal immigration even though the administration has increased the number of immigrants deported to their home countries. The Republican hopefuls disagree among themselves on the steps to deal with the problem.

For his part, Obama concedes that Congress will not approve a broad immigration overhaul in this election year. But he used his State of the Union speech to call for passage of a bill — the so-called DREAM Act — to allow legal status for some immigrants who have served in the U.S. military or completed college.

As the immigration debates continue, here are some of the major questions being considered:

Major State Immigration Laws in Court

Five states have followed Arizona's lead in giving state and local police a role in enforcing federal immigration law. With some variations, the laws authorize or require police after an arrest, detention or stop to determine the person's immigration status if he or she is reasonably suspected of being unlawfully in the United States. In legal challenges, federal courts have blocked major parts of five of the laws; the Supreme Court is set to hear arguments on April 25 in Arizona's effort to reinstate the blocked portions of its law.

State	Bill, date signed	Legal challenge
Arizona	S.B. 1070: April 23, 2010	*United States v. Arizona* Major parts enjoined; pending at Supreme Court
Utah	H.B. 497: March 15, 2011	*Utah Coalition of La Raza v. Herbert* Major parts blocked; suit on hold pending Supreme Court ruling in Arizona case
Indiana	SB 590: May 10, 2011	*Buquer v. City of Indianapolis* Major parts blocked; suit on hold pending Supreme Court ruling in Arizona case
Georgia	HB 87: May 13, 2011	*Georgia Latino Alliance v. Deal* Major parts blocked; on hold at 11th Circuit
Alabama	HB 56: June 9, 2011	*United States v. Alabama* Major parts upheld; on hold at 11th Circuit
South Carolina	S20: June 27, 2011	*United States v. South Carolina* Major parts blocked; suit on hold pending Supreme Court ruling in Arizona case

Sources: National Conference of State Legislatures, http://www.ncsl.org/issues-research/immig/omnibus-immigration-legislation.aspx; American Civil Liberties Union; news coverage.

Is illegal immigration an urgent national problem?

As the anti-illegal immigration bill HB 56 was being signed into law, Alabama's Republican Party chairman depicted the measure as needed to protect the state's taxpayers and the state's treasury. "Illegal immigrants have become a drain on our state resources and a strain on our taxpaying, law-abiding citizens," Bill Armistead declared as Republican governor Bentley signed it into law on June 9, 2011.[12]

Today, Republican officials continue to defend the law in economic terms. "Unemployment was sky high, especially in areas where there's high concentration of these undocumented workers," says Shana Kluck, the party's spokeswoman. Kluck also points to the cost on public treasuries. "The public-assistance budgets were bursting at the seams," she says. "That's why HB 56 was necessary."

Nationally, groups favoring tighter immigration controls make similar arguments about immigrants' economic impact, especially on jobs and wages for citizen workers. "We need to slow down immigration," says Dan Stein, president of the Federation for American Immigration Reform (FAIR), pointing to the current high levels of unemployment and underemployment.

"Immigration helps to decimate the bargaining leverage of the American worker," Stein continues. "If you use a form of labor recruitment that bids down the cost of labor, that leads you to a society where a small number are very, very rich, there's nobody in the middle, and everyone is left scrambling for crumbs at the bottom."

"The longer this economic doldrum continues, the more likely you are to see some real pushback on immigration levels as such, not just illegal immigration," says Krikorian with the low-immigration group Center for Immigration Studies. The group's research director, Steven Camarota, said if illegal immigrants are forced to go back to their home countries, there is "an ample supply of idle workers" to take the jobs freed up.[13]

Pro-immigration groups say their opponents exaggerate the costs and all but ignore the benefits of immigrant labor. "They never take into account the contributions that undocumented immigrants make," says Mary Giovagnoli, director of the American Immigration Council's Immigration Policy Center.

"We've had an economy that depends on immigration," says Ali Noorani, executive director of the National Immigration Forum. "It would be an economic and social disaster for 11 million people to pick up and leave."

Madeleine Sumption, a senior labor market analyst with the pro-immigration Migration Policy Institute in Washington, acknowledges that immigration may have what she calls a "relatively small" impact on employment and wages for citizen workers. But the costs are more than offset, she says, by the benefits to employers, consumers and the overall economy.

The benefits can be seen particularly in sectors that employ large numbers of immigrants, according to Sumption. "The United States has a large agriculture industry," she says. "Without immigration labor, it would almost certainly not be possible to produce the same volume of food in the country." The health care industry also employs a high number of immigrants, especially in low-end jobs, such as home-health aides and hospital orderlies. "These are jobs for which there is a growing demand and an expectation of an even more rapidly growing demand in the future," Sumption says.

In Alabama, Rubio with the Hispanic coalition and the leaders of the agriculture and construction groups all discount Camarota's contention that citizen workers are available to take the jobs currently being filled by immigrants. "We did not have a tomato crop [last] summer because the immigrants who pick that crop weren't there," Rubio says. "This is hard work, and many people don't want to do it."

Reed, president of the state's builders and contractors' organization, says construction companies similarly cannot find enough workers among the citizen labor force. "Traditionally, in our recruitment efforts we have unfortunately not found those that are unemployed are ready and willing to perform these kinds of jobs that require hard labor in extreme weather conditions," Helms says.

The claimed costs and benefits from immigration for public treasuries represent similarly contentious issues. Low- or anti-immigration groups emphasize the costs in government services, especially education and medical care. Pro-immigration groups point to the taxes that even unlawful aliens pay and the limits on some government benefits under federal and state laws. In an independent evaluation of the issue, the nonpartisan Congressional Budget Office in 2007 found a net cost to state and local governments but called the impact "most likely modest."[14]

The cost-benefit debates are more volatile in stressed economic times, according to David Gerber, a professor of history at the University of Buffalo and author of a primer on immigration. "People get angry when they feel that immigrants are competing for jobs of people in the United States or when they feel that immigrants are getting access to social benefits that the majority is paying for," Gerber says. "In harder times, it makes people angrier than in times of prosperity."[15]

Even so, David Coates, a professor at Wake Forest University in Winston-Salem, N.C., and co-editor of a book on immigration issues, notes that fewer undocumented workers are entering the United States now than in the peak year of 2007, and the Obama administration has been deporting unlawful aliens in significantly greater numbers than previous administrations. Asked whether illegal immigration should be less of an issue for state legislators and national politicians, Coates replies simply: "Yes, in terms of the numbers."

Should state and local police enforce immigration laws?

Alabama's HB 56 was stuffed with more provisions for state and local governments to crack down on illegal immigrants than the Arizona law that inspired it or any of the copy-cat laws passed in four other states. Along with the stop-and-check section, the law includes provisions making it a state crime for an unauthorized alien to apply for work and barring unauthorized aliens from court enforcement of any contracts. Another provision made it illegal to conceal, harbor or rent to an illegal immigrant or even to stop in a roadway to hire workers.

Opponents harshly criticized the enforcement provisions as they were signed into law. "It turns Alabama into a police state where anyone could be required to show their citizenship papers," said Cecillia Wang, director of the ACLU's Immigrant Rights Project. Noorani, with the National Immigration Forum, called the law "a radical departure from the concepts of fairness and equal treatment under the law," adding, "It makes it a crime, quite literally, to give immigrants a ride without checking their legal status."[16]

Today, even with the harboring provision and several others blocked from taking effect, opponents say the law is having the terrorizing effect that they had predicted on immigrants both legal and illegal as well as U.S. citizens of Hispanic background. "We've heard numerous accounts of people who have been stopped under very suspicious circumstances, while driving or even while walking on the street," says Justin Cox, an ACLU staff attorney in Atlanta working on the case challenging the law.

The law "has had the effect that it was intended to have," Cox says, "which was to make immigration status a pervasive issue in [immigrants'] everyday lives."

Unlawful Immigration High Despite Dip

Despite a dip beginning in 2007, an estimated 11.2 million unauthorized immigrants live in the United States, one-third more than a decade ago (top graph). An estimated 8 million are in the civilian labor force, a 45 percent increase since 2000 (bottom graph).

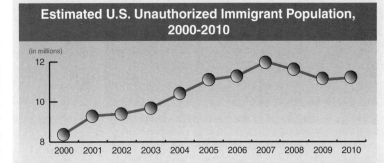

Estimated U.S. Unauthorized Immigrant Population, 2000-2010

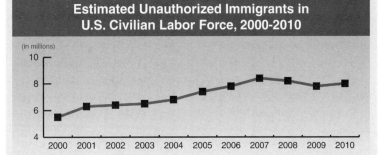

Estimated Unauthorized Immigrants in U.S. Civilian Labor Force, 2000-2010

Source: Jeffrey Passel and D'Vera Cohn, "Unauthorized Immigrant Population: National and State Trends, 2010," Pew Research Center, February 2011, pp. 1, 17, www.pewhispanic.org/files/reports/133.pdf

Supporters of the law are defending it, but without responding to specific criticisms. "We've seen an awful lot of illegal immigrants self-deport," House Majority Leader Hammon said as opponents rallied in Montgomery on Feb. 14. "We're also seeing Americans and legal immigrants taking these jobs."[17]

When questioned by a Montgomery television station about critical documentaries prepared for the progressive group Center for American Progress, Hammon declined to look at the films but attacked the filmmaker. "We don't need an activist director from California to come in here and tell us whether this law is good or not," Hammon said. "The people in Alabama can see it for themselves."[18]

Nationally, immigration hawks view the new state laws as unexceptional. "They're helping the feds to

Republican Alabama Gov. Robert Bentley addresses lawmakers at the state capitol on June 9, 2011, before signing the state's new immigration law. Republican cosponsors of the law, Sen. Scott Beason (left), and state Rep. Micky Hammon (right), both oppose softening or repealing the law. But state business interests want to ease provisions that threaten employers with severe penalties for hiring undocumented workers. They also worry about the perception of the law outside the state.

enforce immigration laws," says Center for Immigration Studies executive director Krikorian. "The question is [whether] local police use immigration laws as one of the tools in their tool kit to help defend public safety."

"Every town is a border town, every state is a border state," Krikorian continues. "Immigration law has to be part of your approach, part of your strategy in dealing with some kind of a significant problem."

FAIR president Stein strongly objects to the Obama administration's legal challenges to the state laws. "It should be a massive, industrial-strength issue that the Obama administration" has attacked the laws on grounds of federal pre-emption. But Giovagnoli with the pro-immigration American Immigration Council says the state laws should be struck down. "Congress has established that immigration enforcement is a federal matter," she says. "The more states get into the mix, the more you create a real patchwork of laws that don't make sense together."

As Krikorian notes, federal law already provides for cooperative agreements between the federal government and state or local law enforcement agencies to enforce immigration laws. U.S. Immigration and Customs Enforcement (ICE), the successor agency to the Immigration and Naturalization Service, touts the so-called 287(g) program on its website as one of the

agency's "top partnership initiatives." The program, authorized by an immigration law overhaul in 1996, permits the federal agency to delegate enforcement power to state or local law enforcement after officers have received training on federal immigration law.[19]

Pro-immigration groups say the training requirement distinguishes 287(g) programs from the broader roles being given state and local police by the new state laws. "State and local law enforcement officers are not trained to do this kind of work," says Cox. "Inevitably, they're going to rely on pernicious stereotypes about what an undocumented immigrant looks like." The result, Cox continues, "is a breakdown of trust between the immigrant community and law enforcement, which ultimately affects all of us. It undermines public safety."

Alabama Republicans, however, insist that the state law fulfills a 2010 campaign pledge that helped the GOP gain control of both houses of the state legislature and that it remains popular despite the criticisms and legal challenges. "We've definitely been criticized," party spokeswoman Kluck acknowledges, but she blames the criticisms on "misinformation." As for possible changes in the law, Hammon and other legislative leaders are guarding details until a bill with proposed revisions can be completed by late March.

Should Congress make it easier for illegal immigrants to become citizens?

With many Republican primary and caucus voters viewing illegal immigration as a major issue, presidential candidate and former Massachusetts Gov. Mitt Romney says he has a simple solution: Get undocumented immigrants to "self-deport" to their home countries and then get in the legal waiting line for U.S. citizenship. But one of his rivals for the Republican nomination, former House speaker Newt Gingrich, pushing stronger enforcement at the border, mocks Romney's belief that 11 million unlawful aliens will go back home voluntarily. Speaking to a Spanish-language television network in late January on the eve of the Florida presidential primary, Gingrich called Romney's plan "an Obama-level fantasy."[20]

Pro-immigration groups agree that Romney's stance is unrealistic. "It's a fantasy to think that people are going to self-deport," says the National Immigration Forum's Noorani. Unlike border-control advocates, however, Noorani and other pro-immigration advocates and experts say the solution is "a path to legal citizenship" for the undocumented.

"We need a functioning legal immigration system, a system that has the necessary legal channels for a person to immigrate here whether for a job or his family," Noorani says. "That doesn't exist here." Without "a solution," Noorani says, "the only ones who are winning are the crooked employer who is more than happy to exploit the undocumented, poor third-country worker."

Immigration hawks quickly denounce any broad legalization proposal as an "amnesty" that they say is neither workable nor deserved. "All amnesties attract future immigration," says the CIS's Krikorian. "All amnesties reward lawbreakers." As evidence, immigration critics point to the broad amnesty granted under the 1986 immigration act to some 3 million immigrants — and its evident failure within a matter of years to stem the flow of illegal immigrants from across the country's Southern borders.

As an alternative to broader proposals, pro-immigration groups are pushing narrower legislation that in its current form would grant conditional legal status to immigrants who came to the United States before age 16 and have lived in the United States for at least five years. The so-called DREAM Act — an acronym for the Development, Relief and Education for Alien Minors Act — had majority support in both chambers of the Democratic-controlled Congress in 2010 but failed to get a Senate floor vote in the face of Republican opposition.

The DREAM Act starts with the assumption that immigrants who came to the United States as children have grown up as Americans and are innocent of any intentional immigration violations. They would be eligible for a conditional permanent residency and could then earn a five-year period of temporary residency by completing two years in the U.S. military or two years in a four-year college or university.

"The intent of the DREAM Act is to provide legal status for individuals who are enlisting in our armed services or pursuing higher education," says Noorani. "Whether they came here at age 5 or 15, I think we only stand to benefit."

"It's a good way to show that if you provide legal status to folks like this, the world is not going to fall apart," says Giovagnoli with the American Immigration Council. "In fact, the country would be better off if these people were in the system."

Similar proposals have been introduced in Congress since 2001. Immigration hawks acknowledge the proposals' appeal and argue over details. "The concept that people who have been here from childhood, that it might be prudent to legalize people in that position, is a plausible one," says Krikorian. But, he adds, "As it exists, it is not a good piece of legislation."

As one change, Krikorian says the eligibility age should be lowered, perhaps to age 10 or below. "The reason they pick 16 is it legalizes more," he says. Paradoxically, Krikorian also says the bill is too narrow by allowing temporary residency only by joining the military or going to college. "What if you're not college material?" he asks.

Krikorian also dismisses the idea of absolving those who arrived as youngsters of any responsibility for immigration violations. "The parents . . . did know what they were doing," he says. The bill needs to be changed, he says, "to ensure that no parent would ever be able to benefit" under family-reunification rules.

Gingrich and some GOP lawmakers favor a narrower version of the DREAM Act that would extend legal status for serving in the military but not for going to college. Supporters oppose the narrower version. "If you read the bill carefully, it would actually allow a fewer number of immigrants to enlist in the military than the original," Noorani says. Krikorian also dismisses the alternative. He calls it "phony," adding that it would help "only a few thousand people a year."

The White House pushed hard for the bill in the Democratic-controlled Congress's lame-duck session in December 2010 but fell short in the Senate. Obama continues to speak out for the bill, most prominently in his State of the Union address. "[I]f election-year politics keeps Congress from acting on a comprehensive plan, let's at least agree to stop expelling responsible young people who want to staff our labs, start new businesses, defend this country," Obama said near the end of the Jan. 24 speech. "Send me a law that gives them the chance to earn their citizenship. I will sign it right away."[21]

BACKGROUND
Constant Ambivalence

The United States is a nation of immigrants that has been ambivalent toward immigration through most of its history. Immigrants are alternately celebrated as the source of diversity and criticized as agents of disunity. Immigrants were recruited to till the soil, build the cities and labor in the factories, but often criticized for taking jobs from and lowering wages for the citizen workforce. The federal government reflected popular sentiment in restricting immigration in the late 19th and early 20th century, only to draw later criticism for exclusionary policies. Today, the government is drawing criticism for liberalized policies adopted in the 1960s and for ineffective border enforcement from the 1980s on.[22]

African slaves were the first source of immigrant labor in America, but Congress banned importation of slaves in 1808. Otherwise, the United States maintained an open-door policy on immigration until the late 19th century. Europe's mid-century agricultural crisis drove waves of German and Irish peasants to the United States in the 1840s and '50s. Many were met by ethnic and anti-Catholic hostility, embodied in the first nativist political movement: the American or so-called Know-Nothing Party. The party carried one state in the 1856 presidential election and then faded from history.

Significant Chinese immigration began with the California Gold Rush of 1849 and increased with the post-Civil War push to complete the transcontinental railroad. Stark warnings of the "Yellow Peril" led to a series of restrictions at the federal level — most notably, the Chinese Exclusion Act of 1882, which suspended immigration of Chinese laborers and barred citizenship for those already in the United States. Significantly for present-day debates, efforts to deport those in the country or to seal the borders against new Chinese immigrants were no more than partly successful.[23]

Congress laid the basis for present-day immigration law and policy in a series of increasingly restrictive enactments from the 1890s through the early 1920s that coincided with the great waves of immigration from Europe, including regions previously unrepresented in the American polity. The Immigration Act of 1891 established the Bureau of Immigration, then under the Treasury Department, and provided for border inspections and deportation of unlawful aliens. Additional laws prescribed admission procedures, created categories of inadmissible immigrants and tightened the exclusion of immigrants from Asia.

The restrictive policies drew support from nativists worried about assimilation, pro-labor groups concerned about the impact on jobs and wages and progressive leaders fearful of the impact on the urban environment. The restrictions culminated in the passage of the first and second Quota Acts in 1921 and 1924, which established the first quantitative limitation on immigration (350,000, lowered to 150,000) and a national-origins system that favored immigrants from Northern and Western Europe. In reporting the bill in 1924, a House committee stated: "If the principle of liberty . . . is to endure, the basic strain of our population must be preserved."[24]

The Quota Acts' exception for Western Hemisphere immigrants combined with the unrest associated with the Mexican Revolution (1910-1929) to produce what Stanford historian Albert Camarillo calls "a tsunami" in immigration across the United States' Southern border. Camarillo says 1.5 million Mexicans — one-tenth of the country's population — relocated to the United States by the end of the 1930s.[25] The influx fueled ethnic prejudice embodied in the derogatory term "wetback" to refer to the Mexican immigrants, most of whom actually entered by crossing arid regions rather than fording the Rio Grande River.

During the Great Depression of the 1930s, the federal and state governments — concerned about the impact on jobs for Anglo workers — sent tens of thousands of Mexicans back to their home country, sometimes with force and little regard for due process. During World War II, however, the government worked with Mexico to establish the so-called bracero program to use temporary immigrant labor for agricultural work. The "temporary" program continued into the 1960s.

Congress liberalized immigration law with a 1952 statute that included restrictionist elements as well and then, dramatically, with a 1965 law that scrapped the Eurocentric national-origins system and opened the gate to increased immigration from Latin America and Asia.

The 1952 law preserved the national-origins system but replaced the Chinese Exclusion Act with very small quotas for countries in the so-called Asia-Pacific Triangle. The act also eliminated discrimination between sexes. Over the next decade, immigration from European countries declined, seemingly weakening the rationale for the national-origins system. Against the backdrop of the civil rights revolution, the national-origins system seemed to many also to be antithetical to American values. The result was the Immigration Act of 1965, which replaced national-origins system with a system of preferences

CHRONOLOGY

Before 1960 *Congress establishes immigration quotas.*

1920s Quota Act (1921), Johnson-Reed Act (1924) establish national-origins quota system, favoring Northern European immigrants over those from Southern Europe, elsewhere.

1952 McCarran-Walter Act retains national-origins system but adds small quotas for some Asian countries.

1960s *Congress opens door to immigration from outside Europe.*

1965 Immigration and Nationality Act of 1965 abolishes national-origins quota system dating from 1920s; allows dramatic increase in immigration from Central and South America, Asia.

1980s-1990s *Illegal immigration increases, becomes major public issue.*

1986 Immigration Reform and Control Act allows amnesty for many unlawful aliens, prohibits employers from employing undocumented workers; enforcement proves elusive.

1996 Illegal Immigration Reform and Immigrant Responsibility Act seeks to strengthen border security, streamline deportation proceedings; creates optional E-Verify system for employers to electronically check immigration status of workers and job applicants.

2000-Present *Illegal immigration increases; immigration reform falters in Congress; state laws to crack down on illegal immigration challenged in court.*

2001 Al Qaeda 9/11 attacks on U.S. soil underscore national security threat from failure to track potential terrorists entering United States (Sept. 11); USA Patriot Act gives immigration authorities more power to exclude suspected terrorists (Oct. 26).

2005-2006 Immigration reform measures fail in GOP-controlled Congress despite support from Republican

President George W. Bush; Congress approves Secure Fence Act, to require double-layer fence on U.S.-Mexico border.

2007 Immigration reform measure dies in Senate; three motions to cut off debate fail (June 7). . . . Arizona legislature passes employer-sanctions law; companies threatened with loss of operating license for knowingly hiring undocumented aliens, required to use federal E-Verify system; signed into law by Democratic Gov. Janet Napolitano (July 2). . . . Unauthorized immigrant population in United States peaks near 12 million.

2008 Democrat Barack Obama elected president after campaign with little attention to immigration issues (Nov. 4); Obama carries Hispanic vote by 2-1 margin.

2009 Obama endorses immigration reform, but without specifics; issue takes back seat to economic recovery, health care.

2010 Arizona enacts law (S.B. 1070) to crack down on illegal immigrants; measure requires police to check immigration status if suspect or detainee is reasonably believed to be unlawful alien; makes it a crime to fail to carry alien registration papers; signed by Republican Gov. Jan Brewer (April 23); federal judge blocks parts of law (July 28). . . . DREAM Act to allow legal status for unlawful aliens who entered U.S. as minors approved by House of Representatives (Dec. 8) but fails in Senate: 55-41 vote is short of supermajority needed for passage (Dec. 18).

2011 Utah, Indiana, Georgia follow Arizona's lead in giving state, local police immigration-enforcement powers (March, May). . . . Federal appeals court upholds injunction against parts of Arizona's S.B. 1070 (April 11). . . . Supreme Court upholds Arizona's employer-sanctions law 5-3 (May 21). . . . Alabama enacts nation's toughest state law on illegal immigrants, HB 56 (June 9). . . . Federal judge blocks some parts of HB 56, allows others to take effect (Sept. 28).

2012 Immigration is flashpoint for Republican presidential candidates. . . . Obama urges passage of DREAM Act (Jan. 24). . . . Alabama, Georgia laws argued before U.S. appeals court (March 1). . . . Supreme Court to hear arguments on Arizona's S.B. 1070 (April 25); ruling due by end of June.

Journalist Reveals His Immigration Secret

"There's nothing worse than being in limbo."

When journalist-turned-immigration rights activist Jose Antonio Vargas traveled to Alabama with a documentary filmmaker, he found a Birmingham restaurant patron who strongly supported the state law cracking down on undocumented aliens. "Get your papers or get out," the patron said.

"What if I told you I didn't [have papers]?" Vargas is heard asking off camera. "Then you need you get your ass home then," the patron rejoined.[1]

Vargas says he is home — in America, where he has lived since his Filipina mother sent him, at age 12, to live in California with his grandparents in 1993. "I'm an American without papers," says Vargas, who came out as an undocumented immigrant in dramatic fashion in a 4,300-word memoir in *The New York Times Magazine* in June 2011.[2]

In the story, Vargas recounts how he learned at age 16 that he was carrying a fake green card when he applied for a driver's license. The DMV clerk let him go. Back home, Vargas confronted his grandfather, who acknowledged the forgery and told Vargas not to tell anyone else.

For the next 14 years, Vargas kept his non-status secret from all but a handful of enablers as he completed high school and college and advanced rapidly from entry-level newspaper jobs to national-impact journalism at *The Washington Post*, *Huffington Post* and glossy magazines. His one attempt at legal status ended in crushing disappointment in 2002 when an immigration lawyer told him he would have to return to the Philippines and wait for 10 years to apply to come back.

Vargas was inspired to write about his life by the example of four undocumented students who walked from Miami to Washington, D.C., in 2010 to lobby for the DREAM Act, the status-legalizing proposal for immigrants who came to the United States as minors. Vargas's story, published by *The Times* after *The Washington Post* decided not to, quickly went viral in old and new media alike.

In the eight months since, Vargas has founded and become the public face for a Web-based campaign, Define American (www.defineamerican.org). "Define American brings new voices into the immigration conversation, shining a light on a growing 21st century Underground Railroad: American citizens who are forced to fill in where our broken immigration system fails," the mission statement reads. "Together, we are going to fix a broken system."

The DREAM Act fell just short of passage in Congress in December 2010 and has gotten little traction since.

Journalist Jose Antonio Vargas disclosed in *The New York Times* in June 2011 that he was an undocumented immigrant.

Getty Images/Justin Sullivan

Broader proposals to give legal status to some of the 11 million unlawful aliens are far off the political radar screen. Vargas is critical of Alabama's law cracking down on illegal immigration but acknowledges the states' frustration with federal policies. "At the end of the day, the federal government hasn't done anything on this issue," he says.

In the meantime, Vargas waits. "There's nothing worse than being in limbo," he says. In the story, he cited some of the hardships for the undocumented. As one example, he cannot risk traveling to the Philippines, so he has yet to meet his 14-year-old brother. But Vargas says he has no plan to "self-deport." "I love this country," he says.

— *Kenneth Jost*

---

[1]"The Two Faces of Alabama," http://isthisalabama.org/. The films by director Chris Weitz were prepared under the auspices of the Center for American Progress. Some comments from Vargas are from a Feb. 15, 2012, screening of the videos at the center.

[2]Jose Antonio Vargas, "Outlaw," *The New York Times Magazine*, June 26, 2011, p. 22. Disclosure: the author is a professional acquaintance and Facebook friend of Vargas.

favoring family reunification or to lesser extents admissions of professionals or skilled or unskilled workers needed in the U.S. workforce.

Quickly, the demographics of immigration shifted — and dramatically. Immigration increased overall under the new law, and the new immigrants came mostly from Latin America and Asia. By 1978, the peak year of the decade, 44 percent of legal immigration came from the Americas, 42 percent from Asia and only 12 percent from Europe.[26]

Cracking Down?

Immigration to the United States increased overall in the last decades of the 20th century, and illegal immigration in particular exploded to levels that fueled a public and political backlash. Congress and the executive branch tried to stem the flow of undocumented aliens first in 1986 by combining employer sanctions with an amnesty for those in the country for several years and then a decade later by increasing enforcement and deportations.

Then, in the wake of the Sept. 11, 2001, terrorist attacks on the United States, Congress and President George W. Bush joined in further efforts to tighten admission procedures and crack down on foreigners in the country without authorization.

Estimates of the number of immigrants in the United States illegally are inherently imprecise, but the general upward trend from the 1980s until a plateau in the 2000s is undisputed. As Congress took up immigration bills in the mid-1980s, the Census Bureau estimated the number of those undocumented at 3 million to 5 million; many politicians used higher figures. The former Immigration and Naturalization Service put the number at 3.5 million in 1990 and 7.0 million a decade later. Whatever the precise number, public opinion polls registered increasing concern about the overall level of immigration. By the mid-1990s, Gallup polls found roughly two-thirds of respondents in favor of decreasing the level of immigration, one-fourth in favor of maintaining the then-present level and fewer than 10 percent for an increase.[27]

The congressional proposals leading to the Immigration Reform and Control Act in 1986 sought to stem illegal immigration while recognizing the reality of millions of undocumented immigrants and the continuing need for immigrant labor, especially in U.S. agriculture. The law allowed legal status for immigrants in the country continuously since 1982 but aimed to deter unauthorized

immigration in the future by forcing employers to verify the status of prospective hires and penalizing them for hiring anyone without legal status. Agricultural interests, however, won approval of a new guest worker program. Some 3 million people gained legal status under the two provisions, but illegal immigration continued to increase even as civil rights groups warned that the employer sanctions would result in discrimination against Latino citizens.

The backlash against illegal immigration produced a new strategy for reducing the inflows: state and federal laws cutting off benefits for aliens in the country without authorization. California, home to an estimated 1.3 million undocumented aliens at the time, blazed the path in 1994 with passage of a ballot measure, Proposition 187, that barred any government benefits to illegal aliens, including health care and public schooling. The education provision was flatly unconstitutional under a 1982 ruling by the U.S. Supreme Court that guaranteed K-12 education for school-age alien children.[28]

The measure mobilized Latino voters in the state. They contributed to the election of a Democratic governor in 1998, Gray Davis, who dropped the state's defense of the measure in court in his first year in office. In the meantime, however, Congress in 1996 had approved provisions — reluctantly signed into law by President Bill Clinton — to deny unauthorized aliens most federal benefits, including food stamps, family assistance and Social Security. The law allows states to deny state-provided benefits as well; today, at least a dozen states have enacted such further restrictions.

The centerpieces of the 1996 immigration law, however, were measures to beef up enforcement and toughen deportation policy. The Illegal Immigration Reform and Immigrant Responsibility Act authorized more money for the Border Patrol and INS, approved more funding for a 14-mile border fence already under construction and increased penalties for document fraud and alien smuggling. It sought to streamline deportation proceedings, limit appeals and bar re-entry of any deportee for at least five years. And it established an Internet-based employer verification system (E-Verify) aimed at making it easier and more reliable for employers to check legal status of prospective hires. The law proved to be tougher on paper, however, than in practice. The border fence remains incomplete, deportation proceedings backlogged and

A Maricopa County deputy arrests a woman following a sweep for illegal immigrants in Phoenix on July 29, 2010. The police operation came after protesters against Arizona's tough immigration law clashed with police hours after the law went into effect. Although the most controversial parts of the law have been blocked, five other states — Utah, Indiana, Georgia, Alabama and South Carolina — last year enacted similar laws.

E-Verify optional and — according to critics — unreliable. And illegal immigration continued to increase.

The 9/11 attacks added homeland security to the concerns raised by the nation's porous immigration system. In post-mortems by immigration hawks, the Al Qaeda hijackers were seen as having gained entry into the United States with minimal scrutiny of their visa applications and in many cases having overstayed because of inadequate follow-up.[29] The so-called USA Patriot Act, enacted in October 2001 just 45 days after the attacks, gave the INS — later renamed the U.S. Citizenship and Immigration Service and transferred to the new Department of Homeland Security — greater authority to exclude or detain foreigners suspected of ties to terrorist organizations. The act also mandated information-sharing by the FBI to identify aliens with criminal records. Along with other counterterrorism measures, the act is viewed by supporters today as having helped prevent any successful attacks on U.S. soil since 2001. Illegal immigration, however, continued to increase — peaking at roughly 12 million in 2007.

Getting Tough

Congress and the White House moved from post-9/11 security issues to broader questions of immigration policy during Bush's second term, but bipartisan efforts to allow legal status for unlawful aliens fell victim to Republican opposition in the Senate. As a presidential candidate, Democrat Obama carried the Hispanic vote by a 2-1 margin over Republican John McCain after a campaign with limited attention to immigration issues. In the White House, Obama stepped up enforcement in some respects even as he urged Congress to back broad reform measures. The reform proposals failed with Democrats in control of both the House and the Senate and hardly got started after Republicans regained control of the House in the 2010 elections.

Bush lent support to bipartisan reform efforts in the Republican-controlled Congress in 2005 and 2006 and again in the Democratic-controlled Congress in his final two years in office. Congress in 2006 could agree only on authorizing a 700-mile border fence after reaching an impasse over a House-passed enforcement measure and a Senate-approved path-to-citizenship bill. Bush redoubled efforts in 2007 by backing a massive, bipartisan bill that would have allowed "earned citizenship" for aliens who had lived in the United States for at least eight years and met other requirements. As in the previous Congress, many Republicans rejected the proposal as an unacceptable amnesty. The bill died on June 7 after the Senate rejected three cloture motions to cut off debate.[30]

Immigration played only a minor role in the 2008 presidential campaign between Obama and McCain, Senate colleagues who had both supported reform proposals. Both campaigns responded to growing public anger over illegal immigration by emphasizing enforcement when discussing the issue, but the subject went unmentioned in the candidates' three televised debates. McCain, once popular with Hispanics in his home state of Arizona, appeared to have paid at the polls for the GOP's hard line on immigration. Exit polls indicated that Obama won 67 percent of a record-size Hispanic vote; McCain got 31 percent — a significant drop from Bush's 39 percent share of the vote in 2004.[31]

With Obama in office, Congress remained gridlocked even as the president tried to smooth the way for reform measures by stepping up enforcement. The congressional gridlock had already invited state lawmakers to step into the vacuum. State legislatures passed more than 200 immigration-related laws in 2007 and 2008, according to a compilation by the National Conference on State

Legislatures; the number soared to more than 300 annually for the next three years.[32]

The numbers included some resolutions praising the country's multi-ethnic heritage, but most of the new state laws sought to tighten enforcement against undocumented aliens or to limit benefits to them. Among the earliest of the new laws was an Arizona measure — enacted in June 2007, two weeks after the Senate impasse in Washington — that provided for lifting the business licenses of companies that knowingly hired illegal aliens and mandated use of the federal E-Verify program to ascertain status of prospective hires. Business and labor groups, supported by the Obama administration, challenged the law on federal preemption grounds. The Supreme Court's 5-3 decision in May 2011 to uphold the law prompted several states to enact similar mandatory E-Verify provisions.[33]

The interplay on immigration policy between Washington and state capitals is continuing. In Obama's first three years in office, the total number of removals increased to what ICE calls on its website "record levels." Even so, Arizona lawmakers and officials criticized federal enforcement as inadequate in the legislative debate leading to SB 1070's enactment in April 2010. Legal challenges followed quickly — first from a Latino organization; then from a broad coalition of civil rights and civil liberties groups; and then, on July 6, from the Justice Department. The most controversial parts of the law have been blocked, first by U.S. District Court Judge Susan Bolton's injunction later that month and then by the Ninth Circuit's decision affirming her decision in April 2011. The legal challenges did not stop five other states — Utah, Indiana, Georgia, Alabama and South Carolina — from enacting similar laws in spring and early summer 2011. Civil rights groups and the Justice Department followed with similar suits challenging the new state enactments.

As the 2012 presidential campaign got under way, immigration emerged as an issue between Republican candidates vying for the party's nomination. The issue posed difficulties for the GOP hopefuls as they sought to appeal to rank-and-file GOP voters upset about illegal immigration without forfeiting Latino votes in the primary season and in the general election. Presumed front-runner Mitt Romney took a hard stance against illegal immigration in early contests but softened his message in advance of winning the pivotal Jan. 31 primary in Florida with its substantial Hispanic vote.

Despite differences in details and in rhetoric, the three leading GOP candidates — Romney, Newt Gingrich and Rick Santorum — all said they opposed the DREAM Act in its present form even as Obama called for Congress to pass the bill in his State of the Union speech.

CURRENT SITUATION

Obama's Approach

The Obama administration is claiming success in increasing border enforcement and removing unlawful aliens while injecting more prosecutorial discretion into deportation cases. But the mix of firm and flexible policies is resulting in criticism from both sides of the issue.

U.S. Immigration and Customs Enforcement (ICE) counted a record 396,906 "removals" during fiscal 2011, including court-ordered deportations as well as administrative or voluntary removals or returns. The number includes a record 216,698 aliens with criminal convictions.[34]

Meanwhile, Homeland Security Secretary Janet Napolitano says illegal border-crossing attempts have decreased by more than half in the last three years. In a Jan. 30 speech to the National Press Club in Washington, Napolitano linked the decline to an increase in the number of Border Patrol agents to 21,000, which she said was more than double the number in 2004.

"The Obama administration has undertaken the most serious and sustained actions to secure our borders in our nation's history," Napolitano told journalists. "And it is clear from every measure we currently have that this approach is working."[35]

Immigration hawk Krikorian with the Center for Immigration Studies gives the administration some, but only some, credit for the removal statistics. "They're not making up the numbers," Krikorian says. But he notes that immigration removals increased during the Bush administration and that the rate of increase has slowed under Obama.

In addition, Krikorian notes that new figures compiled by a government information tracking service indicate the pace of new immigration cases and of court-processed deportations slowed in the first quarter of fiscal 2012 (October, November and December 2011). A report in early February by Syracuse University's Transactional Records Access Clearinghouse (TRAC) shows 34,362 court-ordered removals or "voluntary departures" in the period, compared to 35,771 in the previous three months — about a 4 percent drop.

A separate TRAC report later in the month showed what the service called a "sharp decline" in new ICE filings. ICE initiated 39,331 new deportation proceedings in the nation's 50 immigration courts during the first quarter of fiscal 2012, according to the report, a 33 percent decline from the 58,639 new filings in the previous quarter.[36]

"The people in this administration would like to pull the plug on enforcement altogether," Krikorian complains. "They refuse to ask for more money for detention beds and then plead poverty that they can't do more."

From the opposite perspective, some Latino officials and organizations have been critical of the pace of deportations. When Obama delivered a speech in favor of immigration reform in El Paso, Texas, in May 2011, the president of the National Council of La Raza tempered praise for the president's position with criticism of the deportation policy.

"As record levels of detention and deportation continue to soar, families are torn apart, innocent youth are being deported and children are left behind without the protection of their parents," Janet Murguía said in a May 10 press release. "Such policies do not reflect American values and do little to solve the problem. We can do better."[37]

Latinos disapprove of the Obama administration's handling of deportations by roughly a 2-1 margin, according to a poll by the Pew Hispanic Center in December 2011. Overall, the poll found 59 percent of those surveyed opposed the administration's policy while 27 percent approved. Disapproval was higher among foreign-born Latinos (70 percent) than those born in the United States (46 percent).[38]

Napolitano and ICE Director John Morton are both claiming credit for focusing the agency's enforcement on the most serious cases, including criminal aliens, repeat violators and recent border crossers. Morton announced the new "prosecutorial discretion" policy in an agency-wide directive in June 2011.[39]

TRAC, however, questions the claimed emphasis on criminal aliens. The 39,331 new deportation filings in the first quarter of fiscal 2012 included only 1,300 against aliens with convictions for "aggravated felonies," as defined in immigration law. "Even this small share was down from previous quarters," the Feb. 21 report states. Aliens with aggravated felony convictions accounted for 3.3 percent of deportations in the period, compared to 3.8 percent in the previous quarter.[40]

The administration is also being questioned on its claim — in Obama's El Paso speech and elsewhere — to have virtually completed the border fence that Congress ordered constructed in the Secure Fence Act of 2006.[41] The act called for the 652-mile barrier to be constructed of two layers of reinforced fencing but was amended the next year — with Bush still in office — to give the administration more discretion in what type of barriers to use.

As of May 2011, the barrier included only 36 miles of double-layer fencing, according to PolitiFact, the fact-checking service of the *Tampa Bay Times.* The rest is single-layer fencing or vehicle barriers that critic Krikorian says are so low that a pedestrian can step over them. PolitiFact calls Obama's claim "mostly false."[42]

Meanwhile, the administration is preparing to extend nationwide its controversial "Secure Communities" program, which tries to spot immigration law violators by matching fingerprints of local arrestees with the database of the Department of Homeland Security (DHS). A match allows U.S. Immigration and Customs Enforcement (ICE) to issue a so-called detainer against violators, sending their cases into the immigration enforcement system. The administration touts the program as "a simple and common sense" enforcement tool. Critics note, however, that it has resulted in wrongful detention of U.S. citizens in a considerable but unknown number of cases. One reason for the mistakes: The DHS database includes all immigration transactions, not just violations, and thus could show a match for an immigrant with legal status.[43]

Supreme Court Action

All eyes are on the Supreme Court as the justices prepare for arguments on April 25 in Arizona's effort to reinstate major parts of its trend-setting law cracking down on illegal immigrants.

The Arizona case is the furthest advanced of suits challenging the six recently enacted state laws that give state and local police responsibility for enforcing federal immigration laws. After winning an injunction blocking major parts of the Arizona law, the Obama administration filed similar suits against Alabama's HB 56 as well as the Georgia and South Carolina measures.

Should Congress pass the DREAM Act?

YES Walter A. Ewing
*Senior Researcher, Immigration Policy Center
American Immigration Council*

Written for *CQ Researcher*, March 2012

The Development, Relief and Education for Alien Minors Act is rooted in common sense. To begin with, it would benefit a group of unauthorized young people who, in most cases, did not come to this country of their own accord. Rather, they were brought here by their parents. The DREAM Act would also enable its beneficiaries to achieve higher levels of education and obtain better, higher-paying jobs, which would increase their contributions to the U.S. economy and American society. In short, the DREAM Act represents basic fairness and enlightened self-interest.

More than 2 million young people would benefit from the DREAM Act, and their numbers grow by roughly 65,000 per year. They came to the United States before age 18, many as young children. They tend to be culturally American and fluent in English. Their primary ties are to this country, not the countries of their birth. And the majority had no say in the decision to come to this country without authorization — that decision was made by the adult members of their families. Punishing these young people for the actions of their parents runs counter to American social values and legal norms. Yet, without the DREAM Act, these young people will be forced to live on the margins of U.S. society or will be deported to countries they may not even know.

Assuming they aren't deported, the young people who would benefit from the DREAM Act face enormous barriers to higher education and professional jobs because of their unauthorized status. They are ineligible for most forms of college financial aid and cannot work legally in this country. The DREAM Act would remove these barriers, which would benefit the U.S. economy.

The College Board estimates that over the course of a working lifetime, a college graduate earns 60 percent more than a high school graduate. This higher income translates into extra tax revenue flowing to federal, state and local governments.

The DREAM Act is in the best interest of the United States both socially and economically. It would resolve the legal status of millions of unauthorized young people in a way that is consistent with core American values. And it would empower these young people to become better-educated, higher-earning workers and taxpayers. Every day that goes by without passage of the DREAM Act is another day of wasted talent and potential.

NO Mark Krikorian
*Executive Director, Center for
Immigration Studies*

Written for *CQ Researcher*, March 2012

The appeal of the DREAM Act is obvious. People brought here illegally at a very young age and who have grown up in the United States are the most sympathetic group of illegal immigrants. Much of the public is open to the idea of amnesty for them.

But the actual DREAM Act before Congress is a deeply flawed measure in at least four ways:

• Rather than limiting amnesty to those brought here as infants and toddlers, it applies to illegal immigrants who arrived before their 16th birthday. But if the argument is that their very identity was formed here, age 7 would be a more sensible cutoff. That is recognized as a turning point in a child's psychological development (called the "age of reason" by the Catholic Church, hence the traditional age for First Communion). Such a lower-age cutoff, combined with a requirement of at least 10 years' residence here, would make a hypothetical DREAM Act 2.0 much more defensible.

• All amnesties are vulnerable to fraud, even more than other immigration benefits. About one-fourth of the beneficiaries of the amnesty granted by Congress in 1986 were liars, including one of the leaders of the 1993 World Trade Center bombing. But the DREAM Act specifically prohibits the prosecution of anyone who lies on an amnesty application. So you can make any false claim you like about your arrival or schooling in America without fear of punishment. A DREAM Act 2.0 would make clear that any lies, no matter how trivial, will result in arrest and imprisonment.

• All amnesties send a signal to prospective illegal immigrants that, if you get in and keep your head down, you might benefit from the next amnesty. But the bill contains no enforcement provisions to limit the need for another DREAM Act a decade from now. That's why a serious proposal would include measures such as electronic verification of the legal status of all new hires, plus explicit authorization for state and local enforcement of immigration law.

• Finally, all amnesties reward illegal immigrants — in this case including the adults who brought their children here illegally. A credible DREAM Act 2.0 would bar the adult relatives of the beneficiaries from ever receiving any immigration status or even a right to visit the United States. If those who came as children are not responsible, then those who are responsible must pay the price for their lawbreaking.

The ACLU's Immigrants Rights Project, along with Hispanic and other civil rights groups, has filed separate challenges on broader grounds against all six laws. Federal district courts have blocked parts of all the laws, though some contentious parts of Alabama's law were allowed to take effect.

District court judges in the Indiana, South Carolina and Utah cases put the litigation on hold pending the Supreme Court's decision in the Arizona case. Alabama and Georgia asked the Eleventh U.S. Circuit Court of Appeals to postpone the scheduled March 1 arguments in their cases, but the court declined.

Judge Charles R. Wilson opened the Atlanta-based court's March 1 session, however, by announcing that the three-judge panel had decided to withhold its opinion until after the Supreme Court decides the Arizona case. "Hopefully, that information will help you in framing your arguments today," Wilson told the assembled lawyers.[44]

Wilson and fellow Democratic-appointed Circuit Judge Beverly B. Martin dominated the questioning during the three hours of arguments in the cases. Both judges pressed lawyers defending Alabama and Georgia on the effects of their laws on the education of children, the ability of illegal aliens to carry on with their lives while immigration courts decided their cases and what would happen if every state adopted their approach to dealing with immigration violations. The third member of the panel, Richard Voorhees, a Republican-appointed federal district court judge, asked only three questions on technical issues.

Opening the government's argument in the Alabama case, Deputy Assistant U.S. Attorney General Beth Brinkmann said the state's law attempts to usurp exclusive federal authority over immigration. "The regulation of immigration is a matter vested exclusively in the national government," Brinkman said. "Alabama's state-specific regulation scheme violates that authority. It attacks every aspect of an alien's life and makes it impossible for the alien to live."

Alabama Solicitor General John C. Neiman Jr. drew sharp challenges from Wilson and Martin even before he began his argument. Wilson focused on the law's Section 10, which makes it a criminal misdemeanor for an alien unlawfully present in the United States to fail to carry alien registration papers.

"You could be convicted and sent to jail in Alabama even though the Department of Homeland Security says, 'You're an illegal alien, but we've decided you're going to remain here in the United States?' " Wilson asked.

Neiman conceded the point. "If the deportation hearing occurred after the violation of Section 10, then yes," Neiman said. "Someone could be held to be in violation of Section 10 and then later be held not removable."

Wilson also pressed Neiman on the potential effects on the federal government's ability to control immigration policy if states enacted laws with different levels of severity. "These laws could certainly have the effect of making certain states places where illegal aliens would be likely to go," the state's attorney acknowledged.

Representing the ACLU in the separate challenge, Immigrants Rights Project director Wang sharply attacked the motive behind the Alabama law. The law, she said, was written to carry out the legislature's stated objective "to attack every aspect of an illegal immigrant's life so that they will deport themselves." *

In Washington, lawyers for Arizona filed their brief with the Supreme Court defending its law, SB 1070, in early February. Among 20 *amicus* briefs filed in support of Arizona's case is one drafted by the Michigan attorney general's office on behalf of 16 states similarly defending the states' right to help enforce federal immigration law. A similar brief was filed by nine states in the Eleventh Circuit in support of the Alabama law.

The government's brief in the Arizona case is due March 19. Following the April 25 arguments, the Supreme Court is expected to decide the case before the current term ends in late June.

Meanwhile, legal challenges to other parts of the state's law are continuing in federal court in Arizona. In a Feb. 29 ruling, Bolton blocked on First Amendment grounds a provision prohibiting people from blocking traffic when they offer day labor services on the street.[45]

OUTLOOK
A Broken System

The immigration system is broken. On that much, the pro- and low-immigration groups agree. But they disagree

---

* The appeals court on March 8 issued a temporary injunction blocking enforcement of two provisions, those prohibiting unlawful aliens from enforcing contracts in court or entering into business transactions with state or local government agencies.

sharply on how to fix it. And the divide defeats any attempts to fix it even if it can be fixed.

Pro-immigration groups like to talk about the "three-legged stool" of immigration reform: legal channels for family- and job-based immigration; a path to citizenship for unlawful aliens already in the United States; and better border security. Low-immigration groups agree on the need for better border controls but want to make it harder, not easier, for would-be immigrants and generally oppose legal status for the near-record number of unlawful aliens.

Public opinion is ambivalent and conflicted on immigration issues even as immigration, legal and illegal, has reached record levels. The nearly 14 million new immigrants, legal and illegal, who came to the United States from 2000 to 2010 made that decade the highest ever in U.S. history, according to the low-immigration Center for Immigration Studies. The foreign-born population reached 40 million, the center says, also a record.[46]

Some public opinion polls find support for legal status for illegal immigrants, especially if the survey questions specify conditions to meet: 66 percent supported it, for example, in a Fox News poll in early December 2011. Three weeks earlier, however, a CNN poll found majority support (55 percent) for concentrating on "stopping the flow of illegal immigrants and deporting those already here" instead of developing a plan for legal residency (42 percent).[47]

Other polls appear consistently to find support for the laws in Arizona and other states to crack down on illegal immigrants — most recently by a 2-1 margin in a poll by Quinnipiac University in Connecticut.[48] "Popular sentiment is always against immigration," says Muzaffar Chishti, director of the Migration Policy Institute's office at New York University School of Law and himself a naturalized U.S. citizen who emigrated from his native India in 1974.

Pro-immigration groups say the public is ahead of the politicians in Washington and state capitals who are pushing for stricter laws. State legislators "have chosen to scapegoat immigration instead of solving tough economic challenges," says Noorani with the National Immigration Forum. "There are politicians who would rather treat this as a political hot potato," he adds, instead of offering "practical solutions."

From the opposite side, the Federation for American Immigration Reform's Stein says he is "pessimistic,

disappointed and puzzled" by what he calls "the short-sighted views" of political leaders. Earlier, Stein says, "politicians all over the country were touting the virtues of engagement in immigration policy." But now he complains that even Republicans are talking about "amnesty and the DREAM Act," instead of criticizing what he calls the Obama administration's "elimination of any immigration enforcement."

Enforcement, however, is one component of the system that, if not broken, is at least completely overwhelmed. In explaining the new prosecutorial discretion policy, ICE director Morton frankly acknowledged the agency "has limited resources to remove those illegally in the United States."[49] The nation's immigrant courts have a current backlog of 300,225 cases, according to a TRAC compilation, double the number in 2001.[50]

Employers' groups say the system's rules for hiring immigrants are problematic at best. In Alabama, Reed with the contractors' group says employers do their best to comply with the status-verification requirements but find the procedures and paperwork difficult. The farm federation's Helms says the same for the rules for temporary guest workers. "We're working at the national level to have a more effective way to hire legal migrant workers to do those jobs that it's hard to find local workers to do," he says.

The rulings by the Supreme Court on the Arizona law will clarify the lines between federal and state enforcement responsibilities, but the Center for Immigration Studies' Krikorian says the decision is likely to increase the politicization of the issue. A ruling to uphold the law will encourage other states to follow Arizona's lead, he says, but would also "energize the anti-enforcement groups." A ruling to find the state laws pre-empted, on the other hand, will mobilize pro-enforcement groups, he says.

The political and legal debates will be conducted against the backdrop of the nation's rapidly growing Hispanic population, attributable more to birth rates than to immigration.[51] "Whoever the next president is, whoever the next Congress is, will have to address this issue," says Giovagnoli with the American Immigration Council. "The demographics are not going to allow people to ignore this issue.

"I do believe we're going to reform the immigration system," Giovagnoli adds "It's going to be a lot of work. Even under the best of circumstances, it's a lot of work."

NOTES

1. Quoted in Kim Chandler, "Alabama House passes Arizona-style immigration bill," *The Birmingham News*, April 6, 2011, p. 1A.

2. The case is *Arizona v. United States*, 11-182. Background and legal filings compiled on SCOTUSblog, www.scotusblog.com/case-files/cases/arizona-v-united-states/?wpmp_switcher=desktop.-

3. See Human Rights Watch, "No Way to Live: Alabama's Immigration Law," December 2011, www.hrw.org/news/2011/12/13/usalabama-no-way-live-under-immigrant-law.

4 Quoted in David White, "Hundreds rally at State House seeking immigration law repeal," *The Birmingham News*, Feb. 15, 2012, p. 1A.

5. See "Unauthorized Immigrant Population: State and National Trends, 2010," Pew Hispanic Center, Feb. 1, 2011, pp. 23, 24, www.pewhispanic.org/files/reports/133.pdf. The U.S. Department of Homeland Security estimates differ slightly; for 2010, it estimates nationwide unauthorized immigrant population at 10.8 million.

6. For previous *CQ Researcher* coverage, see: Alan Greenblatt, "Immigration Debate," pp. 97-120, updated Dec. 10, 2011; Reed Karaim, "America's Border Fence," Sept. 19, 2008, pp. 745-768; Peter Katel, "Illegal Immigration," May 6, 2005, pp. 393-420; David Masci, "Debate Over Immigration," July 14, 2000, pp. 569-592; Kenneth Jost, "Cracking Down on Immigration," Feb. 3, 1995.

7. Quoted in David White, "Illegal immigration bill passes," *The Birmingham News*, June 3, 2011, p. 1A.

8. See Dana Beyerle, "Study says immigration law has economic costs," *Tuscaloosa News*, Jan. 31, 2012, www.tuscaloosanews.com/article/20120131/news/120139966. For Beason's statement, see http://scottbeason.com/2012/01/26/beason-statement-on-the-impact-of-hb-56-on-alabama-unemployment-rate/.

9. Samuel Addy, "A Cost-Benefit Analysis of the New Alabama Immigration Law," Center for Business and Economic Research, Culverhouse College of Commerce and Business Administration, University of Alabama, January 2012, http://cber.cba.ua.edu/

New%20AL%20Immigration%20Law%20-%20Costs%20and%20Benefits.pdf; Hammon quoted in Brian Lyman, "Studies, surveys examine immigration law's impact," *The Montgomery Advertiser*, Feb. 1, 2012.

10. See Alan Gomez, "Immigrants return to Alabama," *USA Today*, Feb. 22, 2012, p. 3A; Jay Reeves, "Immigrants trickling back to Ala despite crackdown," The Associated Press, Feb. 19, 2012.

11. The decision in *United States v. Alabama*, 2:11-CV-2746-SLB, U.S.D.C.-N.D.Ala. (Sept. 28, 2011), is available via *The New York Times*: http://graphics8.nytimes.com/packages/pdf/national/112746memopnentered.pdf. For coverage, see Brian Lyman, "Judge allows key part of immigration law to go into effect," *The Montgomery Advertiser*, Sept. 29, 2011; Brian Lawson, "Judge halts part of immigration law," *The Birmingham News*, Sept. 29, 2011, p. 1A. The Alabama Office of the Attorney General has a chronology of the legal proceedings: www.ago.state.al.us/Page-Immigration-Litigation-Federal.

12. Quoted in Eric Velasco, "Immigration law draws praise, scorn," *The Birmingham News*, June 10, 2011, p. 1A.

13. Steven A. Camarota, "A Need for More Immigrant Workers?," Center for Immigration Studies, June 2011, http://cis.org/no-need-for-more-immigrant-workers-q1-2011.

14. "The Impact of Unauthorized Immigrants on the Budgets of State and Local Governments," Congressional Budget Office, Dec. 6, 2007, p. 3, /www.cbo.gov/sites/default/files/cbofiles/ftpdocs/87xx/doc8711/12-6-immigration.pdf.

15. David Gerber, *American Immigration: A Very Short Introduction* (2011).

16. Quoted in Velasco, *op. cit.*

17. Quoted in White, *op. cit.* Hammon's office did not respond to several *CQ Researcher* requests for an interview.

18. "Alabama's Illegal Immigration Law Gets Hollywood's Attention," WAKA/CBS8, Montgomery, Feb. 21, 2012, www.waka.com/home/top-stories/Alabamas-Illegal-Immigration-Law-Gets-Attention-From-Hollywood-139937153.html. The four separate videos

by Chris Weitz, collectively titled "Is This Alabama?" are on an eponymous website: http://isthisalabama.org/.

19. See "Delegation of Immigration Authority 287(g) Immigration and Nationality Act," www.ice.gov/287g/ (visited February 2012).

20. See Sandhya Somashekhar and Amy Gardner, "Immigration is flash point in Fla. Primary," *The Washington Post*, Jan. 26, 2012, p. A6.

21. Text available on the White House website: www.whitehouse.gov/the-press-office/2012/01/24/remarks-president-state-union-address.

22. General background drawn from Gerber, *op. cit.*; Otis L. Graham Jr., *Unguarded Gates: A History of America's Immigration Crisis* (2004). Some country-by-country background drawn from Mary C. Waters and Reed Ueda (eds.), *The New Americans: A Guide to Immigration Since 1965* (2007).

23. Roger Daniels, *Guarding the Golden Door: American Immigration Policy and Immigrants Since 1882* (2004), pp. 19-22.

24. Quoted in Graham, *op. cit.*, p. 51.

25. Albert M. Camarillo, "Mexico," in Waters and Ueda, *op. cit.*, p. 506.

26. Figures from *INS Statistical Yearbook*, 1978, cited in Daniels, *op. cit.*, p 138.

27. Polls cited in Daniels, *op. cit.*, p. 233.

28. See *Plyler v. Doe*, 452 U.S. 202 (1982).

29. See Graham, *op. cit.*, Chap. 17, and sources cited therein.

30. "Immigration Rewrite Dies in Senate," *CQ Almanac 2007*, pp. 15-9 — 15-11, http://library.cqpress.com/cqalmanac/cqal07-1006-44907-2047763.

31. See Julia Preston, "Immigration Cools as Campaign Issue," *The New York Times*, Oct. 29, 2008, p. A20, www.nytimes.com/2008/10/29/us/politics/29immig.html; Mark Hugo Lopez, "How Hispanics Voted in the 2008 Election," Pew Hispanic Research Center, Nov. 5, 2008, updated Nov. 7, 2008, http://pewresearch.org/pubs/1024/exit-poll-analysis-hispanics.

32. "Immigration Policy Report: 2011 Immigration-Related Laws and Resolutions in the States (Jan. 1- Dec. 7, 2011)," National Conference of State Legislatures, www.ncsl.org/issues-research/immigration/state-immigration-legislation-report-dec-2011.aspx.

33. The decision is *Chamber of Commerce v. Whiting*, 563 U.S. — (2011). For coverage, see Kenneth Jost, *Supreme Court Yearbook 2010-2011*, http://library.cqpress.com/scyb/document.php?id=scyb10-1270-72832-2397001&type=hitlist&num=0.

34. See "ICE Removals, Fiscal Years 2007-2011," in Mark Hugo Lopez, *et al.*, "As Deportations Rise to Record Levels, Most Latinos Oppose Obama's Policy," Pew Hispanic Center, Dec. 28, 2011, p. 33, http://pewresearch.org/pubs/2158/latinos-hispanics-immigration-policy-deportations-george-bush-barack-obama-administration-democrats-republicans. The report notes that ICE's statistics differ somewhat from those released by DHS, its parent department.

35. "Secretary of Homeland Security Janet Napolitano's 2nd Annual Address on the State of America's Homeland Security: Homeland Security and Economic Security," Jan. 30, 2012, www.dhs.gov/ynews/speeches/napolitano-state-of-america-homeland-security.shtm.

36. "Share of Immigration Cases Ending in Deportation Orders Hits Record Low," *TRAC Reports*, Feb. 7, 2012, http://trac.syr.edu/immigration/reports/272/; "Sharp Decline in ICE Deportation Filings," Feb. 21, 2012, http://trac.syr.edu/immigration/reports/274/. For coverage, see Paloma Esquivel, "Number of deportation cases down by a third," *Los Angeles Times*, Feb. 24, 2012, p. AA2, http://articles.latimes.com/2012/feb/24/local/la-me-deportation-drop-20120224.

37. Text of La Raza statement, www.nclr.org/index.php/about_us/news/news_releases/janet_murgua_president_and_ceo_of_nclr_responds_to_president_obamas_speech_in_el_paso_texas/. For coverage of the president's speech, see Milan Simonich, "In El Paso, President Obama renews national immigration debate, argues humane policy would aid national economy," *El Paso Times*, May 11, 2011.

38. Lopez, *op. cit.*, p. 16.

39. U.S. Immigration and Customs Enforcement: Memorandum, June 17, 2011, www.ice.gov/doclib/secure-communities/pdf/prosecutorial-discretion-memo

.pdf. For coverage, see Susan Carroll, "ICE memo urges more discretion in immigration changes," *Houston Chronicle*, June 21, 2011, p. A3.

40. "Sharp Decline," *op. cit.*

41. For background, see Reed Karaim, "America's Border Fence," *CQ Researcher*, Sept. 19, 2008, pp. 745-768.

42. "Obama says the border fence is 'now basically complete,' " PolitiFact, www.politifact.com/truth-o-meter/statements/2011/may/16/barack-obama/obama-says-border-fence-now-basically-complete/. The original rating of "partly true" was changed to "mostly false" on July 27, 2011.

43. See "Secure Communities," on the ICE website: www.ice.gov/secure_communities/; Julia Preston, "Immigration Crackdown Snares Americans," *The New York Times*, Dec. 14, 2011, p. A20, www.nytimes.com/2011/12/14/us/measures-to-capture-illegal-aliens-nab-citizens.html?pagewanted=all.

44. Coverage of the hearing by contributing writer Don Plummer. For additional coverage, see Brian Lawson, "11th Circuit won't rule on Alabama/Georgia laws until after Supreme Court rules on Arizona," *The Huntsville Times*, March 2, 2012; Jeremy Redmon, "Court to rule later on Georgia, Alabama anti-illegal immigrant laws," *The Atlanta Journal-Constitution*, March 2, 2012.

45. See Jacques Billeaud, "Judge blocks day labor rules in AZ immigration law," The Associated Press, March 1, 2012.

46. Steven A. Camarota, "A Record-Setting Decade of Immigration, 2000-2010," Center for Immigration Studies, October 2011, www.cis.org/articles/2011/record-setting-decade.pdf.

47. Fox News poll, Dec. 5-7, 2011, and CNN/ORC International poll, Nov. 18-20, 2011, cited at www.PollingReport.com/immigration.htm.

48. Quinnipiac University poll, Feb. 14-20, 2011, cited *ibid.*

49. ICE memo, *op. cit.*

50. "Immigration Court Backlog Tool," Transactional Records Access Clearinghouse, http://trac.syr.edu/phptools/immigration/court_backlog/ (visited March 2012).

51. "The Mexican-American Boom: Births Overtake Immigration," Pew Hispanic Center, July 24, 2011, www.pewhispanic.org/files/reports/144.pdf. The report depicts the phenomenon as "especially evident" among Mexican-Americans; it notes that Mexican-Americans are on average younger than other racial or ethnic groups and that Mexican-American women have more children than their counterparts in other groups. For background, see David Masci, "Latinos' Future," *CQ Researcher*, Oct. 17, 2003, pp. 869-892.

BIBLIOGRAPHY
Selected Sources
Books

Coates, David, and Peter M. Siavelis (eds.), *Getting Immigration Right: What Every American Needs to Know*, Potomac, 2009.
Essays by 15 contributors representing a range of backgrounds and views examine, among other issues, the economic impact of immigration and proposed reforms to address illegal immigration. Includes notes, two-page list of further readings. Coates holds a professorship in Anglo-American studies at Wake Forest University; Siavelis is an associate professor of political science there.

Daniels, Roger, *Guarding the Golden Door: American Immigration Policy and Immigrants Since 1882*, Hill and Wang, 2004.
A professor of history emeritus at the University of Cincinnati gives a generally well-balanced account of developments and trends in U.S. immigration policies from the Chinese Exclusion Act of 1882 through the immediate post-9/11 period. Includes detailed notes, 16-page bibliography.

Gerber, David, *American Immigration: A Very Short Introduction*, Oxford University Press, 2011.
A professor of history at the University of Buffalo gives a compact, generally positive overview of the history of immigration from colonial America to the present. Includes two-page list of further readings.

Graham, Otis L. Jr., *Unguarded Gates: A History of America's Immigration Crisis*, Rowman & Littlefield, 2004.

A professor emeritus at the University of California-Santa Barbara provides a critical account of the United States' transition from an open-border policy with relatively small-scale immigration to a system of managed immigration that he views today as overwhelmed by both legal and illegal immigration. Includes notes.

Reimers, David M., *Other Immigrants: The Global Origins of the American People*, New York University Press, 2005.

A New York University professor of history emeritus brings together new information and research about the non-European immigration to the United States, emphasizing the emergence of "a new multicultural society" since 1940. Individual chapters cover Central and South America, East and South Asia, the Middle East, "new black" immigrants and refugees and asylees. Includes extensive notes, six-page list of suggested readings.

Waters, Mary C., and Reed Ueda (eds.), *The New Americans: A Guide to Immigration Since 1965*, Harvard University Press, 2007.

The book includes essays by more than 50 contributors, some covering broad immigration-related topics and others providing individual portraits of immigrant populations by country or region of origin. Includes detailed notes for each essay, comprehensive listing of immigration and naturalization legislation from 1790 through 2002. Waters is a professor of sociology at Harvard University, Ueda a professor of history at Tufts University.

Articles

"Reap What You Sow," *This American Life*, Jan. 27, 2012, www.thisamericanlife.org/radio-archives/episode/456/reap-what-you-sow.

The segment by reporter Jack Hitt on the popular public radio program found that Alabama's law to encourage undocumented immigrants to self-deport was having unintended consequences.

Kemper, Bob, "Immigration Reform: Is It Feasible?," *Washington Lawyer*, October 2011, p. 22, www.dcbar.org/for_lawyers/resources/publications/washington_lawyer/october_2011/immigration_reform.cfm.

The article gives a good overview of recent and current immigration debates, concluding with the prediction that any "permanent resolution" will likely prove to be "elusive."

Reports and Studies

"No Way to Live: Alabama's Immigrant Law," Human Rights Watch, December 2011, www.hrw.org/reports/2011/12/14/no-way-live-0.

The highly critical report finds that Alabama's law cracking down on illegal immigrants has "severely affected" the state's unlawful aliens and their children, many of them U.S. citizens, as well as "the broader community linked to this population."

Baxter, Tom, "Alabama's Immigration Disaster: The Harshest Law in the Land Harms the State's Economy and Society," Center for American Progress, February 2012, www.americanprogress.org/issues/2012/02/pdf/alabama_immigration_disaster.pdf.

The critical account by journalist Baxter under the auspices of the progressive Center for American Progress finds that Alabama's anti-illegal immigration law has had "particularly harsh" social and economic costs and effects.

Passel, Jeffrey S., and D'Vera Cohn, "Unauthorized Immigrant Population: National and State Trends, 2010," Pew Hispanic Center, Feb. 1, 2011, www.pewhispanic.org/files/reports/133.pdf.

The 32-page report by the Washington-based center provides national and state-by-state estimates of the unauthorized immigrant population and the number of unauthorized immigrants in the workforce.

For More Information

American Civil Liberties Union, Immigrant Rights Project, 125 Broad St., 18th floor, New York, NY 10004; 212-549-2500; www.aclu.org/immigrants-rights. Seeks to expand and enforce civil liberties and civil rights of immigrants.

American Immigration Council, 1331 G St., N.W., 2nd floor, Washington, DC 20005; 202-507-7500; www.american immigrationcouncil.org. Supports sensible and humane immigration policies.

America's Voice, 1050 17th St., N.W., Suite 490, Washington, DC 20036; 202-463-8602; http://americasvoiceonline.org/. Supports "real, comprehensive immigration reform," including reform of immigration enforcement practices.

Center for Immigration Studies, 1522 K St., N.W., Suite 820, Washington, DC 20005-1202; 202-466-8185; www .cis.org. An independent, nonpartisan research organization that supports what it calls low-immigration, pro-immigrant policies.

Define American, www.defineamerican.com/. Founded by journalist and undocumented immigrant Jose Antonio Vargas, the web-based organization seeks to fix what it calls a "broken" immigration system.

Federation for American Immigration Reform, 25 Massachusetts Ave., N.W., Suite 330, Washington, DC 20001; 202-328-7004; www.fairus.org. Seeks "significantly lower" immigration levels.

Migration Policy Institute, 1400 16th St., N.W., Suite 300, Washington, DC 20036; 202-266-1940; www.migration policy.org. A nonpartisan, nonprofit think tank dedicated to analysis of the movement of people worldwide.

National Council of La Raza, 1126 16th St., N.W., Suite 600, Washington, DC 20036-4845; 202-785-1670; www .nclr.org. The country's largest national Hispanic advocacy and civil rights organization.

National Immigration Forum, 50 F St., N.W., Suite 300, Washington, DC 20001; 202-347-0040; www.immigration forum.org. Advocates for the values of immigration and immigrants to the nation.

Pew Hispanic Center, 1615 L St., N.W., Suite 700, Washington, DC 20036; 202-419-4300; www.pewhispanic.org/. Seeks to improve understanding of the U.S. Hispanic population and to chronicle Latinos' growing impact on the nation.

15

Preventing Disease

Nellie Bristol

Mayor Chip Johnson, of Hernando, Miss., supports a wide range of projects designed to make residents healthier while saving taxpayers money. In his six years in office he has developed bike paths and lanes while pushing to require developers to build sidewalks and city engineers to plan roads with walkers and bicyclists in mind. A wellness program he approved for city employees reduced health insurance costs 15 percent. "For us, that's a lot of money," he said.

From *CQ Researcher*, Jan. 6, 2012

S oon after his election as mayor, Chip Johnson began trying to transform Hernando, Miss., into an oasis of healthy living.

In impoverished Mississippi, that was a challenge worthy of the surgeon general. The state ranks highest in the nation in cardiovascular deaths, obesity and infant deaths and second worst in diabetes.[1]

But if residents exercised and ate right, Johnson figured, future illnesses might be prevented, at the same time saving taxpayers money and making the city of 14,000 a more attractive business environment.

Six years later, Johnson has developed bike paths and lanes with $800,000 in federal, state and private grants, while pushing to require developers to build sidewalks and city engineers to plan roads with walkers and bikers in mind. He even started a farmers market that accepts food stamps.[2]

As a Republican, Johnson believes that health and fitness decisions are personal, but he also knows those decisions shape demand for tax-supported health services, influence overall medical costs and help determine the business climate. "We want to recruit corporations to Hernando," he said. "They're not stupid. When they make their decisions, they look at health care costs."[3]

Hernando, a fast-growing bedroom suburb for nearby Memphis, Tenn., is atypical in Mississippi because of its higher rate of affluent and professional residents. Even so, Johnson's efforts are seen as a guide for fostering healthy habits in any community, rich or poor.

Public health experts argue that a locally based, multipronged approach like Hernando's is the only way for communities to

More Than 30 States Have High Obesity Rates

At least one-fourth of adults in 33 states are obese.* In nine states, mainly in the South, 30 percent or more of adults are obese. At least 20 percent are obese in another 16 states. Overall, more than one-third of American adults (more than 72 million people) and 17 percent of children are obese.

Percentage of Adults Who Are Obese, by State, 2009

* Obesity is defined as a body mass index (BMI) of at least 30, or about 30 lbs. over- weight for a 5'4" person.

** No data available

Source: "Obesity: Halting the Epidemic By Making Health Easier," Centers for Disease Control and Prevention, 2011, p. 2, www.cdc.gov/chronicdisease/ resources/publications/aag/pdf/2011/Obesity_AAG_WEB_508.pdf

reverse the major risk factors for chronic disease: poor eating habits, lack of exercise, smoking and alcohol use, which contribute to cardiovascular and lung disease, diabetes and some cancers.

While there is no hard evidence yet that Johnson's initiatives have improved the town's health, a wellness program Johnson approved for the city's 115 employees helped lead to a 15 percent reduction in health insurance costs. "For us, that's a lot of money," he said.[4]

While Johnson is working to get his town on a better health trajectory, the public health picture nationwide doesn't seem to be improving.

The annual health rankings released recently by the United Health Foundation, an advocacy and philanthropy group, showed that positive health trends in 2011, such as reductions in smoking, preventable hospitalizations and cardiovascular deaths, were offset by increases in obesity,

diabetes and childhood poverty. "The country's overall health did not improve between 2010 and 2011," the foundation said.[5]

Negative health trends are taking a toll on the nation's resources. Chronic diseases are responsible for more than three-quarters of U.S. health care costs.[6] The bill is even higher for government health programs, with chronic disease accounting for 96 percent of Medicare spending for the elderly and 83 percent of Medicaid spending for the poor.[7]

Worldwide, chronic, noncommunicable disease is expected to cost the global economy $47 trillion over the next two decades (in today's dollars).[8] The U.N.'s World Health Organization (WHO) estimates that at least 80 percent of heart disease, stroke and Type 2 diabetes cases and more than 40 percent of cancer could be prevented or better managed through smoking cessation, healthy eating and better fitness.[9]

Public health experts say reducing chronic disease requires efforts by a broad range of government and private-sector actors. They advocate government actions such as public health messages, limits on salt, sugar and fat in commercial foods and increased sidewalk construction to encourage exercise. They also are encouraging:

• Packaged-food manufacturers to reduce marketing of sugary breakfast cereals and other unhealthy products to children;

• Restaurants to cut portion sizes and post calories counts;

• Communities to build more playgrounds, and,

• The medical system to offer inexpensive or free preventive services and link patients to local support programs.

Some physicians even call for removing severely obese children from their parents.[10] "It should only be used as a last resort," said David Ludwig, a child obesity expert at Harvard University. "It's also no guarantee of success, but when we have a 400-pound child with life-threatening complications, there may not be any great choices."[11]

While many view that idea as extreme, even modest steps can be highly controversial.

Critics of the preventive health movement say, for example, that the "obesity epidemic" has been overblown by public health officials and is a ruse to allow meddling in personal choices and affairs. "This epidemic has been constructed to the benefit of the medical industry that has in part medicalized the treatment of obesity over the years," said University of Houston sociologist Samantha Kwan.[12]

Julie Guthman, an associate professor of community studies at the University of California, Santa Cruz, agrees. "I'm not convinced obesity is the problem it's made out to be," she says. She argues, for example, that a common tool used to determine obesity — the body mass index (BMI) — doesn't effectively take into account muscle mass. She also says the correlation between body weight and sickness is not fully proven.

"People who are overweight or slightly obese actually seem to have longer life expectancy than people who are of so-called normal weight," she says. "There's a lot of panic without really understanding the dimensions of the problem."

Former Gov. Sarah Palin, R-Alaska, took on the issue by bringing cookies to a school in Pennsylvania in reaction to the news report that the state school board was considering limiting sweets brought to the classroom. "I wanted these kids to bring home the idea to their parents for discussion," she said. "Who should be deciding what I eat? Should it be the government or should it be parents? It should be the parents."[13]

Palin also took on the high-profile Let's Move program developed by first lady Michelle Obama to attack childhood obesity, which has more than tripled since 1980.[14] "Instead of government thinking that they need to take over and make decisions for us according to some politician or politician's wife's priorities, just leave us alone, get off our back and allow us as individuals to exercise our own God-given rights to make our own decisions, and then our country gets back on the right track," Palin said.[15]

The food industry also is pushing back, fighting government requirements to limit certain foods, such as potatoes, in school lunches, reformulate products and curtail some types of advertising to children. Industry officials say they prefer a voluntary approach.

But many people think Americans' increasing weight and sedentary lifestyles call for action. A group of retired generals, admirals and other senior U.S. military leaders declared in 2010 that an "alarming" 75 percent of 17-24-year-olds are unfit for military service, citing obesity

Smoking Kills Nearly Half a Million Annually

About 443,000 Americans die each year from smoking, including deaths from secondhand smoke. Smoking-induced lung cancer and heart disease each accounts for about 30 percent of the deaths. Tobacco use is the single most preventable cause of disease, disability and death in the United States.

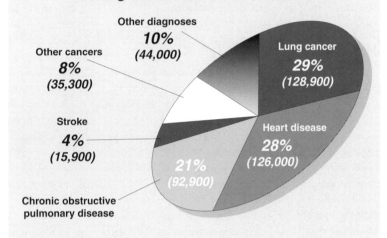

Annual Smoking-Related Deaths, by Disease, Including Secondhand Smoke, 2000-2004

Source: "Tobacco Use: Targeting the Nation's Leading Killer," Centers for Disease Control and Prevention, 2011, p. 2, www.cdc.gov/chronicdisease/resources/publications/aag/pdf/2011/Tobacco_AAG_2011_508.pdf

as a contributing factor. They urged a ban on junk food in schools, improvement in school lunches and greater access for children to obesity-reduction programs.[16]

"If we don't take steps now to build a strong, healthy foundation for our young people, then it won't just be our military that pays the price — our nation as a whole will suffer also," they wrote.[17]

As lawmakers, employers and individuals struggle to find the best ways to prevent or delay chronic disease, here are some of the issues being discussed:

Does preventing disease save money?

Reducing health care costs is a perennial national priority. Health spending in the United States totaled $2.5 trillion in 2009, or an average of $8,086 per person. Spending on health constitutes 17.6 percent of the U.S. gross domestic product (GDP), more than twice the 7.2 percent of GDP in 1970, according to the Kaiser Family Foundation.[18] And unless changes are made, health care costs are expected to keep growing.

The subject is of special concern to congressional lawmakers, particularly in a time of high budget deficits. Medicare, the federal health care program for the elderly and disabled, accounts for 20 percent of national health expenditures. Medicaid, the joint state/federal program for low-income people, makes up 15 percent of national health expenditures. Altogether, the federal government share of national health spending is 27 percent.[19]

Some lawmakers have zeroed in on disease prevention as a cost-cutting measure, reasoning that preventing people from getting sick would save money on future care. But strictly in economic terms and not improvements in longevity and quality of life, the reality is much more complicated.

"Studies have concluded that preventing illness can in some cases save money but in other cases can add to health costs," wrote Joshua Cohen, deputy director of the Tufts University Center for the Evaluation of Value and Risk in Health, and other researchers. "Whether any preventive measure saves money or is a reasonable investment despite adding to cost depends entirely on the particular intervention and the specific population in question." For example, the authors continued, "drugs used to treat high cholesterol yield much greater value

for the money if the target population is at high risk for coronary heart disease, and the efficiency of cancer screening can depend heavily on the frequency of the screening and the level of cancer risk in the screened population."[20]

To try to quantify the cost effectiveness of certain disease-prevention services, the Robert Wood Johnson Foundation studied preventive services provided in medical settings, including immunizations and screening for a variety of risk factors such as hypertension and high cholesterol. The researchers drew several conclusions, including that preventive services can reduce prevalence of specific diseases and help people live longer and that many preventive services offer good value for scarce health care dollars.

But they also found that most preventive care does not result in cost savings. "Costs to reduce risk factors, screening costs and the cost of treatment when disease is found can offset any savings from preventive care," they wrote. "Additionally, living longer means people may develop other ailments that increase lifetime health care costs."[21]

In fact, the review of 17 medications/immunizations and screening services found only two that reduced costs: childhood immunizations and counseling of adults on the use of low-dose aspirin to prevent cardiovascular disease. However, a number of other services were found to be cost effective. That is, they didn't directly save health care dollars, but the benefits were sufficiently large compared to the costs to make them valuable services for improving health. These included flu shots for adults, counseling on the use of folic acid for pregnant women and a variety of screening tests, including those for colorectal, breast and cervical cancer, hypertension and cholesterol.

The picture is more positive for what are known as community-based prevention efforts. The Trust for America's Health, a disease-prevention advocacy group, evaluated 84 studies of prevention activities targeted at communities rather than individuals. To be included in the review, interventions could not require medical treatment and had to be proven to reduce disease through improving physical activity and nutrition and preventing smoking and other tobacco use. Programs included, for example, establishment of farmers markets, calorie and nutrition labeling, nutrition education for young mothers and raising cigarette and other tobacco taxes.

Overall, the group found that an investment of $10 per person per year in proven community-based disease-prevention programs could save more than $2.8 billion annually in health care costs in one to two years, more than $16 billion annually within five years and nearly $18 billion annually in 10 to 20 years.[22] The group concluded: "a small strategic investment in disease prevention could result in significant savings in U.S. health care costs."

As lawmakers confront rising health care costs, spiraling obesity rates and an aging population, more focus should be placed on evaluating the cost effectiveness of disease intervention, including prevention efforts, some experts say. But such efforts are fraught with controversy. The U.S. Preventive Services Task Force, which makes recommendations about interventions based on a calculation of benefit to risks, has come under fire in recent years for endorsing more limited use of widespread services such as mammography and prostate cancer screening.

Putting a dollar value on activities aimed at prolonging life has attracted even more heat. The 2009 economic stimulus legislation, for example, included funding for an Obama administration-supported comparative-effectiveness analysis of medical services, but references to calculating cost effectiveness were dropped following objections in Congress.[23]

But some, including Cohen at Tufts, argue that while costs shouldn't be the only consideration, they should be taken into account. "At any given time, we can only spend so much money as a country on health care, so it's not a question of whether we should be spending money only on those things that save money," he says. "If we do things that are less cost effective — have a smaller benefit per dollar invested — we will be taking away, on some level, from those things that are

more cost effective, and we will be decreasing overall population health."

Should government encourage behavior change?

Whose responsibility is it to stop Americans from dying from preventable diseases? The question stirs passions deeply tied to opinions on the role of government in society. Many supporters of government involvement say the most effective approach does not focus necessarily on individuals, but rather on creating environments that "make the healthy choice the easy choice."

But not everyone sees the value of getting the government involved. For example, some argue the obesity "epidemic" is overstated and that the government is overstepping when it tells people what to eat.

Nonetheless, government at all levels is actively trying to improve nutrition and increase access to daily exercise. Specific policies adopted include higher taxes on cigarettes

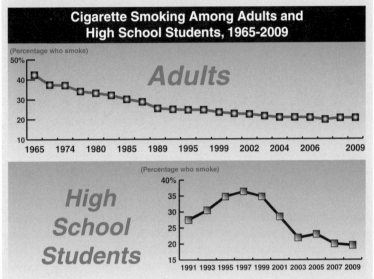

Smoking Declined Among Adults, Students

About 20 percent of adults and high school students smoke cigarettes. The percentage has declined by half for students since the mid-1990s and for adults since 1965.

Cigarette Smoking Among Adults and High School Students, 1965-2009

Source: "Tobacco Use: Targeting the Nation's Leading Killer," Centers for Disease Control and Prevention, February 2011, www.cdc.gov/ chronicdisease/resources/publications/AAG/osh_text.htm#chart2

Smoking and Obesity Are Biggest Killers

Some 555,000 people died in the United States in 2000 from smoking or obesity. Alcohol abuse was a distant third in the list of behaviors leading to death.

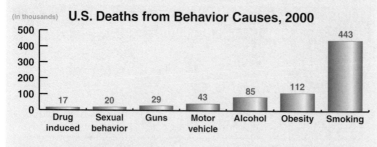

(in thousands) **U.S. Deaths from Behavior Causes, 2000**

Source: "Preventing Chronic Disease: The New Public Health," Alliance for Health Reform, September 2011, p. 2, www.allhealth. org/publi cations/Public_health/Preventing_Chronic_Disease_New_Public_Health_108.pdf

to reduce smoking, trans-fat bans to lower the risk of heart disease and healthier school lunch menus.

Many experts concerned about unhealthy eating say the government should better educate consumers about what is in their food, create more access to fresh fruit and vegetables and ban unhealthy foods in schools. "Where the government comes in is when industry is not acting responsibly," said Margo Wootan, director of nutrition policy at the Center for Science in the Public Interest, a consumer advocacy group, and that leaves a lot of potential room for government action, she adds. "The food industry has resisted every meaningful policy I've ever worked on — menu labeling, trans fat labeling, getting soda and candy bars out of schools. The industry's job is not to promote American health, it's to make money."

Scott Kahan, associate director of the Johns Hopkins University Weight Management Center, in Baltimore, said government has long had a role in improving health, starting with upgrading sanitation and water quality. It also steps in when the public is faced with infectious disease, including flu outbreaks. "When we look at how we improved the infectious disease problem in America, structural interventions, policy interventions and government interventions were a really important part of that," he says.

Today, he continues, the nation faces a different set of diseases with different causes, but the need for government action is no less. "We live in an environment right

now that in many ways could be called toxic, that's not unlike the toxic infectious environment of a hundred years ago," he says. "In this case, it's sort of a toxic environment around the foods that we eat." The unhealthiest, most high-calorie foods tend to be the cheapest and most heavily marketed, he says, often to young children. As a result, "It's going to be extremely important for government and also the private sector to come together to continue to evolve a set of policies and practices that make the healthier choice just a little bit easier and make the unhealthy choice not so easy."

Former Gov. Parris Glendening, D-Md., now president of the Leadership Institute at Smart Growth America, a coalition of urban advocacy groups, says making changes to the "built environment" to encourage healthier living "is a very legitimate role for state and local governments." Smart growth revolves around the concept that communities should have easy, preferably car-free access to jobs and shopping, and that public policy should encourage sidewalks, bike paths and public transportation to increase daily exercise and reduce air pollution, both of which improve health.

Smart-growth supporters point to a study in Charlotte, N.C., showing that building a light-rail system led users to walk more and lose weight. "The built environment can constrain or facilitate physical activity," said lead investigator John M. MacDonald of the University of Pennsylvania. "Understanding ways to encourage greater use of local environments for physical activity offers some hope for reducing the growth in the prevalence of obesity."[24]

Diane Katz, a research fellow in regulatory policy at the Heritage Foundation, a conservative think tank, says there is nothing wrong with politicians or other leaders encouraging constituents to adopt healthier lifestyles, although she thinks the deficit and other issues should take priority.

But Katz rejects efforts to insert the government into individual food decisions. "Nutrition regulations are commonly justified to defeat an obesity 'epidemic,' " she says, but "both the extent of the problem and the risk it poses are often exaggerated, the product of special-interest propaganda or dubious research." She adds: "Underlying government constraints on food choice is the presumption that individuals are incapable of making dietary decisions and government will do a far better job of it — a conceit that insults the most fundamental principles of limited government and personal freedom."

Katz turns Kahan's argument on its head, saying that since infectious-disease threats are now reduced, health officials have focused on eating and exercise habits because they need to "concoct new menaces to occupy their time."

Meanwhile, many sectors of the food industry are fighting government involvement. Several battles have erupted recently in the policy realm, including one over serving potatoes and pizza in school cafeterias. The Department of Agriculture recently proposed, based on Institute of Medicine recommendations, to limit the amount of tomato paste that could be considered a serving of vegetables and reduce the starchy vegetables that could be served in schools.[25] Congress altered the tomato paste recommendations spurred by industry groups including, reportedly, the American Frozen Food Institute and Schwan's Food Service, which provides pizzas to schools. Senators from large potato-growing states, Republican Susan Collins of Maine and Democrat Mark Udall of Colorado, worked with the National Potato Council to protest limits on starchy vegetables.[26]

Some companies have begun changing their products to ward off further government action. ConAgra Foods, for example, pledged in 2009 to reduce sodium in about 80 percent of its products by 2015. Kraft Foods said in 2010 it would reduce sodium in its North American products by an average of 10 percent by 2012.[27]

PepsiCo also has been a healthy-products leader. In 2010 it announced 11 goals to improve public health, including product reformulation and changes in marketing.[28] Derek Yach, a former WHO official and now senior vice president of global health policy at PepsiCo, says the government's role is to send the right signals and messages to consumers about healthy eating while industry continues to create healthier products. But that may not be enough to change consumer tastes, he says.

"Even if we put out better products," Yach says, "there's no guarantee they're going to be enjoyed and consumed or whether they're going to displace things with higher salt, sugar and fat, which have been the dietary norm for decades."

Should the health care system focus more on wellness?

The U.S. health care system is designed primarily to treat the sick, not encourage people to stay healthy.

Financial incentives reward health care providers for performing services and procedures, usually after illness has taken hold. But the vast majority of diseases start years and sometimes decades before an affliction drives a patient to a doctor's office. That leaves many experts arguing that caregivers and patients must be given the tools and incentives to stop chronic diseases before they begin.

Are You Getting Enough Exercise?

To maintain good health, the federal Centers for Disease Control and Prevention recommends the following guidelines:

Recommended physical activity — Moderate-intensity activities — such as brisk walking, bicycling, vacuuming, gardening or anything that causes small increases in breathing or heart rate — for at least 30 minutes per day, five days a week; or vigorous-intensity activities — such as running, aerobics, heavy yard work or anything that causes large increases in breathing or heart rate — for at least 20 minutes per day, three days a week.

Insufficient physical activity — More than 10 minutes total per week of moderate or vigorous-intensity activities, but less than the recommended levels.

Inactivity — Less than 10 minutes total per week of moderate or vigorous-intensity activities.

Leisure-time inactivity — No reported physical activity or exercise in the previous month.

Source: "Physical Activity Statistics: Definition," Centers for Disease Control and Prevention, May 2007, www.cdc.gov/nccdphp/dnpa/physical/stats/definitions.htm.

Several obstacles stand in the way, however:

- An imbalance in the types of services for which physicians are paid;
- A fragmented health system that doesn't give patients comprehensive care;
- A lack of physician training in disease prevention, and;
- An overreliance on technology.

Physicians traditionally have been paid for ordering diagnostic tests, prescribing drugs, performing surgery or conducting other procedures, not for spending time getting to know patients and their potential health risks. As doctors become busier, time with patients has gotten shorter.

"Physicians whom we talk to on a regular basis who truly want to do more health-behavior counseling or coaching with their patients are simply unable to do so because they aren't paid by federal government plans or private insurers to do that kind of preventive medicine work," says Paul Bonta, associate executive director of the American College of Preventive Medicine. Preventive health experts want a system that would pay care providers to delve deeper into lifestyle issues that may be causing disease and to counsel patients on diet modification or smoking cessation.

Other changes also could help, says Georges C. Benjamin, executive director of the American Public Health Association. Insurers should pay for cancer screening without requiring contributions from the patient. In addition, he says, physicians who ensure that patients receive immunizations, blood-pressure screening and other preventive procedures should be financially rewarded.

Preventive health advocates also say physicians need to play matchmaker, linking patients with community programs that offer unique support. "The majority of prevention, especially wellness, probably happens outside the medical system," says Elizabeth Tilson, medical director at Community Care of Wake and Johnston counties in North Carolina. "If you think about it, you may only get into the medical system once or twice a year. The vast majority of the time patients are out in their world."

Medical professionals often aren't aware of community-based support services, such as stop-smoking clinics or nutrition counseling, or don't help patients connect with them, advocates say.

A model of a more comprehensive approach is the "medical home," in which a health care provider tracks a patient's entire care and helps the patient find appropriate programs and specialists. At Martin's Point, a medical center in Portland, Maine, physicians monitor patient care through electronic medical records, and health educators help patients address medication or social issues connected with their disease.[29]

Bonta agrees that physicians need more help in providing ongoing services through their offices or referring patients to community resources. "Often, the patient will go to the physician's office, and the physician will say, 'Start exercising more, we need to get your weight down,' and the patient leaves the office and has no idea how to go about exercising more," he says. "Until we reach the point where we are able to educate or inform physicians about all the work that's going on within their communities, we can't make meaningful inroads in facilitating the behavior change that's needed."

Medical training also needs improvement, says Michael Parkinson, former president of the American College of Preventive Medicine and now a health consultant. He says the centuries-old "false dichotomy" between medical care and "wellness" was made worse in the United States in the early 20th century by the first schools of public health, which Parkinson says split off disease-prevention activities from medical school curricula. As a result, he says, most physicians are not trained in prevention.

Moreover, he adds, the model is outdated in a society in which three-quarters of health care costs could be mitigated through lifestyle changes.

Parkinson says it's unfair to ask doctors who have never been trained in disease prevention and never paid for preventive services to be held responsible for reversing the country's obesity epidemic.

Parkinson also argues that the medical system directs most health spending toward drugs and surgery after disease is present rather than focusing on low-tech strategies of improved diet and exercise. The "medical-industrial complex essentially now consumes nearly 20 percent of the U.S. gross domestic product, and what it lives on is an inherent bias we have for quick fixes with high technology at low or no cost" to consumers, he says.

The payment system also disconnects consumers from the costs of their care, Parkinson says. Patients need to understand, for example, that losing weight could lessen their back pain and risk of arthritis and perhaps help them avoid costly surgery and pharmaceuticals, he says. Those who choose more expensive options should be responsible for some of the extra costs, he adds.

While the increased focus on disease prevention appears to have universal support in the medical field, the shift could create new "winners and losers" in health care reimbursement, Tilson says. "I don't think that conceptually or philosophically anybody is against helping to reimburse for prevention. I just think it's a pure financial argument. There is just not enough money right now," she says.

Investing more in wellness could mean less money for new technologies and could heighten tensions between general practitioners and specialists. Primary-care physicians have argued for years that they aren't afforded the same prestige granted to specialists and can make as little as a fourth of the annual salary of an orthopedist or surgeon.[30] But shifting the advantage to preventive-care practitioners could make today's high earners unhappy.

BACKGROUND

Preventable Diseases

B uilding on the success of the smallpox vaccine, inoculations have been developed for many diseases, and the number keeps growing. In the 19th century, vaccines were developed for rabies and plague. The 20th century saw a host of new vaccines, including those for diphtheria, pertussis, measles and polio.[31] In 2006, a vaccine was approved that prevents the human papilloma virus, which can cause cervical and other cancers.[32]

While immunizations are considered by many to be the most important public health advance ever, some people are concerned about the safety of vaccines and about the growing number of inoculations children receive, which now cover more than a dozen diseases and can require multiple doses.[33]

As public health and medical advances in the early 20th century began to drastically reduce the prevalence of infectious disease and prolong lives, developed countries began to face a different type of disease burden:

High school and college-level students struggling to lose weight play soccer during fitness training at Wellspring Academy, in Reedley, Calif. More than one-third of American adults and 17 percent of children are obese.

noncommunicable disease. The significance of cancer, heart disease and other chronic conditions began to be recognized in the 1930s, but according to James Marks, senior vice president and director of the health group at the Robert Wood Johnson Foundation, people didn't think they could be stopped. "Many people thought for a long time that chronic diseases like heart disease and cancer were inevitable and that there wasn't much we could do about them," he says. Doctors made efforts to control high blood pressure and cholesterol levels, but only in extreme cases. Slowly, evidence accumulated showing that some diseases were preventable, including lung cancer and heart disease.

A major milestone in preventing chronic disease came in the form of the U.S. surgeon general's 1964 report on tobacco. Cigarette smoking increased dramatically in the first part of the 20th century, bringing with it a precipitous increase in lung cancer. Annual per capita cigarette consumption jumped from 54 cigarettes in 1900 to 4,435 in 1963. In 1930, the lung cancer death rate for men was 4.9 deaths per 100,000, a rate that increased to 75.6 per 100,000 in 1990.[34]

The ill effects of smoking became more apparent during the 1930s, '40s and '50s as more studies suggested smoking was causing the epidemic rise of lung cancer. In

1957 the U.S. Public Health Service officially declared that evidence pointed to a causal relationship between smoking and lung cancer.[35] In 1964, Surgeon General Luther Terry issued a landmark report on smoking and health that cited cigarette smoking as responsible for a 70 percent increase in the mortality rate of smokers compared to nonsmokers.[36]

The report also estimated the average smoker had a nine- to 10-fold risk of developing lung cancer compared to nonsmokers, and heavy smokers had at least a 20-fold risk. It also connected smoking during pregnancy with lower-weight newborns. In 1965, Congress required health warnings on all cigarette packages. In 1969, cigarette advertising was banned on radio and television. Per capita cigarette consumption began to fall, reaching 1,619 in 2006.[37]

As evidence accumulated showing the hazards of secondhand smoke, jurisdictions began imposing smoking bans. The first was in Minnesota in 1975. The state's Clean Indoor Air Act limited smoking to designated areas in public place and at public meetings.[38] More bans followed, and now 3,487 U.S. municipalities restrict smoking.[39] Twenty-five states had comprehensive indoor smoking bans by 2010.[40] Airplanes were divided into smoking and no-smoking sections in 1973; in 1987 Congress began banning smoking on planes.[41]

While lung cancer was the most obviously preventable disease, evidence began to grow in the 1950s and '60s that other conditions could be controlled as well, particularly heart disease. The seminal Framingham Heart Study, launched in 1948 by the National Heart, Lung and Blood Institute, provided the telling data. Researchers recruited 5,209 men and women between the ages of 30 and 62 from Framingham, Mass., to identify risk factors for heart disease and stroke through extensive physical exams and lifestyle interviews.[42]

The study identified high blood pressure, blood triglyceride and cholesterol levels, age, gender, physical inactivity and psychosocial issues as possible drivers of disease. Other studies contributed as well, creating a solid body of evidence that diet, physical activity, smoking and alcohol abuse contribute to chronic diseases including stroke, heart disease, diabetes and cancer.

Focusing on the diseases as well as improvements in medical care began to have an effect. After peaking in the early 1990s, cancer rates have generally fallen since 1998.[43] From 1950 to 1996, deaths from heart disease fell by 56 percent, and deaths from stroke declined 70 percent.[44]

Obesity

As some risk factors for chronic diseases came more under control, including high cholesterol and blood pressure, another major health threat emerged: obesity. In 1960, 13 percent of American adults were obese. By 2008, the figure had risen to 34 percent. During the same period, the percentage of extremely obese adults rose from slightly less than 1 percent of adults to 6 percent.[45]

Excess weight is associated with a variety of diseases, including heart disease, Type 2 diabetes, some types of cancer, hypertension and stroke. In addition to health consequences, obesity is costly. Medical spending is 42 percent higher for obese people than for those of normal weight.[46] Diagnosed diabetes increased 164 percent from 1980 through 2009, according to the Centers for Disease Control and Prevention (CDC).[47] The disease can cause kidney problems and blindness and require lower-limb amputations.[48]

For many years, the afflictions associated with obesity, including diabetes and cardiovascular disease, were attributed to increased wealth and personal choice. But health experts now say a variety of social, policy and commercial factors are fueling the epidemic and must be addressed by policymakers and the private sector. Contributors to the nation's obesity epidemic include high fat, sugar and salt levels in packaged and fast foods, increased portion sizes and a car-based transportation system.

The public-health response focuses on several areas: increased consumption of fruits and vegetables; increased physical activity; breastfeeding; and decreased consumption of sugary drinks and energy-dense foods, such as meat, processed foods and sweets.

But reducing disease risk factors that are so embedded in society, personal in nature and driven by commercial interests from food manufacturers to tobacco companies has proven daunting. Jeffrey Levi, executive director of the Trust for America's Health, a Washington-based health advocacy group, says addressing current health conditions represents a shift for public health experts. Prevention traditionally focused on infectious disease, "breaking a chain of infection in some way," he says. Current health efforts, by contrast, focus on more intimate personal

CHRONOLOGY

1700s-1800s *Modern vaccine development begins; germ theory attributes diseases to specific organisms and shows they are contagious.*

1789 Smallpox vaccine developed by British physician Edward Jenner.

1854 British physician John Snow traces cholera outbreak in London to a water pump, giving a major boost to the science of epidemiology.

1885 Rabies vaccine developed by French scientist Louis Pasteur.

1897 Plague vaccine developed by Russian microbiologist Waldemar Haffkine.

1900-1950 *U.S. mortality rates plunge with improvements in clean-water technologies, housing, other living standards.*

1917 Cholera vaccine developed by Haffkine, who performs the first human tests of the injection on himself.

1923 Diphtheria vaccine developed by German scientist Emil Adolf Behring.

1924 Tetanus vaccine developed by P. Descombey.

1948 Framingham Heart Study begins; identifies risk factors for chronic disease.

1950-1970 *Risk factors for chronic diseases begin to be identified and addressed.*

1952 Polio vaccine developed by U.S. medical researcher Jonas Salk.

1964 Surgeon General Luther Terry issues landmark report saying cigarette smoking increases mortality rate of smokers by 70 percent compared to nonsmokers.

1965 Congress requires health warnings on cigarette packages.

1967 World Health Organization (WHO) calls for global eradication of smallpox.

1969 Cigarette advertising banned.

1970-1990 *Smallpox eradicated, but new diseases such as HIV/AIDS take hold.*

1973 Airplane cabins divided into "smoking" and "no-smoking" sections.

1975 First indoor clean-air law limits smoking to designated areas in public spaces.

1980 WHO declares smallpox eradicated. . . . First cases of HIV/AIDS appear in the United States.

1989 Congress bans smoking on commercial flights.

1990s-2000s *Cancer rates peak and begin to fall; obesity rates rise.*

1992 Environmental Protection Agency declares secondhand tobacco smoke a Class A carcinogen.

1998 States get a $246 billion windfall after settling a lawsuit against tobacco companies, but little of the money funds smoking-cessation programs.

2000 Government sets goal of reducing childhood obesity rate, estimated at 15 percent, to 5 percent by 2010.

2003 Study links urban and suburban sprawl with weight gain.

March 2010 President Obama signs the Patient Protection and Affordable Care Act, which includes a $15 billion Prevention and Public Health Fund.

May 2010 White House Task Force sets goal of eliminating childhood obesity in a generation; nutrition labeling of chain-restaurant menus becomes law, effective in 2011.

2011 House of Representatives votes to repeal Prevention and Public Health Fund (April); Obama's deficit-reduction proposals include a $3.5 billion cut in the fund (September); House Republicans propose an $8 billion reduction (December).

Poor Countries Struggle to Curb Preventable Illnesses

"The world is essentially sleepwalking into a sick future."

Malaria and HIV often get the headlines in stories about global health problems, but the biggest threats in poor countries are the same ones afflicting the wealthy and well-fed: lack of exercise, smoking and diets brimming with fat, salt and sugar.

Chronic, or noncommunicable, disease recently became the world's leading killer, accounting for 63 percent of deaths in 2008, according to the U.N.'s World Health Organization (WHO).[1]

The effects of modern lifestyles — including greater reliance on automobiles, pollution, increases in smoking and unhealthy diets are spreading preventable cancers, diabetes and respiratory and heart disease to every corner of the globe. The illnesses are having the greatest impact, however, where poverty is rampant and health systems are inadequate.

The vast majority of cancers in the developing world, for example, are detected in their late stages, but effective treatments are lacking in general. In Uganda, 96 percent of those who die from cancer never see a health care provider.[2] Moreover, in many developing countries, even pain medications for cancer often are unavailable.

Chronic diseases are killing people at earlier ages in developing countries than in the developed world. Nearly 30 percent of deaths from noncommunicable diseases occur among people under age 60 in low- and middle-income countries, compared to 13 percent in high-income countries.[3]

"In wealthy countries, deaths from heart disease and strokes have declined significantly," said Margaret Chan, WHO's director-general. "But this gives a distorted picture. For some countries, it is no exaggeration to describe the situation as an impending disaster — a disaster for health, for society and most of all for national economies."[4]

In September the United Nations unanimously called chronic diseases "a challenge of epidemic proportions" and set out a plan to develop global and national goals for disease reduction, particularly in low- and middle-income areas.[5]

Included in draft targets are recommendations to reduce smoking and decrease salt levels in food.[6] The WHO also developed a list of low- or no-cost disease-prevention steps that countries could adopt, such as promoting public awareness about diet and physical activity.[7]

In addition, the U.N. is working to accelerate implementation of the WHO Framework Convention on Tobacco Control, an international health treaty developed in 2003 that promotes tobacco regulation.[8]

As in the United States, attacking chronic diseases requires a multiprong approach, including strengthening health systems, changing government policies in areas such as urban planning and school physical education requirements and encouraging the involvement of business.

behaviors like food choices, "not something public health people traditionally have been terribly comfortable with."

Community Prevention

Federal policies now support the concept of community prevention — developing local efforts to address the leading preventable causes of death and disability, obesity and tobacco use. The health reform bill passed by Congress in 2010 included a Prevention and Public Health Fund totaling $15 billion over its first 10 years. In addition to supporting preventive health initiatives, it funds public health infrastructure and workforce

improvements, including research and disease tracking.[49] The fund also supports first lady Michelle Obama's Let's Move campaign, which aims to drastically curtail rising rates of childhood obesity through physical activity and improved nutrition.[50]

But not everyone is convinced. Critics said that by providing greater access to preventive services and disease screening, the reform act would in fact increase health costs. In addition, they said there was no guarantee that changes in communities would decrease health costs. Republican senators tried to remove the fund from the Senate version of the bill. Sen. Michael Enzi, R-Wyo., called the

The global food industry has resisted stiffer government regulations, but some companies are participating in voluntary efforts. In 2008, the International Food and Beverage Alliance, which includes such giants as Coca-Cola, Kraft and Kellogg's, committed to five actions over five years to make products healthier: Reformulating food content, providing nutrition information to consumers, advertising responsibly, raising awareness of nutritious diets and promoting physical activity.[9]

But some U.N. officials say such voluntary efforts are too weak to adequately address global health problems.

"World leaders must not bow to industry pressure," said Olivier De Schutter, U.N. Special Rapporteur on the Right to Food, a watchdog role at the international organization. "It is crucial for world leaders to counter food-industry efforts to sell unbalanced processed products and ready-to-serve meals too rich in trans fats and saturated fats, salt and sugars. Food advertising is proven to have a strong impact on children and must be strictly regulated in order to avoid the development of bad eating habits early in life."[10]

Despite the rapid growth in chronic illnesses around the globe, international aid aimed at helping developing countries improve their health systems has been weak. Only an estimated 3 percent of health-related development assistance is devoted to chronic disease.[11] That isn't expected to change any time soon as major donors, including the United States, face their own economic woes and continue to focus on current funding commitments, primarily to fight AIDS, tuberculosis, malaria and afflictions facing children and pregnant women.

Some view the focus as shortsighted. Without a stronger effort to reduce chronic diseases globally, said Ann Keeling, chair of NCD Alliance, an international coalition that focuses on the problem, "the world is essentially sleepwalking into a sick future."[12]

— *Nellie Bristol*

[1]"Global Status Report on Noncommunicable Diseases 2010," World Health Organization, www.who.int/nmh/publications/ncd_report2010/en/.

[2]"Chronic Disease in Developing Countries: Poor Countries are Developing the Diseases of the Rich, with Lethal Consequences," *The Economist*, Sept. 24, 2011, www.economist.com/node/21530099.

[3]World Health Organization, *op. cit.*

[4]Maddy French, "Why Non-Communicable Diseases Hit the Developing World So Hard," *The Guardian*, June 29, 2011, www.guardian.co.uk/journalismcompetition/why-non-communicable-diseases-hit-the-developing-world-so-hard.

[5]"Political Declaration of the High-level Meeting of the General Assembly on the Prevention and Control of Non-communicable Diseases," U.N. General Assembly, Sept. 16, 2011, www.un.org/ga/search/view_doc.asp?symbol=A%2F66%2FL.1&Lang=E.

[6]Nellie Bristol, "The UN Weighs Solutions to the Plague of Noncommunicable Disease," *Health Affairs*, November 2010.

[7]World Health Organization, *op. cit.*

[8]"Tobacco Control for Global Health and the Development/NCD Summit," Framework Convention Alliance, www.fctc.org/index.php?option=com_content&view=article&id=503:tobacco-control-and-global-health&catid=258:tobacco-control-and-global-health.

[9]"Who We Are," International Food and Beverage Alliance, www.ifballiance.org/about.html.

[10]"World Leaders Must Take Binding Steps to Curb Unhealthy Food Industry-UN Expert," UN News Centre, Sept. 16, 2011, www.un.org/apps/news/story.asp?NewsID=39578&Cr=non+communicable+diseases&Cr1=.

[11]Bristol, *op. cit.*

[12]Kate Kelland, "UN Summit Talks Stalled," Reuters, Aug., 17, 2011, www.idf.org/un-summit-talks-stalled-reuters-interview-ncda-chair-ann-keeling.

prevention fund "new pork barrel spending," adding, "The bill will pave sidewalks, build jungle gyms and open grocery stores, but it won't bring down health care costs or make quality [health] coverage more affordable."[51]

Doctors and public health experts increasingly focus on "evidence-based medicine," or scientifically proven medical interventions. They use the same strategies for disease prevention as well. The U.S. Preventive Services Task Force reviews evidence and makes recommendations to physicians about which screening tests, counseling, immunizations and preventive medications should be recommended to patients.[52]

The panel's findings are sometimes controversial. For example, in 2009 it raised the age at which it recommended that women with an average risk for breast cancer should routinely receive mammograms. The change spurred a fierce debate among doctors, women, insurers and politicians. "Their justification: These new guidelines capture 81 percent of mammography's benefits [and] save a lot of resources, with only a 3 percent drop in survivorship from the most common cancer to affect women," said Marisa Weiss, president and founder of BreastCancer.org, a nonprofit cancer awareness and information site.

Get Out of Your Car, Urban Planners Urge

"Complete Streets" program promotes bicycling and walking.

State and local lawmakers are trying to accomplish what years of preaching by the President's Council on Physical Fitness and other public health authorities have largely failed to do: Get people moving.

Twenty-five states and 314 city, country or regional jurisdictions have adopted so-called Complete Streets policies, pledging to consider installing bike lanes and sidewalks in future road-construction and major road-rehabilitation projects, according to the National Complete Streets Coalition, a Washington, D.C.-based advocacy group.[1]

The coalition, which encourages people to ditch their cars and build exercise into their daily lives, claims many benefits for the approach beyond disease prevention: improved pedestrian safety, greater use of better-connected commercial centers, fewer traffic jams and better air quality.

"We have this huge infrastructure investment in transportation, and the only thing we do with it is focus on moving cars," says Barbara McCann, the coalition's director.

New Jersey Transportation Commissioner James Simpson is a strong advocate of the approach. The state has its own Complete Streets policy, and 13 municipalities and one county have adopted versions. "A local Complete Streets policy raises awareness among residents, elected officials and the private sector," Simpson wrote. "When projects are proposed, pedestrian, bicycle and transit accommodations are no longer an afterthought — they become an integral feature of the overall investment plan."[2]

But Complete Streets policies don't have universal support. The St. Cloud, Minn., City Council initially rejected a proposal on a tie vote earlier this year because of concerns about redundancy with current policies, effects on new development and costs.[3] The council subsequently approved the proposal, however, when a supportive council member was able to vote a few weeks later.[4]

The New York State Association of Counties recently opposed a Complete Streets proposal in the General Assembly, saying budgets are too tight to give it priority and that the "diversion of effort and funding" mandated by the provision "would further the deterioration of our infrastructure."[5]

In Congress, Complete Streets bills have been introduced in the last three sessions, but none has moved forward.

The Complete Streets approach emerged in the late 1990s, when, McCann says, the President's Council on Physical Fitness was failing in its effort to get more people to exercise. The council brought its concerns to McCann, a writer and transportation expert working on ways to make streets friendlier to walkers and bikers.

"They said, 'OK, we have been trying to get people to go to the gym for years, and it's not working,'" McCann says. "'There's just a totally flat line on the number of people who are willing to make a special time of day to exercise.'"

The movement got a major boost in 2003 when a report by Smart Growth America, a Washington group that supports better urban planning, equated suburban sprawl — and its reliance on driving rather than walking — with weight gain. "The results show that people in more sprawling counties are likely to have a higher body-mass index," a

"But what really is the cost?," Weiss asks. "And who is paying the price? It could be you, your mom, daughter, sister, aunt or grandmother or all of us."[53]

CURRENT SITUATION

Public Health Targets

Despite the steady decline in smoking — from 42 percent of adults in 1965 to about 21 percent in 2009 — tobacco remains the primary cause of preventable death in the United States — 443,000 annually.[54] Smoking also is a major focus for public health efforts.[55]

The combination of obesity and inactivity ranks as the nation's second-leading killer, causing 112,000 deaths a year, according to the CDC.[56] While smoking-cessation policies have made progress through increased taxes and smoke-free regulations, public policy to control obesity has proved more difficult.

summary of the research says. In addition, the research showed a "direct relationship" between sprawl and chronic disease, with the odds of high blood pressure increasing 6 percent for every measured increase in sprawl.[6]

Some criticized the study's methods and conclusions, however. "This is just another attempt by the report's sponsors to spin research showing only trivial weight differences between city and suburban residents into a national crisis requiring land use restrictions," wrote researchers at the Heritage Foundation, a conservative think tank in Washington.[7]

Even McCann concedes that making a direct connection between planning policy and health has been elusive. "Just on the research side, we aren't quite 100 percent there yet on having a direct link between policy and body weight, but there's certainly a chain that's very clear," she says.

Nonetheless, McCann says the connection makes sense on an intuitive level to many planners, and they've started to respond to it. "We're having tremendous success at the state and local level because they really get it," she says.

McCann argues that despite current fiscal constraints, Complete Streets policies are not necessarily more expensive, but simply require engineers to think about a variety of users when planning transportation routes.

"In a way," McCann says, "you're trying to go back to the way communities used to be built."

— *Nellie Bristol*

Getty Images/Spencer Platt

Bike riders in Brooklyn's Prospect Park West got to keep a controversial bike lane after a judge in August 2011 rejected efforts by local residents to remove the lane. Mayor Michael Bloomberg has sought to make the city more bike and pedestrian friendly.

[1]"Complete Streets Atlas," National Complete Streets Coalition, www.completestreets.org/complete-streets-fundamentals/complete-streets-atlas/.

[2]James Simpson, "Opinion: N.J. Complete Streets Policy Paves Way for Road Safety," *The Times of Trenton*, Nov. 18, 2011, www.nj.com/times-opinion/index.ssf/2011/11/opinion_nj_complete_streets_po.html.

[3]Kari Petrie, "MN: St. Cloud Votes No to Complete Streets Policy," *St. Cloud* [Minn.] *Times*, Sept. 13, 2011, www.masstransitmag.com/news/10356650/mn-st-cloud-votes-no-to-complete-streets-policy.

[4]Kari Petrie, "St. Cloud Leaders OK Complete Streets Policy," *St. Cloud* [Minn.] *Times*, Nov. 7, 2011, www.sctimes.com/article/20111108/NEWS01/111070061/St-Cloud-leaders-OK-complete-streets-policy.

[5]Noah Kazis, "NY Counties Oppose Complete Streets Bill Without Understanding It," Streetsblog.org, Feb. 8, 2011, www.streetsblog.org/2011/02/08/ny-counties-oppose-complete-streets-bill-without-understanding-it/.

[6]Barbara A. McCann and Reid Ewing, "Measuring the Health Effects of Sprawl: A National Analysis of Physical Activity Obesity and Chronic Disease," Smart Growth America, September 2003, www.smartgrowthamerica.org/report/HealthSprawl8.03.pdf.

[7]Wendell Cox and Ronald Utt, "Sprawl and Obesity: A Flawed Connection," Heritage Foundation, Sept. 19, 2003, www.heritage.org/research/reports/2003/09/sprawl-and-obesity-a-flawed-connection.

In order to create environments that support healthier habits, the Obama administration is strongly supporting community prevention efforts. The Prevention and Public Health Fund put $298 million of $750 million doled out in fiscal 2011 toward community efforts. "Prevention is something that can't just happen in a doctor's office," said Health and Human Services Secretary Kathleen Sebelius. "If we are to address the big health issues of our time, from physical inactivity to poor nutrition to tobacco use, it needs to happen in local communities." Funds were targeted toward reducing tobacco use, improving nutrition and increasing physical activity and coordinating efforts to prevent diabetes, heart disease and cancer.[57] The grants support, for example, a network of national telephone "quit lines" for smokers, and increased HIV testing opportunities.[58]

Food and the Workplace

Employers as well as the federal government are grappling with the right approach to curbing chronic diseases. As the

Getty Images/Justin Sullivan

Smoking has declined from 43 percent of U.S. adults in 1965 to about 22 percent in 2009, but tobacco remains the nation's primary cause of preventable deaths — nearly half a million annually. Poor diet, lack of physical activity, smoking and alcohol abuse contribute to deadly chronic diseases including stroke, heart disease, diabetes and some cancers. About 4,000 U.S. communities and at least 25 states restrict smoking.

insurance providers for nearly two-thirds of Americans under age 65, employers bear a heavy cost for an unhealthy workforce.[59] The cost to employers for all expenses related to health and lost productivity in 2002 was an average of $18,618 per employee. These costs include health insurance premiums, workers' compensation, short-term disability, long-term disability, sick leave and unpaid leave. Expenditures were 228 percent higher for employees with multiple risk factors for heart disease than for employees without the risk factors. Employees who smoke, get inadequate exercise, have high blood pressure and/or poor nutrition cost employers more in health care expenses, absenteeism and overall productivity.[60]

Workplace wellness programs, which try to control costs and improve employees' health, have become popular in recent years. Features include work-site health fairs, screenings and coaching and weight-management programs. Some employers are even developing programs that pay workers to change unhealthy habits.[61] The CDC is conducting a $9 million initiative to encourage workplace wellness programs, which it said could yield an average $3 return for every $1 spent over a two- to five-year period.[62]

Producers of fast food and packaged foods high in fat and sugar also are being targeted in the fight against chronic disease. An earlier Congress and the Obama administration have called on food companies to shift advertising aimed at children to healthier products.[63] Draft guidelines released in April would set voluntary limits on the amount of sodium, sugar and fats in foods advertised to children. Companies spend about $2 billion a year on advertising foods marketed to kids. In 2009, 86 percent of those products were high in calories, sodium, sugar or saturated fat, compared with 94 percent in 2003, when the industry began a self-regulatory program. But experts say the reduction in unhealthy ingredients isn't moving fast enough.[64]

The food and beverage industry is resisting the guidelines, which are now stalled and may be substantially revised. Industry representatives say they are trying gradually to reformulate their products because they worry that quick changes would result in lost customers.[65] "The food industry and the advertising industry have spent billions on reformulating food, changing advertising and putting together public service announcements," said Dan Jaffe, executive vice president for government relations at the Association of National Advertisers. "There is more to be done, but the critics are never going to be satisfied."[66]

Restaurants also are being asked to change. The Food and Drug Administration is drafting regulations to implement calorie count requirements for chain restaurants, a provision included in the health reform act signed into law in 2010.[67] CDC Director Thomas Frieden said the move "empowers people. It gives them information. It also is important because it gets the restaurants to think twice before they put up a 1,500-calorie breakfast. So it both makes the choices healthier and it makes the options healthier by getting some reformulation on the part of the restaurant industry." Nonetheless, Frieden said, calorie labeling remains only a "modestly effective intervention" that can be overrun by things like low prices. He cited a restaurant chain that discounted a high-calorie foot-long sandwich that resulted in an increase in calories consumed per customer.[68]

Unhealthy foods are being attacked in others ways as well. In 2004, restaurants in affluent Tiburon, Calif., voluntarily stopped using cooking oil with trans fats, making it the first "trans fat free" city in the country.[69] Other jurisdictions followed, notably, New York City in 2006.[70]

Other Initiatives

In other federal efforts, the CDC and the Centers for Medicare and Medicaid Services (CMS) recently started

Should Americans be penalized for unhealthy behaviors?

YES
Michael Parkinson
Past President, American College of Preventive Medicine

Wendy Lynch
Co-Director, Center for Consumer Choice in Health Care, Altarum Institute

Written for *CQ Researcher*, December 2011

Should they be penalized? They already are — and dramatically so. The health and pocketbooks of all Americans already have been hurt by our collective failure to clearly align financial and other incentives — both "carrots" and "sticks" — to help individuals improve health and reduce preventable disease. In truth, those who do not take an active role in their health and health care already are penalized by poor health and higher costs. When we shield consumers from the consequences of their own inaction — by shifting the entire excess cost to their fellow plan members — we compromise their safety and health while costs continue to escalate.

So, let's pose the same question from a reverse perspective: Should we give consumers an opportunity to save money by doing things that are known to improve health and lower costs? We would say yes.

Unsustainable cost trends not only place an unbearable burden on our national debt but also strain the budgets of each family. Some of the overarching drivers of cost are preventable chronic illnesses, medical errors and use of unnecessary or ineffective treatments. All of these cost drivers can be reduced when consumers take an active role in their own care. We can support that active involvement by creating an "environment" (culture, physical spaces, policies and programs) that promotes and sustains better individual choices and actions.

Over a lifetime, one's own behaviors contribute more to health and health care needs than medical treatments will. Individuals who are engaged in their care are less likely to experience errors such as incorrect medications and are more likely to choose appropriate care. Thus, anything that encourages prevention and rewards wise health care choices not only saves money but also averts harm.

Our preferred method of giving people an opportunity to save money is through a funded Health Savings Account. That money serves as a pool of funds to cover expenses before a deductible is reached. If the consumer does not need health care, or can find less expensive alternatives, it accumulates. But consumers can choose to spend it if they want or need to. In this way, each family can choose whether it is worth protecting money (and health) by preventing disease and making wise care choices. That is not punishment, it is personal choice.

NO
Jeffrey Levi
Executive Director, Trust for America's Health; Chair, Advisory Group on Prevention, Health Promotion, and Integrative and Public Health

Written for *CQ Researcher*, December 2011

It is not government's place to ensure that citizens do every last push-up or sit-up. Each of us is personally responsible for making healthy choices for ourselves and our children to prevent illness and promote well-being in our own lives.

However, local, state and federal policymakers can help kids and everyone else, too, by making healthy choices easy choices by providing accessible, safe places to walk, jog, bike, swim, take an exercise class or play sports. In addition, government can improve nutrition and physical-education programs in schools and launch initiatives to reduce tobacco use, especially among children and adolescents.

Ensuring a healthy citizenry isn't about taking punitive measures but, rather, encouraging people to be what they want to be: healthy, productive and happy.

Thankfully, with the creation of the Prevention and Public Health Fund, included in the Affordable Care Act, government has sent the message that it is going to do its best to help people stay healthy in the first place, rather than wait for them to get sick. This is the best, most commonsense way to reduce health care costs and spur economic growth.

A hallmark program of the prevention fund is the Community Transformation Grants (CTGs), which provide communities with the resources needed to work together at the local level to create health initiatives tailored to their specific needs. This can involve small-business owners, faith leaders, youth leaders, employers, community groups, parents, law enforcement officials, schools, and health care providers. Through the CTGs, communities are empowered to create the programs and initiatives that they know will help make the healthy choices easier for all.

You catch more flies with honey than vinegar, as the saying goes. It is government's role to support individuals and communities as they choose to stay active and fit, not penalize them if they fail to do so.

Through support and encouragement, we can spare millions of Americans from developing serious, preventable diseases and, in so doing, shift the paradigm from a sick-care system that focuses on treating disease after it happens to a health care system, where we keep people healthy in the first place.

Office of Mayor Chip Johnson

The road to healthier living — and a more business-friendly community — leads to the farmers market in Hernando, Miss. "We want to recruit corporations to Hernando," said Mayor Chip Johnson. "They're not stupid. When they make their decisions, they look at health care costs."

the task. "Beyond wagging their finger at you and saying, 'you really need to lose weight,' most doctors really don't have the cognitive therapy, the motivational skills to do that." Nonetheless, he says, "the physician initiating and asking about how you're doing on weight and saying how important it is to reverse your diabetes is very, very pivotal."

Getting the imprimatur of a health care payer as large as Medicare is an important step in better engaging the health care system to address lifestyle issues, he adds. The coverage changes, he says, "are important landmarks to progress because what Medicare has finally said is the physician and the delivery system have an important role, not a sole role, but a very important role to both initiate and sustain behavior change, which is the only way we're going to get out of this crisis."

OUTLOOK

Two Steps Forward . . .

The importance of chronic disease prevention is gaining attention as more people realize both its health and fiscal costs.

Employers are developing new ways to help employees change unhealthy behaviors. Meanwhile, policymakers are paying more attention to the way social environments and commercial forces affect lifestyle choices.

In the policy realm, the Patient Protection and Affordable Care Act — the Obama administration's signature health care law — has given unprecedented attention and funding to prevention activities. "In addition to establishing the Prevention and Public Health Fund, the act also requires Medicare and some private insurers to cover certain preventive services, such as cancer screening, without patient co-pays.

However, the fund is threatened by federal budget cuts, and the health care law's legality is being challenged in the Supreme Court, which will decide that issue this year.

Jud Richland, president and CEO of Partnership for Prevention, a coalition of business, nonprofit and government groups, says even if the health care law is repealed or struck down, insurers are likely to continue to support clinical preventive services but that many community intervention programs are likely to lose funding if the prevention fund is raided or killed.

the Million Hearts Campaign aimed at reducing heart attacks and strokes over the next five years. The program focuses on improving access to effective, quality care, increasing clinical attention to heart attack and stroke prevention, promoting heart-healthy lifestyles and consistent use of high-blood-pressure and cholesterol medications.[71]

Medicare also is focusing more on prevention. CMS announced in November that the program would begin covering obesity screening and counseling in a primary-care setting for beneficiaries whose body mass index (BMI) is 30 or more. Under the change, beneficiaries are entitled to a face-to-face counseling session with a health care provider each week for a month followed by sessions every other week for an additional five months. Participants who lose at least 6.6 pounds during the first six months of counseling are entitled to additional visits every month for six months.[72]

Earlier in the month, CMS announced Medicare coverage of intensive behavioral therapy for cardiovascular disease. The program includes promotion of aspirin use, screening for high blood pressure and intensive behavioral counseling to promote a healthy diet to fight known risk factors for cardiovascular and diet-related chronic disease.[73]

Preventive medicine expert Parkinson is concerned that the level of payment is too low and that many physicians may not have the skills necessary to adequately perform

On the state and local levels, lawmakers could continue to enact policies limiting trans fats, requiring menu labeling and mandating other health-related measures. Richland notes that indoor clean-air laws took years to be passed but became popular once implemented. "The momentum's going in the right direction" for other preventive health laws, he says.

New technologies may encourage prevention as well. Smart-phone applications are coming on line that will help people keep track of their blood pressure, count calories or get fitness coaching.[74] A recent report by ABI Research said the market for health and fitness apps will reach $400 million by 2016.[75]

Nonetheless, despite years of messages about good diet and exercise, experts worry Americans could continue to fall short in those areas.

After dropping consistently for several decades, the proportion of Americans who smoke has stayed relatively steady since 2004.[76] Fewer than 20 percent of adults participate in adequate leisure-time aerobic and muscle-building activity.[77] Only 26 percent eat vegetables three or more times a day.[78]

Overall, the United Health Foundation found that reductions in smoking, preventable hospitalizations and cardiovascular deaths were offset last year by increases in obesity, diabetes and childhood poverty.[79]

A massive culture shift is needed, says North Carolina preventive medicine physician Tilson. "It's hard to get people to change behaviors, especially when their entire environment and culture is against them every step of the way," she says. "It's really hard to be healthy in our society right now."

Tilson says her own office reflects that difficulty. Despite having a workplace wellness plan that promotes a healthy diet and adequate exercise, she says, staff members frequently bring in baked goods, and product sales representatives bring cookies and candy for the staff.

"Even our closest friends undermine us," she says. Love and support is "equated with giving sugar."

NOTES

1. "America's Health Rankings," United Health Foundation, November 2011, http://statehealthstats.americashealthrankings.org/#/state/US/MS/2011.

2. "Healthy Americas for A Healthier Economy," Trust for America's Health, October 2011, http://healthyamericans.org/report/90/.

3. *Ibid.*

4. *Ibid.*

5. "United Health Foundation's America's Health Rankings Finds Preventable Chronic Disease on the Rise; Obesity, Diabetes Undermining Country's Overall Health," United Health Foundation, Dec. 6, 2011, www.americashealthrankings.org/mediacenter/mediacenter1.aspx.

6. "Chronic Diseases: The Power to Prevent, The Call to Control: At a Glance 2009," Centers for Disease Control and Prevention, Dec. 17, 2009, www.cdc.gov/chronicdisease/resources/publications/AAG/chronic.htm.

7. "An Unhealthy Truth: Rising Rates of Chronic Disease and the Future of Health in America," Partnership to Fight Chronic Disease, www.fightchronicdisease.org/.../UnhealthyTruths_UPDATED.pptx.

8. "Non-Communicable Diseases to Cost $47 Trillion by 2030, New Study Released Today," World Economic Forum, Sept. 18, 2011, www.weforum.org/news/non-communicable-diseases-cost-47-trillion-2030-new-study-released-today.

9. "Preventing Chronic Diseases: A Vital Investment," 2005, World Health Organization, p. 9, www.who.int/chp/chronic_disease_report/full_report.pdf.

10. Dan Harris and Mikaela Conley, "Childhood Obesity: A Call for Parents to Lose Custody," ABC News, July 14, 2011, http://abcnews.go.com/Health/childhood-obesity-call-parents-lose-custody/story?id=14068280.

11. *Ibid.*

12. "Obesity 'Epidemic' May Be Overstated," UPI.com, March 27, 2009, www.upi.com/Health_News/2009/03/17/Obesity-epidemic-may-be-overstated/UPI-50681237311372/.

13. Andy Barr, "Sarah Palin Brings Cookies, Hits 'Nanny State,' " *Politico*, Nov. 10, 2010, www.politico.com/news/stories/1110/44936.html.

14. "Childhood Obesity Facts," Centers for Disease Control and Prevention, www.cdc.gov/healthy youth/obesity/facts.htm.

15. Nell Katz, "Sarah Palin: Americans Have 'God-Given Right' to be Fat?" CBS, Nov. 30, 2010, www .cbsnews.com/8301-504763_162-20024104-1039 1704.html.

16. "Too Fat to Fight: Retired Military Leaders Want Junk Food Out of America's Schools," Mission: Readiness: Military Leaders for Kids, 2010, http://cdn.mission readiness.org/MR_Too_Fat_to_Fight-1.pdf.

17. *Ibid.*

18. "Fast Facts," Kaiser Family Foundation, http://facts .kff.org/.

19. "National Health Expenditure Data," Centers for Medicare and Medicaid Services, www.cms.gov/ NationalHealthExpendData/25_NHE_Fact_sheet.asp.

20. Joshua T. Cohen, *et al.*, "Does Preventive Care Save Money? Health Economics and the Presidential Candidates," *The New England Journal of Medicine*, Feb. 14, 2008.

21. Sarah Goodell, *et al.*, "Cost Savings and Cost-Effectiveness of Clinical Preventive Care," Robert Wood Johnson Foundation, September 2009, www .rwjf.org/files/research/48508.costsavings.preventive care.brief.pdf.

22. "Prevention for a Healthier America: Investments in Disease Prevention Yield Significant Savings, Stronger Communities," Trust for America's Health, July 2008, http://healthyamericans.org/reports/prevention 08/Prevention08.pdf.

23. Uwe E. Reinhardt, "Cost Effectiveness Analysis and US Health Care," Economix, *The New York Times*, http://economix.blogs.nytimes.com/2009/03/13/ cost-effectiveness-analysis-and-us-health-care.

24. "Public Transit Systems Contribute to Weight Los and Improved Health, Study Finds," *ScienceDaily*, June 28, 2010, www.sciencedaily.com/releases/2010/ 06/100628203756.htm.

25. Jill U. Adams, "'Pizza Vegetable' Controversy is a Hot Potato: A Law Blocking New Regulations of Tomato Paste, Spuds and Salt in School Meals Causes a Stir," *Los Angeles Times*, Nov. 28, 2011,

www.latimes.com/health/la-he-school-lunch-nutri tion-20111128,0,4859084,print.story.

26. *Ibid.*

27. Derek Yach, *et al.*, "The Role and Challenges of the Food Industry in Addressing Chronic Disease," *Globalization and Health*, 2010, 6:10, www.globalization andhealth.com/content/6/1/10.

28. *Ibid.*

29. Julie Rovner, "Future of Primary Care? Some Say 'Medical Home,'" NPR, Aug. 26, 2010, www.npr .org/templates/story/story.php?storyId=129432707.

30. Parija B. Kavilanz, "Family Doctors: An Endangered Breed," CNNMoney, July 18, 2009, http://money .cnn.com/2009/07/16/news/economy/healthcare_ doctors_shortage/index.htm.

31. "Immunization Timeline," Keepkidshealthy.com, www.keepkidshealthy.com/welcome/immunizations/ immunization_timeline.html.

32. Rita Rubin, "First-ever Cancer Vaccine Approved," *USA Today*, June 8 2006, www.usatoday.com/news/ health/2006-06-08-cervical-cancer-vaccine_x.htm.

33. Shari Roan, "Despite Concerns, Most Parents Get Their Kids Vaccinated," *Los Angeles Times*, June 9, 2011, http://articles.latimes.com/2011/jun/09/ news/la-heb-child-vaccines-20110609. For background see the following *CQ Researcher* reports: Nellie Bristol, "HPV Vaccine," May 11, 2007, pp. 409-432; Kathy Koch, "Vaccine Controversies," Aug. 25, 2000, pp. 641-672 and Sarah Glazer, "Increase in Autism," June 13, 2003, pp. 545-568 (updated July 22, 2010).

34. "Achievements in Public Health, 1900-1999: Tobacco Use-United States, 1900-1999," *MMWR*, Centers for Disease Control and Prevention, Nov. 5, 1999, 48(43); 986-993, www.cdc.gov/mmwr/ preview/mmwrhtml/mm4843a2.htm#fig1.

35. "The Reports of the Surgeon General: the 1964 Report on Smoking and Health," National Library of Medicine, http://profiles.nlm.nih.gov/ps/ retrieve/Narrative/NN/p-nid/60.

36. *Ibid.*

37. "Smoking and Tobacco Use, Consumption Data," Centers for Disease Control and Prevention, www

.cdc.gov/tobacco/data_statistics/tables/economics/consumption.

38. Martiga Lohn, "Minnesota Lawmakers Approve Smoking Ban," The Associated Press, May 13, 2007, http://articles.boston.com/2007-05-13/news/29226864_1_bars-and-restaurants-public health experts smoking-ban-limited-smoking.

39. "Overview List-How Many Smoke Free Laws?" American Nonsmokers' Rights Foundation, www.no-smoke.org/pdf/mediaordlist.pdf.

40. Mike Stobbe, "Will Every U.S. State Have a Smoking Ban by 2010?" The Huffington Post, April 21, 2011, www.huffingtonpost.com/2011/04/21/cdc-predicts-every-us-wil_n_852125.html.

41. Glenn Kramon, "Smoking Ban Near on Flights in the US," The New York Times, April 17, 1988, www.nytimes.com/1988/04/17/us/smoking-ban-near-on-flights-in-us.html.

42. "History of the Framingham Heart Study," Framingham Heart Study, www.framinghamheartstudy.org/about/history.html.

43. "Trends Progress Report," National Cancer Institute, http://progressreport.cancer.gov/doc_detail.asp?pid=1&did=2009&chid=93&coid=920&mid=#trends.

44. "Achievements in Public Health 1900-1999: Decline in Deaths from Heart Disease and Stroke, United States 1900 to 1999," Centers for Disease Control and Prevention, www.cdc.gov/mmwr/preview/mmwrhtml/mm4830a1.htm.

45. Cynthia Ogden, et al., "Prevalence of Overweight, Obesity and Extreme Obesity Among Adults: United States, Trends 1960-1962 through 2007-2008," Centers for Disease Control and Prevention, June 2010, www.cdc.gov/NCHS/data/hestat/obesity_adult_07_08/obesity_adult_07_08.pdf.

46. Nellie Bristol, "US Target Disease Prevention in Health Reforms," The Lancet, Dec. 12, 2009, http://download.thelancet.com/pdfs/journals/lancet/PIIS0140673609621073.pdf.

47. "Crude and Age Adjusted Percentage of Civilian, Noninstitutionalized Population with Diagnosed Diabetes, United States 1980-2009," Centers for Disease Control and Prevention, www.cdc.gov/diabetes/statistics/prev/national/figage.htm.

48. For background, see the following CQ Researcher reports: Barbara Mantel, "Preventing Obesity," Oct. 1, 2010, pp. 797-820; Alan Greenblatt, "Obesity Epidemic," Jan. 31, 2003, pp. 73-104; and Adriel Bettelheim, "Obesity and Health," Jan. 15, 1999, pp. 25-48.

49. "Affordable Care Act: Laying the Foundation for Prevention," HealthReform.gov, www.healthreform.gov/newsroom/acaprevention.html.

50. Let's Move, www.letsmove.gov.

51. Ibid., http://articles.chicagotribune.com/2009-08-05/news/0908050021_1_health-care-bike-paths-additional-pork-barrel-projects.

52. "Recommendations for Adults," U.S. Preventive Services Task Force, www.uspreventiveservicestaskforce.org/adultrec.htm.

53. Lauren Cox, "Stop Annual Mammograms, Govt. Panel Tells Women Under 50," ABC News, Nov. 16, 2009, http://abcnews.go.com/Health/OnCallPlusBreastCancerNews/mammogram-guidelines-spur-debate-early-detection/story?id=9099145.

54. "Trends in Tobacco Use," American Lung Cancer Association, July 2011, www.lungusa.org/finding-cures/our-research/trend-reports/Tobacco-Trend-Report.pdf.

55. "Tobacco Use: Targeting the Nation's Leading Killer At a Glance 2011," Centers for Disease Control and Prevention, www.cdc.gov/chronicdisease/resources/publications/AAG/osh.htm.

56. "Frequently Asked Questions about Calculating Obesity-Related Risk," Centers for Disease Control and Prevention, undated, accessed Jan. 2, 2012, www.cdc.gov/PDF/Frequently_Asked_Questions_About_Calculating_Obesity-Related_risk.pdf.

57. "HHS Announces $750 million Investment in Prevention," Department of Health and Human Services, www.hhs.gov/news/press/2011pres/02/20110209b.html.

58. "The Affordable Care Act's Prevention and Public Health Fund in Your State," Department of Health and Human Services, www.healthcare.gov/news/factsheets/2011/02/prevention02092011a.html.

59. "Employer-Sponsored Health Insurance: Trends in Cost and Access," Agency for Healthcare Research and Quality, www.ahrq.gov/research/empspria/empspria.htm.

60. "Promoting Workplace Health," The Healthy States Initiative, January 2008, www.healthystates.csg.org/NR/rdonlyres/B6FC0AB2-A14A-4321-AAF8-778E57AA9752/0/LPBWorkplaceHealth_screen.pdf.

61. Lenny Bernstein, "Do Programs that Pay People to Lose Weight Really Work?," *The Washington Post*, Oct. 10, 2011, www.washingtonpost.com/lifestyle/wellness/do-programs-that-pay-people-to-lose-weight-really-work/2011/10/06/gIQAiIABbL_story.html.

62. "Affordable Care Act Helps Improve the Health of the American Workforce, Increase Workplace Health Programs," Centers for Disease Control and Prevention, press release, Sept. 30, 2011, www.cdc.gov/media/releases/2011/p0930_improve_healthcare.html.

63. William Neuman, "Ad Rules Stall, Keeping Cereal a Cartoon Staple," *The New York Times*, July 23, 2010, www.nytimes.com/2010/07/24/business/media/24food.html.

64. Gretchen Goetz, "Obama Urged to Push Kids' Food Marketing Regs," *Food Safety News*, Sept. 29, 2011, www.foodsafetynews.com/2011/09/academics-urge-obama-to-push-child-food-marketing-regulations.

65. Barbara Mantel, "Preventing Obesity," *CQ Researcher*, Oct. 1, 2010, pp. 977-1000.

66. *Ibid.*

67. Jonathan Berman, "Proposed FDA Regulations to Require 'Chain Restaurants' to Post Nutrition Information," Sept. 27, 2011, www.mondaq.com/unitedstates/x/146784/Healthcare+Food+Drugs+Law/Proposed+FDA+Regulations+To+Require+Chain+Restaurants+To+Post+Nutrition+Information.

68. Eli Y. Adashi, "CDC Director Talks About the Nation's Biggest (and Winnable?) Health Battles," *Medscape Internal Medicine*, Nov. 5, 2010, www.medscape.com/viewarticle/731362.

69. Jim Staats, "Tiburon's Trans Fat Ban Started National Movement," *The Marin Independent Journal*, Feb. 3, 2007, www.marinij.com/fastsearchresults/ci_5155266.

70. Thomas J. Lueck and Kim Severson, "New York Bans Most Trans Fats in Restaurants," *The New York Times*, Dec. 6, 2006, www.nytimes.com/2006/12/06/nyregion/06fat.html.

71. "Million Hearts: About the Campaign," Department of Health and Human Services, htttp://millionhearts.hhs.gov/about-mh.shtml.

72. Robert Lowes, "Medicare Decision to Cover Obesity Counseling Mostly Praised," *Medscape News*, Nov. 30, 2011, www.medscape.com/viewarticle/754531.

73. "Decision Memo for Intensive Behavioral Therapy for Cardiovascular Disease," Centers for Medicare and Medicaid Services, Nov. 8, 2011, www.cms.gov/medicare-coverage-database/details/nca-decision-memo.aspx?NCAId=248.

74. Carla Carter, "Smartphone Apps Keep Health at Your Fingertips, From Fitness to First Aid," *USA Today*, Feb. 2011, http://yourlife.usatoday.com/health/story/2011/02/Smartphone-apps-keep-health-at-your-fingertips-from-fitness-to-first-aid/44130448/1.

75. Chris Gullo, "By 2016: $400M Market for Health, Fitness Apps," *Mobihealthnews*, Nov. 28, 2011, http://mobihealthnews.com/14884/by-2016-400m-market-for-health-fitness-apps/.

76. "Trends in Current Cigarette Smoking Among High School Students and Adults, United States, 1965-2010, Centers for Disease Control and Prevention, www.cdc.gov/tobacco/data_statistics/tables/trends/cig_smoking/index.htm.

77. "Exercise or Physical Activity," Centers for Disease Control and Prevention, www.cdc.gov/nchs/fastats/exercise.htm.

78. Kim Severson, "Told to Eat Its Vegetables, America Orders French Fries," *The New York Times*, Sept. 24, 2010, www.nytimes.com/2010/09/25/health/policy/25vegetables.html?pagewanted=all.

79. "America's Health Rankings Finds Preventable Chronic Disease on the Rise; Obesity, Diabetes Undermining Country's Overall Health," United Health Foundation, Dec. 6, 2011, www.americashealthrankings.org/mediacenter/mediacenter1.aspx.

BIBLIOGRAPHY

Selected Sources

Books

Duffy, John, *The Sanitarians: A History of American Public Health*, University of Illinois Press, 1990.
A preeminent historian of medicine examines public health in the United States.

Faust, Halley, and Paul Menzel, eds., *Prevention vs. Treatment: What's the Right Balance?*, Oxford Press, 2012.
A preventive medicine physician (Faust) and a philosophy professor (Menzel) review a range of issues on preventive care, including spending on prevention and preventive care's apparent lack of emphasis in the medical field.

Guthman, Julie, *Weighing In: Obesity, Food Justice and the Limits of Capitalism*, University of California Press, 2011.
An associate professor in the Community Studies Department at the University of California, Santa Cruz, takes on the "obesity epidemic," challenging many widely held assumptions about its causes and consequences.

Articles

Kliff, Sarah, "What if Prevention Doesn't Save Money?" *The Washington Post*, Dec. 12, 2011, www.washington post.com/blogs/ezra-klein/post/what-if-prevention-doesnt-save-money/2011/12/11/gIQAM60OnO_blog .html.
A health care reporter considers whether preventive services reduce medical costs.

Konrad, Walecia, "Preventing Sickness, With Plenty of Red Tape," *The New York Times*, Sept. 20, 2011, p. D5, www.nytimes.com/2011/09/20/health/policy/ 20consumer.html.
Ambiguity persists among consumers and insurers as to what qualifies as preventive care.

Landro, Laura, "Improving Global Health: Focus on Chronic Disease," *The Wall Street Journal*, Nov. 21, 2011, http://online.wsj.com/article/SB1000142405 2970203699404577042540087339770.html.
Health care experts discuss medical challenges in developing countries.

Lazar, Kay, "Employers Seeing Pluses in Keeping Workers Healthy," *The Boston Globe*, May 31, 2011, p. 1, articles.boston.com/2011-05-31/bostonworks/ 29604741_1_wellness-programs-health-promotion-programs-professor-of-health-economics.
More employers are embracing wellness programs to foster healthier lifestyles.

Stewart, Kirsten, "Mixed Messages on Health Prevention Baffle Consumers," *The Salt Lake Tribune* (Utah), May 26, 2011, www.sltrib.com/sltrib/home2/5187 6215-183/cancer-health-prevention-burt.html.csp.
Medicare beneficiaries are taking advantage of new federal regulations that give them free wellness checkups, but few are lining up for high-cost procedures.

Williams, Misty, "Costs Inspire Wellness Plans, Higher Deductibles," *The Atlanta Journal-Constitution*, Nov. 24, 2011, p. A1.
Rising out-of-pocket health care costs are encouraging more and more Atlanta-area workers to join wellness programs.

Reports

"F as in Fat: How Obesity Threatens America's Future," Trust for America's Health, 2011, Robert Wood Johnson Foundation, http://healthyamericans.org/ report/88/.
Adult obesity rates increased in 16 states in the past year and did not decline in any state. Twelve states now have obesity rates above 30 percent.

"Global Status Report on Noncommunicable Diseases, 2010," World Health Organization, 2011, www.who.int/nmh/publications/ncd_report2010/ en/.
WHO presents the latest global figures on noncommunicable diseases and recommendations for addressing them.

"Healthier Americans for a Healthier Economy," Trust for America's Health, November 2011, http:// healthyamericans.org/report/90/.
Six case studies examine how health affects the ability of states and cities to attract and retain employers and how wellness programs can improve productivity and reduce health spending.

"Measuring the Health Effects of Sprawl: A National Analysis of Physical Activity, Obesity and Chronic Disease," Smart Growth America, September 2003, www.smartgrowthamerica.org/report/Health Sprawl8.03.pdf.
An advocacy group discusses research showing connections among urban sprawl, weight gain and high blood pressure.

"Preventing Childhood Obesity: Health in the Balance," Institute of Medicine, Sept. 29, 2004, www.iom.edu/Reports/2004/Preventing-Childhood-Obesity-Health-in-the-Balance.aspx.

A leading medical advisory group offers a comprehensive national strategy that recommends specific actions for families, schools, industry, communities and the government.

"Preventing Chronic Disease: The New Public Health," Alliance for Health Reform, September 2001, www.allhealth.org/publications/Public_health/Preventing_Chronic_Disease_New_Public_Health_108.pdf.
The United States faces "an epidemic of chronic disease," and preventive steps at the community level are an important antidote, says the nonpartisan organization.

For More Information

Centers for Disease Control and Prevention, 1600 Clifton Rd., Atlanta, GA 30333; 800-232-4636; www.cdc.gov. U.S. agency tasked with protecting public health and safety primarily through disease control and prevention.

National Complete Streets Coalition, 1707 L St., N.W., Suite 250, Washington, DC 20036; 202-207-3355; www.completestreets.org. Advocates for the development of state, local and national policies to encourage making streets safe and accessible to all types of transportation, including walking and biking.

Partnership for Prevention, 1015 18th St., N.W., Suite 300, Washington, DC 20036; 202-833-0009; www.prevent.org. A group of business, nonprofit and government leaders advocating evidence-based disease prevention and health promotion.

Robert Wood Johnson Foundation, Route 1 and College Road East, PO Box 2316, Princeton, NJ 08543; 877-843-7953; www.rwjf.org. Provides research and grants for health-improvement activities.

Smart Growth America, 1707 L St., N.W., Suite 1050, Washington, DC 20036; 202-207-3355; www.smartgrowthamerica.org. Advocates neighborhood planning that allows for sidewalks, bike paths and easy access to public transportation.

Trust for America's Health, 1730 M St., N.W., Suite 900, Washington, DC 20036; 202-223-9870; http://healthyamericans.org. Promotes public health and disease prevention.

United Health Foundation, Mail Stop: W150, 9900 Bren Road East, Minnetonka, MN 55343; www.unitedhealthfoundation.org/Main/Default.aspx. Provides funding and resources for programs that lead to better health outcomes and healthier communities.

World Health Organization, Avenue Appia 20m 1211, Geneva, 27, Switzerland; +41 22 791 21 11; www.who.int/en/. United Nations agency that coordinates international public health efforts.

16

Aging Population

Alan Greenblatt

Activists on Capitol Hill urge lawmakers on April 15 not to cut Medicare, the federal government's health insurance program for the elderly and disabled. The same day, however, the majority-Republican House approved a budget plan that would rein in Medicare costs. Democrats oppose the plan and intend to use it as a campaign issue in 2012. Economists say entitlement programs must be scaled back to control the country's deficit.

From *CQ Researcher*, July 15, 2011

J ames Kempthorne is running out of money. "He saved, or thought he was saving, for retirement," says his son, Dirk, a former Republican governor of Idaho. "He thought he would be okay, even if he lived to be 90."

But on the 4th of July, the senior Kempthorne turned 96. "His savings are gone, and his only source of income is Social Security — Social Security and a couple of sons," Dirk Kempthorne says.

As the proud patriarch of a successful family, James Kempthorne isn't happy about having to rely on his children for help. But he's not alone. Nearly 10 million adult children over age 50 in the United States provide care or financial help to their aging parents.[1]

Such numbers are only going to grow. The oldest members of the baby boom generation — 78 million Americans born between 1946 and 1964 — are turning 65 this year. The sheer number of them means that one will turn 65 every 8 seconds until 2030.[2]

But the population of the "old old" — those over age 85 — is growing, proportionately, faster. America has the largest number of centenarians in the world, at 72,000 — a total that has doubled over the past 20 years and will at least double again by 2020, according to the Census Bureau.[3]

That's the result of good news: increased life expectancy that stems from improved medicine and nutrition and a drastic decline over recent decades in infant mortality.

"I assume that most people would like to live a long, full life, and that's increasingly possible," says John Rother, policy director at AARP, the major advocacy group for seniors, formerly known as the American Association of Retired Persons. "Advances in health care make that more likely for people."

379

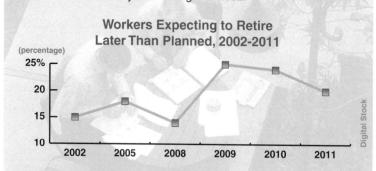

More Americans Expect to Delay Retirement

One-fifth of American workers say they expect to retire later than planned — a lower percentage than in 2009 and 2010, but higher than when the economy was stronger in 2002.

Workers Expecting to Retire Later Than Planned, 2002-2011

(percentage)

Source: Ruth Helman, et al., "The 2011 Retirement Confidence Survey: Confidence Drops to Record Lows, Reflecting 'the New Normal,' " Employee Benefit Research Institute, March 2011, www.ebri.org/pdf/surveys/rcs/2011/ebri_03-2011_no355_rcs-11.pdf.

Still, Rother acknowledges that a good deal of concern exists about the challenges posed by the aging population. The rapid growth in the number of seniors — which will be much higher than population growth among young and working-age Americans — will lead to changes across society, including pressures on the workforce and federal budget.[4]

That's despite the fact that the United States is aging less rapidly than other developed nations, such as Germany, Italy, Spain and Japan. By 2015, the population of working-age people — typically defined as those between ages 15 and 64 — will begin to decline throughout the developed world, with the United States as the sole major exception.

"The demographics are obviously more favorable than just about anywhere else in the rich world," says Richard Jackson, who directs the Global Aging Initiative at the Center for Strategic and International Studies, a think tank in Washington. "We have an aging population, but at the end of the day, when the last of the boomers have passed on to that great Woodstock in the sky, we'll be about as old as Japan and Italy are today. And we'll have a growing population and not a stagnant or a declining one."

But the United States has a major problem those other countries don't have. Spending on health care is far greater here than in other developed countries and will only rise with the aging of the population.[5]

"We look as though our problem is very affordable, relative to other countries," says Neil Howe, president of LifeCourse Associates, a demographics consulting firm in Great Falls, Va., and author of several books about demographics. "The big factor that pushes hugely in the other direction is health care. We are anomalous in that we have a system in which health care costs are growing uncontrollably even before the age wave."

Total enrollment in Medicare, the federal government's health insurance program for the elderly, is expected to rise from 47 million today to just over 80 million by 2030.[6] Richard Foster, Medicare's chief actuary, predicts the program's trust fund could be depleted by 2024.[7]

The growing number of aging Americans also will put enormous strains on Social Security and Medicaid, the state-federal health insurance program for the poor and disabled, which pays for more than 40 percent of nursing home care in the United States.

"What were long-term problems are now at our doorstep," says Maya MacGuineas, director of the Fiscal Policy Program at the New America Foundation and president of the nonpartisan Committee for a Responsible Federal Budget, which advocates greater fiscal discipline.

On April 15, the U.S. House of Representatives approved a budget plan that would attempt to rein in Medicare costs by converting it from an insurance program to a limited subsidy for seniors buying private insurance. The plan is unpopular with the public, according to polls, and Democrats not only oppose it but plan to use it as a campaign issue in 2012.[8]

"We will never allow any effort to dismantle the program and force benefit cuts upon seniors under the guise of deficit reduction," five Democratic senators wrote June 6 to Vice President Joseph Biden, who had been leading negotiations with members of Congress on debt reduction. "Our nation's seniors are not responsible for the fiscal challenges we face, and they should not be responsible for shouldering the burden of reducing our deficits."

But many policy analysts insist some changes to entitlements benefiting seniors, particularly Medicare, will be necessary to bring down the federal deficit.

On average, says Richard W. Johnson, director of the retirement policy program at the Urban Institute, a centrist think tank in Washington, Americans are healthier than 30 years ago. But there's been an increase since the late 1990s in the number of Americans in their late 40s or 50s who are disabled or suffer ailments that make it harder for them to work.

"We're seeing increases in the number of handicapped people in late middle age, mostly because of obesity and sedentary lifestyles," says demographer Phillip Longman of the New America Foundation, a liberal think tank in Washington. "Here we have this generation that's physically unfit and has no savings and whose health care we can't afford at current prices."

Such health challenges are going to make it difficult for many Americans to work longer, which economists argue will be necessary to shore up not only Social Security but also personal retirement savings.

Rother, the AARP policy director, stirred up a great deal of controversy with remarks quoted in *The Wall Street Journal* that suggested the seniors' lobbying group, which had helped torpedo a plan to partially privatize Social Security in 2005, might be willing to accept benefit cuts in the program.[9] The group immediately sought to downplay Rother's comments.

Still, the open debate about cutting entitlement programs, combined with losses in the stock market and the collapse of the housing bubble, have left elder Americans nervous about their financial futures.[10] A "retirement confidence" survey by the Employee Benefit Research Institute found that the percentage of workers "not at all" confident they will be able to afford a comfortable retirement rose from 22 percent last year to 27 percent this year, the highest level in the 21 years the group has conducted the survey.[11]

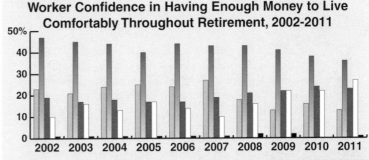

Workers Gloomy About Retirement Prospects

More than one-fourth of American workers are "not at all" confident that they will have enough money to last through retirement. That's nearly a three-fold increase from nine years earlier. Fewer than one in eight workers is "very confident" about a comfortable retirement.

Worker Confidence in Having Enough Money to Live Comfortably Throughout Retirement, 2002-2011

Legend:
- Very confident
- Somewhat confident
- Not too confident
- Not at all confident
- Don't know/refused to answer

Source: Ruth Helman, et al., "The 2011 Retirement Confidence Survey: Confidence Drops to Record Lows, Reflecting 'the New Normal,' " Employee Benefit Research Institute, March 2011, www.ebri.org/pdf/surveys/rcs/2011/ebri_03-2011_no355_rcs-11.pdf.

And it's going to be harder for younger Americans to support the swelling population of seniors. Dowell Myers, a demographer at the University of Southern California, says the ratio of those over 65 to those between 25 and 64 has been constant for 40 years, with 24 seniors for every 100 working-age Americans. But that "dependency ratio" will spike by two-thirds over the next 20 years, to 38 seniors per 100 working-age adults, he says.

"When we come out of this recession, we're going to have fewer new workers and more boomers retiring," Myers says. "That's when we'll feel the changes."

As Americans contemplate the consequences of an aging population, here are some of the questions they're debating:

Should Americans work longer?

In March, the Centers for Disease Control and Prevention announced that the U.S. death rate had hit a new low while life expectancy had once again ticked up. A male born in 2009 could expect to live 75.7 years, while a female could expect to live to 80.6.[12]

Those numbers are a vast improvement over life expectancy in 1935, when Social Security was created. Life expectancy at birth then was just 58 for men and 62 for women.[13]

Cities Struggle to Meet Growing Needs of Elderly

"We have a country that's aging everywhere."

Rockford's not doing well. The Illinois city, about 90 miles northwest of Chicago, was once a leading furniture-making center, but those jobs are mostly gone. As a result, Rockford's unemployment rate was among the highest among U.S. cities during the recent recession.

Most jobs that remain are snatched up by workers 55 and older — about all that's left of Rockford's working-age population. Rockford Mayor Larry Morrissey, who is in his 40s, was elected on a platform of promising economic revitalization that would help bring young people — including natives who've left — back to town.

Without strong cultural amenities or a major university, it's been a tough sell. Lack of jobs presents the biggest obstacle. Even entry-level jobs paying just above minimum wage that once would have gone to teenagers or people in their 20s are now largely held by workers in their 50s. "We have an aging population, and it's getting poorer," said James Ryan, Rockford's city administrator.[1]

Rockford may be an extreme case, but it's not unique. Many former industrial cities in the Northeast and Midwest are growing both older and less affluent. Among the nation's 100 largest metropolitan areas, the ones that have had the highest percentage growth of seniors are struggling places such as Scranton, Pa., Buffalo, N.Y., and Youngstown, Ohio.[2]

"They have higher concentrations of seniors," says William Frey, a demographer at the Brookings Institution think tank who has analyzed 2010 census data on the location of seniors. "The younger people have left."

There are metropolitan areas in Florida that have a high density of people over age 65. But the number of seniors and aging baby boomers who pick up and move to warmer climes in Florida and Arizona is relatively small. Most people retire in their own homes, or at least their own counties.

"You can certainly find lots of upper-middle-class baby boomers who are coping quite well, moving into college towns where there are good social services available and good medical services," says demographer Phillip Longman, a senior research fellow at the New America Foundation. "The vast majority of baby boomers, however, are often stuck underwater in postwar tract housing and more recent exurban construction. They can't get out if they wanted to."

Frey says it's important for communities, particularly in the suburbs that were planned with younger populations in mind, to learn to adapt to aging ones. Every metropolitan area, he says, is seeing marked growth in its senior population — and will see more as boomers age. "The baby boom python keeps rolling along," he says.

In recent years, many local governments and nonprofit groups have tried to come up with programs, such as increased transit, that will help address the needs of populations that are "aging in place."

About 40 localities, including Atlanta, Iowa City, Iowa, and Pima County, Ariz., have passed ordinances mapping out voluntary or mandatory design requirements for new-home construction that would accommodate the needs of seniors and the disabled, sparing more of them from moving to nursing homes. "We could save a lot of money if individuals could continue to live in their own homes and

Those averages were held down by much higher rates of infant mortality. Most people who lived to adulthood could expect to live past 65, even then.

Still, people are living longer — and spending more years in retirement. Those two facts are putting additional strain on both Social Security and Medicare finances. "The typical beneficiary is expecting to receive benefits for almost nine years longer than when the Social Security

program started," says Charles Blahous, a trustee of the Social Security program and research fellow at the conservative Hoover Institution at Stanford University.

Not only are people living longer, but they are retiring earlier. Most men worked, on average, just past 65 during the 1950s. Now, the average retirement age is 62, says Blahous, who was an economic aide to former President George W. Bush.

receive in-home nursing if they need it," says Rep. Jan Schakowsky, D-Ill., who has introduced "inclusive home design" legislation at the federal level.

Helping seniors cope with chronic disease is another way to keep them out of nursing homes. That's why Elder Services of Merrimack Valley in Lawrence, Mass., has been working with seniors and physicians to help coordinate management of prescription drug regimens and other treatments. "We're not a medical facility, but what we have is the ability to draw elders in and educate them on their health care," says Rosanne DiStefano, the facility's executive director.

DiStefano's program has been widely imitated in Massachusetts, as have a number of other innovations designed to help residents adjust to old age. But such programs are having trouble attracting funding in the present budget environment.

Many local governments are providing exercise classes and nutrition assistance for seniors, but a survey by the National Association of Area Agencies on Aging found that finance and funding problems are the biggest challenge localities face in adjusting to an aging population. Thirty percent of local governments say that their overall revenues are in decline.[3]

"If you go community by community, sure, some have developed programs that are better than others," says Robert H. Binstock, a professor of aging and public policy at Case Western Reserve University. "Overall, it's a tremendous problem."

It's not just the lack of programming help offered by governments that is a problem for aging communities, but also a decline in basic services and amenities, Binstock says.

"You've got lots of places that are aging, and the young people are moving out, particularly in rural areas," he says. "You're going to have communities that aren't even going to have grocery stores."

Some states have a youth population that is growing more rapidly than the older population, notably in the

Eighty-year-old Ada Noda, of St. Augustine, Fla., developed health problems and couldn't work, forcing her to declare bankruptcy. Aging trends are seen by many experts as a significant reason for the climb in health care costs. But health economists say medical costs are rising largely because of the increasing availability of expensive treatments.

Southwest, says Frey. But aging populations are growing in many parts of the country not accustomed to accommodating them.

The localities where older residents are starting to predominate, such as Rockford, "are the ones that are going to be most severely hit," says Frey. "We have a country that's aging everywhere, but it's only young in certain spots."

— Alan Greenblatt

[1]Ted C. Fishman, *Shock of Gray* (2010), p. 235.

[2]For background, see Thomas J. Billitteri, "Blighted Cities," *CQ Researcher*, Nov. 12, 2010, pp. 941-964.

[3]"The Maturing of America: Communities Moving Forward for an Aging Population," National Association of Area Agencies on Aging, June 2011, www.n4a.org/files/MOA_FINAL_Rpt.pdf, p. iii.

The age for retiring with full Social Security benefits is slowly rising to 67. Some politicians and economists believe it needs to be raised further. That was the recommendation of President Barack Obama's debt commission last year and is a policy direction lately followed in several European countries.

"What we really need to do is raise the early-entitlement age, which has always been 62 since it was introduced, in

1956 for women and in 1962 for men," says the Urban Institute's Johnson. "The problem with having the early retirement age relatively young is that it does send a signal that 62 is an appropriate time to retire. It's not good for society as a whole, and it's also not good for individuals."

Many people may not be able to retire early, regardless of the official retirement ages set by Social Security.

U.S. Population Growing Grayer

A record 40 million Americans are age 65 or older, nearly double the total four decades ago. The number of seniors has risen every decade since 1880.

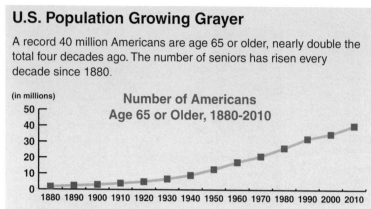

(in millions)

Number of Americans Age 65 or Older, 1880-2010

Sources: "Life Expectancy for Social Security," Social Security Administration, www.ssa.gov/history/lifeexpect.html; "Profile of General Population and Housing Characteristics: 2010," U.S. Census Bureau, 2010,factfinder2.census.gov/ faces/ tableservices/jsf/pages/productview.xhtml?pid=DEC_10_DP_DPDP1&prodTy pe=table.

Americans do a bad job of saving in general, and retirement accounts, in particular, are not as full as they should be. Many people have yet to make up recent stock market losses, and a weak housing market has largely dashed hopes of turning homes into assets that can offer support in retirement.

Fewer private employers are offering guaranteed pension benefits, and pensions and other retirement benefits for government workers are under political pressure as well.[14] The result is that about half of U.S. households are at risk of not being able to maintain their living standards in retirement, according to the Center for Retirement Research at Boston College.[15]

More Americans might need to keep working, and market demand for them to do so may also rise, suggests MacGuineas, of the New America Foundation. "We're actually going to be having labor-market shortages as baby boomers move out of the workforce," she says.

A number of social scientists have speculated about whether boomers will keep working longer for that reason or perhaps out of a desire to keep mentally and socially active. Many have speculated that the next generation of older Americans will want to volunteer or work part time, if not stay in their same job past the normal retirement age. "There's not going to be a shrinking entry-level workforce, but it's not going to be growing" either, says Jackson of the Center for Strategic and International Studies. "There may be demand for older workers."

But not everyone is convinced that many more people will be able to keep working well into their 60s or even 70s. Robert H. Binstock, a professor of aging and public policy at Case Western Reserve University, notes that although people are living longer, they're also afflicted with chronic diseases for longer periods of time. "A lot of them can't do their jobs anymore," he says. "The whole notion that everybody is going to be able to keep doing their job until 70, it's silly."

Blahous, the former Bush administration official, dismisses such arguments. Social Security already makes provisions for disabilities, and people worked, on average, longer a half-century ago, he says. People take early retirement more often, Blahous says, "not because more people are physically breaking down. It's because it's financially beneficial."

But putting aside arguments about whether people are physically capable of working longer, there's also the question of whether they can find work. Alicia Munnell, director of the Boston College Center for Retirement Research, says employers will never say they wouldn't hire older people —"that's against the law" — but they are "very ho hum" about the prospect. Her center has conducted surveys that show employers are worried about issues such as older workers' stamina, ability to learn new skills and adaptability to changing technology.

Thus, although the economics of both entitlement programs and household finances would seem to dictate that more Americans will have to work longer, their chances of doing so might not be as good as they would wish.

"We see employers willing to keep older workers, but they are reluctant to hire [older] people who are new to the payroll," says the Urban Institute's Johnson. "We know that when older people lose their jobs, getting a new job is harder, and the periods of unemployment are longer."

Will spending on health care for the elderly bankrupt the United States?

Health care costs already consume more than double the share of the economy that they did 30 years ago. They are expected to consume $2.8 trillion this year, or

17.9 percent of gross domestic product (GDP), according to the federal Centers on Medicare and Medicaid Services (CMS). That's up from 8.1 percent of the economy in 1975.[16]

Medicare and Medicaid spending have grown at a similar pace. The two programs, which provide coverage for seniors and the poor and disabled, respectively, are on course to grow from about 4 percent of GDP in 2008 to nearly 7 percent by 2035.[17]

The 2010 federal health-care law, known as the Affordable Care Act, was designed to cut Medicare costs by nearly $120 billion over the next five years.[18] But Medicare's actuaries worry that savings from the 2010 law can't all be relied upon. That's because Congress has frequently canceled plans to lower Medicare fees for hospitals and physicians.[19] As a result, the Medicare trust fund is on course to run out of money in 2024 — five years earlier than previously predicted — according to Richard Foster, the chief actuary at CMS.

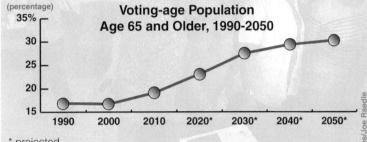

Elderly a Growing Share of Electorate

The proportion of the American electorate age 65 and older has risen modestly over the past 20 years, from 17 percent in 1990 to 19 percent in 2010. But it is expected to grow sharply over the next 40 years, topping 30 percent by 2050.

Voting-age Population Age 65 and Older, 1990-2050

(percentage)

35% — 30 — 25 — 20 — 15

1990 2000 2010 2020* 2030* 2040* 2050*

* projected

Sources: "United States 1990 Census of Population," U.S. Census Bureau, www.census.gov/prod/cen1990/cp1/cp-1-1.pdf; "United States 2000 Census of Population and Housing," U.S. Census Bureau, November 2010, www.census.gov/prod/cen2000/phc-1-1-pt1.pdf; "Projections of the Population by Selected Age Groups and Sex for the United States: 2010 to 2050," U.S. Census Bureau, 2008, www.census.gov/population/www/projections/files/nation/summary/np2008-t2.xls.

Getty Images/Joe Raedle

Rising health care costs are a burden not just for the government but for individuals as well. "We're spending about $8,000 more annually for insurance for a family of four than we did in 2000," says Paul Hewitt, vice president of research at the Coalition for Affordable Health Coverage, an advocacy group in Washington.

Experts say aging trends are a significant reason for the climb in health care costs and an important source of pressure on the federal budget. "It's worth keeping in mind that a significant share of health care growth is demographically based," says Jackson of the Center for Strategic and International Studies. "You're looking at a steep rise in cost just because of the rise in the average age of the beneficiaries — the aging of the aged."

But health economists say aging trends are far from the whole story. Medical costs are rising largely because of the ever-increasing availability of expensive treatments in the health care system — a system that treats young and old alike. "The real problem is not the aging of the population, but the rise of health care costs," says Case Western's Binstock, a former president of the Gerontological

Society of America. "We don't look at the elephant in the room here, which is the enormous profits of the medical-industrial complex."

Most experts agree that major alterations are in order. Some are discouraged that the two major parties seem worlds apart on health care issues. "Both parties have to recognize the need to compromise," says the Urban Institute's Johnson.

That does not appear imminent. Republicans have pledged to repeal the 2010 health care law, considered one of Obama's signature achievements, while Democrats intend to use the GOP's controversial plan to turn Medicare into something resembling a voucher program against them in the 2012 elections.

Even as congressional Republicans seek to slash Medicare and other entitlements, they oppose the Independent Payment Advisory Board, established by the 2010 health care law, which is meant to make recommendations for Medicare spending cuts when its growth exceeds GDP growth by more than 1 percent.

"Cutting providers eventually cuts benefits because they are less available," said Sen. Jon Kyl, R-Ariz., the minority whip. "You don't have as many physicians, for example, to take care of Medicare patients, so either

Walter Breuning celebrates his 113th birthday at a retirement home in Great Falls, Mont., on Sept. 21, 2009. At his death in April 2011 at age 114, he was the last American man born in the 19th century and one of the world's oldest people. The oldest of the 78 million Americans born during the post-World War II baby boom are turning 65 this year, while the share of the population over 85 is growing even faster.

people have to wait a lot longer or they never get to see the physician they'd like to."[20]

But if a political deal is not reached, the consequences could be dire, experts warn. The Congressional Budget Office (CBO) says health care costs, on their current course, could swallow all of GDP by 2082.[21]

The risk of bankruptcy from health costs in particular, says Hewitt, are exactly what bond rating agencies have warned about when they have threatened recently to downgrade U.S. debt — meaning the federal government may not be able to borrow money as cheaply because there's more risk that it won't be able to cover its interest payments.

"Three-quarters of the projected deficits over the next 10 years are new health care spending, according to CBO," Hewitt says. "If you could hold health costs at 2011 levels, you wouldn't have any deficit of note in 2021."

"There's no question that we're on course for health care costs to bankrupt the country," says the New America Foundation's MacGuineas. "You can't have anything growing faster than GDP forever, because it consumes more and more of the economy."

That may be the greatest danger. MacGuineas, like other budget experts, predicts that some sort of change will be made in health care spending, because present trends are not sustainable. But the changes won't come without pain and political difficulty. In the meantime, rising health costs may continue to squeeze spending on other programs.

Will the young and old fight over resources?

When he unveiled his budget in February, New York City Mayor Michael Bloomberg warned that the city faced tough choices because of a budget shortfall of nearly $5 billion. "Everybody expects you to do everything," the mayor said. "That's not the world we live in."[22]

Bloomberg felt he had no choice but to threaten layoffs of more than 4,000 school teachers. At the same time, however, his budget contained a new initiative: the construction of 10 "megacenters" for senior citizens.

Both ideas were ultimately rejected by the city council. Still, says the Urban Institute's Johnson, "That was striking. It seems to be the essence of the potential for intergenerational combat."

The idea that aging boomers will drain the nation's resources through entitlements such as Social Security and Medicare — and that younger generations are not just going to resent but protest it — has seeped into popular culture. It forms the premise, for example, of satirical novels such as Christopher Buckley's *Boomsday* and Albert Brooks' *2030*.

While older voters demand full funding for Social Security and Medicare, younger voters may worry that the growth of those expensive programs is crowding out spending on areas that benefit them more directly, such as education and transportation. Or the young might want to see entitlements cut in order to chop deficits that they'll eventually have to repay.

"I think it's amazing we've gotten this far without younger generations getting more agitated about constantly investing in seniors, with no similar promises made for productive investments for young people," says MacGuineas.

Voting schisms along generational lines have become apparent in some recent elections. "You had this overwhelming tilt of millennials to the Democrats and Obama in 2008," says Howe, co-author of *Millennials Rising*, about the generation born between 1982 and 2002. "Obama and McCain" — Sen. John McCain, Obama's GOP opponent —"were dead even among those 30 and over."

Older Americans voted disproportionately for GOP candidates in 2010. But Democrats won a special election in May in a traditionally Republican congressional district in upstate New York. The election was widely interpreted as a referendum on the House GOP's plan to turn Medicare into a form of voucher program, with seniors turning out in force to reject the idea and the Republican candidate.

"Over the years, until very recently, there's been very little evidence that older people vote on the basis of old-age benefits as a bloc," says Binstock at Case Western Reserve. "It's only in 2010 and the 26th District in New York that you begin to see some signs of this, particularly in relation to Medicare."

Howe and others say boomers, throughout their adult lives, have not voted as a predictable bloc. If they start to in old age, however, they would be formidable. As the population ages, the electorate — the group of people actually voting — is growing older at a disproportionate rate.

The percentage of the voting-age population that is over 65 is expected to climb by more than 10 percent over the next 25 years.[23] And, because older voters tend to go to the polls more regularly, their share of the electorate will climb even more, Binstock predicts.

Some political scientists are skeptical that there will be a young person's revolt, or even noticeable friction between the generations. "I don't buy the generational-conflict theory," says Alan Abramowitz, a political scientist at Emory University. "Programs that benefit the elderly, such as Social Security and Medicare, also benefit their children and grandchildren. If you cut benefits for the elderly, one consequence will be to shift costs onto their children and reduce income available to pay for, among other things, education for their children."

Others echo this point, noting that old-age entitlements keep seniors from being a financial burden on their children, while older voters will want to see young people succeed through education — in part, to help pay the taxes that fund their entitlements.

"Older people really do care about their grandchildren and obviously have a financial stake in having a productive workforce," says Rother, the AARP vice president. "Younger people need to look forward to a secure retirement, and they obviously can't vote to limit Medicare without having repercussions for them later."

Still, some observers say resentment among the young is only likely to grow as entitlements take up an increasingly large share of a strained federal budget. And some worry that the intergenerational compact may be frayed by the fact that the older Americans who receive entitlements are predominantly white, while the school and working-age populations will be increasingly made up of minorities, including Hispanics and Asians.

"Despite the rumblings, I think the population may come to appreciate that old-age benefits are actually things that benefit all generations," Binstock says. "However, I do think that the growing Latino population may very well come to resent paying taxes to support an older white generation."

BACKGROUND

Living Longer

For most of human history, journalist Ted C. Fishman points out in his book about global aging, *Shock of Gray*, people who lived past 45 had beaten the odds. Life expectancy barely budged from 25 years during the Roman Empire to 30 years at the dawn of the 20th century.[24]

Until the Industrial Revolution, people 65 or older never comprised more than 3 or 4 percent of the population. Today, they average 16 percent in the developed world — and their share is expected to rise to nearly 25 percent by 2030.[25] (The share of Americans over 65 will be nearly 20 percent by then.) Demographers call such shifts from historic norms the "demographic transition."

A confluence of factors has led to the current transition. Aging was once largely synonymous with death. Older people were both rarer and more vulnerable to sudden death due to such things as infectious diseases and poor sanitation. But even as modern medicine has conquered diseases that afflict the old, it has done even more to address infant mortality.

With fewer people dying young, life expectancy has increased. And healthier babies have coincided with other societal and economic factors to bring birthrates down. As prosperity grows, death rates fall. And the advent of pensions and other social-insurance programs has meant that parents no longer have as great a need for large families to support them as they age.

Meanwhile, women's roles have changed. Many now balance reproduction with concerns and responsibilities outside the home. Contraceptives are more widely available, while abortion has become legal and available.

Finally, as American society has urbanized, fewer families need to have multiple children to help work in the fields.

"Fertility Splurge"

In the 1930s, demographers predicted that after a long period of decline in birthrates dating back to the Industrial Revolution, the U.S. population would stagnate and was unlikely to rise above 150 million by century's end. But birthrates shot up immediately after World War II, quickly rising to more than 4 million births per year.

All told, about 76 million children were born in the United States between 1946 and 1964, generally considered the period of the baby boom. (Several million have died, but immigrants have more than made up for those numbers, bringing the baby boom total to 78 million.) "Simply put, the baby boom was a 'disturbance' which emanated from a decade-and-a-half-long fertility splurge on the part of American couples," concluded the Population Reference Bureau in 1980.[26]

Childbearing long delayed — first by the Great Depression of the 1930s and then by war — was put off no longer. Women married younger and had their first babies at an earlier age than at any time in modern history.[27] The fertility rate, which refers to the average number of children born to women of child-bearing years, had averaged 2.1 children per woman during the 1930s but peaked at 3.7 in the late 1950s.[28]

The number of babies being born certainly surprised the General Electric Co. in January 1953. It promised five shares of stock to any employee who had a baby on Oct. 15, the company's 75th anniversary. GE expected maybe eight employees would qualify. Instead they had to hand over stock to 189 workers.[29]

The time was ripe, economically, for many more people to have children than had done so during the Depression. GDP expanded rapidly, from $227 billion in 1940 to $488 billion in 1960. Median family income and wages climbed steadily because of tight labor markets, while inflation remained low. The Servicemembers' Readjustment Act of 1944, commonly known as the GI Bill of Rights, helped more people in the middle class buy their first homes and get college educations,

significantly increasing their lifetime earnings. "Never had so many people, anywhere, been so well off," observed *U.S. News & World Report* in 1957.[30]

The Baby Bust

Perhaps because of the advent of the birth control pill in 1960 and the fact that more women had careers, boomers were slower to become parents than their parents had been. Between 1965 and 1976 — the era of the so-called baby bust — fertility among whites dropped below replacement levels.[31]

After just two decades of a "fertility splurge," Americans went back to marrying later and producing fewer children. In 1990, only 32 percent of women 20-24 were married, compared to 70 percent in 1960. Social scientists began to posit that it was the baby boom that was exceptional in American history, not the subsequent bust.[32]

But the baby bust was followed by the uptick known as the "echo boom," when many boomers became parents, racking up 64 million live births between 1977 and 1993.[33]

Meanwhile, boomers continued to dominate many aspects of American life and culture. Some criticized them as frivolous, blaming their personal habits and quests for self-fulfillment for every social ill from divorce rates to teen drug use. Others defended them for fighting for greater rights for women and gays, among others. The debate about boomers' values became a recurring motif in politics — especially after Bill Clinton, who would become the first boomer president, emerged on the national stage in 1992. Political scientists have noted that boomers failed to coalesce behind a single political party, with many growing more fiscally conservative during the 1980s but remaining socially liberal, with views on race, AIDS, drugs and women's rights distinctly different from their parents' generation.

But the mere fact of their massive numbers made them hard to ignore — and created policy challenges as they aged. "This year, the first of about 78 million baby boomers turn 60, including two of my dad's favorite people, me and President Clinton," President George W. Bush said during his 2006 State of the Union address. "This milestone is more than a personal crisis. It is a national challenge. The retirement of the baby boom generation will put unprecedented strains on the federal government."[34]

CHRONOLOGY

1940s-1960s *High postwar birth rates fuel suburban growth.*

1946 First of the 78 million American baby boomers are born.

1956 Women are allowed to collect early benefits under Social Security at age 62. The same deal is offered to men in 1962.

1959 More than 50 million Americans are under age 14, representing 30 percent of the population.

1960 Sun City opens in Arizona, pioneering the retirement community idea.

1960 Seventy percent of women ages 20-24 are married.

1965 Forty-one percent of Americans are under age 20. . . . Medicare and Medicaid, the main government health programs for the elderly, poor and disabled, are created.

1980s-1990s *Boomers set aside youthful rebellion to take a leading role in wealth creation and politics.*

1983 Congress approves a gradual increase in the age at which Americans can collect full Social Security benefits, from 65 to 67.

1986 The Age Discrimination Employment Act is amended to eliminate mandatory retirement ages.

1990 Proportion of married women ages 20-24 drops to 32 percent.

1992 Bill Clinton elected as the first boomer president.

2000s *Oldest boomers, enter their 60s, raising concerns about the cost of their retirements.*

2000 For every American 65 or older, there are 3.4 workers contributing payroll taxes to Social Security — a ratio that will shrink to 2.0 by 2030.

2003 Congress passes an expansion of Medicare that offers a prescription drug benefit to seniors. . . . Pima County, Ariz., becomes the first local government to

require all new homes to be designed to accommodate seniors and the disabled.

2005 The pregnancy rate of 103.2 per 1,000 women aged 15 to 44 years old is 11 percent below the 1990 peak of 115.8.

2006 President George W. Bush, one of the oldest boomers, turns 60. . . . The Pension Protection Act allows workers to dip into their pensions while working past 62.

2007 Federal Reserve Chairman Ben S. Bernanke predicts Social Security and Medicare will swallow 15 percent of annual economic output by 2030. . . . The Federal Aviation Administration proposes increasing the retirement age for pilots from 60 to 65. . . . The nation's earliest-born boomer, Kathleen Casey-Kirschling, applies for Social Security benefits.

2010s *The number of older Americans continues to rise, but the U.S. enjoys more growth among school and working-age populations than other rich nations.*

2010 The number of workers 55 and over hits 26 million, which is a 46 percent increase since 2000. Congress enacts the Affordable Care Act, designed to expand health coverage, including a doubling of the eligible population under Medicaid.

2011 March 16: The Centers for Disease Control and Prevention announces that life expectancy for Americans at birth increased in 2009 to 78.2 years. . . . April 15: The House passes a budget that would convert Medicare into a voucher program for those now under 55. . . . May 24: Democrats win a special election in a traditionally Republican district in upstate New York; the race is seen as a referendum on the House GOP Medicare proposal.

2015 Working-age populations are projected to start declining in the developed world, with the United States as the major exception.

2025 Population growth is expected to stall in every developed country except the United States, which is also expected to be the only developed nation with more children under age 20 than elderly over age 65.

Minority Youths Are Rising Demographic Force

Trend has major implications for aging whites.

White America is aging, while its young people are increasingly dominated by members of ethnic and racial minorities. As a result, the days when the United States will no longer be a white-majority nation are coming sooner than demographers had long expected.

That could lead to a political struggle over resources, some social scientists contend. There could be a generational battle over governmental priorities — one with racial or ethnic overtones.

Younger members of minority groups may not want to fund entitlement programs that chiefly benefit a mostly white cohort of older Americans. Conversely, the elderly — who hold disproportionate political power thanks to higher rates of voter turnout — may seek to protect such programs at the expense of investments in government programs that chiefly benefit the young.

"Over time, the major focus in this struggle is likely to be between an aging white population that appears increasingly resistant to taxes and dubious of public spending, and a minority population that overwhelmingly views government education, health and social-welfare programs as the best ladder of opportunity for its children," political journalist Ronald Brownstein wrote in the *National Journal* last year.[1]

In a number of places, minorities already outnumber whites — at least among schoolchildren. The population of white children declined by 4.3 million from 2000 to 2010,

while that of Hispanic children rose by 5.5 million, according to the 2010 decennial census.

Indeed, the number of white children decreased in 46 states between 2000 and 2010. Whites now make up a minority among those younger than 18 in 10 states and 35 large metropolitan areas, including Atlanta, Dallas and Orlando. In Texas, 95 percent of the growth of the youth population occurred among Hispanics.

"What a lot of older people don't understand is that, to the extent we have a growing youth population, it's entirely due to minorities," says William Frey, a demographer at the Brookings Institution who has analyzed the 2010 census data on children. Twenty-three states have seen a decline in the total number of children. "In the baby boom generation, about 20 percent never had children, which is about double the rate of the previous generation of elders," says Phillip Longman, a policy researcher at the New America Foundation think tank in Washington.

"Now, you're talking about this aging population that doesn't have any family support and doesn't have any biological relations," he says. "It's not so much that they're white as they forgot to have children."

This opens one of the big questions regarding the differences between an older, white population and a younger population made up more from minorities. In his 2007 book *Immigrants and Boomers*, demographer Dowell Myers worried that there is little kinship — or sense of shared identification — between the groups.

Combined spending for Social Security, Medicare and Medicaid will consume 60 percent of the federal budget by 2030, Bush said, presenting future Congresses with "impossible choices — staggering tax increases, immense deficits or deep cuts in every category of spending."

Bush had spent a good chunk of 2005 touting a plan to revamp Social Security, meant to be the signature domestic achievement of his second term. But the

plan — which would have allowed workers born after 1950 to put part of their payroll taxes into private investment accounts in exchange for cuts in traditional benefits — went nowhere. A *Washington Post*/ABC News Poll found that 58 percent of those surveyed said the more they heard about Bush's plan, the less they liked it.[35]

More recent attempts to overhaul the major entitlement plans benefiting seniors have proved no more popular. A House Republican plan to convert Medicare from

But Longman says such concerns may be overstated. "Thirty years ago, I predicted that would be a big thing, the conflict between generations made even worse by the fact that it has an ethnic and racial component to it as well," he says.

Longman argues now, however, that racial lines are getting blurrier. Just as the definition of who was "white" expanded in the first half of the 20th century to include groups such as the Irish and Italians, Hispanics will increasingly be seen as "white," Longman says. "I just think the melting pot continues," he says.

Polls indicate that younger Americans are readier to embrace racial diversity than their elders, while more describe themselves as multiracial. Still, racial animosities and differences persist, and they may become exacerbated as the white population ages and the minority population grows larger.

The public-school system is one place where tensions could rise. Gaps on average reading and math test scores posted by Hispanics and non-Hispanic whites have been narrowing, but remain wide. "Despite the closing white-Hispanic gaps on civics performance, the fact is we're still seeing gaps in the double digits," said Leticia Van de Putte, a Texas state senator who sits on the board that oversees National Assessment of Educational Progress testing.[2]

Because school funding relies partly on property tax assessments in most places, such disparities may be perpetuated by racial segregation. Although the 2010 census showed a decline in residential segregation, black and Hispanic children are more likely to live in a segregated neighborhood than black and Hispanic adults, according to Frey.

"White parents with children may be more likely to locate in select neighborhoods and communities, perhaps those with better schools, or superior public amenities related to childrearing," he writes.[3]

It will be in the interest of the aging white population to see that young people, including Hispanics and other minorities, fulfill their educational potential, says Myers.

Minorities are fueling the nation's growing youth population. Above, black and Hispanic students at the Harlem Success Academy, a New York charter school.

Otherwise, they will be caught short as the working-age population, which pays the bulk of the taxes that support programs that benefit seniors, is made up largely of minorities. "The person you educated 20 years ago, that's who is going to buy your house," he says.

— *Alan Greenblatt*

[1] Ronald Brownstein, "The Gray and The Brown: The Generational Mismatch," *National Journal*, July 24, 2010, www.nationaljournal.com/magazine/the-gray-and-the-brown-the-generational-mismatch-20100724.

[2] "State Senators React to Hispanic Achievement Gains," *Hispanic Tips*, May 5, 2011, www.hispanictips.com/2011/05/05/state-senators-react-to-hispanic-achievement-gains-on-latest-naep-civics-report-card-that-showed-substantial-gains-in-the-performance-of-hispanic-students-at-grades-four-eight-and-12/

[3] William Frey, "America's Diverse Future," The Brookings Institution, April 2011, p. 10, www.brookings.edu/~/media/Files/rc/papers/2011/0406_census_diversity_frey/0406_census_diversity_frey.pdf.

an insurance program into a credit that would help seniors buy private insurance is an example. A survey conducted in May by the Pew Research Center for the People & the Press found opposition to the plan was especially high among "people who say they have heard a lot about this proposal — fully 56 percent are opposed, while 33 percent are in favor."[36]

"The politics of this is, the baby boom is a generation that's always been pretty willing to vote themselves good

fiscal deals," says MacGuineas of the New America Foundation.

"Sandwich" Generation

Boomers will add to the rising number of seniors — but their parents, in many cases, will still be around. Those 85 and over now make up the fastest-growing segment of the U.S. population, according to the National Institute on Aging. That means that even as boomers enter what

A nurse examines stroke victim Elvira Tesarek at her home in Warren, R.I., in May 2011. Nearly 1,300 elderly and disabled adults in the state have been able to return home under a pilot program designed to cut spending on Medicare.

has traditionally been considered old age, they are "sandwiched" between still-living parents and their own children and grandchildren.

The percentage of adults who are providing personal or financial care to a parent has tripled since 1994, according to the MetLife Mature Market Institute. "Nearly 10 million adult children over the age of 50 care for their aging parents," said Sandra Timmermann, the institute's director. "Assessing the long-term financial impact of caregiving for aging parents on caregivers themselves, especially those who must curtail their working careers to do so, is especially important, since it can jeopardize their future financial security."[37]

"Boomers are quite different from earlier generations as they're approaching this age," says William H. Frey, a demographer at the Brookings Institution, a centrist think tank in Washington. For example, boomer women "are much more likely to have lived independent lives, been head of households and worked."

But there's a great deal of economic inequality within the baby boom generation, he notes, which means many retirees will have a hard time making ends meet.[38] In addition, Frey says, boomers didn't have as many children as their parents' generation, so they "can't rely on them for support."

Not everyone views the aging of America as bad news. An aging population, says Eric Kingson, a professor of social work at Syracuse University, is a sign that society has successfully fostered an economy that helps people lead long, prosperous lives. "Population aging is not just about the old," he says. "It's about how all of our institutions are going to change."

CURRENT SITUATION

Financial Insecurity

Even as federal officials debate the affordability of Social Security and Medicare as the population ages, individual Americans are increasingly concerned about their own ability to support themselves during retirement.

Even before the financial crisis of 2008, income and wealth inequality was growing among seniors. "Back in 2004, the top 5 percent of the baby boomers controlled more than half of the assets," says Diane Oakley, executive director of the National Institute on Retirement Security in Washington. "The bottom half had less than 3 percent of the assets."

She hopes lower-income Americans have been able to save more for retirement since then, but stock market losses and the collapse of the housing bubble make that unlikely.

In a recent poll, "78 percent say they can't save enough on their own to be secure in retirement," says Brian Perlman, president and CEO of Mathew Greenwald & Associates, a market research firm in Washington. "People's beliefs are that it's harder and harder to do that."

The risk for retirement has shifted more onto individuals, Oakley says. From 1980 to 2008, she says, the percentage of private-sector workers covered by defined-benefit pension plans — which offer a guaranteed income throughout retirement — dropped from 38 percent to 20 percent.

Meanwhile, defined-contribution plans, such as 401(k) plans, have grown. These plans, which shift the burden for retirement savings onto individuals, have certain tax advantages, but like any personal savings account, they can be drained dry. Unlike defined-benefit plans, the money is gone once 401(k) assets are depleted.

Americans are not contributing enough to 401(k)s to build up sufficient retirement nest eggs. According to Towers Watson, a human-resources consulting firm, only 57.3 percent of Americans have enough in their retirement accounts to replace one year's worth of working salary. Only 10.9 percent had more than four times their current salary saved up.[39]

Because most people are going to be retired more than a few years, that presents a problem. For most, Social Security will represent the bulk of their retirement income, but benefits average only about $14,000 per year.

"Only about half of workers are in any kind of retirement plan through their employers," says the Urban Institute's Johnson. "People don't make the most of their 401(k) plans — they don't contribute the maximum, or at all."

Automatic Enrollment

Most workers have to sign up for 401(k) plans, but Johnson favors automatic enrollment. Automatic enrollment plans would allow employers to deduct part of each paycheck and put the money toward employees' retirement, unless a worker made the express decision to opt out.

"We've run some simulations," Johnson says. "If most people behave as we expect they would, based on past experience, automatic enrollment would increase retirement incomes for low- and moderate-income people by about 20 percent."

The Obama administration supports the idea of automatic enrollment. The administration would like employers, even if they don't offer 401(k) accounts of their own, to enroll their workers in some kind of retirement account.

"The basic idea is that an employer would simply do payroll deduction," says J. Mark Iwry, senior adviser to Treasury Secretary Timothy Geithner. "When we do automatic enrollment in 401(k)s, the [participation] rate goes up from two-thirds or three-quarters to more than 90 percent."

But the idea of enrolling workers automatically into retirement savings accounts may run into opposition in Congress because of budget concerns. Obama's deficit commission last year recommended lowering the cap on annual contributions allowed to such retirement savings accounts.[40]

Aside from putting more money aside for retirement, individuals will also come to rely more on income earned later in life — whether by staying in their old job longer or finding a new one after "retiring," many economists believe.

"If people want to have a secure retirement, they really should work longer," says Alicia Munnell, director of the Center for Retirement Research at Boston College. "There's an enormous benefit in terms of what your Social Security benefits and 401(k) accounts will be. And then, you have [fewer] years over which to spread your savings. All we're talking about, basically, is three to four more years. We're not talking about into your 90s."

Government Cutbacks

Most government workers can count on a relatively comfortable retirement. In contrast to private-sector employees, about 90 percent of state and local government workers are enrolled in defined-benefit programs.

But the disparity between the plans offered to government workers and those at private companies, along with severe budget problems confronting state and local government workers, is increasing pressure on retirement benefits in the public sector, too.

The gap between what states had promised to pay out in pensions and retirement health benefits and the assets they have to pay them had grown to more than $1.26 trillion by the end of the 2009 budget year, according to the Pew Center on the States.[41] Some economists say the gap is even larger.

About a dozen states have altered their pension systems over the past couple of years, according to the National Conference of State Legislatures. Most have made moves such as putting new employees into 401(k)-style accounts, rather than enrolling them in defined-benefit plans.

Math and Politics

But some governors and lawmakers have sought changes in retirement coverage for current workers as well. The battle over retirement benefits has turned political, most notably in Wisconsin, where legislation to strip most public employees of collective bargaining rights led to weeks of large-scale protests at the capital.

State and local retirement accounts might be more than $1 trillion in the red, but union leaders say it's unfair to blame government workers because legislatures

> **"We are draining money out of services and pouring them into retirement benefits. However you define unsustainable, it's unsustainable."**
>
> **— Mayor Chuck Reed
> San Jose, Calif.**

failed to make scheduled payments to pension funds over the years.

Better to blame Wall Street, they say, for racking up record profits even as large-scale investment losses have blown a hole through pension accounts. "They've blamed public employees for problems they've never caused in the first place," says Randi Weingarten, president of the American Federation of Teachers.

Patrick O'Connor, an alderman in Chicago, agrees that unions have a point when they accuse government officials of not properly funding promised benefits. Still, he argues, cities and states have no choice but to cut back on benefits that are no longer affordable.

"Government can't blame the unions in total," O'Connor says. "Government is what put the benefits in place. But I don't think anybody who looks at pension plans thinks they can be funded at the levels they're at."

In San Jose, Calif., Mayor Chuck Reed declared a state of "fiscal emergency" in May, hoping he can persuade voters to give him additional powers that would allow him to change retirement-benefit formulas.[42]

Reed warns that he will have to lay off two-thirds of the city's work force if he can't achieve significant savings in retirement-benefit costs. What consumed $65 million of the city's budget a decade ago already accounts for $250 million and half the city's current budget shortfall. Retirement costs could rise to as much as $650 million annually over the next few years, Reed says.

In Reed's mind, it's simply a math problem. "We are draining money out of services and pouring them into retirement benefits," Reed says. "However you define unsustainable, it's unsustainable."

Public-employee unions concede that Reed's complaints are borne out of real problems with San Jose's finances. They don't agree that his approach is the best way to address those problems, however. And union leaders in San Jose, like their colleagues elsewhere, think stripping public employees of promised benefits will undermine one of the few pockets of retirement security.

"It's perfectly understandable that workers in the private sector are worried about their retirement security," says John Liu, New York City's comptroller. "But to scapegoat public employees will fuel a race to the bottom in our country."

Yet, further cutbacks appear inevitable, even for government workers who have long counted on benefits that would allow them to retire free of financial anxiety. State officials appear to have lost some of their initial enthusiasm for moving to 401(k)-style plans, however, because of the enormous upfront costs in switching from traditional pensions. In Kentucky, increased costs are estimated at $8 billion over 15 years. Nevada would run through $1.2 billion in just two years.[43]

Even the well-funded Pentagon is worried about whether it can afford to fund retirement benefits, including health care, at the levels soldiers and sailors have come to expect.

Retiree pay will cost the Department of Defense about $50 billion next year, according to the Obama administration's proposed fiscal 2012 budget. Military health costs, which have doubled over the past decade, will run even more, with a fair share going to coverage of military retirees.

"We in the Department of Defense are on the same path that General Motors found itself on," retired Marine Maj. Gen. Arnold Punaro, who advises the Pentagon on financial operations, told NPR. "General Motors did not start out to be a health care company that occasionally built an automobile. Today, we're on the path in the Department of Defense to turn it into a benefits company that may occasionally kill a terrorist."[44]

Robert Gates, who stepped down as Defense Secretary June 30, said the military may have to consider moving to a 401(k)-style plan. Financial problems make some sort of change to the Pentagon's pension and retirement health formulas inevitable, he told *Defense News*. "We are way behind the private sector in this."[45]

Should the retirement age be raised?

YES   Andrew G. Biggs
Resident Scholar, American Enterprise Institute

Written for *CQ Researcher*, July 2011

Social Security's retirement age should not be increased for anyone on the verge of retirement, but there's a good case for doing so over coming decades, as the Baby Boomers retire and the population ages.

In 1950, the average retiree claimed Social Security benefits at age 68.5 and lived to around 76. Today, a typical retiree claims benefits at 63 and will live an additional two decades. Americans today live almost one-third of their adult lives in retirement, supported by an increasing tax burden on their kids and grandkids. This isn't simply unfair to future generations. It is also a waste of human talent.

Are there some people who can't work longer? Of course. And for them, early retirement or disability benefits remain an option. But it would be strange in today's service economy if Americans, who work mostly in offices, could not work as long as prior generations who toiled in mines, mills and farms.

Indeed, our longer lives are also healthier lives. According to the National Center for Health Statistics, among individuals ages 65-74 the share describing themselves as in fair or poor health dropped from 25.1 percent in 1983 to 18.5 percent in 2007. Overall, 75 percent of individuals over 65 report being in good, very good or excellent health.

It's easy to scare people — for instance, President Obama's Commission on Fiscal Responsibility and Reform would increase the retirement age to 69. But this would apply only to people who haven't even been born yet and at retirement would live on average to age 88 — almost 10 years longer than they did when Social Security started in the 1930s.

It is true that life expectancies have risen faster for high-earners than for low-income Americans. This is why almost every reform plan that raises the retirement age also makes Social Security more progressive, by boosting benefits for low-earners while trimming them for the rich.

One option is to let the retirement age rise to 67 as scheduled, then increase it in future years as life spans rise. If life expectancies increase quickly, then the retirement age will follow; if life spans stay constant, the retirement age won't need to increase further. By itself, this would fix nearly one-quarter of Social Security's deficit.

Mathematically, we can't fix the entire entitlement deficit by raising taxes. And Medicare is far more likely to require tax increases than Social Security. So it only makes sense to reduce costs where we can. Increasing the retirement age is a reasonable response to longer lives.

NO   Nancy Altman and Eric Kingson
Co-chairs, Strengthen Social Security Campaign

Written for *CQ Researcher*, July 2011

To reduce unemployment during the 1961 recession, and in recognition that many Americans were unable to work until age 65, Congress allowed men to claim reduced Social Security benefits at age 62, just as it had for women in 1956. Speaking in support, Democratic Ohio Rep. Charles Vanik said that "if 2 million male workers eventually retire under this program, 2 million job opportunities will be created."

Ironically, with unemployment topping 9 percent, many in Congress today favor increasing Social Security's full retirement age. This is the wrong policy today, would have been wrong in 1961 and will be wrong in the future.

A retirement age increase is mathematically indistinguishable from a benefit cut, and ill-advised because benefits are too low. Congress has already increased the retirement age from 65 to 67, a 13 percent cut for people born after 1960. A further increase, from 67 to 69, would be another 13 percent cut for retired workers, no matter whether they claim benefits at age 62, age 70, or any age in between, and translates into lower benefits for many spouses and widow(er)s. Benefits are modest, averaging about $14,000, and the retirement prospects for persons in their 40s and early 50s are already dimmed by diminishing pension protections, shrinking 401(k) and IRA retirement savings, unemployment and declining home values.

Retirement-age increases especially burden lower-wage and minority workers, who often have no choice but to retire early. It is well-known that many workers must stop work because of serious health and physical challenges; still others face age discrimination and job loss. Sixty-two percent of Latino males and 53 percent of older black male workers are in physically demanding or difficult jobs, compared with 42 percent of their white male counterparts. By retiring early, they claim permanently reduced benefits. A hardship exemption for these categories of workers has never been found to be politically feasible or workable.

Lower-wage workers, on average, have seen little or no increase in life expectancy. Over the past quarter-century, the life expectancy of upper-income men increased by five years while life expectancy among lower-income men increased by only one year and that of lower-income women actually declined.

For all these reasons, Congress should follow the will of the American people, who reject increasing the retirement age. Congress should consider eliminating Social Security's projected shortfall by scrapping the cap on earnings subject to Social Security's FICA contributions, as the American people strongly favor.

OUTLOOK

Political Prospects

Given the costs associated with aging — particularly those involving medical care — some economists are growing pessimistic about the country's long-term budget health. By the time the last of the boomers have turned 65, in 2029, there will be nearly twice as many people enrolled in Medicare as there are today, according to AARP.

"Social Security has pretty much anticipated the aging population and built up a very large trust fund," says Rother, AARP's policy director. "Medicare is the place where the stress shows."

Health care costs are bound to be driven higher by an older population. Some worry Congress won't be able to agree on ways to significantly reduce growth in entitlement programs and thereby reduce the federal deficit.

"I just think the two parties are kind of locked in cement on this stuff," says Hewitt of the Coalition for Affordable Health Care.

The question of whether Congress will change entitlements really depends on the attitudes of the voting public, he says. "I frankly don't think that fiscal conservatives are going to be able to hold the line, because baby boomers in the end are going to decide they don't want to defund their retirement," Hewitt says.

Myers, the USC demographer, says politicians will need to appeal to older voters to make big policy changes. Older Americans may love their entitlements, but they'll have to be convinced that younger, working-age people need money left over for productive investments in areas such as education and infrastructure — and shouldn't be saddled with crippling debt, Myers says.

"The only winning political strategy is not to fight [older voters] but persuade them it's in their interest," Myers says. "I believe they control the electorate for the next 20 years, and we don't have 20 years to wait."

Budget realities will force changes to entitlement programs in the next decade, says MacGuineas of the New American Foundation. And, she says, waiting until financial markets force fiscal changes, as has been happening in European countries such as Greece, won't be pleasant.

"There's no question that by 2020, changes will have been made," she says. "What I'm worried about is that changes may have been forced upon us — changes made because of markets will be much more painful."

Not everyone thinks some kind of fiscal crisis is inevitable. Blahous, the Hoover Institution fellow and Social Security trustee, says he's pessimistic, but not because he worries the country will face "economic Armageddon."

Instead, Blahous worries that continuing unbridled growth in major entitlement programs will mean "we'll have more expensive government than we've ever had before," he says. "People's after-tax income will not have the growth we've seen in the past."

There are some positive predictions. The Urban Institute's Johnson says widowhood is becoming less common. "Men are living longer, and the differences between men and women's mortality is lessening. Widowhood is still associated with poverty."

Still, Johnson expects income inequality among the aged to continue to grow and more older Americans will need to work longer. Others say policy changes to health coverage are inevitable, despite the political opposition engendered both by President Obama's 2010 health care-expansion law and the House GOP's current effort to limit Medicare growth.

"We're going to be moving more and more toward managed care," says Binstock, the Case Western Reserve health policy professor, "in the sense that there'll be a fixed budget in terms of care for older people." Older people will be hurt as a result, Binstock contends.

But the New America Foundation's Longman isn't convinced. A move toward some form of managed care will lead to better health outcomes than the current U.S. health system, which is prone to ill-informed treatment and mistakes, he says.

"I would hope in 10 years, we have turned the corner on the health care thing," Longman says. "The idea that we're going to let people go get any care they want from anybody they want, that's not going to work."

Longman says the outlook is "gloomy" but that it won't be impossible to turn things around. As long as health care is restructured and "as long as today's young people don't forget to have children," the U.S. should be able to care for its growing senior population, he says.

But fewer people are having children — and certainly fewer are having multiple children, notes Fishman, the author of *Shock of Gray.* "We're about a generation away from children having no brothers and sisters, no aunts and uncles, no cousins," he says. "People may be looking continuously for more family supports, but the family just won't be there."

The prospect of fewer children and longer life expectancy means the median age will continue to rise. No matter the difficulties posed by the aging of the baby boom generation, they won't be solved by that generation's passing.

"The boomers may seem like a large cohort of older people," Fishman says, "but the median age is increasing and that won't turn around."

NOTES

1. "Double Jeopardy For Baby Boomers Proving Care For Their Parents," MetLife Mature Market Institute, June 2001, p. 2, www.metlife.com/assets/cao/mmi/publications/studies/2011/mmi-caregiving-costs-working-caregivers.pdf.

2. For background, see Thomas J. Billitteri, "Rethinking Retirement," *CQ Researcher*, June 19, 2009, pp. 549-572.

3. Matt Sedensky, "Number of 100-Year-Olds is Booming in U.S.," The Associated Press, April 26, 2011, http://news.yahoo.com/s/ap/20110426/ap_on_re_us/us_centenarian_boom.

4 For background, see Marcia Clemmitt, "National Debt," *CQ Researcher*, March 18, 2011, pp. 241-264.

5. For background, see the following *CQ Researcher* reports: Marcia Clemmitt, "Health-Care Reform," June 11, 2010, pp. 505-528, updated May 24, 2011; Beth Baker, "Treating Alzheimer's," March 4, 2011, pp. 193-216; Alan Greenblatt, "Aging Baby Boomers," Oct. 19, 2007, pp. 865-888; and Marcia Clemmitt, "Caring for the Elderly," Oct. 13, 2006, pp. 841-864.

6. Richard Wolf, "Medicare to Swell With Boomer Onslaught," *USA Today*, Jan 1. 2011, http://abcnews.go.com/Politics/medicare-swell-baby-boomer-onslaught/story?id=12504388.

7. From remarks at "The 2011 Medicare Trustees Report: The Baby Boomer Tsunami," American Enterprise Institute, May 16, 2011.

8. See, for instance, "CNN Poll: Majority Gives Thumbs Down to Ryan Medicare Plan," CNN.org, June 1, 2011, http://politicalticker.blogs.cnn.com/2011/06/01/cnn-poll-majority-gives-thumbs-down-to-ryan-plan/.

9. Laura Meckler, "Key Seniors Association Pivots on Benefit Cut," *The Wall Street Journal*, June 17, 2011, http://online.wsj.com/article/SB100014240527023041864045763897609554034 14.html.

10. For background, see Thomas J. Billitteri, "Middle-Class Squeeze," *CQ Researcher*, March 6, 2009, pp. 201-224.

11. Employee Benefit Research Institute, "The 2011 Retirement Confidence Survey: Confidence Drops to Record Lows, Reflecting 'the New Normal,' " March 2011, www.ebri.org/pdf/surveys/rcs/2011/EBRI_03-2011_No355_RCS-11.pdf.

12. "U.S. Death Rate Falls for 10th Straight Year," Centers for Disease Control, March 16, 2011, www.cdc.gov/media/releases/2011/p0316_deathrate.html.

13. "Life Expectancy for Social Security," Social Security Administration, www.ssa.gov/history/lifeexpect.html.

14. For background, see Kenneth Jost, "Public-Employee Unions," *CQ Researcher*, April 8, 2011, pp. 313-336; and Alan Greenblatt, "Pension Crisis," *CQ Researcher*, Feb. 17, 2006, pp. 145-168.

15. For background, see the center's Web page on its "National Retirement Risk Index" publications at http://crr.bc.edu/special_projects/national_retirement_risk_index.html.

16. See Annual Report of the Medicare Trustees, Center for Medicare and Medicaid Services, May 13, 2011, www.cms.gov/ReportsTrustFunds/downloads/tr2011.pdf.

17. "Choosing The Nation's Fiscal Future," National Academies Press (2010), p. 79, available at www.ourfiscalfuture.org/wp-content/uploads/fiscalfuture_full_report.pdf.

18. "Strengthening Medicare: Better Health, Better Care, Lower Costs," Centers for Medicare and Medicaid Services, www.cms.gov/apps/files/medicare-savings-report.pdf.

19. Matthew DoBias, "Medicare's Actuary Paints a Darker Picture Than Trustees," *NationalJournal.com*, May 23, 2011, www.nationaljournal.com/healthcare/medicare-s-actuary-paints-a-darker-picture-than-trustees-20110523.

20. Emily Ethridge, "Republicans Decry Medicare Cost-Control Panel While Seeking Broad Cuts," *CQ HealthBeat*, June 8, 2011.

21. "CBO'S 2011 Long-Term Budget Outlook," Congressional Budget Office, www.cbo.gov/doc.cfm?index=12212.

22. Jonathan Lemire and Erin Einhorn, "Mayor Bloomberg Unveils $65.6 Billion Budget," *New York Daily News*, Feb. 17, 2011, http://articles.nydailynews.com/2011-02-17/local/28628742_1_president-michael-mulgrew-mayor-bloomberg-teacher-layoffs.

23. "As Boomers Wrinkle," *The Economist*, Dec. 29, 2010, www.economist.com/node/17800237?story_id=17800237.

24. Ted C. Fishman, *Shock of Gray* (2011), p. 13.

25. Richard Jackson and Neil Howe, *The Graying of the Great Powers* (2008), p. 7.

26. Paul C. Light, *Baby Boomers* (1988), p. 10.

27. Herbert S. Klein, "The U.S. Baby Bust in Historical Perspective," in Fred R. Harris., ed., *The Baby Bust: Who Will Do the Work? Who Will Pay the Taxes?* (2006), p. 115.

28. Light, *op. cit.*, p. 23.

29. Steve Gillon, *Boomer Nation: The Largest and Richest Generation Ever and How It Changed America* (2004), p. 1.

30. *Ibid.*, p. 6.

31. Klein., *op. cit.*, p. 173.

32. Jeremy Greenwood, Ananth Seshadri and Guillaume Vandenbroucke, "The Baby Boom and Baby Bust." *American Economic Review*, 2005, p. 183.

33. William Sterling and Stephen Waite, *Boomernomics: The Future of Money in the Upcoming Generational Warfare* (1998), p. 3.

34. President George W. Bush, State of the Union address, Jan. 31, 2006, www.washingtonpost.com/wp-dyn/content/article/2006/01/31/AR2006013101468.html.

35. Jonathan Weisman, "Skepticism of Bush's Social Security Plan Is Growing," *The Washington Post*, March 15, 2005, p. A1, www.washingtonpost.com/wp-dyn/articles/A35231-2005Mar14.html.

36. "Opposition to Ryan Plan Among Older, Attentive Americans," Pew Research Center, June 6, 2011, http://people-press.org/2011/06/06/opposition-to-ryan-medicare-plan-from-older-attentive-americans/.

37. Sheryl Nance-Nash, "Caring for Aging Parents Will Cost Boomers $3 Trillion," *AOL DailyFinance*, June 15, 2011, www.dailyfinance.com/2011/06/15/caring-for-aging-parents-will-cost-boomers-3-trillion/.

38. For background, see Marcia Clemmitt, "Income Inequality," *CQ Researcher*, Dec. 3, 2010, pp. 989-1012.

39. See, "Retirement Attitudes," Towers Watson, September 2010, www.towerswatson.com/assets/pdf/2717/TowersWatson-Retirement-Attitudes_NA-2010-17683.pdf.

40. "Will Congress Slash Your 401(k) Tax Break," Reuters Wealth, June 16, 2011, http://blogs.reuters.com/reuters-wealth/2011/06/16/will-congress-slash-your-401k-tax-break/.

41. William Selway, "U.S. States Pension Fund Deficits Widen by 26%, Pew Center Study Says," Bloomberg, April 25, 2011, www.bloomberg.com/news/2011-04-26/u-s-states-pension-fund-deficits-widen-by-26-pew-center-study-says.html.

42. Elizabeth Lesly Stevens, "San Jose Mayor Declares State of 'Fiscal Emergency,'" *The Bay Citizen*, May 21, 2011, www.nytimes.com/2011/05/22/us/22bcstevens.html.

43. Stephen C. Fehn, "States Overhaul Pensions But Pass On 401(k)-Style Plans," *Stateline*, June 21, 2011, www.stateline.org/live/details/story?contentId=582585.

44. Tamara Keith, "Health Care Costs New Threat to U.S. Military," NPR, June 7, 2011, www.npr.org/2011/06/07/137009416/u-s-military-has-new-threat-health-care-costs.

45. Vago Muradian, "Q&A: Robert Gates, U.S. Defense Secretary," *Defense News*, June 13, 2011, p. 32, www.defensenews.com/story.php?i=6792060&c=FEA&s=INT.

BIBLIOGRAPHY

Selected Sources
Books

Fishman, Ted C., *Shock of Gray*, Scribner, 2010.
The author, a former financial trader, uses statistics and sketches of representative individuals to portray how aging is presenting fiscal, health and economic challenges to countries including Japan, China and the United States.

Gillon, Steve, *Boomer Nation: The Largest and Richest Generation Ever and How It Changed America*, Free Press, 2004.
The History Channel's Gillon writes a sympathetic history of the boomers, whose birth, he says, is the "single greatest demographic event in American history."

Pearce, Fred, *The Coming Population Crash and Our Planet's Surprising Future*, Beacon Press, 2010.
A former New Scientist news editor traces the history of population changes, looking at past state-sponsored efforts at population control and the implications for possible population decline in decades to come.

Articles

"As Boomers Wrinkle," *The Economist*, Dec. 29, 2010, www.economist.com/node/17800237?story_id=17800237.
Aging baby boomers will resist any cuts to their entitlements.

Brownstein, Ronald, "The Gray and the Brown: The Generational Mismatch," *National Journal*, July 24, 2010; www.nationaljournal.com/magazine/the-gray-and-the-brown-the-generational-mismatch-20100724.
The United States is seeing a divergence in attitudes and priorities between a heavily nonwhite population of younger people and an overwhelmingly white cohort of older people.

Fehr, Stephen C., "States Overhaul Pensions But Pass on 401(k)-Style Plans," *Stateline*, June 21, 2011, www.stateline.org/live/details/story?contentId=582585.
Pensions for state government workers are badly underfunded, but officials are still wary of switching employees to retirement savings accounts.

Hare, Kristin, "Older Americans Are Working Longer," *St. Louis Beacon*, April 24, 2011, www.stlbeacon.org/issues-politics/172-Economy/109733-retiring-retirement-americans-are-working-longer-.
Ten years ago, 4 million people age 65 and older were working or looking for jobs. By March, that number had increased to 7 million.

Johnson, Kirk, "Between Young and Old, A Political Collision," *The New York Times*, June 3, 2011, www.nytimes.com/2011/06/04/us/politics/04elders.html.
Is there such a thing as a Medicare voting bloc? Some political scientists suggest there increasingly could be pitched political battles between generations over government resources.

Ludden, Jennifer, "Boomers Take the 'Retire' Out of Retirement," NPR.org, Jan. 1, 2011, www.npr.org/2011/01/01/132490242/boomers-take-the-retire-out-of-retirement.
As baby boomers reach age 65, many are optimistic, but a bit more than half may not be able to maintain current living standards in retirement.

Rucker, Philip, "NY Race Is Referendum on GOP Medicare Plan," *The Washington Post*, May 15, 2011, www.washingtonpost.com/politics/ny-special-election-becomes-referendum-on-gop-medicare-plan/2011/05/15/AFnoVR4G_story.html?hpid=z3.
Democrats successfully test a strategy they intend to use in 2012, castigating Republicans for looking to overhaul Medicare.

Studies and Reports

Arno, Peter S., and Deborah Viola, "Double Jeopardy for Baby Boomers Caring for Their Parents," MetLife Mature Market Institute, June 2011, www.metlife.com/assets/cao/mmi/publications/studies/2011/mmi-caregiving-costs-working-caregivers.pdf.
Nearly 10 million adult children over age 50 care for their aging parents.

Cohn, D'Vera, and Paul Taylor, "Baby Boomers Approach 65 — Glumly," Pew Research Center, December 2010, http://pewsocialtrends.org/files/2010/12/Boomer-Summary-Report-FINAL.pdf.
As they approach 65, boomers continue to be accepting of changes in social trends and aren't ready to concede they have reached old age.

Frey, William, "America's Diverse Future," Brookings Institution, April 2011, p. 10, www.brookings.edu/~/media/Files/rc/papers/2011/0406_census_diversity_frey/0406_census_diversity_frey.pdf.
The 2010 census showed that the number of white and black children shrank, while there was significant growth among Hispanics and Asians younger than 18.

Jackson, Richard, and Neil Howe with Rebecca Strauss and Keisuke Nakashima, "The Graying of the Great Powers: Demography and Geopolitics in the 21st Century," Center for Strategic and International Studies, 2008, www.agingsociety.org/agingsociety/publications/public_policy/CSISmajor_findings.pdf.
The report offers a comprehensive survey of aging trends in the developed and developing world.

For More Information

AARP, 601 E St., N.W., Washington, DC 20049; (888) 687-2277; www.aarp.org. The largest advocacy organization for older Americans.

American Society on Aging, 71 Stevenson St., Suite 1450, San Francisco, CA 94105; (415) 974-9600; www.asaging .org. Founded as the Western Gerontological Society; offers programs and online learning for professionals in health care, social services, government and other fields who seek to improve the quality of life for older adults.

Boston College, Center for Retirement Research, Hovey House, 140 Commonwealth Ave., Chestnut Hill, MA 02467; (617) 552-1762; crr.bc.edu. Conducts research on issues related to retirement, particularly finance and health.

Center for Strategic and International Studies, Global Aging Initiative, 1800 K St., N.W., Washington, DC 20006; (202) 887-0200; csis.org/program/global-aging-initiative. Conducts research and education programs on long-term economic, social and geopolitical implications of demographic change in the United States and abroad.

Employee Benefit Research Institute, 1100 13th St., N.W., Suite 878, Washington, DC 20005; (202) 659-0670; www .ebri.org. Conducts research on employee benefits, including pensions and defined-contribution plans such as 401(k)s.

National Association of Area Agencies on Aging, 1730 Rhode Island Ave., N.W., 4th Floor, Washington, DC 20036; (202) 872-0888; www.n4a.org. Umbrella organization for local area aging agencies.

National Institute on Aging, Building 31, Room 5C27, 31 Center Dr., MSC 2292, Bethesda, MD 20892; (301) 496-1752; www.nia.nih.gov. Leads the federal government's scientific effort to study the nature of aging.

National Institute on Retirement Security, 1730 Rhode Island Ave., N.W., Suite 207, Washington, DC 20036; (202) 457-8190; www.nirsonline.org. Studies retirement-income issues such as pensions.

Urban Institute, Program on Retirement Policy, 2100 M St., N.W., Washington, DC 20037; (202) 833-7200; www .retirementpolicy.org. Conducts research on issues relevant to retirement, such as Social Security, long-term care and unemployment rates among older Americans.

UCLA, Center for Policy Research on Aging, 3250 Public Policy Building, Box 951656, Los Angeles, CA 90095; (310) 794-5908; www.spa.ucla.edu. Studies major policy and political issues surrounding aging; devotes particular attention to issues relating to ethnic populations.

ⓈSAGE research**methods**

The essential online tool for researchers from the world's leading methods publisher

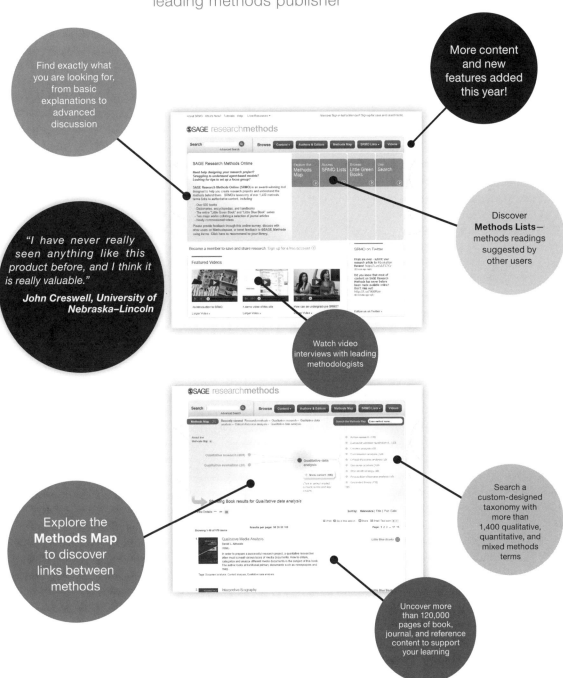

Find exactly what you are looking for, from basic explanations to advanced discussion

More content and new features added this year!

Discover **Methods Lists**— methods readings suggested by other users

"I have never really seen anything like this product before, and I think it is really valuable."

John Creswell, University of Nebraska–Lincoln

Watch video interviews with leading methodologists

Explore the **Methods Map** to discover links between methods

Search a custom-designed taxonomy with more than 1,400 qualitative, quantitative, and mixed methods terms

Uncover more than 120,000 pages of book, journal, and reference content to support your learning

Find out more at
www.sageresearchmethods.com